THE WAR OF THE AMERICAN REVOLUTION
Day by Day

Volume One

The Preliminaries
and the Years 1775,
1776, 1777, and 1778

by

The Rev. Frederick Wallace Pyne, Ph.D.

HERITAGE BOOKS
2009

HERITAGE BOOKS

AN IMPRINT OF HERITAGE BOOKS, INC.

Books, CDs, and more—Worldwide

For our listing of thousands of titles see our website
at
www.HeritageBooks.com

Published 2009 by
HERITAGE BOOKS, INC.
Publishing Division
100 Railroad Ave. #104
Westminster, Maryland 21157

International Standard Book Numbers
Paperbound: 978-0-7884-4799-0
Clothbound: 978-0-7884-8107-9

DEDICATION

This Book is dedicated to my Wife and Companion

ANN RAMMES PYNE

my faithful friend and supporter
who on many, many travels and journeys
has been by my side to almost all the
places and events
of the War of the American Revolution,
and tolerates my endless fascination
with those heroes who gave us
a country of Freedom and Liberty.

TABLE of CONTENTS

TABLE of MAPS and PICTURES

FOREWORD

A BOOK THAT EVERY AMERICAN SHOULD READ

A Chronological History of the Revolution is a very good way to discover one of the most forgotten aspects of our War for Independence - how long it lasted. It was exactly eight years from April 19, 1775, when the first shots were fired on Lexington Green, to April 19, 1783, when Washington ordered Congress's proclamation of the war's end to be read to his troops at New Windsor, New York.

As you will discover in these pages, that proclamation was not quite the end of the contest. The British army did not evacuate New York City for another six months. George Washington did not resign his commission as Commander in Chief until December 23, 1783.

The war's awesome duration is by no means a minor point. It underscores how stubbornly the Americans pursued the goal of independence. In these pages you will see how often they might have become discouraged and given up the exhausting contest. But they knew the value of the prize for which they were contending. It was enshrined in that momentous word - liberty.

Frederick Pyne has done a remarkable job of showing all sides of the bitter, often divisive struggle. Above all he has captured the innumerable moments of high courage and decisive acts that make the drama one of the most unforgettable stories in the history of the world.

Thomas J. Fleming

Manhattan, New York
Author of *Liberty! The American Revolution*
President, American Society of Historians

PREFACE

Civil War aficionados have E. B. Long's book, *The Civil War Day by Day: an Almanac, 1861-1865*, and Robert Denney's, *The Civil War Years: A Day-By-Day Chronicle*. They provide a great deal of information in an easy and convenient format. One can quickly look up an event by date or name, and explore in depth the information provided.

There are many books on the Revolution, some encyclopedic in content, but none that provides the reader with a full chronological each-and-every-day by day account of the entire course of that war. The values of a chronological detailing of the war are several. For instance, a time line conveys the fact that nearly sixteen months elapsed, from the shots fired at Lexington and Concord on 19 April 1775 to the approval of the language in the Declaration of Independence by the Continental Congress on 4 July 1776.

Another, and equally useful, reason for a chronological work on our American Revolution is the element of concurrency--that is, a work that allows the reader to see the several things that were occurring at or near the same time in different places. For example, as Benedict Arnold was struggling up the Kennebec River and preparing a siege of Quebec in the late fall and early winter of 1775, Richard Montgomery was attacking Fort Chambly and Montreal, while Philip Schuyler was trying to find supplies and reinforcements for Fort Ticonderoga, and the British under Henry Clinton would soon be leaving Boston on an expedition to Charleston, South Carolina, as George Washington at Cambridge, Massachusetts was concerned about creating one army while disbanding another, during the siege of Boston.

As a descendant of one of the Signers of the Declaration of Independence, I naturally have a great interest in this period of American history. Feeling that a need for a true and complete chronological history of the Revolution cried for fulfillment, I launched upon this work. The result, in this Volume 1 is a daily citation of events throughout the period from the first shots at the Green of Lexington on 19 April 1775 to the travails of the John Adams party traveling through Spain to get to Paris, France, on 31 December 1779.

Perhaps we remember that the American Revolution began with the battles of Lexington and Concord, and the linear retreat of the British back to Boston on 19 April 1775, pursued by a gathering horde of militia. In early May 1775 some loosely organized militia under Ethan Allen and Benedict Arnold captured Fort Ticonderoga and raided into Canada. Then came the Battle of Bunker Hill on 17 June 1775. In the meantime, the Second Continental Congress assembled in Philadelphia.

Now, no pusillanimous discussion of petitions, no arguments about non-importation, no hand-wringing or hat-holding over how to deal with our British foes! No, indeed, we must now address ourselves to the more serious problems of defending our lives and properties.

The militia from New England besieging the British, requested advice and support, and urged the Continental Congress to assume responsibility for these forces outside Boston. The Congress, on 14 June 1775, authorized the raising of ten companies of expert riflemen. The next day they appointed Colonel George Washington of the Virginia Militia to command "all the forces raised or to be raised for the defense of these United Provinces." He left to join his "army" in Cambridge, Massachusetts, arriving on 3 July 1775.

What did he find? A mess! The army was in the greatest confusion, almost every aspect of its organization and direction needed to be straightened out. This army needed reorganizing, enlarging, strengthening. There was no regular guard nor outpost provision, no effort at proper food preparation, storage, distribution, or purchase. The smell was terrible. No thought had been given to field sanitation, latrines, clean water supply, or a laundry system. There was also little or no discipline. One of Washington's first acts was to determine the precise strength of his army. The New England colonies believed they had gathered as many as 24,000 men. Washington was told, upon arrival, that maybe 19,000 men were at hand. When he finally received a report, it said he had only 13,743 foot troops available for duty.

Washington's next major problem was supply. There was no standard ration. There was no such thing as a uniform, and no system to take care of replacements, repair, or new supply--so they wore what they had. Powder was a critical item. Few American powder mills existed. Almost all of what was available was captured or imported from France, the West Indies, or Spain. When the British made motions indicating an advance out of Boston in late July, there was scarcely enough powder to issue nine cartridges to each man. Small arms were grossly defective. There was no common weapon, no armor artificer, or maker of muskets to correct and repair weapon failures. There was also no musket resupply system, no parts, no maintenance. Housing was in local homes, public buildings, and tents. By November, there was a shortage of blankets and fuel.

Washington was in desperate need of a good officer corps. In an Army without uniforms, there was no distinction between grades. He set up a simple system of rank identification: corporals, a green knot of cloth on the right shoulder; sergeants, a red knot; field grade officers, red cockade in their hats; yellow for Captain; green for Lieutenant; sashes for General officers: light blue for commanding General; purple for Major General; pink for Brigadier General; green for Aides.

From the top down there was soon a great overturning in the camp: officers on the lines every day, inspections, clean-up, guard and outpost, order and regularity, training, military discipline, daily returns of men, equipment and supplies. A complete reorganization of the army was ordered, dividing it into three great divisions.

Militia were enlisted for the short term. This army was not built for a future or for even a few months ahead. The troops that had come early on soon felt that they had done their part, and left. It was now someone else's turn to take over. This kept the army at minimum strength through the summer and fall, but a problem that would soon threaten the very existence of the army arose out of the impending termination of its period of enlistment. By 31 December 1775, the engagement of every man in the camp would expire, and the whole army would fade away.

Thus, as the year approached its end, Washington was faced with the necessity of recruiting his army anew. He appealed to the Congress for a more widely representative army--troops from the other colonies--a more truly "continental" force. His goal was a force of 20,000 men enlisted in a new Continental Army, in formations authorized by and responsible to the Congress, not each colony. The Congress in Philadelphia responded by enacting Articles of War, and providing for enlistments of one year--to the end of 1776.

Outside Boston, Washington had to disband one army and create another in the presence of the enemy. He intended that the Continental Army should rise above its origins in part-time militia soldiering to become an instrument of national resolve; disciplined and skilled. Every week that went by produced an improvement in military knowledge, skill, and deportment. While not enough of the militia troops enlisted for the next year to make up the full 20,000-man army he was hoping for, enough did to provide a solid backbone to the fledgling American Continental Army. Washington had turned a rabble into an army!

With the arrival of the fifty-nine pieces of artillery Knox brought down from Fort Ticonderoga in February 1776, along with barrels of powder, flints, lead, and ball, Washington was able to make Boston untenable for the British, who abandoned the city on 17 March 1776.

Washington took his new army to New York, was defeated at Long Island, driven across New Jersey, and then made an attack on Trenton in a brilliant move that saved the cause for independence.

Still, towards the end of 1776, Washington had the same problem of disbandment as the year before. Now, however, the Congress authorized three-year enlistments, or for the duration, which at least provided the general with a more permanent force.

With this Continental Army, supported as needed by militia, Washington defeated the British, we won our independence, and became a great nation upon the earth. The rag, tag, and bobtail troops had done the impossible!

At times of great stress in our nation's history, Americans have always found the courage, strength, spirit, and will to move on to victory. It was so with George Washington, and it is so with us today. Perhaps it is appropriate to come forward to early 1941. The British were alone in a death struggle with Germany, and we were nearly a full year away from Pearl Harbor, but reaching out with our prayers and goods to help. President Franklin Delano Roosevelt, in his Four Freedoms speech on 6 January 1941, said "This nation has placed its destiny in the hands, heads, and hearts of its millions of free men and women, and its faith in freedom under the guidance of God. Freedom means the supremacy of human rights everywhere. Our support goes to those who struggle to gain those rights and keep them. Our strength is in our unity of purpose. To that high concept there can be no end but victory!" Let us then grasp that same concept and relive the days of our struggle to victory in the War of the American Revolution. Just how many days were there between the engagements at Lexington and Concord and Washington's return home? There were 3,172 days between those two events-- nearly nine years.

In many of the sketches will be included some quotations from the Journals of the Continental Congress, as well as from many of the persons of those days. Please, remember that spelling was not as formalized as it is currently, and the reader needs to be aware of these differences, that if noted on each occasion would swamp the work with "sics."

So, Dear Reader, you will find five numbered chapters in this Volume 1; one on The Preliminaries that led us into a war with the mother country, and then each day set forth in four additional chapters (one for each year of the Revolution for this volume, beginning with 1775 through 1778), with an indication of what transpired that day. Each chapter will close with a short precis or summary. Twenty-eight maps and pictures, three appendices, and a bibliography listing the more than four hundred and fifteen sources used during the research, and a complete index round out the work on this Volume 1.

Frederick W. Pyne
Buckingham's Choice
Adamstown, MD 21710
4 July 2008

GLOSSARY

While writing this book, some reviewers suggested including an 18th century military glossary. It is purposely placed with the front matter, so readers might learn about these terms, expressions, and usages.

Abatis
A defensive obstacle of sharpened heavy stakes, points toward the enemy, placed close together, in line and depth, as a part of, and usually in front of fortification.

Approach
The offensive works leading toward the enemy's fort; includes parallels, trenches, saps.

Artificer
Technical personnel skilled in the mechanic arts who make, repair, and recondition all sorts of weapons or articles of war.

Artillery
Generally of three types: Cannon that fire in a flat trajectory; Howitzer fires in a high trajectory; Mortar fires in an arching trajectory.

Bateau
Flat bottomed heavy boat, propelled by oars, poles, or sail, with tapered ends. Used to carry men and supplies on rivers and lakes.

Battalion
A term frequently used interchangeably with regiment to mean a body of three-ten companies, being about 240-700 men. Generally commanded by a colonel, with a lieutenant colonel and a major as the field officers.

Brevet
An honorary rank awarded for bravery. In lieu of the awards and metals presented today. Did not convey command or pay--only the honor.

Brig
A class of sailing vessel with two square rigged masts. Smaller than a ship.

Chevaux -de-frise
A portable defensive obstacle made of large logs bristling with sharpened spikes. Used on land and underwater to hinder movement of the enemy.

Corps
Not the major division of an army, used during and since the Civil War, but a small specialized body.

Counter sign
Password given to all troops in an encampment in response to a challenge. A security measure.

Dragoon	Mounted infantry. Capable of rapid movement, used as a screening unit.
Enfilade	To place units so that their fire attacks the entire length of the enemy line or flank. What one round may miss, it might hit another near or next to it.
Fascine	A bundle of faggots or sticks, portable, used to fill in spaces in a embankment.
Fleche	A small earthen outwork to defend a fortification.
Gabion	A portable wickerwork defense basket Can be filled with dirt or stones.
Gondola	A flat bottomed boat with pointed ends, rigged for both oars and sails.
Jäeger	A German or Hessian soldier equipped with a short barreled rifle. Used in wooded areas and as points.
Parade	That part of a military encampment, fortification, or winter quarters where troops assemble.
Parole	Has two meanings: one is the word given in daily orders in camp or garrison to know friend from foe. The other is the promise and pledge made by a prisoner of war regarding any allowed absence to return, unless exchanged.
Parallels	At a siege the trenches dug to approach the fort, city, or defensive place of the enemy. They are usually numbered as the first parallel, second parallel, each one closer to the enemy's position.
Privateer	Commander of a private vessel given a letter of authorization to seize vessels of the enemy.
Reconnoiter	To examine the ground upon which one expects to do battle. To view the enemy positions.
Redoubt	An outlying earthen trench-like small fortification protecting the main defensive position.
Sappers	Troops trained for tunnel and digging work, who make saps, or tunnels under forts.

I. The Preliminaries

The end of the Great War for Empire (as historians are beginning to refer to what has been styled the French and Indian War or the Seven Years' War), denoted by the Treaty of Paris on 10 February 1763, brought a wonderful sense of relief to the Americans in the colonies. It also brought a wonderful sense of pride in being English to these Colonists in America. The phrase, "the scratch of a pen" used by the great narrative historian, Francis Parkman, is descriptive of the great changes wrought by this event. References for this preliminary period are listed in the Bibliography and the end of this chapter.

No matter that one might be of Welsh, Scots, Irish, English, German, Swiss, Swedish, French, or Dutch extraction--the idea of English habits of speech, of newsprint, of trading, of owning land, or of governance and freedom seemed to be more useful and important to colonists than their former situations.

However, these did not totally wipe away some of the little irritations of class and supposed superiority that the mother country exhibited to her colonies, creating problems that were offensive. In fact, these problems grew worse year by year, as the English Parliament heaped unwonted burdens upon its colonial citizens.

Let us then make a summary list, year by year, of these events that were the preliminaries to our War of the American Revolution.

1763: First was the Proclamation Line, an Act of Parliament of 7 October 1763 which made the ridge of the Appalachian Mountains the dividing line between settlers and Indians. No settlement is to be permitted west of that line, all currently residing there are to "remove themselves" to the east, and all further purchases from the Indian's side of the line are forbidden. A couple is overheard talking to their neighbors about this problem--let's listen. We are John and Elizabeth Greene. We live in the western part of Pennsylvania, in an area of Lancaster County that is far removed from the county seat. We are hopeful that a new county will be erected in a few years, with local government closer to us. Right now, in 1764, we have recently heard about this new Proclamation Line. It was posted at the nearby tavern and our neighbor told us about it yesterday. It seems that the Parliament in England has imposed upon us a requirement that disallows any settlement west of the Appalachians, and forces us to move back to the east side of the mountains. We are very disturbed! My husband had been out here during the old French War, both as a drover with the Braddock Expedition, and later with cutting the Forbes road over the mountains. He liked the nice land he saw. It is free, or nearly so, to those with the energy and vision to work and protect it. Sure, we had trouble with the Indians the first winter we came, but they have now all pretty well been beaten back. We'll be damned if we'll give up and come back east! To the devil with the Parliament and the Indian Commissioners!

1764: The Revenue Act of 5 April 1764, more popularly called the Sugar Act. Its purpose was to raise revenues from America to defray the costs of the Old French War. Duties were laid on molasses, British textiles and imported wines. It also doubled the duty on foreign goods shipped to America, and expanded the list of dutiable goods, while banning certain imports into America.

1765: The infamous Stamp Act of 22 March 1765. A direct tax on all newspapers, broadsides, licenses, ship's papers, and legal documents, by means of documentary stamps required to be purchased from appointed stamp agents. Let's listen in on Sarah Weston, as she describes her concerns about this Act. I own and run a nice inn and tavern in Edenton, North Carolina. My husband and I started this some 10 to 12 years ago, and it has enjoyed a fine reputation, especially among the lawyers and young professionals who come here for the Court Sessions. He died and left the place to me--it is my sole means of support I am Sarah Catherine Weston. During these past weeks here during the August court session of 1765, I have heard frequent and sometimes violent arguments about this new enactment of the Parliament--the Stamp Act. As I understand it, every deed, every issue at law or equity, all newspapers, all licenses (including my own tavern, food and liquor permits), every document of any sort whatsoever will require a documentary stamp of some prescribed denomination to be affixed before it becomes legal. This affects the cost of doing business to almost everyone everywhere, and is widely seen as an unapproved tax imposed by the British upon us, without our prior knowledge or consent. It is an abomination-- away with it!

1766: While the Parliament did abandon the Stamp Act in the face of massive opposition, they could not resist slapping the Declaratory Act of 18 March 1766 on the colonies. It asserted that the Parliament had full authority to make laws binding the American colonists "in all cases whatsoever." This becomes a real sore point within the decade!

1767: Sometimes called the Intolerable Acts, the Townsend Acts of 29 June 1767 laid import duties on glass, lead, paints, paper, and tea. Hear what a pair of small dry goods shopkeepers have to say about this action. We are Caroline and Josepha Howland, sisters of Philadelphia. We have a fine dry goods and import business. Now, in the fall of 1767, comes news of the Townsend Acts. These are a series of enactments that impose import duties on glass, paints, lead, paper, and tea. How is one supposed to conduct business when some outside official thrusts his nose into your affairs--puts his hand in your pockets-without your consent? We are very much opposed to these new attempts by a legislative body 3,000 and more miles away telling us--no, dictating to us--how and what will be taxed or dutied to provide revenue for their purposes, not ours. This must stop!

1768: The Quartering Act of 1 October 1768 is passed. Two Regiments of British troops arrived in Boston and are quartered in both public buildings and private homes. We should hear what a New Yorker thinks of this. My name is Abigail Delafield. I keep a small house in the City of New York, and have just read about the Quartering Act passed by Parliament this past autumn of 1768, requiring--requiring, mind you--that homeowners in Boston provide bed and board to British troops sent over for our protection by order of Parliament. Well, I don't mind telling you, I think that is disgraceful! While I don't happen to live in Boston, I realize that same thing could just as well happen here in New York, or anywhere else, for that matter. Can you imagine having to put up with a bunch of rowdy, slovenly, ill-mannered soldiers in your own home, without your consent, and with minimum (and sometimes no) reimbursement for your food outlay and preparation?

1769: Governor Botentort of Virginia, in response to actions of the Virginia Assembly in condemning the Parliament regarding both taxes and transportation of accused persons to England for trial, dissolved the Assembly on 17 May 1769. Members met the next day in Williamsburg's Raleigh Tavern. This would happen again with another, later Royal Governor.

1770: The famous Boston Massacre of 5 March 1770 occurs when the British guard fired upon a crowd in King Street, killing three and wounding nine persons. This news is widely and quickly spread throughout the colonies. Listen to a woman from a nearby colony express her views. I am Hannah Trowbridge and live in Newport, Rhode Island. Just yesterday, March 5, 1770, some British soldiers, quartered up in Boston, fired on a group of citizens in King Street. The broadside today reported that three men were killed, and nine other persons were wounded by this attack upon the citizenry of Boston. It is an affront! It is a massacre! It is a destruction of our rights as British citizens, and an attack upon our very lives and our freedom! These acts and enactments, year after year, are increasingly seen as separating us from our former pride in English law and monarchy. If King and Country can no longer look upon us as proper citizens and equals in the eyes of the Law, then perhaps some other, more acceptable means of governing may have to be found!

<u>1771:</u> A North Carolina enactment, called the Johnson Bill of 15 June 1771, made "rioters" guilty of treason. This led to the Battle of the Alamance, where frontier folk were obliged to take an oath of allegiance to the government.

<u>1772:</u> A serious threat to any local self-rule was the Crown Salaries Act of 13 June 1772. Governor Hutchinson of Massachusetts announced that he and all judges would henceforth receive their salaries directly from the crown, thus rendering the executive and the judiciary independent of the legislative, with accountability only to the crown--not to the people or their legislative assembly.

<u>1773:</u> Parliament passed the Tea Act on 10 May 1773 in efforts to support the East India Tea Company. This required the payment of a small duty for tea shipped to America. Refusing to pay any duty on imported tea, a group of Bostonians, loosely dressed as Indians, on the night of 16 December 1773, boarded three tea ships in the harbor and dumped 342 chests overboard. No other property was damaged. Listen to the reaction from as far away as South Carolina. We are Susan and James Manigault. We run a fine drapery and furniture business here in Charleston. Mrs. Mainigault takes care of the drapery and cloth end of the business, and I make, repair, and sell quality furniture. Just the other day, the packet boat from New England brought news of the Boston Tea Party. It seems that a group of merchants and citizens of that town, disgusted with the imposition of a tax on East India Company imported tea, dumped 342 chests of it from three ships into the harbor. Nothing else was damaged. We here, throughout the southern colonies, fully support our northern brothers in this action! The Parliament continues to pay little or no attention to our requirements. None of them, I believe, have ever set foot on this side of the Ocean, so what can they know of our needs?

<u>1774:</u> The Boston Port Bill of 31 March 1774. An angry Parliament, in response to the Boston Tea Party, prohibited the loading or unloading of any ships, except military stores, in any part of Boston Harbor, thus closing down the commerce of the city. Let us hear from a lady in Maryland, and her reaction to the news of this action. My name is Julia Williams Stockton. I manage a growing seamstress business in Baltimore, Maryland. We are very much in support of the Sons of Liberty springing up all around us. Last year, the tea ship *Peggy Stewart* was unloaded in Chesapeake Bay. An express rode into town last night, and today, Thursday, June 7, 1774, the broadside came out to inform us about Parliament's enactment of the Boston Port Bill, wherein, in response to the Boston Tea Party, the entire harbor was closed to any loading or unloading of ships of any kind, size, or flag. In other words, the Port of Boston was shut down! Goods, foodstuffs, money from towns and villages all around this area are being assembled to help

relieve the poor, blockaded people of Boston. It is a terrible thing, is it not, that our British brethren should treat us so miserably?

Following the Boston Port Bill, the parliament, not content with that action, comes up with the Massachusetts Government Act of 20 May 1774. That Act annulled the Massachusetts Charter, by appointing the House of Representatives, rather than allowing an election. They were appointed by the King to serve "at pleasure," thereby removing any true local representation in the colony. Other colonies quickly came to the support of Massachusetts and Boston, sending food, money, and other goods. Calls for intercolonial meetings came from several sources.

The First Continental Congress met in Philadelphia at Carpenter's Hall, from 5 September 1774 to 26 October 1774. Twelve of the Colonies (Georgia could not make it) sent 56 delegates. They endorsed the so-called Suffolk Resolves, which declared the Coercive Acts unconstitutional, urged the formation of a locally elected government for Massachusetts, advised the people of the colonies to arm themselves and form their own militia, and recommended strong economic sanctions against Britain. They also called for the convening of another congress at Philadelphia on 10 May 1775, if Britain had not by then addressed the issues and grievances set forth by the Americans in the various petitions, resolutions, and letters that had already been dispatched. The territory of the thirteen colonies along the eastern seaboard of the Atlantic coast is somewhat uncertain, but is generally accepted as the Appalachian ridge. The bounds of each colony are also somewhat indistinct. [See Fig. I-1, p. 6].

The Massachusetts Provincial Congress, a shadow group that soon became the de facto government of the Colony, on 26 October 1774, adopted a comprehensive military program based upon the existing militia system. It directed militia officers to reorganize their commands into more efficient units and to conduct new elections (so as to remove Tory leaning people, and replace them with Patriots). They were also to set aside the most able-bodied and agile men to the number of about one quarter of any force who were also willing to undergo additional training and drill, and be ready to respond in an emergency, thus creating minute companies, also known as Minutemen. Supplies are collected. Weapons, ammunition and military stores are located throughout the colony.

1775: Reaction in Britain to news arriving from America about local New England colonial organizations, committees of various sorts, and militia drilling was rapid and firm. A declaration by both Houses of Parliament on 6 February 1775

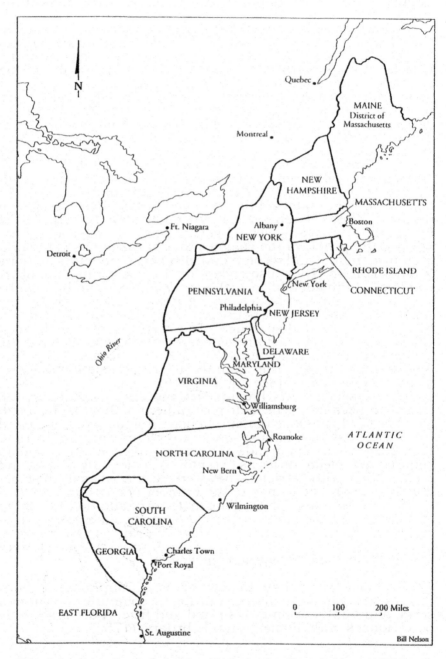

Fig. I-1: American Colonies Before the Revolution, 1775

labeled the Colony of Massachusetts to be in rebellion. This was quickly followed on 20 March 1775 by the New England Restraining Act, which forbade all the New England colonies to trade with any nation or place other than Britain, and also barring all of them from the North Atlantic fisheries.

On 5 April 1775, the Massachusetts Provincial Congress, wishing to augment its militia with a more permanent force, adopted regulations for a Constitutional Army. An army, not just a loose group of village and town militia companies! Delegates were also sent to the other New England colonies to urge their participation in what quickly comes to be known as the New England Army. Having done the most that they feel is possible, including the appointment of general officers and the election of field grade officers, the Provincial Congress adjourns on 15 April 1775.

Thus, we now have viewed, year by year, the Preliminaries to our War of the American Revolution. Things were all set for the lighting of the powder keg!

How did we Americans, feeling so proud to be British subjects and supporters of King and Country at the end of the French and Indian War in 1763, come to a view that abandoned that feeling? In fact, we threw over King and Country, set up a whole new state, formed new governments, and became completely independent of Great Britain. Was that not a fearful thing? What forms of governance could or would we create to fill the void of monarchical rule under which we had lived for more than a century? If the confrontation should come to arms, how will we find, train and arm the troops required to defend our homes? Even if we should attempt to separate ourselves, would not royal authorities come down upon us like wolves on sheep? How could we beat the strongest navy and the best army in the world?

I have often wondered what it was, and how it came to be, that the settlers who became colonial Americans arrived at views, brought down to us today, that we now consider the proper mode of dealing with our neighbors, with our fellow citizens, and even with other peoples in other countries. Most of these views are embodied in our Constitution.

Some of these views are: that what you believe could be different from what I believe; that your choice of religious practice could be different from mine; that your political views could be different from mine, and I will fight to the death to protect your right to those differences. Perhaps it is possible that we can also do very nicely, thank you, without monarchial, and without hereditary rule.

Maybe it was the sense of responsibility that coming to and taming a wilderness provided. Perhaps it was the self-sufficiency that was required to survive in that new environment. Perhaps it was the love of independence and liberty that came from doing things for oneself, rather than relying upon some authority.

It may also be that the mother country, Great Britain, was itself a major contributor to the split. Why is it that they could not have come to some understanding and accommodation to the needs and requirements of the colonists? It has been said that this failure of effort and imagination on the part of the leaders in England may have been "the greatest blunder in the history of British statecraft."

John Adams had said something about this: "The revolution was in the hearts and minds of the people, before the war." Perhaps it was so.

Works cited in the Bibliography will prove useful to readers seeking fuller information and deeper insights into this dozen years between the Great War for Empire, ending with the treaty of Paris in February 1763, and the opening fights at Lexington-Concord that begins the era of the War of the American Revolution. These works are: Anderson, Fred, *Crucible of War: The Seven Years War and the Fate of Empire in British North America, 1754-1776*; Borneman, Walter R., *The French & Indian War; Deciding the Fate of North America*, Bridenbaugh, Carl, *Cities in Revolt*; Carp, Benjamin L., Rebels Rising: *Cities and the American Revolution*; Phillips, Kevin, *The Cousin's Wars, Religion, Politics, and the Triumph of Anglo-America*; Taylor, Alan, *The Divided Ground: Indians, Settlers, and the Northern Borderland of the American Revolution*; Ellis, Joseph J., *American Creation; Triumphs and tragedies at the Founding of the Republic*, (Alfred A. Knopf, New York, 2007).

II. The Year 1775

19 April 1775:

Wednesday. As early as Saturday, 15 April, the flank companies of the 5th, 10th, 18th, 23rd, 38th, 43rd, 52nd, and 59th Regiments of the British Army quartered in Boston, Massachusetts are ordered relieved of their normal duties. Boats are taken from the British vessels in the harbor, repaired, and placed in readiness for use. All this activity alerts the Patriots that something might be afoot, so they patrol and watch for suspicious movements of these British troops in their midst. By dark of Tuesday evening on 18 April, Lieutenant General Thomas Gage informs Lord Percy that the object of a British mission is to seize and destroy military stores located at Concord. The troops assigned to this mission, to the number of about 700, are rowed across the Charles River to Lechmere's Point (now East Cambridge) where they wade ashore. Paul Revere and William Dawes are sent out to raise the alarm between Boston and Concord as early as 10 o'clock that night. Dr. Samuel Prescott joins Revere and Dawes after midnight. Only Prescott reaches Concord. Revere is seized by a British patrol and Dawes is forced to return to Lexington. [See Fig II-2, p. 10]. Other riders are sent out to alert the population in other places and the word spreads very rapidly throughout Massachusetts, and the other New England colonies, and shortly into all the other colonies.

In the dark of the pre-dawn hours of the morning, Lieutenant Colonel Francis Smith and Marine Major John Pitcairn lead this British contingent through Menotomy to Lexington. There, on the Green, as the dawn is just breaking, Pitcairn, leading the advance, finds Captain John Parker with 77 militiamen, [See Appendix 1, p. 1027], lined up in battle order. Pitcarin orders the rebels to "Throw down your arms." Parker orders his men to disperse. The Americans start to turn and move away. A shot is fired. The British regulars fire a volley and charge with their bayonets. Just about then, Smith arrives on the scene with the balance of the troops, and order is restored. Eight militiamen are dead, and nine others wounded. One British private is slightly wounded, and Pitcairn's horse has two minor flesh wounds. This is the Battle of Lexington! [See Fig. II-3, p. 11].

After telling his Officers that their mission is to find and destroy arms in Concord, and firing a victory salute, Smith marches his column out of Lexington toward their destination. Arriving about 7 o'clock, the units disperse to the South Bridge, the North Bridge, and the jail and inn in the town center. Limited stores are found and burnt. Near the North Bridge, groups of patriots assemble and are fired on by the British, under Lieutenant Gould. Colonel Buttrick, commanding the patriot militia, orders a return firing . Nine regulars, including four officers, fall in this first volley. It seems that the vaunted British redcoats can be overcome! This is the "shot heard 'round the world".

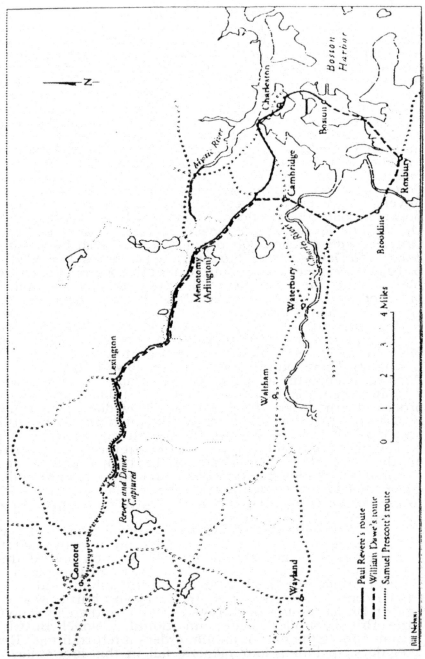

Fig. II-2: Routes of the Alarm Riders

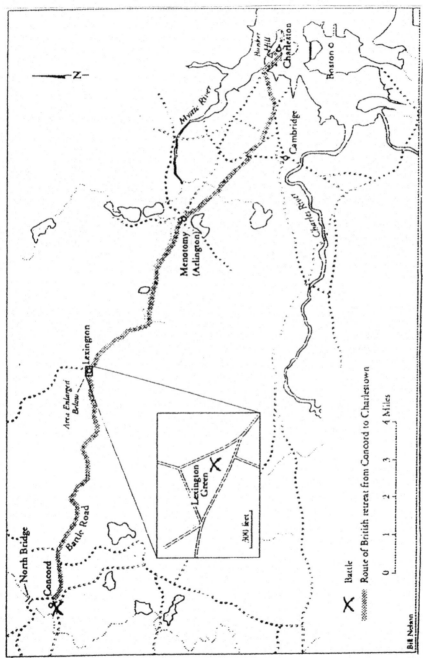

Fig. II-3: Battles of Lexington and Concord, 19 April 1775

By noon, Smith, aware that he is being surrounded and outnumbered, organizes his command for departure. He has found little--certainly nothing worth the deaths on both sides and the patriot anger he is leaving behind. The Lexington Alarm causes arousal of militia groups from many other towns throughout New England, some as far away as Connecticut and Rhode Island. The British column is soon under attack by musketry from behind stone fences, trees, and homes, by hundreds of Patriot militia. It is a gauntlet run of nearly 18 miles back toward Boston. A relief column under Lord Hugh Percy is sent out and helps to rescue Smith's troops from possible annihilation at Lexington, where they rest and reorganize.

The combined British force continues on shortly after 2 o'clock in the afternoon, but they are still under attack by what are now thousands of men creating a moving ring of fire from Patriot muskets. On and on the column moves; hungry, thirsty, running out of ammunition, tired--bone tired--on beyond Lexington, Munroe Tavern, Menotomy, toward the bridge over the Charles River near Cambridge. There is nearly a mile and a half of continuous fierce firing, battle, smoke, running, shouting, the Americans each trying to get in a shot or two; the regulars trying to keep the Patriots at a distance.

Percy decides it is better to get his force close to British ships and their guns as quickly as possible. The Patriots have pried up the boards of the Charles River bridge and thrown them in the river. In order to avoid the bridge, and get away from the intense rebel fire on a route that would be shorter and much safer, Percy takes a side track onto the Charlestown Peninsula, and the troops hunker down in the shadow of the British fleet. It is now about 8 o'clock, nearing dusk. It rains that night. The British regulars lie down, sprawled upon the ground on and near Bunker Hill. Their loss for the day is about 14% of those engaged. The Patriot's loss, about 3 %. It has been a long day.

20 April 1775:

Thursday. During the next morning, the British take the wounded and tired troops from the Lexington and Concord raid, off the Charlestown Peninsula, and ferry them back to hospitals or their barracks in Boston for rest and refitting.

The alarms that were spread so rapidly by many riders, have reached very far in a short period of time. Israel Bissel is one of these post riders. He is sent by Colonel Joseph Palmer to request that "all persons are desired to furnish him with horses, as they may be needed" for him to carry the news to Connecticut and beyond.

Some militia companies collect themselves under their elected leaders and come to the Boston area as a unit; other men come as individuals in response to the call. The British regulars, both those on the Charlestown Peninsula and those in Boston itself, find themselves quickly surrounded and enclosed by the large and growing New England Patriot militia. Israel

Putnam of Connecticut arrives at Cambridge. He has ridden about 100 miles in 18 hours!

In Williamsburg, Lord John Murray, Earl of Dunmore, Royal Governor of Virginia, orders the Royal Marines to take gunpowder from the public magazine.

21 April 1775:

Friday. Israel Bissel, one of several post riders carrying news of the British raids on Lexington and Concord, leaves New London, Connecticut, just after midnight. Spreading the word quickly, he rides all night, getting fresh horses as he goes, and grabbing a little food and drink as opportunity affords. He is through Lyme, Saybrook, Guilford, along the shore of Long Island Sound, as he continues west. He is in Branford by 10 o'clock in the morning, and New Haven by noon.

New Hampshire militia march to Cambridge as they learn about the fights at Lexington and Concord.

Patriots in South Carolina seize all the gunpowder from the State House and from the Hobcaw and Cochran's Magazines in Charleston, although they have yet to hear of Lexington and Concord.

In response to Dunmore's order, about 3 o'clock this morning, a patrol of Royal Marines, under Captain Henry Collins of the armed schooner *Magdalen*, comes from Burwell's Ferry, on the James River, and quietly removes and carries back to the vessel 15 half-barrels of Virginia militia gunpowder stored in the magazine. Since this magazine had been constructed at the public expense, and the munitions in it belong to Virginia, the taking of it, in secret, is highly disapproved of by most Virginians. The incident sparks a distaste of the Royal Governor, and engenders further discontent among the citizens of the colony.

22 April 1775:

Saturday. In Boston, British General Thomas Gage, pens a report to the Earl of Dartmouth, noting the arrival of several vessels, and describing the British defeat and retreat from Concord, wherein he says "... that they were at length a good deal pressed. Lord Percy then arrived opportunely to their assistance with his Brigade and two pieces of cannon, and not withstanding a continual skirmish for the space of fifteen miles, receiving fire from every hill, fence, barn, &ca. His Lordship kept the enemy off, and brought the troops to Charlestown, from whence they were ferried over to Boston. Too much praise cannot be given Lord Percy for his remarkable activity and conduct during the day ... I have likewise the honor to transmit your Lordship a Return of the killed, wounded, and missing. The whole country was assembled in arms with surprising expedition and several thousand are now assembled about this Town threatening an attack, and getting up artillery."

Governor Dunmore threatens to free enslaved Negroes if any British officials come to any harm resulting from Patriot actions of any sort whatsoever.

23 April 1775:
    Sunday. Because the militia that first responded to the Lexington Alarm had been called up for only short term service, the Massachusetts Provincial Congress, the de facto government of the colony outside British control of Boston, meeting in Watertown, authorizes the raising of 13,600 men, and appeals to the other New England colonies of Connecticut, Rhode Island, and New Hampshire for aid. (At this time, Maine is a district of Massachusetts and Vermont is disputed territory claimed by New York and New Hampshire), These colonies vote to send 9,500 men to Cambridge. Each will provide three regiments, while Massachusetts provides 24 regiments, all under the command of Artemas Ward. Known as the Eight Months Army, this force comes to over 12,000 men!
    Today, Sabbath or no, Israel Bissel is riding into and through New York City about 4 o'clock in the afternoon, with the striking news of the British incursion to Lexington and Concord. On receipt of this news, a group of patriots seize the arsenal and arm themselves with 600 muskets.

24 April 1775:
    Monday. In Worcester, Massachusetts, about 40 miles west of Boston, John Hancock and Samuel Adams arrive by coach, having escaped from Lexington on the very day of the fight, on their way to the Second Continental Congress assembling in Philadelphia.
    The Fredericksburg, Virginia officers of the Independent Militia Company write to complain of the theft of the gunpowder from the public magazine at Williamsburg. "That a submission to so arbitrary an exertion of Government may not only prejudice the common cause by introducing a suspicion of a defection of this Colony from the noble pursuit but will encourage the tools of despotism to commit further acts of violence."

25 April 1775:
    Tuesday. The Rhode Island Assembly votes to raise an army of 1,500 men in support of the request of the Massachusetts Provincial Congress for assistance in the siege of Boston. In a short while Connecticut and New Hampshire will also add their militia strength to the effort. Thus, this lose body of militia becomes known as the New England Army.
    In the early hours of the morning, Israel Bissel, riding fast, brings his news of the fights in New England to Germantown and Philadelphia. Later in the day nearly 8,000 people at a town meeting in Philadelphia resolve to defend their property, liberty, and lives with arms.
    Patriots in Baltimore, Maryland seize military supplies from the local arsenal. These kinds of actions—Americans throwing over the authority of a monarch many miles away, who seems to have little or no real interest in their welfare, and to grasp the reins of governance for themselves, happen all over the colonies.

26 April 1775:
Wednesday. Major Pitcairn prepares his report of the action on 19 April 1775 for Lieutenant General Thomas Gage. It is not pretty!

In Connecticut, the Provincial Assembly votes to raise troops for an army of 6,000 men to assist in the New England confrontation with the British at Boston.

The New York Committee of 60 proposes an expansion of their numbers to 100. They feel that this will provide for both a wider representation of the populace, and will also give more weight to their proposals and proclamations.

27 April 1775:
Thursday. In Williamsburg, Virginia, Peyton Randolph, a strong patriot and delegate to the Continental Congress, writing for the Corporation of the City of Williamsburg, to Mann Page, a member of the House of Burgesses, recites the business of the theft of the gunpowder from the magazine, and hopes that "matters may be quieted for the present." Notice how there is still a major concern that the issue of control, sharing power, and loyalty to the King is present in the language of these patriots.

28 April 1775:
Friday. The New York Committee of 60 (soon to be formally expanded to 100), seeking a more permanent revolutionary governing body, asks for replacement of the current ineffective Provisional Congress.

By sundown, the shocking news of the British regulars and American Patriots fighting at Lexington and Concord has reached the Potomac River.

In Williamsburg, Virginia, an express rider canters into town late at night, waking the populace with the news of the British raids on Lexington and Concord, and the militia's successful reaction in chasing them back to Boston.

29 April 1775:
Saturday. As a Captain of Connecticut militia, Benedict Arnold, arrives in Cambridge, Massachusetts, with his company of Patriots.

In Orange County, New York, a general association is formed to assure the execution of measures advocated by the Continental Congress and the New York Provincial Congress.

30 April 1775:
Sunday. Fired with a desire to do something, and having served in the French and Indian War in upper New York, Benedict Arnold is soon talking to the Massachusetts Committee of Safety about the idea of capturing Fort Ticonderoga, an area he knows well. He points out that this British Fort, still has a goodly number of artillery pieces, badly needed by the patriot forces. There are also flints and gunpowder, and best of all, very few enemy troops.

1 May 1775:
    Monday. The New York Committee, now expanded to 100, recommends that each man arm himself with a weapon and seek training in its use and care, and learn something of military discipline.

2 May 1775:
    Tuesday. The Committee of Public Safety in Cambridge, Massachusetts concludes its discussion with Benedict Arnold, intending to prepare orders for the capture of Fort Ticonderoga.
    In Virginia, governor Patrick Henry calls out the colony's Militia to protect the Capital at Williamsburg from British raids or incursions. The recent actions of Royal Governor Dunmore have so angered and disturbed the populace that there is a great uncertainty regarding any future acts he might order.

3 May 1775:
    Wednesday. The Massachusetts Committee of Safety appoints Benedict Arnold a Colonel of Militia with authority to raise "not exceeding 400 men" in western Massachusetts for an attack upon Fort Ticonderoga, to "reduce the same.," taking possession of "the cannon, mortars, stores, & ca..."
    In London, the Earl of Dartmouth instructs the colonial Governor of North Carolina, Josiah Martin, to raise militias and organize an association of loyalists. Evidence of just how far out of touch those in London are with the situation in America, is the fact that, at the same time, patriot militia are gathering around him, Martin sends to Thomas Gage in Boston, back in March, for arms and ammunition. Martin is also now getting his family ready to leave for New York, and will himself leave by the end of the month.

4 May 1775:
    Thursday. The Pennsylvania Assembly rejects Lord North's proposal for conciliation.
    Cadwallader Colden, of New York, writes to both Lord North and Lord Dartmouth in London, to inform them of the "state of annarchy [sic] and Confusion into which this Province has run since the actual Commencement of Hostilities."
    The Rhode Island legislature passes a resolution renouncing allegiance to King George III of England.

5 May 1775:
    Friday. Benjamin Franklin, with his grandson Temple, arrives in Philadelphia after a six week crossing on the packet boat from England. Both will be wonderful future assents for the emerging new American nation. Franklin, because he knows Britain and the British well, Temple, because he has become quite a linguist.
    A Naval action off Martha's Vineyard, Massachusetts takes place in which the British sloop of war *Falcon*, of 16 guns, captures two American sloops--which are soon recaptured by two hastily fitted out American vessels.

6 May 1775:
Saturday. Benedict Arnold learns that Ethan Allen is raising a force at Castleton, Vermont, for the purpose of an attack on Fort Ticonderoga, and hurries there to claim command under the authority of his Massachusetts Commission.

New Jersey Governor William Franklin, in a letter to the Earl of Dartmouth, reports that the fight at Lexington on 19 April greatly diminished any chance of accommodation or reconciliation with the colonies.

Benjamin Franklin, having arrived back in America the day before, is informed that the Pennsylvania Assembly has selected him as one of its deputies to the Second Continental Congress, which is expected to meet in Philadelphia four days hence.

7 May 1775:
Sunday. Benjamin Franklin, writes to his son, William Franklin, the Royal Governor of New Jersey, to encourage him to support the idea of American independence. Considering just how fixed is the young Franklin's view of monarchy and its trappings, it is interesting to note that the father still had hopes of "rescuing" the son to the patriot cause.

The news of the fight at Lexington, Massachusetts, reaches North Carolina.

8 May 1775:
Monday. The brigantine *Industry* brings news of the battles at Lexington and Concord fifteen days earlier, up in Massachusetts, to Charleston, South Carolina.

The Bucks County, Pennsylvania Committee of Safety urges the Townships to form militia groups.

Benedict Arnold arrives at Castleton and tries to wrest the leadership of the expedition against Fort Ticonderoga from Ethan Allen on the basis of his Massachusetts Commission. Since Arnold has no troops, Allen rejects his claims for a full command, but does allow Arnold to assume a sort of joint command. They travel southwest towards Fort Ticonderoga.

9 May 1775:
Tuesday. Arriving at Hand's Cove, across from Fort Ticonderoga, late at night, the Allen-Arnold group searches for boats to carry them across Lake Champlain. They can locate only two craft, so select only a portion of their force to cross early in the morning.

10 May 1775:
Wednesday. Patriot militia forces under Ethan Allen and Benedict Arnold with only the 83 troops that they can carry in the two boats they have collected, row across the narrow portion of Lake Champlain at Fort Ticonderoga, in the very early morning. The boats are sent back for more men, but there is no time to waste if surprise is to be achieved. Because the south wall of the fort is in a ruinous condition, the men swarm through and over the ruins to the curtain at the main gate.

There a single sentry points his musket, which flashes in the pan. The sentry runs onto the place d'Armes shouting "alarm" with the Americans close behind, yelling like Indians. Allen and Arnold dash up the staircase in the west barracks to the door of the Post Commander's Quarters, shouting for him to come out. Captain William De la Place, with a small force of only 42 total personnel, is not in a position to refuse to surrender. Thus is captured this important post with all its military stores of artillery and gunpowder, items that will prove most useful in the near future.

The Committee of Safety of Tryon County, New York, meets in the Cherry Valley Church, where Articles of Association are drafted. Similar documents are being prepared throughout the colonies. Their purpose is to determine one's political leaning. Signing such a document, indicates support for the patriot cause; refusing to sign brands one as a Tory.

Dr. Myles Cooper, loyalist president of King's College (later Columbia University), is threatened by a New York group of rebels, but, with the help of Alexander Hamilton, a young student at the college, manages to elude the mob.

The Second Continental Congress assembles in Philadelphia. Peyton Randolph is elected President and Charles Thomson, Secretary.

11 May 1775:
Thursday. Patriots seize gunpowder in the Royal Magazine in Savannah, Georgia.

A group of 30 soldiers under Samuel Herrick from the Ethan Allen group at Hand's Cove capture the village of Skenesboro (now Whitehall, New York) along with its mills and shipyard.

12 May 1775:
Friday. The New England delegates to the Second Continental Congress try to persuade the Congress to adopt the New England army around Boston. They argue that these four colonies are acting to protect themselves from British aggression, and in doing so are acting to defend all the colonies. Adoption of the troops around Boston would remove the regional cast of the conflict and also broaden the base for support of any military action.

Under Seth Warner, patriots from Ethan Allen's group capture the British post at Crown Point, consisting of a garrison of one sergeant, eight privates, and ten women and children. All of them are taken without resistance.

13 May 1775:
Saturday. The Provincial Congress of Massachusetts appoints a committee to establish a postal system.

Captain John Brown and Captain Eleazer Oswald arrive at Fort Ticonderoga with a small schooner and several bateaux captured at Skenesboro, along with 50 recruits and a few prisoners. This is particularly pleasing to Benedict Arnold, who now has some troops of his own to command. Also, Arnold is a sailor, Allen is not. Therefore there is no objection to Arnold's having command of a naval squadron for an expedition to the Canadian post at St. John's, north on the Richelieu River.

In the Mohawk Valley, at his home in Johnson Hall, Sir John Johnson, who had disbanded his adherents nearly four months ago and given his parole that he would remain under the orders of the Continental Congress, breaks his parole, and with a body of supporters flees to Canada.

14 May 1775:

Sunday. The New York Committee of 100, orders the citizens of Staten Island and nearby New Jersey to halt the illicit sale of provisions to the British ships, a few of which are still in the harbor.

Near Fort St. John's, Canada, about 50 patriots under Benedict Arnold prepare plans to make a surprise attack upon the garrison of 15 British soldiers. Arnold has some vessels that will serve to carry most of his men, and any of the captured number of the enemy, if he can achieve the surprise he needs.

15 May 1775:

Monday. In Philadelphia, James Duane, a delegate from New York, introduces a letter from the New York Committee of 100, reporting a concern that British troops are on their way to the city, and requesting Congressional advice. Not really having a good idea of just what to do about the situation, Congress appoints a committee to consider defensive needs. On the committee is a Virginia delegate: George Washington.

In Richmond, Virginia, the Convention issues instructions to the Colony's delegation in Philadelphia to propose independence. While most patriots are certainly annoyed, even angry at the English Parliament, the idea of actually separating themselves from the mother country is too radical a step at this early stage in the conflict. This is the first occasion when an official colony body recommends such an action.

16 May 1775:

Tuesday. Congress forms itself into a Committee of the Whole, to take into consideration the "State of America." Now they start using expressions like America instead of Separate Colonies, and United Colonies instead of naming them all. A sense of common purpose, with common problems to be solved, and common goals to be achieved appears. Delegates from widely separated colonies, who have grown up in different geographic climes, and have very different political and social backgrounds had difficulty opening themselves up to others. Now, they are a bit more trustful of each other.

Richard Henry Lee of Virginia makes a motion that the Congress "raise an army". There is opposition, but there is also support. No action is taken on this motion, but it is clear that there is growing congressional support for some form of united defensive military posture.

The Committee for Westmoreland County, in Hannastown, Pennsylvania, sends resolutions declaring that it is the duty of Americans to resist British oppression and form a defense association.

At Fort Pitt a Committee of Virginians, acting in the name of the inhabitants of Augusta County, Virginia, (this area was in dispute between Pennsylvania and Virginia at the time), also hold a meeting, with similar resolves.

17 May 1775:
Wednesday. The New York Provincial Congress this day assumes the functions of government. This type of action has and will be ongoing for all the 13 colonies, as each becomes the de facto governing body of the area each virtually controls.

Benedict Arnold, approaching with 35 men who have rowed through the night and early morning in two bateaux, surprises and captures the Canadian post of St. John's (St. Jean) on the Richelieu River. The garrison includes a Sergeant, 14 men, and a 70-ton sloop (HMS *George III*, 16 guns), with a crew of seven. Because Arnold learns that the fort at Chambly, just 12 miles away, is expecting 200 reinforcements to arrive shortly, he leaves with the more valuable supplies and heads south for Crown Point.

Ethan Allen also wishes for something after his capture of Fort Ticonderoga, so he bethinks to take himself to try St. John's, and follows Arnold's route up the lake with 90 men in four bateaux. The two expeditions-- Arnold's coming south and Allen's heading north-meet about six miles south of St. John's. Allen is informed that the place has already been taken, its garrison is in irons in the hold of Arnold's vessel, and the post abandoned. Allen, however, feels he could re-occupy it and hold it. He fails.

18 May 1775:
Thursday. News of the capture of Fort Ticonderoga reaches the Continental Congress. The impact of this aggressive military move (no longer a strictly defensive posture), is to snap the delegates into a more assertive view of their duties toward providing support for military action. They conclude that it is quite possible, nay probable, for British forces to come down from Canada and attack the colonies. It is apparent that the line of the Hudson/Champlain Valley is the most critical route for either offense or defense. Therefore, they instruct local communities in Albany and New York City to move military supplies to safety, and to call upon New England for any assistance that might be required in defending Ticonderoga.

Royal Governor Josiah Martin of North Carolina reports to his superiors in London that he is powerless to prevent the people of his colony from forming an army and a government. Yet, this is the same man who assures the British that there are large numbers of Loyalists ready to rise to assist in putting down the rebels.

19 May 1775:
      Friday. Six transports of British Marines arrive in Boston, with new regiments to reinforce Thomas Gage.

20 May 1775:
      Saturday. The Committee of Safety for Cambridge, Massachusetts, votes to refuse to admit slaves into the army being formed.
      In North Carolina, the Mecklenburg Accords, proposing Independency are signed.

21 May 1775:
      Sunday. John Adams writes to colleagues in Massachusetts that many delegates have become convinced the British are hostile. "I can guess that an Army will be posted in New York and another in Massachusetts at Continental Expense."
      Ethan Allen, after a repulse by the reinforced British garrison at St. John's, returns to Fort Ticonderoga.
      The British are rather closely confined to Boston by the siege-like ring of patriot militia all around them. They are in need of forage, vegetables, fresh meat, and provisions. While their fleet does give them the opportunity to control much of the water areas around Boston, they have little means to effect any land excursions. In other words they find themselves in a sort of stand-off. Gage sends four sloops and 30 men to bring in a supply of hay from Grape Island in the harbor. The Americans send three companies to oppose them. There is a brief skirmish, and the British make off with only a few tons of hay. The Americans burn all the rest.
      The Pennsylvania Assembly passes a Declaration of Rights.

22 May 1775:
      Monday. Henry Laurens of Charleston, South Carolina writes that the events at Lexington and Concord have created in South Carolina, "an amazing readiness to contribute to the common cause."

23 May 1775:
      Tuesday. The Second Provincial Congress of New Jersey confirms its allegiance to the Continental Congress.
      New York issues a Declaration of Rights.

24 May 1775:
      Wednesday. John Hancock, delegate from Massachusetts, is elected to be president of the Second Continental Congress, replacing Peyton Randolph who has to return to Virginia.
      Abigail Adams writes to her husband, John, who has gone to Philadelphia for the Second Continental Congress, telling him of the difficulties soldiers and civilians are having because of the

shortage of food stuffs. These shortages are the result of the massive number of troops constantly coming and going to besiege the British in Boston. Just too many mouths to feed.

25 May 1775:
Thursday. The British frigate *Cerebus* arrives in Boston Harbor with additional reinforcements for Thomas Gage, including three Major Generals: William Howe, Henry Clinton, and John Burgoyne.

At the Second Continental Congress, the Committee of the Whole presents a report recommending the following: King's Bridge, which links Manhattan Island with the mainland must be fortified; so also must the Hudson Highlands, which protect the connection between New England and the middle colonies; New York's militia must be brought into a state of readiness and the New York Provincial Congress must raise 3,000 men to serve until 31 Dec 1775.

26 May 1775:
Friday. A British naval surgeon visits an American encampment and makes note that the Americans are "a drunken, canting, lying, praying, hypocritical rabble without order." Probably at least partially correct.

The Continental Congress seems to be betwixt and between, not knowing whether to seek reconciliation with Great Britain or make serious preparations for fighting. They resolve both to begin preparations for military defense, **and** to prepare what is called the "Olive Branch Petition" to King George III. The resolution declares that the current government is to be styled, "United Colonies of America".

27 May 1775:
Saturday. The British send a 100-man marine detachment in eight barges with an armed naval escort--the schooner *Diana* and a sloop--to raid Hogg Island and Noodle Island in Boston harbor and secure the sheep and cattle that graze on the islands. Local citizen-spies have informed the Americans of this impending attack. Colonel Israel Putnam is sent with 300 men to defend the livestock and prevent their capture. The British force lands first at Noodle Island and chases a company-sized American defense force back to Hogg Island. There the British are confronted by Putnam's main force and return to their barges. [See Fig.III-9, p. 99].

28 May 1775:
Sunday. The British schooner *Diana* runs aground at Hogg Island as the fight continues with the Americans, who are trying to protect the horses, cattle, and sheep at pasture. Americans swarm aboard, capture four 4-pounders and twelve swivels from her, and set her on fire. There has been considerable firing on both sides--four Americans are slightly wounded and 20 British killed.

In the City of Philadelphia, more than 2,000 men turn out for military exercises. This shows real spirit and impresses observers, but it is not the only locale where such actions take place. In little villages and larger cities all throughout the colonies, small groups of militia do the same thing.

Word of the British raids on Lexington and Concord finally arrives in London. A group of cabinet members hasten out of the city to bring the word to King George III, who is with his family at the Royal residence in Kew.

29 May 1775:

Monday. Josiah Martin, Royal Governor of North Carolina, packs up his belongings in preparation for shipment to New York and the protection of the British Navy.

Congress, adopts a resolution urging Canadians to join with them in the revolution against British oppression.

The New York Provincial Congress orders all citizens to sign a General Association, similar to the resolution adopted by Orange County on 29 April 1775.

30 May 1775:

Tuesday. Deputy Quartermaster General William Sherrett complains to his superiors of the serious shortage of food and fuel in Boston.

American forces go back to both Hogg and Noodle's Islands, and carry off several hundred sheep and some cattle left by the British after their skirmishes three days earlier. The Americans also take 800 sheep and some more cattle off of Deer Island.

31 May 1775:

Wednesday. Congress receives a report from Benedict Arnold that the British post at St. John's on the Richelieu River above the northern end of Lake Champlain has been reinforced and troops are massing there. Fearing a possible attack upon Fort Ticonderoga near the southern end of Lake Champlain, Arnold asks the Congress to send troops to defend the fort.

In the Mohawk Valley of New York, Guy Johnson, British Superintendent of Indian Affairs, recruits a large group, including the Butler brothers (John and Walter), Joseph Brant, two of Sir William Johnson's sons, and more than 200 other Indians and whites. They depart from the Valley and head for Canada. Much mischief will later develop from some or all of this group.

A Committee in Charlotte, North Carolina, adopts the Mecklenberg Resolutions, challenging any Royal authority in the colonies, and declaring that any person who accepts a royal commission will be an enemy of the people.

Governor Josiah Martin of North Carolina flees New Bern to take refuge on the British ship *Cruzier* in the Cape Fear River. Never mind that he, as well as others of the Royal Governors of the south, held a view that there were large numbers of Loyalists, waiting to assist defeating the rebels.

1 June 1775:
Thursday. The Continental Congress, concerned over the recently arrived news of the defeat at St. John's and also about any possible attacks by the British on Fort Ticonderoga or New England, resolves that "No further expedition or incursion ought to be made ... against or into Canada." As they are also asking the Canadians to join in the revolution (as they had two days ago), perhaps they thought it best not to be seen as encouraging any aggressive moves in that direction.

2 June 1775:
Friday. The Provincial Congress of South Carolina asserts solidarity with the other colonies.
Massachusetts requests that the Continental Congress assume responsibility for (or adopt) the New England Army at Boston.
Congress creates an Army Pay Department.
The British schooner *Margaretta,* accompanied by the sloops *Polly* and *Unity,* enters the port of Machias, in the district of Maine, for the purpose of loading lumber for the garrison at Boston.

3 June 1775:
Saturday. In Williamsburg, a small group of young patriots attempt to enter the public magazine and make off with some arms. In an ensuing struggle with British soldiers, three of the young men are injured. This, however, is an example of the spirit and elán found among very many Americans, who wish to fight for their rights and liberties, without arms, and take enormous risks to secure the means of soldiering.

4 June 1775:
Sunday. The business with the Canadians seems not to be going well. Ethan Allen sends out a reconnoitering patrol and expresses surprise when they are fired upon and pursued by some Canadians.

5 June 1775:
Monday. Probably as a result of the young men being injured two days ago in Williamsburg, a larger mob of people gather and break into the town magazine. They make off with 400 of the muskets stored there.

6 June 1775:
Tuesday. Those British troops still remaining in New York City are evacuated to transports riding at anchor in the harbor. American Lieutenant Colonel Marius Willet and a small group of the Sons of Liberty seize five wagon loads of weapons after confronting British soldiers, who they found trying to take the arms with them from the city. The Patriots need and must have arms if they are to defend their homes and liberties from the tyranny of the British.

7 June 1775:
    Wednesday. The Provincial Congress of New York approves of the efforts by Patriot officials in Albany to raise a body of troops for the cause. But, as yet not certain of their authority, nor their right to do such a thing, request that no more troops be raised in this manner until further orders. This is a good example of the desire, but hesitancy among the Patriot leaning citizens in many places throughout the colonies.

8 June 1775:
    Thursday. With all the problems he has stirred up, and thus fearing major trouble from the Patriot forces of the Colony of Virginia, John Murray, Governor Dunmore of Virginia flees to the British warship HMS *Fowey* anchored off the York River near Yorktown. This seems to be a bit safer place than Norfolk.

9 June 1775:
    Friday. The Provisional Congress of South Carolina places a prohibition on exports of rice and corn, and begins stockpiling supplies for the future.

10 June 1775:
    Saturday. At the Continental Congress, John Adams proposes the idea of a Continental Army. While no further action is taken on the proposal, the thought begins to ferment among the delegates.

11 June 1775:
    Sunday. A militia body from Brigadier General David Wooster's Connecticut troops raid the Turtle Bay warehouses and magazine, and are able to make off with shot, cannon balls, horse harness, and other needed military supplies.
    American patriots, determined to prevent the British force at Machias, Maine, from accomplishing their mission of obtaining lumber, try to capture a group of them as they worship at church. Midshipman James Moore and some of the officers of the *Margaretta* manage to escape and return to their ship in the harbor. A pursuit by the Americans results in the capture of the sloop *Unity*.

12 June 1775:
    Monday. Further action and a skirmish at the port of Machias, by the Americans yields the capture of the British schooner HMS *Margaretta*.
    Gage issues a proclamation, written by Burgoyne, offering a pardon to all persons who would lay down their arms and return to a state of full loyalty to King and Country, except for "Samuel Adams and John Hancock, whose offenses are of too flagrant a nature to admit of any other consideration than that of condign punishment." It further announces martial law throughout the province, even though the British control nothing outside the limits of the town of Boston. The

preposterous, flamboyant, and pontifical style of the piece arouses both resentment and derision on both sides of the Atlantic.

Rhode Island, through their Assembly, establish a small naval force, commissioning two small vessels: the *Katy* (ten four-pounders, and the *Washington*). The Assembly names Abraham Whipple as commander of this colony naval force.

13 June 1775:

Tuesday. Patriots get wind that Gage is thinking of occupying Dorchester Heights.

14 June 1775:

Wednesday. The Continental Congress, in response to the Massachusetts request of 2 June 1775, agrees to adopt the patriot New England Army surrounding Boston, making it a truly Continental Army. To make it more an American Continental Army, the Congress, also calls for the raising of ten companies of Light Infantry (basically riflemen) to serve in the siege of Boston, thus extending the military participation beyond New England. These companies are allocated as follows: six from Pennsylvania, two from Maryland, and two from Virginia. The enlistment period is set for one year, to expire on 1 July 1776.

15 June 1775:

Thursday. The Second Continental Congress commissions George Washington to be the "Commander of all the forces raised or to be raised" in defense of liberty. He thus becomes the Commander-in-Chief of the American Army in the War of the American Revolution.

Artemas Ward and the Massachusetts Provincial Congress, having learned of British General Gage's proposed plan of seizing Dorchester Heights and of re-occupying the Charlestown Peninsula and nearby areas in order to give his troops some elbow room, determines that the Americans need to fortify Bunker Hill on the Charlestown Peninsula. The patriots, therefore, pre-empt the British move by arranging to send a force to the peninsula. The area had been evacuated earlier by the British shortly after their return from the raid at Concord on 19 April 1775. If the Americans can seize, fortify, and hold a place on the Charlestown Peninsula, they will be in a position to command much of Boston inself.

Naval Commander Abraham Whipple captures two British ships in Providence River, Rhode Island.

16 June 1775:

Friday. George Washington gives his acceptance speech to the Continental Congress. In it he declares himself "not equal to the Command I am honored with." He further declines any salary, but will keep "an exact account of my expenses; those I doubt not they will discharge and that is all I desire."

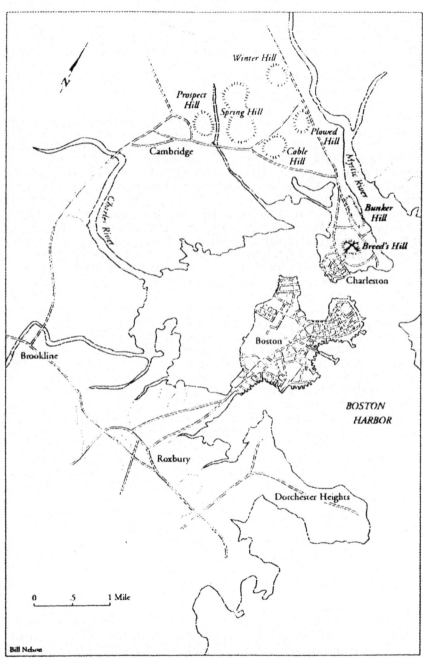

Fig. II-4: Bunker Hill, 17 June 1775

The Continental Congress authorizes a number of senior officer positions (but not the persons) for the new army it is creating: five staff offices, including an adjutant general, a commissary of musters, a paymaster general, a commissary general, and a quartermaster general; also secretaries, aides, and engineers.

The Massachusetts Provincial Congress appoint Colonel Richard Gridley as chief engineer officer to design a defense for Bunker Hill.

Before this day is over, orders are issued for three regiments of Massachusetts State troops, under the command of Colonels William Prescott and Israel Putnam, to assemble near the Charlestown Neck for duties of entrenchment and to erect works for defense against any British attack from that direction.

As darkness falls, about 1,800 patriot troops march onto the Charlestown Peninsula. Colonel Gridley, the engineer officer with the New England army marks and lays out the lines for a defense work on Breed's Hill. This is a slightly lower elevation than the originally intended Bunker Hill, but it is also closer to the British ships in the harbor and to the town of Boston. Thus, it is Breed's Hill that becomes the location of the fortified position the Americans create and defend, not Bunker Hill.

The Americans are astute diggers in the earth. It seems that when their legs are protected from enemy fire, they are quite capable of protracted defense against the disciplined attacks of the British infantry. The methodology of these British infantry attacks are generally to form long, well dressed lines from which battalions of troops march to drums towards an enemy. The British troops are armed with smooth-bore muskets, the effective maximum range of which is about 50–60 yards. It is not the fire of the musket that the British rely upon–that serves only to cover the battlefields with smoke, perhaps kill a few of the enemy, but mainly to allow the still forward marching battalions to get ever closer to the enemy. It is the bayonet, a 16 inch long knife-like extension of the musket, that will do the damage. If the Americans, protected by their earthwork, can shoot down enough British soldiers, before they reach the redoubt they are digging, perhaps they will win the fight.

The digging parties are assigned to specific areas of the marked out lines. Work begins just as soon as the tools are in the hands of the soldiers. Picks, shovels, mattocks, and the outlines of an entrenchment quickly appear. Work goes by shifts, as soon as one party needs a break, a new team steps in to continue. Thus it goes all night long.

17 June 1775:

Saturday. The Prescott-Putnam force have worked through the night to erect an earthwork redoubt on Breed's Hill and extend their breastwork toward the Mystic River. When the sun comes up this morning, the British are thunder struck at what these provincials have done!

Lieutenant General Thomas Gage gives orders to capture or

destroy the American forces dug in on Breed's Hill, placing Major General William Howe in command of about 2,500 regulars for this purpose. They make amphibious landings at Moulton's Point, just north of Charlestown.

The British make two frontal assaults on the American redoubt on Breed's Hill, as well as upon the fence rail extension down to the beach near the Mystic River. The Patriot force is able to withstand these attacks with a withering fire, and throw the ranks of the British troops back down the hill. However, as no reinforcements arrive and no replenishment of ammunition is brought forward, they are not able to stand up to a third assault, and many flee back across the Charlestown Neck. Maj. Gen. Joseph Warren of the Massachusetts militia is shot and killed in this third attack. The results of this bloodbath, called the Battle of Bunker Hill: British, 226 officers and men killed, 828 wounded; American, 145 killed, 304 wounded. A British officer says, "One more such victory and we shall be undone." [See Fig. II-4, p. 27].

George Washington, having verbally accepted the offer, receives the formal commission of the Congress as Commander-in-Chief of a new Continental Army. In efforts to create a more complete structure for the army they had adopted, the Second Continental Congress appoints two major generals, Artemas Ward and Charles Lee, and an adjutant general, Horatio Gates, to assist Washington in his command position.

18 June 1775:
Sunday. Boston shipbuilders refuse to continue with any work on a brig under construction for the British Crown.

In Philadelphia, John Hancock writes to Elbridge Gerry in Watertown, Massachusetts, "Ten Companies of fine Riflemen ... are ordered to proceed immediately to your Army; these are clever fellows." Indeed they are—very few New Englanders have ever seen a performance with a rifle—almost all of them have and use muskets only.

19 June 1775:
Monday. The Congress appoints two more major generals: Philip Schuyler of New York and Israel Putnam of Connecticut. [See Appendix 4, p. 1035]

Gage orders all Boston residents to surrender any firearms they may have, or be considered enemies of His Royal Majesty's government.

Margaret Mansfield, Benedict Arnold's wife, whom he had married in 1767, and by whom he had three sons, dies in Connecticut.

20 June 1775:
Tuesday. George Washington receives his instructions from the Congress. He is requested to "... proceed to Boston, take charge of the army of the united colonies, destroy or capture all armed enemies, prepare and send to the Congress an accurate

strength return, and listen to the advice of a council of war."

Washington, in his first military role as Commander-in-Chief, and at the request of the local politicos, reviews the Philadelphia militia.

Thomas Jefferson of Virginia arrives in Philadelphia, is recognized as a duly elected delegate, and takes a seat in the Continental Congress.

21 June 1775:
Wednesday. Horatio Gates at his home, "Traveller's Rest," near Shepherdstown (in what is now West Virginia) receives orders from Washington to report immediately to Boston.

Nathanael Greene is chosen Brigadier General of the Rhode Island forces.

22 June 1775:
Thursday. The Congress, wishing to complete the general officer list to manage their newly created army, appoints eight brigadier generals: Seth Pomeroy, Richard Montgomery, David Wooster, William Heath, Joseph Spencer, John Thomas, John Sullivan and Nathanael Greene. Having established its structure and purpose, Congress votes to raise money to support the Continental Army.

The response to the Congressional call for six companies of riflemen from Pennsylvania has been so great that two additional companies are organized and a regiment formed.

23 June 1775:
Friday. George Washington and Philip Schuyler leave Philadelphia to travel to their respective areas of responsibility: Washington to Boston, Schuyler to Albany. They are accompanied by Major General Charles Lee, Major and Aide-de-Camp Thomas Mifflin, and Lieutenant Colonel and Secretary Joseph Reed. A detachment of the Philadelphia Light Horse escorts the group.

24 June 1775:
Saturday. The Washington cavalcade, in its march towards Boston, reaches Brunswick, New Jersey.

The New York Provincial Congress assumes the power of taxation throughout the province.

Near New York, George Washington writes to the President of Congress, reporting that an express from the army camp around Boston had papers addressed to the president of Congress, took the liberty to open them, because the New York patriots needed to know the status there, as did he, "You will find Sir by that letter a great want of powder in the provincial army; which I sincerely hope the Congress will supply as speedily as in their power. I propose to set off for the provincial camp tomorrow and will use all possible dispatch to join the forces there."

25 June 1775:
  Sunday. As the Washington cavalcade approaches New York City, it is discovered that a serious problem of conflict could arise. This is because the Royal Governor, Tryon, is also arriving this day. The Washington group is advised to head up the west side of the Hudson River and to cross at the ferry slip at Hoboken. They land in New York City about 4 o'clock in the afternoon.

  While it had been discussed that Major General Philip Schuyler was to command in the northern areas, Congress had not formalized this arrangement. They now name him to command the New York Department.

  The Pennsylvania Delegates, with authority from the Pennsylvania Assembly, appoint the field officers for the colony's regiment of riflemen.

26 June 1775:
  Monday. The New York Provincial Congress makes a formal address to the American Commander-in-Chief, attesting their devotion to the continental cause without giving unendurable offence to those who fear military rule. Washington declares that after the "establishment of American Liberty" he will return to his role as a private citizen. Shortly after 3 o'clock the Washington group is traveling again, over King's Bridge, to spend the night in Westchester County.

27 June 1775:
  Tuesday. The Washington cavalcade, slowed by citizens wishing to see him and welcome him, arrives only as far as New Rochelle, New York.

  The Continental Congress, reversing its position of 1 June, authorizes the invasion of Canada, because they believe that it will be an easy task, and it will deny the British any advantage of proximity in attacking from the north.

  At Fort Ontario (present day Oswego, NY), Guy Johnson holds a Council of nearly 1,500 Indians, urging them to support and remain loyal to England.

28 June 1775:
  Wednesday. Philip Schuyler leaves the Washington group and heads north towards his duties at Albany. The remainder of the group, also leaving behind the Philadelphia Light Horse, head east towards New Haven, where Washington is asked to review a Company of Yale student militia.

  The Massachusetts Congress provides for the raising of soldiers to protect the coast of the province.

29 June 1775:
  Thursday. Washington sets out for Wethersfield, Connecticut, anxious to get to Boston and his assignment.

  Governor Dunmore, Royal Governor of Virginia, concerned about his safety, and apprehensive of the large numbers of patriot rebels he observes, sails from Yorktown down the York River to Norfolk, where he feels he will be better protected by the British warships at anchor in that roadstead.

30 June 1775:

Friday. Washington arrives at Springfield, Massachusetts, and is joined there by Dr. Benjamin Church and Moses Gill of the Provincial Congress of Massachusetts.

Having previously asked Washington and Schuyler to offer suggestions for regulation of the army it was creating, the Continental Congress, adopts a full set of Articles of War.

1 July 1775:

Saturday. Traveling today with Church and Moses, Washington learns a good deal about conditions in the Boston area. The entourage reaches Marlborough, Massachusetts, where it stops for the night.

The Continental Congress, in an effort to counter British employment of native Americans or Indians, resolves to enter into an alliance "with such Indian Nations, as will enter into same ..."

2 July 1775:

Sunday. George Washington, arriving in Cambridge, Massachusetts, is quartered in the Wadsworth House, home of the President of Harvard College, Samuel Langdon.

Robert Beverly, a Virginia planter, writes to a business contact in London that, "Our publick affairs are so far from being carried on with Certainty in these Times of Anarchy, that the wisest heads amongst us know not in what Train Things are to remain ..."

3 July 1775:

Monday. In a formal ceremony, General George Washington takes command of all the American forces around Boston, and sets up his headquarters at Cambridge. There are about 14,000 troops, in a loosely configured semi-circle around Boston. He faces a major job of re-organization, sanitation and the instillation of discipline.

4 July 1775:

Tuesday. Washington issues general orders to the army, announcing that they and those who enlist, "are now Troops of the United Provinces of North America." He expresses hope "that all Distinctions of Colonies will be laid aside, so that one and the same Spirit may animate the whole, and the only Contest be, who shall render, on this great and trying occasion, the most essential service to the Great and common cause in which we are all engaged."

The Continental Congress approves a resolution denouncing trade restraining acts as "unconstitutional, oppressive, and cruel."

The Provincial Congress of Georgia meets and takes control of the management of the Province.

5 July 1775:
Wednesday. In Philadelphia, having slowly and thoughtfully prepared the Olive Branch Petition (that they had begun back on 26 May 1775), which most carefully appeals directly to the King for reconciliation, and lays the primary blame for the problems between the colonies and the Mother Country upon the Parliament. The Congress adopts the language of the petition and forwards it to England.

Benjamin Franklin, writes to his former long-time friend in England, William Strahan, "You are a Member of Parliament, and one of that Majority which has doomed my Country to destruction. You have begun to burn our Towns, and murder our People. Look upon your hands! They are stained with the blood of your relations! You and I were long Friends: You are now my Enemy, and I am yours."

6 July 1775:
Thursday. Congress issues the "Declaration of the Causes and Necessity of Taking up Arms." In it are several new and wonderful expressions: "United Colonies," "Our cause is just," "Our Union is perfect," "being with one mind," "resolved to die as freemen rather than live as slaves," "We fight not for glory or for conquest," and "in defense of the freedom that is our birthright." The Declaration details the reasons for the colonists fighting the British, and prays for reconciliation on reasonable terms.

7 July 1775:
Friday. Governor James Wright of Georgia calls for a day of fasting and prayer, requested by the Provincial Congress.

In Philadelphia, Benjamin Franklin writes to Joseph Priestley, in England, "... that propositions of attempting an accommodation were not much relished; and it has been with difficulty that we have carried another humble petition to the crown, to give Britain one more chance, one opportunity more, of recovering the friendship of the colonies; which, however, I think she has not sense enough to embrace, and so I conclude she has lost them forever..."

8 July 1775:
Saturday. A skirmish ensues between patriot forces at Roxbury, Massachusetts, and a British patrol out foraging.

In Chatham County, Georgia, local militia capture the British vessel *Philippa* and its gunpowder, which is sent to the patriot army around Boston.

9 July 1775:
Sunday. In London, England, the London Common Council has offered a petition indicating that Parliament had no

authority to tax the American colonies. King George III declares the petition "most decent and moderate in words," but subversive in its denial of Parliament's authority to tax.

George Washington, who has been quartered at the Wadsworth House on the Harvard College Campus, wishes to move to more private and roomier space for his headquarters and staff and prepares to leave.

10 July 1775:

Monday. George Washington moves into the Vassal House in Cambridge, which becomes headquarters for the American Army during the remainder of the siege of Boston.

Georgia commissions a vessel for naval service to capture British supply vessels, and is successful in overcoming one that is shipping 5,000 pounds of gunpowder, which bounty is promptly sent to the Continental Army.

11 July 1775:

Tuesday. Delegate George Read, although from Delaware, secures the inclusion of a ninth Company, that had been recruited from Lancaster County, Pennsylvania, into the newly forming Pennsylvania Regiment of Riflemen.

Georgia's Provincial Congress assures Governor James Wright that, although the colony has aligned itself with the other American colonies, it still retains a great regard for England and is pledged to work toward reconciliation.

12 July 1775:

Wednesday. Patriots attack Fort St. John on the Richelieu River, but do not have enough forces, nor cannon to succeed, and so begin a siege.

Americans capture Fort Charlotte in McCormick County, South Carolina.

Governor Dunmore of Virginia reports to London that rebels have occupied his residence, converted the capitol into a barracks, mobilized a force in Yorktown, and intercepted official mail. He writes, "the People of Virginia manifest open Rebellion by every means in their power, and declare at the Same time that they are his Majesty's Most dutyfull [sic] subjects..."

The Continental Congress establishes commissions on Indian relations for three areas: the North, Middle, and South Region of the colonies.

13 July 1775:

Thursday. At headquarters in Cambridge, General Orders state "As the army will be forthwith form'd into brigades: The Adjutant General will at orderly time this day, deliver to the Adjutant of each Regiment, a number of printed returns, one of which, must be immediately fill'd up, and sign'd by the Commanding Officer of each Regiment, and sent as soon as possible to the Adjutant General; by the Adjutant of each Regiment; on the back of the return, it will be necessary to mention; where and in what manner, the regiment is a present posted." The parole is given as Georgia, and the countersign as Huntingdon.

The Continental Congress approves an Address to the Six Nations (The Iroquois), urging the Indians, "to remain at home and not join either side, but keep the hatchet buried deep." Similar speeches are ordered to be presented to other tribes.

14 July 1775:
Friday. John Wilkes, Mayor of London, and members of the Common Council, offer a petition to King George calling for reconciliation with the colonies and an end to all military operations in America. The King will later state that he "owed it to the rest of the law-abiding people to oppose the petition." It is interesting to note how the King and Council operate in opposition to many people in Britain who wish a better diplomatic approach and some accommodation to America.

15 July 1775:
Saturday. In Wilmington, North Carolina, the Committee of Safety passes a resolution calling for as many men as possible to join Colonel Robert Howe (no relation to the British Howe brothers) in his attempt to overthrow the British detachment occupying Fort Johnston, guarding the mouth of the Cape Fear River.

In Philadelphia, the Congress authorizes foreign vessels to import essential war materials.

16 July 1775:
Sunday. Abigail Adams, writing to her husband, delegate John Adams, reports that she was visited by General George Washington. Abigail reports that Washington was charming and polite, and as to his appearance, carriage, and demeanor, "... not the half was told me ... dignity with ease, and complacency, the Gentleman and Soldier look agreeable blended in him."

In Montreal, Sir John Johnson arrives from the Mohawk Valley of New York with nearly 200 supporters.

17 July 1775:
Monday. At headquarters in Cambridge, General Orders state "There is reason to apprehend, that the General Orders are not regularly published to the non-Commission Officers, and Soldiers of the army; as pleading ignorance of Orders, will not for the future be admitted in excuse of any delequincy. It is once more ordered, that the Adjutants of the several corps, will be exact in seeing the orders, read every evening to the men off duty, of their respective corp, as they may depend upon answering before a Court Martial, for any neglect in obeying this order. There being a great neglect in sending in the returns to the Adjutant General, as directed by the General Orders of Friday last; the General assures commanding officers of corps, from whom the returns are expected, that he will not for the

future, pass over the slightest neglect, in sending returns to
headquarters, at the time directed by the General Orders; if
there is any remissness in the Adjutant, the Colonels will
confine the transgressors." The parole is given as Boston, and
the countersign as Salem.

The third Virginia Convention meets in Richmond and orders
the formation of two regiments as well as minutemen and militia
companies.

18 July 1775:
Tuesday. Patriots in North Carolina occupy Fort Johnston,
near Wilmington. Royal Governor Josiah Martin seeks refuge on
a British warship.

The Continental Congress requests, by resolution, that all
the colonies establish minutemen units in their militia.
Company officers are to be appointed by their men, and the
regimental officers by provincial authorities. One-fourth of the
militia units of each colony are to be minute-man organizations.
Congress also resolves that each colony, at its own expense,
should provide armed vessels for the protection of its harbors
and coastal towns.

The first of the rifle companies authorized by Congress
arrives in Cambridge, this one from Berks County,
Pennsylvania.

Maj. Gen. Philip Schuyler, arriving at the northern outlet of
Lake George (at the place where it spills down to form the sluice
feeding Lake Champlain) about 10 o'clock in the evening finds
a single sentry on duty at the head of the carrying place to Fort
Ticonderoga. The sentry tries without success to wake the three
other soldiers on duty. Schuyler walks into the Fort,
unimpressed with its security. He immediately organizes the
soldiers there to hold Fort Ticonderoga, which had been
captured in May and secures it for use by the American cause,
as may be needed.

19 July 1775:
Wednesday. The Congress appoints commissioners to treat
with and seek peace with the Indian tribes.

At Cambridge, Massachusetts, Washington is making
progress in his efforts to improve discipline, order, and
cleanliness in the American army around Boston. He gives Brig.
Gen. Horatio Gates a free hand as Adjutant General in
establishing administrative procedures. Gates develops printed
forms for compiling strength returns.

20 July 1775:
Thursday. American patriots in New York raid royal stores in
Turtle Bay, New York (now East 42nd Street), which are sent to
Cambridge and Lake Champlain.

New York observes a Day of Fasting and Devotion, in
accordance with the recommendation of the Continental
Congress.

21 July 1775:
    Friday. An American patrol, under Major Joseph Vose, sets off in whaleboats for a raid to Nantasket Point on Brewster Island in Boston Harbor, Massachusetts. The patrol confiscates lamps, oil, gunpowder, and boats, and burns the wooden parts of the lighthouse.
    In Philadelphia, the Continental Congress hears the proposal of Benjamin Franklin for Articles of Confederation. It will take some while before any such Union is finalized and ratified by all the colonies.

22 July 1775:
    Saturday. Seeking better organization of the army he has inherited, Washington divides the forces around Boston into three divisions: one under Maj. Gen. Charles Lee, one under Maj. Gen. Artemas Ward, and one under Maj. Gen. Israel Putnam.

23 July 1775:
    Sunday. To further regularize his army, and especially in light of the lack of uniforms, Washington orders commissioned officers to wear cockades in their hats, as follows: pink (or red) for field rank [Colonel, Lieutenant Colonel, Major], yellow or buff for Captains, green for Lieutenants and Subalterns. He directs sergeants to wear red tabs (or strips of cloth) on the right shoulder.
    From Cambridge, Washington writes to Brig. Gen. John Thomas expressing concern over Thomas's request to resign, "... after suggesting those reasons which occur to me against your resignation, your own virtue and good sense must decide upon it. In the usual contests of empire and ambition, the conscience of a soldier has so little share, that he may very properly insist upon his claims of rank; ... but in such a cause as this, where the object is neither glory nor extent of territory, but a defense of all that is dear and valuable in life, surely every post ought to be deemed honorable in which a man can serve his country. What matter of triumph will it afford our enemies, that in less than one month, a spirit of discord should shew (sic) itself in the highest ranks of the army, not to be extinguished by any thing less than a total desertion of duty? How little reason shall we have to boast of American Union and Patriotism, if at such a time and in such a cause smaller and partial considerations cannot give way to the great and general interest. These remarks can only affect you as a member of the great American body, but as an inhabitant of Massachusetts Bay, your own province and the other colonies have a peculiar and unquestionable claim to your services, and in my opinion you cannot refuse them without relinquishing in some degree that character for public virtue and honor which you have hitherto supported. If our cause is just, it ought to be supported, but where shall it find support, if Gentlemen of merit and experience, unable to conquer the prejudices of a competition,

withdraw themselves in the hour of danger. I admit, Sir, that your claims and services have not had due respect, it is by not means a singular case; worthy men of all nations and Countries have had reason to make the same complaint, but they did not for this abandon the public cause, they nobly sniffled the dictates of resentment, and made their enemies ashamed of their injustice. For the sake of your bleeding country, your devoted province, your charter rights, and by the memory of those brave men who have already fell in this great cause, I conjure you to banish from your mind every suggestion of anger and disappointment ..."

24 July 1775:
    Monday. The Virginia Convention passes a resolution to cease the export of flour, wheat, and other provisions from the colony to any other country.
    Joseph Trumbull is appointed Commissary-General of the Continental Army.

25 July 1775:
    Tuesday. Dr. Benjamin Church is named the first Surgeon-General of the Continental Army.
    Captain Michael Doudel leads his company from York, Pennsylvania, into the lines at Cambridge. His is the first Continental unit (outside of New England troops, and the Berks County Rifle Company) to reach the Boston area.

26 July 1775:
    Wednesday. The Maryland Convention meets in Annapolis, where it votes to support the Continental Congress. It also resolves to organize 40 Companies of Minutemen.
    Benjamin Franklin is named Postmaster-General, and charged with establishing an American Post Office.

27 July 1775:
    Thursday. Congress takes further action in creating support systems for the colonies military forces, establishing the Army Medical Department.
    Seth Warner is elected leader of the Green Mountain Boys of Vermont.
    Thomas Gage, the British Commander at Boston, gives over command of the army to Major General William Howe and becomes the Civil Governor.

28 July 1775:
    Friday. The Pennsylvania Committee of Safety orders Robert Morris to import from Holland and Spain the medicines required by the harbor defense force. Morris is a principal in the mercantile firm of Morris & Willing and becomes a strong supporter of the cause of the American Revolution, including becoming the treasurer of the Continental Congress.

29 July 1775:
   Saturday. In Philadelphia, the Continental Congress establishes the Army Chaplain Department and the Advocate General Department. These adjunct departments begin to flesh out the bare bones of the heretofore militia oriented American Army.

30 July 1775:
   Sunday. John Adams writes to his wife Abigail that the Continental Congress proposes to adjourn soon because the delegates seem to feel that they should take a recess "during the sultry month of August."

31 July 1775:
   Monday. Another raid on Brewster Island, in Boston Harbor, as a follow-on to the raid of 21 July 1775, because the British have begun trying to rebuild the lighthouse. The American forces, 300 strong under Major Benjamin Tupper, are successful in killing or capturing the entire British force of 32 marines, an officer, and ten carpenters, demolishing their work, and driving off the British warships.
   Congress rejects a plan of reconciliation proposed by the British Prime Minister, Lord North, because the plan is sent to prominent private individuals, instead of the Congress, and because it falls far short of addressing the major issues of taxes and local control over laws.

1 August 1775:
   Tuesday. The Second Continental Congress adjourns to reconvene on 5 September 1775. The delegates need time to visit their home colonies, hear the views of the citizens, and digest the important events of the last four months. It is expected when Congress reconvenes in September that Georgia will include a delegation. Heretofore, the colony has been represented unofficially by individuals.
   Elbridge Gerry, Chair of the Committee of Supply of the Massachusetts Provincial Congress, writes a letter to George Washington reporting that the supply of gunpowder for the army besieging Boston is only 36 barrels, not the 308 barrels earlier reported. Washington is shocked.
   A letter to a gentleman in Philadelphia, from Fredericktown, Maryland, reports seeing Captain Michael Cresap's Rifle Company, which has come from over the mountains with 130 men, give a demonstration of their weapons. "Nineteen out of twenty shots could be placed within an inch of a ten-penny nail at a distance of 100 yds!"
   In Williamsburg, Virginia, the House of Burgesses gives consideration to proposals for independency.

2 August 1775:
   Wednesday. Headquarters, Cambridge, General Orders state "Capt. Oliver Parker of Col. Prescott's Regiment, tried by a

General Court Martial whereof Col. Glover was President. for "defrauding his men of their advance pay, and by false returns, imposing upon the Commissary, and drawing more rations than he had men in his company, and for selling the provisions he by that means obtained, is by the Court found guilty of the whole charge against him and sentenced to be cashiered, mulcted [fined] of all his pay and rendered incapable of future service." The parole is given as Halifax, and the countersign as Geneva.

In South Carolina, William Drayton and William Tennet, in response to orders of the Council of Safety, leave Charleston traveling the interior regions of the colony to secure support and affection to the patriot cause.

3 August 1775:
Thursday. Washington calls a Council of War partly to address the issue of the critical need for gunpowder reported to him in a letter from Elbridge Gerry. The discrepancy between what had been earlier listed, and what was, in fact, in hand, resulted from inexperience and lack of understanding of reportorial methods. It seems that the early report included not only all the powder that had been collected by the colonies, but also what had been expended in the months since then. So, Washington has a crisis at hand. He cannot afford to let the news of the low state of gunpowder reach the British. He has only enough for perhaps nine rounds apiece for each of his soldiers. One needs little imagination to envision the disaster that might develop should the information regarding the pitifully poor state of the American gunpowder situation reach British ears. The British issue powder for 60 rounds per man as a standard fighting rule. Surely they will attack immediately, if they learn of the rebel shortage of this critical commodity.

Washington requests Governor Nicholas Cooke of Rhode Island to immediately dispatch a fast vessel to Bermuda, slip-in, and quickly and quietly remove the provincial supply of gunpowder known to be stored in the magazines there. Because Bermuda is actually a series of small islands, it is possible for one who knows the waters to do just that.

From the British Camp at Charlestown, Lord Rawdon writes to the Earl of Huntingdon, expressing his view "... that the skirmish on the 19th of April was, as you predicted, a very foolish affair. Our men were even unprovided with sufficient ammunition. And the two pieces of cannon which were sent out with the Brigade under Lord Percy were only supplied with four and twenty rounds, when they had to fight every yard of their way for almost as many miles. I have in former letters given you an account of this action [the Battle of Bunker Hill]; it well be sufficient to say that we found it a much more difficult piece of work to dislodge them than any of us imagined."

4 August 1775:
Friday. In London, King George III congratulates himself on securing German troops, "much cheaper than if raised at home,

and when not further wanted saves the expense of half pay." These German Troops are from six different German- speaking principalities. (The reader should understand, that at this time, 1775, there was no such political entity as Germany. Such a nation does not come into being until 1871.) These principalities are Anhalt-Zerbst, Brunswick, Hesse-Cassel, Hesse-Hanau, Anspach-Bayreuth, and Waldeck. Perhaps because the majority of these mercenary troops and their successive Commanders (von Heister, von Knyphausen, and von Lossberg) were all from a Hesse area they, of course, became known collectively to the American colonists as Hessians.

Captain Michael Cresap's company of Maryland riflemen have gotten as far as Lancaster, Pennsylvania, and give another demonstration of their amazing marksmanship with the rifle.

5 August 1775:
Saturday. An American patriot from Charleston, South Carolina, writes to London, "Be assured peace will never be firmly established between Great Britain and America, until the latter receives an ample recognition of her rights, and a full satisfaction for the blood that has or may be shed."

6 August 1775:
Sunday. The Virginia Convention appoints Patrick Henry to the post of Commander of the First Regiment of the colony's militia. He is later named Commander-in-Chief of the regular forces of the colony.

John Paul Jones is instructed to sail into Bermudian waters and cruise about to "annoy" or capture British commerce.

7 August 1775:
Monday. In Paris, King Louis, XVI agrees to send Julien Achard de Bonvouloir to America on a fact-finding mission. Bonvouloir is also instructed to assure the Americans that France has no aspirations for a reconquest of Canada.

8 August 1775:
Tuesday. Captain Daniel Morgan and his Virginia riflemen arrive in Cambridge, Massachusetts.

Washington writes to the New York Legislature, expressing concern over a New York vessel, providing the enemy with provisions, and reporting upon his efforts to gain intelligence, "Gentn: It must give great concern to any considerate mind, that, when this whole continent, at a vast expense of blood and treasure, is endeavoring to establish liberties on the most secure and solid foundations, not only by a laudable opposition of force to force, but denying itself the usual advantages of trade; there are men among us so basely sordid as to counteract all our exertions, for the sake of a little gain. I have been endeavouring by every means in my power, to discover the future intentions of our enemy here. I find a general idea prevailing thro' the army and in the Town of Boston, that the troops are soon to leave the Town and go to some other part of the continent. New York is the place generally intentioned as their destination."

9 August 1775:
Wednesday. Captain Michael Cresap and his Company of Maryland riflemen arrive in Cambridge. These riflemen and their weapons are new to most of the New Englanders, who are equipped with smooth bore muskets. The use of a rifled weapon, ie. one with spiral groves in the barrel, gives a tighter fit and a spin to the ball, making it much more accurate and at greater distances.

10 August 1775:
Thursday. Two American schooners, returning to Salem from the West Indies, are chased by British Captain John Linzee of the sloop HMS *Falcon* (16 guns). Linzee is forced by shore gunfire to release a captured patriot sloop and to retreat with the loss of two barges he was protecting, and the 35 men from Gloucester Harbor, Cape Ann, Massachusetts, he had captured and is required to free.

11 August 1775:
Friday. Around Boston, Washington warns the British commander, Thomas Gage, about the treatment of prisoners, "... I shall regulate my conduct towards those gentlemen who are or may be in our possession, exactly by the rule you shall observe towards those of ours now in your custody, if severity and hardship mark the line of your conduct, painful as it may be to me, your prisoners will feel its effects."
At Jackson's Creek Meeting, South Carolina, the Rev. William Tennent preaches to a large congregation, including remarks about the state of the colony. He wins over the leading men of the area to support the Revolution.

12 August 1775:
Saturday. The Massachusetts House of Representatives instructs inhabitants of the colony, "... not to fire a gun at beast, bird, or mark, without real necessity." The recommendation is made to encourage the conservation of gunpowder.

13 August 1775:
Sunday. In London, Lord Sandwich announces that the British Navy has engaged the 6,000 tons of shipping needed to transport Regiments from Ireland to America.
At Gloucester, Massachusetts, a skirmish takes place between patriots and a British naval foraging party. The British are beaten off by the Americans.

14 August 1775:
Monday. Americans raid storage magazines in Bermuda, carrying off more than 100 barrels of gunpowder.

In Cambridge, Washington writes to Governor Nicholas Cooke of Rhode Island, expressing concern over the shortage of gunpowder and wondering about the possibilities of securing some from the French West Indies or Bermuda, "The voyage is short, our necessity great, the expectation of being supplied by the inhabitants is by a sudden stroke. There is a great difference between acquiescing in the measure and becoming principals, the former we have great reason to expect the latter is doubtful. The powder by all our information is public property, so that as you observe it may be settled with by our other accounts."

15 August 1775:
Tuesday. Lord William Campbell, Royal Governor of South Carolina, appeals to the House of Assembly for aid, admitting that, "... thy powers of Government are wrested out of my hands. I can neither protect, nor punish; therefore with the Advice of His Majys Council I apply to you & desire that in this dreadful emergency You will aid me with all the assistance in your power, in enforcing the Laws, & protecting His Majys Servants ..."

16 August 1775:
Wednesday. In New Jersey, the Provincial Congress resolves to organize a military force consisting of 48 battalions, one ranger company, and 63 companies of militiamen.

17 August 1775:
Thursday. British military officials in Cork, Ireland, recruit men for military service in America.
At headquarters, Cambridge, General Orders state "The Commanding Officer of Artillery is to see that all the ordnance stores, are faithfully collected, and put under the care of the Commissary of the Artillery; and that the Commissary of Artillery, is to see that all the powder, lead, and flints are placed in the magazine appointed to receive them. The Army being regularly brigaded, and a Major of Brigade appointed and fix'd to each Brigade: they are to keep an exact roster of duty for all Officers, Non-Commissioned Officers, and Soldiers of their respective Brigades." The parole is given as Exeter and the countersign as Falkland.

18 August 1775:
Friday. The Dutch renew their embargo on the export of military stores to America.
In Cambridge, General Orders state "John Conner of Capt. Olivers Company, Col. Doolittles Regiment, tried at a General Court Martial for 'stealing a cheese', the property of Richd. Cornell, is found guilty of the charge and adjudged to receive thirty-nine lashes upon his bare back. The General approves the sentence, sand orders it to be executed at the reliving the main guard, at the head of the two guards." The parole is given

as Gloucester and the countersign as Hartford.

19 August 1775:
    Saturday. Two Philadelphia printers have written a letter to
a London publisher that is printed in the London Chronicle,
"This province has raised 1,000 riflemen, the worst of whom will
put a ball into a man's head at a distance of 150 or 200 yards,
therefore advise your officers who shall hereafter come out to
America to settle their affairs in England before their
departure."

20 August 1775:
Sunday. By this time, about 1400 of the riflemen authorized by
the Congress have arrived at the Army encampment around
Boston. With a huge crowd of spectators on hand, Washington
publicly has these men give a demonstration of their amassing
marksmanship.
    A 7 inch diameter pole is set up in a field, as all the other
troops and visitors assemble on the sidelines. The riflemen are
placed at a distance of 200 yards from this pole target, and the
firing begins. The pole is riddled near in half!
    The British in Boston fear these long-range shooters, and
attempt to stay under cover or out of range. British Major
General William Howe writes back to England about "the
terrible guns of the rebels." The mere presence of such a force
buys some time for Washington to prepare, train, and organize
his forces.

21 August 1775:
    Monday. General George Washington, while he has brought
some small semblance of order and discipline to the troops in
his army around Boston, is well aware of the fact that he has a
long way to go to build a force that will go the distance and win
a war against a much more disciplined and well-trained army.
This is a major concern for him at this time. He is also aware
that the "Eight-Month Army" he has inherited will cease to exist
by the end of the year. Congress is currently adjourned, and he
has not yet been able to secure support for the idea of a longer
term of service for soldiers. Washington has urged a
commitment of at least three years, preferably "until the end of
the war," but negative reaction to long terms of military service
is strong. How will it be possible to procure, train, and organize
a "new" army while disbanding an "old" army--all in the face of
a well-armed and attentive foe. Another problem Washington
has in this connection is the manner of conveying his thoughts
to the delegates in Congress and those who influence them. It
is too easy to have mail miscarry. Thus, much of what
Washington wishes to present to the Congress, must go by
means of couriers—selected horsemen who will personally
deliver the letters, reports, and comments from headquarters to
the specified persons.

22 August 1775:
Tuesday. King George III, disgusted with his rebellious colonies, prepares a proclamation to present to Parliament, declaring the Americans to be in a state of open rebellion.

At Cambridge, Washington writes to Joseph Palmer, a Massachusetts businessman, "In answer to your favor of yesterday I must inform you, that I have often been told of the advantages of Point Alderton with respect to its command of the shipping going in and out of Boston Harbor. My knowledge of this matter would not have rested upon enquires only, if I had found myself at any time since I came to this place, in a condition to have taken such a post. But it becomes my duty to consider, not only what place is advantageous, but what number of men are necessary to defend it; how they can be supported in case of attack; how they may retreat if they cannot be supported; and what stock of ammunition we are provided with for the purpose of self-defense, or annoyance of the enemy. Would it be prudent then in me, under these circumstances, to take a post 30 miles distant from this place when we already have a line ... at least ten miles in extent?"

23 August 1775:
Wednesday. In parliament, King George III, has his proclamation regarding the colonies presented by Lord North. In it, the King declares all the American Colonies to be in a state of rebellion, and "out of his protection."

The colonial governments of both Virginia and Massachusetts discuss the manufacture of saltpeter and encourage the increase of production of gunpowder.

In New York City, Patriots plan to remove 21 cannon from the Battery, under fire of the British man-of-war, HMS *Asia*, in the harbor.

24 August 1775:
Thursday. Toward the end of August the gunpowder crisis in the patriot camp has eased somewhat. At this time, Washington has 184 barrels of gunpowder, as well as thousands of flints and several tons of lead.

The New York Provincial Congress resolves that the cannon in the Battery at the foot of Manhattan Island be dismantled and taken to a patriot secured location. Captain John Lamb with 60 men sets about this work. British Captain George Vandeput of the HMS *Asia* (64 guns) sends a barge of armed men to investigate. A brief exchange of fire ensues. In the city, a number of townsfolk, believing that the place might be sacked and burned, and not knowing just who might be fighting whom or how violent they might become, make an exodus across the Hudson River to New Jersey.

25 August 1775:
Friday. Lord North, British Prime Minister, advises King George that, "The cause of Great Britain is not yet sufficiently

popular," predicting difficulty in reaching military enlistment goals.

In Albany, New York, the Northern Indian Department holds a council with the Iroquois, in which the Indians agree to remain neutral in the fight between the colonists and the British.

26 August 1775:

Saturday. The Rhode Island Assembly resolves to have their delegates to the next Continental Congress session ask if they may build a fleet of vessels, at continental expense, "for the protection of these colonies."

At Fort Ticonderoga, Brig. Gen. Richard Montgomery, second-in-command under Maj. Gen. Philip Schuyler, assumes command of the field forces. Montgomery is urged by the Congress to invade Canada, and perhaps seek Canadian support as a fourteenth Colony.

During the night, Brigadier General John Sullivan leads a fatigue party of 1,200 men, with a guard of 2,400, including 400 Pennsylvania riflemen, to Ploughed Hill near the base of the Charlestown Peninsula, and closer to the British positions on Bunker's Hill. The purpose is to build fortifications at this site to harass the British and to command the Mystic River. [See Fig. II-4, p. 27].

27 August 1775:

Sunday. By daylight John Sullivan's detachment has completed an entrenchment that threatens the British on Bunker Hill. An artillery duel ensues, in which the Americans sink one British floating battery and damage another.

Benjamin Franklin writes to Silas Dean agreeing with his opinion that the colonies need a navy. "I hope the next Winter will be employed in forming one. When we are no longer fascinated with the idea of a speedy Reconciliation, we shall exert ourselves to some purpose. Till then Things will be done by halves."

28 August 1775:

Monday. This morning a British column forms on Bunker Hill, and the Americans, fearing an attack on their newly erected entrenchment at Ploughed Hill, sound the alarm--but nothing other than an exchange of fire develops.

A South Carolina native states that, "Everything here is suspended but warlike preparations ... The Country is unanimous." He is perhaps a bit sanguine in his views, since he may be unaware that there are some loyalist sympathizers in the interior parts of his colony.

Richard Montgomery is under orders from Philip Schuyler to begin an advance on Canada. He learns that the British at Fort St. John on the Richelieu River have nearly completed two large sailing vessels that could dominate the lake. Starting from Fort Ticonderoga, he travels north toward Ile aux Noix (Isle of Nuts), a low-lying Island at the head of the river as it spills out of Lake Champlain, with about 1,200 men in two sailing vessels, and several gondolas, bateaux, rowing galleys, and canoes.

29 August 1775:
Tuesday. George Washington expresses a concern that false claims of shortages of wood, hay, and oats have inflated the cost of these items to the Commissary Department, and requests the legislature to place a fixed price upon these items. Gouging of prices and even peculation by a few suppliers of goods to the service must be controlled, and the perpetrators brought to justice.

Patriots in New York City, organized into militia units, attack a mixed force of loyalists and British regular troops. While the attack is inconclusive, it is a foretaste of the bitter rivalry between these two politically antagonistic bodies.

30 August 1775:
Wednesday. Washington writes to the President of the New York Provincial Congress attacking ship owners who secretly slip into and deliver provisions to the British enclosed in Boston. He also emphasizes his need for gunpowder, noting that although his troops have seized a hill advancing towards the enemy, their "poverty [of ammunition] prevents our availing ourselves of the Advantage of the situation."

British Captain Wallace of the HMS *Rose* bombards the coastal town of Stonington, Connecticut, on Long Island Sound, after a foraging expedition from his ship has been repulsed by the townspeople. No homes are burned, since he is using only round shot, but several are shattered, and casualties are suffered by the townfolk.

31 August 1775:
Thursday. In New York, the Provincial Congress enters into a contract with Joseph Hallett for importing 15 tons of gunpowder and 1,400 muskets.

1 September 1775:
Friday. Richard Penn and Arthur Lee, representing the Continental Congress, present the Olive Branch Petition to the Earl of Dartmouth. This petition is one more attempt made by the colonists to peacefully settle their differences with Great Britain. The petition is couched in the most obsequious language, reiterating their grievances, while professing their attachment to the King. George III refuses even to receive the petition. Such a snub to an official document, prepared by a representative body of his people, is seen in America as clear evidence that it is the King himself who is the enemy.

2 September 1775:
Saturday. Because the British Navy generally actively patrols and thus has control over the waters around Boston, it is very

difficult to keep them from bringing in supplies with which to provision their troops. Washington, is anxious to exert pressure on this control, take advantage of opportunities, and "tighten the noose." He appoints Captain Nicholas Broughton to take command of the armed schooner *Hannah* for the purpose of seizing vessels carrying soldiers, ammunition, weapons, and supplies to and from the city. His instructions are, "You, being appointed a Captain in the Army of the United Colonies of North-America, are hereby directed to take command of a detachment of said army and proceed on board the schooner *Hannah*, at Beverly, lately fitted out and equipped with arms, ammunition, and provisions, at the continental expense. You are to proceed, as commander of said schooner, immediately on a cruise against such vessels as may be found on the high seas or elsewhere, bound inwards and outwards, to or from Boston, in the service of the Ministerial Army, and to take and seize all such vessels laden with soldiers, arms, ammunition or provisions, for or from said army, for which you shall have a good reason to suspect are in such service."

Brig. Gen. Richard Montgomery and his troops arrive at Isle La Motte, near the northern outlet of Lake Champlain, about ten miles south of the Canadian border, near where the Lake narrows to form the Richelieu River, flowing north. Montgomery is trying to reach the British at Fort St. John and to destroy the large vessels they are building there. High winds and rain hold them at Isle La Motte for two more days, when Major General Philip Schuyler arrives.

3 September 1775:
    Sunday. Since the fighting at Lexington, back on 19 April, the patriot forces have not had a specific banner of any kind to call their own or to fly over their encampments. This is remedied by the adoption of the Grand Union Flag–13 alternate red and white stripes, with the Union Jack in the canton.

    Washington writes to Reuben Colburn, a shipbuilder,to "go with all expedition to Gardinerstown (in the District of Maine) upon the River Kennebec and without delay proceed to the construction of two hundred Batteaus ..." This is a part of the effort to get the ball rolling on a thrust into Canada, in support of Brigadier General Richard Montgomery, but via a more easterly route. This Kennebec route will become known as "Arnold's Trek."

4 September 1775:
    Monday. A Rhode Island patriot submits a proposal to the Committee of Safety to build a submersible craft. He claims that this craft will be able to travel unseen under the water and approach British warships with the purpose of destroying them.

    Philip Schuyler catches up with Richard Montgomery, at Ile La Motte, and gives approval to the plan of action to attack and destroy the British vessels at Fort St. John. Thus joined together, they lead the expedition north during the twilight hours, arriving at Ile aux Noix.

5 September 1775:
    Tuesday. Stripped down to fighting trim, their baggage, tents, and supplies left on Ile aux Noix, Schuyler and his men head further north to Fort St. John. As they go ashore, a flank party under Major Thomas Hobby moves off towards the fort, but is ambushed by about 100 Indians, led by a New York Tory, Captain Tice. During the night, a spy brings news to Schuyler that the fort is heavily fortified with troops and cannon, that no Canadians will join with them, and that the Americans would be wise to return to Ile aux Noix and make ready a means of keeping the British boats from entering onto Lake Champlain. The Americans withdraw.
    In Charleston, South Carolina, the Council of Safety adopts a proactive program for the defense of the province, calling upon the militia to stand "in readiness as in a time of Alarm."
    In General Orders, Washington writes, "A Detachment consisting of two Lieut Colonels, two Majors, ten Captains, thirty Subalterns, thirty Sergeants, four drummers, two fifers, and six hundred and seventy-six privates to parade tomorrow at eleven o'clock, upon the Common in Cambridge, to go upon Command with Colonel Arnold of Connecticut; one Company of Virginia riflemen and two Companies from Colonel Thompson's Pennsylvania Regiment of riflemen, to parade at the same time and place, to join the above Detachment." These troops are all made ready for an expedition to Quebec.
    In Philadelphia, the Continental Congress, is scheduled to reconvene, but, there not being a sufficient number present to conduct business, adjourns from day to day, until next week on 12 September 1775.

6 September 1775:
    Wednesday. General Washington prepares a letter to the residents of Bermuda, defending the American struggle to secure its rights and urging them to deliver to him the contents of their powder magazines. In return, he promises to ask the Continental Congress the release of provisions needed by them.
    Washington's final draft of an "Address to the Inhabitants of Canada", calls for their support of the American conflict with Britain. Benedict Arnold will take it with him on a expedition now in the works.

7 September 1775:
    Thursday. In New York City, the Provincial Congress orders the Quakers to submit a list of all male members of their society aged 16 to 60 who are living within the city and county. The Quakers refuse on the grounds that the request violates their religious beliefs.
    The American schooner *Hannah,* Captain Nicholas Broughton, out of Beverly, Massachusetts, captures the British

supply ship *Unity* after a brief fight off Cape Ann, and takes her into Gloucester, Massachusetts, as a prize.

8 September 1775:
      Friday. The Schuyler-Montgomery detachment at Ile aux Noix has the Richelieu River boomed (obstructions in the water) to prevent passage of any British vessels south onto Lake Champlain. They also fortify the place, so that they now have an excellent defensive position. Reinforcements also arrive, so that Schuyler now has about 1,700 men.

9 September 1775:
      Saturday. Plans are laid to stop the British-built vessel, *Royal Savage*, in the Richelieu River, from going south onto the lake. At the same time a party of 700 men are to go again to Fort St. John and invest it.
      At Cambridge, Washington writes to Governor Jonathan Trumbull, "Our state of ammunition disables us from availing ourselves of our present stations as I would wish to do, and requires every assistance that can be given it. You will therefore on receipt of this be pleased to forward whatever can be spared from the necessities of the Colony, and the more expedition you can use, the more acceptable it will be."

10 September 1775:
      Sunday. As the American assault party of now 800 men approach Fort St. John, the party is divided into a flanker-covering section and the main section of 500 men under Lieutenant Colonel Rudolphus Ritzema. Apprehensive of another possible Indian ambush, the flankers collide with the main column in the dark and panic. Richard Montgomery soon has them in hand, but as the day comes on, and word arrives that the *Royal Savage* is ready for sailing, too many of the men are demoralized, and it is decided to give up the attempt. Instead, they embark in their bateaux for Ile aux Noix, thus ending another unsuccessful assault on Fort St. John.
      In the American encampment surrounding Boston, at Prospect Hill, disorderliness among poorly disciplined riflemen leads to several courts-martial. Thirty-three men are convicted of disobedience and mutinous behavior, and are fined 20 shillings each.

11 September 1775:
      Monday. In New York, a group of conscientious objectors (probably the Quakers who refused to furnish lists of names and military age data for their male members on 7 September) sends the Committee of Safety £152 in support of the cause of the American Revolution. Thus it can be seen, that while the Quakers, in general, adhere to their tenets of faith, most of them also wish to support the principles of the American Revolution, and do so with their purses.
      Colonel Benedict Arnold gathers his forces and prepares to

set off from Cambridge with about 1,100 volunteers for his expedition to Quebec.

12 September 1775:

Tuesday. In London, Lord Dartmouth announces that 10,000 stand of arms and six light artillery pieces will be sent to North Carolina where Governor Josiah Martin claims a large body of loyalists will oppose the rebels with force.

The Second Continental Congress reconvenes in Philadelphia after an adjournment of nearly one and a half months. This is a delay of a full week from the intended re-assembly, because not all the delegations are able to arrive on the scheduled date. Twelve colonies are represented.

Philip Schuyler falls ill, and has to remand his command over to Richard Montgomery, while he returns to Albany to recover.

13 September 1775:

Wednesday. In Boston, British Admiral Graves, orders Captain Vandeput, of the HMS *Asia* in New York Harbor, to seize and keep in safe custody any delegates to the Continental Congress and any "Rebel General Officers, or the chief radical leaders in New York."

In Philadelphia, Georgia sends a contingent of delegates, so now the Congress includes representatives from all the 13 Colonies.

14 September 1775:

Thursday. Fort Johnston, on James Island near Charleston, South Carolina, is attacked by patriot forces.

Washington gives orders and instructions to Benedict Arnold for his planned expedition up the Kennebec River and on to Quebec. [See Fig. II-6, p. 55]. In them, Washington tells Arnold, "... to use expedition, since the Winter season is now approaching; discover the real sentiments of the Canadians; abuse no inhabitants .., and conciliate those people and Indians you meet; pay full value for all provisions ..."

15 September 1775:

Friday. The British Charge d'Affairs in Paris is ordered to protest the shipment of 30 tons of gunpowder to Philadelphia by the Governor of St. Domingo, a French possession. It seems that General Washington's pleas to the Caribbean has borne fruit.

Captain Eleazer Oswald, acts as Colonel Arnold's secretary during the march to Quebec. With Arnold, he sets out this morning from Cambridge. At Salem, they procure two hundred pounds of ginger and engage a teamster to transport it and two hundred and seventy blankets to Newburyport.

An American detachment captures Fort Johnston in Charleston. The Royal Governor of South Carolina, Lord William Campbell, takes flight and seeks refuge aboard the British sloop of war HMS *Tamer*.

16 September 1775:
    Saturday. In South Carolina, patriot leader William H. Drayton, with the Rev. William Tennent and about 1,000 militia, are confronted by loyalist (Tory) leaders Colonels Thomas Fletchall and Moses Kirkland, whose larger body of soldiers has taken the field. In order to avoid shedding blood over issues not yet clarified as to loyalties, Drayton persuades the Tories to disperse and the two sides sign a treaty of neutrality for the interior community of Ninety-Six.

17 September 1775:
    Sunday. Rather than pull his outposts back and concentrate his meager forces around Montreal and Quebec, the British Commander in Canada, Guy Carleton, adopts a "forward Policy." He reinforces the post at Fort St. John and the garrison at Fort Chambly, both on the Richelieu River, about 11 miles apart. This, he hopes, will at least slow down any American incursion, and give him time to strengthen his major cities. [See Fig. II-6, p. 69].

18 September 1775:
    Monday. The Continental Congress resolves to appoint a Secret Committee (later changed to Committee of Commerce) to seek foreign aid and import military supplies, specifically: up to 500 tons of gunpowder, 20,000 musket locks, 10,000 stand of arms and 40 brass six-pounders.
    Near Fort St. John, Canada, having posted 350 men in boats on the Richelieu River to prevent the British ship *Royal Savage* from moving south onto Lake Champlain, Richard Montgomery lands the rest of his men to begin a siege of the fort.

19 September 1775:
    Tuesday. The British government halts the practice of using flint stones as ballast in ships sailing to America, because they do not wish to give opportunity to American raiders to capture and make use of such a valuable cargo. British Admiral Thomas Graves is ordered to search all incoming ships, American or foreign, and dump all flint stone ballast they find into deep water, or confiscate all flints suitable for use in firearms for their themselves.
    Arnold's detachment for the Quebec Expedition weighs anchor at 7 o'clock in the morning from Newburyport, Massachusetts, and sails across the Atlantic shore of Maine to Gardinerstown, up the embayment of the Kennebec River. [See Fig. II-5, p. 55]. Dr. Senter is a part of this expedition, and he keeps a diary, noting "Our fleet consisted of 11 sail of shipping, sloops and schooners, containing, upon average 100 troops, as our army consisted of 1100 men, officers included."
    In Philadelphia, the Congress appoints a Secret Committee empowered to make contracts for the purchase of foreign war supplies.

20 September 1775:
    Wednesday. In Canada, Ethan Allen informs Richard Montgomery that he, Allen, has 250 Canadians under arms and more volunteers coming in all the time.
    At headquarters, Cambridge, General Orders state "No person is to presume to demand a Continental Commission, who is not in actual possession of the like Commission, from the proper authority of the Colony he is at present engaged to serve, which must be produced, at the time application is made for a Continental Commission. If, from unavoidable circumstances, any gentleman has served from the beginning of the campaign, in the rank of a Commissioned Officer, and has not yet received a Commission, being justly entitled thereto, such officer's pretensions will be duly weighed and consider'd; and upon sufficient proof of the justice of his claim, a Commission will issue accordingly." The parole is given as Falmouth and the countersign as Gloucester.

21 September 1775:
    Thursday. General Washington writes to Congress to President John Hancock, describing the many problems facing the Army. These include the serious problem of the expiration of many of the soldiers' enlistments, the need for winter clothing, and the lack of funding. The temporary character of the army besieging Boston is a major difficulty with which Washington has to contend, "The Connecticut and Rhode Island troops stand engaged to the 1st December only, and none longer than to the 1st January. A dissolution therefore, of the present army will take place unless some early provision is made against such an event. The necessities of the troops having required pay, I directed those of Massachusetts should receive a month's pay, on being mustered and returning a proper roll, but a claim was immediately made for pay by Lunar Months, and several Regiments have declined taking up their warrants on this account. As this practice was entirely new to me, tho' said to be warranted by former usage, the matter here now waits the determination of the Hon. Congress. For the better regulation of duty, I found it necessary to settle the rank of Officers and to number the Regiments, and as I had not received the commands of the Congress upon the subject, and the exigence of the service forbade any farther delay ..."

22 September 1775:
    Friday. Admiral Thomas Graves advises the British Admiralty against relying on America for supplies and provisions for the fleet during the coming winter. All necessary items will have to be shipped from England.

23 September 1775:
    Saturday. Having arrived the day before at Gardinerstown, Arnold's Expedition departs up the Kennebec River on their long and difficult trek to Quebec. The first efforts are to forward men,

provisions, and bateaux to Fort Western, on the east shore of and about thirty miles up the Kennebec River. Senter reports in his journal "Arrived at Ft. Western at 10 o'clock in the morning, We were now come to a rapid in the river, beyond which our transport could not pass, nor could they all get up as far as this. The batteaux were all made of green pine boards, which rendered them somewhat heavy."

24 September 1775:
        Sunday. The British Cabinet gives notice that it is their intention to "carry on the war against America with the utmost vigor, and to begin the next campaign as early as possible in the spring. The outlines of the plan to be pursued are: an army of eighteen thousand men to be employed in New England, and another army of twelve thousand men are to act in Virginia and the middle Provinces."
        Arnold notes in his journal "Despatched Lieutenant Steel, with six men, in two birch canoes, to Chaudiére Pond, to reconnoitre, and get all the intelligence he possibly can from the Indians ..."

25 September 1775:
        Monday. Ethan Allen must abort a poorly timed and much too early an attempt upon Montreal. Without sufficient men or resources, neither an attack nor investment proves successful. Attempting to rush the town in a surprise attack, Allen and 40 of his men are captured by the British. Allen is placed in chains and taken to a prison ship.
        At Fort Western, Arnold divides his army into four divisions, sending each off about a day apart. In his journal he notes "Despatched the three companies of rifles with forty-five days provisions, under the command of Captain Morgan, as an advanced party, with orders to proceed to the great carrying place, and to cut a road over to the Dead River."

26 September 1775:
        Tuesday. In the Continental Congress, John Hancock writes to Washington on behalf of the Congress asking him to prepare winter quarters for the troops at Cambridge. Edward Rutledge of South Carolina makes a motion to have Washington discharge "all Negroes as well as slaves or Freemen in his Army." The motion fails!
        Peace negotiations with the Indians at Fort Pitt begin, hosted by Virginia Indian agents. These agents, as negotiators, will hold off frontier Indian warfare for more than a year.
        Arnold notes in his journal "The second division, consisting of the three Companies, viz: Hubbard's, Topham's, and Thayer's, under the command of Colonel Greene, embarked."

27 September 1775:
        Wednesday. Ethan Allen's impetuosity, imprudence, and inability to provide for supply and support have not been helpful

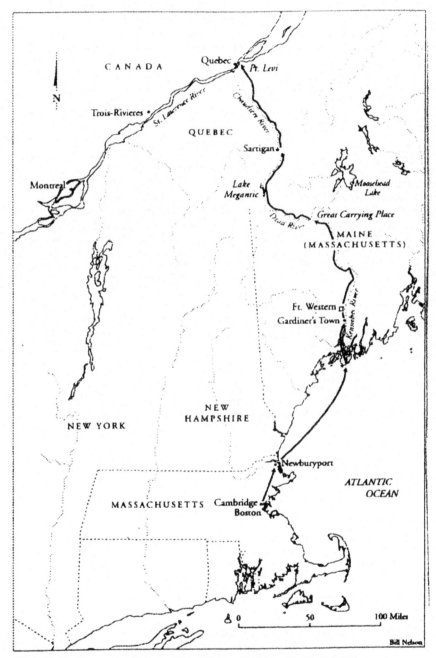

Fig. II-5: Route of Arnold's Expedition, Fall, 1775

to the patriot cause. His capture has encouraged the Canadians not to join with the Americans; it suggested to many of the Indians that they would rather be on the winning side, and has been a major stumbling block for Brigadier General Richard Montgomery in his efforts to conquer Canada for America.

At Fort Western, Major Return Jonathan Meigs, notes in his journal "At three o'clock, P.M. I embarked on board my battoe (sic) with the third division of the army, consisting of 4 companies of musketmen, with 45 days' provision, and proceeded up the river ..."

28 September 1775:

Thursday. In the camps around Boston, Washington is concerned about health, sanitation, and discipline. In several of his General Orders he recommends inoculation. This is because one of the most serious problems is smallpox--a debilitating disease, highly infectious, causing death in up to 40% of its victims. To assist in controlling this problem, Washington has encouraged the practice of inoculation. This was, at the time, a highly contentious procedure, because few people had any real understanding of the etiology of the disease. Before Dr. Edward Jenner discovered vaccination, inoculation was the only known defense against smallpox. However, those inoculated persons were still infectious, although at a very much lower level than those who caught the disease naturally.

29 September 1775:

Friday. As Montgomery continues to try to successfully attack Fort St. John, he must contend with the after effects of Ethan Allen's disastrous incursion against Montreal, but is having great difficulty with recruitment, discipline, the weather, and supplies.

On the Kennebec River, Meigs writes in his journal "In the morning continued our route up the river. At 11 o'clock A.M., arrived at Fort Halifax, which stands on a point of land between the river Kennebec and the river Sebastecook."

30 September 1775:

Saturday. At Stonington, Connecticut, patriot militia beat off a British raiding party.

Meigs notes in his journal "Proceeded up the river 7 miles, and encamped, where Colonel Arnold joined us at night, and encamped with us.

1 October 1775:

Sunday. Lt. Gen. Thomas Gage orders two detachments from the British Post at St. Augustine, East Florida, to Boston, leaving only about half a regiment in all of the province of East Florida. Only ninety soldiers are left at St. Augustine, and the balance are scattered in stations at New Smyrna, Matanzas,

Cowford, Lookout Tower, and St. John's River.

2 October 1775:
    Monday. At Portsmouth Harbor, New Hampshire, the British supply ship *Prince George*, transporting much needed flour from Bristol, England to Boston, mistakenly enters Portsmouth, and is taken by force by American patriots.
    Meigs writes in his journal "In the morning proceeded up the river, and at 10 o'clock arrived at Scohegin Falls, where there is a carrying place of 250 paces, which lies across a small island in the river."

3 October 1775:
    Tuesday. The Committee of Safety for New York orders repair to the barracks and hospital at Albany, "with all possible dispatch and in the cheapest ... manner, so as to make them ready for the reception of the troops of the Continental Army."
    At Norridgewock Falls, on the Kennebec River, Meigs's bateau fills with water going over the falls. He losses his kettle, butter, and sugar. These items cannot be replaced at this remote location.

4 October 1775:
    Wednesday. The Massachusetts House of Representatives orders the overseers of Harvard College "to inquire into the principles" of its staff and to "dismiss those who, by their past or present conduct, appear to be unfriendly to the liberties and privileges of the Colonies."
    Meigs notes in his journal "I proceeded up the river about one mile, and crossed the river, where there is a carrying place of one mile and a quarter: here I came up with the second division, commanded by Col. Greene."

5 October 1775:
    Thursday. The Continental Congress appoints a committee to prepare a plan for the fitting out of two armed vessels to intercept enemy transport ships.
    Meigs notes "All day at the carrying place. At evening moved one company up the river one mile, where they encamped, waiting for the other companies of my division."

6 October 1775:
    Friday. The Arnold Expedition takes several days to get all the four divisions of the force over the carrying place at Carratuncas. The Kennebec River here is confined between two rocks about 500 feet apart, so the water is very rapid.
    The Continental Congress passes a resolution calling for the arrest of all loyalists who are dangerous to "the liberties of America."
    In Bermuda, Captain Whipple, who has been sent to procure gunpowder, is well received by the people, but finds

no powder there to take back to the besieging American forces.

7 October 1775:
Saturday. After refusing to provision a British ship, Bristol, Rhode Island, is bombarded and burned. Townspeople eventually surrender 40 sheep.

At headquarters, Cambridge, General Orders state "The Court having duly considered the evidence are of opinion that Lieut. Col. Brown is not guilty of any fraud, in endeavouring to have Harrington and Clarke muster'd, in the manner he did. But the Court are of opinion, that Col. Brown is guilty of employing Harrington for fourteen days, and Clarke for eighteen days, out of camp, upon his own business, yet are inclined to think it was done rather thro' ignorance, than a fraudulent intent, and therefore adjudge that he be fin'd four pounds, lawful money, for the said offense. Lt Col Brown to be released, as soon as he has paid his fine to Dr. Foster, Director of the Hospital, who   will apply it to the use of the sick, in the General Hospital under his care. The General hopes, the stigma fixed on Lieut. Col. Brown by the above sentence, will be a sufficient warning to all Officers, not to be guilty of the like offence, especially as the General is confident, no General Court Martial will, for the future, admit a plea of ignorance, in excuse of so atrocious a crime." The parole is given as Uxbridge and the countersign as Williamsburg.

8 October 1775:
Sunday. At headquarters, Cambridge, George Washington and his General Officers meet in a Council of War, and agree that the new army must contain at least 20,372 men, enlisted for a full one-year term. This conclusion is passed on to the Congress, who must decide just how such a force will be provided.

At Carratuncas on the Kennebec River, Arnold's army is working to get all the divisions over this carrying place. It is difficult work, because the river is running fast, in many places it is shallow, and it is raining.

9 October 1775:
Monday. British Maj. Gen William Howe writes to Lord Dartmouth with his view that the British army should be evacuated from Boston, and moved to Rhode Island, where it "would be better connected, and the corps would act with greater effect."

10 October 1775:
Tuesday. Lt. Gen. Thomas Gage, being recalled by Germain because it is believed that Gage lacks the vigor and initiative to prosecute the war, departs from Boston for a return to England. He is succeeded as Commander-in-chief by Major General William Howe.

Arnold notes in his journal "At 9 A.M. arrived at Curratunck (sic) falls ... here mountains begin to appear on each side the river, high, & snow on the tops ..."

11 October 1775:

Wednesday. John Hancock writes to Philip Schuyler, Commander of the Northern Department, expressing the hope of Congress that endeavors in Canada will result in convincing the Canadians to join in union with the 13 Colonies, form a Provincial Convention, and send delegates to the Continental Congress. One wonders at these views of the Congress toward Canada, who, only a few months ago were being very chary about involving any Canadians in this colonial revolt.

Meigs reports in his journal "I crossed the great carrying place, as far as the third pond. There had the pleasure to discover Lieut. Steele and party, who had been sent forward on a reconnoitering command, as far as the Chaudiere Pond. They discovered nothing with regard to the enemy. I returned back to the second pond and lodged with Col. Greene."

12 October 1775:

Thursday. The Irish Parliament finalizes an address to King George III, pledging their "unfeigned zeal and unshaken loyalty" for the King and the British government.

At Cambridge, Washington writes to the President of Congress, "With respect to the reduction of the pay of the men, which may enter into the consideration of their support, it is the unanimous opinion of the General Officers, that it cannot be touched with safety at present. I had given orders for the equipment of some armed vessels to intercept the enemy's supplies of provisions and ammunition. Our last accounts from Col. Arnold are very favorable; he was proceeding with all expedition, and I flatter myself, making all allowances he will be at Quebec the 20th instant. The latest and best accounts we have from the enemy are, that they are engaged in their new work across the South End of Boston, preparing their barracks for winter, keeping about 500 men at Bunker's Hill to be relived each week. There is some discussion of stirring up the Indians in the southern colonies, which I transmit for your information."

13 October 1775:

Friday. Congress authorizes the creation of a navy for the Continental forces. It votes to outfit two ships, one of which is to be of ten guns--a rather small Navy, but a start. Prior to this, vessels used for protection or for capturing British supply ships either have been army authorized and outfitted, part of locally authorized expeditions, individual colony efforts, or privateers, rather than Continental authorized naval units. Such individual ship manning and privateer efforts will continue throughout the War of the American Revolution, alongside Continental naval forces.

Meigs notes "Col. Enos arrived this day at the great carrying place, with the 4th division of the army, consisting of three companies of musketmen."

14 October 1775:

Saturday. In London, Secretary of State Lord Suffolk, receives intelligence that the colony of Pennsylvania is preparing an armed fleet and floating batteries to prevent the passage of the King's ships through the Delaware River. Suffolk recommends that the Admiralty dispatch a vessel to destroy the floating batteries.

15 October 1775:

Sunday. The investment of Fort St. John goes forward, but first it seems that the post at Fort Chambly must be captured in order to isolate St. John from any support from the north. Efforts are prepared to move a detachment around the fort, and proceed down the Richelieu River with cannon and troops to force the surrender of Chambly, a stone fort guarding the river near some shallow falls.[See Fig. II-6, p. 69]. Brigadier General Montgomery is anxious to complete the capture of both places so as to move on Montreal as soon as possible.

The Arnold expedition is working to cross the three ponds (or small lakes) at the great carrying place. It is extremely hard work. One man is severely injured by a falling tree, blown down by the wind.

16 October 1775:

Monday. The maritime minister of France sends orders to officials in port towns urging them to prevent American ships from loading war munitions.

Arnold notes in the Journal being kept for him "Early in the morning continued our route over the Savanna (sic) which is divided by a small wood ... The road excessive wet and miry, being up to our knees ..."

To provide a semblance of a proper navy for use of the patriots, two schooners, the *Lynch* and *Franklin* are being fitted out. That means they are being prepared with a new set of sails, heavier decking to carry the weight of guns, and more anchors to allow for kedging. They are under the command of Captain Brought and Selman. Their orders are, "The honorable Continental Congress having received intelligence that two north country brigantines of no force sailed from England some time ago for Quebec, laden with six thousand stand of arms, a large quantity of powder and other stores. You are hereby directed to make all possible dispatch for the River St. Lawrence and there to take such a station as will best enable you to intercept the above vessels. You are also to seize and take any other transports laden with men, ammunition, clothing, or other stores for the use of the Ministerial Army or Navy in America, and secure them in such places as may be most safe and convenient."

17 October 1775:
    Tuesday. In Wilmington, North Carolina, the colony's Committee of Safety orders the creation and sale of certificates proving one's loyalty to the American cause. To encourage the sale of such certificates, the committee orders that no business be conducted with any citizen of the colony unless they produce one of the certificates.
    During this night, 135 Americans, under Major John Brown, ambush a supply train headed for Fort Chambly, about 11 miles north of Fort St. John on the Richelieu River. This allows the Americans to begin a siege of the place.

18 October 1775:
    Wednesday. A British naval squadron, under the command of Lieutenant Henry Mowat, bombards and burns the waterfront of Falmouth (now Portland, Maine). Mowat has given the inhabitants some time to evacuate the place, but many later complained that not enough time was allowed for them to remove their belongings and also the older people in some families. (See sketch for 24 October 1775.)
    The British at Chambly sally forth to disrupt the siege attempts by the Americans, but American Colonel Timothy Bedel arrives with 500 reinforcements to help Brown drive them back, and an investment begins.
    A three-man committee from the Continental Congress meets with Washington and representatives of Connecticut, Rhode Island, and Massachusetts, because those states are the location and source of men, food, and forage; to draw up a plan for the reorganizing, supply, and continuance of the Continental Army.
    At the Dead River, Meigs reports in his journal "In the morning ordered eight men to kill two oxen, which we had drove with great difficulty to this place, and to bring forward five-quarters to the detachment that was gone forward, and to leave three-quarters under a guard for Col. Eno's division. Then I proceeded up the river with my division about 20 miles."

19 October 1775:
    Thursday. Fort Chambly is fully invested, and the Americans bring up their cannon to batter down the walls and force a surrender.
    In New York, the Royal Governor, William Tryon, retires to, and seeks refuge on, the British warship HMS *Duchess of Gordon* in the harbor. He will stay there until the British return in 1776. The patriots in New York take this flight as an act of abdication of his responsibilities as governor.
    Meigs notes "This day I received orders from Col. Arnold to proceed with my division with the greatest expedition, to Chaudiére River, and when arrived there, to make up our cartridges, and wait for the rear division, and furnish a number of pioneers, under command of Mr. Ayers, to clear the

carrying place."

20 October 1775:

Friday. The Congressional Committee meeting with Washington regarding the planning for the Continental Army agrees that the forces so raised should be supplied with provisions by the New England colonies. Washington is granted authority to impress wagons, vessels, horses, and other necessary items. He also urges that when the current eight-months army of New England militia units service ends, he will require a new Continental army, and requests a term of three year or the duration of the war.

The siege of Chambly ends after a few cannon shots are fired by the Americans into the thin-walled stone fort. British Major Stopford surrenders with 88 officers and men, and a large store of gunpowder, musket cartridges, three mortars, and 125 stand of arms are taken by the American victors.

21 October 1775:

Saturday. Upon the recommendation of the Continental Congress and with news of an imminent attack, the Provincial Congress of New York orders all sulfur and brimstone supplies in New York City to a safe place up on the Hudson River.

Dr. Senter notes in his journal about the weather and the problems the troops are having to contend with on Arnold's Expedition "The storm had increased excessively, and had now raised the river to a quick running current. The wind increased to an almost hurricane the latter part of the day."

Arnold reports in his journal "... slept very comfortably until 4 o'clock in the morning, when we were awakened by the freshet which came rushing on us like a torrent, having rose 8 feet perpendicular in 9 hours, and before we could remove all our baggage & forced us from our comfortable habitation ..."

22 October 1775:

Sunday. Peyton Randolph, a Virginia Delegate, and former President of the Continental Congress, dies this day in Philadelphia.

In London, William Legge, Second Lord Dartmouth and Secretary for the Colonies, prepares instructions for Major General Howe in Boston to dispatch an expedition to the southern colonies, perhaps Charleston. The impetus is the British belief that local Loyalist support will rise up to help defeat the patriots.

Arnold's Expedition, heavily rained upon, blown about, and wet to the skin, spends the whole day drying out their baggage and clothes.

23 October 1775:

Monday. The Congressional Committee meeting with Washington agrees to accept the Penobscot, Stockbridge, and

St. John Indian tribes' offers of assistance, allowing them to be employed in the Army, if necessary. The Committee decides, however, to exclude Negroes.

Arnold notes in his journal that "... we had the misfortune of oversetting 7 battoes (sic) loosing (sic) all the provisions." Dr. Senter reports in his journal "The number of bateaux were now much decreased. Some stove to pieces against the banks, while others became so excessive leaky as obliged us to condemn them."

24 October 1775:

Tuesday. A Falmouth resident, Pearson Jones, pens a report of the incident of the British naval bombardment of the town on 18 October 1775. He severely criticizes the British for their inhumanity, their willful destruction of property, and the endangerment of lives.

Washington writes to the Falmouth Committee of Safety explaining why he cannot send detachments from his army to protect them, as they have requested. To do so is a ploy the British continue to employ--hoping to lure Washington into committing forces to dispersed places in fights he is not likely to win, and also to weaken his central command.

The conflict between Governor Dunmore of Virginia and the rebel patriot forces reaches the shooting stage, when the frustrated Royal Governor sends naval forces to destroy Norfolk, Virginia. Captain Squire sails six of his tenders into Hampton Creek, and starts to bombard the town. He also sends landing parties ashore to apply the torch. Patriot riflemen drive off the boats and kill several British seamen.

Arnold sends back the sick men of his army. He also orders Colonels Greene and Enos to send back as many of their poorest soldiers in their detachments, as will leave 15 days ration for the remainder. Dr. Senter reports in his journal "Approaching necessity now obliged us to double our diligence. Three miles only had we proceeded ere we came to a troublesome water-fall in the river ... Not more than the last mentioned distance before we were brought up by another. As the number of falls increased, the water became consequently more rapid." He also found men without food, eating candles for supper.

25 October 1775:

Wednesday. At dawn, American Colonel William Woodford arrives at Norfolk with 100 Culpeper militia and deploys them to repel any renewed attack by the British upon the town. The American riflemen are able to shoot the British sailors, gunners, and topmen in such numbers that the British are ordered to withdraw. Two of the British sloops run aground and are captured. Five vessels are sunk and one boat is captured with seven sailors aboard. There are no American casualties.

Dr. Senter notes in his journal "Every prospect of distress now came thundering on us with two fold rapidity. A storm of snow had covered the ground of nigh 6 inches deep, attended with very severe weather." Senter also recapitulates the order of marching and the reasons therefore: Morgan with the first division, the pioneers, and the least provisions, who are to blaze the way, cut paths, mark out carrying places, and reconnoiter the route; Greene with the second division to improve the route, carry more provisions, and assist at the carrying places; Meigs with the third division to bring on more provisions and further improve the route; Enos with the fourth or last division with all the balance of the provisions, and the easiest travel of the army, since much of the work was to have been done by the earlier divisions on the route. Yet, in this time of trial and difficulty, it is Enos who turns back. Lt. Col. Roger Enos, commander of the 2nd Connecticut Regiment, with his men, quits the expedition and returns down the river. The defection of Enos' entire section, added to the loss of men from injury, sickness, or accident, reduces Arnold's force to continue on to Quebec to less than 700 men.

26 October 1775:

Thursday. Patriot forces attack the British at Hampton, Virginia.

The Continental Congress passes a resolution recommending that all colonies export goods to the West Indies in exchange for the import of arms, ammunition, sulfur and saltpeter.

At Cambridge, Washington writes to Philip Schuyler, "Colonel Allen's misfortune will I hope, teach a lesson of prudence and subordination to others, who may be too ambitious to outshine their General Officers, and regardless of order and duty, rush into enterprizes, which have unfavorable effects to the public, and are destructive to themselves. Dr. Franklin, Mr. Lynch and Col. Harrison, delegates from the Congress have been in the capital camp for several days, in order to settle the plan of continuing and supporting the army. This Commission extended to your Department; but upon consideration, it appeared so difficult to form any rational plans that nothing was done upon that head. If your time and health will admit I should think it highly proper to turn your thoughts to this subject, and communicate the result to the Congress, as early as possible. We have had no event of any consequence in our Camp for some time, our whole attention being taken up with preparations for the winter, and forming the new army, in which many difficulties occur. The enemy expect considerable reinforcements this winter and from all accounts are garrisoning Gibraltar and other places with foreign troops, in order to bring the former garrisons to America. The Ministry have begun the destruction of our sea port towns by burning a flourishing town of about 300 houses to the eastward, called

Falmouth. This they effected with every circumstance of cruelty and barbarity, which revenge and malice would suggest. We expect every moment to hear other places had been attempted and had been better prepared for their reception. The more I reflect upon the importance of your expedition, the greater is my concern, least it should sink under insuperable difficulties. I look upon the interests and salvation of our bleeding country in a great degree to depend upon your success."

27 October 1775:
Friday. In Philadelphia, the Society of Friends (Quakers), asks the Pennsylvania Assembly "... to guard against any proposal or attempt to deprive us and others of the full enjoyment of liberty of conscience." Quaker religious beliefs prohibit members from bearing arms or supporting armed conflict through personal service or financial obligation.

Suspicious of the actions of American Surgeon General, Dr. Benjamin Church, General Washington, places him under arrest to be held for trial as a spy.

Meigs notes in his journal "In the morning continued our route across the carrying place ..." at the height of land. Arnold makes the Chaudiere River the place of rendezvous for the scattered troops of the divisions of his army. Dr. Senter notes in his journal "Our bill of fare for last night and this morning consisted of the jawbone of a swine destitute of any covering. This we boiled in a quantity of water, and with a little thickening constituted our sumptuous eating."

28 October 1775:
Saturday. Major General William Howe, the new Commander-in-Chief of the British Army in America, issues a proclamation to the American residents of Boston forbidding any person from leaving the city on pain of death. He also orders citizens to organize into military companies in order to aid in the defense of their city.

Meigs reports arriving at the Chaudiere River. Senter notes in his journal "The provisions were ordered into one fund, in order that every man might be acquainted with what he had to depend upon to carry him into the inhabitants, computed at about a hundred miles."

29 October 1775:
Sunday. Four armed American vessels sail from Cambridge as part of a fleet created to cruise the coast in search of enemy transports carrying arms and provisions.

Most of Arnold's army marches 18 miles, out of the height of land and down the Chaudiere River.

30 October 1775:
Monday. Congress establishes the Naval Committee. It is the first real administrative Committee on standing naval

affairs for the colonies. Two additional ships are authorized, one to carry 20 guns, the other 36.

Captain Henry Dearborn keeps a journal of his experiences during the Arnold Expedition to Quebec. He reports in it that "We marched very early in the morning, our provisions to be very scant, some companies had but one pint of flour for each man and no meat at all."

In Montreal, Guy Carleton, in an effort to relieve Fort St. John, sends a force of about 800 men, under Lt. Col. Allan McLean, to cross the St. Lawrence River. However, a force of Green Mountain Boys and troops of the 2nd New York, under Seth Warner have occupied the opposite bank of the river and create such a hot fire that the British effort is turned back. The siege of St. John continues.

On the Arnold Trek, Dr. Senter writes in his journal "In this state of uncertainty we wandered through hideous swamps and mountainous precipices with the conjoint addition of cold, wet, and hunger, not to mention our fatigue—with the terrible ... famishing ..."

31 October 1775:
　　Tuesday. Washington tries to encourage re-enlistment in the new army establishment by reserving new supplies for those who agree to commit to another full year of service. He also promises each man time to visit his family during the coming winter.

Dearborn notes in his journal "We started out very early this morning, I am still more unwell ... Carried our canoe over a carrying place ... We went down about 28 miles."

1 November 1775:
　　Wednesday. The Continental Congress learns of King George's rejection of the Olive Branch Petition they had completed back on 23 Aug 1775, and of his declaration that all the American colonies are in rebellion. They also receive reports that the British troops soon to be sent to subdue them will be accompanied by German mercenaries from several of the German principalities.

The Congress resolves to ban the export of produce and livestock, except horses, from the colonies unless the proceeds of the shipments are used to purchase military stores.

Meigs notes in his journal "This day I passed a number of soldiers who had no provisions, and some that were sick, and not in my power to help or relieve them, except to encourage them. One or two dogs were killed, which the distressed soldiers eat with good appetite, even the feet and skins."

2 November 1775:
　　Thursday. American troops, under the Command of Brig. Gen. Richard Montgomery, finally end the siege after 55 days with the surrender and capture of Fort St. John, Canada. British Major Preston surrenders 600 defenders. For the

Americans, it is a very expensive victory in both time and personnel, since it delays any attack upon Montreal and the capitol city of Quebec. [See Fig. II-6, p. 67].

The trial of Dr. Benjamin Church finds him guilty. He is convicted of treason, dismissed from the service, expelled from Massachusetts, and imprisoned. Eventually he is allowed to sail for the West Indies, but his ship disappears en route.

3 November 1775:
Friday. In Cambridge, Washington deplores the destruction of "So many valuable Plantations of Trees" by the soldiers to be used for firewood. He writes that, "from Fences to Forest Trees to fruit Trees, is a Nationwide advance to houses, which must next follow ..."

Meigs reports "At 12 o'clock we met provisions, to the inexpressible joy of our soldiers, who were near starving. After refreshing ourselves, marched a few miles and encamped."

In Saluda County, South Carolina, an America militia force seizes the ammunition stored at Mine Creek.

4 November 1775:
Saturday. The Continental Congress agrees to underwrite the cost of raising three battalions for the defense of South Carolina and one for the colony of Georgia. Congress also recommends that South Carolina create a new form of government, more representative of the republican form, than the currently used monarchial form.

The Congress also comes to agree with General Washington and his General Officer recommendation of 8 October 1775, as to the size and makeup of the new Continental Army. It thus authorizes a reorganization of a force of at least 20,372 men, enlisted for one full year (a three year-term was felt to be too long), beginning on 1 January 1776.

At Sartigan on the Chaudiere River, Dr. Senter writes in his journal "The five miles march last evening brought us to the Colonel's quarters (Arnold), and this morning the savages assembled.. and waited on the Colonel to know our reasons for coming among them..." Arnold makes a speech to the Indians, which seems to get 50 of them to assist in transporting parts of the army farther down the river.

5 November 1775:
Sunday. In General Orders this day, Washington admonishes the troops at Cambridge for celebrating the anti-Catholic Guy Fawkes Day while the Congress and the army are attempting to win French Canadian support for the cause of the revolution.

King George III receives numerous expressions of support for his repressive policies towards the American colonies from communities in England and Scotland. Lord North has organized this endorsement campaign.

Brig. Gen. Richard Montgomery begins his march towards

Montreal. It has taken a long time to train his troops, organize them into a good fighting unit, and bloody them in short fights with the British. The delay in reducing Fort St. John has cost him dearly as winter approaches. [See Fig. II-6, p. 67]

The Congress appoints Esek Hopkins as Commodore of the small, four-vessel Continental fleet outfitting in Philadelphia: *Columbus* (10 guns); *Alfred* (14 guns); *Andrew Doria* (20 guns); *Cabot* (36 guns). Hopkins will make good use of this group of vessels as he raids British shipping.

6 November 1775:

Monday. The Governor of Jamaica reports to London that, "the North Americans are simply supplied with Gun Powder and many other Military Stores by the French in Hispanola, which is sold at an advanc'd price by the inhabitants who I find import great quantitys [sic] from Old France, finding it such an advantageous article of Commerce. But I do not learn that they get any out of the Royal Stores or Magazines."

Rhode Island passes a law making the death penalty the punishment for any citizen proved to have assisted England in suppressing the revolution.

7 November 1775:

Tuesday. In Philadelphia, the Continental Congress, not satisfied with some of the language, further amends the Articles of War.

In Virginia, Governor Dunmore, based on the British vessel HMS *William* at Norfolk, issues a proclamation declaring Virginia under martial law. It has little or no effect, since he is not able to control the courts, the militia nor the towns.

In Rhode Island, the General Assembly, which had been suspended by the Royal Governor, Joseph Wanton, on 3 May 1775, for "unpatriotic activities," acts to depose the governor. This clears the way for a representative form of government.

The Arnold Expedition, works its way down the Chaudiere River towards Point Levis on the St. Lawrence. The going is a bit easier on the lower reaches of the river, and with some food, water, and rest, they are slightly recovered from their near famished condition.

8 November 1775:

Wednesday. General George Washington is confronted with some serious problems in army organization, supply, discipline, and training. How to encourage experienced troops to enlist for the next year? How to assemble and train a capable officer corps? How to overcome the serious problem of local and provincial differences and rivalries? He writes to the Congress, "Connecticut wants no Massachusetts men in her corps. Massachusetts thinks there is no necessity for a Rhode Islander ..."

9 November 1775:

Thursday. At Phipp's Farm, (Lechmere Point), patriot militia drive off a British raiding party of nine companies of Light Infantry and 100 grenadiers, seeking cattle to supply the Boston garrison. Americans, fearing that this was more than a foraging party, stage a counterattack, under command of Colonel William Thompson and his Pennsylvania riflemen. The British quickly withdrew with only ten cows.

The Congress learns of the rejection of the Olive Branch Petition by King George III.

Colonel Benedict Arnold, having sailed out of Newburyport, Massachusetts on 19 September 1775, and after a most arduous and frustrating trek to Quebec up the Kennebec River and over the Heights of Land, finally leads about 600 of his weary men to the St. Lawrence River at Pointe Levis, nearly opposite the city of Quebec. [See Fig. II-5, p. 55]

10 November 1775:
        Friday. Congress adopts resolutions to encourage domestic production of saltpeter, to raise two battalions of Marines, and to dispatch two agents to Nova Scotia to secure information on the sentiments of the populace regarding joining with the Americans in resisting British control, and in their state of military readiness.

11 November 1775:
        Saturday. The Continental Congress retains the missionary, Samuel Kirkland, engaging him to spread the "Gospel amongst the Indians" and confirm "Their affections to the United Colonies ... thereby preserving their friendship and neutrality."

Governor Carleton at Montreal has only about 150 troops and a few militia remaining in the town. The walls of the town will only stop musketry, not cannon, and in some places have fallen into disrepair. It is not a hopeful situation, when facing Brig. Gen. Montgomery's American force of more than 1,000 men. Carleton therefore puts on shipboard his valuable military stores, destroys the rest, and sails away under fire from American shore batteries.

In Quebec, the American leader of the Green Mountain Boys, Colonel Ethan Allen, who had so impetuously and imprudently attacked Montreal in a rash action on 25 September 1775, and was captured, has been removed by slow degrees to this place. Now he is placed on the ship, HMS *Adamant*, in chains, for transportation to England.

In Charleston Harbor, South Carolina, American Captain Simon Tufts on his vessel *Defense* clashes with two British vessels, *Tamer* and *Cherokee*, while on a mission to blockade Hog Island Creek.

12 November 1775:
        Sunday. Upon hearing of England's rejection of the Olive Branch Petition, Abigail Adams writes, "Let us separate. They are unworthy to be our Brethren. Let us renounce them and instead of supplications as formerly for their prosperity and

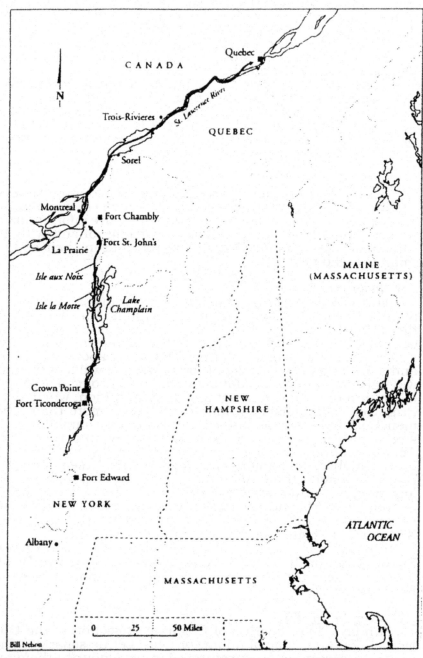

Fig. II-6: Montgomery's Battles in Canada, 1775

happiness, let us beseech the almighty to blast their councils and bring to Nought all their devices."

At Hog Island Channel in Charleston Harbor, Captain Simon Tufts successfully sinks several hulks he had towed there to create a blockage.

An attack upon the British post at Montreal by American Brigadier General Richard Montgomery's American forces begins. [See Fig. II-6, p. 70].

13 November 1775:
Monday. The Massachusetts General Court authorizes owners of merchant vessels to engage in privateering under authority and license of the state.

Montgomery's attack upon Montreal, after an easy battle, leads to the city's surrender by a deputation of its citizens, capture by American forces, and its occupation. However, Governor Guy Carleton has already departed with some of the military stores and men down river toward Quebec.

Colonel Arnold's expedition, having procured more than 20 birch bark canoes and a dozen dugouts, manages to cross the St. Lawrence River under cover of darkness, avoiding the British vessels in the harbor, to the Quebec, or north, shore. [See Fig. II-5, p. 55].

14 November 1775:
Tuesday. A skirmish takes place between about 150 patriot militia, under Colonel William Woodford, and 350 loyalists, under Governor Dunmore at Kemp's Landing, Virginia. The Loyalists are holding and guarding a bridge when the patriots attack. The loyalists defeat the attackers, and pursues them for a short distance.

King George III informs Lord North that he has contracted to raise as many as 4,000 German soldiers from various principalities on the continent for use by Great Britain in the war in America. These become known as the Hessians, that the British rent from six different German leaders during the war, in total nearly 29,000 such troops.

15 November 1775:
Wednesday. Virginia Royal Governor Dunmore issues a proclamation offering freedom to "all indentured Servants, Negroes, or others, [appertaining to rebels] ... that are able to bear arms, they joining His Majesty's Troops."

Arnold expedition, having crossed the St. Lawrence River, occupies the Plains of Abraham and tries to bluff the garrison at Quebec into surrender, without success.

16 November 1775:
Thursday. In Quebec, a Council of War decides to defend the city by securing troops from naval vessels.

In Cambridge Washington writes to Philip Schuyler, "Dear Sir: I wrote to you this day by express and informed you therein the great necessity I was in for ordinance stores and ammunition, and that I would send you Henry Knox, Esqr. To

New York, to procure there, as much as can be spared: from thence to proceed to you. That Gentleman will deliver you this letter. I recommend him and the business he goes upon to your attention. Should he find more money than he carries with him necessary, you will please to supply him."

Washington gives Henry Knox the following written instructions, "You are immediately to examine into the state of artillery of this army, and take an account of the Cannon, Mortars, Shells, Lead and Ammunition, that are wanting. When you have done that, you are to proceed in the most expeditious manner to New York; there apply to the President of the Provisional Congress, and learn of him whether Colonel Reed did any thing, or left any orders respecting these articles, and get him to procure such of them as can possibly be had there. The President, if he can, will have them immediately sent hither: if he cannot you must put them in a proper channel for being transported to this camp with dispatch, before you leave New York. After you have procured as many of these necessaries as you can there, you must go to Major General Schuyler, and get the remainder from Ticonderoga, Crown Point, or St. John. If it should be necessary, from Quebec, if in our hands. The want of them is so great, that no trouble or expense must be spared to obtain them. I have wrote to General Schuyler, he will give every necessary assistance that they may be had and forwarded to this place with the utmost dispatch. I have given you a Warrant to the Pay-Master General of the Continental Army, for a thousand dollars to defray the expense attending your journey, and procuring these articles; an account of which you are to keep and render upon your return. Endeavor to procure what flints you can."

17 November 1775:

Friday. *The Virginia Gazette* carries a letter from a reader advising planters to warn their slaves that the British government are worse enemies than their masters; that if Americans are defeated, the slaves will be sold in the West Indies, and to advise the slaves to look for an improved status in the next world.

Colonel Richard Gridley is relieved as Chief of Artillery of the New England Army. Though his prior experience has made him valuable in the fighting, he is a sickly man and cannot continue to command. Henry Knox is named as his replacement.

18 November 1775:

Saturday. Colonel Henry Knox, now Chief of Artillery, with his brother, William, sets out towards New York City and Fort Ticonderoga for an expedition intended to bring selected cannon back to the Boston area for use in properly completing the siege of the city, and forcing the British to leave. The Knox brothers leave Cambridge and reach Marboro (Marlborough), Massachusetts. Soon they will be in Worcester, where Henry would see his wife, Lucy Knox.

Lord Germain, who has recently become the new Secretary

of State for America, succeeding Lord Dartmouth, informs Maj. Gen. William Howe that 20,000 soldiers are to be supplied for the spring campaign and five regiments are to be dispatched to the Carolinas by the end of November.

At the walls before Quebec, Benedict Arnold's detachment, fearing an attack upon them from a larger British force and being without artillery, in a Council of War decides to withdraw from their position on the Plains of Abraham.

19 November 1775:

Sunday. In the interior parts of South Carolina, William H. Drayton has not had great success in rallying large numbers of patriots to his forces. The Tories in the area are bold and rather numerous and decide to return to the vicinity of Ninety-Six in Greenwood County, South Carolina. In doing so the Tories find a patriot detachment under Major Andrew Williamson with about 550 men, and drive them into Ninety-Six with a larger force of more than 1,000 men.

Arnold's detachment marches up the St. Lawrence River about 20 miles to Pointe aux Trembles, where they are quartered in a village. It has been a long and extremely difficult trek from Fort Western, and now here they are, removed from their objective, Quebec, and no closer to a means of attacking the place than they were ten days ago. Arnold, who seeks action, is frustrated by his inability to come to grips with the defenders of Quebec. [See Fig. II-5, p. 55].

Adverse winds slow the British movement down river from Montreal, under the command of Governor Guy Carleton. The Americans take advantage of this, set up batteries on the banks of the St. Lawrence River, and begin a bombardment of the British flotilla. Colonel John Brown demands the surrender of the British Flotilla, to which they are forced to agree. Armed vessels, several small craft, and stores are captured. However, Guy Carleton and a few officers manage to slip away and escape ashore, and thence walk down river to enter Quebec.

20 November 1775:

Monday. At Cambridge, Washington writes to Joseph Reed, complaining of Reed's wish to resign as his Aide-de-Camp, remarks that he needs him very badly. He then goes on to discuss other matters "Dr. Church is gone to Governor Trumbull, to be disposed of in a Connecticut gaol, without the use of pen, ink, or paper, to be conversed with in the presence of a magistrate only, and in the English language. So much for indiscretion, the Doctor will say. Your accounts of dependence upon the people of Great Britain, I religiously believe. It has long been my political creed, that the ministry durst not have gone on as they did, but under the firmest persuasion that the people were with them. The weather has been unfavorable, however, for the arrival of their transports; only four companies of the seventeenth regiment and two of the artillery are yet arrived, by our last advices from Boston. Arnold, by a letter which left him the 27th ultimo, had then only got to the Chaudiére Pond and was scarce of provisions. His rear division, under the command of the noble Colonel Enos, had, without his privity or consent, left him with three companies; and his expedition, I fear, in a bad way."

A siege of Ninety-Six, South Carolina, soon develops, with the defending Tories outnumbering the patriots. There are a few casualties on both sides. It seems to be a stand off.

21 November 1775:
Tuesday. At headquarters, Cambridge, General Orders state "John Davidson of Capt. Bancrafts Company, and Thomas Knolton of Capt. Towns Company, Col. Bridge's Regimt. , tried at the General Court Martial of which Col. Aaron Cleveland was President, for 'quitting their post when upon duty.' The Court were of opinion that the prisoners are guilty of the crime laid to their charge, and do adjudge them to be punish'd with fifteen lashes each, but on account of the youth and ignorance of their duty, the Court recommend the prisoners for mercy. The General is pleased, upon the recommendation of the Court, to pardon the prisoners, but at the same time desires, it may be noticed, that such a crime will not meet mercy in future." The parole is given as Gloucester and the counter sign as Hampshire.

After two days of inconclusive and desultory fighting, a truce is arranged between the two sides at the fortified settlement of Ninety-Six, South Carolina, and the forces again separate.

22 November 1775:
Wednesday. Congress resolves to permit the colonies to export a fixed amount of provisions to Bermuda, where inhabitants are faced with starvation, in return for salt, which is badly needed in the colonies. Unlimited quantities of food can be exported from the colonies, if the return cargoes contain the desired military supplies.

In South Carolina, a force of loyalists, assembling at Reedy River, are dispersed by patriots.

23 November 1775:
Thursday. Richard Montgomery writes, "Till Quebec is taken, Canada is unconquered." He concludes that an attack of the city is inevitable, and prepares the troops for such an operation. One of his main difficulties is heavy cannon. He has none.

In Virginia, the numerous skirmishes, and a few larger battles between patriot detachments and Tories under Governor Dunmore, result in the British capture of the town of Norfolk.

24 November 1775:
Friday. At headquarters, Cambridge, Washington writes to Aaron Willard, a Massachusetts business man. The Continental Congress desires that two persons be sent to Nova Scotia to inquire into the state of and disposition of the inhabitants thereof toward the American cause. "I do hereby constitute and

appoint you the said Aaron Willard, Esq. to be one of the persons to undertake this business, and as the season is late, and this work of great importance, I entreat and request that you will use the utmost dispatch, attention, and fidelity in the execution of it. The necessity of acting secretly, is too apparent to need recommendation. You will keep an account of your expenses, and upon your return will be rewarded in a suitable manner, for the fatigue of your journey and the services you render your country, by conducting and discharging this business with expedition and fidelity."

The Pennsylvania Assembly brands as public enemies all individuals who refuse to accept provincial bills of credit.

In Virginia, in response to Lord Dunmore's Proclamation of 7 November, *The Virginia Gazette*, publishes the following: "Here you have a proclamation that will at once show the *baseness* of lord Dunmore's heart, his *malice* and *treachery* against the people who were *once* under his government, and his *officious* violation of all law, justice, and humanity; not to mention his *arrogating* to himself a power which neither he can assume, nor any power upon earth invest him."

25 November 1775:
Saturday. Colonel Henry Knox and his brother William Knox arrive in New York City en route to Fort Ticonderoga.

The South Carolina Congress resolves that "the colony is in a state of actual alarm" and sends additional militia forces into the interior to reinforce those fighting against the loyalists.

Congress formally declares that British vessels are subject to capture, and sets up Admiralty Courts to deal with prizes and prize money.

26 November 1775:
Sunday. In his absence, George Washington instructs his manager at Mount Vernon plantation to "Let the Hospitality of the House, with respect to the poor, be kept up. Let no one go hungry away."

27 November 1775:
Monday. Richard Montgomery begins a march from Montreal towards the city of Quebec.

Captain John Manley, of the American schooner *Lee*, captures the British brig *Nancy* off the Massachusetts coast, and brings her into Cape Ann for unloading. She yields a most important cargo of much needed military stores: 2,000 muskets, 100,000 flints, 30,000 round shot, 30 tons of musket shot, and a 13" brass mortar, renamed "Congress".

28 November 1775:
Tuesday. The Continental Congress, having earlier set up a Naval Committee, now formally establishes by adoption "Rules for the Regulation of the Navy of the United Colonies"--a true naval branch for the Continental Navy of the United Colonies.

Henry Knox and his brother leave New York City on

horseback and ride hard north toward Albany.

The Congress resolves to appoint a Committee of Secret Correspondence, not to be confused with the "Secret Committee" formed on 18 September 1775 for commerce and trade. It is a five- man committee that is the embryo of what becomes the Committee on Foreign Affairs and even later the Department of State.

Samuel Nicholas is commissioned as a Marine. He is the first officer of the new Marine Corps authorized by the Congress on 10 May 1775.

29 November 1775:

Wednesday. Congress appoints the members of a secret committee to explore and seek out possible assistance (supply, fiscal, military, political) from European nations in the fight against Britain.

At Cambridge, Washington writes to the Massachusetts Legislature, "The necessity of giving furloughs to the soldiers of the present, who inlists (sic) into the new army, by way of encouragement and to afford opportunity of providing necessaries for themselves and families, was so strongly impress'd upon me, that I have consented to fifty of a Regiment being absent at a time. This will be a reduction of at least 1500 men from the strength of our lines; to t his I am to add, that contrary to my expectations and assurances given, I now find that the Connecticut Regiments cannot be induced to stay beyond their limited term. Such a considerable diminution of our force, at a time when so capitol a change is taking place in the face of an enemy, increasing in strength, cannot but be attended with extreme hazard, if some expedient is not fallen upon to supply the deficiency. In perusing a Resolve of your Honble. Body, I perceive it to be determined, that your troops are to be paid by the Lunar (28 days to the month) from the time of their enlisting to the first of August. I cannot help observing as my opinion, that it will throw the rest of this army into disorder and that as the Continental Congress have explicit terms resolved that it is the Calendar Months that they mean to pay by; that the difference between the two must be considered as a Colonial not a Continental charge."

30 November 1775:

Thursday. At Pointe aux Trembles, Arnold's men are beginning to recover somewhat from the cold, lack of food, and lack of shoes they have suffered during their famous trek up the Kennebec River. Sheltered in houses, and finding ample cattle in the villages near their quarters, they are building an adequate food supply. They have made coverings for their feet from the hides of cattle slaughtered for meat. Arnold now feels that his men are ready for an attack upon Quebec. He takes a small patrol to reconnoiter possible routes of attack.

1 December 1775:

Friday. Brigadier General Montgomery, and his men sail down the St. Lawrence River towards Quebec and a union with

Colonel Arnold's detachment, so that the joint command can invest and attack the city.

Henry Knox reaches the welcome sight of Albany. There he confers with Philip Schuyler about ways and means of transporting the guns he hopes to transfer to the army around Boston.

2 December 1775:

Saturday. In Philadelphia, Thomas Jefferson proposes a resolution in the Congress calling for the exchange of Ethan Allen, captured by the British at Montreal, for a British officer of equal rank.

On the St. Lawrence River, Richard Montgomery, this evening, with more than 300 men arrives at the American encampment at Pointe aux Trembles (now Neuville) to reinforce Benedict Arnold's detachment. Montgomery also brings artillery, a good supply of ammunition, clothing, and provisions.

3 December 1775:

Sunday. Montgomery, having joined forces with Arnold, plans to march toward Quebec and lay siege to the city.

At Cambridge, the captain of an American schooner brings in a captured enemy vessel carrying 5,000 pounds of dry goods.

The British revive a fear of smallpox by sending victims of the disease from Boston into the patriot lines.

The first official Continental Flag, (13 alternate red and white strips with the British Union in the canton--now called the Grand Union Flag) is raised aboard the *Alfred,* a 24-gun ship, commanded by John Paul Jones.

4 December 1775:

Monday. In an effort to prevent Connecticut troops from leaving the service, Major General Charles Lee threatens to cut off provisions for three weeks to those who do not re-enlist, and posts a notice to innkeepers between Cambridge and Hartford asking them to refuse service to deserters. Soldiers react to the notice by posting one of their own stating, "General Lee is a fool and if he had not come here we should not know it."

Henry Knox and his brother arrive at Fort George this evening, at the foot of Lake George. Not wishing to sail up the lake at night, they spend the night there. Henry is quartered with a young British Lieutenant, John André, making his way south.

5 December 1775:

Tuesday. Recruitment and retention woes continue for Washington, as Massachusetts sets a monthly pay schedule of twenty-eight days (lunar, instead of calendar), adding a thirteenth month of pay per year to each soldier's salary. He writes the Massachusetts Council, "...it aims the most fatal stab to the peace of this army that ever was given, that Lord North himself could not have devised a more effective blow to the recruiting service."

At Pointe aux Trembles, somewhat restored in strength and morale, Arnold and Montgomery march their combined force of now nearly 1,000 men back to Quebec, with the artillery and stores following in bateaux on the river.

Leaving Fort George about 10 o'clock this morning, Henry Knox and brother William sail down (North) Lake George, reaching the landing dock for Fort Ticonderoga about 5:30 in the afternoon--a good and fast passage.

6 December 1775:
Wednesday. West Indian sugar planters and London merchants draft a petition to the House of Commons asking for concessions for rum trade in the forthcoming Parliamentary bill stopping all trade with America.

Royal Governor William Tryon of New York manages to have the public records in the city seized and transferred to the British ship in the harbor, HMS *Duchess of Gordon*. He claims this is for the safety of such records.

7 December 1775:
Thursday. Dr. Benjamin Gale writes to Silas Deane, a Connecticut delegate to the Continental Congress, regarding the progress of construction on a submarine invented by David Bushnell.

At Cambridge, Washington writes to the President of Congress, "I am credibly informed that James Anderson, the Consignee, the part owner of the ship, *Concord*, and its cargo, is not only unfriendly to American liberty, but actually in arms against us, being Captain of the Scotch Company in Boston. Whether your being acquainted with this circumstance or not, will operate against the vessel and cargo, I will not take upon me to say, but there are many articles on board absolutely necessary for this army, which whether a prize or not, they must have."

8 December 1775:
Friday. The French Foreign Minister, Count de Vergennes, announces that King Louis XVI will renew his order to French ports forbidding the loading of munitions on American ships. Despite issuing the original order in October, commerce in war goods has not diminished.

The combined Arnold expedition and Montgomery troops, now under Montgomery's command, begin an investment of and siege of the City of Quebec.

9 December 1775:
Saturday. The Congress promotes Richard Montgomery to the rank of Major General.

At Great Bridge, Virginia, a fight ensues between American militia forces under Colonel William Woodford, numbering about 870 men, and loyalist adherents to the crown with some British troops, under Captain Samuel Leslie, numbering about 410 men. The British are defeated in a surprise action, lasting less than 25 minutes. There are 62 British casualties. One American is slightly wounded in the hand. The patriot forces occupy Norfolk. Lord Dunmore and the remaining British take refuge on ships in the harbor.

At Fort Ticonderoga, Henry Knox has carefully selected a total of 59 pieces of artillery, including mortars, a barrel of excellent flints, and 23 boxes of lead. The total weighs more than 120,000 pounds! It is all hauled down to the loading dock and lashed to a scow, a piragua, and bateaux. By 3 o'clock this afternoon the boats shove off for the south end of Lake George. [See Fig. III-8, p. 91]

10 December 1775:
    Sunday. A group of British Marines and sailors, under the command of Captain James Wallace of the HMS *Rose*, raid the town of Jamestown, Rhode Island.
    Richard Montgomery, now before Quebec, has laid siege of the city for two days. During the night, as a heavy snowstorm blankets the ground, Montgomery's artillery (6 and 12- pound guns) begins battering the city and its walls, but, unfortunately, do little damage, because they are not of a heavy enough weight to do the job.

11 December 1775:
    Monday. The Virginia and North Carolina patriots who had routed loyalist troops at Great Bridge on Saturday, burn a portion of Norfolk, to deny any further use of the shelter or stores therein to the British, still lurking on ships in the harbor.
    Congress approves a $3,000 appropriation to support American diplomats in Europe.

12 December 1775:
    Tuesday. To provide much needed fuel for the colony, the Massachusetts Council allows decayed barns, stores, and houses to be torn down, as well as any public buildings, if needed.
    At headquarters, Cambridge, General Orders state "The Honorable the Continental Congress having been pleased to appoint Henry Knox, Esqr. Colonel of the Regiment of the Artillery, upon the new establishment; he is to be obeyed as such. The Colonels or commanding officers of the five Connecticut Regiments, upon the new establishment; to deliver to the adjutant General tomorrow at orderly time, an exact list of the Commissioned Officers of their respective Corps, together with a return of the men they have each of them inlisted (sic) for the above regiments; as an express is immediately to set out to Governor Trumbull, who has demanded the same, to lay them before the Assembly of the Colony." The parole is given as Effingham and the countersign as Fuller.

13 December 1775:
    Wednesday. The Continental Congress agrees with the report of the committee appointed to devise ways and means

for fitting out a naval armament, and authorizes the Naval Construction Act of 1775. This act provides for the fitting out of thirteen vessels as follows: one in New Hampshire, two in Massachusetts, two in Rhode Island, one in Connecticut, two in New York, four in Pennsylvania, and one in Maryland. The vessels are to be: five of 32-guns, five of 28-guns, and three of 24-guns. The materials for fitting them out are to be furnished by the colonies. The cost allowed is $66,666.67 each, on average

14 December 1775:
Thursday. In Cambridge, Washington writes to the President of Congress, "I will make application to Genl. Howe and propose and exchange for Mr. Ethan Allan. I am much afraid I shall have a like proposal to make for Captain Martindale of the armed brigantine *Washington* and his men, who it is reported was taken a few days past by a man - of- war and carried into Boston. We cannot expect to be always successful. About 150 more of the poor inhabitants are come out of Boston, the smallpox rages all over the town, such of the military as had it not before, are now under inoculation. This I apprehend is a weapon of defense, they are using against us. What confirms me in this opinion is, that I have information that they are tearing up the pavements, to be provided against a bombardment."
With reinforcements from Williamsburg and North Carolina, American forces fully occupy all of Norfolk, which had been held by the British after they captured it on 23 November 1775.

15 December 1775:
Friday. At headquarters, Cambridge, General Orders state "The quartermasters of all the Regiments, are as soon as possible, go deliver to the Deputy Commissary General, Mr. Elisha Avery, all the cider barrels, butter firkins, and candle boxes in the possession of their respective corps; as those articles are very much wanted for the public service." The parole is given as Rockingham and the countersign as Richmond.
Following the patriot capture and occupation of Norfolk from the British, the *Virginia Gazette* reports that Lord Dunmore will bombard the city if frontier riflemen enter the fight.

16 December 1775:
Saturday. At Cambridge, Washington writes to the Massachusetts Legislature, "Not being able to discover from the (Congressional) Resolves themselves, or the letter which accompanied them, whether a copy had been transmitted to you by the President, or to be handed in by me, I thought it best to err on the safe side; especially as the Quartermaster General has just informed me, that he is exceeding scarce of hay and can get none under six pounds lawful a ton."

A representative of the Delaware Indian tribe visits the Continental Congress where he is thanked by John Hancock for keeping the Delawares neutral in the conflict between Britain and America.

17 December 1775:
Sunday. Montgomery, still at the walls of Quebec, has had no success in communicating with Carleton, who refuses to receive his letters, parley, or negotiate with him in any way.

At Cambridge, Washington writes to Maj. Gen. Artemas Ward, "Sir: The applications for liberty to go to the lines are so frequent that they cause much trouble. You will, therefore, Sir, grant passes to such as you may think proper. At the same time I would recommend to you that the officer who will attend upon these occasions be a person of sense, and one who will carefully attend to the conversation of those who meet on the lines."

18 December 1775:
Monday. At Cambridge, Washington writes to Sir William Howe, "Colonel Allen, who with his small party, was defeated and taken prisoner near Montreal, has been treated, without regard to decency, humanity, of the rules of War; that he has been thrown into irons and suffers all the hardships inflicted upon common felons. I think it my duty, Sir, to demand and to expect from you an Ecclaireissement [clarification] on this subject. And further assuring you that whatever treatment Colonel Allen receives; whatever fate he undergoes, such exactly shall be the treatment and fate of Brigadier [Richard] Prescott, now in our hands."

A company of foot rangers raids Sullivan Island, South Carolina, where Royal Governor Campbell has retained slaves and loyalists.

19 December 1775:
Tuesday. The New York Provincial Congress orders the purchase of 1,000 copies of the proceedings of the Continental Congress in Low Dutch and in German to be distributed to the residents of the colony.

On Sullivan's Island, near Charleston, patriots who have raided the Tory forces, burn the Pest House, denying its use to any Loyalist adherents.

In Philadelphia, Benjamin Franklin writes to Charles William Frédérick Dumas, in The Hague, Holland, "That you may be better able to answer some questions which will probably be put to you concerning our present situation, we inform you that the whole content is very firmly united, the party for the measures of the British ministry being very small and much dispersed; that we have had on foot the last campaign an army of near twenty-five thousand men, wherewith we have been able, not only to lock up the king's army in Boston, but to spare considerable detachments for the invasion of Canada, where we have met with great success, as the printed papers sent herewith will inform you ..."

20 December 1775:
Wednesday. At headquarters, Cambridge, General Orders state "In consequence of a complaint exhibited by the colonels and commanding officers of corps, in the brigade upon Winter Hill ... his Excellency is pleased to order a Court of Enquiry to sit tomorrow at eleven in the forenoon, to examine into the cause thereof. Major General Putnam, with Brigadiers Sullivan, Greene, and Heath, to compose the Court of Enquiry. All evidences and persons concerned to attend the Court." The parole is given as Fairfax and the countersign as Woodford.

The Continental Congress orders a temporary cease fire between the colonies of Connecticut and Pennsylvania in their dispute over the conflicting land claims in the Wyoming Valley of Pennsylvania. This issue will surface again, until resolved by the courts towards the end of the war.

21 December 1775:
Thursday. In London, the British Parliament passes a bill calling for the confiscation of all American vessels, whatever they may carry or wherever they may be found, and the impressment of their crews into the service of the English Navy.

22 December 1775:
Friday. Under Colonel Thompson, 500 patriot rangers and militia surprise and capture a force of loyalists under William Cunningham at Great Cane Brake in Greenville County, South Carolina. Nearly 30 inches of snow is falling, as the patriots round up the Loyalists and force them to sign a paper pledging not to take up arms again, on pain of property loss. This is sometimes called the Snow Campaign.

Esek Hopkins, the first captain in the Continental Navy, is officially commissioned as a commodore.

The British Parliament passes the American Prohibitory Act, which prohibits all trade and intercourse with any of the thirteen colonies, and authorizes the seizure of American vessels as prizes.

23 December 1775:
Saturday. King George III, with the passage of an Act of Parliament, now issues a Royal Proclamation to give it the full weight of Royal approval, closing the American colonies to all commerce and trade. This to take effect on 1 March 1776. Also in December, Congress is informed that France may offer support to the Americans in the war against Britain.

In England, Ethan Allen, captured at Montreal, arrives as a prisoner, after an ocean voyage from Quebec.

24 December 1775:
Sunday. In a campaign against loyalists in the upcountry of South Carolina, American patriot forces are impeded by a heavy snowstorm that will dump an additional 15 inches during the next several days.

The Georgia Council of Safety attempts to stop several vessels from loading lumber on the Sapelo River planned for export to the West Indies.

25 December 1775:
   Monday. Brigadier General Montgomery (not yet knowing that he has been promoted) has been preparing for an attack upon Quebec, and awaits an opportunity for a dark night. Not everyone, however, wants to be in the attack force, or at least is not animated sufficiently to hazard the attempt. Since it is Christmas, Montgomery allows the troops the luxury of extra wine and food.

26 December 1775:
   Tuesday. The Continental Congress calls for another three million dollars in bills of credit to be issued to help defray the costs of building a navy and supplying the army. The 13 Colonies pledge for the redemption of the bills of credit by levying taxes in each colony.
   Richard Montgomery writes to Philip Schuyler to report the reluctance of some men to support an attack upon Quebec, which he states is now required to reduce the place. The siege has had little or no effect. Montgomery also notes that after he had addressed the troops , "in a very sensible Spirited manner ... the fire of patriotism kindled in their breasts." The attack was to be made on the Lower Town, on a dark and stormy night.
   In the afternoon, Colonel Henry Knox and a small advanced party of his "Artillery Trek" reaches Albany and discusses with Philip Schuyler, plans and the needs for the future transport of the "noble train of artillery" still located between Glens Falls and Saratoga.

27 December 1775:
   Wednesday. A group of 34 prisoners taken by the British near Montreal are moved to the HMS *Solebay* to be transported to Boston.
   In Falmouth, England the HMS *Adamant* arrives with its cargo of captives, including Colonel Ethan Allen, who is the only officer in this group of prisoners and Indians.
   Before the walls of Quebec, the weather dark and stormy seems right for an attack, but it is discovered that a deserter has delivered the proposed plan to Carleton, and the attack is abandoned.

28 December 1775:
   Thursday. The Continental Congress resolves that troops raised in Virginia be enlisted on the same terms and pay as the forces enlisting in the Continental Army at Cambridge. As the actual armed conflict between the Colonies and England continues, a truly national force becomes desirable.
   In Philadelphia, the French agent, Archard de Bonvouloir, appears before Congress and gives informal assurances that his country has a strong interest in the American Revolution, and may possibly be persuaded to support an alliance.

29 December 1775:
    Friday. At headquarters, Cambridge, General Orders state "The General was in great hopes that a sufficient sum of money, would have been sent from Philadelphia, to have paid the troops for the month of October, November, and December, but is sorry to inform them, that there is no more yet arrived than will allow one month's pay."
    Washington writes to the Massachusetts Legislature, explaining the pay situation of four independent companies, "I do not think myself authorised to direct pay for them, without first laying the matter before Congress, which I shall do, by inclosing an exact transcript of your representation of the case, with this simple remark, that they were not Regimented, and were doing duty at some distance from these Camps; I did not know whether to consider them, as a part of the Continental Army, And therefore had not ordered them payment heretofore." The parole is given as Providence and the countersign as Salem.
    In Schenectady, New York, the Committee of Correspondence asks local Magistrates to post notices and otherwise inform the populace to prevent the firing of guns on New Year's Day in order to conserve gunpowder.

30 December 1775:
    Saturday. Washington's recruitment officers are allowed to discuss enlistment in the American Army with free Negroes who want to join. While there have been black soldiers as patriots in the militia and eight-month army, this new process formalizes the acceptance of black soldiers in the new army. Washington's army, to begin on the first of the year 1776, will be a better organized and truly continental one, with soldiers from all the colonies.
    At Cambridge, Martha Washington writes to her friend Elizabeth Ramsay, discussing her trip and the situation she finds, "... some days we have a number of cannon and shells from Boston and Bunkers Hill, but it does not seem to surprise any one but me; I confess I shudder every time I hear the sound of a gun ... I have been to dinner with two of the Generals, Lee and Putnam ... to me that never see any thing of war, the preparations are very terrable indeed, but I endever [sic] to keep my fears to myself as well as I can. This is a beautiful country, and we had a very pleasant journey through New England, and the pleasure to find the General very well. We came within the month from home to the Camp."

31 December 1775:
    Sunday. At the walls before Quebec, the nights of 29 and 30 December had been clear and mild--not the required dark and stormy weather the Americans are seeking for their attack upon the Lower Town. But, the last day of the year is perfect–a snow fall driven by a fierce wind. The British garrison has about 1,800 men under Governor Carleton. The assignments having all been made, the troops assembles (about 800 men) and each party goes to its duty. Montgomery and Arnold each

lead a contingent. The fighting is heavy and lasts about three hours. Montgomery is killed, and Arnold wounded. Daniel Morgan is surrounded, and forced to surrender. The American losses are about 426. The British lose five killed and thirteen wounded.

Having spent some days in planning with Philip Schuyler, Henry Knox is now ready with 124 pair of horses, more than 32 span of oxen, and with sledges and sleighs to proceed upon his artillery trek across the Mohawk River, down to Albany, across the Hudson River, and thence across the Berkshire Mountains of Massachusetts to Cambridge, where General Washington is anxiously awaiting their arrival. [See Fig. III-8, p. 91].

And so ends the first year (or the best part of a year) of a revolution, in which many folks are still hoping for some solution to the difficulties and problems between the mother country, England, and her colonies on the Atlantic seaboard. But think for a moment. Aren't many of our young men, with musket in hand, still encamped around Boston in a siege-like surround of armed British troops?

And are not other young American colonists still in and around Quebec fighting other British troops, or merely surviving in the cold? If we colonials are and have been in actual physical combat with British regiments sent over here by Parliament under the King's order, just how sanguine is the view that any such accommodation between the Colonies and the Mother Country might come to fruition?

There are many folks in the colonies who have more and more tended to think that, while some form of accommodation might sound great, perhaps it is a bit unreal to expect that any such eventuality will ever come to be. It is just that many folks are so used to English ways, habits, goods, and usages that the idea of throwing all that over seems difficult to imagine.

What happens if we have no court system like the one we're used to? How do we manage without all the judges, governors, Royal officers, and the goods and services we now get from Britain? Who will protect us from raids by the Indians or the Spanish when we no longer have our wonderful British Navy and Army to protect us? And, if we are to try to throw this all over, how will we ever defeat them? No, it's all too difficult for now.

Perhaps the next year will see some resolution. For those readers interested in more detailed accounts of this year of 1775, excellent works by several authors are listed in the Bibliography, including: Fischer, David Hackett, *Paul Revere's Ride*; French, Allen, *The day of Lexington and Concord*; Hamilton, Edward Pierce, *Fort Ticonderoga: Key to a Continent*; Fleming, Thomas J., *Now we are Enemies: The Story of Bunker Hill*; Ketchum, Richard M., *Decisive Day: The Battle of Bunker Hill*; Roberts, Kenneth, *March to Quebec Journals of the Members of Arnold's Expedition*; Lefkowitz, Arthur S., *Benedict Arnold's Army*; French, Allen, *The First Year of the American Revolution*.

III. The Year 1776

<u>1 January 1776:</u>

Monday. The Americans withdraw from Quebec. Arnold erects defenses of frozen snow. Carleton has captured more than 400 men, and the Americans have lost another 60 in killed and wounded. The British loss--five killed and 13 wounded.

At Cambridge, the Eight Month Army is discharged, leaving Washington with the serious and daunting problem of recruiting a new Continental Army. How can Washington keep up the siege of Boston without enough troops to man the lines? The Orderly Book for headquarters has this comment written in it "This day giving commencement to the new army, which in every point of view is entirely Continental, the General flatters himself that a laudable spirit of emulation will now take place, and pervade the whole of it."

Governor Dunmore of Virginia, having angered the rebels in Williamsburg and then aroused the entire colony by his willful actions, has reached Norfolk. Just outside this community he is attacked by Virginia militia, flees to a British ship in the harbor, and fires upon the town.

The Grand Union Flag (13 alternate red and white stripes and the Union Jack in the upper left corner) is adopted as the official flag of Washington's army.

In New Jersey, the Committee of Safety of Elizabethtown having approved of a raid, 60 patriots in four boats slip along side a British supply ship, *Blue Mountain Valley*, and capture it as a prize.

<u>2 January 1776:</u>

Tuesday. In retaliation of Lord Dunmore's firing upon Norfolk, rebels set fire to the homes of prominent Tories and much of the remainder of the town in a fire that lasts for 50 hours.

Knox's artillery trek has gotten as far as the Mohawk River, and in crossing the ice, one of the heavy cannon crashes through and sinks. It takes some time to haul it out and proceed.

<u>3 January 1776:</u>

Wednesday. In Philadelphia, the Continental Congress is deeply disturbed that a majority of the inhabitants of Queen's County, New York, have refused to send deputies to the Convention of that County. Feeling these people are unwilling to support the cause of the Revolution, either because they hope to avoid serving if America should win or have an easy time if England should, the Congress declares these people to be out of the protection of the United Colonies, and that no person is to have commerce or communication with them.

The Knox artillery train, having crossed the Mohawk River, continues its march south toward Albany. [See Fig. III-8, p. 91].

4 January 1776:
Thursday. In London, Lord George Germain, who has replaced the British Secretary for the Colonies, William Legge, Earl of Dartmouth, writes to the Lords of the Admiralty that it is "... the King's intention that every effort should be made to send relief to Quebec as early as possible."

The Congress resolves to form an additional battalion to be raised in the County of Cumberland, Pennsylvania. They also resolve that one company in each of the five battalions previously ordered shall consist of expert riflemen, and that the Pennsylvania Committee of Safety see that these resolutions are carried into effect.

5 January 1776:
Friday. New Hampshire adopts the first of the written constitutions among the colonies. John Adams has advocated this approach, because he feels it will go a long way to strengthen each colony's political position, as well as reinforce the idea of "independency."

Colonel Henry Knox reports to General Washington that his artillery train has reached Albany. The citizens of the town are delighted to see so much heavy ordnance, and will seek help to ferry (drag) these large weapons across the ice of the Hudson River.

The Marine Committee of Congress orders Esek Hopkins to collect his fleet of small warships for the purpose of sweeping British cargo vessels from the Chesapeake Bay.

6 January 1776:
Saturday. The instructions to Major General William Howe, first prepared by Lord Dartmouth and continued by George Germain, Viscount Sackville, regarding an Expedition to the south, have been delivered to Howe, who is pleased to pass them on to his second-in-Command, Henry Clinton.

Young Alexander Hamilton, an ardent patriot, forms a provincial company of artillery in New York.

In Philadelphia, the Continental Congress adopts a resolution, declaring, among other things, that it has "... no design to set up as an independent nation."

With a cold spell that freezes the ice on the Hudson River, Knox is able to pass his artillery train over the river to the east side at Greenbush, opposite Albany, New York.

7 January 1776:
Sunday. Henry Knox organizes his artillery trek into separate groups of guns with oxen and teams of men, each a mile or two apart from the others. No one group being too large or unwieldy, but close enough to support each other in case of need, and assisting each other by improving the track or road as they go. Thus arranged they march south down the east side of the Hudson River, on the Old Post Road to Kinderhook and Claverack. [See Fig. III-8, p. 91].

8 January 1776:
Monday. In the lines around Boston, Major Thomas Knowlton leads a successful raid upon the British in the Town of Charlestown. The raid interrupts a performance of a play written by Maj. Gen. John Burgoyne.

9 January 1776:
Tuesday. At headquarters, Cambrigde, General Orders include thanks to Major Thomas Knowlton for the resolution and leadership he provided upon his raid last evening upon the British works at Bunker Hill. General Orders go on to say "It is almost certain that the enemy will attempt to revenge the insult, which was cast upon them last night; for which reason the greatest vigilance , and care, is recommended: as it also is, that the outposts be always guarded by experienced officers, and good soldiers ..." The parole is given as Knowlton and the countersign as Charlestown.
The Continental Congress requests that New York take measures to defend the entrances to that large harbor.

10 January 1776:
Wednesday. A 47-page pamphlet, written by a recent English emigrant, Thomas Paine, and called *Common Sense*, is published. It costs two shillings (a moderately large sum in 1776: about $8 in 2008 money), and does not have the author's name attached to it, but appears anonymously. It has been printed by Robert Bell in Philadelphia. Extremely popular and widely copied, the pamphlet will sell about 120,000 copies within the next three months! It offers many well-thought-out arguments about why Americans should cease their pusillanimous approach of reconciliation or accommodation, and seek complete independence from Britain. Paine uses ordinary "street" language--no references to history, nor to legal or philosophical writers. He sets forth what he feels are two deeply flawed elements in the unwritten English Constitution: monarchy and hereditary rule. These, he says, are bad news because, even if one should luck out by having a competent monarch by accident of birth on some occasion, what is the guarantee that his heir will be? And what is it that automatically makes him ruler material in the first place? No, indeed, redesign the structure and machinery of government. In short, overthrow these bad elements of monarchy and hereditary rule, and build something upon more republican principles. Revolt, separate yourselves from Britain, establish your own form of government. Paine's language includes this thought, "We have it in our power to begin the world anew. America shall make a stand, not for herself alone, but for the world." They are wonderful words, and inspire very many people to reconsider the accommodation approach. Perhaps it just might be possible to create something by way of governance, that is more egalitarian, more republican, more people oriented and directed.

Henry Knox selected 59 of Fort Ticonderoga's guns for the wintry, 300-mile trip to Boston. Hauled by sledge, his "noble train of artillery" was dogged by one mishap after another, including a "cruel thaw."

Fig. III-7: Over the Berkshires, January 1776

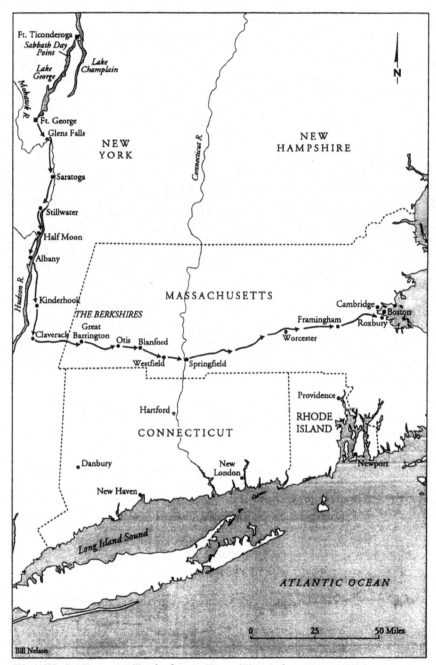

Fig. III-8: Knox's Trek from Fort Ticonderoga, 1776

In North Carolina, Royal Governor Josiah Martin, aboard the British sloop HMS *Scorpion,* issues an appeal to all loyalists to gather near Wilmington on the Cape Fear River, and support a British army offensive in the south.

At Quebec, the remaining American forces try to survive the cold and bitter weather, and the humiliation of a massive defeat. With Richard Montgomery killed in the action of New Year's Eve, the command of the force devolves upon Benedict Arnold, who is promoted to Brigadier General.

Colonel Henry Knox's artillery train reaches the Berkshire Mountains. [See Fig. III-7, p. 90, and Fig. III-8, p. 91].

11 January 1776:
        Thursday. At headquarters, Cambridge, Washington writes to the President of Congress, reporting upon his concern for the future aims of the British, and believing them to be New York, says, "I have sent Major General Lee to New York. I have given him letters recommentory (sic) to Governor Trumbull, and to the Committee of Safety of New York. The evening of the 8th. Instant a party of our men under the command of Major Knowlton were ordered to go and burn some houses which lay at the foot of Bunkers Hill and at the head of Charlestown; they were also ordered to bring of the guard which we expected consisted of an officer and thirty men. They crossed the Mill Dam about half after eight o'clock, and gallantly executed their design, having burnt eight houses, and brought with them a sergeant and four privates of the 10th Regiment."

In Williamsburg, the Virginia Convention passes a Resolution to create a small State naval force "... for the protection of the several rivers in this Colony."

12 January 1776:
        Friday. In Rhode Island, the British raid Prudence Island, but are driven away the next day.

13 January 1776:
        Saturday. Josiah Bartlett, a delegate from New Hampshire to the Continental Congress, reports in a letter to John Langdon that the copies of *Common Sense* have been "greedily bought up and read by all ranks of people". Other editions are being rapidly published by other printers in Philadelphia, as well as many other places, and its price has dropped to 18 pence (or about $3.60 in 2008 money).

14 January 1776:
        Sunday. At Cambridge, Washington writes to Joseph Reed, "The reflection on my situation, and that of this army, produces many an uneasy hour when all around me are wrapped in sleep. Few people know the predicament we are in, on a thousand accounts; fewer still will believe, if any disaster happens to these lines, from what cause it flows. I have often thought how much happier I should have been, if, instead of accepting the command under such circumstances, I had taken

my musket on my shoulder and entered the rank, or, if I could have justified the measure to posterity and my own conscience, had retired to the back country, and lived in a wigwam."

In or near Westfield, Massachusetts, the passing of the artillery train of Henry Knox brings out great curiosity from the locals, who want to touch the large weapons and wonder at the weight and size of them.

15 January 1776:
Monday. Knox's artillery train, coming out of the Berkshires, is now able to make somewhat better time, and approaches Springfield on its way east. [See Fig. III-8, p. 89]

16 January 1776:
Tuesday. Connecticut appoints new delegates to the "General Congress of the United Colonies": Roger Sherman, Oliver Wolcott, Samuel Huntington, and William Williams. Their letter of appointment is read in the Congress.

At headquarters, Cambridge, Washington writes to the New Hampshire Legislature, "The alarming and almost defenceless state of our lines, occasioned by the slow progress of raising recruits for the New Army and the departure of a great number of the militia, which has been called in for their support, til the 15th instant, from this and New Hampshire Governments; rendered it necessary for me to summon the General Officers in Council, to determine on proper measures to be adopted for their maintenance and preservation. In order that each Regiment may consist of a proper number of officers and men, I herewith send you a list for their regulation ..."

Knox's artillery train passes through Springfield, Massachusetts.

17 January 1776:
Wednesday. The Continental Congress resolved that the colonels of the several battalions (regiments) being raised are to appoint places of rendezvous, find quarters for recruits, assure that recruits are healthy, able, sound, and not under 16 years of age.

The Knox artillery train heads east from Springfield toward Worcester. Henry Knox pushes on to Cambridge in order to report to Washington, and learn from him the desired location of the pieces he is bringing with him.

18 January 1776:
Thursday. At Cambridge, Brigadier General William Heath records in his Memoirs that "Col. Knox, of the artillery, came to camp. He brought from Ticonderoga a fine train of artillery, which had been taken from the British, both cannon and mortars, and which were ordered to be stopped at Framingham."

In Savannah, Georgia, Joseph Habersham raises a group of patriots who capture the Royal Governor, James Wright, and place him under house arrest.

19 January 1776:
Friday. In Delaware (sometimes also called "The Lower Three Counties"), the Council of Safety begins its deliberations over the makeup of the officers to form a continental regiment. There are to be eight companies in the battalion (or regiment, these terms were frequently used interchangeably). Additionally, there are also to be battalion officers and staff officers.

20 January 1776:
Saturday. Sir Henry Clinton sets sail from Boston with a body of troops to rendezvous at the mouth of the Cape Fear River, North Carolina, with another force coming from Cork, Ireland. Clinton's orders are to restore the King's authority in the four southern colonies. He is also expected to join up with a body of North Carolina Loyalists the British hope are assembling near Wilmington on the Cape Fear River in response to Gov. Josiah Martin's appeal.
Philip Schuyler, of the Northern Department, leads a force that grows to nearly 3,000 New York militia to Johnson Hall (near what is now Johnstown, New York), and forces Sir John Johnson, with about 700 loyalists to surrender and disarm. This action ends effective loyalist resistance in the Albany County area.

21 January 1776:
Sunday. At headquarters, Cambridge, General Orders state "The Colonel or commanding officer of each Regiment, is forthwith to send out one, or two, prudent and sensible Officers, to buy up such arms as are wanted for his regiment. All recruits who shall furnish their own arms shall be paid one dollar, for the use of them ..." The parole is given as Granby and the countersign as Monckton.
In Philadelphia, Delegate Silas Deane of Connecticut writes to his wife, reporting that he needs to stay for awhile "... to close the Naval Accounts and assist in getting forward the preparations for the fleet ..."

22 January 1776:
Monday. In New Jersey, the Elizabethtown Committee of Safety orders a raid upon the British transport and supply ship *Blue Mountain Valley*, anchored about 40 miles south of and off Sandy Hook. A raiding party under Elias Dayton and William Alexander proceeds late this night to capture the vessel.

23 January 1776:
Tuesday. The Elizabethtown raiding party of about 60 volunteers, in whaleboats and other rowed vessels, having rowed during the early hours of darkness the nearly 40 miles toward Sandy Hook to find the vessel, succeed in capturing the British transport and supply ship *Blue Mountain Valley*, and the all the provisions aboard her.

24 January 1776:
    Wednesday. After an exhausting trek across the Berkshire Mountains, Colonel Henry Knox delivers his 59 pieces of ordnance to Cambridge, Massachusetts. He has brought 43 cannon and 16 mortars all the way from Fort Ticonderoga! [See Fig. III-8, p. 89].
    In the bitter cold of a New England winter, on the road toward Cambridge, from Braintree, John Adams travels with his servant and companion, Joseph Bass, to see General Washington. After a short visit they will ride off on a trip to Philadelphia that will take two weeks, because Adams needs to return to the Continental Congress. The reader can put himself in place of John Adams as he rides along, and imagine what it would have been like. Today that trip, on an Interstate Highway, might take about seven hours. In 1776 there were no Holiday Inns nor Hilton Hotels, no warm vehicles, no easy stopping places nor fast food restaurants. It took a lot of effort, time, and money to go from place to place. The wonder is that so much traveling was done!

25 January 1776:
    Thursday. In Philadelphia, the Congress resolves to procure a monument from Paris or another part of France and erect it in Philadelphia in memory of Richard Montgomery.

26 January 1776:
    Friday. Richard Smith writes in his Diary that in the Congress a letter was read from Maj. Gen. Charles Lee, reporting upon his travel to New York City to see to its defense. After considerable discussion on the matter, a committee is appointed to meet with Lee and review with him and the New York Committee of Safety the measures to be taken in this matter.

27 January 1776:
    Saturday. In Philadelphia, the New York delegates to the Congress write to the New York Committee of Safety reporting information and requesting cooperation in the matter of Charles Lee's march into the city, and the means of protecting the city by armed vessels.

28 January 1776:
    Sunday. At Cambridge, George Washington writes to John Manley, commending him on his recent naval action as he engaged with his undermanned schooner two British vessels and their cargoes, and took the prizes into Plymouth.

29 January 1776:
    Monday. In Philadelphia, the New York Delegates, William Floyd and Henry Wisner, write to Maj. Gen. Philip Schuyler expressing concern over the unsuccessful attempt of Richard Montgomery at Quebec. They further state that the Congress is determined to gain possession of Canada, if possible. To that

end they have ordered seven battalions to the Northern Department.

30 January 1776:
Tuesday. In Philadelphia, Delegate Thomas McKean, of Delaware, writes to Philip Schuyler informing him of some data revealed by a prisoner, to the effect that about 200 Scots settlers in the Royal Scotch Emigrants Regiment in the Mohawk Valley are assembling, and that they should be apprehended as prisoners of war to be exchanged for those American soldiers who had been captured at Quebec. It makes no sense to allow adherents to the Crown to wander loosely about the countryside.

31 January 1776:
Wednesday. Richard Smith writes in his diary, noting that the Massachusetts Delegation felt that their powers in the Congress might expire, since new delegates have not yet arrived. But the appointments of the replacements having been published in two newspapers, the Congress was quite willing to accept them.

At Cambridge, George Washington writes to Joseph Reed, "I hope my countrymen of Virginia will rise superior to any losses the whole navy of Great Britain can bring on them, and that the destruction of Norfolk, and the attempted devastation of other places, will have no other effect, than to unite the whole country in one indissoluble bond. A few more of such flaming arguments, as were exhibited at Falmouth and Norfolk, added to the sound doctrine and unanswerable reasoning contained in the pamphlet *Common Sense*, will not leave numbers at a loss to decide upon the propriety of a separation."

1 February 1776:
Thursday. In New York the Committee of Safety rescinds its order of placing troops under its direction, and remands them to the control of Maj. Gen. Charles Lee. This issue of "control" over troops will, throughout the war, rear its head in various places to the disadvantage of American forces. It must be remembered that there has been no regular army of Americans in the New World. This is a new, and not altogether cheerfully accepted, idea.

2 February 1776:
Friday. In Philadelphia, President of the Congress, John Hancock, writes to Colonel William Alexander (Lord Stirling), commending him upon his recent action in capturing the British vessel *Blue Mountain Valley*.

3 February 1776:
Saturday. Josiah Bartlett, a Delegate from New Hampshire, writes to John Langdon, another delegate from New Hampshire and a ship builder and merchant, noting that the Secret Committee has made a contract for $10,000 for importing sail

cloth and blankets. He sends a copy of the contract to Langdon for his information and action.

4 February 1776:
Sunday. American Maj. Gen. Charles Lee and an advance contingent of the Continental Army arrive in New York City from the Boston area to occupy and begin the process of defending the city from British attack.

British Maj. Gen. Henry Clinton and his part of an expedition for the southern colonies, puts into New York harbor at Sandy Hook. There he consults with the New York Royal Governor William Tryon (formerly also Royal Governor of North Carolina), who has taken refuge aboard ship. Clinton is hopeful that Tryon's knowledge and experience in North Carolina will prove useful for a British southern campaign.

5 February 1776:
Monday. At headquarters, Cambridge, General Orders state "The Colonels upon the old establishment, will this day and tomorrow receive the Warrants for their Pay-Abstracts, for the months of November and December, of which all persons concern'd are to take notice, and govern themselves accordingly. For the future, when a Warrant is granted, and pay'd for any sum upon account of pay, of the Regiments, or Corps, to any of the Commanding Officers thereof, there will be no allowance afterwards, for any neglect, or supposed mistake. It is the duty of every Colonel, and Captain, to be exact in their abstractions and returns, and the consequences of being otherwise, must fall upon themselves." The parole is given as Newport and the countersign as Cooke.

In New York, Andrew Allen and Thomas Lynch, Delegates from the Congress, are to meet with Lord Drummond, a representative of the Crown, to discuss issues of agreement towards some "accommodation." Lynch enquires after the character of Drummond from William Smith.

6 February 1776:
Tuesday. John Hancock writes to Philip Schuyler commending his zeal in recent operations in the Northern Department. He encloses Resolves of the Congress regarding the problem of specie (cash), needed in that department.

7 February 1776:
Wednesday. In New Jersey, American Colonel William Alexander, Lord Stirling, with 1,000 men, arrives in New York City to serve under Charles Lee.

8 February 1776:
Thursday. John Hancock writes to John Bull, noting that the Congress has ordered $250,000 to be sent to George Washington, that Bull is to take charge of that money, and that he should engage two persons to accompany him in carrying that large sum to Washington's Headquarters.

9 February 1776:
   Friday. In Philadelphia, Delegate Richard Smith notes in his diary that a packet of letters containing the signals of the men of war and transports of the British Navy has been found in a captured British vessel. Copies of this useful information are promptly forwarded by copies to the American Navy and to all delegates of each colony.

10 February 1776:
   Saturday. At Cambridge, Washington writes to the Committee of Safety of New York, "Being in the greatest want of arms at this alarming and important crisis, for the army under my command, without the most distant prospect or hope of getting more from these Governments, than what I already have; I beg leave to solicit the favors of your Committee of Safety in this instance, and earnestly request, that they will use their exertions to get and send to me, in the most expeditious manner, all that they can possibly procure."
   The North Carolina Delegation writes to the their state Council of Safety reporting that a wagon load of materials is being sent to Edenton, North Carolina, with drums, colors, fifes, gun powder, and pamphlets.

11 February 1776:
   Sunday. From Ipswich, Massachusetts, Sarah Hodgkins writes to her husband Joseph in Camp at Prospect Hill, "I received two letters from you on ordination day after meeting which was a great comfort to me to hear that [you] were well. But there seems to me to be something wanting. I wanted you home & that would have crowned all. It is very cold tonight. I hope you are provided with a comfortable lodging. I think a lot about you both by night & by day[,] but I desire to commit you to God who has hitherto preserved you ... but I must conclude. I remain your most affectionate companion till death."
   In Savannah, during the night, the Royal Governor of Georgia, James Wright, who is under house arrest by the patriot militia, manages to escape his captors, and takes refuge aboard the British ship HMS *Scarbourough*, anchored in the Savannah River.

12 February 1776:
   Monday. At headquarters, Cambridge, General Orders state "The General being informed that several of the militia are coming in without arms, orders that the Brigadiers, to whose brigades they are joined, do examine into this matter, and discharge every man who has not arms as they come in, keeping an account thereof, to deliver when called for. It is with no small degree of astonishment, that the General observes by the returns of last week, that seventeen men have been dismissed the service, out of which number Col. Whitcomb alone has discharged seven. He is, therefore, called upon, to be at headquarters tomorrow morning, at 10 o'clock, to account for his conduct in this instance. At the same time it is declared and particular attention will be paid to it, that if any Colonel,

of Commanding Officer of a Regiment, presume in future to discharge a man without proper authority, for so doing, he will be put in arrest and tried for disobedience of orders." The parole is given as Plymouth and the countersign as Portsmouth.

After some delay because of contrary winds, Sir Henry Clinton, with the part of the British expedition to retrieve the southern colonies, leaves the sheltered anchorage of Sandy Hook to continue his journey south.

13 February 1776:

Tuesday. At Philadelphia, Josiah Bartlett, a delegate from New Hampshire, writes to John Langdon, reporting upon actions in the Congress, and assuring Langdon that his efforts to build a frigate for the Marine Committee have the full support of that committee.

14 February 1776:

Wednesday. Congress sends a resolution to the journeymen and carpenters building the Continental frigates, who, in a rush of patriot excitement, have marched off to fight around New York. Commending their spirit and zeal, the resolution notes that the public will be more essentially served by them in their capacities as workmen on the frigates.

Action at Dorchester Neck, Massachusetts. The Americans fight a short skirmish, forcing the British patrol to flee, thus securing passage to the area of Dorchester Heights for the American troops, who will soon wish to make use of it, for placing the artillery brought by Henry Knox.

15 February 1776:

Thursday. In Cambridge, Washington writes to Governor Jonathan Trumbull, "I am much obliged and return you my sincere thanks, for ordering the powder from Providence to this Camp, at this time of necessity, and will most cheerfully pay for it, or replace it, when in my power, as shall be most agreeable to you. And also for the arms you are good enough to promise to send me as they are exceedingly wanted."

In Boston Harbor, the British make a raid upon Prudence Island.

16 February 1776:

Friday. At the siege around Boston, George Washington, having determined to seize Dorchester Heights, and having ordered a skirmish that cleared the enemy patrol from the approach road, holds a council. [See Fig. III-9, p. 103]. He had hoped to make a bolder move upon Boston itself, but the Council of War votes against this idea, because it is felt that direct attacks on the well- entrenched and fortified British post would be much too bloody and difficult for the patriot troops. However, Henry Knox's ability to transport the artillery from Fort Ticonderoga, and the arrival of the guns at Cambridge, gives hope that this artillery will prove most useful. If placed upon the heights on the Dorchester Peninsula, they can effectively bombard both Boston and the British ships in the harbor, forcing the British either to attempt an attack upon the American positions, which might be easily defeated, or to abandon Boston.

17 February 1776:
Saturday. From Philadelphia, Esek Hopkins, commanding the first Continental Navy squadron puts to sea. He has six ships with him: *Alfred* (24 guns); *Columbus* (20 guns); *Andrew Doria* (14 guns); *Cabot* (14 guns); *Providence* (12 guns), and *Wasp* (8 guns). Hopkins, although directed by the Congress to break the British blockage of the Chesapeake Bay, sails down the Delaware Bay and on to Nassau, in the Bahamas. There, he hopes to capture badly needed supplies stored in the British forts and poorly guarded.

Maj. Gen. Henry Clinton arrives with his part of the British southern expedition at Hampton Roads, Virginia to visit with Governor Lord Dunmore, who has taken refuge aboard ship.

18 February 1776:
Sunday. In Cambridge, Washington writes to the President of Congress, enclosing information on a council of war during which Washington advanced reasons for an assault upon Boston but the council did not concur, "The result will appear in the enclosed Council War, and being almost unanimous, I must suppose to be right although, from a thorough conviction of the necessity of attempting something against Ministerial Troops, before a reinforcement should arrive and while we were favour'd with the ice, I was not only ready, but willing and desirous of making the assault; under firm hope, if the men would have stood by me, of a favourable (sic) issue, not withstanding the enemy's advantage of ground, artillery, & ca."

John Adams writes to James Warren, reporting upon the characters and abilities of the three Delegates chosen by the Congress for the committee to visit Canada.

19 February 1776:
Monday. In Philadelphia, at the Dutch Reformed Church, the Rev. William Smith delivers an oration in memory of Richard Montgomery and the officers and men who fell with him at Quebec on 31 December 1775.

20 February 1776:
Tuesday. Joseph Hewes, Delegate from North Carolina, writes to Samuel Johnston, telling him that a wagon load of supplies is being forwarded to him, for use by militia as they prepare to defend the area around Wilmington, believed to be the target of the British expedition under Henry Clinton.

21 February 1776:
Wednesday. The Secret Committee writes to Philip Schuyler, noting that eight tons of gunpowder have been sent with all

possible dispatch for Canada to be delivered to Schuyler's headquarters at Albany for further transport, as needed.

22 February 1776:
Thursday. In Philadelphia, James Duane, a delegate from New York, makes note of the debates in the Congress, most of which are centered upon the issue of the continental army: its pay, its means of and duration of enlistment, and its use of one colony's troops in another colony.

23 February 1776:
Friday. At headquarters, Cambridge, General Orders state "Lieut. Thomas Cummings tried at a General Court Martial for 'behaving in a scandalous and infamous manner, unbecoming the character of an officer and gentlemen'–is sentenced to be cashiered. The General approves the sentence and orders it to take place immediately." The parole is given as Canterbury and the countersign as St. Asaph.
Richard Smith writes in his diary that a number of items were discussed in the Congress, and that Carter Braxton of Virginia arrived and took his seat.

24 February 1776:
Saturday. At Army headquarters in Cambridge, General Orders set forth that all Brigadier Generals are ordered to see that the regiments in their brigades turn in their respective weekly returns (tabulations of numbers of personnel in each rank present and fit for duty, on leave, sick, or extended duty elsewhere) on time, and that they shall be examined by the Brigadier General and signed by him. The parole is given as Hopkins and the countersign as Alfred.

25 February 1776:
Sunday. Colonel Alexander Lillington, of North Carolina, with 150 Wilmington minutemen reaches the area of Moore's Creek Bridge, nearly 20 miles northwest of Wilmington, near the banks of the Black River. He is joined there by Colonel John Ashe with 100 Volunteer Rangers.
Captain Andrew Shaw arrives in Nassau, with news that eight vessels in the fleet of Commodore Esek Hopkins are gathering off Cape Delaware with the intention of attacking New Providence. Actually, Hopkins has only six vessels, and he is planning to sail to Nassau.

26 February 1776:
Monday. Colonel Richard Caswell arrives at Moore's Creek Bridge, North Carolina, with his force of about 750 patriot troops. Together with the contingents of Lillington and Ashe, they total 1,000 men. This group sets about creating earthworks for their protection and shelter against Tory fire that is soon expected from the west and removes some of the planking from the bridge, leaving only the stringers upon which to cross. They rest that night on their arms.
A Tory force of about 1,700 Scottish Loyalists, under Brig.

Gen. Donald McDonald has reached within six miles of Moore's Creek Bridge, and camps there.

At Cambridge, a council of war concludes that, with the artillery Knox has brought from Fort Ticonderoga, the American forces are in an excellent position to dominate the British garrisoned in Boston, under William Howe. So it is that an agreement is reached to take possession of Dorchester Heights on the night of 4 March, that being the eve of the anniversary of the Boston Massacre.

27 February 1776:
  Tuesday. The Tory force advances upon the Moore's Creek Bridge, in the very early hours of the day. Scouts have reported earthworks on the west side of the bridge. As they advance with claymores (large, heavy swords) only, they find that the rebel forces are not in the entrenchments, and assume that the attack will be easy and perhaps the rebels have abandoned the field. To their chagrin, as they charge the bridge, they are met by rebel infantry fire along with two artillery pieces. The attack is shattered in minutes. The patriots counterattack and pursue the terror-stricken Tories. About 30 Tories are killed or wounded, 850 are taken prisoner. The patriots capture 1,500 rifles, 350 muskets, 150 swords, 13 wagons and, most importantly, £15,000 in specie!

  Because of still further delays resulting from bad weather, Henry Clinton finally leaves Hampton Road, setting forth on the Southern expedition.

28 February 1776:
  Wednesday. At headquarters, Cambridge, General Orders state "The Commanding General at Roxbury, will as soon as possible, establish a detail of duty at that post, as similar to that in yesterday's orders, as the circumstances of his command will admit; which, when fix'd is to be transmitted to the Commander-in-Chief, for his inspection and approbation." The parole is given as Harrison and the countersign as Lynch.

  George Washington writes a "Thank You" note to Negro poet Phyllis Wheatley, who has written a poem in his honor.

29 February 1776:
  Thursday. At headquarters, Cambridge, General Orders give the parole as Franklin and the countersign as Carroll. "The Commanding officers of brigades are to order all spears, in the several posts, and redoubts, to be examined, cleaned, and collected in the proper places, and make a return of the number fit for service in each brigade, and where deposited."

  Richard Smith writes in his diary, noting that William Whipple, a delegate from New Hampshire, has arrived and taken his seat in the Congress.

1 March 1776:
  Friday. France, under King Louis XVI, and Spain, under Carlos (Charles) III, are both desirous of revenge against Britain, resulting from losses to Great Britain in former wars.

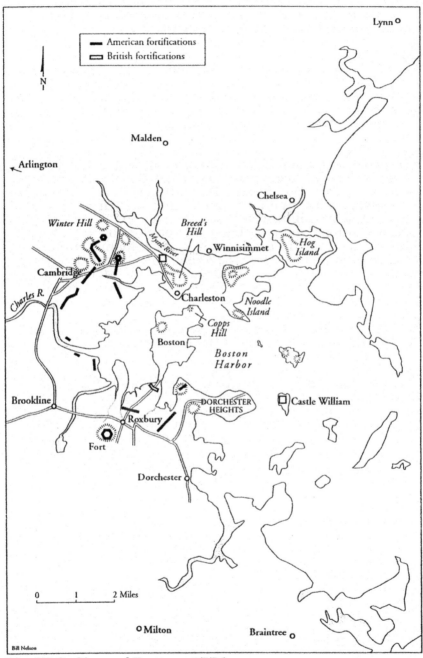

Fig. III-9: Siege of Boston, 1776

Yet, though they are anxious to punish the British, both countries are reluctant to side openly with the loosely organized American patriots and their anti-monarchial sentiments. With these concerns in mind, the two countries begin talks to explore possible joint actions.

2 March 1776:
      Saturday. At the Siege of Boston, George Washington, orders a diversion of American gunnery, by a bombardment from the Cambridge lines toward the Boston Back Bay area to suggest to the British that an attack might be made in that quarter. [See Fig. III-9, p. 103].

3 March 1776:
      Sunday. Commodore Esek Hopkins with a small fleet of American vessels, attacks the British island of New Providence (Nassau), in the Bahamas. He launches a successful amphibious assault upon the forts, and captures a goodly quantity of useful military stores.
      Henry Clinton, soon to be accompanied by Royal Gov. Josiah Martin of North Carolina and Gov. William Campbell of South Carolina, arrives off Cape Fear. Clinton decides not to land after learning of the Loyalist defeat at Moore's Creek Bridge. He awaits the arrival of the other part of the expedition from Cork, Ireland, under Admiral Sir Peter Parker and Maj. Gen. Charles Cornwallis.
      In Philadelphia, Congress votes to send a commercial Agent to France. Silas Deane is appointed to the post.

4 March 1776:
      Monday. Brig. Gen. John Thomas, with 2,000 men, carries out the plan for the fortification of Dorchester Heights approved at the Council of War meeting on 16 February, and on this single night completes the work of entrenchment. The guns Henry Knox has laboriously dragged from Fort Ticonderoga are ready for work, thundering all along the American lines toward the British lines in Boston proper. British artillery answers to little effect. [See Fig. III-9, p. 103].

5 March 1776:
      Tuesday. In Boston, the British do not seem to understand what all the firing the previous night is about--maybe just the "rebels" making noise? But at first light, as a sentry peers through the dawn mists, he sees the new works on Dorchester Heights. With this, it becomes apparent to the British high command that their position is untenable, unless those positions on the heights overlooking the City can be overrun. (An important aspect of artillery in those days was its ability to extend its range when at an altitude above the objective.) William Howe orders an attack for the next day.

6 March 1776:
      Wednesday. The British plan to attack Dorchester Heights is turned back because of a fierce and sudden storm.

Two British warships and a transport move up the Savannah River in Georgia and take eleven rice-laden merchant ships. The troops land at Hutchinson's Island, opposite the city of Savannah.

7 March 1776:
Thursday. After warnings by the patriots for the British to withdraw from Hutchinson's Island, the rebels set fire to two of the merchant ships, which drift toward the British transport in the river and cause a panic. When Colonel John Bull arrives with 400 Carolina patriots, the British abandon their plan to attack the town of Savannah. This action drives Royal Gov. James Wright from the colony.

In Boston, William Howe concludes that the harbor and waterfront need to be protected from American fire, but the guns of the British ships cannot be elevated enough to reach the emplacements on Dorchester Heights. Aware of American preparations for counterattack, and recalling the slaughter at Bunker Hill, Howe decides to evacuate Boston.

Charles Lee, whom Washington had sent to New York for the purpose of preparing the defenses of that place, is ordered to Charleston, South Carolina. In temporary command of the growing number of American forces around the New York area is Brigadier General William Alexander, Lord Stirling.

8 March 1776:
Friday. At headquarters, Cambridge, General Orders state "The General Court Martial, of which Colo. Phinney was president, to assemble tomorrow morning, at eleven o'clock, at Pomeroy's Tavern in Cambridge. His Excellency, the General, returns his thanks to the militia of the surrounding districts, for their spirited and alert march to Roxbury, last Saturday and Sunday, for the noble ardour (sic) they discovered in defense of the cause of liberty, and their country." The parole is given as Henry and the countersign as Loyal.

As the civilian inhabitants of Boston learn that the British intend to evacuate the city, they come to plead with Howe not to burn the place on his departure.

9 March 1776:
Saturday. At headquarters, Cambridge, Washington writes to Governor Jonathan Trumbull, "Sir: The important post of Dorchester Hill, which has long been the object of our particular attention, and which for various weighty reasons I had hitherto delayed taking possession of, I have the pleasure to inform you is now so well secured, that I flatter myself it will not be in the power of the enemy to disposess [sic] us. A detachment of twenty-five hundred men, under command of Brig. General Thomas on Monday evening last, begun the works there, which they have carried on ever since without the least molestation from the enemy. I thought it necessary to draw off their attention from the grand object, and accordingly ordered a brisk cannonade and bombardment of the Town, which had the desired effect for they had no suspicion of our

real design, 'til Tuesday morning, when they discovered our troops in possession of the hill."

At the siege of Boston, American troops, attempting to occupy Nook's Hill, are driven off by British artillery fire.

10 March 1776:
Sunday. At headquarters, Cambridge, General Orders give the parole as Tilghman and the countersign as Mercer.

In Chesapeake Bay, the British sloop of war HMS *Otter* defends against American patriots attacking from the shore.

11 March 1776:
Monday. Benjamin Franklin writes to Philip Schuyler, Commander of the Northern Department, informing him of the appointment of three Congressional Commissioners to Canada for purposes of seeking support. He asks Schuyler to do what he can to facilitate and expedite their journey from Albany north.

12 March 1776:
Tuesday. Henry Clinton and his Southern expedition has reached the Cape Fear River and he is joined by Josiah Martin, Royal Governor of North Carolina, and William Campbell, Royal Governor of South Carolina.

13 March 1776:
Wednesday. After a few days of cat and mouse thrusts against the British sloop of war *Otter*, patriot forces from two Maryland militia companies and a Maryland ship *Defence* attack and drive away the intruder from near the shore of Chariton Creek, Northampton County, Virginia.

14 March 1776:
Thursday. In Cambridge, Washington writes to Maj. Gen. Charles Lee, "You have doubtless heard before this time of our being in possession of Dorchester Hill, which important business was executed in one night without any loss. The enemy were thrown into utmost consternation when they perceived, the next morning, what had been effected the preceding night, and made preparations to dislodge us. Three thousand men under command of Lord Percy were draughted (sic) for this service; but a very heavy storm of wind and rain frustrated their design. Failing in this attempt, they have thought it most prudent to quit the Town, and have been for several days past very busily employed in embarking their troops, and stores, on board transports, most of which are now in Nantasket Road, waiting for a fair wind to sail somewhere. It is most probable their destination is for New York. The vast importance of that place is doubtless a capital object with them. It is most certainly so to us; and in consequence of their shameful retreat I shall begin to march part of this army immediately and follow with the remainder, as soon as their accommodations on the road, will permit."

Congress sends advice to all the colonies to disarm all loyalists. It also orders the defense of New York City by 8,000 men.

15 March 1776:

Friday. In Boston, William Howe, who has been approached by a number of citizens asking that he not burn the city, offers a counter proposal. The British will not burn Boston if they are allowed to evacuate the city without interference. This proposal is quickly passed to George Washington, and a tacit agreement is reached under which the British will not be molested in their packing up to leave.

16 March 1776:

Saturday. The loading of the many ships, and the transportation of numerous Tories and their belongings at Boston has taken much time. It has been ten days since the decision was reached to evacuate the city. Nearly 9,000 men and officers, more than 1,100 Loyalists and almost 1,000 women and children of the soldiers have to be accommodated on board, and personal items stowed away on some 125 vessels.

17 March 1776:

Sunday. The British embark to leave the city of Boston, but the ships remain in the outer harbor awaiting wind and tide. This day, which for many years in Boston and its environs has been known and celebrated as Evacuation Day, is also St. Patrick's Day, and thus a double celebration. Soldiers immune to smallpox are carefully selected to take over in the city. However, efforts to keep out all the other non-immune people who wish to re-enter the city are quite ineffective, and an epidemic soon breaks out.

The Bibliography lists the classic work on this matter of the Public Health of Boston in its early years; John Ballard Blake, *Public Health in the Town of Boston, 1630 -1822.*

John Sullivan leads his men into the abandoned Charlestown lines. Israel Putnam takes his troops into Boston itself, to find the city a scene of desolation--except that, from a military point of view, large caches of Royal stores have been unaccountably left behind.

18 March 1776:

Monday. General George Washington enters Boston today, and instead of some dramatic speech, calls for a church service, and asks Dr. Eliot, dean of the Boston Clergy, to preach a sermon of thanksgiving.

19 March 1776:

Tuesday. At Cambridge, George Washington writes to John Hancock, "The town, although it has suffered greatly, is not in so bad a state as I expected to find it; and I have a particular pleasure in being able to inform you; Sir, that your home has received no damage worth mentioning. Your furniture is in tolerable order, and the family pictures are all left entire and untouched."

In Philadelphia, the Congress approves the use of privateers, "... to cruise on the enemies of these united colonies." In a few days it will authorize these vessels by more official means.

20 March 1776:
Wednesday. At headquarters, Cambridge, General Orders state "Whitcomb's, Phinney's, and Hutchinson's Regiments are to march into Boston this day, and remain there until further orders. They are to guard the Town, and public stores there, and do all such fatigue, and other duties, as the General commanding there, thinks proper to order. Every possible precaution will be taken to destroy the infection of the small pox." The parole is given as Dorchester and the counter sign as Salem.

The Continental Army completes its occupation of Boston.

21 March 1776:
Thursday. In Philadelphia, James Duane sends a letter by Carpenter Wharton to the New York Provincial Committee regarding the contracting of military rations for the Middle Department; that area around New York city, outside the control of British forces, most of New Jersey, Pennsylvania, Delaware, and Maryland--as distinct from the Northern Department, which is all of the rest of New York state, and New England; or the Southern Department, which includes all the colonies south of the Potomac River.

22 March 1776:
Friday. Benjamin Franklin writes to Charles William Frédéric Dumas, saying in a brief note that the bearer, Mr. Deane, will inform him of things happening in Philadelphia, as he cannot put them in writing, for fear of capture.

23 March 1776:
Saturday. While some colonies have a small naval presence, and a few individual vessels have done some pursuit and capture of British ships, no central (ie., Congressional) orders have been issued for such matters. On this date, the Congress authorizes privateering by the issue of Letters of Marque and Reprisal.

24 March 1776:
Sunday. At Cambridge, Washington writes to the President of Congress, reporting upon the British evacuation of Boston and noting that their fleet is still in Nantasket Road. He also reports that he has caused a large and strong work to be thrown up on Fort Hill to command the whole harbor in case the enemy should choose to return. He indicates that Major General Ward and Brigadier General Frye are desirous of leaving the service and he lays the matter before Congress to allow them to resign their commissions. He also seeks guidance

and directions on a line of conduct to be pursued regarding how he should handle any British peace commission or commissioners that should arrive in Boston, which he has just occupied

25 March 1776:
    Monday. In Cambridge Washington writes to Joseph Reed, in which he reports that he is puzzled over the British evacuation of Boston noting that they have blown up, burnt, and demolished the fortifications on Castle Island and are now all still in Nantasket Road. He does not know what they are doing, he believes they might be trying to fit themselves better for a sea voyage. Perhaps they are reloading the vessels which were originally loaded in great haste and disorder; and they have yards, booms, and bowsprits yet to fix. "We have detached six regiments to New York, have many points to look to, and, on Monday next, ten regiments of militia, which were brought in to serve till the first of April, stand disengaged. I am fortifying Fort Hill in Boston, and demolishing the lines on the Neck there, as it is a defense against the country only. I can spare no more men til I see the enemy's back fairly turned, and then I shall hasten towards New York."
    Congress votes thanks and a gold medal to General George Washington for his achievements during the siege of Boston, resulting in complete British evacuation of the place.

26 March 1776:
    Tuesday. The Congressional Committee of Observation for the Canada Expedition (sometimes referred to as the Canada Mission) leaves Philadelphia. Three congressmen have been appointed as envoys to negotiate with the Canadians: Benjamin Franklin, Samuel Chase, and Charles Carroll. Carroll's cousin, Fr. John Carroll, has been included, and also Brig. Gen. the Baron Frederick William Woedtke, whom Congress assigned to the northern army, accompany the party to travel as far as Fort Ticonderoga.
    South Carolina adopts a state constitution, and an independent government.

27 March 1776:
    Wednesday. William Howe, whose army has been embarked aboard transports in the outer Boston harbor, with his entire force and many Loyalists, sails today for Halifax, Nova Scotia. With the exception of Henry Clinton's force off the North Carolina coast, there are, for the time being, no British forces in the 13 American colonies.
    At headquarters, Cambridge, Washington is arranging to send off more troops to the New York area. The very difficult operations required of moving rather large bodies of troops for any distance, entails many, many detailed pre-arrangements.

28 March 1776:
    Thursday. The Committee on Military Supplies writes to the Maryland Convention urging the establishment of public works

for the finding, making, and shipping of salt petre and gunpowder.

29 March 1776:
Friday. In Cambridge, Washington sends Orders and Instructions to Maj. Gen. Israel Putnam, "As there are the best reasons to believe that the enemy's Fleet and Army, which left Nantasket Road last Wednesday evening, are bound to New York, to endeavor to possess that important Post. It must be our care to prevent them from accomplishing their designs. To that end, I have detached Brig. Gen. Heath with the whole body of riflemen, and five Battalions of the Continental Army by the way of Norwich in Connecticut to New York. These, by an express arrived yesterday from Genl. Heath, I have reason to believe are in New York. Six more Battalions under General Sullivan march this morning by the same route and will, I hope, arrive there in eight or ten days at farthest. The rest of the army will immediately follow in Divisions, leaving only a convenient space between each Division, to prevent confusion, and want of accommodation upon their march."

The Canada Mission party, having traveled by coach along the poor roads of New Jersey, arrives in New York City.

30 March 1776:
Saturday. At headquarters, Cambridge, General Orders state "A detachment from the Regiment of Artillery, to be ready to march on Monday morning, with the Brigade of Brig. Gen. Greene. The Colonels commanding the Regiments of this Brigade, may each of them receive a warrant for five hundred pounds, lawful money upon application at Headquarters." The parole is given as Dedham and the countersign as Putnam.

John Adams writes to Norton Quincy, joyfully reporting upon the capture of the city of Boston and its harbor.

31 March 1776:
Sunday. At Army headquarters in Cambridge, General Orders notes that five regiments in Brigadier General Joseph Spencer's Brigade are to march out of camp for New York at sunrise on Thursday next (5 Apr 1776). Washington writes to Augustine Washington, "The enemy left all their works standing in Boston and on Bunker's Hill; and formidable they are. The town has shared a much better fate than was expected, the damage done to the houses being nothing equal to report. But the inhabitants have suffered a good deal, in being plundered by the soldiery at their departure." The parole is given as Moore, and the countersign as Newborn.

From Braintree, Massachusetts, Abigail Adams writes to her husband John, remarking upon her views of Virginia, "I am willing to allow the Colony great merit for having produced a Washington but have been shamefully duped by a Dunmore. I have sometimes been ready to think that the passion for Liberty cannot be equally strong in the breasts of those who have been accustomed to deprive their fellow creatures of theirs. Of this I am certain that it is not founded upon that generous and christian principal of doing to others as we would have others do unto us. I feel very differently at the approach of spring to what I did a month ago. We knew not then whether we could plant or sow with safety, whether when we had toiled we could reap the fruits of our own industry, whether we could rest in our own Cottages, or whether we should be driven from our sea coasts to seek shelter in the wilderness, but now we feel as if we might sit under our own vine and eat the good of the land. I feel a gaieti de Coar [by which she means gaieté de coeur or happiness of heart] to which before I was a stranger. I think the Sun looks brighter, the Birds sing more melodiously, and Nature puts on a more cheerful countenance. We feel a temporary peace, and the poor fugitives are returning to their deserted habitations."

1 April 1776:
    Monday. In Cambridge, Washington writes to the President of Congress, concerning a spy report on the Province of Nova Scotia which had been somewhat of an object throughout the war but nothing was ever launched against it. "This letter will be delivered to you by Jonathan Eddy, Esq. The gentleman from Nova Scotia who I mentioned to you. He seems desirous of waiting on the Honorable Congress in order to lay before them the State of Public Affairs and the situation of the inhabitants of that Province; and as it might be in his power to communicate many things personally which could not be so well done by letter, I encouraged him in his design and have advanced him fifty dollars to defray his expenses. The Acadian accompanies him, and as they seem to be solid, judicious men, I beg leave to recommend them both to the notice Congress."
    Brigadier General David Wooster arrives at Quebec with American reinforcements, and takes over command from the wounded Benedict Arnold.

2 April 1776:
    Tuesday. At headquarters, Cambridge, General Orders state "General Ward to send a regiment tomorrow morning, at ten o'clock, out of Boston, to relieve Col. Leonard's regiment upon Dorchester Heights." The parole is given as Hartford and the countersign as Kingsbridge.
    The Canada Mission party is at the Albany pier of New York City, preparing to leave to travel up the Hudson River for Albany and the north.

3 April 1776:
    Wednesday. At Cambridge, Washington writes to Brig. Gen. Arnold, "The chief part of the troops are marched from hence towards New York. I will set off to-morrow." Harvard College confers the honorary degree of Doctor of Laws on Washington, "...who by the most signal smiles of Divine Providence on his military operations, drove the Fleet and Troops of the enemy with disgraceful precipitation from the town of Boston."
    The Congress completes "Instructions to the Commanders of private ships or vessels of war that have Commissions of

Letters of Marque and Reprisal, authorising [sic] them to make captures of British vessels and cargoes." These authorizations make such private vessels into privateers, giving them the cover of legality to cruise and capture on the high seas.

4 April 1776:
Thursday. Washington has been concerned as to just where the British, who have evacuated Boston, may be going next. He believes that their next blow might fall upon New York City, so he wants to leave a garrison at Boston, to protect it against any enemy incursion, but take the remainder of his American forces to the New York area and prepare defenses against any British attack there. He has already sent some of his troops in that direction. This night will be his last stay in the Vassal House he has occupied since 10 July 1775.

The American frigate *Columbus* (20 guns), part of Esek Hopkins Squadron, captures the small British schooner HMS *Hawk* (six guns) with little resistance.

5 April 1776:
Friday. Washington moves to Providence, Rhode Island, and stays at Stephen Hopkins' House.

The American frigate *Alfred* (24 guns) fights the British bomb brig HMS *Bolton* (10 guns), which puts up little resistance, since her guns were designed for land bombardment, not naval action.

6 April 1776:
Saturday. A Squadron of five Continental ships, including the *Alfred* (24 guns) under Captain Esek Hopkins, encounters the British frigate HMS *Glasgow* (20 guns), under Captain Tryingham Howe off Block Island, Rhode Island, on a return from Nassau. The lone British vessel gives a good account of herself in the ensuing fight, inflicting heavy damage on the *Alfred.*

7 April 1776:
Sunday. At Albany, Philip Schuyler writes to George Washington, reporting that "The Regiments destined for Canada arrived incomplete, sickness and desertion have reduced them much more, so that our Army in country will be greatly short of what was intended."

8 April 1776:
Monday. George Washington, traveling by horseback, as is his usual mode, is in Norwich, Connecticut, at the Leffingwell Inn, slowly working his way from the Boston area to New York.

9 April 1776:
Tuesday. In Philadelphia, the Continental Congress takes under consideration the issue of prisoners of war, and resolves that: 1.) A list of prisoners in each Colony be made out and transmitted to the House of Assembly, Convention, Council or

Committee of Safety of each colony respectively; 2.) That each Colony cause a strict observance of the terms of such prisoners so none escape and that they be treated properly.

Washington is in New London, Connecticut, at the Nathaniel Shaw House on his way toward New York.

10 April 1776:
Wednesday. Congress agrees that it is not the business of that body to relieve fiscal difficulties of colleges. It resolves that it is neither seasonable nor prudent to contribute monies out of the public treasury for such a purpose, and denies requested relief for Dartmouth College.

Washington, still working his way toward New York, is this day in Old Lyme, Connecticut, with his headquarters at John McCurdy's House.

11 April 1776:
Thursday. Washington arrives at New Haven, Connecticut, making his headquarters at Isaac Beer's. Washington writes to Captain Samuel Mackay, who has requested relief from his condition of prisoner of the British by means of an exchange, "I could wish that it was in my power, consistent with the duty I owe my country to grant you the relief you desire. I have made repeated applications to General Howe for an Exchange of Prisoners, but he has not thought proper to return any answer. It has been in his power to set you at liberty, and if you are still a prisoner the blame must lay entirely upon him. Whenever it is in my power to release you, by a mutual exchange, I shall do it with the greatest pleasure."

12 April 1776:
Friday. In Halifax, North Carolina, the Fourth Provisional Congress instructs its delegates in the Continental Congress to stand for Independence. This is the first colony to take such an action, and the resolutions containing the instructions become known as the Halifax Resolves. This is a bold and forward step. While, the continuation of the war has begun to impact many people that an accommodation is not possible, to recommend actual separation and total independence is viewed as radical.

13 April 1776:
Saturday. In Philadelphia, the Continental Congress passes a resolution regarding any Peace Commission: "... unless such commissioner or commissioners shall produce a commission to treat with the Continental Congress ... be required to return immediately..."

Washington, with two aides, William Palfrey and Stephen Moylan, and his Adjutant-General, Horatio Gates, arrives at New York. Washington makes his headquarters in New York City at William Smith's House.

14 April 1776:
Sunday. Carter Braxton, writes to Landon Braxton stating that "...independency & total separation from Great Britain are

the interesting subjects of all ranks of men & often agitate our body." He requests advice and information so as to help him in his office as a Delegate from Virginia.

At New York, the headquarters Orderly Book contains the following "The General compliments the officers, who have successively commanded at this Post, and returns his thanks to them, and to all the officers, and soldiers, under their Command for the many Works of Defense, which have been so expeditiously erected, and doubts not but that same Spirit of Zeal for the service will continue to animate their future conduct."

15 April 1776:

Monday. At Providence, Rhode Island, two new American warships are launched: the *Warren* (32 guns), and the *Providence* (28 guns).

In Philadelphia, the Continental Congress issues a resolution recommending that all the colonies reject Royal authority, and form an independent state government.

16 April 1776:

Tuesday. Samuel Adams writes to James Warren stating his strong support of "Independency." Regarding the notion of possible reconciliation, he says, "We know that it has been the constant practice of the King & his junto ever since this struggle began to endeavor to make us believe their designs were pacifick (sic) while they have been meditating the most destructive plans & they insult our understanding by attempting thus to impose upon us even while they are putting these plans into execution."

17 April 1776:

Wednesday. Washington is in New York City at Abraham Mortier's House.

The American sloop of war *Lexington* (16 guns), commanded by Captain John Barry, engages the British warship HMS *Edward* (8 guns).

18 April 1776:

Thursday. From Fort George, on Lake Champlain, New York, Samuel Chase writes to John Adams, reporting on the situation of the Canada expedition. He says that Colonel Arthur St. Clair will be bringing his regiment from Fort Edward to Fort George. He expresses concern about the rate of desertions.

19 April 1776:

Friday. From New York, George Washington writes to the Congress reporting the receipt of letters from Philip Schuyler, and in particular noting that four regiments, ordered to begin their march from Boston to New York, have not done so because the colonels of those regiments failed to make out the abstracts for their pay. He points out that the lack of proper

training and ability found in too many Continental officers is
woefully apparent.

20 April 1776:
    Saturday. In Philadelphia, Delegate William Whipple of New
Hampshire writes to John Langdon reporting on the business
of Naval officers. He notes that earlier there had been a great
scarcity of candidates, now, however, there is an abundance of
them. Thus, the Committee for selection can be very critical,
and the quality of Naval officers will improve.

21 April 1776:
    Sunday. From the north end or outlet of Lake George,
Samuel Chase writes again to John Adams, noting that the
investment of Quebec seems to be going well, except that too
many troops are sick in hospital. He reports that Colonel
Arthur St. Clair's regiment is expected at this place on Tuesday
next (23 April 1776).

22 April 1776:
    Monday. Washington leaves New York to travel toward
Philadelphia, in order to consult with the Congress.
Washington feels that the British have an attack upon New
York in mind. To defend the city, he has brought troops from
Boston to New York, approved the plans of Charles Lee for
redoubts and fortifications, and has his forces actively engaged
in creating additional outworks for better defense of the city.
The Congress would very much like to see New York defended,
and the British beaten off. Washington has doubts about the
ability of the forces available to him to do any such thing.
Therefore, a conference has been called by the Congress to
establish what might be done, and what might not. But,
because Washington is very solicitous of the views and superior
position of the Congress, he is not likely to press contrary
opinions.

23 April 1776:
    Tuesday. John Hancock writes to Nathaniel Shaw, Jr.,
stating that he (Shaw) is appointed Agent for the Congress for
Continental prizes entering the ports of the Colony of
Connecticut, and authorizes him to employ one or more
deputies as may be necessary to the conduct of the business
entrusted to him.

24 April 1776:
    Wednesday. John Hancock, president of the Congress,
writes to Moses Hazen, discussing the improper behavior of
some troops in the American service towards the Canadians,
that had been reported to the Continental Congress. Hancock
further notes that the Commanding Officer in Canada
(Brigadier General David Wooster) has been enjoined to be very
attentive to military discipline. This problem of discipline is
serious. No soldier is to act or speak in unkindly ways.

25 April 1776:
    Thursday. At headquarters, New York, General Orders state "Complaints having been made to the General, of the injuries done to farmers, in their crops, and fields, by soldiers passing over, and trampling upon the young growth, in a wanton and disorderly manner; he expressly orders the officers commanding, either upon duty, or in quarters in the country, to take especial care to put a stop to such practices, and endeavour (sic) to convince their men, that we come to protect, not to injure the property of any man." The parole is given as Johnstone and the countersign as Lutterell.
    Washington arrives in Philadelphia, to review with the Congress the status, needs, and future of the army he commands, and to report his views of the defense of New York City, and seek the advice of the delegates.

26 April 1776:
    Friday. John Hancock writes to Philip Schuyler, deploring the poor treatment of Canadians by American troops, repeating again the admonition he had sent to Moses Hazen, regarding military discipline among the soldiers in their dealings with Canadian citizens and soldiery. One does not win hearts and minds by force!

27 April 1776:
    Saturday. John Adams writes to Maj. Gen. Horatio Gates, noting that too many folks believe in utter nonsense. A belief in "accommodation" with Great Britain is equally specious. He also reports a very favorable opinion of Robert Morris, whom he regards as a solid, stable, patriotic, and sensible man.

28 April 1776:
    Sunday. In New York, Washington writes to Colonel Richard Gridley, "It gives me much concern to hear from every one that comes from Boston, that those works that were laid out for it's defense, are in little more forwardness, than they were when I left that Town. Who am I to blame for this shameful neglect, but you, sir, who was to have them executed? It is not an agreeable task to be under the necessity of putting any gentleman in mind of his duty; but it is what I owe the public. I expect and desire, Sir, that you will exert yourself in compleating (sic) the works with all possible dispatch, and do not lay me under the disagreeable necessity of writing to you again upon this subject."
    John Adams writes to John Penn, a delegate from North Carolina, noting that many folks are now leaning heavily toward some physical and political break with Great Britain. He is glad to hear from Penn that in Virginia and North Carolina, "... all fondness for the King and Nation is gone."

29 April 1776:
    Monday. The Iroquois complain that there is a lack of traders serving their needs for blankets, clothing, and ammunition, and call for a council with the Americans at

Albany. Most of the Indian sachems still adhere to a neutrality in this war, but a lack of a ready supply of trade goods will be a factor in many of them uniting with the British.

The Pennsylvania Committee of Safety writes to Captain Harvey of the Ship *Union*, Captain Curwin of the Ship *Hope*, and Captain Osman of the Ship *Sally*, ordering them to proceed down the Delaware River under protection of the Pennsylvania ship *Montgomery* and the Continental ship *Reprisal* to capture HMS *Roebuck* aground on Brandywine Shoal.

30 April 1776:
Tuesday. In Philadelphia, John Hancock writes to the Massachusetts Council to report that, "... nothing is so much wanted at this juncture as a supply of specie ..." This problem of a lack of ready money will continue to plague the Congress, the Army, the colonies, and most individual citizens, throughout the entire period of the Revolution.

1 May 1776:
Wednesday. In New York, Washington writes to Maj. Gen. Charles Lee, "General Howe's retreat from Boston was precipitate, beyond anything I could have conceived. The destruction of the stores at Dunbar's Camp after Braddock's defeat [he is recalling a much earlier occasion] was but a faint image of what was seen at Boston; artillery carts cut to pieces in one place; gun carriages in another; shells broke here; shot buried there, and everything carrying with it the face of disorder and confusion, as also of distress."

Brigadier General John Thomas relieves recently promoted Major General David Wooster in command of the American forces at Quebec.

2 May 1776:
Thursday. The French are quite willing, nay anxious, to take the English down a peg or two--their loss to Great Britain in the Seven Years War has left the French seeking a means of revenge. This squabble between the American Colonies and Britain seems to the French like a good opportunity to strike back. However, they wish to be careful about how they go about doing so. What if America should not win? What if Great Britain should choose to attack the French for any aid they might give the Americans? Thus, while they want to have the Americans succeed, and want to help them defeat England, they need to find a way to do this without being seen as doing so. A "front" trading company is set up, "Roderique Hortalez et Cie," administered by a secret agent, Pierre de Beaumarchais, avoiding direct dealings by the French government that is to work with the patriots. Through this company, military goods and money can and does flow to America.

3 May 1776:
Friday. The planned British Expedition to the south had included a portion of troops to be sent from Cork, Ireland to

join with the portion under Henry Clinton. This Cork element now arrives off the coast of North Carolina in a fleet of ships and transports under Admiral Peter Parker, with troops under the command of Maj. Gen. Charles Cornwallis. With the two halves of the expedition in hand, Henry Clinton decides to attack Charleston, South Carolina.

In London, King George III appoints Admiral Lord Richard Howe, and his brother Maj. Gen. William Howe as peace commissioners, to see if they can deal with the rebelling colonists and restore loyalty to the crown. These brothers are, respectively, the Navy and Army commanders of the British forces now gathering in England and at Halifax, Nova Scotia, to descend on America.

4 May 1776:

Saturday. Congress has sent a number of reinforcements to the Northern Army in efforts to support the forlorn attempts to induce Canada to join with them as a fourteenth Colony. Repeated failures throughout this winter and early spring do not seem to have impressed upon them that the Canadians are, in general, not at all warm to the idea. Since American efforts at persuasion have not worked, why would efforts at fighting succeed? Brig. Gen. John Thomas, Commander of American forces at Quebec, now decides to raise the rather weak siege of the place, and withdraw. [See Fig. III-10, p. 119].

In Rhode Island, the General Assembly passes an Act declaring Independence from Royal authority, and the colony becomes the, "State of Rhode Island and Providence Plantations."

5 May 1776:

Sunday. At New York, Washington writes to the President of Congress, expressing his concern over the shortage of arms, "In the hands of the Committee of Safety at Philadelphia, there are, ... not less than two or three thousand stand of arms for Provincial use. A number might be borrowed by Congress; provided they are replaced with continental arms. As they are brought into the magazine in that City. At a crisis so important as this, such a loan might be attended with the most signal advantages while the defenseless state of the regiments, if no relief can be had, may be productive of fatal consequences. I enclose a copy of a return ... from the troops in the Highlands, ... Colonel Ritzema's Regiment only 97 firelocks and seven bayonets belonging thereto, and that all the regiments from the eastward are deficient from twenty to fifty of the former."

From Elizabethtown, New Jersey, John Jay writes to Philip Schuyler, introducing Henry Brockholst Livingston, and commending him to Schuyler for some employment. Livingston soon becomes an Aide-de-Camp to Schuyler.

6 May 1776:

Monday. Near Quebec, Guy Carleton and 900 men rout the 250 American besiegers under John Thomas on the Plains of Abraham. Carleton coordinates this attack with the timely approach of a British fleet on the St. Lawrence River. This fleet, under Maj. Gen. John Burgoyne, with more than 6,000 troops sailed up the River as soon as the ice had gone out. Since Thomas has already concluded to withdraw, he now begins a retreat towards Montreal. [See Fig. III-10, p. 119].

In New York, Washington writes to the New York Committee of Safety, "Gentlemen: I beg you leave to refer to your examination of Joseph Blanchard and Peter Puillon, who were yesterday apprehended, the former on suspicion of carrying on a correspondence with persons on board the King's ships, the latter of having supplied them with some provisions, in violation of, and contrary to, the regulations which have been adopted for preventing such practices. There are witnesses against both, which are ordered to wait on you; and also some papers found in possession of Mr. Blanchard which, though previous to your resolves in point of date, indicate an intimacy between him and Colonel Fanning, the Secretary, to whom, I am told, he has written since their publication, and his knowledge of them."

In Philadelphia, the congress responds to Washington's request of 24 March 1776 regarding the manner of handling any peace commission and requesting directions, by resolving as follows: "It may be one of those delusive contrivances by which they lull us into hopes of reconciliation ... if commissioners are intended to be sent from Great Britain to treat of peace, that the practice usual in such cases will be observed, by making previous application for the necessary passports or safe conduct ... Congress will then direct the proper measures ..."

7 May 1776:
	Tuesday. At Philadelphia, the Board of Treasury writes to the conventions of the states of New Hampshire, New Jersey, New York, Maryland and Rhode Island, requesting the census or enumeration of the inhabitants of each state be taken and the results turned into the Congress, as requested in a Resolution of 26 December 1775.

8 May 1776:
	Wednesday. On the Delaware River, 13 Pennsylvania galleys attack two British warships close to the mouth of Christiana Creek, near Wilmington. The British are forced to withdraw down the river.

	In Rhode Island, the legislature appoints Nathanael Greene to be a Brigadier General. He will develop, mature, and become one of Washington's greatest generals, taking over the terrible supply situation from a failing Mifflin, and later a small southern army from a defeated Gates.

9 May 1776:
	Thursday. William Floyd, a delegate from New York, writes to John McKesson, noting that "The preparations our enemies on the other side of the water, from intelligence we have, appear to be very considerable."

10 May 1776:
   Friday. In New York, George Washington writes to Lund Washington, discussing many items of personal money matters, "There is another matter, which I think justice to myself requires a mention of, and that is with respect to the sterling balance which it will appear I was owing Mr. Custis upon last settlement. It was then, and ever since has been, my intention to assign him as many bonds, carrying interest, as would discharge his balance. But my attendance upon Congress in the Fall of 1774, and the Spring of 1775, put it out of my power to attend the General Courts at this Sessions; consequently no Order could be taken, or account rendered, of the matter; and now, by the rise of exchange, if I was to turn current money bonds into sterling, I should be a considerable sufferer... The many matters, which hang heavy upon my hands at present, do not allow me time to add, but oblige me to request, as I have wrote fully to Colonel Mason on this subject, that you will shew him, and, if necessary let him have this letter."
   John Paul Jones is given his first command, as he receives orders for the sloop of war *Providence* (12 guns).

11 May 1776:
   Saturday. At Philadelphia, Oliver Wolcott, a delegate from Connecticut, writes to his wife, Laura, telling her to have courage in the face of danger, and to bear up under the press of disasters that sometimes come by the very nature of war.

12 May 1776:
   Sunday. At headquarters, New York, General Orders state "The carpenters, boat builders, and painters, who were selected for public service this morning, by Major Genl. Putnam, are to parade tomorrow morning at sunrise, in the street opposite to Genl. Putnam's where they will receive his orders." The parole is given as Madrid and the countersign as Paris.
   In Philadelphia, Samuel Adams writes to James Warren that the Congress, concerned about the defense of New England, agrees "... that the troops in Boston should be augmented to 6,000."

13 May 1776:
   Monday. At Philadelphia, President John Hancock writes to General George Washington, noting that he has caused the sum of $400,000 to be forwarded for the use of the troops in New York and Massachusetts.

14 May 1776:
   Tuesday. The Secret Committee writes to Philip Lacey, captain of the brig *Polly*, telling him sail to the Chesapeake, and there to place himself under the command of the Continental Fleet, now sailing south on Chesapeake Bay. Also "... to avoid enemy ships, get out to sea, and then pursue your orders to capture enemy shipping."

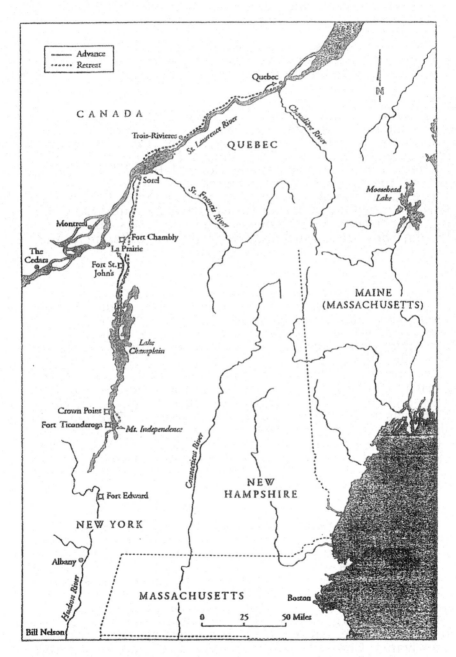

Fig. III-10: American Defeat and Retreat in Canada, 1776

15 May 1776:
Wednesday. In Richmond, the Virginia Convention instructs its delegates in the Continental Congress to propose independence.

The Congress passes a Resolution that each colony "... institute such forms of Government as to them shall appear necessary to promote the happiness of the people."

16 May 1776:
Thursday. About 40 miles upstream from Montreal, at a place called The Cedars, a patriot force of about 300 men, retreating from Quebec, is approached by British troops and Indians. (The site is under the command of Major Butterfield, to whom it has devolved while Colonel Bedel has gone to Montreal to bring back reinforcements.)

The Continental Congress commissioners to Canada, Charles Carroll and Samuel Chase, write to Philip Schuyler, urging the forwarding of provisions for the American army in Canada. They are in particular need of food stuffs, including pork.

17 May 1776:
Friday. The American troops at The Cedars, are surrounded by the British and Indian party of about 600 under Captain Foster. Both sides keep up a loose fire for two days. The British have no cannon, but the Americans, are under Major Butterfield, who is timid and wishes to surrender. [See Fig. III-10, p. 121].

At Nantasket Roads, in the outer harbor of Boston, American Captain James Mugford, on the schooner *Franklin*, with a crew of 21 men, captures the British transport, *Hope*, which was sailing for Boston, laden with a large cargo of military stores including seventy-five tons of gunpowder. The British on board are quite unaware that the city had been evacuated by the British garrison two months earlier, and are somewhat chagrined at having been taken so easily, and their cargo unloaded in their open view.

18 May 1776:
Saturday. Delegate James Duane of New York writes from Philadelphia, to John Jay, expressing doubt that either the Maryland or Pennsylvania assemblies will listen to recommendations of the Continental Congress regarding Independence and separation. Duane indicates that a wait of a few weeks might be helpful in turning aside the weak-hearted, and thus allow a better "union of the Colonies."

In Williamsburg, Virginia, the Convention receives a petition from the frontier outpost at Harrodsburg, charging the Transylvania Company with efforts to set up a separate government, so as to avoid the constraints of Virginia laws regarding dealings with the Indians, the purchase of lands, and the regularization of settlement.

19 May 1776:
    Sunday. At The Cedars, American Major Butterfield, knows that an American reinforcement is only about three or four miles away. When a flag is sent to him for surrender by British Captain Foster, Butterfield, nevertheless, quickly agrees to give up his post.

20 May 1776:
    Monday. In New York, Washington writes to Benjamin Franklin, "On the morning of the 17 inst. with much concern and surprise I received the melancholy account of our troops being obliged to raise the siege of Quebec with the loss of their cannon, a number of small arms, provisions, &c. I had hoped before this misfortune, that the troops there would have maintained their posts, and on the arrival of the two Brigades detached from hence ... would terminate in a favourable (sic) and happy issue. To what cause to ascribe the sad disaster, I am at a loss to determine ..."
    In Philadelphia, delegate John Adams, writes to James Warren, reporting that a delegation from Georgia has arrived. Adams adds that "... every post and every day rolls in upon us Independence like a torrent."

21 May 1776:
    Tuesday. At Johnson Hall, New York, Colonel Elias Dayton arrives with 300 men to arrest Sir John Johnson, who since his agreement to disarm in January, has been discovered to support the Loyalist efforts and rearm many Tories. Schuyler now needs to take Johnson into custody, and dispatched Dayton for that purpose. Johnson, however, learns of the force to arrest him, and escapes to Canada. He leaves his pregnant wife with two children behind. They are taken into custody and held in Albany.

    John Hancock writes to George Washington from Philadelphia, offering his large home in Boston to the General and Mrs. Washington. Hancock does this not only because the general is to consult with the Congress, but also because Hancock wants to afford Martha Washington a comfortable place from which to recover from the smallpox inoculation she is willing to undergo.

22 May 1776:
    Wednesday. Brig. Gen. Benedict Arnold, with 900 Americans, confronts the British force that had received the surrender of the Americans at The Cedars, three days before. Arnold enters into a cartel to exchange the prisoners.
    At Amboy, New Jersey, Washington writes to Maj. Gen. Israel Putnam, "You will please to give every assistance which General Schuyler requires, that may be in your power, and least, ... in trenching tools of every kind will be wanted, more powder, lead, and cannon ball, and guns for the vessels on Lake Champlain, rigging, sail-cloth, and sail makers ..."

23 May 1776:
Thursday. In New York, General Orders state "The sail makers in the different regiments, are all to parade in front of the General's Quarters, tomorrow morning at six o'clock. The order for doubling the sentries at night to be strictly attended to." The parole is given as Amboy and the countersign as York.

Robert Treat Paine, a member of a committee concerned with production and supply of gunpowder, leaves Philadelphia to inspect a number of powder mills. This matter of gunpowder continues to concern several of the senior officers in the army.

24 May 1776:
Friday. John Hancock, in his capacity as President of the Congress, writes to Philip Schuyler, transmitting specie, resolves of the Congress regarding affairs in Canada, and his own good wishes.

25 May 1776:
Saturday. In Philadelphia, the Continental Congress resolves to commission Indians for military service. This has been discussed a number of times in the past, always with negative results, but now receives the approval of most delegates.

26 May 1776:
Sunday. The Secret Committee of the Congress meets today, and conducts a good bit of business, including the transmittal of gunpowder to the several departments, the reporting of funds, and the receipt of contracts.

27 May 1776:
Monday. In New York, the Third Provincial Congress declares independence from Royal authority, and takes steps to create a new government for the province.

General Orders give the parole as Killingly and the countersign as Pomfret.

28 May 1776:
Tuesday. Robert R. Livingston writes from Philadelphia to his sister Catherine Livingston at the family home at Clermont on the Hudson River, "We have reason to believe that our enemy will make great efforts this summer, I hope however by the blessing of God to see them repelled & this country after a glorious struggle emancipated from the tyranny of an inhuman prince. But enough of politicks [sic], only let me give you one caution before I leave it, never let your spirits forsake you, believe that many evils are incident to war but at the same time believe that a just cause can not fail of success."

29 May 1776:
Wednesday. In New York, a committee of mechanics urges the New York delegates in the Continental Congress to vote for independence.

30 May 1776:
   Thursday. John Adams writes to Samuel Cooper, in response to a letter from him of 20 May 1776, wherein Cooper reports the results of an election in Boston. Adams also expresses how thrilled he is by an account of naval actions in Boston Harbor that Cooper had written about to him.

31 May 1776:
   Friday. Samuel Chase writes to Philip Schuyler from Chambly reporting upon actions, as the Americans continue their retreat from Canada.
   In Philadelphia, George Washington writes to Augustine Washington, "Since my arrival at this place, where I came at the request of Congress, to settle some matters relative to the ensuing campaign I have received your letter... I am very glad to find that the Virginia Convention have passed so noble a vote [their unanimous resolution to instruct their delegates in Congress to propose independence], and with so much unanimity. Things have come to that pass now, as to convince us, that we have nothing more to expect from the justice of Great Britain. To form a new government, requires infinite care, and unbounded attention; for if the foundation is badly laid the superstructure must be bad. Too much time therefore, cannot be bestowed in weighing and digesting matters well."

1 June 1776:
   Saturday. Vice Admiral Sir Peter Parker, of the Royal Navy, sails his squadron into the well-defended harbor of Charleston, South Carolina. Not realizing that the patriot forces have been preparing for a possible British attack upon this southern city (they had been warned the British fleet was assembling along the North Carolina coast), Parker runs into a most difficult fire storm from Fort Moultrie on Sullivan's Island on the north jaw of the harbor mouth, and Fort Johnston on the south jaw. Any surprise is lost, and the attack goes awry.

2 June 1776:
   Sunday. At Fort Chambly, Canada, Brig. Gen. John Thomas, who had been Commander of American Forces in Canada, dies of smallpox. Brig. Gen. John Sullivan takes over the command of these forces.

3 June 1776:
   Monday. Dr. Lewis Beebe takes a count of the men in the barns at Chambly, suffering from smallpox. He puts the number at just over 300. The reader must understand that smallpox, was an all-pervasive disease that afflicted nearly everyone. It was so common in the 18th Century that the chance of going through life without being exposed was extremely thin. An emerging new technique was preventive inoculation against natural smallpox. The technique generally was to pass a thread through some opened or erupted pustules from a smallpox-infected person. Then with a very small

incision place the infected thread therein and bind or sew it in place. The inoculated person would develop a mild case of smallpox, and thereafter be immune. The mortality rates from inoculated persons ran to about one percent, while for naturally infected persons it was as much as eighteen percent. In spite of this very significant improvement in the general health of the troops, there was still a good bit of opposition, based on religious, political, and medical factors. As for religion, there were those who felt that these epidemics were God's punishment for a community's sins, and any impious attempt to circumvent them was against God's will. The political objections could hardly be separated from the religious, at least in New England. Who was going to support inoculation, if it was seen as an offence against God? In the medical community there was the understanding that inoculation did contain a certain element of risk. Besides, not all physicians were as careful or knowledgeable about the procedure as they should have been. See also the sketch for 13 July 1776. The Bibliography lists Dr. John B. Blake's paper, *Inoculation in Colonial America.*

4 June 1776:
  Tuesday. George Washington leaves Philadelphia to return to New York City.
  At Charleston, Maj. Gen. Charles Lee arrives from New York on orders from the Continental Congress to assist in the defense of the city, and to provide experienced leadership to the patriot groups being attacked by British land and naval forces.

5 June 1776:
  Wednesday. In Philadelphia, the Continental Congress completes a great deal of business related to the army. It also resolves that the master of the sloop *Betsey and Ann,* that had come from Bermuda with a load of salt, be allowed to exchange it for provisions much wanted in Bermuda, so long as he takes an oath to avoid all English men of war.

6 June 1776:
  Thursday. Washington returns to New York City and sets up his headquarters at Abraham Mortier's House.

7 June 1776:
  Friday. Richard Henry Lee, Delegate from Virginia at the Continental Congress in Philadelphia, introduces the famous resolution on instructions of the Virginia Convention, "Resolved, that these united colonies are, and of right ought to be, free and independent states, that they are absolved from all allegiance to the British Crown, and that all political connection between them and the State of Great Britain is, and ought to be, totally dissolved." While it is not an entirely new idea, it is certainly a shocking one to some of the delegates present.

Off the coast of Massachusetts, the American privateer, *Yankee Hero* (12 guns) under Captain Tracy is attacked by British frigate HMS *Milford* (32 guns), under Captain John Burr. Tracy has only a portion of his ship's complement aboard, but puts up a gallant fight against vastly superior odds before being forced to strike colors.

8 June 1776:
Saturday. Congress resolves itself into a committee of the whole (a parliamentary technique often used to allow full debate on an issue), in order to formally debate and consider Lee's proposal of independence the day before.

At Trois Rivières, Canada, a force of 2,000 Americans under Brig. Gen. William Thompson, plans to seize this place, believing it to be garrisoned by about 700 British and Canadians. Instead the place is held by about 7,000 British troops under Guy Carleton and Maj. Gen. John Burgoyne. In a three- day running fight, the Americans are dispersed, closely pursued by the British, and retreat towards Sorel and Montreal. Thompson and 235 other Americans are captured during this action.

At Montreal, the Americans evacuate the place and retreat towards St. John, under Benedict Arnold, with about 300 men. [See Fig. II-10, p. 121].

9 June 1776:
Sunday. In New York, Washington writes to Maj. Gen. Philip Schuyler, "As there is but too much probability that Sir John Johnson may attempt to ravage the frontier Counties, and to excite the disaffected to take arms against us, I think it will be advisable that Colo. Dayton should remain as you request, as long as you apprehend a necessity for it. It is not in my power to spare any more men from hence, either for the communication, or to assist in repairing Ticonderoga. The detachments already gone to Canada have weakened the force necessary for defense of this place, considering its importance."

British Maj. Gen. Henry Clinton finally lands his troops on Long Island, just outside the harbor at Charleston, South Carolina.

10 June 1776:
Monday. In Versailles, King Louis XVI approves a loan of 1,000,000 livres to Roderique Hortalez et Cie, the front trading company that will supply military goods and money to the War of the American Revolution. The front is designed to hide any notion of direct action by the government of France in aiding the American rebels.

At Halifax, Nova Scotia, British Maj. Gen. William Howe, and a large force assembled there, leave for New York City.

In Philadelphia, after additional debate by the Congress upon Richard Henry Lee's resolution for independence, the motion is set aside (tabled) for later action on 2 July 1776. Part of the reason for this delay is to give some of the fence sitters a chance to rethink their position.

11 June 1776:

Tuesday. In New York, the Provincial Congress advises its delegation in the Continental Congress to abstain from voting on independence, because there is still a moderately strong Loyalist sentiment among some New Yorkers. In a reaction to this hesitancy on the part of the Provincial Congress, a mob in the City captures some Tories, whom they strip, ride on rails, or put in jail.

In Philadelphia, the Continental Congress appoints a five-person committee to draft a statement or declaration regarding independence. The members of this Committee are John Adams, Benjamin Franklin, Thomas Jefferson, Roger Sherman, and Robert Livingston.

12 June 1776:

Wednesday. In Philadelphia, the Continental Congress plans for a national union of all the colonies, and appoints John Dickinson as Chairman of a committee to draft Articles of Confederation toward this end. Also, the Congress takes action to consider negotiations of national treaties with foreign powers. Finally, the Congress creates a Board of War and Ordnance to oversee and manage affairs connected with the army; it will later grow into the War Department.

In Richmond, Virginia, the Virginia Convention adopts George Mason's Bill of Rights. These principles of Rights will become points of argument in the development of both state and national constitutions over the next several years.

13 June 1776:

Thursday. In Canada, the Americans are in serious trouble. As the British pursuit from Trois Rivières and Montreal approaches the American forces at Sorel, Brig. Gen. John Sullivan withdraws to St. John on the west shore of the Richelieu River. There he is joined by Benedict Arnold and a residue of his troops from the Montreal garrison. This will not be the last halt for the Americans in Canada. [See Fig. III-10, p. 121].

14 June 1776:

Friday. The Congress resolves that Philip Schuyler be directed to hold a conference with the Six Nations for the purpose of engaging them "in our interest." Congress also gives approval to Schuyler's preparations to take post at Fort Stanwix, and to erect a fortification there.

15 June 1776:

Saturday. At St. John, Canada, seeking to protect his retreating troops, John Sullivan , sends Benedict Arnold with a detachment to Fort Chambly to act as a rear guard and hold off or delay the British who have been in pursuit.

16 June 1776:

Sunday. At Fort Chambly, Canada, Benedict Arnold fights a rear guard action against pursuing British troops, as the Americans continue to fall back toward their bases in New York State.

At headquarters, New York, General Orders state "The Continental Congress have been pleased to come to a Resolution on June 10, 1776, that the pay of Continental troops, in the middle department be henceforth the same as that of the troops in the eastern departments. The General therefore directs, that when the pay abstracts for any of the corps of the middle department are made out, the Colonels or commanding officers thereof, will take care that the pay of the men, from the 10th of June, be the same as those of the eastern Regiment." The parole is given as Hanover and the countersign as Ireland.

17 June 1776:

Monday. The Congress, directs that Philip Schuyler make a good road, clear creeks for navigation, and see that other activities are performed that will improve and make easy the transport of men, supplies, and support between Albany and Fort Edward, and on to the lakes, that "... shall be sufficient to make us indisputably masters of the lakes ..."

18 June 1776:

Tuesday. The various units of forces raised in South Carolina for the defense for that colony are resolved by the Congress to be considered as continental forces, and allowed the same pay, rations, and disbursements as other continental units.

19 June 1776:

Wednesday. In Canada, the retreating Americans leave Fort St. John on the Richelieu River just before the British arrive, and pull away up the river to Ile aux Noix. Here they will stay, many of them dying of smallpox, malarial fever, or dysentery, for nearly a week, before departing to travel farther south up the river to Lake Champlain and Crown Point, and thence on still farther south to safety at Fort Ticonderoga. [See Fig. III-10, p. 119]. This American army is badly discouraged, poorly trained (or not at all), sick, without great leadership, wanting in the elán required by any military force to succeed in missions across large areas, and the will to complete those missions.

20 June 1776:

Thursday. In Connecticut, the General Assembly absolves itself of any allegiance to King George III, and proclaims Independence.

In New York, Washington writes to Colonel James Clinton, sending an order, with a warrant of arrest, to him to personally escort a prisoner, Fletcher Matthews, a Tory found to be enlisting Loyalists. "Sir: On the execution of the inclosed warrant with expedition, care and exactness, much may depend. I therefore desire you will perform the service therein required, yourself. In the instant he is seized, inform him that there are indubitable evidences of his being concerned in a scheme of inlisting (sic) men for the King's service and note his answers. Communicate this matter to no person living til you perform the office required of you."

21 June 1776:
    Friday. In Philadelphia, the Royal Governor William Franklin of New Jersey appears under arrest before the Continental Congress. After examination, he is removed to Connecticut under the control of Governor Jonathan Trumbull.

22 June 1776:
    Saturday. John Hancock writes to James Athearn, informing him that two privateers from Philadelphia have taken three Jamaican ships. Hancock requests that the captains of these American privateers be assisted in dealing with the prizes and cargoes of the captured vessels, since they are strangers to Martha's Vineyard, where the vessels have been taken.

23 June 1776:
    Sunday. William Whipple writes to Joshua Brackett enclosing some recent resolves of the Congress, and explaining how the adjudication of captured vessel prizes is to be handled.

24 June 1776:
    Monday. Concerned about the all too frequent and arbitrary means by which some of the westering pioneers cheat and steal lands from the Indians in the Kentucky area, the Virginia Convention passes a resolution declaring that purchases of such lands will not be considered valid unless approved by the legislature.
    At Ile aux Noix on the Richelieu River, John Sullivan, with the residue of a sickly, beaten, discouraged, and poorly disciplined American army, barely manages to repulse a British attack, and so decides to leave and retreat further to south to Crown Point.

25 June 1776:
    Tuesday. Off Sandy Hook, New Jersey, the first three ships of a mighty armada of the British fleet arrive. Within five days the fleet, under the command of British Admiral Molyneux Shuldham, convoying Maj. Gen. William Howe and his troops from Halifax, Nova Scotia, will arrive.

26 June 1776:
    Wednesday. At headquarters, New York, General Orders state "Agreeable to a resolve of the Honorable the Continental Congress, no certificates of expenses are to be given in future by any but Brigadiers, Quartermasters, and their Deputies, or a Field Officer on a march, or other officer commanding at a detached post. The commanding officers of the several

regiments, whether in camp, or detached posts are as soon as possible to return into the Adjutant General's Office the names of their several officers; their ranks and dates of their respective commissions–in order that the same may be forwarded to Congress." The parole is given as Falmouth and the countersign as Georgia.

At Cherokee Indian Town, South Carolina, Captain James McCall, and his South Carolina Rangers, skirmishes with Indians. McCall is taken prisoner.

27 June 1776:

Thursday. At and near Crown Point, New York, the remainder of the American army retreating from Canada, in several smaller groups, has found some shelter at places along the shore of Lake Champlain, but most of the army has settled here.

28 June 1776:

Friday. Admiral Shudham's fleet crosses the bar and approaches the Narrows of New York Bay between Long Island and Staten Island.

At Sullivan's Island, South Carolina, a British fleet of eight warships under Admiral Peter Parker is repulsed and severely damaged in Charleston Harbor by American artillery under Colonel William Moultrie. This British defeat ends British operations with regular forces in the Carolinas for two years.

The five-member drafting committee of the Declaration of Independence, having finished its work, asks Thomas Jefferson to present the results to Congress for debate and action. This draft is read, and ordered to "Lie on the table"–no further action until some later date.

29 June 1776:

Saturday. In Richmond, the Virginia Convention adopts a state constitution, setting up an independent government for this former colony, and rejecting all monarchial rule. Patrick Henry is duly elected Governor of the state.

30 June 1776:

Sunday. British Maj. Gen. William Howe, with 9,300 troops, begins disembarking onto Staten Island. This process will take about a week in order to get all the troops off-loaded and into tentage.

1 July 1776:

Monday. After a series of retreats, lost skirmishes, disease, and lack of supply, a sorrowfully weak and discouraged Northern American army finally arrives back at Fort Ticonderoga, from whence it had started with such elán on 28 August 1775, under Brig. Gen. Richard Montgomery.

In Philadelphia, the Continental Congress, meeting as a Committee of the Whole, spends a part of the day debating the issue of independency that was presented on 7 June, but there still being a few members who object to so radical a move, and hoping to attract others with a more positive view, concludes by a motion to postpone any vote upon the matter until the next day.

2 July 1776:
    Tuesday. The Continental Congress takes up the issue of independency, and votes to approve Richard Henry Lee's Resolution of 7 June 1776, "That these united colonies are, and of right ought to be free and independent states; that they are absolved from all allegiance to the British crown, and that all political connexion [sic] between them, and the state of Great Britain, is, and ought to be, totally dissolved."
    It is a near run thing. New York has to abstain, because its delegation has no instruction from the state convention, although that will come in a few more days. Let us be clear about what happened in the Congress this day: Some have thought that it was the day of the Declaration of Independence---not so. There was no agreed Declaration of Independence to approve or to sign. What happened this day is only the approval of the Resolution for independence. Each day has its own little drama to reveal. Is that not the very purpose of this book? Read on, and find out what happened and on what day it happened as to a Declaration of Independence, and when and by whom it was signed.

3 July 1776:
    Wednesday. In Philadelphia, John Adams writes to his wife Abigail, "Yesterday the greatest Question was decided, which ever was debated in America, and a greater perhaps, never was or will be decided among men. A Resolution was passed without one dissenting Colony 'that these united Colonies , are, and of right ought to be free and independent States, and as such, they have , and of Right ought to have full Power to make War, conclude Peace, establish Commerce, and to do all the other Acts and Things, which other States may rightfully do.' You will see in a few days a Declaration setting forth the Causes, which have impelled us to this mighty Revolution, and the Reasons which will justify it, in the Sight of God and Man."
    After some other business, and agreeable to the order of the day, the Continental Congress resolves itself again into a Committee of the Whole, to take into further consideration the language set forth in the draft of the declaration. This Committee of the Whole is a technique used to allow open debate upon an issue. They invest a good bit of the balance of the day on reviewing and modifying the draft prepared by the five-person committee they had appointed to prepare a statement upon independency---a Declaration of Independence. This is also not a day in which anyone approved or signed any such document. They are just adjusting the language so as to satisfy the entire Congress. The southerners, for example, want nothing to do with changing the current operation of slavery--- so all that language disappears.

Fig. III-11: Independence Hall

4 July 1776:

Thursday. The Congress again does some business early in the day. Then, agreeable to the order of the day, resolves itself into a Committee of the Whole to complete the debates upon the language upon the declaration they did not finish yesterday. After more debate and final acceptance of the language in the revised draft, the Congress fully agrees upon the work, and votes to approve. [See Fig. III-11, p. 133]. They then order it to be "authenticated and printed." This first printing is done by John Dunlap in his shop in Philadelphia as a fast broadside version for quick dissemination—perhaps 500 copies. The Congress also votes that copies "... be sent to the several assemblies, conventions and communities or councils of safety and to the several commanding officers of the continental troops, that it be proclaimed in each of the United States and at the head of the army."

Thus, this date, the 4th of July, becomes the day we celebrate as Independence Day! But, also keep in mind, dear reader, that nobody signs any Declaration of Independence this day. The only thing that is signed is the fact that the language in the document has been approved, and that it is to be printed --and that is signed by the President of the Congress, John Hancock (who signs all resolutions and actions), and the Secretary to the Congress, attesting to its correctness (authenticating), Charles Thompson. But nobody has signed any full and printed Declaration of Independence on this day, simply because there is no such printed document yet available to sign. That will have to wait until tomorrow. Read on!

Before completing the business of the day, Congress resolves that a committee be formed to bring in a design for a seal for the United States of America—named to this first committee for a seal are Benjamin Franklin, John Adams, and Thomas Jefferson.

5 July 1776:

Friday. With a printed copy of John Dunlap's Declaration available, one copy is placed in the Journal of the Congress, on a page left blank for that purpose, attached to the page by a wafer (a small, round bit of paper) and glued. This page is signed by the President of the Congress, John Hancock, and witnessed by the Secretary, Charles Thompson. NO one else-- repeat--no one else, signs either the page or the printed document on this day!

6 July 1776:

Saturday. Concerned about the defeats in Canada, the Congress adds three members "to the committee to enquire into the miscarriages." They are: William Floyd of New York, Caesar Rodney of Delaware, and Abraham Clark of New Jersey.

7 July 1776:

Sunday. In Paris, Silas Deane arrives to assume his duties as a commissioner from America.

At headquarters, New York, General Orders state "A working party of one hundred and fifty men properly officered to go to Kings Bridge tomorrow, to march at six o'clock from the parade; they are to take two days provision with them, after which they will draw out the stores there–to take their arms and tents with them and when they get there Genl. Mifflin will give them orders." Washington writes to Colonel James Clinton, "I hope you will be able to get arms sufficient for the men under your command who are destitute; but if not, you are to dismiss all those whom you can not equip. I mean to confine myself to the militia wholly, as it is equally absurd and unjust, to keep men in continental pay, who will be of no service in time of action, for want of arms. It is, in fact, amusing ourselves with the appearance of strength, when at the same time we want the reality." Washington also writes to Governor Jonathan Trumbull, "The situation of our affairs calls aloud for the most vigorous exertions and nothing less will be sufficient to avert the impending blow. From four prisoners taken the other day, we are informed Genl. Howe has already about ten thousand men, being joined by the Regiments from the West Indies and some of the Highland troops in his passage hither; that he is in daily expectation of the arrival of Admiral Howe and that nothing would be attempted til he came, having some from Halifax, in consequence of advises received a few days before, from England, that the Admiral was ready to sail with a fleet of one hundred and fifty ships, with a large reinforcement to join him here. These armies when united, you will readily conceive will be extremely formidable and such as will require a large and numerous one on our part, to oppose them." The parole is given as Goshen and the countersign as Hartford.

8 July 1776:
    Monday. The Declaration of Independence is read to the public in places as scattered as Philadelphia, Easton, Trenton, and White Plains, and in many other places throughout July and on into August. It is also printed in a number of local newspapers and in broadsides.
    At Gwynn Island, Chesapeake Bay, patriots capture Lord Dunmore's base camp and scatter his fleet and forces. After a brief raid up the Potomac River, Dunmore will withdraw to New York, and then, finally back to England.

9 July 1776:
    Tuesday. George Washington, from his headquarters in New York City, orders officers of the several brigades of the Continental Army in and around New York to pick up copies of the Declaration of Independence at the adjutant-general's Office. The Orderly Book reports this in these words "The Honorable Continental Congress, impelled by the dictates of duty, policy, and necessity, having been pleased to dissolve the connection which subsisted between this Country and Great Britain, and to declare the United Colonies of America free and independent States."

The several brigades are to be paraded in hollow squares at their place of encampment and in a "loud voice" publicly have the entire Declaration read to them. Washington is interested in having all the troops know just what it is the new nation has been founded upon, and what his men are being asked to defend.

New York had been the hold-out on independence, their delegation abstaining as instructed. Now, however, the Provincial Congress formally adopts a resolution for independence, so now they can join with the other 12 Colonies. The Declaration of Independence becomes the "Unanimous Declaration." We have since changed the name of the place where these momentous debates took place from the Pennsylvania State House to Independence Hall. [See Fig. III-11, p. 132].

In New York City, patriots pull down the equestrian statue of King George III in Bowling Green, and break it up in pieces to melt the lead for ammunition.

10 July 1776:
Wednesday. In New York, Washington writes to the President of Congress, "Agreeably to the request of Congress, I caused the *Declaration* to be proclaimed before all the army under my immediate command: and have the pleasure to inform them, that the measure seemed to have their most hearty assent; the expressions and behavior, both of officers and men, testifying their warmest approbation of it."

In Philadelphia, the Congress, having carefully reviewed the circumstances of the surrender, and subsequent treatment as prisoners, of the Americans captured at The Cedars on 19 May 1776, concludes that terrible things had been done to them. They had been turned over to the nearly 500 Indians with Captain Foster. Two were murdered the night of the surrender, and others later. Others were nearly starved, mistreated, and their baggage plundered. The Congress resolves that all these actions, done while under the officers of his Britannic Majesty, are considered to have been done by his orders. They further resolve that effective and immediate measures must be taken to bring the offenders to condign punishment. If not, the Americans may be forced into equal retaliation. A copy of the full report and the resolutions of the Congress is transmitted to Washington, for him to copy and forward to both Major General William Howe and Major General John Burgoyne.

11 July 1776:
Thursday. At New York, Washington writes to Philip Schuyler, "General Howe's fleet from Halifax has arrived, in number about one hundred and thirty sail. His army is between nine and ten thousand, being joined by some regiments from the West Indies, and having fallen in with part of the Highland troops in his passage. He has landed his men on Staten Island, which they mean to secure, and it is in daily

expectation of the arrival of Lord Howe, with one hundred and fifty ships, with a large and powerful reinforcement."

In Philadelphia, John Hancock writes to George Washington to inform him of a number of resolves of the Congress, but also to report that the militia of Pennsylvania are en route to join his army. The Congress generally favors a view that New York City should be defended. The reality that some of the American military people hold, is that it is a difficult place to defend.

12 July 1776:
Friday. In New York harbor, the British send two frigates, HMS *Phoenix* (44 guns) and HMS *Rose* (20 guns), up the Hudson River, to test the American defenses, and to see if they can cut or interdict waterborne communications between northern New York and the City. They are successful.

At Staten Island, British Vice Admiral Richard Howe, Fourth Viscount Howe, an older brother of William Howe, arrives with additional ships (about 150) and troops (11,000). To the many European nations that have been bested by British sea power: the French, Spanish, Dutch, Russians and Danes, it seems as though the English are more skillful, more resourceful, and more in their element at sea than others, in the same way that a seal or shark is a better swimmer than a horse or a bear. Thus, Americans are hard put to devise ways to defend against, or at least deflect, this awesome naval power.

In Philadelphia, John Dickinson presents the results of his Committee's work on a draft of a national union, the Articles of Confederation. It will be a long struggle to get this document ratified by all 13 Colonies.

13 July 1776:
Saturday. The Howe brothers are a part of an effort by the British to offer some reconciliation and pardon to the Americans. On this day, Vice Admiral, Lord Richard Howe, sends Lieutenant Samuel Reeves, under a flag of truce, to the American post at Perth Amboy, New Jersey to deliver dispatches to Brig. Gen. Hugh Mercer. Mercer sends the unsealed letters to Washington, who, in turn, forwards them to Congress. It turns out the British really have very few powers and little to grant the Americans. The American viewpoint is that they (the Americans) have done nothing that needs to be pardoned, nor are they interested in reconciliation, now that independence has been declared.

In Boston, Abigail Adams and her four young children are inoculated against smallpox.

14 July 1776:
Sunday. On the Hudson River, the British again send two frigates up the river to explore and test the currents and possible resistance. The move is completely unopposed all the way to the Tappan Zee, because the Americans have no means of preventing such movements. Although this is a clear

indication of the   weakness of American defenses on Manhattan, it goes unheeded.

15 July 1776:
   Monday.   In New York, Washington writes to Maj. Gen. Philip Schuyler, concerning the congressional resolution of 24 June 1776 that he order an enquiry into the officers of the Canadian expedition, "I am very sensible of the general enquiry requested by Congress must be a work of difficulty and delicacy; but as they seem to desire it very earnestly, I hope it is not impracticable. I should hope, upon a conference with Generals Gates and Arnold, some plan may be devised to comply with it. I am persuaded you will leave nothing unattempted on your part for this purpose."
   In Philadelphia, as the resolution of the New York Provincial Congress becomes known to that state's delegates, they vote to fully support the Declaration of Independence, from which they had to abstain earlier.
   At Lyndley's Fort, near Rayborn Creek, in Laurens County, South Carolina, a group of American patriots, under John Downs, have taken refuge in the fort and are attacked by a party of Indians and Loyalists. Reinforced by 150 militia, the patriots beat off and rout the attackers in a skirmish.

16 July 1776:
   Tuesday. Lord Dunmore, the Royal Governor of Virginia, is a sore loser! Still holding out in Chesapeake Bay before leaving for New York, and in command of a small British flotilla, he attempts to seize St. George's Island, Maryland, in the Potomac River near its mouth at the Chesapeake Bay. The landing force is driven off by a local patriot militia.

17 July 1776:
   Wednesday. The Congress highly approves of George Washington's action in refusing to receive a letter from Lord Howe, because Howe has addressed him as "George Washington, Esqr." They further direct that no letter or message Washington or other commanders of the American troops shall be received, on any occasion, from the enemy, unless it is addressed to them in the full title and character they respectively sustain.

18 July 1776:
   Thursday. The Provincial Congress of New Jersey changes its name to the Convention of the State of New Jersey.
   In Boston, the Declaration is read aloud to the public at the State House.

19 July 1776:
   Friday. In Philadelphia, now that the Declaration is a unanimous statement of all thirteen states, and learning just how important their action on this matter has become to the people of the country, the Congress votes to have the document

properly engrossed (printed on parchment), and formally signed by all the delegates on some designated occasion. This quality printing is done by Timothy Matlack in his shop in Philadelphia. It is this printing that we generally recognize as our Declaration of Independence. It still will not be signed, however, until the appointed day of 2 August 1776.

20 July 1776:
    Saturday. In New York, Joseph Reed prepares a Memorandum on an earlier meeting between George Washington and James Patterson, part of which states, "Gen. W. Then observed that the Conduct of several of the [British] Officers would well have warranted a different treatment from what they had received—some having refused to give any Parole & others having broke it when given by escaping or endeavoring to do so. Col. P. Answered that as to the first they misunderstood the matter very much & seemed to have mistook the Line of Propriety exceedingly—and as to the latter Gen. Howe utterly disapproved & condemned their conduct—that if a Remonstrance was to be made such violations of good faith would be severely punished—but that he hoped Gen. W. was too just to draw public inferences from the misbehavior of some private individuals that bad men were to be found in every class & Society—that such behavior was considered as a dishonor to the British Army."
    In Philadelphia, Benjamin Franklin writes to Lord Richard Howe, a senior member of the Conciliation Committee, seeking to find a means of "accommodation" with the colonists, in which missive Franklin says that British actions "... have extinguished every spark of remaining affection for that parent country we once held so dear."
    In the face of continued rebuffs and evidences of American unwillingness to lean toward "accommodation" without Crown recognition of independence, it is amazing to observe how nearly pathetic are the continued British attempts to seek accord, even though they have no powers to grant what is required by the Americans as a first principle.

21 July 1776:
    Sunday. At headquarters, New York, Washington writes to the Secret Committee of the New York Legislature, "It is impossible for me personally to reconnoitre all the different posts under my command. [I am] so sensible of the importance of the fortresses in the Highlands, that I ordered Lord Stirling to visit them, which he did early in the summer, and reported to me their situation at that time; and through his representations, I continued two gentlemen in continental pay, who were acting as Engineers, under orders from the authority of this State. I have repeatedly pressed Col. [James] Clinton to spare no pains to put them on the best footing possible, and indeed, I had reason to suppose they were in tolerable order to receive the enemy. I will this day send up Mr. Machin, a Lieutenant of the [artillery] train, who has just returned from

overseeing the works at Boston; he is as proper a person, as any I can send, being an ingenious faithful hand, and one that has had considerable as an Engineer."

At Charleston, South Carolina, after lingering for three weeks, Admiral Peter Parker and Maj. Gen. Henry Clinton abandon any hopes of success in their enterprise and set sail for New York.

22 July 1776:

Monday. The Congress resolves the issue of prisoner exchange, concluding that the Commander-in-Chief of each department be empowered to negotiate prisoner exchanges on the following basis: one continental officer for one enemy of equal rank, either land or sea service; one soldier or sailor for one; and one citizen for one. They also resolve into a Committee of the Whole to take into consideration the Articles of Confederation, but come to no conclusion. This deliberation on the Articles will drag on for some while.

23 July 1776:

Tuesday. After his repulse at St. George's Island on 16 July 1776, Lord Dunmore's expedition sails up the Potomac River, destroying several plantations owned by patriots. Then he goes up the Occoquan Creek as far the falls, where a landing party destroys the mill. They withdraw upon the arrival of Prince William County militia.

24 July 1776:

Wednesday. In Boston a group of more than 100 women assemble with a cart and some hand trucks at the warehouse of Thomas Boylston to demand the keys so that they can open the building and take out the coffee he has been hoarding as a means of driving up the price. Several marketplace riots take place in a number of locales in the weeks after the Declaration of Independence, as merchants take advantage of temporary shortages of sugar and coffee to hike prices. Generally, these affairs are resolved as the goods are seized and sold at a reasonable price, but it points out how some people, even then, would use, or try to create, shortages of an item to sell it at a falsely high price.

25 July 1776:

Thursday. In debates upon some of the Articles of Confederation, a number of the delegates in the Congress note just how ridiculous it is for some states to be putting forward their claims as set forth in the language of some early grants of "... to the South Sea" (meaning the Pacific Ocean).

26 July 1776:

Friday. At headquarters, New York, General Orders state "Complaints have been made that some of the soldiers ill treat the country people, who come to market. The General most positively forbids such behavior, and hopes the officers will exert themselves to prevent it. Good policy as well as justice, demands that they should have all possible encouragement as the health of the soldiers much depends upon supplies of vegetables. Those who have been guilty of such practices, will do well to consider what will be our situation, at this season, if we drive off the country people, and break up the market. The healthy will soon be sick, and the sick must perish for want of necessaries. No   favour will be shewn to any offenders hereafter." The parole is given as Cambridge and the countersign as Darby,

The Congress continues its debate upon the Articles of Confederation. This issue will take quite a while before it is to be accepted by all the States.

27 July 1776:
Saturday. In Philadelphia, Samuel Adams writes to Benjamin Kent, including the following wise thought, "The Colonies were not then all ripe for so momentous a change. It was necessary that they should be united, and it required time and patience to remove old prejudices, to instruct the unenlightened, convince the doubting and fortify the timid."

28 July 1776:
Sunday. Having received the orders from General George Washington, in response to the instructions of Congress, to read the newly printed Declaration of Independence to each brigade in the Army, Colonel Arthur St. Clair (pronounced Sinclair), at Fort Ticonderoga, has his whole brigade (consisting of the 2nd, 3rd, 5th, and 7th Pennsylvania Regiments) paraded on the Place d'Armes as he reads the entire Declaration to the troops. At the end of the reading he says, "God save the free and Independent States of America," and asks for three "Huzzahs!"

29 July 1776:
Monday. In North Carolina, to discourage the Cherokee Indian alliance with the British, Brig. Gen. Griffith Rutherford, with 2,400 North Carolina militia, begins a long invasion which will destroy 32 Indian towns and villages. Rutherford is joined in this effort by Major Andrew Williamson's South Carolina troops and Colonel William Christian's Virginia troops. Following this invasion, Cherokee power is broken in North Carolina.

30 July 1776:
Tuesday. The Congress takes into consideration the Report on the Causes of the Miscarriages in Canada, and concurs that a combination of short enlistments, lack of specie, and the spread of smallpox are major contributors. They also resolve that Major Butterfield, who has surrendered his post at The Cedars be court-martialed. Note, however, that a good part of the responsibility for this miscarriage rests with the Congress.

31 July 1776:
Wednesday. In New York, Washington writes to Maj. Gen. Philip Schuyler, "It gives me great satisfaction to hear, that taking post at Fort Stanwix, has not given umbrage to the Indians; and also that those that were at Philadelphia, and this place, have returned to their several Nations. From this circumstance, I am hopeful, you w ill be able to engage them in our interest, and with the assistance of the reward allowed by Congress, to excite their efforts to make prisoners of our enemies. I would have you press the matter strongly in both instances, and though you should not succeed, I flatter myself, you will secure their neutrality. That will be an important point to gain."

Congress orders that five tons of fine musket powder be sent immediately to General Washington in New York.

1 August 1776:
Thursday. At American Army headquarters, in General Orders, Washington expresses his "... great concern that jealousies, arguments, fights among the troops from different States, regions, and locales have arisen, and that such behavior is injurious to the cause in which we are engaged." He further notes that the honor and success of the army ought to be supported with "... one hand and one heart. That we are all united to oppose the common enemy, and all distinctions sunk in the name of an American ... ought to be our only emulation, and he will be the best soldier and best patriot, who contributes most to this glorious work, whatever his station, or from whatever part of the continent he may come."

Henry Clinton returns from his failure at Charleston, along with Sir Peter Parker's battered squadron of nine warships, and enters the harbor of New York.

At Essenecca Town, South Carolina, Major Andrew Williamson leads a party of Americans in a skirmish with Indians and Tories, under Alexander Cameron. Early this morning the patriots are ambushed, but Colonel Leroy Hammond leads a mounted charge against the enemy, 13 of whom are captured. The American, Francis Salvador, a plantation owner and elected member of the South Carolina Provincial Congress, is killed in the action.

2 August 1776:
Friday. Having voted for the Resolution of Independence on 2 July 1776, and then approved the specific language in the Declaration of Independence on 4 July 1776, the Continental Congress concludes that a quality, engrossed copy should be prepared and signed. This date has been assigned for the signing. Most, but not all, of the men we know today as the "Signers" actually put pen to paper, while a few more added their signatures later. In total, there are 56 of these Signers. [See Fig. III-11, p. 133, also See Appendix 2, p. 451].

In North Carolina, the town of Forks of the Tar River is renamed Washington--it is the first town to be named for the American Commander-in-Chief.

3 August 1776:
Saturday. At Tappan Zee, New York, Lt. Col. Benjamin Tupper, with five small boats, attacks the British frigates that have passed unscathed upstream in mid-July from Staten Island and are now anchored in this wide part of the Hudson River. The attack fails.

4 August 1776:
Sunday. John Adams writes to Brig. Gen. Nathanael Greene, responding to his of 14 July 1776. Both men are in close agreement upon the pay structure of the Continental officers, feeling that the current pay allowance is much too low. However, Adams points out that not all the delegates to the Congress have the same views that he and Greene have on this touchy subject.

5 August 1776:
Monday. The Congress resolves, "That the Commanders of all ships of war and armed vessels of these states ... be permitted to inlist [sic] into service on board said ships and vessels, any seamen who may be taken ..."

6 August 1776:
Tuesday. In Philadelphia, Congress resolves that Philip Schuyler be directed to apply to John Burgoyne, proposing a general exchange of prisoners on the terms agreed by the Congress; and, particularly, of delivering Brig. Gen. Prescott, now a United States prisoner, for Brig. Gen. Thompson, now a British prisoner.

7 August 1776:
Wednesday. Off the New Hampshire coast, the American privateer *Hancock*, under Captain Wingate Newman, captures the British transport *Reward*, and brings her into Portsmouth, New Hampshire, as a prize. Her cargo includes turtles intended for Lord North.

8 August 1776:
Thursday. At headquarters, New York, Washington writes to Brig. Gen. William Livingston, "You will have heard of the unexpected arrival of the Carolina Army [Henry Clinton's return from his failed expedition against Charleston] on Staten Island, which added to the Hessians and foreign troops under Lord Howe, exhibit a force justly alarming. When I compare it with that which we have to oppose them, I cannot help feeling anxious apprehension. I have therefore wrote to Connecticut, and to the Convention of your Province [New Jersey], to call the militia immediately, but as it may take some time, and the necessity admit of no delay, I have thought it proper to apply to

you also, under the Resolution of Congress of last June, copy of which was sent you when Lord Howe's fleet first arrived, to beg you would use your utmost exertions to forward this most necessary measure. The consequences to the American interest of any failure here, are so obvious, that I need not enlarge upon them, your own good judgement will suggest every thing proper."

At Oconore, South Carolina, Americans under Major Andrew Williamson attack and kill several Indians in a skirmish.

9 August 1776:
Friday. At headquarters, New York, General Orders state "An ammunition cart is provided for each Regiment with spare cartridges; these carts are immediately to join the several regiments to which they belong and keep with them in some safe place near the regiment. The Commissary General to deliver to the Colonel of each regiment, rum in proportion of half a pint to a man; the Colonel to make a return of the number of men for this purpose, and to see that it is properly dealt out, by putting it under the care of a very discreet officer." The parole is given as Lexington and the countersign as Maryland.

The Congress advances $10,000 to Colonel John Haslet for the use of the Delaware battalion, he to be accountable for that sum.

10 August 1776:
Saturday. The Congress orders that Isaac Cooper, a ship joiner, not go to New Jersey, because his service is wanted more in Philadelphia. This is a good example of some of the minutiae in which the Continental Congress all too frequently gets mired.

At the Tugaloo River, South Carolina, Andrew Pickens leads a party of patriots in a skirmish against the Cherokee Indians. After successfully defeating the Indians, Pickens troops burn the nearby Indian towns of Estatoe and Tugaloo.

11 August 1776:
Sunday. In New York, Washington writes to the New York Legislature, "It is true, when the proceedings of your Honorable body for the raising of levies, were first communicated to me, and it was mentioned by the Committee who brought them, that it was expected they would be paid by the States. I did not think myself authorised to take into service so large a number of men, and therefore could not say the states would pay them. But the situation of our affairs being much changed and requiring their service, I cannot but consider them as much entitled to Continental pay as any troops in this army. In this light I am persuaded Congress will view them. It is so obvious and so equitable, that no application from me can be necessary."

In New Jersey, William Livingston, is elected as the first State Governor, replacing the appointed Royal Governor, William Franklin.

12 Augsut 1776:
Monday. The main contingent of reinforcements for the British forces in America arrives from Europe, with much of their camp equipage, to join with the brothers Howe in New York harbor. This British force now totals about 32,000 troops, 10,000 seamen, and nearly 400 transports and 30 vessels of the line. It is the largest military force ever assembled in the New World up to that time.

At Tamassy, South Carolina, Americans under Major Andrew Williamson and Andrew Pickens lead an expeditionary force to attack a Cherokee war party. They engage the Indians in an hot fight. Both sides lose men, but the Indian losses are nearly twice those of the patriots. The Indian Town of Tamassy is burned.

13 August 1776:
Tuesday. At headquarters, New York, General Orders state "The enemy's whole reinforcement is now arrived, so that an attack must, and will soon be made. The General therefore again repeats his earnest request, that every officer, and soldier, will have his arms and ammunition in good order, keep within their quarters and encampment, as much as possible; be ready for action at a moments call; and when called to it, remember that liberty, property, life, and honor, are all at stake; that upon their courage and conduct, rest the hoped of their bleeding and insulted country; that their wives, children, and parents, expect safety from them only, and that we have every reason to expect heaven will crown with success, so just a cause." The parole is given as Weymouth and the countersign as York.

The Congress, always short of specie, orders the printing of $5,000,000 in bills of various denominations.

14 August 1776:
Wednesday. Congress, passes a resolution stating acceptance and encouragement to those German troops who might consider deserting in order to gain the freedom and free exercise of their religion in these states.

15 August 1776:
Thursday. In New York, Major General Nathanael Greene, whom Washington had named as Commander of the American forces on Long Island, writes to his chief that he is "... confined to my bed with a raging fever." This may loom as a disastrous leadership problem in the very near future. Who will replace him as commander of the forces to face the expected British invasion? To have this problem added to Washington's burden at this crucial time in the preparation for a battle is bad news.

16 August 1776:

Friday. At Tappan Zee, New York, the Americans try again to assault the British frigates anchored there, this time using fire rafts. Although the attempt fails, the Captain of the HMS *Phoenix* is so alarmed at these attacks that he orders the squadron to return downstream and rejoin the British fleet off Staten Island.

Aboard the HMS *Eagle*, off Staten Island, William Howe, writes to Benjamin Franklin, "I can have no difficulty to acknowledge that the powers I am invested with were never calculated to negotiate a reunion with America under any other description than as subject to the crown of Great Britain. But I do esteem those powers competent not only to confer and negotiate with any gentlemen of influence in the Colonies upon the terms, but also to effect a lasting peace and reunion between the two countries were the temper of the Colonies such as professed in the last petition of the Congress to the King."

17 August 1776:

Saturday. At headquarters, New York, Washington issues a Proclamation to and for the citizens, "Whereas a bombardment and attack upon the city of New York, by our cruel and inveterate enemy, may be hourly expected; and as there are great numbers of women, children, and infirm persons, yet remaining in the city, whose continuance will rather be prejudicial than advantageous to the army, and their persons exposed to great danger and hazard; I do, therefore recommend it to all such persons, as they value their own safety and preservation, to remove with all expedition out of the said town, at this critical period. Trusting that, with the blessing of heaven upon the American arms, they may soon return to it in perfect security. And I do enjoin and require all the officers and soldiers in the army under my command to forward and assist such persons in their compliance with this recommendation."

In New Jersey the Delegation to the Continental Congress receives and lays before the Congress a resolution of that state's convention that empowers one, and one only delegate, if he were the only such present, to represent that state in the Congress.

18 August 1776:

Sunday. At New York, Washington writes to Governor Trumbull of Connecticut, "The whole of the British forces on America, except for those in Canada, are now here, Clinton's arrival being followed the last week by that of Lord Dunmore, who now forms part of the army we are now to oppose. His coming has added but little to their strength."

In Philadelphia, John Morton writes to Persifor Frazer, bemoaning the difficulties of quickly gathering troops to send to, and defend, New York. He reports that the militia of Chester County have marched out, and others are expected. He is concerned, though, that the British seem to have nearly or more than 30,000 troops encamped on Staten Island.

19 August 1776:

Monday. In New York, Washington is trying to learn what the enemy is planning to do. Surely, they have ample forces, and control of the waters around the City. What are they going to do, what are they waiting for, and how shall he counter it? Washington receives a message from Brig. Gen. Hugh Mercer, that an American sea captain who had recently been on Staten Island has reported that the British intend to attack Long Island.

20 August 1776:

Tuesday. In New York, Nathanael Greene's doctor diagnoses his "raging fever" as "a putrid and billious [sic] fever" (probably typhus) and fears "his life endangered." Washington must now name a substitute commander for the Long Island forces. He chooses Major General John Sullivan.

21 August 1776:

Wednesday. In Elizabeth, New Jersey, Brigadier General William Livingston sends another message to Washington that he has learned that the British are planning a three-pronged attack on Bergen Point, Elizabeth Town Point, and Amboy from their base on Staten Island.

22 August 1776:

Thursday. William Howe begins to embark 20,000 British and Hessian troops and sends them across New York harbor from Staten Island to the beaches at Gravesend on the western end of Long Island. There they will arrange to attack the American position in front of the heights of a small village called Brooklyn.

23 August 1776:

Friday. On Long Island, the transport of British and Hessian troops to Gravesend and Flatbush continues, and is largely completed this day.

In New York, Washington writes to the President of Congress, "Sir: I beg leave to inform Congress that yesterday morning and in the course of the preceding night, a considerable body of the enemy, amounting by report to eight or nine thousand, and these all British, landed from the transport ships mentioned in my last, at Gravesend Bay on Long Island, and have approached within three miles of our lines, having marched across the low cleared grounds, near the woods at Flatbush where they are halted, from my last intelligence. I have been obliged to appoint Major General Sullivan to the command on the Island, owing to General Greene's indisposition, he has been extremely ill for several days and still continues bad. You will receive the treaty between the Commissioners and the Indians of the Six Nations and the others at German Flats, which General Schuyler requested me to forward."

24 August 1776:
Saturday. In Philadelphia, Benjamin Franklin writes to Thomas McKean, a delegate from Delaware, regarding the business of the German mercenary troops that the Congress is hoping to encourage to desert. He offers the thought that letters in the German language with a little tobacco, floated across the waters to Staten Island, might induce some of them to do just that.

25 August 1776:
Sunday. John Adams writes to Colonel Henry Knox, agreeing with him that more mortars, howitzers, and field pieces are needed, but knows not where to find them. Adams discusses the need for quality officers, and seeks advice upon candidates for promotion.

26 August 1776:
Monday. At Valley Grove, Long Island, in a preliminary action of the Long Island campaign, Henry Clinton leads a night march to Jamaica Pass to try to flank the American defenses.
At headquarters, New York, General Orders state "Six hundred men properly officered, from General [Erastus] Wolcott's Brigade, to parade tomorrow morning, at six o'clock on the grand parade, without arms for fatigue: four hundred to take directions from General McDougall, and two hundred from Lieut. [Nicholas] Fish; the same number to be continued 'til the works are completed; to leave work at young flood and go on again at the ebb. The General is very anxious for the state of the arms and ammunition, the frequent rains giving too much reason to fear they may suffer; he therefore earnestly enjoins officers and men to be particularly attentive to it and have them in the best order." The parole is given as Newcastle and the countersign as Paris.

27 August 1776:
Tuesday. In the early hours, the British advance forces, under Henry Clinton, have gotten to within a few hundred yards of Jamaica Pass, without being detected. Washington moves over to Brooklyn Heights to be closer to any action the massive British forces might begin. While Henry Clinton is making his flanking maneuver, Howe sends Brig. Gen. James Grant on a secondary attack upon the American forces on their right flank under Brig. Gen. William Alexander, attracting their attention away from the Jamaica Pass flanking maneuver. (The Battle of Long Island, as it has been called, is actually a battle in and near the then tiny village of Brooklyn. It is a complete British victory. Many Americans flee from the field without opposing the enemy at all. William Alexander (Lord Stirling),

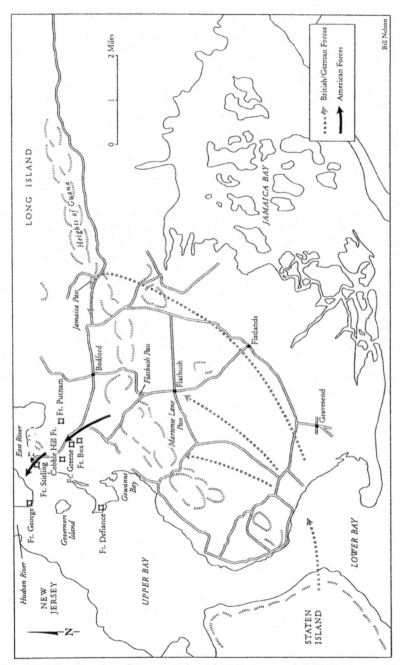

Fig. III-12: Battle of Long Island, 27 August 1776

holding the American left, closest to the Narrows, tries to hold off the British right, but after a most gallant fight, is driven back, and defeated. The British, however, do not immediately follow up their victory, as might have been expected, perhaps because of concerns about possible massive counterattacks. [See Fig. III-12, p. 149].

28 August 1776:
   Wednesday. The Congress, resolves the important business of regularizing gunpowder. Qualified inspectors are to be appointed to test and mark each and every cask of such material with the letters U.S.A.; and every manufacturer of gunpowder is to mark each such cask with the first letters of his name.

29 August 1776:
   Thursday. In Philadelphia, the Congress resolves, "That a Committee of three be appointed to devise ways and means of regulating the post office, and establishing advice boats between the southern colonies and Philadelphia, so as to facilitate and expedite the conveying of intelligence from one part of the continent to another." Appointed to this committee are: Thomas Heyward, Thomas Jefferson, and Robert Morris.
   John Adams writes to William Tudor, "The strange uncertainty, in which we are still involved, concerning the late skirmishes, upon Long Island, have given rise to the foregoing observations. [Wherein Adams is distressed over the poor quality of reports coming from American officers.] My friends have been a little negligent, in not writing me a line, upon this occasion. I think we have suffered in our reputation for generalship, in permitting the enemy to steal a march upon us. We have not been sufficiently vigilant in obtaining information of the motions and numbers of the enemy after their landing on Long Island, in reconnoitering them and in keeping out advanced guards and patrolling parties. Our officers don't seem sufficiently sensible of the importance of an observation of the King of Prussia, that stratagem, ambuscade, and ambush are the sublimest chapter in the art of war."

30 August 1776:
   Friday. This night, George Washington and his entire army is rowed back across the East River to Manhattan Island to the escape the clutches of the British forces that would otherwise surely destroy them.
   In Princeton, New Jersey, the election of William Livingston, as Governor, is approved by the convention, and arrangements for his formal inauguration are prepared.

31 August 1776:
   Saturday. Washington has his headquarters in New York City. General Orders state "Both officers and soldiers are informed that the retreat from Long Island was made by the unanimous advice of all the general officers." The reasons of

this council for evacuating Long Island are: 1.) The advanced party had met with a defeat; 2.) The loss sustained in the death of captivity of valuable officers and their battalions or a large part of them occasioned confusion and discouragement among the troop; 3.) Heavy rains which fell for two days and nights injured the arms and spoiled much of the ammunition, and a the soldiery being without cover were worn out; 4.) The enemy had several large ships that attempted to get up the East River to cut off our communication; 5.) Smaller enemy vessels might come between Long Island and Governor's Island which would further cut off communication; 6.) Parts of our lines were weak, being only abbattied with brush and affording no strong cover so that there was reason to apprehend that they might be forced causing confusion in our troops who would have been cut to pieces, or made prisoners; 7.) The divided state of the troops made defense very precarious and defending long and extensive lines difficult and dispiriting; 8.) The enemy had ships of war in the Sound at Flushing Bay and the troops landing there would move across Long Island in order to cut off and prevent all communication. But the British, with their control of the waters around the Island, threaten to enter the city at any point at any time." Washington stays in the city until 14 September. The parole is given as Harlem and the countersign as Flushing.

1 September 1776:
    Sunday. Washington, needing to reorganize his army, rearranges it into three grand Divisions, or wings with Major General Israel Putnam, Major General Nathanael Greene, and Major General William Heath as the commanders.

2 September 1776:
    Monday. In Philadelphia, John Adams writes to William Tudor, Judge Advocate of the Continental Army, "So! The fishers [British commissioners seeking peace], have set a seine, and a whole school, a whole shoal [shallow as well as school–here Adams is using a pun] of fish, have swam into it, and been caught. The fowlers have set a net and a whole flock of pigeons [gullible Americans who believe the British ploy], have alighted on the bed, and the net has been drawn over them. But the most insolent thing of all, is sending one of those very pigeons, as a flutterer [John Sullivan who brought Lord Howe's proposal for a private conference with some delegates] to Philadelphia, in order to decoy the great flock of all."
    The Congress today hears a lengthy report from the committee on specie, concerning various values of coins or other specie. This is a matter of great moment to the Congress, and a tabular presentation of all the gold and silver coins circulating throughout the colonies is prepared. The table reduces all other coins to the value of the Spanish milled dollar, or piece of eight.

3 September 1776:
    Tuesday. In Philadelphia, Delegate Josiah Bartlett writes to Delegate William Whipple regarding the continued efforts of the

Reconciliation Committee under Lord Richard Howe, pointing out the real lack of power to negotiate that these British gentlemen claim to have, and that the Congress would be wise to tread very softly on this whole matter. However, the Congress finds itself in a bit of a pickle: here the British are extending (or seeming to extend) an olive branch, yet America is not having any of it. Nevertheless, the Congress has formed a committee to meet with Lord Howe and hear the British presentations. The committee is made up of John Adams, Benjamin Franklin, and Edward Rutledge.

4 September 1776:
Wednesday. In Princeton, New Jersey, William Livingston, the elected Governor, is inaugurated in Nassau Hall. He is the first elected governor of the state, replacing the former Royal Governor, William Franklin.

In Philadelphia, John Adams writes to Samuel Cooper, "Our generals, I fear have made a mistake in retreating from Long Island. I fear they will retreat from the city of New York next. These are disagreeable events. I don't like these measures. I wish there was more firmness. But let not these things discourage. If they get possession of New York, Long Island, and Staten Island—these are more territory than their whole army can defend this year."

5 September 1776:
Thursday. The Congress resolves that Maj. Gen. John Sullivan be requested to inform Lord Howe that the representatives of the free and independent states of America cannot, with propriety, send any of its members to confer with the British Commissioners in their private capacity. If, however, the British have any authority to treat with representatives of the Congress on matters of peace, inform the Congress of that authority and it shall think it proper to make notice of the same.

6 September 1776:
Friday. In New York, Washington writes to Maj. Gen. William Heath, "The present posture of our affairs, the season of the year, and many other reasons which might be urged, renders it indispensably necessary that some systematic plan should be form'd, and, as far as possible pursued by us. I therefore desire that immediately upon receipt of this letter you will let Genls. Mifflin and Clinton know that I desire to see them with you, at this place, at eight o'clock tomorrow morning. Let them know the business they are called together for, in order that their thoughts may be turned as much as possible to the subject. Do not fail to bring exact returns of the two brigades with you, and the two Jersey Regiments at Fort Washington; a perfect knowledge of our strength indispensably necessary to the determining upon any plan."

Washington also writes to Sir William Howe, "By a letter from Major General Sullivan, while on Long Island, and which he acquainted me was wrote by your permission, I was informed, it would be agreeable to exchange that gentleman for Major General Prescott, and Brigadier Lord Stirling for any Brigadier of yours in our possession. In consequence of this intelligence, I have wrote to Congress, requesting that General Prescott may be sent here, that the proposal may be carried into execution. We have no Brigadier of yours a prisoner with us, except General McDonald, taken in North Carolina, whom I am willing to exchange for Lord Stirling, and shall be glad to know your pleasure on the subject."

In Philadelphia, the Congress instructs and charges the committee to meet with the British Peace Commissioners, to accept no terms other than recognition of Independence.

7 September 1776:
Saturday. In New York City, Washington calls a Council of War to review matters regarding the defense of the city, and what other choices might be available in the face of an enemy who control the waters around the city, and is poised to attack the city. Israel Putnam's wing has about 5,000 men, stationed to guard the lower end of Manhattan Island at and near Fort George (near the present site of the Battery). Nathanael Greene is stationed near the middle of Manhattan Island to guard the areas around Kips Bay and Turtle Bay. [See Fig. II-14, p. 163]. William Heath, with a force of about 9,000 men, is stationed at Harlem Heights, near the northern part of Manhattan Island. It is a spread out force trying to defend too much terrain with too little resources. On the coming Thursday, another Council will convene to further visit this problem.

David Bushnell of Connecticut, has built a small submersible craft called *The American Turtle*, with which he hopes to damage British ships. In the early hours of this day, with Sargent Ezra Lee at the controls, the turtle tries to attack the HMS *Eagle* (64 guns) in New York harbor, without success.

8 September 1776:
Sunday. George Washington writes to the Congress, reporting upon his disposition of the troops he has at hand in the New York City vicinity. He also writes to the New York Legislature, "I have just received the Resolve of your Convention, respecting the removal of the bells belonging to the different Churches and public edifices in this City, to Newark in the Province of New Jersey. The measure I highly approve of, and shall accordingly have it carried into execution. I have been conversing with Genl. [James] Clinton, concerning the defense of the Forts in the Highlands, who agrees with me in sentiment, that the force already there is by no means sufficient; I should therefore conceive it would be greatly in advancement of the service, if you would cause a reinforcement of the militia, amounting to about 600 men, to be sent there from the counties of Ulster and Orange or any other that may be most proper and convenient. They may be usefully and importantly employed, as well in defense of the Highlands, in case they should be attacked, as in erecting new works and fortifications, by which they may be rendered more secure."

9 September 1776:
    Monday. In Philadelphia, the Continental Congress adopts by resolution the name "United States of America" for the new nation. It will now no longer be styled the united colonies, nor are any of the former colonies to use the term colony in describing themselves. All are now states, and the nation is the United States of America. However, it takes a little while for all these new designations to sink in and be used on a regular basis.

10 September 1776:
    Tuesday. The Congress passes a resolution in response to Washington's recent reports, informing him that it is not the sense of Congress that "... respecting New York that the army or any part of it should remain in that City a moment longer than he shall think proper for the public service that troops be continued there."

11 September 1776:
    Wednesday. This morning, Lord Richard Howe sends his barge from Staten Island, to Perth Amboy to bring the three Americans appointed by the Congress to hear the proposals of the Peace Commissioners from Great Britain; John Adams, Edward Rutledge, and Benjamin Franklin. The meeting is most civil and is reported in several official and unofficial sources. After a very pleasant cold luncheon, the two sides meet in a conference room at Lord Howe's headquarters on Staten Island. It is without results, because the Americans can only negotiate with the British, upon the acceptance of independence, and since that is the one point upon which the British have no authority to discuss. The conference is doomed to failure before it starts.

12 September 1776:
    Thursday. In New York City a second Council of War is called by Washington to review again the issue discussed on 7 September 1776. On this occasion, cooler heads prevail, and by a vote of ten to three it is recommend that the city be abandoned as indefensible, and a potential trap for some parts of the Army. A hasty and speedy retreat to safer and higher ground is deemed immediately needful.

13 September 1776:
    Friday. At headquarters, New York, General Order state "The visiting officer has again reported that the men from Col. Silliman's, Col. Lewis's, and Col. Thompson's Regiments, go upon guard, deficient in ammunition and with bad arms. The General hopes the officers of those Regiments will immediately attend to it." The parole is given as Newark and the countersign as Amboy.
    The Committee of the Treasury reports, "That there is due to John Bates for 266 camp kettles, delivered to Gustavus Risburg, assistant to the deputy quarter master general for the flying camp 354 60/90 dollars." This odd fraction of ninetieths

appears many times in Congressional authorizations. Perhaps it is a means of noting small change, because, as Continental Currency was printed, the smallest denominations were 1/6, ⅓, ½, ⅔ of a dollar. The dollar gets its name from the Dutch pronunciation of the German thaler, daalar, which the Americans called the dollar.

14 September 1776:
Saturday. At New York Washington writes to the President of Congress, noting that he has received the resolution regarding New York City. "I thank them for the confidence they repose in my judgment, respecting the evacuation of the City. I could wish to maintain it, because it is known to be of importance. But I am fully convinced that it cannot be done, and that an attempt for that purpose, if persevered in, might and most certainly would be attended with consequences the most fatal and alarming in their nature."

George Washington removes from New York City to Harlem Heights and makes his headquarters at the Jumel Mansion near present 161st Street.

15 September 1776:
Sunday. In the early morning today, British vessels bring 4,000 troops to Kips Bay (present 34th Street). The warships pound the patriot defenses there, after which the British regulars assault the beach and quickly defeat the undisciplined militia, who panic in the face of a withering fire. Washington cannot stop the fleeing men. The American troops at the tip of Manhattan Island are apprised of the attack, and quickly march north to avoid being cut off by a British force that could slice the island in two at its middle. American forces take up new defensive positions north of McGown's Pass, near 140th Street. British Maj. Gen. William Howe pushes his forces north to about what is now 90th Street at Horn's Hook. [See Fig. III-14, p. 167].

16 September 1776:
Monday. American troops have marched north up Manhattan Island, and the British troops have marched north and east across the island. Washington orders a reconnaissance toward the British lines. American Lt. Col. Thomas Knowlton makes contact with two British light infantry battalions. He is soon reinforced and pushes the British troops back. British Brig. Gen. Alexander Leslie comes up with reinforcements, including Hessian troops and artillery. Knowlton is killed in the fight, and the Americans fall back to their defensive positions. This is the Battle of Harlem Heights.

In Philadelphia, the Congress, aware of the weakness of the American army, authorizes a new force of 88 battalions (or regiments), with enlistments to be for the duration of the war. It never happens. This is much too ambitious a plan, and the Congress and Washington soon must accept a more modest military establishment.

17 September 1776:

Tuesday. At headquarters, Harlem Heights, General Orders state "The General most heartily thanks the troops commanded yesterday by Major [Andrew] Leitch, who first advanced upon the enemy, and the others who so resolutely supported them. The behavior of yesterday was such a contrast, to that of some troops the day before, as must shew what may be done, where officers and soldiers will exert themselves. Once more therefore, the General calls upon officers, and men, to act up to the noble cause in which they are engaged, and to support the Honor and Liberties of their Country. The gallant and brave Col. [Thomas] Knowlton, who would have been an honor to any country, having fallen yesterday, while gloriously fighting, Capt. [Stephen] Brown is to take the command of the party lately led by Col. Knowlton." The parole is given as Leitch and the countersign as Virginia. In Philadelphia, the Congress approves a policy known as the Plan of 1776, in which it proclaims freedom of the seas and defines the rights of neutrals. It becomes a model for most 18th century treaties.

18 September 1776:

Wednesday. At headquarters, in the Morris house, Washington writes to the President of Congress, "The evacuation of New York, and retreat to the Heights of Harlem in the manner they were made, would be succccded by some other interesting event, I beg leave to inform them, that as yet nothing has been attempted upon a large and general plan of attack. The enemy appeared in several large bodies upon t he plains, about two and a half miles from hence; I rode down to our advanced posts to put matters in a proper situation, if they should attempt to come on. When I arrived there, I heard a firing which I was informed was between a party of our Rangers under the command of Lieutenant Colonel Knowlton and an advanced party of the enemy. The parties under Colonel Knowlton and Major Leitch unluckily began their attack too soon, it was rather in flank than in rear. In a little time Major Leitch was brought off wounded, having received three balls thro' his side, and in a short time after Col. Knowlton got a wound, which proved mortal. Their men however persevered and continued the engagement with the greatest resolution."

In Philadelphia, the Congress is concerned over the issue of some officers holding down multiple positions as a commander of a unit, or the second in command, might also serve as a quartermaster for another unit; and approves a resolution "That no officer in the continental army shall be allowed to hold more than one commission, or to receive pay but in one capacity at the same time."

19 September 1776:

Thursday. In New York, Sir William Howe issues a proclamation promising in the King's name pardons and favors to all who would now return to the British allegiance.

The Board of Treasury reports that they have examined the vouchers brought into their office by Joseph Hewes, one of the

Naval Committee "...have expended the sum of one hundred and thirty four thousand three hundred and thirty three and 27/90 dollars in fitting out eight armed vessels."

Near Franklin, North Carolina, Colonel Andrew Williamson's column of patriots is ambushed, about nine miles south at what is called the Black Hole of the Coweecho River, by a body of Cherokee Indians. The patriots suffer heavy casualties, but are able to attack and clear the pass.

20 September 1776:
     Friday. In Philadelphia, Congress revises the Articles of War to include changes recommended by Washington, based in part on the experiences of the past year. The original "Articles" had been largely a copy of the British model.

In New York City, during the night, a fire breaks out. How or by whom it was started no one has ever discovered, but it rages all night and into the following day, destroying 493 buildings. It burns a swath across the city from Broadway west to the Hudson River.

21 September 1776:
     Saturday. In Dover, Delaware, a state constitution is approved. It is introduced and heralded as a model of democracy and republican government.

22 September 1776:
     Sunday. Nathan Hale is executed as a spy without a trial. The British are anxious to demonstrate to patriots that resistence to royal authority is not going to be tolerated, to cower and discourage the rebels. Such behavior by the British has exactly the opposite effect upon most Americans.

23 September 1776:
     Monday. On Montresor's Island, New York, American Lt. Col. Michael Jackson is sent with a detachment of 240 men in boats to try to retake the island, occupied by the British since 10 September 1776. The attack fails due to lack of support by two-thirds of the detachment, which recalcitrants were later held for court martial.

24 September 1776:
     Tuesday. The Congress provides additional Instructions to its agents in France toward the conclusion of a Treaty. The Americans are quite anxious to have the French help, but are a bit wary of possible French demands, including a view that they just might be interested in reclaiming territory lost in the Great War for Empire.

25 September 1776:
     Wednesday. At headquarters, Harlem Heights, General Orders state "The Brigadiers who are in want of tents for their brigades, are to meet at the Quartermaster-generals's this afternoon four o'clock, and divide such as are on hand among them. Such regiments of militia, as have returned, to the

Quartermaster-General the articles belonging to the public they have received; and to their respective brigadiers, the ammunition they have drawn, of which they are first to produce certificates, are discharged, and may return home, as soon as they think proper. The General hopes the commanding officers, and all others, of those regiments, will take care that no other men mix with them when going off– and that particular care be taken, that no horses be carried away by the men, but what are certainly and properly employed in that service." The parole is given as Cumberland and the countersign as Pitt.

The committee formed to have care of the journals of Congress is to collect them from the various printers and assemble them for sale. The Congress wishes to have their debates and resolutions available to and open to the people. How different this is from the views of hierarchal governments.

26 September 1776:

Thursday. In Philadelphia, Congress appoints three commissioners to be representatives of the United States to negotiate with European powers: Silas Deane, Benjamin Franklin, and Arthur Lee, who is already in Europe. Thomas Jefferson, who is also named, has declined this office. Deane will become something of a problem and will be removed.

27 September 1776:

Friday. At headquarters, Harlem Heights, Washington writes to the President of Congress, referring to Howe's proclamation of 19 September 1776, "I received yesterday the enclosed declaration by a gentleman from Elizabethtown, who told me, many copies were found in the possession of the soldiers of Canada, that were landed there a day or two ago by General Howe's permission. I shall not comment upon it. It seems to be founded on a plan that has been artfully pursued for some time past. The account of the troops in Canada comes from a person among the prisoners sent from Canada. It was anonymous, nor do I know the intelligencer; according to him, the enemy in that quarter are stronger than we supposed and their naval force much greater on the Lakes than we had any ideas of."

The Congress recommends that the Convention of the State of Pennsylvania cause all deserters from their troops to be apprehended and sent back to Washington's headquarters.

28 September 1776:

Saturday. At Harlem Heights, Washington writes to the President of Congress, commenting upon a replacement for Col. Hugh Stephenson, of the Rifle Regiment, who has died. "I recommend to the particular notice of Congress, Captain Daniel Morgan, just returned among the prisoners from Canada, as a fit and proper person to succeed to the vacancy occasioned by his death. The present field officers of the Regiment cannot claim any right of preference to him, because he ranked above them as a Captain when he first entered the service. His conduct as an officer on the expedition with General Arnold last fall, his intrepid behavior in the assault on Quebec when the brave Montgomery fell; the inflexible attachment he professed to our cause during his imprisonment and which he perseveres in, added to these his residence in the place Col. Stephenson came from and his interest and influence in the same circle and with such men as are to compose such a regiment; all in my opinion entitle him to the favor of Congress, and lead me to believe, that in his promotion, the States will gain a good and valuable officer for the sort of troops he is particularly recommended to command."

The legislature and convention of Pennsylvania adopts a state constitution. This provides the legal basis for governing with and by the election of persons of their own choosing.

29 September 1776:
Sunday. In Philadelphia, Benjamin Rush writes to Colonel Anthony Wayne, noting that Colonel John Shea has resigned the command of the 3rd Pennsylvania Regiment, leaving Wayne now the senior Colonel in the Pennsylvania Line. Rush further offers some advice, suggesting better communications with the Congress, that might lead to possible future promotion to Brigadier General.

30 September 1776:
Monday. Congress recommends to the legislatures of each state "... that they appoint examiners of surgeons [sic], and that no surgeon shall receive a commission to act as such in the army who shall not produce a certificate from such examiners to prove his qualifications to the office."

1 October 1776:
Tuesday. Congress resolves that the President, John Hancock, write letters to all the state conventions and assemblies requesting each state deliberate and select the men and take measures to be to see that a full representation from each state is included in the Continental Congress, and that it be speedily completed.

2 October 1776:
Wednesday. The Congress directs that the Board of War sell to John Bayard, Alexander Henderson, and Matthew Irwin 1,600 pounds of gunpowder and 800 pounds of lead for use in their privateers, *General Lee* and *Colonel Parry*.

3 October 1776:
Thursday. At headquarters, Harlem Heights, General Orders state "Genl. Putnam will please to point out proper places for huts, to shelter the picquet-guard and direct the officers who command these guards, to see that the men are employed every day at work thereon 'til they are completed; and this, for the sake of their own health and convenience, it is hoped they will do as soon as possible, as the wether will soon grow too uncomfortable to lay without shelter. As the new Articles for the government of the Army, are to take place on Monday next, it is expected that the officers will make their men acquainted with

them as soon as possible, that crimes may not pass unpunished on any pretense of ignorance." The parole is given as Ireland and the countersign as Florida.

In Philadelphia, Congress authorizes a domestic loan of $5,000,000 at four percent interest.

4 October 1776:

Friday. Privateers are having difficulty securing the prize monies they feel due them, and petition the Congress to resolve the problem. In response to the petition, the Congress resolves that the officers and men of the *Andrew Doria* shall have all the prizes taken by them laid before the Marine Committee for review and their approbation. If the Marine Committee concurs with the facts of the capture and the value of the prizes, they are directed to pay to said officers and men one-half of what may be estimated to be due them.

5 October 1776:

Saturday. At headquarters, Harlem Heights, Washington writes to Governor William Livingston, "Sir: The Congress having directed me, by resolve ... to procure as soon as possible, an exchange of the officers taken on Long Island, for the same number of British officers and privates, now prisoners in the United States; it becomes necessary, for me to be informed of the numbers and ranks of the prisoners in the different States, in order to carry the same into execution. You will, therefore, oblige me, by having made out and transmitted to me, an exact return of the number of officers in New Jersey, their ranks, names, and the corps to which thdey belong. The numbers of the non-commissioned officers and privates without their names will be sufficient. They should also be collected from the different places where they are stationed, and brought together to some convenient place, from which they can be sent to General Howe when the cartel is fully settled."

Congress agrees to advance five months pay to the officers, and three months pay to the men who were taken prisoner in Canada and sent to the United States by Sir Guy Carleton.

6 October 1776:

Sunday. In Harlem Heights, Washington writes to Maj. Gen. Benjamin Lincoln, "As I Am credibly informed that the inhabitants along the Sound carry on a frequent communication with the enemy on Long Island, you are hereby instructed to collect all the boats, and other small craft on the Sound, from Hare Neck downwards to any extent you shall think proper, and convey them to any place you shall conceive to be most convenient."

In Philadelphia, Caesar Rodney, a delegate from Delaware, writes to John Haslet, reporting that he (Rodney) will be leaving the Congress, but encouraging Haslet, who had inquired about possible employment with the national government, to check into possible future political positions in the government of Delaware.

7 October 1776:
    Monday. In Philadelphia, the Congress approves a resolution to establish a commissary of prisoners, that each state shall appoint a commissary, whose duties are to include: a listing of all prisoners under their care, their condition, number, and grade.

8 October 1776:
    Tuesday. Congress resolves that it be recommended to the assemblies and conventions of the states from Virginia to New Hampshire, inclusively, to take the most effectual measures for completing, by 10 November, their proportions of the levies to be raised during the war.

9 October 1776:
    Wednesday. At headquarters, Harlem Heights, Washington writes to Governor Jonathan Trumbull, "As our present army is upon the eve of their dissolution; it behoves us to exert every nerve, to enlist immediately for the new one. Without, I am convinced we shall have none to oppose the enemy, and who will have it in their power, to spread havoc and devastation wheresoever they will. I would therefore submit it to your consideration, whether it might not be proper, as soon as you have made choice of your officers and which I think should be effected as early as possible, to a point a committee, with power to repair to this place and make such arrangements, as may be necessary with respect to those who are now in the service, in order that they may begin to recruit out of the present corps, without any loss of time."
    The Congress makes a number of resolutions today regarding general and regimental hospitals, surgeons, medicines, apothecaries, bedding, and many other matters affecting soldier health and care. The concern for medical support for the army is quite real and unfortunately all too poorly handled. Too many physicians are untrained.

10 October 1776:
    Thursday. At Harlem Heights, Washington writes to Maj. Gen. Philip Schuyler, "We are again deprived of the navigation of this [Hudson] River by three Ships-of-War, two of 44 and the other of 20 guns, with three or four tenders passing our chevaux-de-frise yesterday morning, and all our batteries, without any kind of damage or interruption, not withstanding a heavy fire was kept up from both sides of the river. I have given directions to compleat (sic) the obstructions as fast as possible, and I flatter myself, if they allow us a little time more that the passage will become extremely difficult, if not entirely insecure. Their views I imagine are chiefly, to cut off our supplies and probably to gain recruits."
    The Marine Committee reports upon the ranking of 24 captains of vessels in the Navy of the United States. A tabular presentation of the 24, with the name of the vessels, is approved by the Congress; which also empowers the Marine Committee to settle the rank of the lieutenants of the Navy.

11 October 1776:
     Friday. Benedict Arnold has been sailing and rowing his fleet of little vessels (a sloop, two schooners, four galleys, and eight gondolas) around the northern parts of Lake Champlain for nearly a month, looking around and picking the best spots to defend against what is surely a much larger naval force under the British. He selects and stations his fleet behind Valcour Island, between it and the western shore of the lake. Arnold arranges his vessels in a half-moon configuration, facing south, so as to force the British fleet to round the southern tip of Valcour Island, and then sail north to meet him. Arnold will then have the advantage of surprise, because the hills of the island will screen him from the British until they have passed the southern tip, and also because they will have lost way in turning into the channel between the island and the mainland. [See Fig. III-13, p. 163].

12 October 1776:
     Saturday. On Lake Champlain, Sir Guy Carleton, with a stronger fleet and more guns, does as Arnold had planned. He sails right past Valcour Island, and has to double back to attack the Americans.
     While, Carleton has more guns than Arnold, he also is not able to make use of the larger and heavier ones, because the vessels on which they are mounted cannot effect an entrance into the narrow channel. Carleton is temporarily held off by Arnold's small flotilla, but the British gunboats get in close and do great damage. The American vessel *Philadelphia* is badly holed and sinks. The American *Royal Savage* is grounded and later set afire. As dusk sets in, the British withdraw to the mouth of the channel, feeling that they have won the fight, and the job will be finished the next day. Arnold, with what remains of his fleet, slips away during the darkness of night, rowing south hugging the west shore.

13 October 1776:
     Sunday. Battle of Throg's Neck, New York. Howe wishes to avoid the American defenses on Harlem Heights. To do so he makes an amphibious landing behind the rebel lines and debarks about 4,000 troops at this point (now known as Ft. Schuyler Park). They land unopposed, but find that this nearly island-like point has only two places to cross as they try to movement farther north and east. [see Fig. III-14, p. 167].

14 October 1776:
     Monday. Arnold's little naval force has retreated up Lake Champlain to within a few miles of Crown Point. The British forces, in close pursuit of Arnold, have been on a lengthy chase of Arnold's weakening flotilla up (South) Lake Champlain, and attack his remaining vessels. Arnold puts up a terrific, but losing fight. Two more of his vessels sink, but all the men escape. Two more are driven ashore in a sinking condition. Arnold's fleet is reduced to the *Congress* and four gondolas.

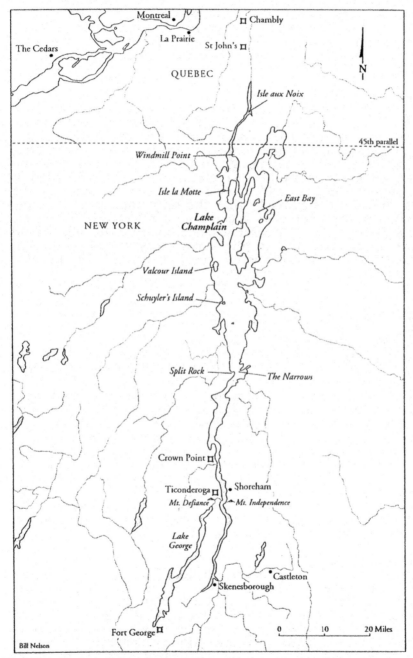

Fig. III-13: Arnold at Lake Champlain, 12 October 1776

Arnold takes on the British *Inflexible, Maria,* and *Carleton,*even though they are all larger vessels with heavier guns. It is a lost cause, and Arnold, finally, burns all five of his remaining boats, leaving their colors flying. He then leads what remains of his men, on foot, overland for nearly ten miles to Crown Point. Later he will march farther south to Fort Ticonderoga, as Carleton moves to Crown Point. [See Fig. III-13, p. 163].

15 October 1776:
    Tuesday. At headquarters, Harlem Heights, General Orders include, "... the General in most pressing terms exhorts all officers commanding divisions, brigades, and regiments to have their officers, and the men, under their respective command, properly informed of what is expected from them; that no confusion may arise in case we should be suddenly called to action, which there is no kind of doubt, is near at hand, and he hopes, and flatters himself, that the only contention will be, who shall render the most acceptable service to his country, and his posterity. The General also desires, that the officers will be particularly attentive to the men's arms and ammunition, that there may be no deficiency, or application for cartridges, when we are called into the field."
    The Congress orders that the sum of $1,753 30/90 be advanced to Lieutenant Francis Nichols for the purpose of paying the soldiers of his company returned from Quebec.

16 October 1776:
    Wednesday. At Harlem Heights, Washington writes to Governor Jonathan Trumbull, "By some deserters who came ashore from their shipping at Frog's Point, and who I think in this instance are deserving of credit; I am acquainted that there are now between Hellgate and Frog's Point five Ships-of-War: *Fowey* (24 guns), *Le Brune* (32 guns), *Carysfort* (28 guns, *Niger* (32 guns), *Halifax* (16 guns), and that the *Mercury* and one other ship are cruising off Block Island'; whether their number may be augmented or diminished in a short time, is more than I can say; though I must observe, that the enemy's frigates of 28 guns are not deterred from passing through Hell Gate."
    Charles Lee has been ordered back from Charleston to the New York area. Washington holds a council of war to discuss the "Enemy's intentions to surround us."

17 October 1776:
    Thursday. At headquarters, Harlem Heights, Washington writes to the New York Legislature, "Judging it a matter of the utmost importance, to secure the passes thro' the Highlands, I have sent Monsr. Imbert [Captain Jean Louis Imbert], a French gentleman, who has been placed in the army, as an Engineer by Congress, in order to take your directions respecting the passes and such works as you may esteem necessary tp preserve them. As the situation of affairs in this State is rather alarming, I would beg leave to recommend your earliest attention to this business, and that no time may elapse before the works are

begun. I have no acquaintance with Monsr. Imbert, and his abilities in his profession remain to be proved. However, I trust under your care and advice, that whatever maybe essential will be immediately done."

Congress appoints a committee of four to review resolutions of Congress relating to the capture and condemnation of prizes, and to report any alterations or additions that should be made. Named to the committee are: George Wythe, Edward Rutledge, Robert Treat Paine, and Samuel Huntington.

18 October 1776:
    Friday. Frustrated at Throg's Neck, William Howe, moves his operations to Pell's Point, New York. The British press the American forces. Washington leaves Morrisania, and travels to King's Bridge. The landing at Pell's Point is resisted by the Americans, who exchange fire with the British, before falling back. Many volleys are fired on each side, as the defenders withdraw to a new position, which the British do not attack as it grows dark. The main American Army in New York retreats 15 miles toward White Plains. [See Fig. II-14, p. 167].

    In Philadelphia, Congress gives a commission to Thaddeus Kosciusko, a Polish volunteer, as Colonel of Engineers. A difficulty the American army faces is the lack of, or a serious shortage of trained engineer officers. Thus, they seek non-American personnel for these positions.

19 October 1776:
    Saturday. In Philadelphia, Delegate Edward Rutledge from South Carolina writes to Robert R. Livingston expressing deep concern for the lack of quality representation by men of character and ability from some states. He reports that New York is all too frequently not properly represented, and hopes for better men in the Congress in the future.

20 October 1776:
    Sunday. Washington establishes his headquarters at King's Bridge, New York, as he prepares to defend the areas of Westchester County from the expected British incursions.

    Washington writes to Joseph Trumbull, "I must therefore request and entreat your every possible exertion to have large quantities of provisions carried to the interior parts of the country, with the utmost expedition, out of the reach of the enemy, for trying to penetrate from the Sound and to form a line in our rear, from whence proper supplies may be immediately drawn for the subsistence of our troops. "

21 October 1776:
    Monday. The British occupy New Rochelle, New York, without opposition.

    The Congress agrees upon a standard form of oath, to be taken by all and every officer to the effect that they owe no allegiance to King George III, and that they will "...support, maintain, and defend the said United States ... with fidelity and honor. So help me God."

22 October 1776:
    Tuesday. The American main army, numbering 14,500 present and fit for duty, arrives at White Plains.
    Action at Mamaroneck, New York, as American Colonel John Haslet fights British Colonel Robert Rogers Rangers in a skirmish.

23 October 1776:
    Wednesday. Washington leaves King's Bridge to go about five miles north of White Plains, where he makes his headquarters at Elijah Miller's House. New York City is now completely evacuated by the Americans.
    At headquarters, White Plains, General Orders state "It has been observed with some concern, that scouting parties go out without any advanced, or flanking parties, both which are absolutely necessary for their safety and success, and which they must have on all occasions. The commanding officers of regiments should on all marches, draw provisions for the wagoners, who attend them, and give them all possible assistance." The parole is given as Denton and the countersign as Chester.

24 October 1776:
    Thursday. Congress resolves "... that an order for £ 50 (equal to $ 133 1/3) be drawn on the treasurer in favor of R. Peters, Secretary to the Board of War, to pay for a light waggon (sic) purchased for use of the Congress. This order says that one English pound sterling has a value of 2.6667 American dollars or one Spanish milled dollar or a piece of eight. That, however does not take into account the real purchase value of the variety of specie available more than two centuries ago, nor of the availability (or lack thereof) of the goods or services one wishes to purchase. Recent authors have attempted to tabulate such values without great success. An English officer or soldier might be able to use his pound sterling in specie to purchase 4-6 times what one American dollar would buy. But, that too would depend upon the availability of the item being purchased. Mark Boatner in his wonderful *Encyclopedia of the American Revolution*, (3rd Ed., 1994, p. 842) states, "Authorities disagree so radically on actual figures ... I have deliberately avoided an attempt to give them here ..." And so do I--because I agree with that view! It is nearly impossible to determine, with any accuracy, the value of monies from the past, related to goods in the present. Nothing beats a thorough, deep, and good grasp of History, which might help.

25 October 1776:
    Friday. The Congress recommends to the several assemblies and conventions of the United States that they procure full supplies of firearms, bayonets, brass or other field pieces, powder, lead, flints, medicines, entrenching tools, tent cloth, blankets, and other clothing, for such of their militia as are deficient therein.

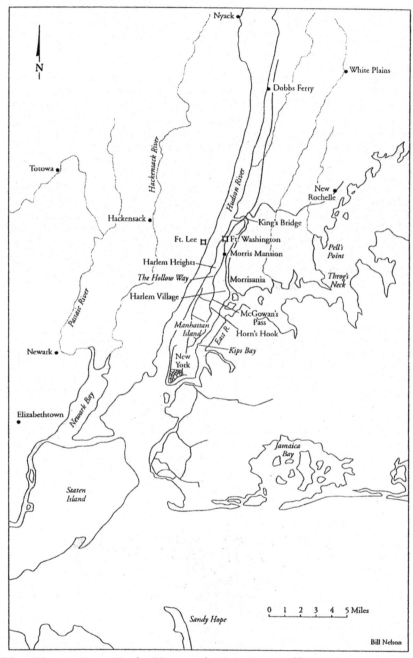

Fig. III-14: New York City and Vicinity, Fall 1776

26 October 1776:
    Saturday. From Elizabethtown, New Jersey, Delegate Abraham Clark writes to Elias Dayton reporting that he has been overburdened with work both in the Congress and in the State Assembly to which he was also elected. Members of his family have been quite ill, and he also is not well.

27 October 1776:
    Sunday. In Philadelphia, Delegate William Hooper from North Carolina writes to Joseph Hewes saying that with John Penn (also from North Carolina) leaving to return, he is left with the duty of representing his state. He would rather be helping with the development of the state constitution, but feels that his current obligation is to the Continental Congress.

28 October 1776:
    Monday. The Battle of White Plains, General Washington moved his troops rapidly to secure White Plains before British Maj. Gen. William Howe. Howe is not in a hurry. He moves from Throg's Neck and Pell's Point, awaits reinforcements at New Rochelle, and with about 13,000 troops moves toward White Plains. He attacks Washington on Chatterton's Hill. They move through heavy musket fire but continue to climb up the hill in a bayonet charge that dislodges the defenders who withdraw in good order.

29 October 1776:
    Tuesday. Congress recommends to the state of North Carolina that they fortify and secure, at their expense, the entrance to the Cape Fear River, near Wilmington, by erecting batteries and other works of defense and by placing obstructions in proper parts of the river to block enemy ships.

30 October 1776:
    Wednesday. Washington establishes a few units of Dragoons (horse mounted infantrymen, capable of traveling fast and light--great for scouting, carrying messages, Express Riders---the cavalry of small and poor armies who do not have large bodies of mounted troops) to provide much needed reconnaissance and screening.

31 October 1776:
    Thursday. In Philadelphia, the Congress appoints a committee of five to prepare an effectual plan for suppressing the internal enemies of America, and preventing a communication of intelligence to our other enemies, both internal and external. Chosen for this committee: Samuel Adams, George Wythe, Richard Henry Lee, James Wilson, and George Ross.

1 November 1776:
    Friday. Washington withdraws from White Plains to North Castle, New York. British Commander William Howe had planned another attack upon the rebel forces, but heavy rains

interfered, and the Americans have withdrawn anyway, so the attack was called off. The two armies settle upon their arms, bury their dead, and tend to the sick and wounded.

2 November 1776:
    Saturday. The Treasury Board is directed to prepare all the necessary materials and to have them ready for a new emission of five millions of dollars, to be issued when the Congress shall order.
    At Fort Washington, Ensign William Demont, the adjutant of the 5th Pennsylvania Regiment garrisoning the post under the command of Colonel Robert Magaw, deserts to the enemy with plans of the place.

3 November 1776:
    Sunday. At Crown Point, British Brig. Gen. Guy Carleton abandons this post after a long chase, because it is too late in the season to continue and also because his supply and communication line is too long and difficult. So it is that Arnold's fleet of gondolas and other vessels, much smaller in number and size and weight of gunnery than those of Carleton, delays the British enough to force them to retire.

4 November 1776:
    Monday. Matthew Thornton, a delegate from New Hampshire, attends and presents his credentials to the Continental Congress.
    William Howe receives the traitor Demont's plans of Fort Washington from Earl Percy.

5 November 1776:
    Tuesday. At headquarters, White Plains, General Orders state "The General is very sensible that the time of service of many of the militia, will soon expire, but as this is the most interesting and critical part of the campaign, and their departure would greatly discourage the other troops, and injure the service; he doubts not their love to their Country, will induce them to prolong their stay, until the close of the campaign, which must happen soon." The parole is given as Mamaroneck and the countersign as Goshen.
    William Howe orders the British army to withdraw from White Plains and march southwest to the Hudson River and Kings Bridge, New York.

6 November 1776:
    Wednesday. Congress hears a report of a Court of Enquiry [sic] appointed by Maj. Gen. Philip Schuyler at Albany regarding the disposition of certain goods and vessels taken by the patriot forces at Sorel in Canada last summer while under orders from Brig. Gen. Richard Montgomery. Were these to be considered as prizes and handled in the same manner, or as booty to be distributed in that manner? The question is passed to the Marine Committee for resolution.

7 November 1776:
    Thursday. At White Plains, Washington writes to Maj. Gen. Nathanael Greene, "The enemy after having encamped in full view of us and reconnoitering our situation for several days, thought proper on Tuesday morning to decamp. They have bent their course to Dobbs Ferry inclining towards Kings Bridge. What their real designs are, we, as yet are strangers to, but conjecturing that too little is yet done by General Howe to go into Winter Quarters, we conceive that Fort Washington will be an object for part of his force , whilst New Jersey may claim the attention of the other part. To guard against the evils arising from the first, I must recommend to you to pay every attention in your power and give every assistance you can to the garrison opposite to you. To guard against the latter, it has been determined in a Council of War, to throw over a body of troops, so soon as we can with more precision ascertain the destination of the enemy into the Jerseys."
    The Congress appoints Richard Bache to be Postmaster General in the absence of Benjamin Franklin, who is going to France.

8 November 1776:
    Friday. At Halifax, Nova Scotia, a group of 180 local rebels led by Jonathan Eddy and John Allen begin a siege in an effort that will last more than two weeks and will be an unsuccessful attempt to wrest control of the place from the British. This is yet another example of the lukewarm, on again, off again, efforts of the Congress and various patriot groups to see if Nova Scotia can be added to the colonies.
    At headquarters, White Plains, General Orders state "The Court Martial of which Genl. [Alexander] McDougall is President, to sit immediately for the trial of Maj. [Jonathan William] Austin in arrest, upon charges of 'Burning the houses at White Plains, contrary to General Orders.' Capt. [Joseph] Poole of Col. Cary's Regt., Genl. Fellow's Brigade, tried by the same Court Martial, and convicted of 'Shamefully abandoning his post'– ordered to be cashiered. The General approves each of the above sentences; and orders the former to join his regiment, and the latter to depart the army immediately." The parole is given as Philadelphia and the countersign as Portsmouth.

9 November 1776:
    Saturday. Concerned over the problem of a too easy and free communication and transportation of supplies of foodstuffs, forage and other essentials between the enemy in New York and Staten Island from Elizabethtown, Newark and other points in New Jersey adjacent thereto, to the great detriment of the American cause, the Congress requests the Governor of New Jersey to "... take most speedy and effective measures to stop all communication between his state and the enemy's quarters that are not directed by proper authority."

10 November 1776:
    Sunday. In Philadelphia, Richard Henry Lee writes to Robert Carter saying that he feels the British have vastly overextended themselves. While they may have kept Canada, which Lee feels is more due to the smallpox than American arms, he is very upbeat, and feels the British have paid dearly for their trifle of conquests.

11 November 1776:
    Monday. Washington is at Peekskill, New York, where he makes his headquarters. He writes to the President of Congress, "I left White Plains about 11 o'clock yesterday. All peace then. The enemy appeared to be preparing for their expedition to Jersey, according to every information. What their designs are, or whether their present conduct is not a feint I cannot determine. The Maryland and Virginia troops under Lord Stirling have crossed the river as have part of those from the Jersey, the remainder are now embarking. The troops judged necessary to secure the several posts thro' the Highlands, have also got up. I am going to examine the passes and direct such works as may appear necessary, after which and making the best disposition I can, of things in this quarter, I intend to proceed to Jersey, which I expect to do tomorrow."
    In Annapolis, Maryland, the legislature adopts a Constitution for the state.

12 November 1776:
    Tuesday. The Congress, is trying to raise the 88 battalions it has authorized. As an inducement the Congress concludes that those who enlist for the duration of the war shall have entitlement to 100 acres of land, while those who enlist only for three years will not have such entitlement.

13 November 1776:
    Wednesday. Washington removes to the east side of the Hudson River, and sets up headquarters at Fort Lee, New Jersey. He has been out of touch with the garrison and troops at Fort Washington on the opposite side of the river, and thus has little knowledge of their situation. Fort Washington has been constructed of earth and wood and does not have built into it many of the defensive features needed to resist a siege. There are no ditches, casements, proper walls, and few adequate redoubts or outer works. More importantly the fort lacks a good food supply, little fuel, and almost no water to allow it to sustain any kind of a determined siege. Nathanael Greene has transferred some additional troops to reinforce Robert Magaw, bringing that garrisons strength to about 2,900 men.

14 November 1776:
    Thursday. The Board of War is ordered to confer with the Council of Safety of the State of Pennsylvania so as to cooperate with them in devising ways and means of calling forth the

strength of this and neighboring states, for the defense of the City of Philadelphia, against any attempts the enemy may make toward its possession.

15 November 1776:
Friday. At Fort Washington, Howe has brought a strong force of nearly 8,000 men to attack the small outposts near this fort, and soon has the place closely surrounded. He sends his adjutant, Colonel James Patterson, under a white flag calling for Magaw to surrender. Magaw gives Patterson a written refusal.

The Congress fixes the rate of pay for the Naval officers of the Continental Navy, and also determines the ranking of ships captains relative to Army ranks as follows: a ship of 40 or more guns is to be equal to Colonel; of 20-40 guns to be equal to Lieutenant Colonel; of 10-20 guns to be equal to Major; Lieutenants in the Navy to be equal to Captains in the Army.

16 November 1776:
Saturday. The Battle of Fort Washington, New York. Howe has battled George Washington up the Hudson valley, and defeated him at White Plains. This leaves American Colonel Robert Magaw isolated in a fortification on what is now Washington Heights, (at West 184th Street), with about 1,200 troops. It has been decided by an American War Council to hold the fort, and Magaw has been reinforced with 1,700 troops to bring his strength up to nearly 2,900 troops.

Washington crosses the river from Fort Lee, in company with Nathanael Greene, Israel Putnam, and Hugh Mercer, to consult with Magaw, and inspect the fort for themselves. Seeing that they could do nothing, however, they depart.

William Howe, sends Knyphausen with 3,000 Hessian troops to attack the fort from the north. Cornwallis and other British units, numbering nearly 5,000 men, attack the fort and its outlying defenses from the south and east. Fort Washington cannot hold out against such determined assaults. Magaw is forced to surrender to the British and Hessians who capture Fort Washington, and the remaining nearly 2,400 American soldiers. [See Fig. III-14, p. 167].

In St. Eustatius, the Dutch garrison at Fort Orange fires a salvo of 11 guns, to return the salute of the American vessel, the *Andrew Doria* under Captain Isaiah Robinson, who is flying the Grand Union ensign from his quarter staff. It is the first salute to this new flag of the Americans.

17 November 1776:
Sunday. From General Greene's quarters at Fort Lee, Washington writes to Governor Jonathan Trumbull, "... with much concern I beg leave to inform you of an unfortunate event that has taken place. About 12 o'clock the enemy made a general attack upon our lines around Fort Washington; which having carried, the garrison retired with the Fort, Col. Magaw, finding there was no possibility of a retreat across the North

finding there was no possibility of a retreat across the North River, over to Fort Lee, surrendered the post. We do not yet know our own loss or that of the enemy in forcing the lines; but I imagine it must have been considerable on both sides, as the fire in some parts was of long continuance and heavy; neither do I know the terms of capitulation. The force of the Garrison before the attack was about 2,000 men. The importance of the North River, and the sanguine wishes of all to prevent the enemy from possessing it, have been the causes of this unhappy catastrophe."

In Philadelphia, John Witherspoon, a delegate from New Jersey, writes to Benjamin Rush expressing great dissatisfaction with Dr. John Morgan, who seems to have been a something less than a well- qualified physician. Morgan is later dismissed as Physician-in-Chief of the Continental Army.

18 November 1776:

Monday. Washington is at Hackensack, New Jersey at Peter Zabriskie's home, where he makes his headquarters. He does not hesitate to take action after the loss at Fort Washington. Orders are issued to remove as much of the stores from Fort Lee as possible, and to extract all the troops from that post, now no longer of any defensive value.

19 November 1776:

Tuesday. At Hackensack, Washington writes to the President of Congress, "I have not been yet able, to obtain a particular account of the unhappy affair of the 16th (loss of Fort Washington), nor of the terms on which the garrison surrendered. As Fort Lee was always considered as only necessary in conjunction with that on the East side of the River, to preserve the communication across, and to prevent the enemy from a free navigation, it has become of no importance by the loss of the other."

The British make a night crossing of the Hudson River at Closter, New Jersey, upstream of Fort Lee. Their purpose is to be able to attack and defeat any American troops posted at Fort Lee, and thus gain freer access up the Hudson River.

20 November 1776:

Wednesday. The British capture abandoned Fort Lee as the Americans retreat towards the Raritan River, New Jersey. The Americans lose the cannon at Fort Lee, a good deal of baggage, about 250 tents, nearly 1,000 barrels of flour, and other quarter master stores. The fleeing American army arrives in Hackensack by dusk.

21 November 1776:

Thursday. Washington writes to the President of Congress, "Yesterday morning a large body of the enemy landed between Dobb's Ferry and Fort Lee. Their object was evidently to inclose (sic) the whole of our troops and stores that lay between the North and Hackensack Rivers, which form a very narrow neck of land. Upon the first information of their having landed and of their movements, our men were ordered to meet them, but finding their numbers greatly superior and that they were extending themselves to seize on the passes over the river, it was thought proper to withdraw or men, which was effected and their retreat secured."

Washington begins the long retreat across New Jersey, closely followed by British Maj. Gen. Charles Cornwallis. Washington on this date, is safely across the Passaic River, about eight miles west of Hackensack, New Jersey. [See Fig. III-15, p. 177].

22 November 1776:
Friday. By dawn, Washington and his army are marching out of Acquackanoc, along the west side of the Passaic River towards Newark.

The Congress sends blank commissions to General George Washington, for his use in reviewing and selecting good officers for the new three-year regiments. He is to be assisted in this effort by a three-person committee: William Paca, John Witherspoon, and George Ross. This officer selection is an important part of Washington's efforts to improve the quality and ability of his officer corps.

23 November 1776:
Saturday. Washington, and the retreating American Army, now reported at a strength of 5,140 fit for duty, have reached Newark. The British pursuit seems somewhat lethargic. So the Americans are able to watch and rest for several days, until 28 November 1776. Washington is greatly concerned, since the term of more than 2,000 of his troops will expire on 1 December 1776, and of nearly another 1,000 on 1 January 1777. How is he to manage a defense without soldiers? It becomes a constant and nagging problem for him and the Continental Congress.

Washington writes to the President of Congress, "The situation of our affairs is truly critical, and such as requires uncommon exertions on our part. From the movements of the enemy, and the information we have received, they will certainly make a push to possess themselves of this part of the Jerseys. In order that you my be fully apprized of our weakness, and of the necessity there is of our obtaining early succors, I have by the advice of the general officers here, directed General Mifflin to wait on you."

24 November 1776:
Sunday. George Washington and his army continue a retreat across New Jersey, as he tries to find sites from which he can hold up, delay, and damage the columns of Lord Cornwallis that are pursuing him. Local militia are greatly desired because they can assemble quickly, and allow the more stable Continental forces to prepare defenses. Washington's headquarters are set up at Newark, from which he writes to Colonel David Forman, "Sir: Having received information, that there is danger of an

insurrection of Tories in the County of Monmouth, and it being
highly necessary that the most speedy check should be given to
a measure of so pernicious a tendency; you are hereby ordered
to march, with the Regiment under your command, into the
said County of Monmouth, and on your arrival there, you are
authorized to apprehend all such persons, as from good
information appear to be concerned in any plot or design
against the Liberty or Safety of the United States. And you are
further authorized, immediately to attack any body of men
whom you may find actually assembled or in arms for the
purpose aforesaid. And if you should find their numbers
superior to your force, you have full authority to call in and take
command of such number of militia of the State of New Jersey,
as you may judge sufficient."

25 November 1776:
    Monday. With great concern over the safety and security of
the seat of government, the Congress requests the Council of
Safety of Pennsylvania to call forth all the associators in the city
of Philadelphia and its liberties (nearby areas outside the
jurisdiction of the city), and the counties of Philadelphia,
Chester, Bucks, and Northampton to continue in the service of
the United States for six weeks beyond any service time for
which they may have enlisted or been called upon.

26 November 1776:
    Tuesday. In Philadelphia, Congress resolves that the number
and kind of artillery to be on prize ships be determined, and
that all brass pieces belonging to the states be sent with all
expedition to General Washington in New Jersey.

27 November 1776:
    Wednesday. Governor William Livingston of New Jersey,
writes to George Washington, "I can easily form some idea of the
difficulties under which you labour (sic) and particularly of one
for which the public can make no allowances because your
prudence and fidelity to the cause will not suffer you to reveal
it to the public, and instance of magnanimity superior perhaps
to any that can be shown in battle. But depend upon it, my dear
Sir, the impartial world will do you ample justice before long.
May God support you under that fatigue both of body and mind
to which you must be constantly exposed."
    At his headquarters in Newark, Washington writes to Maj.
Gen. Charles Lee, "Dear Sir: My former letters were so full and
explicit, as to the necessity of your marching, as early as
possible, that it is unnecessary to add more on that head. I
confess I expected you would have been sooner in motion. The
force here, when joined by yours, will not be adequate to any
great opposition. At present it is weak, and it has been more
owning to the badness of the weather, that the enemy's
progress has been checked, than any resistance we could make.
They are now pushing this way, part of 'em have passed the
Passaic. Their plan is not entirely unfolded, but I shall not be

surprised, if Philadelphia should turn out the object of their movement. The distress of the troops, for want of cloaths (sic), I feel much, but what can I do?"

Congress requests the four New England governments to take the most effective measures to have 10,000 pairs of shoes and 10,000 pairs of stockings purchased in those states, and sent forward with all possible expedition to Washington's headquarters for the use of the soldiers under his command.

28 November 1776:

Thursday. Washington is at Brunswick, New Jersey, where he sets up headquarters. The patriot army evacuates Newark and retreats south to Elizabethtown.

The vanguard of the British troops enter Newark from the north, as Washington's rear guard is leaving to the south. While the British are desirous of catching Washington's army, they are also careful of the effective defensive measures the American artillery presents and do not rush forward into potential danger.

29 November 1776:

Friday. The main American forces reach Brunswick by noon. General George Washington, already there, now makes the decision to continuc on through the center of New Jersey, sending his sick and wounded west to the area of Morristown. He writes to the President of Congress, "On Thursday morning I left Newark, and arrived here yesterday with the troops that were there. It was the opinion of all the generals who were with me, that a retreat to this place was requisite and founded in necessity." {See Fig. III-15, p. 177].

30 November 1776:

Saturday. At Brunswick, in Cochrane's Tavern, Washington is up early. The only reinforcements he has received are a few stragglers from the flying camp. More importantly, tomorrow, 1 December, the enlistments of about two thousand of his soldiers will expire. The British force, much larger than his, is but a few hours away. Washington writes to the President of Congress, "I have now no assurances, that more than a very few of the troops composing the flying Camp will remain after the time of their engagement is out; so far from it, I am told, that many of General Ewing's brigade, who stand engaged to the 1st of January, are now going away. If those go, whose service expires this day, our force will be reduced to a mere handfull."

Washington also writes to The Board of War, "I met Captain Thomas Hesketh (of the 7th Foot, British Army) on the road, and as the situation of his family did not admit of delay, I permitted him to go immediately to New York, not having the least doubt but General Howe will make a return of any officer of equal rank, who shall be required."

He also writes to Governor William Livingston, "Pennsylvanians are enlisted till the first of January, I am informed that they are deserting in great numbers; I therefore entreat, that you would without loss of time, give orders to the

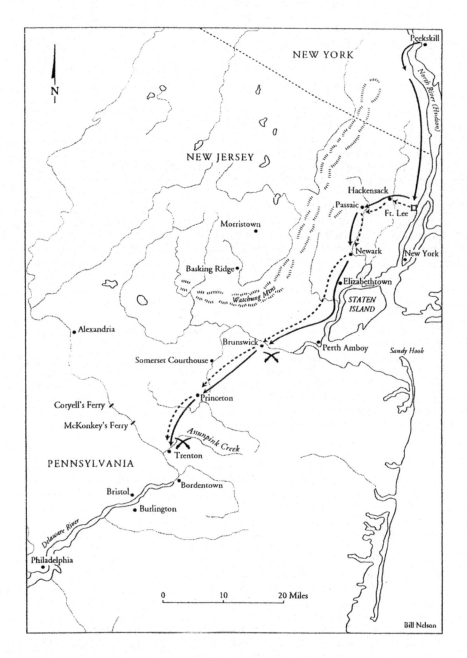

Fig. III-15: Retreat Across New Jersey, Fall 1776

officers of militia on the roads and the ferries over Delaware, to take up and secure every soldier that has not a regular discharge or pass. In order to effect this, proper guards should be immediately posted. I thank you most sincerely for your feelings for me at this time and upon this occasion; I will not, however despair; but look forward with a hope that such reinforcements will yet arrive to my assistance, as will enable me to prevent our common enemy from making much further progress."

The Howe brothers issue a Proclamation of Pardon. It is an offer of amnesty to those persons who return allegiance to the King, and will swear an oath of fidelity to the British Crown. All are invited to do so within sixty days. For this they will be given a full pardon for whatever they might have done, and will receive a certificate guaranteeing their lives and their property.

1 December 1776:

Sunday. A brief rear guard action takes place at Brunswick, as Captain Alexander Hamilton with his artillery covering the crossings of the Raritan River, holds up the advance of the British Light Dragoons. Washington barely escapes this pursuit of his forces by the British. He writes to Charles Lee, "The enemy are advancing, and have got as far as Woodbridge and Amboy, and, from information not to be doubted, they mean to push for Philadelphia. The force I have with me is infinitely inferior in numbers, and such as cannot give or promise the least successful opposition."

A large portion of Washington's troops have come to the end of their one-year enlistment, and simply head home. The General and his little Army, now reduced to less than 3,000 men, retreat toward Princeton. The British are held on the north side of the Raritan River until the bridge is repaired, thus allowing the Americans to escape.

2 December 1776:

Monday. At Princeton, Washington writes to the president of the Congress, "I arrived here this morning with our troops between eight and nine o'clock. When the enemy first landed on this side of the North (Hudson) River, I apprehended that they meant to make a push this way, and knowing that the force which I had, was not sufficient to oppose 'em, I wrote to Genl. Lee to cross with the several Continental Regiments in his Division, and hoped he would have arrived before now."

Washington leaves Princeton later in the morning and is near Trenton by the afternoon. American Major General Charles Lee, encamped near Castle Hill, New York, crosses to the west side of the Hudson River but is slow in acting upon Washington's call for support in fighting or in helping him escape the British. The British are able to march into Brunswick, but fearing the American artillery and seeing the American defense posture, do not continue the pursuit, and remain there until 6 December.

3 December 1776:
    Tuesday. George Washington is at Trenton. He writes to The President of Congress, "Immediately on my arrival here, I ordered the removal of all military and other stores and baggage over the Delaware; a great quantity is already got over." He continues to request Charles Lee to hasten to join him, and help defend New Jersey and Pennsylvania against any further British incursions. This delay in Lee's response to Washington's repeated requests for military support and reinforcement irks the Commander-in-Chief.

4 December 1776:
    Wednesday. At Auray, Brittany, France, Benjamin Franklin writes to Silas Deane at Paris, reporting that he has just arrived at Quiberon Bay aboard the *Reprisal*, and is awaiting a favorable wind for Nantes. He goes on to note, "I find myself here as near to Paris as I shall be at Nantes, but I am obliged to go there to provide myself with money for my journey, and to get my baggage, which was left on the ship. I shall endeavor to join you as soon as possible. I propose to retain my incognito until I ascertain whether the court will receive ministers from the United States. I have several letters for you from the committee, which I do not send forward because I know they contain matters of consequence, and I am not certain of their safety in that way."
    In New Jersey, American units come into Kingston, Rocky Hill, and Princeton. Some are quickly forwarded to Trenton; others remain for a few days at their destination to recover from the long retreat.
    At Trenton, Washington writes to the President of Congress, "I received a letter from Genl. Lee. On the 30th ulto. He was at Peekskill and expected to pass with his division two days after. From this intelligence you will readily conclude that he will not be able to afford us any aid for several days. By Colo. [Samuel] Griffin who went from Brunswick on Sunday morning with a Capt. [Richard] Symes to pass him by our guards, and w ho was detained by Lord Cornwallis till Monday evening on account of his situation. The amount of Genl. [Henry] Clinton's force from what he could collect from the officers, was about six thousand, as to their destination he [Symes] could not obtain the least information. By him I also learned, the enemy were in Brunswick and that some of their advanced parties had proceeded two miles on this side. The heavy rain that has fallen has probably checked their progress and may prevent their further movement for some time."

5 December 1776:
    Thursday. At Trenton, Washington writes to the President of Congress, "By last advices, the enemy are still at Brunswick; and the account adds, that General Howe was expected at Elizabethtown with reinforcements, to erect the King's standard, and demand submission of this State. As nothing but necessity

obliged me to retire before the enemy, and leave so much of the Jerseys unprotected, I conceive it to be my duty, and it corrisponds [sic] with my inclination, to make head against them, as soon as there shall be the least probability of doing it with propriety; that the country might in some measure be covered. Because I was disappointed in my expectation of militia, and because on the day of the approach of the enemy and probably the reason of the attack, the term of the Jersey and Maryland brigades service expired and neither of them would stay an hour longer. These, among ten thousand other instances, might be adduced to shew {sic} the disadvantages of short enlistments, and the little dependence upon militia in times of real danger; but as yesterday cannot be recalled, I will not dwell upon a subject which no doubt has given much uneasiness to Congress, as well as severe pain and mortification to me. "

Washington is trying to gather his forces together, and orders units still in the Princeton vicinity to march toward Trenton to join with the troops already there.

6 December 1776:

Friday. At Trenton, Washington writes to the President of Congress, "I have not received any intelligence of the enemy's movements. From every information they still remain at Brunswick, except some of their parties who are advanced a small distance on this side. Today I shall set out for Princeton myself, unless something should occur to prevent me, which I do not expect."

In Richmond, the Burgesses organize the western part of the state of Virginia and name it Kentucky County.

7 December 1776:

Saturday. Action at Tappan, New York: A group of Tories pillage the Town, abuse patriot citizens, and cut down the Liberty Pole.

American forces at and near Trenton, New Jersey, have been collecting all the boats up and down the Delaware River, and this day cross over into Pennsylvania.

General Washington's army, having successfully retreated across New Jersey, avoiding any major battles with the British, but delaying them in their pursuit, is now on the western side of the Delaware River, which acts as a moat or partial barrier to further attacks by the pursuing British, since no boats are available to the British for making an armed crossing.

8 December 1776:

Sunday. General George Washington crosses the Delaware River at Trenton with the rear guard of the army this morning. He makes his headquarters at the Falls of the Delaware, Pennsylvania, at Summerseat. About 11 o'clock, the British march down towards the east side of the river, expecting to find boats within reach. But all have been collected by the American troops for some considerable distance up and down the river.

Howe and Cornwallis are pleased that they have chased the rebels out of New Jersey. Howe lays plans to garrison the posts they have captured and go into winter quarters. [See Fig. III-16, p. 183].

Maj. Gen. Charles Lee still has not taken action in response to Washington's repeated orders to join with him. It seems that Lee is not quite sure Washington is the best leader of the American army, and might be hoping that a disaster would lead the Congress to appoint him (Lee) to fill the position of Commander-in-Chief.

The British occupy Newport, Rhode Island, with a force of about 6,000 troops under Major General Henry Clinton.

9 December 1776:

Monday. Washington's small and shrinking army has crossed the Delaware River, but has been reduced by soldiers leaving as their tours of duty expire. Washington pleads with men to stay on for a few more weeks, without notable success. He is now down to about 2,500 troops.

At Trenton, Washington writes to the President of Congress, "I had removed the troops to this side of the Delaware; soon after, the enemy made their appearance, and their van entered just as our rear guard quitted. We had removed all our stores, except a few boards."

Thomas Paine has been with the American troops since the abandonment of Fort Lee, and marched with them through all the long retreat across New Jersey. He notes for future use in his *American Crisis*, "I shall not now attempt to give all the particulars of our retreat to the Delaware. Suffice it, for the present to say, that both officers and men, though greatly harassed and fatigued, frequently without rest, covering, or provision, the inevitable consequences of a long retreat, bore it with a manly and a martial spirit. All their wishes were one, which was, that the country would turn out, and help them drive the enemy back. There is a natural firmness in some minds, which cannot be unlocked by trifles, but, which, when unlocked, discovers a cabinet of fortitude and I reckon it among those kind of public blessings which we do not immediately see, that God hath blessed him (Washington) with in interrupted health, and given him a mind that can even flourish upon care."

10 December 1776:

Tuesday. At the Falls of the Delaware, Washington writes to Lund Washington, "I wish to heaven it was in my power to give you a more favorable account of our situation than it is. Our numbers, quite inadequate to the task of opposing that part of the army under the command of General Howe, being reduced by sickness, desertion, and political deaths (on or before the first instant, and having no assistance from the militia), were obliged to retire before the enemy, who were perfectly well informed of our situation, till we came to this place, where I have no idea of being able to make a stand, as my numbers, till joined by the Philadelphia Militia, did not exceed three thousand men fit for duty."

British prisoners sent from New Jersey are ordered to Fredericktown, Maryland, to be conveyed there by Captain Mountjoy Baily with a guard force of 18 troops.

11 December 1776:

Wednesday. Maj. Gen. Israel Putnam is directed to order parties of active, spirited men, with proper guides, to cross from Philadelphia into New Jersey, under the conduct of good officers, to harass and to gather intelligence of the motions and situation of the enemy, and report daily through Putnam to Congress.

At Trenton Falls Washington writes to Maj. Gen. Charles Lee, "Dear Sir: Your favor of the 8th. instr. By the light horsemen reached me last night. Having wrote you fully respecting my situation just before it came to hand, it is unnecessary to add much now. I shall only say that Philadelphia, beyond all question, is the object of the enemy's movements and that nothing less than our utmost exertions will be sufficient to prevent Genl. Howe from possessing it. The force I have is weak and entirely incompetent to that end. I must therefore entreat you to push on with every possible succour you can bring. Your aid may give a more favourable complexion to our affairs. You know the importance of the City of Philadelphia and the fatal consequences that must attend the loss of it."

12 December 1776:

Thursday. In Philadelphia, Congress vests Washington with near dictatorial powers to recruit additional troops, as the British appear to continue to advance towards the city. Congress packs up on this date and prepares to flee to Baltimore. They also authorize a Regiment of Dragoons, upon recommendation of Washington. This becomes the first Cavalry unit in the United States Army.

Charles Lee, now a few miles west of Morristown, New Jersey, finally decides to obey Washington's order to join him, and orders Maj. Gen. John Sullivan to march via Easton, Pennsylvania, the next day. However, Lee decides to spend a night at a tavern near Basking Ridge, New Jersey.

13 December 1776:

Friday. The British army, under William Howe, now goes into winter quarters in New York City. Some of the British troops are quartered on Staten Island, and Brunswick, New Jersey. A few are positioned to guard British supply lines across New Jersey. Most of the places captured by the British and Hessian forces in the long retreat of Washington's army across New Jersey, are garrisoned by Hessian units. [See Fig. III-16, p. 183].

At Trenton Falls, Pennsylvania, Washington writes to the President of Congress, "The apparent designs of the enemy being to avoid this ferry, and land their troops above and below us, have induced me to remove from this place, the greater part

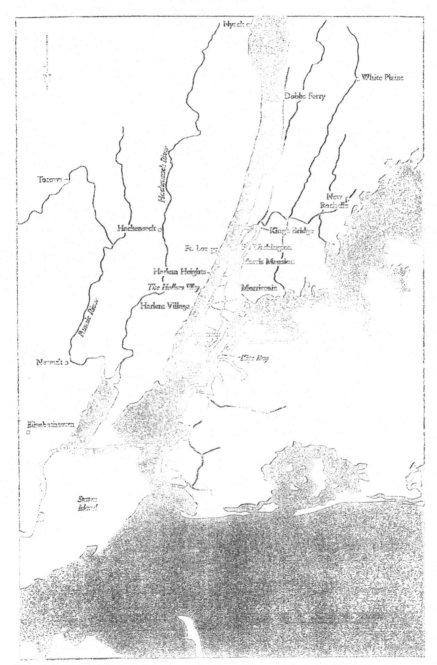

Fig. III-16: British Occupation of New York, 1776

of the troops and throw them into a different disposition of the river, whereby I hope not only to be more able to impede their passage, but also to avoid the danger of being enclosed in this angle of the river. As General [John] Armstrong has a good deal of influence in this state and our present force is small and inconsiderable, I think he cannot be better employed than to repair to the counties where his interest lies to animate the people, promote the recruiting service, and encourage the militia to come in."

A British Patrol captures American Maj. Gen. Charles Lee at the Basking Ridge tavern in which he had chosen to spend the night. This is a most foolish move on Lee's part. He made arrangements for very few guards, and should have been with his troops in any event.

14 December 1776:
    Saturday. German Colonel Johann Rall, assigned to command the Hessian Brigade, arrives at Trenton this morning. William Howe breakfasts with his officers at Trenton, and leaves later in the day for Princeton and New York. Washington is at the same time across the Delaware River, in Pennsylvania, staying at the house of Thomas Barclay in Trenton Falls, and later moves his headquarters further north to be closer to the main body of his troops.

15 December 1776:
    Sunday. In Hunterdon County, New Jersey, Captain John Mott, a former Quaker, who had married "out of meeting" and is now a militia officer, defends his home against six Hessian invaders. When they break down the door of his home, Mott defends his family using the fireplace poker and tongs, killing three Hessians, before the others flee. The story of this intrusion and others like it quickly spreads among the New Jersey communities who are experiencing similar affronts by the British and German occupiers. This helps to arouse the militia in the state to assist in containing the British occupation, and denies the British the forage they so desperately need.

    American Colonel David Chambers leads a group of Amwell Township militia east of Coryell's Ferry to attack an outpost of British foraging parties.

16 December 1776:
    Monday. On the Delaware River, David Chambers sends back across the River three prisoners captured in his raid yesterday to George Washington for questioning.

    At headquarters, near Coryell's Ferry, Washington writes to Maj. Gen. William Heath, "I am now to acquaint you, that from information received of the enemy's movements, it appears to me, that they intend leaving this part of the country, and to retire towards Brunswick and the towns continuous to it, perhaps for the purpose of going into Winter Quarters. I entirely agree with you in sentiment, that your troops cannot be better employed than in surprising any of the enemy's posts either at Hackensack or the parts adjacent ..."

17 December 1776:
Tuesday. At the Falls of the Delaware, Washington writes to Lund Washington, "Hither to, by our destruction of the boats, and vigilance in watching the fords of the river, we have prevented them from crossing; but how long we will be able to do it God only knows, as they are still hovering about the river. And if every thing else fails, will wait till the 1st of January, when there will be no other men to oppose them but militia, none of which but those from Philadelphia, are yet come. The unhappy policy of short enlistments and a dependence upon militia will, I fear, prove the downfall of our cause, though early pointed out with an almost prophetic spirit! Our cause has also received a severe blow in the captivity of Gen. Lee. Taken by his own imprudence, going three or four miles from his own camp, and within twenty of the enemy, notice of which by a rascally Tory was given a party of light horse seized him in the morning after traveling all night, and carried him off in high triumph....our only dependence now is upon the speedy enlistment of a new army. If this fails, I think the game will be pretty well up, as, from disaffection and want of spirit and fortitude, the inhabitants, instead of resistence, are offering submission and taking protection from Gen. Howe in Jersey."
A British patrol of dragoons is sent north, up the Delaware River toward Pennington and McConkey's Ferry, and are attacked by a band of Hunterdon County Militia. It is becoming quite unsafe for small bands, patrols, squads, or platoons of British or Hessian troops to reconnoiter, forage, or man outposts in or near the Jersey shores of the Delaware River.

18 December 1776:
Wednesday. The North Carolina Convention adopts a constitution for the state.
In the Delaware River Valley, another British dragoon is killed in an action by about 100 American militia forces, who seek to contain, remove, or destroy these occupiers of the West Jersey areas near the Delaware River.

19 December 1776:
Thursday. When William Howe left Trenton for wintering in New York, he ordered a number of posts to be established in the New Jersey areas that his troops had captured. In particular, he ordered the Hessian regiments to garrison the posts on the east side of the Delaware River. So it is that these posts are occupied by German speaking officers and men who have no understanding of the language or abilities of the American people around them whom they are to patrol and contain.
While out foraging, three grenadiers from a party of the Lossberg Regiment are captured by New Jersey militia.

<u>20 December 1776:</u>

Friday. George Washington makes a visit to a camp eleven miles upriver from the Falls of the Delaware. He returns to William Keith's home at the Upper Falls of the River.

The Second Continental Congress, fearful that the British might try to capture Philadelphia, have fled the city and will reconvene in Baltimore, Maryland, as the Third Continental Congress.

John Sullivan joins Washington with the units of Charles Lee's troops.

Colonel Johann Gottlieb Rall, in command at Trenton, sends a reinforced patrol of Jägers and dragoons four miles north, toward Howell's Ferry, where they are confronted by a body of about 150 Hunterdon County militia, commanded by Captain John Anderson. In the fight that ensues, the Americans lose three or four men, and have to leave the field. However, the nearly constant patrolling and watchfulness required by the occupying Hessian forces, quickly wears them out. They are very tired troops.

<u>21 December 1776:</u>

Saturday. Benjamin Franklin arrives in Paris. He joins Silas Deane and Arthur Lee to form the commission for negotiating treaties with European nations.

At headquarters, Bucks County, Washington writes to Governor Jonathan Trumbull, "When I reflect, upon what our situation in this quarter will be, in ten days from this time; I am almost led to despair. As I said before, I cannot count upon those troops whose time is to expire upon the first of January. I am then left with a few southern regiments, almost reduced to nothing by sickness and fatigue, to oppose the main body of Gen. Howe's army, laying close upon my front, and most assuredly waiting for the dissolution of out army, to make as easy a conquest of the province of Pennsylvania, as they have done of Jersey. I do not find the militia of Pennsylvania inclined to give me as much assistance, as they are able to do, were they willing; tho' I am endeavouring (sic) to bring them out by every means, and am making use of both threats and persuasions to gain my end."

<u>22 December 1776:</u>

Sunday. In Philadelphia, the Secret Committee writes to William Bingham, Captain of the schooner *Lewis*, with instructions on how to dispose of his cargo to the benefit of the Continental service. Bingham is to bring his cargo into a convenient port, and there off-load it in the care of a commissary officer.

In Morristown, New Jersey, Brig. Gen. William Maxwell is placed in charge of all the Continental and militia forces there to harass the British and prevent the locals from seeking the proffered protection from the King's forces.

23 December 1776:
Monday. The Congressional representatives in Europe are authorized to borrow up to two million pounds sterling, as Congress seeks foreign loans to continue the war..

While on a patrol in the vicinity of Mount Holly, New Jersey, German Captain Johann von Ewald, Commander of a Hessian Jäger Company and the British 42nd Regiment is attacked by nearly 800 colonials, under the command of Colonel Griffin. After a few shots are exchanged, the Americans leave the area, overwhelmed by British and Hessian artillery.

24 December 1776:
Tuesday. General George Washington is at the Upper Falls of the Delaware River at the Thompson-Neely House, desperately trying to locate and gather his scattered soldiers and issue orders for reinforcement of his little band of troops. He has divided his small corps into three detachments: one at and around Bristol; another near the Trenton Ferry, nearly opposite Trenton; and the remainder, under his own command to patrol the Ferry crossing north of Trenton. He also knows he has to make a try at some sort of action, or his troops, most of whose enlistments soon expire, will all depart. A thrust of some kind, even if not fully successful, may restore American spirit and cause the state militia to turn out to help.

Washington is beginning to mature the outlines of a plan he has hatched. This evening he rides over to the headquarters of Nathaniel Greene at Samuel Merrick's house. There, at a council of officers that includes John Sullivan, Hugh Mercer, William Alexander, Henry Knox and the Rev. Dr. MacWhorter, a plan is developed to attack the Hessian garrison at Trenton--a plan Washington has been mulling over for the past several days. John Cadwalader is to attack Mount Holly and Bordentown, James Ewing to cross at Trenton Ferry and take position south of the Assunpink Creek, while Washington will attack from the north.

In North Carolina, Robert Caswell is elected Governor by the Provincial Congress under the new state constitution.

25 December 1776:
Wednesday. In London, Major General John Burgoyne is at Brook's Club in the company of his friend, Charles James Fox. The betting book there records an entry that Burgoyne wagers 50 guineas with Fox that by the following year he will return victorious from America. He will not make it.

Having determined upon a plan of attack on the Hessian garrison and other posts on the Delaware River, Washington issues his orders. All the attacks are to be in coordination with his own attack from the north. Both the Cadwalader and Ewing attacks fail, because they are unable to cross the ice-choked Delaware River. The troops under Washington's command, who are to attack Trenton, leave their encampment about 2 o'clock in the afternoon and march to the ferry landing.

This night, with the able assistance of Colonel John Glover's Marbleheaders, Washington crosses the Delaware River at McKonkey's Ferry (now Washington's Crossing) with a part of his army (about 2,400 men) to attack the Hessians stationed at Trenton, NJ. [See Fig. III-17, p. 189].

26 December 1776:
      Thursday. On this morning after Christmas, the troops of George Washington's attack force are rowed and poled over the Delaware River in Durham boats. In spite of the bitter cold, the ice choked river, and a storm of rain, sleet and snow, they make it to the New Jersey side with artillery and horses about 3 o'clock.

There are two roads, nearly parallel to the river leading southwesterly into Trenton. Nathanael Greene is assigned the upper, or most northerly road, the Pennington Road. John Sullivan marches along the road nearer the river, the River Road. Washington is greatly concerned about the slow transport across the river and the difficulties in assembling the troops on the Jersey side, as well as the slowness of travel on the icy roads. It is much later in the early morning than he had hoped for. He had wished to attack the Hessians at or near dawn, and now he knows he will not reach the town of Trenton for several hours. He is disturbed that the element of surprise will be lost if he cannot make a dawn attack.

The story that the Hessians were all drunk and drowsy on this day after Christmas, is largely a fiction. After more than a week of constant patroling, fatigue duty, interior guard duty, foraging for grains, corn, and food, message carrying, and scouting duties, they are all physically exhausted and not as alert and combat ready as is desired. There has been little opportunity for rest among these troops. Besides, their Commander, Colonel Johann Gottlieb Rall, is not awed by the rebels. He dismisses them as a group of undisciplined rabble who present little threat to his trained and well-ordered troops. Although his post at Trenton is isolated, and therefore a candidate for attack, Rall fails to follow orders to fortify and prepare defenses at the place for which he is responsible. He spends a good part of the night in gaming at cards and jesting with his officers.

As the Americans approach Trenton on the Pennington Road, a guard challenges them. But, his musket flashes in the pan. He is overwhelmed and captured. The two wings of the American force converge on the garrison about 8 o'clock, the Greene Division quickly firing a battery of cannon down the main King and Queen Streets. At nearly the same time the Sullivan Division delivers a flanking fire into the Hessian troops, who have turned out rapidly. Hessian guns attempting to go into action are silenced by Captain Alexander Hamilton's artillery company. The Hessians attempt to counterattack, but are stopped before they get into bayonet range. Americans push the Hessians east to surrender about 9:30 o'clock. Having captured nearly 920 prisoners, who are quickly rowed back

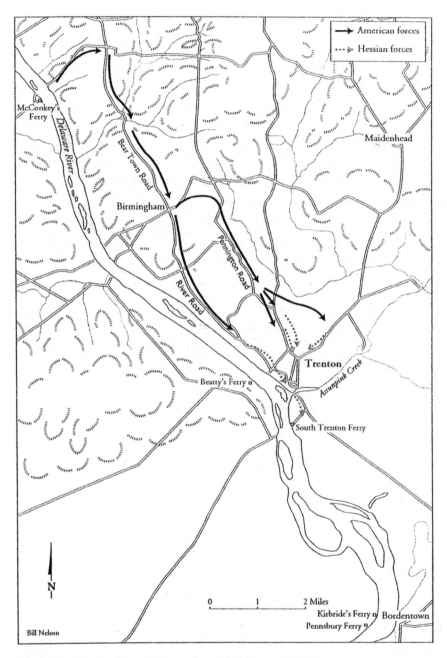

Fig. III-17: Battle of Trenton, 26 Dec. 1776

across the Delaware River at the two Trenton ferries, the Americans tend to the wounded. [See Fig. III-17, p. 189].

27 December 1776:
    Friday. The Americans who have won the Battle of Trenton, without the support of either Cadwalader or Ewing, withdraw across the river. Washington returns over the Delaware, and makes his headquarters at Newtown, Pennsylvania, at Mrs. John Harris's home.
    At headquarters, Newtown, Washington writes to John Hancock, President of Congress, "I have the pleasure of congratulating you upon the success of an enterprise, which I had formed against a Detachment of the enemy lying in Trenton, and which was executed yesterday morning. Finding from our disposition, that they were surrounded, and that they must inevitably be cut to pieces if they made any further resistance, they agreed to lay down their arms."
    In Baltimore, the Congress resolves to raise 16 regiments At Large (not all from any one state, but mixed locales, without any state designation) . These will not be numbered units, but will be designated by the names of their Colonels.

28 December 1776:
    Saturday. The Congress, concerned about the possibility of another British advance upon the Lake Champlain route toward Albany, requests that Philip Schuyler build two floating batteries on the lake to cover the boom. They also order that the committee for supplying cannon be directed to procure ten six-inch brass howitzers, with shells, and a proper attrail (the trail part of a cannon used for transport and stability while firing) for use by the Northern Army and that a Fort be constructed on the east side of the lake opposite Fort Ticonderoga, on Mount Independence.

29 December 1776:
    Sunday. At Newtown, Washington writes to the President of Congress, "I am just setting out to attempt a second passage over the Delaware, with the troops that were with me on the morning of the 26th. I am determined to effect it, if possible but know that it will be attended with much fatigue and difficulty, on account of the ice, which will neither allow us to cross on foot or give us an easy passage for the boats. Genl. [John] Cadwalader crossed from Bristol on the 27th. And by his letter of yesterday, was at Bordentown with about eighteen hundred men. In addition to these Gen. Mifflin sent over five hundred from Philadelphia on Friday, three hundred yesterday evening from Burlington, and will follow today with 700 or 800 more. I have taken every precaution in my power for subsisting of the troops, and shall without loss of time and as soon as circumstances will admit of, pursue the enemy in their retreat, try to beat up more of their quarters and in a word, in every instance adopt such measures as the exigency of our affairs

requires and our situation will justify. What was done, occasioned the enemy to leave their several posts on the Delaware with great precipitation. The peculiar distresses to which the troops who were with me were reduced, by the severities of cold, rain, snow, and storm; the charge of the prisoners they had taken ... would not authorize a further pursuit at that time."

In Baltimore, the Congress resolves itself into a Committee of the Whole for the purpose of taking into consideration the report of the committee on a plan for obtaining foreign assistance.

30 December 1776:
Monday. General George Washington re-crosses the Delaware River and occupies the town of Trenton, setting up headquarters at the home of a Loyalist, John Barnes.

In Baltimore, the Congress resolves to send commissioners to Austria, Prussia, Spain, and Tuscany for the purpose of soliciting support and assistance.

31 December 1776:
Tuesday. At Trenton, Washington writes to Maj. Gen. William Heath, "Your exertions to secure the arms, accoutrements, ammunition &c can't be too great. It must be done. You need not take any notice of the order for stopping a dollar from those who had arms found 'em. The stoppage would be of little consequence to the states, and an injury to individuals, many of whom perhaps had it not in their power to procure arms. Before this, I expect some of Colo. Knox's officers will have got to Peekskill, having been sent to recruit for the artillery and with proper instructions respecting that department and that also of the artificers."

Requiring troops for a few weeks more, Washington uses persuasion to get a majority of his men to re-enlist. British forces, aroused by his defeat and capture of Trenton, march under Charles Cornwallis towards Washington and his army.

Washington writes to Robert Morris, "Our affairs are at present in a most delicate, tho' I hope a fortunate situation. But the great and radical evil ... here again shows its hateful influence. Tomorrow the Continental Troops are all at Liberty. I wish to push our success to keep up the panic and in order to get their assistance have promised them a bounty of 10 dollars if they will continue for one month. But here again a new difficulty presents itself—we have not money to pay the bounty, and we have exhausted our credit ... Sir, to give us assistance, do it; borrow money where it can be done. We are doing it upon our private credit. Every man of interest and every lover of his country must strain his credit upon such an occasion."

The year 1776 proves a most momentous one for the War of the American Revolution! A new Continental Army is created, albeit only for a one-year period.

Boston is evacuated by the British, who have occupied it for several years, the idea of independency grows into an actual approval of a resolution by the Continental Congress, followed by a Declaration and a statement of purpose, which, until recognized by England, will cause the war to continue.

An attempt is made to defend New York City, the American army is defeated, the City occupied by the British. Washington is then outflanked by the British Army, placed always on the defensive, pushed across Westchester County, and escapes to New Jersey.

The American forts on both sides of the Hudson River, Fort Washington and Fort Lee, are lost to the British, one by attack and the other by being abandoned as untenable. These are major losses to the American army.

However, General Washington manages to stay a few steps ahead of the British, and keeps a small and dwindling army intact, as he makes the long retreat across New Jersey. This force in being requires the British to react, rather than plan any strategy that might effectively win the physical contest.

Washington keeps his small army intact--and that threatens the British and their German allies. Across New Jersey, he manages to keep ahead of his pursuers, gets to the Delaware River, crosses, secures all the boats to deny any to the enemy. He worries about how he will, yet again, build one army while discharging another at the end of the year.

At near year's end, the British seek to go into winter quarters, hold the territory they have captured, and rest their troops while thinking about the next campaign period. Washington, aware that he must strike a blow, succeeds with his brilliant crossing of the Delaware River and attack upon the Hessians at Trenton.

The Bibliography lists works that give a good overview of this year of 1776, both its glory and its disappointments: Fleming, Thomas J., *1776: Year of Illusions*,; McCullough, David, *1776: America and Britain at War*; Mires, Charlene, *Independence Hall in American Memory*; Taylor, Robert T, Editor, *Papers of John Adams*, v. 5; Lefkowitz, Arthur S., *The Long Retreat: The Calamitous Defense of New Jersey, 1776*; Fitzpatrick, John C., Editor, *The Writings of George Washington*, v. 6.

IV. The Year 1777

1 January 1777:

Wednesday. The German officers captured at the Battle of Trenton on 26 December 1776 are taken to Major General Israel Putnam, who receives them hospitably. They are housed temporarily in Philadelphia.

Lord Charles Cornwallis marches down hurriedly from New Brunswick to Princeton with reinforcements and a strong desire to defeat the rebel forces at Trenton. Washington, with good and reliable intelligence, dispatches Brig. Gen. Matthias Alexis Roche de Fermoy to execute delaying actions against the British on their move toward Trenton. A defensive covering position is set up by the Americans at Five-Mile Run, about one mile south of Maidenhead, New Jersey.

2 January 1777:

Thursday. Near mid-morning, the British advance guard runs into the American covering force at Five-Mile Run. Fermoy returns to Trenton, and the command devolves upon Colonel Edward Hand, who with his Pennsylvania riflemen seriously delays the enemy attack, and forces it to waste time in deploying at each fold in the ground. Hand falls back, taking advantage of every ground cover he finds, setting up another defense position at Shabakunk Run. Again he slows the British advance, costing them large losses of both troops and time. He then falls back to Stockton Hollow, near the outskirts of Trenton, and sets up still another defense position. With each re-deployment, the British are slowed, until they finally reach Trenton.

General George Washington has his troops encamped south of the Assunpink Creek. The running battle has been called the Second Battle of Trenton. Cornwallis arrives late in the day, with plans to attack the Americans in the morning. General Washington is well aware that he cannot stand up to the superior numbers and discipline of Cornwallis' troops. Providentially, Washington learns of a back way around Cornwallis' flank. That night, Washington's troops leave their campfires burning, fooling the enemy into believing that they have dug in for battle tomorrow and are bedding down for the night, while they are actually slipping away toward Princeton.

3 January 1777:

Friday. Earl Cornwallis, on his way, has left Lieutenant Colonel Charles Mawhood as a rear guard at Princeton, as Cornwallis, with the main body of the British forces rushes on toward Trenton. In the morning Cornwallis is very surprised to discover that the American force he felt that he had in the bag last evening, has disappeared. How is it possible, he wonders, that a worn-out, force of rebels could vanish so completely, and where had they gone?

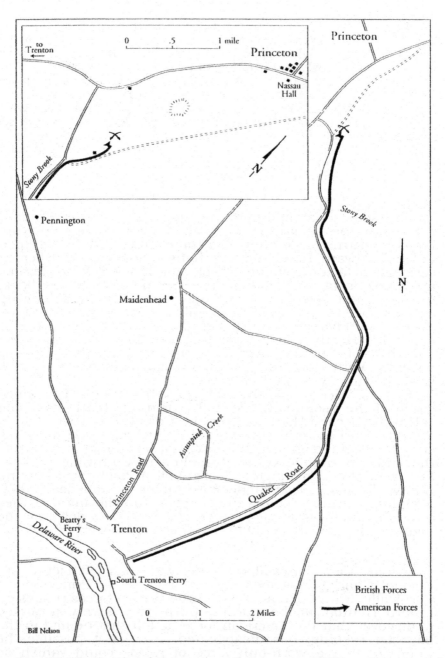

Fig. IV-18: Battle of Princeton, 3 January 1777

Washington, using the back roads he had scouted, has marched his entire force towards Princeton in the wee hours of the morning. His advance stumbles into Mawhood's Brigade marching toward Trenton.

The Battle of Princeton [See Fig. IV-18, p. 194] results in a victory for the Americans as they recover from an early attack by Mawhood. Brigadier General Hugh Mercer blunts the British attack, is fatally wounded in the defense of his position, and dies a few days later.

Sweeping across Stony Brook Road, up the Back Road, Americans forces pursue Mawhood's troops into Princeton and then northeast as they retreat towards Brunswick. British losses are about 550, including nearly 300 prisoners. The Americans lose about 50 men. A further strike at Brunswick is deemed too much of a stretch, and the last American troops withdraw from Princeton in the afternoon, just as the British vanguard appears on the other side of town. Following a short exchange of fire, the Americans march toward Morristown, New Jersey, leaving their pursuers unable to follow, because the Americans have destroyed the bridge over the Millstone River. American forces spend the night encamped near Somerset Courthouse, which the rear guard does not reach until nearly 11 o'clock in the evening.

4 January 1777:

Saturday. At Maidenhead, New Jersey, Captain John Stryker, leading a body of Somerset County mounted militia, attacks a British convoy and captures a number of supply wagons.

Near Brunswick, New Jersey, Thomas Rodney, a Colonel of Delaware militia, who has been keeping a diary, writes, "At daylight this morning our army was put in motion and passed on towards Brunswick and crossed the Raritan over a bridge 6 miles about that Town, but the General found the army was too much fatigued to attempt Brunswick as the enemy's main body were so close after us, he therefore changed his course and went on to a place called Pluckemin situated among the mountains of Jersey about 10 miles from the last place. Here he was obliged to encamp and await the coming up of nearly 1,000 men who were not able through fatigue and hunger to keep up with the main body, for they had not had any refreshment for two days past and as all our baggage had been left at Trenton the army in this situation was obliged to encamp on the bleak mountains whose tops were covered with snow, without even blankets to cover them. Most of this army were militia and they bore all this with a spirit becoming Freemen and Americans." While this is a militia officer writing these words, it is instructive that he has a view of such troops as steadfast and faithful.

At Baltimore, Maryland, the Congress resolves that Benjamin Brannon be appointed a signer of the continental bills of credit.

5 January 1777:
    Sunday. From Paris, William Lee writes to the Committee
of Foreign Affairs, reporting that he is of the opinion that the
King of Prussia is supportive of the independence of America,
and awaits only the example of the French court to act. Lee is
also uncertain of the Spanish position, saying they seem to be
interested, but invest a great deal of time delaying any
decision.
    At Rahway, New Jersey, a small American militia body
attacks a British foraging detachment, forcing them to
abandon collecting hay and straw. These constant harassing
skirmishes severely hamper British efforts to provide forage
for their animals.

6 January 1777:
    Monday. In Philadelphia, the German officers captured at
Trenton leave, under guard, for Baltimore where the Congress
is in session.
    At Morristown, New Jersey, General George Washington
makes his headquarters at the Arnold Tavern on the west side
of the green. The American Army will winter at an
encampment near here.
    In northeastern New Jersey, American detachments
capture the villages of Hackensack and Elizabethtown.
    Thus, Washington has driven Sir William Howe and his
forces out of the state, except for the posts at Perth Amboy
and New Brunswick, each garrisoned by a body of about
5,000 men.

7 January 1777:
    Tuesday. At Baltimore, the Congress resolves itself into a
committee of the whole to take into consideration a
proposition for setting on foot an expedition against Nova
Scotia. They debate this problem, come to a resolution and
write a report which is to lie on the table until tomorrow.

8 January 1777:
    Wednesday. From Versailles, King Louis XVI writes to
Charles III, King of Spain, "England our common and
inveterate enemy has been engaged for three years in a war
with her American Colonies. We had agreed not to meddle
with it, and viewing both sides as English, we made our trade
free to the one that found most advantage in a commercial
intercourse. In this manner America provided herself with
arms and ammunition, of which she was destitute. I do not
speak of the succors of money and other kinds which we have
given her, the whole, ostensibly, on the score of trade.
England has taken umbrage at these succors, and has not
concealed from us that she would be revenged sooner or later.
She has already, indeed, seized several of our merchant
vessels, and refused restitution. We have lost no time on our
part. We have fortified our most exposed colonies and placed

our fleets upon a respectable footing, which has contributed to aggravate the ill humor of England. America is triumphant [The King is referring to the evacuation of Boston], and England cast down; but the latter has still a great unbroken maritime force, and the hope of forming a beneficial alliance with her Colonies, the impossibility of their being subdued by arms being now demonstrated. They [by which he means the English] will fall upon us in as great strength as if the war had not existed. This being understood, and our grievances against England notorious, I have thought, after taking the advice of my council ..., and having consulted upon the propositions which the insurgents [by which he means America] make that it was just and necessary to begin to treat with them, to prevent their reunion with the mother country."

The Congress, in Baltimore, takes up the issue of an expedition upon Nova Scotia, and resolves, "That the council of the State of Massachusetts Bay be desired to attend to the situation of the enemy in the province of Nova Scotia, and, if they are of opinion that an advantageous attack in the course of the winter or early spring may be made on Fort Cumberland and the said province, whereby the enemy's dockyard and other works ... they are hereby impowered to conduct the same in behalf of these united States ..."

9 January 1777:
Thursday. The Congress resolves that the directors of the military hospitals throughout the army make returns in each of the departments of the kind and quantity of medicines, instruments, and hospital furniture that remain on hand.

10 January 1777:
Friday. The Congress resolves to send $300,000 to Ebenezer Hancock, the Deputy Paymaster General in the Eastern Department, for the purpose of paying the bounties and defraying the expenses of raising the new levies in that department.

11 January 1777:
Saturday. Concerned about a problem of some post riders and deputy post masters, who, it is said, are being disaffected to the American cause, the Congress resolves that the Postmaster General list the names of such persons in these positions. The purpose of this resolution is so that authorities may identify such post riders, and determine how best to deal with them. Such persons, who may be disaffected, carrying mail, much of which may have sensitive military or political intelligence is extremely dangerous to the cause of American Independence. If such information should fall into the hands of the British, very serious consequences could develop. Congress has a very sore spot when it comes to Loyalists.

They are seen as enemies, and are to be controlled in ways
that prohibit them from assisting the British.

12 January 1777:
    Sunday. At York, Pennsylvania, John Witherspoon and
James Lovell write to the American commissioners in Paris,
expressing concern over the loss of important papers,
intended to be delivered by Captain John Folger. Suspecting
Folger of theft and spying, they order that he be confined. The
entire issue of transporting sensitive diplomatic materials
across the ocean comes under review. Such papers are so
important, and their contents so critical to secrecy that the
Congress must devise some means of seeing that they are
handled with great care.

13 January 1777:
    Monday. The Congress at Baltimore, empowers the Marine
Committee, still in Philadelphia, to purchase the prize sloop of
war captured by the *Andrea Doria*, with her guns, apparel,
and furniture, and fit her out as a Continental cruiser.
    From Hartford, Connecticut, John Adams writes to his
wife Abigail, on his way to return to the Congress, reporting
that the riding has been so hard, and the weather so cold
they could push no farther. He also notes they are cheered by
information that Washington has gained another victory.

14 January 1777:
    Tuesday. By the evening of this day, Captain Lewis
Farmer, in command of the German prisoners captured at
Trenton, with about 50 German officers, non-commissioned
officers, and soldiers, arrives in Baltimore, where he is able to
quarter his charges until further disposition is made for them.

15 January 1777:
    Wednesday. At Morristown, Washington is pleased that
the local New Jersey militia now turns out to harass the
enemy in the way the General had in mind. Only a few weeks
earlier, when the British were seemingly invincible and in
control, many people applied to them for the pardons Howe
held out. But the British and Hessian atrocities, combined
with Washington's recent victories have reanimated patriot
hearts. Most of the state is back in American hands, and its
residents now exhibit a renewed commitment to the patriot
cause. New Jersey militiamen, under the capable direction of
Brigadier General Philemon Dickinson, raid, harass, surprise,
skirmish, attack, capture, and demoralize the enemy at every
opportunity. Some historians now call this the "Forage War."
It keeps the enemy off balance at a time of winter rest and
refitting because it is so difficult to engage in actual military
maneuver and travel. At the same, time it fuels the physical
and psychological needs of the Americans.

In Baltimore, this morning Captain Farmer is able to turn his German prisoners, captured at Trenton, over to the Board of War.

16 January 1777:
Thursday. Congress forms a committee of seven to enquire into and report upon the conduct of British and Hessian officers towards the officers, soldiers, and marines in the service of the United States, and any other inhabitants of these states, in their (British or German) control as prisoners of war. The committee is to collect data not only of the conduct of such enemy officers to patriot military personnel, but to determine also how the civil citizen subjects of the states and their property are treated.

17 January 1777:
Friday. Washington instructs Brigadier General William Heath to attack the Hessian garrison at Fort Independence, north of King's Bridge, New York. Four separate columns, totaling nearly 6,000 men, advance upon the position, defended by about 2,000 Hessians. Heath orders the garrison to surrender, and is refused. The Americans are attacked by the Hessian and flee during a rain storm.

18 January 1777:
Saturday. At headquaters in Morristown, Washington writes to Philip Schuyler, "The enemy, by two lucky strokes at Trenton and Princeton, have been obliged to abandon every part of Jersey, except Brunswick and Amboy and the small tract of country between them, which is so intirely exhausted of supplies of every kind, that I hope, by preventing them from sending their foraging parties to any great distance, to reduce them to the utmost distress, in the course of this winter. Colo. Dayton arrived from the northward a few days ago; he informs me that the time of most of his regiment expires in February; but that they are extremely anxious to get down to this part of the country, where many of them have families and connections, who they suppose must have suffered many hardships, as the enemy were for some time in possession of the country and committed every kind of depredation upon the inhabitants; he thinks, if they were brought down here, before they are discharged, that most of them might be induced to inlist (sic) for the war, which would be a thing to be wished for, as I am told they are a fine body of men and well acquainted with this country, which will in all probability by the scene of action next campaign."
At Baltimore, the German prisoners, captured at the Battle of Trenton, depart under Lieutenant John Lindenburger, on their way to Dumfries in Prince William County, Virginia, where they will be imprisoned.

19 January 1777:
    Sunday. From Poughkeepsie, New York, John Adams writes to Abigail, telling her he could not cross the Hudson River at the lower ferry slips because of too much floating ice. Instead, he and his party had to ride north to Poughkeepsie to cross on the ice. Adams also reports that Washington is at Morristown, New Jersey, and Cornwallis at New Brunswick.

20 January 1777:
    Monday. Two miles from Somerset Courthouse, New Jersey, near Abraham Van Nest's mill, militia Brigadier General Philemon Dickinson, commanding about 400 New Jersey troops and 50 or more Pennsylvania riflemen, attack and flank a British detachment of about 550 troops, out from New Brunswick on a foraging expedition. At what is now known as the Battle of Millstone, the Americans defeat the British, taking baggage wagons, horses, cattle, and sheep, and kill or wound 25, while losing only five of their own.

21 January 1777:
    Tuesday. Congress resolves that the 8th Virginia regiment, now in South Carolina, be ordered to return to Virginia, there to be fully recruited and marched when complete, as fast as possible, to join General George Washington at Morristown, New Jersey.

22 January 1777:
    Wednesday. In Baltimore, John Hancock writes to the Maryland Council of Safety, "I have it in Charge from Congress most earnestly to request that you will immediately appoint Subaltern Officers for the several Companies which are now raising in our State in Consequence of your Orders, that the recruiting Service may be expedited as fast as possible, and the Men raised be properly trained. The enclosed Resolve recommending it to you to call forth the Militia from the Counties therein mentioned, and such others as you shall think proper, to reinforce Genl. Washington at this critical Period."

23 January 1777:
    Thursday. At Quibbletown (now Newmarket), New Jersey, a body of 350 Virginia Troops attack two British regiments of nearly 600 men in total, assisting with a forage party, with heavy loss to the enemy. It is not safe for the enemy to send small, unprotected patrols, or forage parties, or even persons out for a ride or a visit without a flag or a large escort of troops, because they will be pounced upon by the Americans.
    At headquarters, Morristown, George Washington writes to Brigadier General John Cadwalader, "March your brigade from hence to Chatham or posts below that. Consult with Genls. Sullivan and Stephen upon the propriety of an attempt

upon any of the enemy's posts or giving them a formidable alarm; and, if you should find a willingness in your officers and men to the undertaking of any practicable scheme, do not omit, in conjunction with the troops at the posts of the Chatham & ca. to prosecute it. Genl. Sullivan is already wrote (sic) to on this head."

Brigadier General Philemon Dickinson writes to Colonel John Nielson, "I have the pleasure to inform you that on Monday last with about 450 men, chiefly our militia I attacked a foraging party near Van Nest Mills consisting of 500 men with 2 field pieces, which we routed after an engagement of 20 minutes. Brought off 107 horses, 49 wagons, 115 cattle, 70 sheep, 40 barrels of flour, 106 bags, and many other things, 49 prisoners."

24 January 1777:
Friday. Aware that certain tribes of Indians, in or near the headwaters of the Susquehanna River, are on their way to Easton, Pennsylvania, for a conference, the Congress resolves that $1,000 be delivered to George Walton and George Taylor, agents, for the purchase of presents for said Indians. And further, the Congress reminds these agents, to tell the Indians to remain peaceable and friendly.

25 January 1777:
Saturday. From the War Office at Baltimore, the Board of War writes to the Executive Committee (the Congress being adjourned, and its President, John Hancock, being ill with the gout), referring to a part of a letter relating to the removal of military stores from Philadelphia to Baltimore. They say such a step would be attended with injurious consequences to the cause, premature, and might render the patriots contemptible in the eyes of the enemy. They further note that Maj. Gen. Israel Putnam is at Princeton with about 6,000 troops, and another 3,000 are in Philadelphia. The British have been largely chased from New Jersey, and are harried whenever they leave their posts at New Brunswick or Amboy.

26 January 1777:
Sunday. In Philadelphia, the Executive Committee writes to John Hancock, enclosing letters and reporting that while there are a goodly number of arms currently at hand, these arms have been put into the hands of militia, and are thus scattered. The Committee suggests some efficacious method be adopted to draw these weapons into public arsenals, from which they may be issued as needed, and repaired and stored while awaiting issue.

27 January 1777:
Monday. In Philadelphia, the Executive Committee again writes to John Hancock, expressing concern over the issuing,

repair, and supply of the small arms belonging to the
continental service. They reinforce the idea of controlling this
musketry, i.e., public arsenals in which to house them,
gunsmiths to repair them, and requirements to deposit them
when not in service.

28 January 1777:
   Tuesday. The Secret Committee informs Congress of a
fraud in the shipping trade of a certain Captain William Bayly,
who sold a valuable cargo of American goods at Hispaniola
intended for St. Eustatia, then made a voyage to France and
traded a second cargo, and thence reloaded with goods, came
to Baltimore. Bayly claimed he sold the vessel, and received
no monies for all these transactions. But he has a residue of
£2,500 cash in hand. The Secret Committee is empowered to
judge and punish this offender in the public interest.

29 January 1777:
   Wednesday. The Congress approves of the actions of the
commissioners for Indian Affairs in the Middle Department,
who acted prudently to call in forces for protection and
defense at Fort Pitt against some tribes of Indians about
whom they have cause to be apprehensive.
   At headquarters in Morristown. George Washington writes
to the Pennsylvania Council of Safety, "I am glad to find, that
your House of Assembly are about framing a law, to make
your Militia turn out more generally; till that is done, the
service falls particularly upon a few individuals; who
complain, with great justice, of risquing (sic) their lives in
defence of those who upon your present plan, do not even
make a pecuniary satisfaction for the exemption of their
persons. But I would wish to see every man ... obliged to turn
out, when the good of his country demands it. For now we
want more men than money."

30 January 1777:
   Thursday. At Morristown, General Orders state "The
commanding officers of the regiments and corps lately come
in, are to make themselves acquainted with the General
Orders, which have been issued for the Government of the
Army at this place, and to attend to them, particularly those
... respecting the assignment of parades, and assembling the
troops in case of alarms." The parole is given as Quebec and
the countersign as Rahway.
   Congress resolves to send $300,000 to Jonathan
Trumbull, Jr. deputy paymaster for the Northern department
for his use in procuring supplies. Trumbull is a fine Patriot,
the son of the Governor of Connecticut, and brother of John
Trumbull, the painter. He is probably responsible for keeping
the Continental Army supplied in these early years.

31 January 1777:
  Friday. In Baltimore, Benjamin Rush writes to his wife Julia, reporting upon the circumstances of his housing arrangements and about the other boarders. He notes, in particular, a French officer, who is one of 21 children!

  From headquarters at Morristown, a circular letter to the states is sent out from Washington, "The great countenance and protection shewn and given to deserters by persons in the different neighbourhoods, from whence they originally come, has made that vice so prevalent in the army, that unless some very effectual measures are fallen upon to prevent it, our new army will scarcely be raised, before it will again dwindle and waste away from that cause alone. I know of no remedy, so effectual, as for the different states immediately to pass Laws, laying a very severe penalty upon those who harbour or fail to give information against deserters, knowing them to be such ..."

1 February 1777:
  Saturday. At Drake's Farm, near Metuchen, New Jersey, a regiment of Virginia Continentals attack a British force gathering hay. It is a trap in which the Americans find themselves up against two brigades. Nevertheless, they fight doggedly, forcing the enemy to flee the field, with a loss of more than 100 casualties, against an American loss of about 35 men.

  The state of Maryland has a problem with Tories in the Eastern Shore counties of Somerset and Worcester. The Congress resolves that the State send artillery and militia to seize, secure, and suppress Tories named in a listing, and all others in the counties who shall appear to have been the leaders of a Tory faction there. Further, that a day be given for all the inhabitants of said counties to assemble at appointed places and take the oath of allegiance required by the state. Any that refuse shall be disarmed.

2 February 1777:
  Sunday. At headquarters, Morristown, Washington prepares orders for Lieutenant Colonel Adam Comstock, "You will proceed to Rhode Island and use your utmost industry and influence in raising the regiment on the Continental establishment to which you was [sic] appointed by the Genl. Assembly of that State, on the condition and terms prescribed by Resolve of Congress on that subject. You will appoint some place to wch [sic] the recruits may conveniently repair to be disciplined, and omit no opportunity of informing me of your success in this business."

  In Baltimore, Maryland, John Adams writes to his wife Abigail, noting that he arrived the previous day, after what he reported as "... the longest journey and through the worst roads and the worst weather that I have ever experienced."

3 February 1777:
    Monday. In Baltimore, John Adams writes to James Warren, reporting upon the situations and conditions of people and places in some of the states, about which he has learned, as follows; the part of New York still in patriot possession seems pretty well united, the Jerseys are lending much assistance (the Forage War), the Pennsylvania Assembly is gradually acquiring the confidence of the people. Delaware has written and adopted a Constitution, Governor Patrick Henry of Virginia has recovered his health, North Carolina has completed the organization of its Government, South Carolina and Georgia have done likewise.

4 February 1777:
    Tuesday. John Adams and James Lovell, delegates from Massachusetts, attend the Congress and take their seats. So does Thomas Burke, a delegate from North Carolina.

5 February 1777:
    Wednesday. A memorial of Gotlieb Klose, native of Silesia and late missionary of the United Brethren to the Negroes on the island of Jamaica, is read, stating that he was transported to Bristol in the snow *Thomas*, Thomas Nicholson, master, by the Continental cruiser *Andrea Doria*. He prays that his effects, consisting of the tools of his trade and clothing, may be restored to him. The Congress grants his prayer.

6 February 1777:
    Thursday. At Morristown, Washington orders that all the soldiers in the camps, who have not previously had the smallpox (giving them immunity), or have not previously been inoculated against the disease, be now inoculated.
    The Congress resolves that the Secret Committee be directed to procure a supply of arms and clothing for the Continental forces raised in the state of Georgia, for the defense of that state. They also prepare forms for the passport of vessels, allowing these vessels to pass and proceed on their voyage, and another for a certificate for vessels, stating that they have been inspected.

7 February 1777:
    Friday. Congress orders that several sums of money be paid to various vendors and suppliers, among these one Robert Aitken, for paper, inkstands, quills, and sealing wax for the use of the Treasury Office amounting to 14 pounds, 0 shillings, 11 pence, or 37 41/90 dollars. (See the sketch for 13 September 1776 for an explanation of the odd fractions.)

8 February 1777:
    Saturday. At Quibbletown, New Jersey, a goodly size force of British and Hessian battalions battle a mixed force of

American Continentals and militia, resulting in a draw. The point, however, is that the enemy is not free to wander or forage about at pleasure. They will be attacked at every opportunity.

From headquarters in Morristown, George Washington writes to Brigadier General Holden Parsons, "... I do not know at this time what can be better done in that quarter, than adopting the plan you propose, of crossing over to the east end of Long Island and destroying the forage. I am so fully convinced of the good effects of the enterprize (sic) that I have ordered it to be done, generally, in the neighbourhood (sic) of the enemy here... General Schuyler seems to be under great apprehension about Ticonderoga, he has too much cause. I intend that the garrison at that place shall come from the Eastern Troops. Your attack therefore upon Long Island must not take up time, lest engaged there th service may suffer more considerably elsewhere."

9 February 1777:
Sunday. From Baltimore, John Hancock writes to Robert Treat Paine in Boston, noting that the removal of Congress from Philadelphia and the consequent slowing down, even stagnation of business is the cause of much delay in the conduct of business in the Congress. Not all the delegates are present and too many committees are short of the men required to complete their reports.

10 February 1777:
Monday. Congress recommends to the Council of Safety of Maryland that it seek to prevent the sailing of all Chesapeake provision vessels, while the enemy's ships of war infest the bay, since it is apprehended that these provisions might fall into the possession of the enemy, to the detriment of the cause, and loss thereof to the army as well as to the citizenry of the area.

11 February 1777:
Tuesday. The Congress appoints a committee of seven to devise ways and means of supporting the credit of the Continental currency. Named to this committee are Benjamin Harrison, Thomas Burke, Roger Sherman, Samuel Chase, William Ellery, Arthur Middleton, and Nathan Brownson.

12 February 1777:
Wednesday. At headquarters in Morristown, Washington writes to Brig. Gen. William Maxwell, "These fellows at Elizabeth Town, as well as all others who wish to remain with us, for no other purpose than to convey intelligence to the enemy, and poison our people's minds, must and shall be compelled to withdraw immediately within the enemy's lines; who are hesitating which side to take and behave friendly to

us, till they determine, must be treated with lenity. Such as
go over to the enemy, are not tp take with them any thing but
thier clothing and furniture, their horses, cattle and forage
must be left behind. Such as incline to share our fate, are to
have every assistance afforded them that can be granted with
safety ..."

The Medical Committee is ordered to write to General
George Washington regarding the inoculation of such troops
as have not had the smallpox, and seek his thoughts on how
best to do this, consistent with the public safety. It should be
recalled that inoculated persons, until they are completely
healed, are still infectious, and are thus a potential danger to
others, and these infectious persons must be confined for a
period.

13 February 1777:
    Thursday. Concerned about deserters from the service, the
Congress orders that those Articles of War that address the
issue of desertion and the Congress' most recent resolution
on this matter, be printed and widely distributed. This, it is
hoped, will give the troops first-hand information about how
they are to conduct themselves as soldiers.

14 February 1777:
    Friday. The Congress, after some discussion, raises the
pay of certain listed staff officers in the Continental service. In
too many cases, it is proving difficult to recruit specialized
people into the Continental Army because the pay and
emoluments are seen as being too low.

15 February 1777:
    Saturday. The committee reviewing the report of the four
New England states presents their report, which is considered
by the Congress. It highly approves of the measure therein
which regulates the price of goods and produce that remedies
"... the evils occasioned by the present fluctuating and
exorbitant prices ..." The Congress therefore recommends that
a similar group be formed by the states of New York, New
Jersey, Pennsylvania, Delaware, Maryland, and Virginia, to
meet at York, Pennsylvania; and another group from North
Carolina, South Carolina, and Georgia to meet at Charleston,
South Carolina, for the same purpose.

16 February 1777:
    Sunday. At Passy, France, Benjamin Franklin, Silas
Deane, and Arthur Lee write to the Committee of Foreign
Affairs, forwarding the Treaties of Amity and Alliance. These
two treaties have two important political values for America.
One, the treaty dealing with amity, is an expression of
friendship between the two nations, and the opening of easy
commerce between them. The other, the treaty of alliance, is a

compact to form as allies against Britain, with the end being the independence of the United States. Franklin, Deane, and Lee hope the Congress will approve the terms of these two treaties and ratify them as soon as possible.

17 February 1777:
    Monday. In Baltimore, the Congress resolves, "That Congress do approve of the attention which General Schuyler has given to secure the friendship of the Six Indian Nations towards these States, and the measures which he is taking to defeat the evil designs of our enemies, who, with unremitting cruelty, are endeavouring to precipitate these Indians into a war against us."

18 February 1777:
    Tuesday. General George Washington is directed to cause an enquiry to be made into the military abilities and conduct of the French gentlemen in the army, and how far they can be usefully employed in the service of these states. He is to dismiss such of them as he shall find unworthy of commissions, or unable to render service in the military line, because of their incomplete command of the English language.

19 February 1777:
    Wednesday. At headquarters, Morristown, Washington writes to George Clinton at New Windsor, New York, "Information ... that many of the inhabitants, living near the Passaick Falls, are busily employed in removing their provision and forage within the enemy's reach, with the design of supplying them, obliges me to beg the favor of you to let me know what success you have experienced in collecting the troops voted by the Convention of the State of New York. The presence of some men in that neighbourhood [sic], would be attended with much good; add to this, the well grounded probability that the enemy will make some movement soon, and you will, I am satisfied, use your utmost exertions to bring a reinforcement to our assistance. At present I cannot check the above mentioned practice, least the detachment sent that way, may be more wanted for other purposes than this. I therefore wish that some of your troops would take that duty off my hands, and that you would further enable me to oppose any designs of the enemy."
    Troops raised in Virginia for the Continental Army are ordered to march to join Washington's army as soon as possible.

20 February 1777:
    Thursday. The Congress feels that the only weapon they have available to "...teach their enemies to regard the Law of Nations and the rights of humanity ..." regarding the

treatment of American prisoners in British captivity is retaliation. Therefore, they order the Board of War to take five Hessian field officers and Colonel Campbell into safe and close custody.

21 February 1777:

Friday. The Board of War writes to General George Washington, reporting that Major General Artemus Ward has declined command of the Eastern Department. Washington is directed to name a successor.

22 February 1777:

Saturday. The Congress orders "That all regiments, companies, or parties of soldiers in their march or in quarters shall be constantly attended by one or more officers of their corps, who shall see that all the regulations ... are strictly complied with, and no injuries or irregularities of any kind committed, as the commanding officer of every party marching or in quarters shall answer the neglect thereof with the forfeiture of his commission."

23 February 1777:

Sunday. At Passy, Benjamin Franklin writes to Arthur Lee, reporting that David Hartley, a British envoy, had informed him that Lord North has brought in two bills before Parliament. One is to renounce all claims of taxation in America. The other to empower commissioners to treat with any person or bodies of men in America on a proposal for peace. Franklin further notes that David Hartley has indicated to him that Lord North desires some accommodation, and would be happy to send emissaries over to Paris to discuss such matters with the American commissioners.

Near Rahway, New Jersey, British Colonel Charles Mawhood, with the Third Brigade and a battalion of grenadiers, makes a sweep into the country to find and defeat a body of American troops. He finds a group of New Jersey militia driving off some cattle and sheep, with a force on a hill behind them. Mawhood attacks the rebel flank, with a company of grenadiers. Suddenly an American force, hidden behind a fence, rises up and fires. The British are outflanked by Continental Brig. Gen. William Maxwell leading a brigade of mixed New Jersey-Pennsylvania troops, including Colonel Edward Hand's regiment of Riflemen. A rifle of those days had an effective range of 150 to 225 yards—about two to three times the effective accurate killing reach of muskets. The British grenadier company soon has no man standing, except its captain, John Peebles, and take to their heels, hobbling and crawling as fast as they can away from the fight. Two additional American regiments appear, and the British are completely defeated, retreating all the way to Amboy, using their forage wagons to carry their wounded. The British loss in this battle is about 85 men. The Americans lose five men killed and nine wounded.

At Amboy, a British Captain, John Peebles, keeps a Diary in which he notes, "The enemy seeing a disposition to march back showed themselves again in our rear which occasioned a counter march to oppose them, but on our facing them they retired with firing a few shot, we moved on again, the men much fatigued & harassed a great many of them quite knock'd up; shortly after we got into the main road the Rebels appear'd in our rear & rear flanks & harassed the Grenadiers that formed the rear guard very much. We were at last obliged to halt & fire some cannon amongst them which set them scampering. As we came near Woodbridge we found a large body of them in a wood posted to oppose us in front. Upon discovering them we fired a few pieces of cannon into the wood and then formed a line in front which moved into the wood & poured in their fire, which made them, the Rebels, quicken their steps to their right ... We then got to the road again & moved on without further molestation & got into Amboy between 7 & 8 o'clock much fatigued."

24 February 1777:
Monday. From headquarters, Morristown, George Washington writes to his brother, John Augustine Washington, "Our scouts and the enemy's foraging parties, have frequent skirmishes; in which they (the enemy) always sustain the greatest loss in killed and wounded, owing to our superior skill in firearms; these, and frequent desertions, tho' not of any great magnitude, serves to waste their army ..."

Congress resolves that all arms or accoutrements belonging to the United States be stamped or marked with the words, "United States."

25 February 1777:
Tuesday. It is represented to the Congress that profaneness in general, and, in particular, cursing and swearing, shamefully prevails in the army. They resolve that General Washington be informed and that he be requested, in concert with his general officers, to take measures for reforming this abuse. A profane army is a poorly disciplined army, and a poorly disciplined army cannot project an image of virtue, and will not win battles, according to the Congress.

26 February 1777:
Wednesday. In Baltimore, William Ellery writes to William Vernon expressing his sorrow that Vernon has had to leave his home, but, says Ellery, "...it is the fortune of war." He goes on to say, "The time is fast approaching when the proud Hierarchy will sink like a Milstone [sic] never to rise any more,

when the Sons of Freedom will triumph over the Minions of arbitrary Power."

27 February 1777:
   Thursday. In Baltimore, the Medical Committee brings in a rather full report which is read and ordered to "lie on the table", meaning the Congress will address the matter at some future time. The Congress, which had left Philadelphia as the British forces were threatening in December 1776, and is currently convened in Baltimore, still for reasons of safety, now concludes that it can safely return to Philadelphia. Therefore, it is resolved that upon adjournment this evening, the Congress will re-assemble to meet in Philadelphia on Wednesday next (5 March 1777). However, the congressmen do not make it, and the next session of the Congress will not be until a week later, on 12 March 1777.
   Robert Morris writes to George Washington, "I do no like to be sanguine, and yet it is necessary in a contest like this we are engaged in to view the best side of the picture frequently. Remember, good Sir, that few men can keep their feelings to themselves, and that it is necessary for example sake, that all leaders should feel and think boldly in order to inspirit those that look up to them. Heaven has blessed you with a firmness of mind, steadiness of countenance, and patience in sufferings, that give you infinite advantages over other men. This being the case, you are not to depend on other people's exertions being equal to your own, one mind feeds and thrives on misfortunes by finding resources to get the better of them; another sinks under their weight, thinking it impossible to resist; and as the latter description probably includes the majority of mankind, we must be cautious on alarming them... But I really think if the brightest side of our affairs were sometimes to be painted by your pen, or sanctified by your name, it would draw forth the exertions of some good men sooner than distress does from others. We have now to lament the absence from the public counsels of America...without any proper appointments to fill their places, and this at the very time they are most wanted ..."

28 February 1777:
   Friday. In Paris, Arthur Lee writes to the Committee of Foreign Affairs, "The journeys I have made both north and south, in the public service, have given me an opportunity of knowing the general disposition of Europe upon our question. There never was one in which the harmony of opinion was so universal; from the prince to the peasant there is but one voice, one wish—the liberty of America, and the humiliation of Great Britain." While Lee has ability, he is probably not the best choice in a diplomatic role, This is because he does not seem to have the personality to deal with many kinds of people, and he can be abusive and unpleasant. This does not fit with the job he is required to do.

1 March 1777:

Saturday. In Baltimore, Richard Henry Lee writes to Robert Morris, enclosing a memoir describing frigates of a new and better design that he hopes will be better than anything the English can have. Such advanced ship designs and construction for America never do come into being during the War of the Revolution.

2 March 1777:

Sunday. In York, Pennsylvania, James Lovell writes to William Bingham, thanking him for his wonderful efforts in saving and forwarding captured British dispatches and letters that fill in much detail not otherwise available to the Committee of Foreign Affairs. Thus it often is that valuable information is obtained during the war.

At Morristown, George Washington writes to Robert Morris, "The freedom with which you have communicated your sentiments on several matters ... is highly pleasing to me. Letters, however, being liable to various accidents, makes a communication of thoughts that way, rather unsafe: but, as this will be conveyed by a gentleman on whom I can depend, I shall not scruple to disclose my mind, and situation, more freely than I otherwise should do. The reasons, my good Sir, which you assign for thinking General Howe cannot move forward with his army are good, but now conclusive. It is a descriptive evidence of the difficulties he has to contend with, but no proof that they cannot be surmounted. It is a view of one side of the picture, against which let me enumerate the advantages on the other, and then determine how we should act in his situation. General Howe cannot, by the best intelligence, I have been able to get, have less than 10,000 men in the Jersies and on board of transports at Amboy. Ours does not exceed 4,000. His are well disciplined, well officered, and well appointed. Ours raw militia, badly officered, and under no government. His numbers cannot, in any short time, be augmented. Ours must very considerably, and by such troops as we can have some reliance on, or the game is at an end. In addition to all this, his coming himself to Brunswick, his bringing troops which cannot be quartered, and keeping them on ship board at Amboy, with some other corroborating circumstances did induce a firm belief in me that he would move, and towards Philadelphia."

3 March 1777:

Monday. At Morristown, General Washington appoints Major General William Heath to succeed Major General Artemus Ward, who has requested to resign. Heath will replace Ward as commander of the Eastern Department. Washington also writes to Ward, accepting his resignation and ordering him to release all duties and responsibilities to Heath.

4 March 1777:
Tuesday. In Philadelphia, Roger Sherman writes to Jonathan Trumbull, reporting that Washington, with a few continental troops, reinforced and backed up by a goodly number of local militia troops, denies the enemy supplies, provisions, forage, and support. This forage war waged in New Jersey keeps the British and Hessian forces confined quite closely to New York, Staten Island, Perth Amboy, and New Brunswick. If they wish to forage, they must add a large guarding force to the foragers. The enemy is denied freedom of movement, one of the principles of war. [See Appendix 5, p. 1037]

5 March 1777:
Wednesday. On his way from Baltimore to Philadelphia, on the East side of the Susquehanna River, John Hancock writes to his wife Dorothy, who is en route, explaining that he has just crossed the river by cutting through the ice but must await the crossing of the horses and baggage.

6 March 1777:
Thursday. In Kingston, New York, the Convention of Representatives, passes an Act allowing for the confiscation of all Loyalist property in the state. Commissions are set up for the purpose of selling off this property to defray the costs of the war.
In Philadelphia, William Ellery writes to Nicholas Cooke, reporting that the Congress approves of a state lottery as a means of slowing or stopping the depreciation of Continental bills. He recommends a Mr. Jackson to Cooke, as a fellow with such lottery tickets for sale, and hopes Cooke will be able to introduce him to persons in Rhode Island who can promote this lottery.

7 March 1777:
Friday. In Philadelphia, John Adams writes to his wife Abigail, noting that he has returned to Philadelphia from Baltimore, that there has been a good deal of snow in Maryland and Pennsylvania, that the lotteries may help with the problem of depreciation by bringing in needed money, and that the Jerseys have risen to give the enemy a most difficult time in a forage War. He is pleased to report that a number of states have completed organizing their governments.

8 March 1777:
Saturday. At Bonhamtown (near Amboy), New Jersey, Brigadier General William Maxwell attacks a British force of 2,000 troops resulting in great loss to the British. While Washington never does have the full allotment of Continental troops he has been requesting, he learns to make effective use of the local militia forces to flesh out his military programs and attack the British wherever they may be found.

9 March 1777:

Sunday. In Philadelphia, John Adams writes to Nathanael Greene, saying that he is a bit disappointed in the recent actions of the army. "I have derived Consolation however, from these Disappointments, because the People have discovered a Capital patience under them, greater than might have been expected. It was not very Surprising to me that our Troops Should fly in certain Situations, and abandon Lines of Such extent, at the Sudden appearance of a formidable Enemy in unexpected Places because I had learn'd from Marshall Saxe, and from others that Such Behavior was not only common but almost constant among the best regular Troops."

10 March 1777:

Monday. From Philadelphia, William Whipple writes to John Langdon, saying that the removal of Congress from that city, and their subsequent return have put matters in a state of confusion, and he has been unable to procure the dimensions for a 74-gun ship. No such ship-of-the-line vessel is ever built in America during the period of the War of the American Revolution. It is always smaller frigates and sloops of war that Americans use to harass the enemy on the seas.

11 March 1777:

Tuesday. In Philadelphia, John Hancock writes to his wife Dorothy in Baltimore, giving her detailed directions for her trip to return to Philadelphia, such as where to stay, how to pay for things, who the guard will be on her journey, and what to bring. He also suggests that she leave gifts for several people in the Baltimore area he wishes to honor.

12 March 1777:

Wednesday. At headquarters, Morristown, Washington issues orders to all the Colonels of the Continental Regiments in the States of New Jersey, Connecticut, Rhode Island, New York, Pennsylvania, Maryland, and Virginia, "Sir: You are hereby required immediately to send me an exact return of the State of your Regiment, and to assemble all the recruits you have in Camp, in the shortest time possible, there to be inoculated, and in all respects prepared for the field; leaving a sufficient number of proper officers to carry on the recruiting service, who are to follow as fast as they are ready."

The Congress being adjourned from its meetings in Baltimore, has been set to reconvene in Philadelphia on 5 March 1777, but there not being a quorum, have adjourned from day to day, until now. Numerous letters and reports are received. A resolution is passed, recommending to the states that they provide blankets to furnish the quotas of soldiers from each state. It is partially the responsibility of the Congress itself, that many matters go unfinished, incomplete, late, or not at all, simply because some delegates do not appear as ordered to help conduct the business of governing.

13 March 1777:
    Thursday. European gentlemen wishing employment with
the Continental Army of the United States but who do not
have a full and complete command of the language are not
felt to be of great use. Therefore, the Congress resolves that
all the American Ministers be advised to discourage such
persons from coming to America with the expectation of
employment in the service, unless they are masters of the
English language.

14 March 1777:
    Friday. In Philadelphia, the Congress resolves that the
bills drawn on behalf of North Carolina be paid and charged
against the $500,000 advanced to that State.

15 March 1777:
    Saturday. The Congress empowers the Marine Committee
to purchase three ships to be armed and fitted out for the
service of the United States. It also resolves that Daniel
Waters and Samuel Ticker be appointed captains in the Navy,
and have command of two of these ships and that "... the
other ship be given to Captain John Paul Jones, until better
provision can be made for him."

16 March 1777:
    Sunday. In Philadelphia, Lewis Morris writes to the New
York convention, reporting that the adjournment of the
Congress from Baltimore to Philadelphia has brought about a
very unequal representation. He is the only delegate from New
York. The Congress once again must adjourn from day to day,
because there is not yet a quorum, and will not be until 19
March 1777.

17 March 1777:
    Monday. At Passy, Benjamin Franklin writes to Arthur
Lee, noting that a person representing a business of Bordeaux
has offered to provide a packet service to America, but
Franklin is not familiar with the captains who will command
them nor the reputation of the business concern who makes
the offer. He also reports that properly authorized bills are to
be paid out of his account, but notes he is unaware of the
purpose or the authorization of too many of these bills.

18 March 1777:
    Tuesday. In Philadelphia, John Hancock writes to Philip
Schuyler, "The number of foreigners already employed in the
Army of these States is a prodigious weight upon the Service,
and the evil is likely to encrease [sic] unless a speedy stop can
be put to it. For this purpose the Congress have not only
determined that no Commissions should be granted to any
foreign Officers, who are ignorant of the English Language (see
the entry and resolve of the Congress for 13 March 1777), but
have directed the Committee of Secret Correspondence to write

to their Agents abroad to discourage Gentlemen from coming to America with expectations of being taken into Service unless they are acquainted with our Language."

At Portsmouth, New Hampshire, the French vessel *Amphitrite* brings into the harbor a cargo of 52 cannons, 12,000 muskets, and 1,000 barrels of gunpowder.

19 March 1777:

Wednesday. The Congress resolves to advance $100,000 each to the States of New Jersey and Pennsylvania.

At headquarters, Morristown, General Orders state "Such of the arms as have been damaged, and can be repaired, are likewise to be accounted for, making a reasonable allowance for the repair. The Commanding Officer of the Regiment will, on application, receive a warrant on the Paymaster-General for the sum necessary–the arms will then be the property of the public ..." The parole is given as Brunswick, and the countersign as Amboy.

20 March 1777:

Thursday. In Philadelphia, Samuel Adams writes to John Scollay, expressing concern over what he sees as the reduction of the public spirit from the time of the Boston Port Bill to the present day. Adams feels that when too many folks are unwilling to forgo light pleasure or deny themselves any thing that can be purchased, regardless of price. He notes that self-denial is a virtue, not so often found these days.

21 March 1777:

Friday. The Congress specifies the number and ranks of commissioned officers to be assigned to units of differing sizes from small companies to large battalions. Too many times, officers have made trouble and difficulty over rank and authority relative to unit size—this congressional action should help to ease the problem.

22 March 1777:

Saturday. At Peekskill, New York, the Americans have a supply depot. Washington, concerned about protecting the Highlands that guard the Hudson River, has ordered troops to build and defend Fort Hill, near Peekskill. Colonel Marinus Willett, with an assortment of troops to the number of 250 from various units, is the local commander. The British raid the depot with a detachment of nearly 500 troops. The fight lasts two days as the overwhelmed Patriots withdraw, burning some of the mills and storehouses. What the Americans do not destroy, the British do, following the Patriot retreat. Willett is a fine officer, and participates in very many of the northern campaigns throughout the Revolution. He is a great asset for the cause.

23 March 1777:
Sunday. At headquarters, Morristown, Washington writes to the President of Congress. "Sir: Colo. Palfrey having expressed a desire to settle the accounts of his office to this time has obtained my permission to repair to Philadelphia and now waits on Congress with his books and vouchers, hoping that a Committee will be appointed to examine and adjust the same. The disadvantages which have arisen to the service and which have been severely felt for want of constant supplies in the Military Chest, are almost incredible and are not to be described, but with difficulty, to those who are not immediately in the Army and privy to the frequent and importunate applications that are made. To prevent inconveniences of the like nature, in future, I have thought it proper, that an estimate of the monthly advances should be formed and laid before Congress. This Colo. Palfrey will do, and tho' it cannot be effected with a degree of scrupulous exactness and precision, yet from his intimate knowledge of the incidental charges and expenses in the common course of things, the calculation I apprehend will be attended with many benefits. It will shew (sic) Congress the necessary provisions of money to be made for ordinary contingencies and enable them to form a rule for their government in the instance of supplies in the Army."

Washington also writes to Governor Jonathan Trumbull. "I wish you may not be deceived in the forwardness of your regiments, for I can assure you, the Returns fall far short of what was given out. [Col. John] Chandler's, [Col. Heman] Swift's and [Col. Charles] Chas. Webb's, by General Parsons, letter of the 6th inst., had only eighty men each. Tho' the latter sent his son down some weeks ago and drew four hundred stand of arms, assuring me that his father had as many men ready. None of the other Regiments were half full, [Col. John] Durkee's had only 140 men. From this state of facts it is evident, that if the most spirited exertions are not made the enemy will take the field before we can draw a sufficient head of men together to oppose them."

Washington is still having problems fleshing out the regimental-sized units he is seeing coming into camp. Too many of these units are well under strength.

General Orders give the parole as Jamaica and the countersign as Kingston.

24 March 1777:
Monday. Congress passes a resolution that informs both the Commander-in-Chief, and the Commanding General of every Department that they are not bound by the majority of voices in any council of war, contrary to their own view or judgement of any particular military situation. It has occasionally happened that a commanding general's opinion is overwhelmed by a majority of the votes of those in a council. An example is Washington's view that Fort Washington should have been abandoned. He was out-voted,

and accepted the majority view. The results of which were a surrender and total defeat of the Americans. Thus, the Congress wants to free such commanders from feeling they have an obligation to adhere to the majority opinion. Such opinions should be sought, but the final decision rests with the commander.

25 March 1777:

Tuesday. In Philadelphia, Robert Morris, on behalf of the Committee of Secret Correspondence, writes to the commissioners in Paris, enclosing a Congressional resolution of Congress, regarding the expense and problems of too many foreign Officers, who come without prior approval, with enlarged recommendations, without a proper and firm understanding of the English Language, expecting high rank. "The necessity of such a resolution and due attention to it, is fully evinced by the heavy expense America has been put to by many Gentlemen received into their Service, who have found it impossible to render themselves useful for want of the language and we think this the most likely means to save others the charge and trouble of a long voyage, as well as the mortification of being disappointed in their expectations. You will therefore serve all such and oblige us by discouraging their coming to America for military employments."

26 March 1777:

Wednesday. In London, Major General John Burgoyne leaves for Plymouth on the southern coast of England to return to North America with a new plan and new orders. He is to go to Canada and invade south along the Champlain-Hudson River route into New York, and reach Albany. The mission is a British effort to divide the colonies east of the Hudson River from those west of the river. To do so will also require a British force to invade north up the river in cooperation with Burgoyne. But no orders to do so are ever issued! This lack of overall command, and its consequence, is a violation of the Principles of war. [See Volume 2, p, 551.]

27 March 1777:

Thursday. In Philadelphia, the Congress adds two members to the Medical Committee. Those chosen are Abraham Clark, a delegate from New Jersey and William Ellery, a delegate from Rhode Island. It is hoped that the addition of two persons will spread the load and improve the efficiency of the Medical services to the troops.

At headquarters, Morristown, Washington writes to Brigadier Geneeral George Weedon, "I have not yet seen any of the recovered soldiers of the third regiment, spoken of as ordered to this place by you. It is next to impossible, I find, to get either officers or men out of comfortable quarters, issue what orders you will for this purpose. Nothing, I am convinced, but the breaking of two or three officers in every regiment, will effect a radical cure of their negligence, inattention, and in fact, down right disobedience, which is now so prevalent among the officers of this army, and this remedy shall most assuredly be administered,"

28 March 1777:
    Friday. At Plymouth, England, Burgoyne boards the frigate HMS *Apollo*, checking upon the loading of his very large component of baggage, as he prepares to sail to Canada.

29 March 1777:
    Saturday. Congress, concerned about the record keeping requirements necessary for possible future prisoner exchanges with the enemy, resolves "That whenever any prisoners shall be taken by the army, or by any detachment of the army of these United States, or by any body of the militia, the commanding officer do furnish the Board of War with lists of such prisoners, together with the cause and manner of their capture and detention."

30 March 1777:
    Sunday. In Philadelphia, John Adams writes to his son, Charles, "I took a walk upon the wharves, to see the navigation. The new frigate called the *Delaware*, is hauled off, into the stream and is ready to sail. She makes a fine appearance. I then went to the house of one Humphreys an ingenious shipwright and found him making a model of a seventy four gun ship. He has nearly completed it. You can see every part of the ship in its just proportion in miniature."

31 March 1777:
    Monday. Congress approves the sentence of death of a general court martial, finding James Molesworth guilty of being a spy, and orders Major General Horatio Gates to see to its execution.
    Notice is received that the ship *Mercury*, out of Nantes, France, has arrived at Portsmouth, New Hampshire with a cargo of 11,987 fusees (sic, types of muskets), 1,000 barrels of powder, 11,000 gun-flints, 48 bales of woolens, and several other items useful to the American army.

1 April 1777:
    Tuesday. The Congress passes a rather lengthy resolution for better regulating the pay of the army. This issue of pay (or rather lack thereof) will cause much unrest and will plague the American army throughout course of the war.
    At Morristown, Washington writes to Governor William Livingston, "I perceive many difficulties in the execution of your militia law, particularly in suffering an appeal to lay before a Court of Judicature. That indulgence will always be claimed, by the person refusing to serve, where the fine is levied; and before the suit is determined, this contest will probably be determined, one way or other. In the mean time the service of the soldiers is intirely [sic] lost. Colo. Forman,

who waits upon you upon public business, informs me, that
he thinks it would be of considerable advantage, to order out
the militia of Monmouth, Middlesex, and Burlington at this
time; and as it was the district in which he would have
commanded, had he accepted of the Brigadiership offered him
by the State; I could wish that he might have the power of
calling them out, vested in him. He thinks very judiciously,
that it will not only serve to distinguish the well affected from
the ill, but it will hinder the Tories from poisoning the minds
of the people, by pointing out to them, the deficiencies of the
law, and how it may be evaded. Colo. Foreman further
informs me, that many people who have absconded, have left
behind them, stocks of horses, cattle and grain, which will
not only be lost to the owners, but to the public, if some mode
is not fallen upon to secure them. If your Council of Safety
think it proper, the Colonel will take possession of such
effects for the public use, and return you an account of
them."

2 April 1777:
    Wednesday. Congress requests that Governor Johnson of
Maryland give orders for the immediate removal of powder
and military stores from Annapolis to Frederick, and the
powder and military stores at Baltimore to Carlisle,
Pennsylvania.

3 April 1777:
    Thursday. In Philadelphia, John Adams writes to his wife
Abigail, saying that, since she seems to be so interested in
"politicks", he will oblige her by sending such information,
and proceeds to tell her what has been going on in the world.

4 April 1777:
    Friday. Congress resolves "That the invitation given, at the
desire of Mr. President Rutledge by Mr. Galphin, to the Creek
Indians, to form a Congress in the ensuing spring, be
approved; that the State of South Carolina be reimbursed the
expenses, which may attend such meeting, and that Mr.
Galphin do use his endeavours [sic] to persuade some of the
Creek chiefs to attend him to Philadelphia, and that this
Congress will defray the charges of their journey."

5 April 1777:
    Saturday. The State of Rhode Island has empowered the
Governor to issue letters of Marque and Reprisal (Privateers).
The Congress resolves that such commissions "... be of the
same force and validity, as if they had been granted by
Congress..." Included with that resolution is that the
Governor shall not grant any more such commissions, that he
is to recall such as he may have issued, and deliver
Continental commissions in their stead.

6 April 1777:
    Sunday. At Passy, Benjamin Franklin writes to Arthur Lee, reporting upon a matter of monies charged against his accounts for the payment of items supporting the public service.

7 April 1777:
    Monday. Philip Schuyler and William Duer, delegates from New York State, take their seats in the Congress. Consideration of the *Report on Hospitals* is brought to the floor and debate resumed on this critically important area of heretofore loose management, with a large number of resolutions resulting.

8 April 1777:
    Tuesday. In Philadelphia, the Congress takes up the problem of the Articles of Confederation, and resolves that since it needs to be addressed as the Committee of the Whole, "... that two days in each week be employed on that subject, until it shall be wholly discussed in Congress."

9 April 1777:
    Wednesday. The Board of War has presented a report, upon which the Congress resolves, "That the commissary general of military stores, be directed immediately to furnish as many rifles [not exceeding 1,000] to be sent to Fort Pitt, as he can procure ..."

10 April 1777:
    Thursday. At the confluence of the Monongahela River and the Allegheny River that forms the Ohio River, a Fort has been built to both protect the settlers in the region and serve as an outpost of civilization in western Pennsylvania.   George Morgan, an Indian agent at this outpost warns the Congress that British and Indian forces threaten the frontier, and that the American forces and leadership is inadequate to defend the area. The Congress therefore resolves "That Brigadier General (Edward) Hand be, and he is hereby, ordered immediately to repair to Fort Pitt, and take measures for the defense of the western frontiers ..."

11 April 1777:
    Friday. In London, England, Henry Clinton is invested as a Knight with the Order of the Bath at a Levee. He thus now commands the title Sir Henry Clinton. The King wishes him to return to America soon, so as to back up William Howe.
    The Congress completes the process of the election of deputy muster masters general. It also approves of a director general of all military hospitals for the armies of the United States, as well as physicians and surgeons for the various departments. A department was usually a geographic area of the country, such as the Hudson Highlands.

12 April 1777:
    Saturday. The Congress, feeling that some officers have been extraordinary in their leadership of the cause, and wishes to specially honor two such leaders, passes a resolve "That 500 dollars be allowed for erecting the monument to General [Joseph] Warren, and a like sum for erecting the monument for General [Hugh] Mercer." (Both fell in battle, see the sketches for 17 June 1775 and 3 January 1777).
    At Morristown, George Washington writes to John Augustine Washington, "To my great surprise we are still in a calm; how long it will, how long it can remain, is beyond by skill to determine. That it has continued much beyond my expectation already, is certain, but to expect that General Howe will not avail himself of our weak state, is, I think, to say in as many words that he does not know how to take advantage of circumstances, and of course, is unfit for the trust reposed in him. The unfortunate policy of short inlistments is daily, and hourly, exemplified. Thoroughly convinced I am, that if the troops which were inlisted last year had been engaged for the war, or even three years, that I could, with them, and such aids as might have been drawn into our assistance, have drove the British Army and their auxiliary troops out of the Jersies in the course of last winter. I do not know but they might also have been driven from New York. Instead of that, we have, at this late day, an army to assemble for self defense. But past errors cannot be rectified, we must guard as much as possible against future evils."

13 April 1777:
    Sunday. Stung by the losses during the forage war of the winter, Lord Cornwallis develops a plan of attack upon the American garrison outposts. At Bound Brook, New Jersey, Hessian Captain Johann von Ewald leads his Jäger Company, supported by other troops in a four-column surprise attack. The Americans are quickly driven back, the surprise being nearly complete. The British, however, do not consolidate their victory, but retire to New Brunswick.

14 April 1777:
    Monday. Congress takes up the problem of effective recruitment, and passes a number of resolutions on that subject. The issue of the provision adequate numbers of troops to the Continental Army is a constant and seemingly never-ending problem. Hardly has one army been assembled, before it is found too small. They also resolve to establish a magazine at Springfield, Massachusetts, sufficient to hold 10,000 stands of arms and two hundred tons of gunpowder.

15 April 1777:
    Tuesday. In Philadelphia, Congress advances $4,000 to Brigadier General Edward Hand to erect such works at Fort Pitt as he shall think necessary. The Congress also passes a resolution regarding the naming of battalions (regiments),

noting that since the Continental battalions are all on one footing, liable to the same kind of services and entitled to equal privileges, therefore, appellations such as "Congress Own" and "Washington's Life Guards" are improper, and not to be continued. Most such units are numbered, and the Officers of said battalions are to take notice and conform themselves accordingly.

16 April 1777:
Wednesday. In Philadelphia, William Ellery writes to Nicholas Cooke, reporting that the Congress wishes to have the whole force of the state of Rhode Island, aided by the combined militia of Massachusetts and Connecticut, attack and destroy the enemy on Rhode Island.

17 April 1777:
Thursday. A committee of four is appointed to devise ways and means of suppressing the spirit of Toryism in the Maryland counties of Somerset and Worcester, and the Delaware county of Sussex. Named to this committee are William Duer, Samuel Adams, James Wilson, and Benjamin Rumsey, all delegates to the Congress.

18 April 1777:
Friday. Ever concerned about possible British attempts to invade up the Hudson River, the Americans place a chain obstruction across the river between Fort Montgomery and Anthony's Nose. It is one of several such devices used in efforts to thwart British naval advances up into the Highlands.
The committee appointed to enquire into the conduct of the enemy, brings in a report which is read to the Congress. It summarizes four main areas of investigation: 1.) The wanton and oppressive devastation of the country and destruction of property by the enemy; 2.) The inhuman treatment of those who were so unhappy as to become prisoners; 3.) The savage butchery of those who had submitted and were incapable of resistance; 4.) The lust and brutality of the soldiers in abusing women. Numbers of affidavits are appended to this report. It is accepted by the Congress and the committee is ordered to publish the same with the affidavits.

19 April 1777:
Saturday. At Kingston, New York, the convention approves a Constitution for the state.
At Woodbridge, New Jersey, the British make another raid on an American garrison, defended by Captain Christopher Marsh. Large forces are not involved, but this skirmish is typical of the many taking place this spring between American patriot groups and British or Hessian units. Washington is very pleased with the manner of such efforts, because he sees this as a ground swell of support, and a denial of the free use of the territory by the enemy.

20 April 1777:

Sunday. From the port of Los Pasajes, Spain, Lafayette, who has used his own monies, along with a group of volunteer officers, including the Baron de Kalb, sail on the tide in the vessel *Victorie*, he has purchased, for America.

In Philadelphia, Richard Henry Lee writes to his brother Arthur, noting that American trade is sorely hindered by the maritime strength of Great Britain. This could be corrected, Lee avers, if the combined fleets of France and Spain were to fall upon the British fleets.

21 April 1777:

Monday. Agreeable to the order of the day, the Congress again gives consideration to the Articles of Confederation. Because there is so much to debate and so many items to review and adjust, this process will take a good while before a draft can be presented to all the states for ratification.

22 April 1777:

Tuesday. The Board of War submits a report, and a resolution upon it is approved, creating a Corps of Invalids to be employed in garrison duty, and as guards for magazines and arsenals, and as a military school for young gentlemen. This is a very early precursor to what will become West Point. All the subaltern officers, when off duty, are to attend this school. Subjects to be taught are Geometry, Arithmetick [sic], vulgar [numerical] and decimal fractions, and the extraction of roots.

23 April 1777:

Wednesday. At Morristown, George Washington writes to Brigadier General George Clinton, "I think this move so probable [Howe's move towards Philadelphia], as it will give them access to a part of the country most notoriously disaffected, that I desire you will post a body of militia of the State of New York, on this side of the North River, in such place as you shall think most safe to prevent them from being surprised, and at the same time proper to intercept Skinners Corps [a British force of Tories], if they should attempt the above mentioned route [from Bergen through Sussex] to be a diversion from Howe's march to Philadelphia. General Heard, with about two hundred Jersey militia, marched this day to take post at Pompton and extend himself towards Hackensack. Colo. [Theunis] Dey will also have some small parties of his regiment in that quarter; if the enemy should move, they [Heard and Dey], by being called upon, may afford some assistance."

The Congress authorizes Dr. James Tilton to go to Dumfries, Virginia, to take charge of all continental soldiers who are, or shall be, inoculated. Note here how important this program of inoculation becomes. To have the Congress approve such an action is wonderful support.

24 April 1777:
Thursday. British Governor of New York William Tryon (although he has no function left to perform), is made Colonel of a body of Loyalists, and makes a raid on the important patriot depot at Danbury, Connecticut. Tryon has more than 2,000 men with him, and easily brushes aside the weak defending force of about 250 militia. The town is captured, many patriot homes are burned, and large amounts of supplies are burned, carried away, or otherwise destroyed. Fearful of a rising militia body, Tryon orders his troops to depart.
    The Congress requests the Executive Council and Board of War of Pennsylvania to call out three thousand militia, half to assemble at Chester, the other half at Bristol, furnished with a proper train of artillery, all as a reinforcement for General George Washington.

25 April 1777:
Friday. In Philadelphia, the Congress resolves that the governor of the state of New Jersey call out such a part of the militia of that state, as General Washington shall judge necessary to reinforce the army under his command.

26 April 1777:
Saturday. The Committee of the Treasury reports a number of monies due various persons for services. Among these are Captain Benjamin Deane for expenses in escorting money to White Plains, including wagon and horse hire---175 30/90 dollars; Levi Hollingsworth for freight and cartage—437 6/90 dollars; Elizabeth Kuntz for attending and provisions for six men under inoculation—89 81/90 dollars.

27 April 1777:
Sunday. Colonel William Tryon's Danbury raiding party, now trying to escape from the gathering horde of patriot militia, orders his troops to march at 2 o'clock in the morning for re-boarding their ships at Compo Beach. Heading for Ridgefield, Connecticut, they encounter Major General David Wooster, Brigadier Generals Benedict Arnold, and Gold Selleck Silliman, with a body of 700 Patriot men. When Tryon attacks, overwhelming the American militia, Arnold retreats in good order to set up another blockage, and further delays the British, while awaiting additional support to defeat them. Arnold prepares a good position from which to attack the British, as they attempt to continue south to reach their transports.

28 April 1777:
Monday. Near Ridgefield, Tryon's troops are in a running fight to get to their ships, as Arnold's men are soon enhanced by 1,200 Continentals under Brigadier General Alexander McDougall, and another 470 New York militia under Colonel Ludington. The raiders are barely able to escape to board

their ships and leave. While Tryon's Danbury Raid proves to be less than totally successful, he does do a lot of damage to supplies the Americans cannot easily nor cheaply replace.

The Congress resolves itself into a Committee of the Whole to consider letters and papers from Horatio Gates and Philip Schuyler regarding the defense of Fort Ticonderoga. Coming to no conclusion, the Congress resolves to address the issue the next day.

29 April 1777:
Tuesday. In London, England, Sir Henry Clinton sets off for Plymouth to board ship for transport to America.

Agreeable to the order of the day, the Congress resolves itself into a Committee of the Whole to continue with the issue of the defense of Fort Ticonderoga. A report is agreed to, and the Congress passes several resolutions: That Washington write to the eastern states requesting a speedy forwarding of the regiments ordered; that New York keep open the lines of communication between Albany and Fort Ticonderoga; that Gates engage as many carpenters as may be needed to complete the boats for the lake; that St. Clair be informed of the approach of the enemy.

30 April 1777:
Wednesday. At headquarters, Morristown, Washington writes to Colonel Alexander Spotswood, "I want to form a Company for my Guard. In doing this I wish to be extremely cautious; because it is more than probable, that in the course of the campaign, my baggage, papers, and other matters of great public import, may be committed to the sole care of these men. This being premised, in order to impress you with proper attention in the choice, I have to request that you will immediately furnish me with four men of your regiment. And, as it is my further wish, that this Company should look well and be nearly of a size, I desire that none of the men may exceed in stature 5 feet ten inches, nor short of 5 feet nine inches; sober, young, active and well made. When I recommend care in your choice, I would be understood to mean men of good character in the regiment, that possess the pride of appearing clean and soldierlike."

Congress resolves that the Carolina troops, on their way to join Washington, are to halt at Dumfries, Virginia, there to pass through inoculation. Because smallpox is such a debilitating disease, with a high rate of mortality, it is considered important to attempt to protect the troops against it. While not perfect, inoculation is better than nothing.

1 May 1777:
Thursday. The Congress appoints a committee of three-- James Wilson, John Adams, and Richard Henry Lee "... to inquire into the laws and customs of Nations respecting neutrality, and to report their opinion whether the conduct of the King of Portugal, in forbidding the vessels of the United

States to enter his ports and ordering those already there to depart at a short stay, is not a breach of the laws of neutrality, and will justify acts of hostility against the subjects of the said King."

2 May 1777:
Friday. At Manheim, Pennsylvania, Robert Morris writes to James Lovell, reporting that he has packets from Simeon Deane, recently returned from France, said packets containing good news regarding the treaties. Morris sends these forward.

At Morristown, Washington writes to Maj. General William Heath, concerning matters of an arsenal wherein he thinks Springfield will be a safer place than Portsmouth, "I have wrote to Mr. Langdon, to send the remainder yet to Springfield, except he has positive orders to the contrary from Congress. And I would advise you, immediately to remove all supernumerary continental stores from the town and neighborhood of Boston to Springfield, for we find, from two recent instances, that the enemy are determined to destroy our magazines where ever they are accessible, and that it is impossible for us to prevent them effectually, except apprised of their design, if our magazines lay near the coast, or even within one day's march of it. I shall also write to Congress and press the immediate removal of the artillery and other military stores from Portsmouth."

3 May 1777:
Saturday. The Congress orders that a number of accounts be paid, among which is $37 to Captain Samuel Griffith, for the expenses of seven men, from Baltimore to Philadelphia, as a guard for money being transported. Another example of the detailed minutiae the Congress allows itself to wallow in.

4 May 1777:
Sunday. In Philadelphia, Charles Carroll writes to his father, reporting that the enemy has raided into Connecticut, and destroyed a goodly quantity of beef, pork, and flour. Carroll also notes that recent intelligence from the northern department indicates that Carleton's advance parties are within 45 miles of Fort Ticonderoga.

5 May 1777:
Monday. At headquarters, Morristown, General Orders provides information that the Commander-in-Chief calls the attention of the troops to Resolutions of Congress, one of which points out that there is to be one physician and surgeon general for each separate department or district and spells out the duty of this office in some detail. The other of which appoints Dr. William Shippen, Jr. as Director General of all the military hospitals for the armies of the United States. The parole is given as Bethlehem and the countersign as Easton.

Washington writes to the president of the Congress, "By Major [Robert] Troup, one of Genl. Gates's Aides, who left Albany on Tuesday last, I am informed, the accounts of all General Carleton's approach towards Ticonderoga were premature. He says Genl. Gates received a letter before he came away, from Brigadier Genl. Wayne of the 24th. ulto., in which he mentions of it, and that three thousand troops had arrived there all in high spirits and health, except nine, and that the post could never be carried, without the loss of much blood. The proceedings of Congress and your letter of the 29th ulto., were the first and only information I had of Mr. Carleton's being on the lake, having heard nothing upon the subject from Genl. Gates or any other person."

Agreeable to the order of the day, Congress resolves itself into the Committee of the Whole to again give further consideration to the Articles of Confederation.

6 May 1777:
Tuesday. At Quebec, British General John Burgoyne arrives to take command of the army he will lead on an invasion of the United States, by way of Lake Champlain and the Hudson River.

Congress resolves that an order for $30,000 be drawn on the commissioner of the loan office for the state of Rhode Island, in favor of Daniel Tillinghast, for the use of ships of war in that State.

7 May 1777:
Wednesday. The Congress elects Ralph Izard as commissioner for the Court of Tuscany, from which it is hoped that still another country will assist the Americans in defeating the British.

In headquarters at Morristown, Washington writes to Alexander McDougal, "I have a long time seen and felt the ill consequences of the want of arrangement in the Commissary-General's department. I don't think that it is to be imputed to any fault in the present principal, but in the amazing extent of that branch, over every part of which it is impossible that he should keep his eye, and I know, that in several instances he has been infamously deceived by his deputies. If you think that the difficulties which you have lately been put to, proceed from any want of attention or activity, in the person who acts as deputy Commissary in your quarter, I think he ought to be called to account. I however beg that you Genel. Clinton will press the Commissaries and Quartermasters, to remove all those stores from the places mentioned by Congress, to Ulster County as quick as possible; as I very much fear, that if the enemy move up the river, before they got over, we shall feel the want of them. The imperfect state of the fortifications of Fort Montgomery, gives me great uneasiness; because I think, from a concurrence of circumstances, it begins to look, as if the enemy intended to turn their views toward the North River, instead of the

Delaware. If the North River is their object, they cannot accomplish it without withdrawing their forces from Jersey, and that they cannot do unknown to us."

8 May 1777:
Thursday. At Piscataway, New Jersey, a fight ensues as American militia close with a British forage detail, and chase them off.

In Philadelphia, the Congress agrees to a new commission for private ships of war (privateers). Some of the language in that commission is "... that we have granted, and, by these presents, do grant, licence [sic] and authority to _____, mariner, commander of the _____, ... mounting _____ carriage guns, ..., in a war-like manner, and by and with the said _____, and the crew thereof, by force of arms, to attack, subdue, and take all ships and other vessels whatsoever, carrying soldiers, arms, gun-powder, ammunition, provisions or any other contraband goods to any of the British armies or ships of war employed against these United States."

9 May 1777:
Friday. The Congress resolves "That a reward of 24 dollars be paid to every non-commissioned officer or soldier who shall come over with his arms from the enemy."

10 May 1777:
Saturday. The Congress resolves to commission Charles Tuffin Armand, Marquis de la Rouerie as a colonel, and that he is to repair to General George Washington. This French officer becomes one of the most effective volunteers assisting the American revolution.

At Morristown, Washington writes to William Heath, "The Board of War have sent orders to the Continental agents at Boston, Portsmouth, and Providence, to remove all the military stores, arms &, in their possession, from those places, to Springfield where they are to be subject to my directions. Upon enquiring of Genl. Knox, what quantity of the artillery lately arrived, will be wanted in this quarter, he desires that the 31 light pieces of Swedish construction and 2 pieces of the heavy may be sent forward, as far as Litchfield in Connecticut, where the officer who conducts them will meet his further orders. The remainder of the cannon are to be lodged at Springfield for the present. The French artificers, who came over with the cannon, are to go to Springfield where they will be taken into employ. I cannot see the necessity of taking twenty men into pay, purposely to guard the magazine at Springfield. There will ever be a number of the Continental troops, under the denomination of invalids or convalescents and some of them may be drawn together for that purpose."

11 May 1777:
Sunday. Richard Peters, Secretary for The Board of War, writes to General George Washington, enclosing resolutions,

and informing him that the Congress wishes to have information on the numbers of men under Washington's command in New Jersey in order to judge whether or not to send Delaware and Pennsylvania militia to join him.

12 May 1777:
Monday. The Congress, learning from its wide-spread correspondence and numerous newspaper accounts, has finally awakened to the fact that the War of the American Revolution is not merely a local argument between the colonies and the Mother country but a world-wide conflict of political ideas that impact many other nations. Thus, they have a committee prepare drafts of commissions and instructions for ministers to be appointed to the Courts of Madrid, Vienna, Berlin, and Tuscany.

13 May 1777:
Tuesday. In Philadelphia, the Congress resolves that Massachusetts be requested to assist some inhabitants of the counties of Cumberland and Sunbury in Nova Scotia, who, attached to the American cause, are suffering for their views. To relieve these patriots and enable such of them as may be desirous of removing to a place of greater safety, Massachusetts is authorized to raise not more than 500 men.

14 May 1777:
Wednesday. At York, Pennsylvania, Richard Henry Lee writes to his brother Arthur Lee, "Your information in regard to our connection with the fictitious house of Roderique Hortalez & Co. is more explicit than any we had before received; but we further expect that all mystery should be removed. Surely there cannot now be occasion for any, if there ever was for half of the past." The trading house of Roderique Hortalez & Co. is a front to hide the assistance France and Spain offer to the Americans, so that no "official" aide is seen to come from these governments. This is a ruse to hold off the British government from complaining that France and Spain are giving aid and comfort to an enemy, or even that Britain might declare war too soon for these countries.

15 May 1777:
Thursday. The Congress passes a resolution regarding the theft of horses belonging either to the public or to private persons on public business.
At Morristown, General Washington has been sorely pressed to find and keep a reasonably sized army intact and ready to fight. But by this date, as units have entered camp and more recruits have joined under-strength units, Washington now has about 8,100 officers and men organized into five divisions of two brigades each. Most of his soldiers have also been inoculated, and the dread disease of smallpox is much less of a concern than it was in the winter.

16 May 1777:
    Friday. In Philadelphia, Roger Sherman, a delegate from Connecticut, writes to Governor Jonathan Trumbull, noting that all the arms in the hands of the agents of the eastern states are ordered to be sent to Springfield, where a "Laboratory" [by which he means an arsenal] is being erected.

17 May 1777:
    Saturday. Philip Schuyler writes to John Pemberton, "Although the profession of Arms is contrary to the religious tenets of Friends, yet as that Society has on many occasions exercised their benevolence to soldiers by making contributions of clothing & provisions to them & by affording them medical relief when in sickness, I cannot entertain a doubt but that the same humane principle continues to influence their conduct."
    Near what is now Jacksonville, a body of patriots, in the northern part of East Florida, are attacked by British regulars, Loyalists, and Indians at the Battle of Thomas Creek, near where the creek empties into the Nassau River. The Americans are overwhelmed and heavily outnumbered by the British. Some flee to the safety of Georgia, but the British turn the flank of the remaining patriot troops, and defeat them.

18 May 1777:
    Sunday. The American forces attempt to invade the British Colony of East Florida. However, Tory sympathizers in nearby Georgia are keeping the British up to date with patriot plans and movements. In a program called the Second East Florida Expedition, American Colonel John Baker marches south from Sunbury, Georgia, with about 100 mounted militia to join with Lt. Col. Samuel Elbert and a body of 400 Continentals. Elbert does not reach Florida until after the battle. At Thomas Creek, East Florida, near the Nassau River (present site of Jacksonville), British forces, under Major James Marc Prevost, having set an ambush, attack, and defeat Baker.

19 May 1777:
    Monday. At headquarters, Morristown, Washington writes to Maj. Gen. Horatio Gates, "Sir: I have just received yours of the 13th, which is in a great measure answered by one which I wrote to you on the 15th. But I cannot help taking notice of some expressions in your letters, which appear to me like an imputation of partiality in favour of this army, to the disadvantage and inconvenience of the northern. Can you suppose, if there had been an ample supply of tents for the whole army, that I would have hesitated one moment in complying with your demand. I told Major [Robert] Troup exactly what I repeated in mine of the 15th. That on account of our loss at Danbury there would be a scarcity of tents; that our army would be a moving one and that consequently

nothing but tents could serve our turn, and that therefore, as there was the greatest probability of your being stationary, you should endeavour to cover your troops with barracks and huts.' Certainly this was not a refusal of tents, but a request that you should, in your contracted situation, make every shift in your power, to do without them, or at least with as few as possible."

In Philadelphia, the Congress, acting on a petition from inhabitants of Cape May, New Jersey, requesting artillery and ammunition so as to defend themselves, orders the Marine Committee to supply six pieces to them.

20 May 1777:
Tuesday. In Georgia, the Carolinas, and Virginia, the Cherokee Indians have been raiding and skirmishing against various patriot militia bands for some while. After suffering a succession of defeats and the burning of their towns east and west of the mountains, including the loss of food supplies, the Cherokees sue for peace, ceding most of their lands east of the Appalachian Mountains to the several states. Much of this ceded land provides opportunities to grant property to soldiers after the war. The expansion will also encourage the later creation of the new states of Alabama and Tennessee.

21 May 1777:
Wednesday. In Philadelphia, William Whipple, a delegate from New Hampshire, writes to John Langdon, a merchant and legislator, noting that the British ships off the Capes of Delaware and Virginia are "very thick," thus making it difficult for packet boats to bring in their cargoes and mail.

22 May 1777:
Thursday. The Congress, after considering a report from the Board of War, resolves that Major General Philip Schuyler be directed to proceed to the Northern Department and take the command there. That department is to include Albany, Fort Ticonderoga, Fort Stanwix, and their dependencies. An earlier resolution to establish headquarters at Albany is repealed. Schuyler is a good officer, with a speciality in the supply and commissary fields. Reared as a gentleman, he sometimes appeared stuffy to persons without education or abilities of an intellectual nature.

23 May 1777:
Friday. The Board of War reports to the Congress that a conference with Major General Benedict Arnold, along with letters, reports, and papers he has laid before them, concludes that his character and conduct, so cruelly aspersed by others regarding his handling of the British attack at Lake Champlain the previous year, are groundless. Arnold has been an excellent leader, succeeding where others have failed, and this is surely a matter of jealousy.

24 May 1777:
    Saturday. Charles Carroll, a delegate from Maryland, writes to his father, reporting that ten ships in Delaware Bay are approaching Newcastle. He guesses that they are looking to water and find livestock. Carroll also remarks that Major General Schuyler leaves soon for Command of the Northern Department. "This measure will greatly displease Gates & perhaps occasion his resignation, but justice is due Schuyler."

25 May 1777:
    Sunday. From Philadelphia, John Adams writes to Abigail Adams, reporting that he rode his horse down to the Delaware River at 4:30 o'clock in the afternoon, and had a wonderful view of both sides of the river as it sweeps down to Delaware Bay. He enquires after the fruit trees and the corn on the Adams' farm. In spite of the busy business of politics, government, regulations, resolutions, orders, money, loans, and foreign affairs, Adams remains a countryman and farmer at heart!

26 May 1777:
    Monday. In Philadelphia, the Congress resolves that $40,000 be advanced to Joseph Trumbull, Commissary-General, by order of the loan officer in Massachusetts Bay.
    At Morristown, Washington writes to Governor Jonathan Trumbull, "Your anxiety for troops to remain in Connecticut, and my inability to grant them, when I examine matters upon a large and, I believe, just scale, distress me much. I assure you, Sir, no requisition has more weight with me than yours, nor will be more readily granted, when circumstances will admit, and where I think, it will not, in its consequences, be injurious to the general good. A capital object in the enemies plans, is, to divide and distract our attention. For this purpose as the division under Lord Percy been kept so long at Rhode Island, expecting from thence, that the apprehension of an invasion, or of their penetrating the country, would prevent any troops coming from the eastward. Could I but assemble all our forces, our situation would be respectable, and such, I should hope, as would compel General Howe to employ his together, or to hazard their destruction. On the other hand, whilst the quotas from the several states are so extremely deficient, should they be divided and act in detachments, there will be just grounds to apprehend our ruin."

27 May 1777:
    Tuesday. The Congress resolves that warrants issue as follows: $250,00 for the Board of War to the pay master general; $250,000 for Massachusetts; $150,00 for Connecticut; $500,000 for the Board of War; $50,00 to Pennsylvania for recruiting. They also vote in a Resolution

formally naming Albany, Ticonderoga, Fort Stanwix, and their dependencies as the Northern Department.

28 May 1777:
    Wednesday. General George Washington leaves his winter headquarters at the Arnold Tavern in Morristown, and moves to Middlebrook, New Jersey. He needs to keep a close eye upon the British in New York, and to prevent their possible attempts to invade up the Hudson River. Washington's ever present concern for the safety of the Hudson River is based upon his understanding that it is the means of connection between the eastern states and the middle states. If the British ever got serious about seizing and holding all the crossings, ferries, towns and villages on the river, America would be hard pressed to remain as a union.

29 May 1777:
    Thursday. The Congress forms a committee of three to estimate the number of teams required to convey provisions for the army under General Washington. This is surely an administrative function that could and should be handled by a competent officer on the quartermaster general's staff.

30 May 1777:
    Friday. In Philadelphia, the Committee on the Treasury reports "That a warrant should be drawn on the treasurer in favour [sic] of John Ommensetter, for the payment of a light waggon [sic], which was pressed at Baltimore, last winter, to bring money to this place, and not returned him, it being employed in the service of the States, and now remains with the waggon [sic] master general in this city, for 133 30/90 dollars."

31 May 1777:
    Saturday. William Ellery and Henry Marchant, delegates from Rhode Island, attend Congress and present their credentials.
    At Middlebrook, Washington writes to Governor Patrick Henry, indicating that he believes Howe, who had stood out to sea, might be headed for Philadelphia, perhaps by way of Delaware Bay. He requests Henry, should the British fleet arrive on the Virginia coast, to assemble the local militia and annoy the enemy. He also adds a post script to his letter "I must beg your attention to my letter on the subject of filling your regiments. It is a matter of the last importance, and their present weak state does not furnish by any means the quota assign'd you. I trust, and am persuaded no exertions will be omitted to effect this salutary and desirable event."

1 June 1777:
    Sunday. At headquarters, Middlebrook, New Jersey, General Orders state "Each Regiment to be paraded at troop and at retreat beating, the rolls carefully called, and

absentees punished. All officers not on duty, to attend the parade, to see that their men are clean and decent, and their arms and accoutrements in order, their ammunition complete, that they behave well in ranks, are silent, steady, and orderly."

2 June 1777:
    Monday. Nicholas Vandyke, a delegate from Delaware, attends the Congress and takes his seat.
    At headquarters in Middlebrook, General Orders state "The Brigadiers and Field Officers of the day are constantly to attend the grand parade, to see that the guards are properly assembled, give the necessary directions respecting them, and have them marched to their several posts in order. The Adjutants to collect the proportion assigned each regiment on their regimental parades, inspect carefully the state of their arms, accoutrements, ammunition, and dress, and march them off in order, to the brigade parades. Decency, and regard to health, especially in this hot season, indispensibly require, that vaults should be immediately dug ..." The parole is given as Killkenny, and the countersigns as Lancaster and Millstone.

3 June 1777:
    Tuesday. At headquarters, Middlebrook, General Orders state "The Brigadiers to have the springs, adjacent to their several encampments, well cleared and enlarged; placing sentries over them, to see that the water is not injured by dirty utensils. Brigadiers to see the order, for the arrangement of officer's ranks, immediately complied with, by appointing a day, for the field officers of each regiment to take it up. The General is surprised, and sorry to find, that a matter about which so much anxiety and embarrassment have been expressed, when put upon a proper footing to be adjusted, meets with so much neglect and delay." The parole is given as Norfolk and the countersigns as New London and Nantes.
    The Congress appoints a committee of three to devise ways and means of supplying the army with shoes, hats, and shirts. While the Congress can appoint committees to examine problems, the problems are solved by actual persons charged with the responsibility of action.

4 June 1777:
    Wednesday. In Berlin, Arthur Lee, Minister of the United States, arrives to begin his duties with the King of Prussia.
    In Philadelphia, the Congress, agreeable to the order of the day, resolves itself into the Committee of the Whole to take into consideration the state of foreign affairs. Not coming to a conclusion, the committee will sit again.

5 June 1777:
    Thursday. In New York, William Howe receives official word from Lord George Germain about Burgoyne's operation

from Canada down the Champlain-Hudson route to Albany. No specific instructions are included for Howe in this matter. At this same time, Howe is preparing for his own invasion of Pennsylvania, and the capture of the rebel capitol of Philadelphia. It seems that Howe does not grasp that these two operations are in any way interconnected. Nor does Germain nor King George. Another example of British lack of strategic insight, and failure to think out the Principles of War. [See Appendix 3, Volume 2].

The Congress agrees to grant delegate Richard Henry Lee, a leave of absence, his health and private affairs requiring his return to Virginia.

6 June 1777:
Friday. The Congress commissions Elias Boudinot as commissary-general of prisoners of war. Boudinot is authorized to appoint two deputies.

At Middlebrook, Washington writes to Charles, Earl Cornwallis, regarding certain matters of prisoner needs and prisoner treatment, "My Lord: I received the favour (sic) of your Lordship's letter of this day. I am sorry, I cannot with propriety comply with Lieut. Col. Sterling's (Thomas Sterling of the 42nd Foot, British Army) request; but as I wish not to obstruct any supplies, you may think proper to send for the comfort and accommodation of your prisoners with us, I am to assure you, that the greatest care will be taken to forward and deliver, whatever money or necessaries may be transmitted for the purpose; and vouchers of its being done will be returned for the satisfaction of the gentlemen from whom they come. Again Lieut. Col. Sterling can send those articles by a flag addressed to Elias Boudinot, Esquire, Commissary for Prisoners, with proper directions for the distribution of them, and they will not, fail to be observed. Every matter of a similar nature is to pass through his hands, and to be transacted by him, as was signified in a late letter of mine to Lieut. Genl. De Heister, to point out the proper channel of conveyance in these cases. I cannot forbear taking this occasion to remark, that it appears to me not a little singular, to find a gallant discharge of duty in an officer assigned as a reason for exercising the greatest barbarity towards him. I confess I should imagine the Eye of generosity, would rather view it as a motive for applause and tenderness."

7 June 1777:
Saturday. The Congress considers a report presented by the Board of War, and resolves "That the clothier-general furnish each non-commissioned officer and soldier inlisted [sic] in the army of the United States, to serve three years, or during the war, with the articles of cloathing [sic] enumerated by resolution of Congress of 8 October last, or other cloathing [sic] of equal value, notwithstanding the same costs more than twenty dollars."

8 June 1777:
Sunday. John Adams writes to Major General John Sullivan, "The information you give me that desertions from the Enemy are plentiful, gives me pleasure, but the resolution of the Militia to turn out and assist you, gives me much more. Nothing however contributes so much to my happiness, as the accounts I hear, that discipline, order, subordination, cleanliness, health and spirits are so rapidly increasing in our Army. All depends upon this."

9 June 1777:
Monday. The Board of War brings in a report on the issue of prisoners of war, to the effect that, if the British transport any of their American prisoners to the realm of Great Britain or to any of the dominions of the King of Great Britain, to be there confined in common jails, or other places of confinement, the Congress can have no other recourse but to treat prisoners currently in its power in the same manner.

10 June 1777:
Tuesday. In Quebec, Sir Guy Carleton sends orders to Major John Butler and Captain Walter Butler to gather their forces and meet with and assist Lt. Col. Barry St. Leger in an attack upon the American post at Fort Stanwix, and then move east along the Mohawk Valley to meet with Maj. Gen. John Burgoyne at Albany, as he comes south from Fort Edward.
The commissary of an army is that branch of the service responsible for food and clothing supplies. In the American Army during the War of the American Revolution, this service is in its infancy and is all too frequently inefficient and ineffective. The result is a poorly clad, poorly supplied soldiery. In Philadelphia, the Congress resumes consideration of the report of the Committee on the Commissary Department, and, with amendments, agrees to a lengthy resolution containing 60 sections. However, it will not be resolutions, nor committee reports that solve the problem, but quality officers, with knowledge of acquisition, transportation, storage, and issue of supplies that count.

11 June 1777:
Wednesday. In Berlin, Arthur Lee writes to the Committee of Foreign Affairs, reporting that he believes a treaty of commerce might be made to work between Prussia and America, although he notes that the Germans, unlike the French and British may not have the "bottoms" (types of vessels) needed to cross the ocean.
At Staten Island, New York, William Howe and his staff arrive from Amboy to complete the assembly of a huge undertaking of assembling about 15,000 troops and their support systems to be used for his strike at Pennsylvania and Philadelphia.

12 June 1777:

Thursday. At City Tavern, Philadelphia, a delegate from Delaware, writes a challenge to a delegate from New Jersey. The letter is laid before Congress, which resolves "That the Conduct of Gunning Bedford in sending a Challenge to Jonathan D. Sergeant, a Member of this House for Words spoken in this house in the Discharge of his Duty, is highly reprehensible and subversive of that Freedom of Speech which is Essential to the Constitution and Authority of this House."

13 June 1777:

Friday. At Fort Chambly, with most of his troops assembled, Burgoyne puts on a review (a form of parade) to honor Sir Guy Carleton.

American Major General Arthur St. Clair arrives at Fort Ticonderoga to take command of this post and its dependencies.

At North Island, in the Bay of Georgetown, South Carolina, Marie Jean Paul Joseph Roch Gilbert du Motier, Marquis de Lafayette, arrives aboard the *Victorie*, and spends two days at the home of Major Benjamin Huger. He and the party with him will proceed to Charleston, and from there to Philadelphia.

14 June 1777:

Saturday. In Philadelphia, the Congress passes a resolution "That the flag of the United States be thirteen stripes, alternate red and white: that the union be thirteen stars, white in a blue field, representing a new constellation."

15 June 1777:

Sunday. New York City, occupied by the British, is deprived of the usual means of trade because most of the seaports in and near the city are controlled by the enemy. The normal routes of trade are slowed or cut-off, and in particular the city is distressed for want of salt. The Congress requests the other states to assist in this matter by providing quantities of salt to the New Yorkers, to the degree that it does not hurt the local supplies.

16 June 1777:

Monday. Burgoyne prepares to leave Fort St. John with his expedition to slice into New York, reach Albany, and divide the middle states from the New England states. Including Indians, and Loyalists, he has a force of nearly 8,000 men.

Having agreed upon the form of the Commissary Department, the Congress orders a series of pay scales for the various officers in that department.

The Lafayette party arrives in Charleston, South Carolina. The vessel in which they had crossed the Atlantic, the *Victorie*, will arrive in a few days.

17 June 1777:
Tuesday. Near Fort Ticonderoga, a British Indian raid
captures two persons, one of whom, James McIntosh, having
lived in the area for a number of years, is able, upon
questioning, to report in some detail upon the strength,
condition, outworks, and positions of the Americans in the
fort.
In northeast New Jersey, William Howe is making thrusts
towards Washington's forces, in the hopes of enticing
Washington into a full scale battle, which Howe expects to
win. Washington does not bite on this bait, blocks Howe's
movements, and discerns in them that Howe is not truly
planning to attack Philadelphia by means of a march through
the Jerseys.

18 June 1777:
Wednesday. In Berlin, the Baron de Schlenburg writes to
Arthur Lee, expressing a willingness to further explore the
idea of a treaty of commerce between Prussia and America.
At headquarters, Middlebrook, New Jersey, General
Orders state "Timothy Pickering, Esqr., is appointed a
Adjutant General to the Continental Army. He is to be obeyed
and respected as such. The General begs Col. Connor to
accept his thanks, for his obliging and punctual discharge of
the office, for the time he has acted as such." The parole is
given as Boundbrook, and the countersigns as Bedford and
Boston.

19 June 1777:
Thursday. Richard Peters, secretary of the Board of War,
writes to General George Washington, reporting that he is
trying very hard to get a good grasp of just what the exact
accounts of receipts and distributions there are in the Army,
but has yet to have an accounting of any precision. He
assures the general he will persevere and says he believes the
greatest quantities of ammunition and stores are at the
arsenal at Springfield.
West of Brunswick, New Jersey, Howe's thrusts at
Washington cease, because they have been successfully
blocked. Howe marches back to Brunswick, and begins to
destroy the fortifications he had erected there as a defense
against American attacks.

20 June 1777:
Friday. On the docks at St. John, Richelieu River, the
British-Hessian invasion army, now assembled and all aboard
the many vessels that have been built, reassembled, or
carried to Fort St. John, forming an armada, gets under way
heading south toward Lake Champlain. Maj. Gen. John
Burgoyne (with the local rank of Lieutenant General) has
about 7,400 troops, plus 400 or so Indians under his
command. This armada will sail, row, and paddle up the river
and onto Lake Champlain, camping ashore each night, as

they proceed toward Fort Ticonderoga. An advance contingent is encamped on both banks of the Bouquet River.

21 June 1777:
Saturday. In Philadelphia, John Adams writes to his wife Abigail, "My dearest friend; It would give pleasure to every body your way but the few, unfeeling Tories, to see what a spirit prevails here. The alarm which Howe [Sir William Howe] was foolish enough to spread by his march out of Brunswick, raised the militia of the Jerseys universally, and in this city it united the Whigs, to exert themselves under their new Militia Law, in such a degree that nobody here was under any apprehensions of danger from Howe's march. It seemed to be the general wish that he might persevere in his march that he might meet with certain destruction. But the poor wretches have skulked back to Brunswick. This is a great disgrace. It will be considered so in Europe. It is certainly thought so by our people, and it will be felt to be so by their own people--the poor Tories especially."

22 June 1777:
Sunday. At Fort Ticonderoga, one of Major General Arthur St. Clair's difficulties is the gathering of intelligence. Because of the large number of Indians serving Burgoyne (the Indians being excellent scouts), it is nearly impossible for any of the American scouting parties to get close enough to the British-Hessian armada or their encampments on shore to learn anything. This is very frustrating to St. Clair, since, without information about the enemy, his strentgh and whereabouts, he is lost as to how best to counter an attack.

At the Raritan River, New Jersey, the British forces, under William Howe, are marching from their former post at Brunswick to Amboy. American artillery lobs shells onto the narrow bridge across the river, as Cornwallis' troops are crossing, but do little damage. Howe still hopes his attempts to entice Washington into a fight will succeed, but, nevertheless, he continues his preparations to attack Philadelphia.

23 June 1777:
Monday. In Montreal, Lieutenant Colonel Barry St. Leger, having gathered the troops he is to command for an expedition through the Iroquois country to the Mohawk Valley, departs. He will travel up the St. Lawrence River, across the eastern end of Lake Ontario to Oswego, New York.

In the British Camp on the west shore of Lake Champlain at the Bouquet River, Burgoyne issues Proclamation, "The forces entrusted to my Command are designed to act in concert and to act upon a common principle, with the numerous armies and Fleets which already display, in every quarter of America, the Power, the Justice, and, when properly sought, the Mercy of the King; the cause in which the British Arms are thus exerted, applies to the most affecting interest of the human heart ... The intention of this address is to hold forth security, not depreciation to the country; to those whose Spirit and principle may induce them to partake the glorious task of redeeming their countrymen from dungeons and re-establishing the blessings of legal government ... The domestic, the industrious, the infirm, and even the timid Inhabitants, I am desirous to protect, provided they remain quietly at their houses, that they do not suffer their cattle to be removed, or their corn or forage to be secreted or destroyed; that they do not break up their bridges or roads, or any other Act, directly or indirectly endeavor to obstruct the Operation of the King's Troops, or supply or assist those of the enemy. I have dwelt upon this invitation ... and let not the people be led to disregard it ... I have but to give stretch to the Indian Forces under my Direction, and they amount to thousands, to overtake the hardened enemies of Great Britain ... If the frenzy of hostility should remain, I trust I shall stand acquitted in the eyes of God and Man, in denouncing and executing the Vengeance of the State against the willful outcast. The messengers of Justice and Wrath await them in the Field, and Devastation, Famine, and every concomitant Horror that a reluctant but indispensable prosecution of Military duty must occasion will bar the way to their return."

At Fort Ticonderoga, one of St. Clair's scouts, a Sergeant Heath, returns from a scout down the lake (north) and reports that the Indians are "thick as mosquitoes". He also notes that near the mouth of Otter Creek (on the east side of the lake) he has seen five British ships, as well as encampments on both sides of the Bouquet River (on the west side of the lake). This confirms to St. Clair that the enemy is close at hand, and he prepares plans for an escape, should that become necessary.

24 June 1777:
Tuesday. The Burgoyne armada rows and sails out of Cumberland Bay to continue south up Lake Champlain, and enter the widest part of the lake. Several journals and diaries from members of Burgoyne's forces report upon the stunning beauty, majesty, and glory of the scene. Imagine, if you will, a smooth, calm stretch of water, surrounded by mountains on both sides, green with foliage reflected upon the water, with hundreds of bateaux, canoes, and sailing vessels of varying sizes, all in neat and ordered rows, moving slowly in unison upon the water. It surely must have been a truly awe inspiring sight!

Near Amboy, New Jersey, a rebel dragoon deserter enters the British camp, and on being interrogated, says that Washington has descended from his encampments in the hills and is deploying his army in the area around Quibbletown (now New Market). Howe is delighted with this bit of information as it is the very thing he hoped would happen, as he tries to lure the Americans away from their fortifications, and forcing them into the open, with a chance to run them to ground, and defeat the main American Army.

25 June 1777:
Wednesday. Having collected all the baggage from the *Victorie*, recovered from his seasickness, and visited with Governor Rutledge, the Lafayette party leaves Charleston for its journey to Philadelphia.

General George Washington makes his headquarters in Quibbletown, New Jersey at the Drake House. He wants to be somewhat closer to Howe, but is still leery of an entrapment. Washington is able to make good use of the New Jersey militia as they hover around Howe's army, set up blockages, and harass the British foragers. Howe wants to attack this American Army.

26 June 1777:
Thursday. In New Jersey, Howe sends two British-Hessian columns towards the rebel forces, one under Maj. Gen. John Vaughan, the other under Cornwallis. They encounter some resistance from William Maxwell's brigade, near Short Hills, but a bayonet charge scatters the rebels. The Americans escape with all their wagons and most of their artillery. Washington returns to his Middlebrook headquarters.

In Philadelphia, the Congress again takes into consideration the issue of the Articles of Confederation, but does not come to a conclusion, although some progress is made.

27 June 1777:
Friday. Washington, under attack by Howe, falls back toward the hills and the fortifications they provide. Having lost the element of surprise and unable to destroy the rebels, Howe decides to return to Amboy.

The Congress hears a report of the Committee of the Treasury, that includes a request for $80,000 to Matthew Irwin for the payment of magazines of provisions laid up in Pennsylvania; 20,000 barrels of flour at Lancaster and York, 11,000 bushels of wheat, 15,000 gallons of whiskey.

28 June 1777:
Saturday. From the War Office, Richard Peters, secretary of the Board of War, writes to George Washington, "The Board are of opinion that the whole of the Artillery imported in the *Amphitrite* should be together, with the Grand Army, & the Officers who came from France should accompany the cannon that they may give the necessary directions concerning them. But as your Excellency is the most capable of judging on the matter, the Board leave it entirely to your discretion desiring that if you should not think the order for the twelve pieces from the commander in chief of the Northern Department a proper one, you will be pleased to order the whole of the Artillery immediately to headquarters."

At Short Hills, New Jersey, near the Metuchen Meeting House, about five miles west of Amboy, Sir William Howe makes a sortie with Lord Cornwallis's division and attacks a post of Maj. Gen. William Alexander (Lord Stirling), causing him to retreat with loss.

29 June 1777:
Sunday. In Berlin, Arthur Lee writes to the King of Prussia, as Prussia and America are struggling to conclude a treaty of commerce. Major problems from the Prussian side including the fact that the Prussians do not have ocean-going vessels of any quality or quantity (since most of their trade is riverine), and that the king is most reluctant to allow American privateers into his ports, fearing it might offend the English. Lee states to the King: "The nations that shall endeavor to obtain a part of it [trade with America] for themselves by furnishing to a young and grateful people the means of resisting their oppressors will be very successful. But those who wish to await in tranquility the event of this war ought not to expect to turn trade from the course in which custom and gratitude before that time will have fixed it. The present, therefore, is the proper time for those to begin who wish to enjoy for the future the commerce of America."

30 June 1777:
Monday. The main body of Burgoyne's British-Hessian invasion force is at Crown Point, about eleven miles north of Fort Ticonderoga. At 7 o'clock in the morning, one of St. Clair's guard boats on Lake Champlain fires a warning shot, indicating that the enemy is within sight. Major General Arthur St. Clair has a total of about 2,500 men under his command. Major General John Burgoyne has a total of more than 7,500 men under his command. This one to three ratio of men, now understood by St. Clair, gives him pause about his ability to defend his post. He thus matures a means of escape, sending some of his arms and supplies up Lake George to safety.
At Amboy, New Jersey, William Howe, some of whose forces have been embarking for Staten Island, sends his remaining units away, thus abandoning the king's last foothold in New Jersey, and giving up his hopes of drawing Washington into a battle.

1 July 1777:
Tuesday. In Philadelphia, John Hancock, the President of the Congress writes to Ralph Izard, enclosing his commission as the envoy of the United States to the Grand Duchy of Tuscany, and provides Izard with the following instructions: "... as it is of the greatest importance to these States that Great Britain be effectually obstructed in the plan of sending German and Russian troops to North America, you will exert all possible address to prevail with the grand duke to use his

influence with the Emperor and the courts of France and Spain to this end."

At Crown Point, Burgoyne splits his forces, sending the Hessians, under the Baron Friedrich von Riedesel, up the east side of the lake towards Mount Independence, and Brigadier General Simon Fraser up the west side of the Lake towards Fort Ticonderoga.

2 July 1777:

Wednesday. Near Fort Ticonderoga, British Brig. Gen. Fraser sends a force of more than 600 men, including Canadians and Indians, around the American left to reach the sawmills and cut the road leading south to Lake George. This will remove a possible escape route for the rebels. The Americans at Fort Ticonderoga, under Major General Arthur St. Clair, are still in a bit of a fog regarding the enemy strength, dispositions, and intentions.

3 July 1777:

Thursday. Around Fort Ticonderoga, British Brig. Gen. Simon Fraser brings up the balance of his corps, including artillery, on the west side of Lake Champlain, to the vicinity of Mount Hope and the Lake George Landing. Von Riedesel's Hessians are having a tough time on the east side of Lake Champlain because the approach from the north to Mount Independence is over difficult ground: East Creek is actually more of a swamp, and there are no roads over which to haul wagons, artillery, and supplies.

General George Washington is back in Morristown, after his cat and mouse manoeuvres with Howe.

4 July 1777:

Friday. At Fort Ticonderoga, two German deserters cross into St. Clair's lines and divulge information about Burgoyne's army, that has been mostly lacking for three weeks.

Meanwhile the Americans capture a British regular soldier. When he refuses to talk, Lieutenant Andrew Hodges, disguised as a bumptious Irishman, is sent to the British soldier's cell--with a bottle of spirits. Hodges befriends the soldier, who eventually talks to him at length. Much of what the soldier tells Hodges confirms what the German deserters have already said. Now that St. Clair knows what the British have in mind and how they are proposing to attack his position, he begins to put into operation plans for evacuation to escape from Fort Ticonderoga, knowing that he cannot defend the place.

5 July 1777:

Saturday. Both the Americans in Fort Ticonderoga and the British nearly surrounding them fire a few artillery rounds without much effect. Just after midnight. Brig. Gen. Fraser dispatches a patrol to investigate the elevation known as Sugar Hill. The Americans call it Mount Defiance. Upon a report that the patrol has reached the top, Fraser, with his engineering officer, Lieutenant William Twiss, hike up the mountain. They quickly decide to bring cannon to the top, and orders are issued for a fatigue party to built an abatis at the summit. Two twelve-pounders are in place by mid-morning.

Fort Ticonderoga and Mount Independence are now totally indefensible. St. Clair immediately puts his evacuation plan into action. Most of the arms, supplies, and troops from Fort Ticonderoga move swiftly over the bridge of planks to Mount Independence. The invalids row and sail up the South Bay towards Skenesborough. Guns are spiked, supplies are moved, men are assembled. By midnight the post is ready to be evacuated.

In New York City, Henry Clinton arrives from his trip to England, now with the new title of Sir Henry Clinton, conferred upon him on 11 April 1777. Howe has been awaiting his arrival, so that he can launch his amphibious operation against the rebel capitol of Philadelphia, while leaving Clinton in charge at New York. But contrary winds keep the British fleet bottled up in the harbor until 21 July.

6 July 1777:
Sunday. In the early hours of darkness, the Americans manage to escape from Fort Ticonderoga and Mount Independence. They move by road and water south and east. Most of the supply train, the baggage, the sick, and the ammunition, under Colonel Pierce Long, go by water up the narrow, almost riverine part of Lake Champlain to Skenesborough (now Whitehall, New York). The main American force marches by the military road to Hubbardton, thence south to Castleton. The rear guard, whose mission is to delay any pursuit by the enemy, is under Colonel Ebenezer Francis.

The British-Hessian forces quickly capture and occupy both Fort Ticonderoga and Fort Independence. Brigadier General Simon Fraser immediately sends nearly one-half of his brigade, about 850 men, in pursuit of the retreating Americans. Nearly ten miles into the march, the British find a company-size body of Americans, well into liquor, who inform him about Colonel Francis. Fraser sends to Burgoyne for reinforcements. Late in the afternoon, having stopped for rest, Fraser is joined by Major General the Baron von Riedesel, with nearly 1,100 men. The Germans bivouac for the night and Fraser moves his troops about three miles farther south before resting for the night.

While Colonel Francis is hurrying southeast to avoid his pursuers, Colonel Pierce Long sails south towards Skenesborough, New York. Not aware that Burgoyne is able to cut quickly through the chain barrier at Fort Ticonderoga, nor that the guard, whose duty is to fire cannon at any such attempt, were drunk and did not hold off the British, Long is in no hurry. He also fails to provide any flanking patrols along the winding course of the river-like southerly extension of Lake Champlain through which he is moving as a rear guard. The result is that Burgoyne is nearly on top of Long and his troops, as they arrive at Skenesborough about 3 o'clock in the afternoon. Long is able to escape the trap of a pincer movement by Burgoyne. He burns everything he cannot carry, and hurries off to Fort Anne, New York. The British capture the abandoned American vessels at Skenesborough, and begin a pursuit of Long's force.

7 July 1777:
Monday. Fraser's troops are up by 3 o'clock in the morning, marching toward Hubbardton, (now in Vermont.) The American advance pickets fire, opening the Battle of Hubbardton. The British attack, but are repulsed by an American counterattack that very nearly succeeds in winning the battle. The Germans arrive in the nick of time to rescue the British and drive off the Americans, who retreat eastwardly toward West Rutland, so as to avoid the British who had captured Skenesborough. The British and German losses in this battle are nearly 200 killed and wounded. The Americans lose about 125 killed and wounded. From Rutland, the Americans march south to Manchester, Vermont, and thence along the Battenkill River to Fort Miller on the west bank of the Hudson River.
Burgoyne sends Lieutenant Colonel Hill after the retreating Americans, under Colonel Pierce Long, who are hurrying south towards Fort Anne. This is a small log fort built near a stream, supported by embankments, used as a rest stop from Fort Edward.

8 July 1777:
Tuesday. At Fort Anne, Colonel Pierce Long is reinforced by Colonel Henry Van Rensselaer. British Lieutenant Colonel Hill, with less than 200 men is camped about a mile north of the blockhouse. A deserter enters Hill's camp in the morning, reporting that the Americans have 1,000 troops. Hill, unwilling to attack such a superior force, and feeling it unsafe to retreat, stays put, calling for reinforcements. An Indian war whoop indicates that the British reinforcements are at hand. The Americans retreat to Fort Edward.

9 July 1777:
Wednesday. At Fort Edward, New York, Philip Schuyler writes to George Washington, "I have not been able to learn what is become of General St. Clair and the army. The enemy followed the troops, that came to Skenesborough, as far as Ft. Ann, where they were yesterday repulsed, not withstanding which Colonel Long, contrary to my express

orders, evacuated that post. I am here at the head of a
handful of men, not above 1500 without provision, little
ammunition, not above five rounds a man, having neither ball
nor lead to make any; the country in the deepest
consternation; no carriages to move the stores from Ft.
George, which I expect every moment to learn is attacked and
what adds to my distress is that a report prevails, that I had
given orders for the evacuation of Ticonderoga, whereas not
the most distant hint of such an intention can be drawn from
any of my letters to General St. Clair, or any other person
whatever."

In Philadelphia, the Congress resolves that the state of
Pennsylvania continue with the defense works on the
approaches to the city at and near Chester on the west, and
at Billingsport on the New Jersey side of the Delaware River,
using the assistance of militia provided to complete them.

10 July 1777:
Thursday. At headquarters in Morristown, Washington
writes to the president of the Congress, "If General Arnold has
settled his affairs and can be spared from Philadelphia, I
would recommend him for this business [transfer to the north
to assist in attacks upon Burgoyne's invasion forces] the and
that he should immediately set out for the northern
department. He is active, judicious and brave, and an officer
in whom the militia will repose great confidence. Besides this,
he is well acquainted with that country and with the routes
and most important passes and defiles in it. I do not think he
can render more signal services, or be more usefully employed
at this time, than in this way. I am persuaded his presence
and activity will animate the militia greatly, and spur them on
to a becoming conduct; I could wish him to be engaged in a
more agreeable service, to be with better troops, but
circumstances call for his exertions in this way, and I have no
doubt of his adding much to the honors he has already
acquired. In consequence of the advices from Genl. St. Clair,
and the strong probability there is, that Genl. Howe will push
against the Highland passes, to cooperate with Genl.
Burgoyne, I shall, by the advice of my officers, move the army
from hence tomorrow morning, towards the North River. If
such should be his intention, we shall not be too early, as a
favourable wind and tide will carry him up in a few hours. On
the other hand, if Philadelphia is his object, he can't get
round before we can arrive there, nor can he well debark his
troops & proceed across the land before we can oppose him."

The Congress, agreeable to the bill of Commissary-General
Joseph Trumbull, presented to it for approval, and following a
short debate, orders that $10,000 be paid to Colonel Robert
Lettis Hooper for the payment of flour and beef for the use of
the army.

11 July 1777:
    Friday. At Philadelphia, John Adams writes to Abigail, "We have had no news from camp for three or four days. Mr. Howe. By the last advices, was maoeuvering [sic] his fleet and army in such a manner as to give us expectations of an expedition somewhere: but whether to Rhode Island, Halifax, or up the North River, or the Delaware, is left to conjecture. I am much in doubt whether he knows his own intentions. A faculty of penetrating into the design of an enemy is said to be the first quality of a General, but it is impossible to discover the designs of an enemy who has no design at all. An intention that has no existence, a plan that is not laid, cannot be divined. Be his intentions what they may, you have nothing to fear from him. He has not force to penetrate the country anywhere."

12 July 1777:
    Saturday. The Congress informs General George Washington that there are about 1,400 patriots in Philadelphia and Billingsport, ready to march at a moment's warning, but await his orders.
    At Fort Miller, New York, the Americans are gathering from their retreat from Fort Ticonderoga. Under the leadership of Schuyler, they rest, recover, are regrouped and reorganized, and begin preparations to meet or slow down the British advance.

13 July 1777:
    Sunday. General Washington is at Pompton Plains, New Jersey, at Van Aulen's House, where he makes his headquarters. Washington writes to Maj. Gen. Philip Schuyler, "Dear Sir: I wrote to you yesterday by express, informing you of what I had done towards furnishing you with such supplies as are in my power to give, and the obstacles that at present lie in the way of granting you others that your situation demands. It is astonishing beyond expression, that you had heard nothing of St. Clair and the Army under him. I am totally at a loss to conceive what has become of them."

14 July 1777:
    Monday. In Philadelphia, the Congress orders that $2,245 2/90 be paid to Colonel Lewis Nicola of the City Guard to pay for four companies from 2 June to 2 July 1777. (See the Sketch on p. 154 of 13 September 1776 for an explanation of these odd fractions.)

15 July 1777:
    Tuesday. The Congress is less than pleased with the stream of foreign officers Silas Deane is forwarding to America. One of these officers is Monsieur du Coudray. A committee of three is to be formed to meet with du Coudray

and inform him, that "... Congress cannot comply with the
agreement he has entered into with Mr. Deane; but that
sensible of the services he has rendered these States, and
having a favorable opinion of his merit and abilities, they will
cheerfully give him such rank and appointments as shall not
be inconsistent with the honour [sic] and safety of these
States, or interfere with the great duties they owe to their
constituents." The issue of what to do with Silas Deane
becomes another matter which the Congress will deal with at
a later date.

16 July 1777:
     Wednesday. At camp near the Clove of the Highlands,
Washington writes to the president of the Congress, "I this
day received advice from Staten Island, that on Sunday
seventy sail of the enemy's ships fell down from the watering
place to the [Sandy] Hook, but whether they have since gone
out to sea, I have not heard. Till I have more certain
information of the state of our affairs to the northward, and of
Genl. Howe's real intentions, I have concluded to halt the
army at this place, from whence I can march either forward or
return, as circumstances may require. I shall be very happy if
the Committee of Congress can arrange the commissary's
department in such a manner, as will satisfy the officers
concerned in the business, and at the same time serve to
supply the army with more regularity, than has been done for
some time past. I can assure you the complaints have been
many of late, and not without foundation."
     Congress advances $100,000 to Anthony Butler, agent to
Major General Thomas Mifflin, quarter master general,
agreeable to the draft on the president of the Congress.
Mifflin is a poor excuse for a supply or commissary officer.
Absent too much of the time, almost never on top of his
supplies, and forever pointing fingers at some other poor
junior officer for his own misdirection.

17 July 1777:
     Thursday. The Congress orders that a letter be written to
the executive powers of the States not represented in the
Congress, informing them "... that the confederation of the
States, and several other important matters, are put off for
want of a full representation of all the States ... to send a
sufficient number of members to represent them as soon as
possible."

18 July 1777:
     Friday. At the site of Fort Stanwix, New York. [See Fig. IV-
20, p. 257], sometimes called Fort Schuyler (now Rome),
American Colonel Peter Gansevoort, with about 550 men, is
actively preparing a stout defense against a British attack.

19 July 1777:

Saturday. The Congress orders Colonel Thomas Proctor, at his request, to bring his Pennsylvania artillery battalion into the Continental service. Likewise they bring into Continental Service the North Carolina artillery company.

20 July 1777:

Sunday. In Philadelphia, Cornelius Harnett, a delegate from North Carolina, writes to William Wilkinson, reporting that he has elected to undergo the procedure of inoculation, at Port Tobacco, Maryland, while en route to return to the Congress. He notes that his arm was very sore and inflamed to the point where he could not wear a coat, but the inflammation has finally worn off.

21 July 1777:

Monday. In New York harbor, the British fleet with William Howe's army, weighs anchor and drops down off Sandy Hook.

General George Washington is at Smith's Clove, a cleft in the mountain chain, just a bit north of the New Jersey-New York line—used as the means of travel to by-pass New York City and move troops and supplies to and from New England. Washington uses this place as headquarters, because it places him close enough to the New Jersey routes to the Delaware to counter any possible moves by Howe in that direction, but also close enough to the Hudson River routes to support Schuyler as needed, in case Howe should move in that direction. Washington is forever trying to keep his army intact and in being, while avoiding a major confrontation.

22 July 1777:

Tuesday. Henry Laurens, a delegate from South Carolina, and Cornelius Harnett, a delegate from North Carolina, attend the Congress and take their seats.

At headquarters, eleven miles into the Clove, New York, Washington writes to Philip Schuyler, "Tho' our affairs, for some days past have worn a dark and gloomy aspect, I yet look forward to a fortunate and happy change. I trust Genl. Burgoyne's Army will meet, sooner or later an effectual check, and as I suggested before, that the success, he has had, will precipitate his ruin. From your accounts, he appears to be pursuing that line of conduct, which of all others, is most favourable to us. I mean acting in Detachments."

23 July 1777:

Wednesday. At Annapolis, Maryland, the Lafayette party arrives from its overland journey from Charleston, and prepares to take ship to Baltimore. They need to get to Philadelphia in order to meet with the Congress and present their papers from Silas Deane, seeking commissions in the American forces.

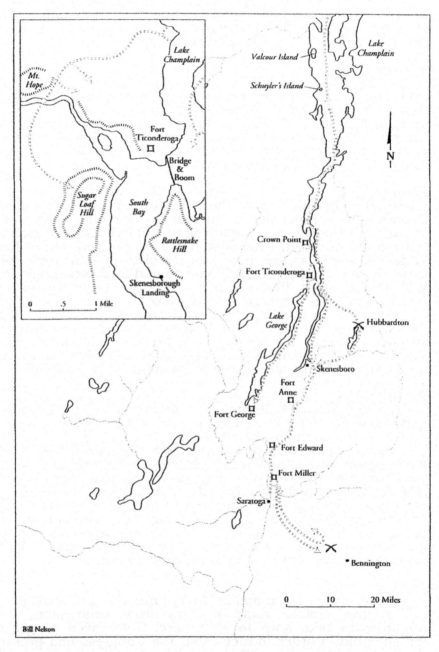

Fig. IV-19: Burgoyne's Route to the Hudson, July 1777

Several naval lieutenants petition the Marine Committee in language that is seen as treasonous, i.e., they seek pay and advancement and threaten not to perform their duties until these issues are addressed. The Congress is insulted, and fears that such combinations of officers seeking to extort monies from the public are dangerous. Thus, they feel it necessary to make an example of them. They are all to be dismissed from the service, their commissions rendered null and void and they are deemed incapable of employment in any of the United States, in any office, civil or military.

At New York Harbor, Sir William Howe, having embarked his army for an expedition on Philadelphia, sets sail from Sandy Hook. He has a force of about 16,000 troops and 267 vessels of all kinds. They disappear over the eastern horizon. He will appear later off the Capes of Delaware.

24 July 1777:
Thursday. George Washington has his headquarters at Ramapo, New Jersey. When he is informed that Howe's fleet has left New York, Washington suspects a descent upon Philadelphia. However, not knowing Howe's intent, Washington sends out patrols and spies to report any movements of the British to him.

25 July 1777:
Friday. British Lieutenant Colonel Barry St. Leger arrives at Oswego, New York, where he is joined by more Indians. His force now totals about 2,000 men. From here St. Leger will march and canoe toward Fort Stanwix.

26 July 1777:
Saturday. General George Washington makes his headquarters near Morristown, New Jersey.

Washington writes to Lord Stirling, "Genl. Greene's division will reach Morristown this evening. Genl. Stephen's and Genl. Lincoln's march thro Chester by the upper road. I have no objection to your Lordships taking the route you mention, and as it will bring you near Newark and Elizabethtown, I have sent orders to Col. Dayton, to endeavour (sic) to procure certain intelligence of the number of the enemy left upon Staten Island and where they are posted. If they only consist of the Green Regiments amounting to about 1,000 men, as a deserter says, a descent may be made to great advantage."

27 July 1777:
Sunday. Sir William Howe's fleet, transporting his forces to attack Philadelphia, is sighted off the Capes of the Delaware.

Burgoyne advances to Fort Edward on the banks of the Hudson River, where he rests his assembling army for some time. Except those soldiers on garrison duty at Fort

Ticonderoga, Burgoyne is gathering his troops from the Hubbarton fight, the Skenesboro, Fort Anne captures, and the Lake George area. He now wants to concentrate his forces and prepare to march farther south. [See Fig. IV-19, p. 250].

28 July 1777:
    Monday. General George Washington makes his headquarters at Flemington, New Jersey.
    Washington writes to the Board of War, "It is not in my power to furnish Genl. Schuyler with any tents. A thousand, of those mentioned in the return, went to his army. I wrote Genl. Putnam, immediately after Genl. Schuyler's application, to forward to his relief, all he could, of a parcel which I heard was then coming from the eastward, how many there were, whether any could be spared or what number has gone, I cannot inform you. So far from being in a situation to assist him in this instance, there are several men in this Army who now want, and who have never been provided with any."

29 July 1777:
    Tuesday. In Philadelphia, the Congress, having received the Silas Deane letters of recommendation from the Lafayette party, and having had an opportunity to review them, are not pleased with this influx of opportunists and receives them coolly.
    Howe's fleet, having sheltered inside the Capes of the Delaware, meet with Captain Andrew Hamond and his frigate HMS *Roebuck*. Hamond has been on a detached command with a squadron off the coasts of Virginia, Maryland and Delaware for nearly 18 months, and thus knows those waters well. A conference is held with the Howe brothers in their flagship, HMS *Eagle*. Hamond points out the difficulties of landing such a large force and supplying it on the likely spots along the Delaware River, which is a fast flowing stream, easily defended. He recommends an approach up the Chesapeake Bay.
    Washington moves with his army to Germantown, Pennsylvania. He still does not have definitive information on the intentions of William Howe, but positions himself so as to be able to block a move, no matter from which direction.

30 July 1777:
    Wednesday. Aware that the British are planning an invasion of the area near Philadelphia, the Congress resolves that the States of Pennsylvania, New Jersey, and Delaware are "... to cause the horses, waggons, carts, cattle, and other live stock contiguous to the bay and river of Delaware, to be removed into the interior parts of the country, whenever the arrival of the enemy's Forces at the capes shall announce the necessity and propriety of such a measure."

31 July 1777:
Thursday. Washington is in Coryell's Ferry, New Jersey, at the Holcombe House.

The Congress accepts the service of the Marquis de la Fayette (the name is spelled many ways, but this is what appears in the journals), and awards him the rank and commission of a major general in the army of the United States.

The intention of Sir William Howe, as to where he might choose to debark his army, is quite confusing to the patriot forces. Having been sighted off the Capes of the Delaware, his fleet is next seen to again put out to sea.

1 August 1777:
Friday. General Washington makes his headquarters at Chester, Pennsylvania, where Lafayette meets with him, and accompanies the general on an inspection tour of the Delaware forts.

At Chester, Washington writes to Maj. Gen. Israel Putnam, "I have this moment received intelligence by express, that the enemy's fleet yesterday morning about 8 o'clock, sailed out of the Capes in an eastern course. This surprising event gives me the greatest anxiety, and unless every possible exertion is made, may be productive of the happiest consequences to the enemy and the most injurious to us. I have desired General Sullivan's division and the two brigades, that left you last, immediately to return and re-cross the River, and shall forward on the rest of the army with all the expedition in my power. I have also written to General [George] Clinton requesting him instantly to reinforce you, with as many militia of the State of New York as he can collect; and you are, on receipt of this, to send on an express to Governor Trumbull, urging it upon him to assist you, with as many of the Connecticut militia as he can get together, and without a moments loss of time. The importance of preventing Mr. Howe's getting possession of the Highlands by a coup de main, is infinite to America, and in the present situation of things, every effort that can be thought of must be used. The probability of his going to the eastward is exceedingly small, and the ill effects that might attend such a step inconsiderable, in comparison with those that would inevitably attend a successful stroke upon the Highlands. Connecticut cannot be in more danger through any channel than this, and every motive of its own interests and the general good, demand its utmost endeavours to give you effectual assistance."

2 August 1777:
Saturday. The advance guard of Barry St. Leger's expedition reaches the vicinity of Fort Stanwix. He does not have enough heavy artillery to batter down the defenses

erected by the Americans, having only two six-pounders and two three-pounders, and is also short of ammunition. They are too late to prevent the arrival of 200 American reinforcements, bringing the defenders strength up to about 750 men. But St. Leger does use some of his Indians to scout the American position, looking for a means of attack.

General George Washington and Lafayette return to Philadelphia from their inspection of the Delaware forts.

3 August 1777:

Sunday. Near Fort Stanwix, New York, St. Leger, now with his full force of Canadians, Tories, and Indians, sets up a siege of the fort. Indians are not much used to sieges, and chafe at the delay in getting to actual fighting. [See Fig. IV-20, p. 256].

In Philadelphia, the Congress resolves that General Washington be directed to order the general whom he shall judge proper to relieve Major General Schuyler in his command to repair with all possible expedition to the Northern Department to assume his duties.

4 August 1777:

Monday. General Washington wishes to be excused from making the appointment of an officer to command the Northern Department, So the Congress proceeds to select Major General Horatio Gates.

5 August 1777:

Tuesday. At Fort Stanwix, the British forces under St. Leger, having the place under siege, but without heavy artillery to batter down the walls, snipe at the fort, but do little damage. St. Leger's Indian allies are restless and urge some form of positive action. He's in a bit of a pickle. While his forces outnumber the American defenders, they have too few troops at hand to make a really tight investment, to clear Wood Creek, and the 16 miles of supply road required to maintain a complete siege.

6 August 1777:

Wednesday. The Congress approves a warrant to issue in favor of the Board of War for $500,000 to be delivered to the paymaster general for the use of the army.

General George Washington is at Germantown, Pennsylvania.

At Fort Stanwix, St. Leger, with a British detachment and a body of Seneca and other Indians under Sir John Johnson and Joseph Brant, still invest this American post.

A rescue expedition, under militia Brig. Gen. Nicholas Herkimer with about 800 patriots, supported by a few Oneida Indians, is ambushed by Brant's Indians east of the Fort at a place called Oriskany. [See Fig, IV-20, p, 256]. As he

American forces are marching west towards the relief of Fort Stanwix, they must pass through a small defile in the pathway. The Indians have already set-up the ambush, posting themselves on both sides of the defile in the forested edges. The Americans march down into the path, which is below the higher ground on each side, unaware that many Indians are hiding in the woods above and on each side of them, waiting for the time to strike.

Before all the Americans enter the defile, a few Indians, too anxious to start a slaughter, fire at the column. The Americans quickly try to scatter and find cover, but there is not much to be found in the defile. A few are able to reach the nearby woods, and fire back at the Indians. The fighting is fierce. Large numbers of patriots are wounded or killed. Numbers of American militia run away, but several groups hold out, fight back, kill many Indians. The combat lasts for several hours. While the remaining Americans are finally able to beat off the attack and retreat in good order, Herkimer is wounded during the battle, helps to direct it while sitting up under a tree, is carried off in a litter, but dies later the next day.

Almost half of the American and Oneida forces are killed, wounded, or captured in this fight. About 170 Loyalists and Iroquois are killed, wounded or missing. This also is the beginning of the demise of the great Six Nations Confederation, since it is the Oneidas who side with the patriots, and most other Iroquois, including the Senecas, engage with the British.

7 August 1777:

Thursday. General George Washington makes his headquarters at Schuylkill Falls, Pennsylvania, from which place he writes to Israel Putnam, "We are as yet intirely in the dark as to the destination of the enemy, the fleet has neither been seen or heard of since they left the Capes of Delaware, of this day week. If they had intended back to the Hook, we must have heard of their arrival there long before this time, as the winds have been constantly fair. As the sickly season has commenced to the southward, and there is no capital object there, I cannot conceive that they are gone that way. I can therefore only conclude, that they intend to go round Long Island into the Sound, or still farther eastward. If they do either of these, it must be upon a plan of co-operating with Genl. Burgoyne, who, as matters are going on, will find little difficulty of penetrating to Albany, for by the last accounts, our Army had fallen down to Saratoga. Congress have thought proper to call down Genl. Schuyler and Genl. St. Clair, to give an account of the causes of our misfortunes to the northward and Genl. Gates goes up to take command. Genl. Schuyler urges the necessity of further reinforcements, alledging that he derives no assistance from the militia."

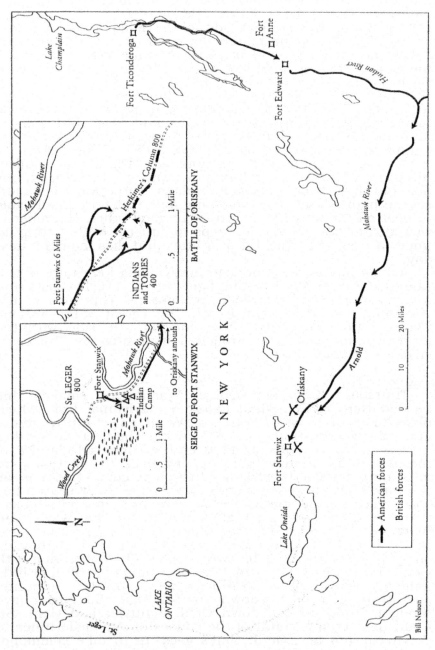

Fig. IV-20: Oriskany and Fort Stanwix, August 1777

8 August 1777:
   Friday. Burgoyne advances parts of his force south from Fort Edward to the site of Fort Miller, near where the Battenkill River flows into the Hudson. Most of his Hessian troops are quartered here. The Americans have abandoned the area, in the face of superior enemy forces, and moved further south.
   In Philadelphia, Benjamin Harrison, Robert Morris, and James Lovell of the Committee of Secret Correspondence write to Charles William Frédéric Dumas, at the Hague, Holland, reporting that they have received a number of his letters and packets and are most grateful for the intelligence he forwards regarding matters in Europe. "But, as we now have Commissioners settled in France, we think it will be needless that you should be at the trouble of making and of forwarding to us from time to time that collection of papers which we formerly mentioned to you. We shall inform our friends at Paris of our opinion on this head, and shall leave it to them to point out the ways in which your zeal for liberty may be most useful to them & us with the least degree of trouble to yourself and injury to your domestic interest."

9 August 1777:
   Saturday. Burgoyne, having learned that there might be a good stock of horses and forage to the east, orders Lieutenant Colonel Friedrich Baum to proceed in that direction. Baum's force leaves Fort Edward and marches toward Fort Miller.
   The Congress resolves that the Board of War be directed to confer with Elias Boudinot, Commissary of Prisoners, and report, as soon as possible, on the manner in which the prisoners under his charge ought to be treated.
   Washington returns to make his headquarters again at Germantown, which he had left just a few days earlier. All this moving around is a function of Washington's concern for the safety of the Hudson River line. He does not know what William Howe might be up to, and wishes to be in a position to move either in the direction of the forts on the Hudson, or the line of approach to Philadelphia in the area of New Jersey.

10 August 1777:
   Sunday. While at the Fort Stanwix siege, Tory Captain Walter Butler, is determined to make a raid upon patriot villages to the east. However, he is instead reinforced by St. Leger with a detachment of 15 men, and given orders to deliver and spread a statement or proclamation from the British authorities. He leaves on this mission down the Mohawk Valley toward German Flats, carrying Lieutenant Colonel Barry St. Leger's proclamation to the people of the Tryon County area. It states that they should declare for the British parliament and King George or else suffer the consequences.

Washington is at Neshaminy Camp, near Crossroads above Hartsville, Pennsylvania, at the Moland House.

11 August 1777:
Monday. Lieutenant Colonel Baum, his battalion reinforced with an additional 100 men, leaves Fort Miller and marches towards Cambridge, New York on a raid to procure horses and forage Burgoyne needs.

At Philadelphia, John Adams writes to Abigail, in which he dwells upon the importance of the female influence upon affairs. "You will find a curious example of this in the case of Aspasia, the wife of Pericles. She was a woman of the greatest beauty and the first genius. She taught him, it is said, his refined maxims of policy, his lofty imperial eloquence, nay, even composed his speeches on which so great a share of his reputation was founded."

12 August 1777:
Tuesday. The Congress takes note that John Penn, former governor of Pennsylvania, and Benjamin Chew, the state's former chief justice, both Tories being made prisoners, both refuse to sign a parole of any kind. The Congress does not look lightly upon persons whose political lean is too far toward Great Britain and its hierarchal system. These two Tories are ordered to Fredericksburg, Virginia, for confinement.

13 August 1777:
Wednesday. New Hampshire militia Major General John Stark, gathering men from New Hampshire and Vermont, is preparing to fight any detachment of Burgoyne's force heading east of the Hudson River. His scouts are aware of Baum's troops heading toward Bennington. Stark orders Lieutenant Colonel William Gregg, who has about 200 men, to intercept them. Gregg arrives at a mill at St. Croix (Sancoick), about nine miles west of Bennington, now late in the day, deploys his troops, and awaits the enemy's appearance. [See Fig. IV-21, p. 261].

Congress issues a warrant in favor of Anthony Butler, agent for Thomas Mifflin, quartermaster general, for $150,000 for the use of that department.

14 August 1777:
Thursday. Baum's advance guard approach the mill and bridge at Sancoick in the early morning. Gregg's men fire, wound one Indian, and withdraw towards Bennington. Baum sends to Burgoyne requesting reinforcements.

Letters from both John Penn and Benjamin Chew, to the president of the Congress requesting that their paroles be admitted are received. It is ordered that such paroles are acceptable and that the order for removing Penn and Chew to Virginia be superseded.

About 9 o'clock in the evening more than 100 sail are seen standing off, and preparing to beat between the capes of the Chesapeake Bay—the fleet carrying Sir William Howe's army is finally discovered.

15 August 1777:

Friday. Lieutenant Colonel Heinrich Breymann, in response to orders from Burgoyne to proceed toward Bennington, marches out of the encampment near Fort Miller to support Baum and wades across the Batten Kill, dragging his cannon. Breymann, however, seems to be in no hurry to march his units to Bennington, nor does he grasp that Baum may be in difficulty. Breymann is very slow to move his troops with any speed to support Baum.

Baum marches his troops from Sancoick another four miles to the Walloomsac River. This is located about five miles west of village of Bennington. There, Baum entrenches his forces and awaits the reinforcements he has requested, because he has learned that the rebel forces are much larger than originally supposed. Also, it is very difficult to march, since it has been raining most of the day and hauling the artillery through the muddy roads is extremely hard and slow work.

Meanwhile, Stark has learned that he is faced with a fairly large body of men, not just the scout of a few Indians. He orders his militiamen to march towards the Walloomsac River, and sends an express to Colonel Seth Warner to quickly bring on his Vermont militia.

Congress remits $400,000 to the state of Georgia for monies advanced.

16 August 1777:

Saturday. Baum urges Breymann to hurry to his assistance, since he is now aware that the American forces are closing in upon him. Breymann sets out in the early morning, but wastes time by halting, dressing ranks, and seeking fresh horses to haul his artillery.

At the Hessian encampment by the New York portion of the Walloomsac River, Lieutenant Colonel Friedrich Baum, with about 800 troops on his raid to Bennington to procure horses, forage, and supplies, is attacked by General John Stark with about 1,500 militia. Stark strikes Baum's force, whose units are poorly placed to support each other by sending Lieutenant Colonel Moses Nichols north and west around the flank and rear of the enemy, and Colonel Samuel Herrick to the south and west in a modified double envelopment. Meanwhile Colonels Thomas Stickney and David Hobart attack the loyalist redoubt located near the

Walloomsac River. The Hessians are severely tested as the Americans swarm over their poorly placed entrenchments.

Later in the day, Seth Warner with more than 500 militia troops from Vermont, arrives to assist Stark's militia in the closing phases of the Battle of Bennington. Stark roundly defeats the Hessian detachment under Baum, in close and desperate fighting, killing more than 200, capturing most of the rest.

As it nears 5 o'clock, Breymann's troops arrive at Sancoick's Mill, about four miles west of the Walloomsac battlefield. There they find some refugees from Baum's detachment. They then march about two miles further east toward the Walloomsac River. Stark and Warner's men are tired from fighting and marching, as they confront this new threat. Breymann's men are equally tired from slogging through rain and mud. The Hessians, however, attack, but soon run low on ammunition. The Americans recover, are reinforced by other units coming west from the earlier battle and begin to swarm around the Breymann troops, who retreat and begin to panic.

Breymann is wounded in the fight, but is still able to lead nearly two-thirds of his detachment in an escape as it becomes dark. Stark orders his men to cease firing, secure the prisoners they have captured, and rejoin the main body of the American forces at Bennington. The loss to the Hessians in this battle, and the loss of elán that frequently follows a defeat, is a blow to Burgoyne's effort to capture Albany.

Most of the Hessian prisoners are bound in pairs and marched to and through the village of Bennington, Vermont, on their way to Boston. They are a great curiosity to the country folk, who have never seen German soldiers before, and think their uniforms, headgear, and heavy swords (those who still have them) a most remarkable sight. Many of the wounded, on both sides, will die during the night and over the next few days. [See Fig. IV-21, p. 261].

17 August 1777:
Sunday. In Philadelphia, Richard Henry Lee writes to Mann Page, "We are not able yet to give you any account of the wandering Howe and his fleet, save that they were seen on the 7th instant off Sinapuxen [sic] steering southward. Our accounts from France say that George [by which he means King George III] depends much on the desperate efforts that Howe & Cornwallis must make to redeem their bankrupt honor."

18 August 1777:
Monday. In Philadelphia, wondering about being a soldier, John Adams writes to Abigail, "It is too late in life, my constitution much too debilitated by speculation, and indeed

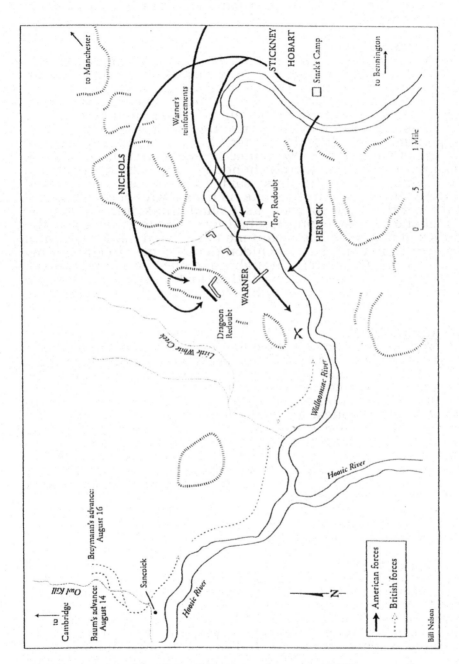

Fig. IV-21: Battles of Bennington, August 1777

it is too late a period of the war, for me to think of girding on a sword. But, if I had the last four years to run over again, I certainly would."

19 August 1777:
    Tuesday. The Congress takes under consideration the issue of the treasury on ways and means of raising funds for the purchase of supplies for carrying on the war.
    At Neshaminy Bridge, Pennsylvania, Washington writes from headquarters to Benjamin Harrison, noting that the Marquis Lafayette may have misunderstood the intent of his appointment or that the Congress did not understand the extent of Lafayette's views, since he seems to believe that his commission is not merely honorary but with a view to a command. "True, he has said that he is young, and inexperienced, but at the same time as always accompanied it with a hint, that so soon as I shall think him fit for the command of a division, he shall be ready to enter upon the duties of it, and in the meantime has offered his service for a smaller command. I ... concluded to ask some direction of my conduct in this matter, through a member [of the Congress], and therefore have imposed this task upon you. Let me beseech you then, my good Sir, to give me the sentiments of Congress on this matter ..."

20 August 1777:
    Wednesday. General Washington is directed to call upon New Jersey for 1,000 militia to relieve an equal number from New York, so that the Yorkers forces may reinforce the Northern Department in repelling Burgoyne.
    In Philadelphia, Benjamin Harrison replies to Washington's request for guidance in the matter of Lafayette, "I remember well a conversation passing betwixt us on the subject of Lafayette, and I told you it was merely honorary, in this light I looked on it, and so did every other member of Congress, he had made an agreement with Mr. Deane, but this he gave up by Letter to Congress, not wishing as he said to embarrass their affairs ..."
    Lafayette joins the army in camp at Neshaminy, Pennsylvania, where he is added to General Washington's "family," i.e, one of his Aides.

21 August 1777:
    Thursday. Henry Laurens writes to John Lewis Gervais, commiserating about what he feels may be a British attack upon Charleston and the south. He is terribly concerned that if the British should capture Charleston they would destroy the southern trade, take the slaves, rice, and indigo, and perhaps supply the West Indies trade with lumber and provisions. This concern over trade, and ways of life are drivers for many of the southern gentlemen. They have great fear over the possible disruption of their current life-styles,

either by the enemy, or even by acts of the Congress. It is only a bit later that it is learned that Sir William Howe's objective is not the southern states, but Philadelphia.

22 August 1777:
        Friday. Sir William Howe's fleet finally arrives in the upper reaches of Chesapeake Bay, after almost a full month's sail from Sandy Hook.
        Congress requests "That the State of Pennsylvania keep 4,000 of their militia to assist in repelling the threatened invasion of the enemy by way of Chesapeake and Delaware bays."

23 August 1777:
        Saturday. Washington is at Germantown, in the home of Spenton.
        Major General Benedict Arnold, with a detachment of about 1,000 men, reaches and relieves Fort Stanwix by evening.
        In Philadelphia, John Adams writes to his wife, Abigail, reporting that the mystery of Sir William Howe's landing is now revealed. The British are at the head of Chesapeake Bay, with 263 sail, and are surely aiming for the city.

24 August 1777:
        Sunday. In Philadelphia, John Hancock writes to General George Washington, with which he conveys letters and packets containing the latest information and intelligence. Not everyone yet seems to have definitive information on the whereabouts of Sir William Howe and his forces. Washington's army, however, is marching south and parades through Philadelphia. His thoughts that Howe might aim for Philadelphia turn out to be correct, and Washington expects to delay or defeat him in this purpose.

25 August 1777:
        Monday. Near Head of Elk, Howe's British transports are disembarking thousands of troops. In his long voyage at sea, Howe's army has lost many horses, his men are weak and require refreshment, and he needs fresh horses and forage for them.
        The Congress orders that the Board of War take speedy and effective measures for having 6,000 stand of arms brought from the magazine at Springfield to headquarters.
        Washington sets up his headquarters at Wilmington, Delaware.

26 August 1777:
        Tuesday. Concerned about the British landing and invasion at Head of Elk, the Congress resolves "That the States of Pennsylvania and Delaware be requested to cause all persons within their respective states notoriously

disaffected, forthwith to be apprehended, and secured, till such time as the respective states think they may be released without injury to the common cause."

27 August 1777:
Wednesday. Washington, accompanied by aides and staff, including the newly arrived Lafayette, rides out of the encampment near Wilmington to make a reconnaissance of the area.

The Congress considers the report of the committee on the matter of the causes of the American evacuation of Ticonderoga and Mount Independence.

28 August 1777:
Thursday. A lengthy resolution regarding the Clothier-General and his means of issue takes up much of the Congress's time this day.

Howe's army moves away from Elkton. Cornwallis marches his corps north, and Lieutenant General Knyphausen marches his corps across the Elk River to Cecil Courthouse. Both corps stay put for five days, foraging for horses and fodder and for the purpose of recovering their strength after the lengthy sea voyage from New York.

29 August 1777:
Friday. In London, England, the War Office, posts the promotion of Sir Henry Clinton, K.B. to the rank of Lieutenant General, and of Sir Guy Carleton, K.B. and of the Earl Charles Cornwallis to the same rank.

Washington and Lafayette, with others, continue to reconnoiter the countryside near and west of Wilmington, keeping a close eye on the roads they feel Howe might use in any advance toward Philadelphia.

At headquarters, Wilmington, Delaware, Washington writes to the President of Congress, "On my return to this place, last evening, from White Clay Creek, I was honored with yours of the 27th. with sundry Resolves of Congress, to which I shall pay due attention. The enemy advanced a part of their army yesterday to Greys Hill, about two miles on this side of Elk, whether with intent to take post there, of to cover, while they remove what stores they found in the town, I cannot yet determine. I do not know what quantity of private property remains, but of the public there were several thousand bushels of corn and oats, which might have been removed also, had not most of the teams in the country been employed by private persons in bringing off very valuable goods. Our light parties yesterday took between thirty and forty prisoners, twelve deserters from the navy and eight from the army have already come in, but they are able to give us very little intelligence. They generally agree that their troops are healthy, but that their horse suffered very much by the voyage. By a letter from Genl. Gates, which you were pleased to transmit me yesterday, he requests, that commissions may be sent to Brigadiers [John] Glover, [Enoch] Poor, and [John] Paterson which I beg the favour of you to do by the return express. The two last lost theirs with their baggage at Ticonderoga, and Genl. Glover had none."

30 August 1777:
    Saturday. Pierre Van Cortlandt of New York writes to Maj. Gen. Horatio Gates, reporting that the Council is desirous of "... securing the families and effects of those who during the present invasion or that of last fall have gone over to the enemy."
    Washington deploys his army behind Red Clay Creek, in efforts to delay Howe's advance.

31 August 1777:
Sunday. In Philadelphia, John Adams writes to William Gordon, bemoaning the loss of Fort Ticonderoga but noting that, while, at present this seems to be a disaster, it might yet put Burgoyne into a difficult situation. Adams further reports, "Mr. Howe has planned his operations in such a manner, as to give us a vast advantage, both of him and Burgoyne. He is at the Head of Elk about 55 miles from this city. Genl. Washington is at Wilmington, about 15 miles on this side of him, with a noble army of continental troops, and a large body of militia, which is constantly and rapidly increasing. Whether the General will be compelled to depart from his Fabian System or not time will discover. A general action, successful to us is destructive to them, and even if they should be successful and keep the field, they will lose so many men, as to be crippled after it. Whereas I think we should be able speedily to reinforce our army, not withstanding the panic and consternation which would follow a defeat."

1 September 1777:
    Monday. The Congress resolves "That three commissioners be appointed immediately to consider of the practicability of burning the enemy's fleet in Chesapeake Bay; that they consult with General Washington on this subject, and, if it appears likely to be effective, that they proceed with all diligence to the execution thereof; that they be authorized to purchase, on the most reasonable terms they can, or employ any vessels that may be convenient for the purpose of fire ships, and that they have power to make use of any continental merchant ships or vessels that may be near the place for the same service ..."

2 September 1777:
    Tuesday. The Auditor-General reports "That there is due to Willing, Morris & Co. for 10,000 quills for the use of the

treasury, war and secretary's offices, the sum of 266 60/90 dollars."

Washington orders Brig. Gen. William Maxwell to keep a close watch on Howe's forces, and warns him that the British are about to resume their march.

3 September 1777:

Wednesday. At Christiana Creek, about five miles northeast of Elkton, in Delaware, Lt. Gen Cornwallis sends German and British light troops to scout out rebel forces near Iron Hill. As they approach the area, they are fired on by troops under the command of Brig. Gen. William Maxwell, who has set up an ambush. Soon a running fight develops, known as the Battle of Cooch's Bridge, in which the Americans, bravely fighting against superior numbers, are pushed back to Washington's main body of American forces dug in at and near White Clay Creek, in a defensive position. [See Fig. IV-22, p. 268].

4 September 1777:

Thursday. The Board of War reports that they have taken into consideration the dispute with regard to the relative rank of four colonels of the New York Continental regiments, "... and find that a committee of the convention of the State of New York, being properly authorized for such purpose, did appoint [the four officers] to their respective regiments, in the following order, viz. Colonel Cortlandt, 2d, Colonel Gansevoort, 3d, Colonel Dubois, 4th, and Colonel Livingston, 5th. As this arrangement must be presumed to have been founded on principles of justice and public utility, the Board of War are of opinion that it would be highly inexpedient to make any alteration in the relative rank of these officers."

5 September 1777:

Friday. In Philadelphia, John Hancock writes to William Livingston, enclosing a Congressional resolution commending the militia of New Jersey for their rapid and effective response to a request for 3,000 men to reinforce General Washington. "The Militia of the State of New Jersey by their late conduct against our cruel enemy have distinguished themselves in a manner that does them the greatest honor, and I am persuaded they will continue to merit on all occasions when called upon the reputation they have so justly acquired."

6 September 1777:

Saturday. In the Northern Department, Major General Horatio Gates has ordered a considerable supply of clothing for his troops, intended as a bounty for them. Some nitpicker of a deputy paymaster general has placed stoppages on the soldiers pay for these extra clothes. The Congress disapproves of the stoppages and directs the money to be returned. The Congressional resolution goes on to say "... that the greatest care ought to be taken to do justice to the soldiers, as well as the public, in this essential article ... such troops as have not been supplied with clothing, ought to be furnished their full bounty without delay ..."

Washington decides to move and reconcentrate his army north of Red Clay Creek, which by now is in a well-defended position. This puts him on and astride the main road into Philadelphia, which he hopes will block Howe.

7 September 1777:

Sunday. In Philadelphia, Eliphalet Dyer writes to Joseph Trumbull, "I think Congress now are in a pretty good temper to do business if this plague fellow Howe, does not disturb us. We are now very sulky and determine not to move for him if we can help it. How long our courage may last I know not. It will not be strange if at this time it should exceed our conduct. We feel very magnanimous, but a few days may decide, before Howe's appearance this way, our removal from this venial City became a serious topic & believe would have been the case had not General Howe appeared, but you know we scorn to fly. Confederation & finances are now the great objects, but ten thousand necessaries are daily crowding in, but there is no design nor art in keeping it off. All are agreed in the object, differ only in the proportion of Representation & taxation." While the mood of some in the Congress may be reflected in Dyer's letter, not all the citizens of the city have such a view. Many Patriots are preparing to leave, while Loyalists hope for occupation by the British.

8 September 1777:

Monday. The Congress yet again takes into consideration the matter of foreign officers. Numbers of them have proceeded upon encouragement of conventions made and signed at Paris by Silas Deane, as "Agent for the United States of North America." The Congress avers that he "... had no authority to make such conventions, and that Congress, therefore, are not bound to ratify or fulfil [sic] them."

Howe's movements continue to puzzle the Americans. He now marches toward the northeast, seeming to threaten Washington's right flank.

9 September 1777:

Tuesday. Washington begins to deploy his troops east of the Brandywine Creek, so as to defend any crossing the British might make, and to be between Sir William Howe with his British and German forces and the city of Philadelphia.

10 September 1777:

Wednesday. General George Washington is at Chadd's Ford, Pennsylvania, at Benjamin Ring's House, from which place he writes to Brig. Gen. Caesar Rodney, "Sir: The New

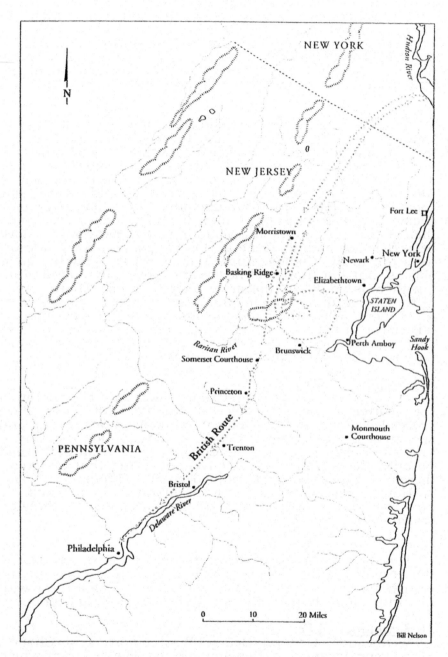

Fig. IV-22: Howe's Route Toward Philadelphia, 1777

Castle County people have no excuse for not joining you now, as the enemy have in a manner left a good part of the country. I have received advice that their advanced guards are within five miles of this place. I wrote you yesterday to follow upon their rear, with all the force you could collect, and I now press it upon you in the most urgent manner; because if we should be lucky enough to give them a stroke at this distance from their ships, you will be ready to intercept them."

11 September 1777:
    Thursday. The Brandywine River is about 15 to 20 miles west of the Schuylkill River and tributary to it. As Washington and Howe are deploying to the best advantage, it is well to note the fords that are used to cross this stream in the area of the Battle of Brandywine.

    From the south to north they are Chadd's, Brinton's, Jones', Wistar's, Buffington's, and Jeffrie's. Washington chooses to keep the river between him and the enemy, and defend the fords on the east side of the river, forcing Howe to attack. Howe prefers his usual flank maneuvers, and orders Knyphaussen to demonstrate in front of Chadd's Ford, keeping Washington busy and his attention fixed on that area, while Howe himself leads the major part of his force around to the north to cross at Jeffrie's Ford. It works all too well. The Americans are surprised, cannot react quickly enough, and several units are pressed so hard they cannot hold. They retreat, and the entire American army follows suit.

    Major General Lafayette is wounded in the leg, and will be removed to the Moravian Hospital in Bethlehem, Pennsylvania for treatment and recovery.

12 September 1777:
    Friday. Washington needs to refit and reorganize his defeated army, and falls back towards the Schuylkill River, making his headquarters near Darby in Delaware County, Pennsylvania.

    General Orders state that "The General expects that each Brigadier or officer commanding a brigade will immediately make the most exact returns of their killed, wounded, and missing." Also included is the parole as Schuykill and the countersigns as Darby and Germantown.

13 September 1777:
    Saturday. Burgoyne moves his army to the west side of the Hudson River on a series of boats, planked over with boards, as a sort of pontoon bridge. He is now short of Indian scouts, being reduced to about 50 or so, the rest having deserted. This means he is much less well-informed regarding the whereabouts and strength of his enemy.

    Washington makes his headquarters at Germantown.

General Orders note that "The officers are, without loss of time to see that their men are completed with ammunition, that their arms are in the best order, the inside of them washed clean and well dried, the touch holes picked, and a good flint in each gun. The strictest attention is expected will be paid to this order as the officers must be sensible their own honor, the safety of the soldier, and the success of the cause depends absolutely upon a careful execution of it. The commanding officer of each regiment is to endeavour (sic) to procure such necessaries as are wanting, for his men. No time is to be lost in doing this."

14 September 1777:

Sunday. In Philadelphia, John Adams writes to Abigail, "How much longer Congress will stay is uncertain. I hope we shall not move until the last necessity, that is, until it shall be rendered certain that Mr. Howe will get the city. It is the determination not to leave this State. Don't be anxious about me, nor about our great and sacred cause. It is the cause of truth and will prevail. If Howe gets the city, it will cost him all his force to keep it, and so he can get nothing else."

Washington's army crosses the Schuylkill River at Levering's Ford, wading in water up to their waists.

Burgoyne reports that he "... is on the west side of North River [by which he means the Hudson]." He will slowly march south on that side of the river.

15 September 1777:

Monday. At Bennington, Vermont, Major General Benjamin Lincoln meets with Brigadier General John Stark and develops a plan to attack Burgoyne's supply line by sending a militia force to attack Fort Ticonderoga.

Howe cannot get into Philadelphia by a direct route, because the Schuylkill River is not fordable at its lower reaches, and he has no boats. The only way to the American capitol is via the upriver fords. Learning that Washington has crossed the river, Howe now hopes he can fight and destroy the American army and at the same time occupy its capitol.

General George Washington keeps moving his forces around the vicinity of Philadelphia, in efforts to deny the city to the British. The battle of Brandywine could have been a fine check to the British advance. Washington makes his headquarters at Buck's Tavern, Pennsylvania.

16 September 1777:

Tuesday. Burgoyne, not certain of the American position, hears the reveille drums from their camp and, now knowing he is close, makes his own camp near Saratoga, New York. He plans to attack, and reconnoiters the American position. By this time Burgoyne's army numbers about 6,800, having lost Germans and Indians on the march. Gates is well entrenched on Bemis Heights, with about 9,400 men. New units of militia are arriving in Gates camp every day, and are quickly posted to places for defense.

Washington brings his army to White Horse, and makes his headquarters at Joseph Malin's house.

17 September 1777:
Wednesday. Major General Benjamin Lincoln, with some 2,300 troops, makes his headquarters at Pawlet, Vermont, about fifteen miles north of Manchester, Vermont. He orders Colonel John Brown, with a detachment of about 400 Massachusetts militia, to make a spoiling raid on Fort Ticonderoga to harass or cut Burgoyne's supply line and release American prisoners found there.

Brown makes a night march north to the narrows of Lake Champlain, above Ticonderoga, crosses the lake, and reaches the high ground above the Lake George Landing to reconnoiter.

Congress gives broad authority to General George Washington to impress "... all such provisions and other articles as may be necessary for the comfortable subsistence of the army under his command."

Washington is at Red Lion Tavern in Pottsgrove, Pennsylvania.

18 September 1777:
Thursday. Early this morning Brown attacks the garrison at the Lake George Landing stage, and the enemy post on Mount Defiance, releasing nearly 120 American prisoners, while capturing more than 260 enemy troops. He then attempts to capture Fort Ticonderoga itself, but the garrison refuses a demand for surrender. Finding the place too heavily fortified, Brown withdraws.

Howe dispatches a light infantry detachment to seize the rebel supply depot at Valley Forge. They arrive in the late afternoon, and, without opposition, capture about 4,000 barrels of flour, 25 barrels of horseshoes, cannonballs, axes, and soap.

Washington and his army are at Warwick Furnace, Pennsylvania, where he continues to look-out for ways to attack Howe. But without adequate cavalry it is very difficult to scout enemy positions and report those movements in a timely manner to higher headquarters.

The president of the Congress receives a letter from Colonel Alexander Hamilton, intimating the necessity of Congress removing immediately from Philadelphia, whereupon the members leave to repair to Lancaster. It is apparent that Sir William Howe's landing at Head of Elk is intended to be a means of moving upon the City, so none of this should have come as a surprise to either the Congress, or the citizens of the city.

19 September 1777:

Friday. At Saratoga, New York, Burgoyne deploys the major part of his troops into three columns in a plan to overwhelm and flank the Americans, who are well entrenched. The Battle of Freeman's Farm, or the First Battle of Saratoga, begins by about noon as the fog burns off the fields.

Gates has a total of more than 10,000 troops, including both militia and Continental units. Burgoyne now has about 6,800 men. He orders a three column attack. In the morning a dense fog surrounds the area, making it difficult for the Americans to notice any movements of the enemy. Scouting parties are sent out, word is carried back to headquarters that the enemy is moving toward the American positions. Arnold dispatches Morgan and Dearborn to the left of the American line with instructions to harass any enemy troops. Shortly after noon, the fog has lifted, as the riflemen from Morgan's regiment reach the southern line of Freeman's Farm, taking cover as they find it, just as they sight British skirmishers at the northern edge of the farm.

The American rifle fire from the trees, the fence line, and the cabin does fearful damage to the officer corps of the British right wing, under Fraser. Many of the British retreat, and the American riflemen, feeling they have the enemy on the run, chase after them in a wild rush. But the British are running toward their own support units, which the riflemen do not see, until nearly on top of them, and then it is the Americans who must retreat in the face of massive British musket fire. There is a lull in the battle, as the two sides try to collect their wounded, and move up support units.

Finally, Gates relents and allows Arnold with Learned and Poor, to reinforce Morgan and Dearborn. They discover that Burgoyne has brought up his own wing of the army with much of his artillery, is reinforced by some of Riedesel's Hessians, and has quickly prepared protection for his heavy weapons. That becomes a focus of Arnold's attacks.

Both armies are fighting fiercely, each trying to gain a few yards or defend a small ditch. Cannons roar and musketry whistles. The entire area is enclosed in the smoke from gunpowder, and the noise from heavy firing. Shouts cannot carry, orders cannot be heard. The British lines push forward with fixed bayonets, expecting that their usual fearsome attack mode will win the day.

The British and Hessians are halted in their advance, and severely mauled by the Americans. Darkness halts the carnage, as each side gathers its wounded. The British have about 570 total casualties, but stay close to where the battle ends. The Americans fall back in good order, with total casualties of about 300 men. [See Fig. IV-23, p. 273.] Washington makes his headquarters at Parker's Ford, Pennsylvania.

20 September 1777:
Saturday. West of Philadelphia, during the night, as American and British troops are dancing around each other following the Battle of Brandywine, Brig. Gen. Anthony Wayne encamps his troops in a secluded place about three miles southwest of the British lines, now known as Paoli, Pennsylvania.

Sir William Howe, learning from some Tory traitors of Wayne's proximity, dispatches Maj. Gen. Charles Grey with two regiments to seek out and destroy the rebels. The night is dark and nearly moonless, with storm clouds blocking any moonlight or starlight. Wayne orders his men to sleep upon their arms. Grey marches stealthily in two divisions towards the encampment, in preparation for attacking in the small hours of the morning, what he hopes will be sleeping and surprised foe.

21 September 1777:
Sunday. At Paoli, about one o'clock in the morning, Grey's regiments are at Wayne's encampment. They rush upon the sleeping Americans with fixed bayonets, without firing a shot, and kill or capture about 150 men in what becomes known as the Paoli Massacre.

Lafayette arrives in Bethlehem for treatment of his leg wound. This is a frequently used hospital/recovery locale for the American army. Lafayette will remain here for several weeks.

22 September 1777:
Monday. At Lake George, New York, Colonel John Brown has captured a large number of vessels from the British at and near Fort Ticonderoga, has embarked his men and the many prisoners they have captured, as well as the Americans they have released, and is moving south toward the head of Lake George.

Howe sends British and Hessian patrols to cross the Schuylkill at Gordon's Ford and Fatland Ford, which they do without opposition. General Washington is at a camp 28 miles from Philadelphia on the Reading Road, where he makes his headquarters. There he receives reports that the British have crossed the river at Gordon's Ford. Washington's army is still scattered, neither Wayne, Maxwell, nor Smallwood having joined up with him.

23 September 1777:
Tuesday. At Diamond Island, New York, on Lake George, about 25 miles north of the head of the lake, Brown, with his Massachusetts Militia Battalion, attacks the British held island, used as a supply depot. The enemy artillery holes the American sloop, and damages a number of other boats. Brown feels it is too tough a nut to crack and heads off to

the head of Lake George and overland to Skenesborough
with his prisoners and the released Americans.

Washington is at a camp about 34 miles from
Philadelphia on the Schuylkill River.

24 September 1777:

Wednesday. At Lancaster, Pennsylvania, Elbridge Gerry,
a delegate from Massachusetts, writes to General George
Washington, informing the general that William Henry of
Lancaster can collect the arms and ammunition from the
inhabitants. However, since neither the Congress nor the
Board of War for the next several days will be able to meet to
give Henry the authority to do so, he requests an
authorization from Washington in answer to Washington's
request.

25 September 1777:

Thursday. In Lancaster, Samuel Chase, a delegate from
Maryland, writes to Thomas Johnson, governor of the state,
reporting that the British have marched around the
countryside, crossed the Schuylkill River by fords, and are
moving towards Philadelphia. Chase believes their advance
parties may reach the city by this night. Chase further
relates that American troops are fatigued by constant
marching since the Battle of Brandywine. Washington,
however, is on the alert for some opportunity to annoy,
attack, or at least snipe at the British forces in any way and
at any place that sees to offer a chance of success.

The British occupy the city of Philadelphia. It is the
largest city in America, and the center of a large trade area.
[See Fig. IV-25, p. 285.]

General George Washington makes his headquarters at
Pottsgrove, again at Henry Keely's.

26 September 1777:

Friday. At Portsmouth, New Hampshire, an out-of-work
Prussian officer, Friedrich Ludolf Gerhard Augustin von
Steuben, disembarks and makes his way to Boston, and
thence to the Congress at York.

27 September 1777:

Saturday. After capturing Philadelphia, the British
complete two artillery batteries south of the city, on the west
bank of the Delaware River. American warships, *Delaware*
(34 guns) and *Montgomery* (18 guns), are sent upriver to
secure any shipping they can seize. A British battery opens
fire, and the Americans reply, but, in their eagerness to
engage the enemy, the American crew on the *Delaware*,
neglect their sails and run aground. She is captured, and
after being floated and refitted, joins the British navy.

General Washington is at Pennypacker's Mill, at
Pennypacker's Mansion.

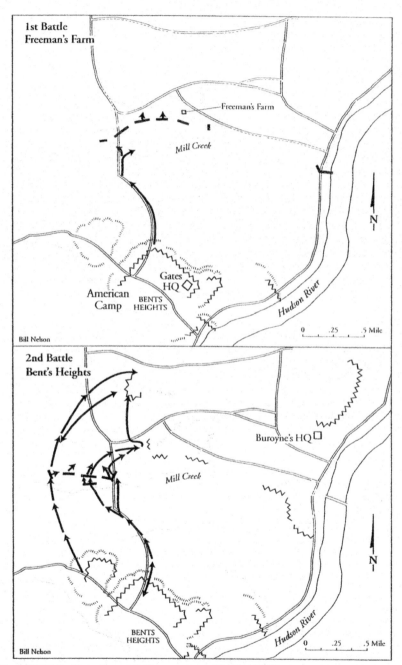

Fig. IV-23: Battles of Saratoga, Fall 1777

The Congress, having left Philadelphia, officially reconvenes in Lancaster, Pennsylvania. However, there is little business conducted, and the members not liking the accommodations, plan to adjourn again the next day to a place further to the west in York.

28 September 1777:
    Sunday. At Lancaster, Eliphalet Dyer writes to Joseph Trumbull, "This State is torn to pieces by factions in Government: Quaker, Dunker, Milese & Moravians in religion whose principles not only prevent them from fighting, but induces them to disaffect others & to give all possible aid to the enemy (Moravians excepted). We had large stores at Reading and at many places back in the Country, at one time General Howe would seem to aim at them, and then make a sudden trek toward the City, though it would appear afterward to be only feints by parties, while his main body lay still and at rest. These appearances put General Washington continually on the march, sometimes one way and sometimes another to counteract his designs by which his troops become fatigued, worn out, and dispirited." Dyer's description of the constant moving about of Washington's army is apt. No rest for the weary.

29 September 1777:
    Monday. Sir William Howe orders Lt. Col. Thomas Stirling with two regiments to occupy Billingsport, New Jersey.
    At York, Pennsylvania, Charles Carroll of Carrollton, a delegate from Maryland, writes to his father, "The Congress not thinking themselves secure from light parties of the enemy at Lancaster, have adjourned to this place, where it will probably remain the whole winter. Howe is in the City, but his shipping cannot come up [the Delaware River] till the fort is taken and the Cheveaux de Frise (sic) are captured and raised."

30 September 1777:
    Tuesday. Because Howe has divided his forces, part occupying Philadelphia, another detachment to occupy Billingsport, and still other forces south of Philadelphia in efforts to open up the Delaware River to British shipping, Washington feels Howe's forces may be ripe for attack. With only a portion of the British and Hessian troops encamped near Germantown, the American Army might profitably attack them. It is this portion of Howe's army that Washington, now receiving reinforcements, plans to attack. With the improvement in his strength and the relative weakness of the British strength by dispersion, Washington has high hopes of inflicting a serious blow upon the enemy.
    George Washington makes his headquarters at Skippack, Pennsylvania, in Peter Wentz's house.

1 October 1777:

Wednesday. The Congress departs from Lancaster, and reconvenes in York, Pennsylvania. They issue warrants of $50,000 each to the states of Rhode Island and Connecticut for the use of the commissioners of the Continental loan offices.

In headquarters at Skippack, General Orders state "The whole army are to strike their tents tomorrow at 8 o'clock, and get ready to march. The regimental Quartermasters are to see that the vaults be dug immediately upon the army's arrival on its new ground: and any soldier caught easing himself elsewhere is instantly to be made prisoner and punished by order of a regimental Court-Martial." The parole is given as Winchester and the countersigns as Warwick and Windsor.

2 October 1777:

Thursday. In York, the Congress confirms the treaty made by Benjamin Franklin and Silas Deane with the Chevalier du Portail on 17 February 1777. Further formal arrangements will soon be made with the French to aid the Americans in their fight for independence.

3 October 1777:

Friday. The Congress hears several letters, among which are two relating to stores and clothing. Because the information in these letters is deemed to be of a sensitive nature, everything in them is to be kept secret.

Having developed a plan to attack Howe at Germantown, Washington orders his troops, in four columns, to march southeast to within about two miles of the enemy outposts. There they are to rest, until all is ready to attack in the pre-dawn darkness.

4 October 1777:

Saturday. At Germantown, Pennsylvania, Howe has had to disperse a good part of his troops for guard duty, occupation duty, and the transport of supplies duty, and so has only about 9,000 men with him. Washington has been reinforced, and has about 11,000 men with him. He feels that he can attack Howe, and prepares a four-prong plan for that purpose; Forman and Smallwood from the far left, Greene attack from the near left down the Lime Kiln Road, Sullivan down the middle on the Skippack Road, and Armstrong on the right down the Ridge Road. Problems ensue. Held up by rough roads and ill-shod shoes, the Americans do not all arrive at their proper places in a timely manner. At dawn there is a dense fog, making it hard to discern what is where and who is who. The American advance seems to be going well, in spite of delays and poor timing. They are pushing the British back, until Lt. Col. Thomas Musgrave uses the Chew House as a fortress. With only about 120 of his troops, he barricades all the doorways and shutters the windows. From the house, his soldiers snipe away at the passing American units. Henry Knox, believing it to be poor policy to leave a fortified position in one's rear, orders his artillery and other forces to attack the stone building. This action further holds up the American advance. Confusion soon prevails, and panic strikes the Americans, who begin to retreat, forcing Washington to order a withdrawal. The British do not pursue. This complicated plan is a violation of the Principles of War. [See Fig. IV-24, p. 279, and Appendix 3, Volume 2, p. 551].

At the British Camp near Saratoga, Burgoyne calls a Council of War. In this council are Phillips, Fraser, and Riedesel. The previous day, their army went on short rations, so everyone knows something has to be done. It has been two weeks since the Battle of Freeman's Farm. No support is to be expected from Sir Henry Clinton in New York. Riedesel, being a realist, holds a view that the army should retreat to Lake George and Fort Ticonderoga, while it still has enough strength to do so. Burgoyne does not agree, he hates to retreat, but may not see the consequences of his foolishness.

Burgoyne will make a reconnaissance in force to test the rebel strength, and, if feasible, make a full attack and if not, then retreat to the Batten Kill.

5 October 1777:
Sunday. In York, the Congress writes to Governor George Clinton and Council of New York, enclosing a resolution of the Congress that New York should erect a monument to the memory of Brigadier General Herkimer, requests that the governor and council take measures for carrying the resolve into execution, for which the Congress has voted $500. "Every mark of distinction shown to the memory of such illustrious men as offer up their lives for the Liberty & Happiness of their Country, reflects real honor upon those who pay the grateful tribute, and by holding up to others the prospects of fame and immortality will animate them to tread in the same path."

6 October 1777:
Monday. Lieutenant General Sir Henry Clinton, wishing to make some demonstration toward assisting Burgoyne, sends a large force, under General Vaughan, up the Hudson River to the forts guarding the Hudson Highlands, about five miles south of West Point. These Forts, Montgomery and Clinton, sit astride Popolopen Creek, which enters the Hudson from the west, and are both under the command of Maj. Gen. George Clinton. Sir Henry Clinton lands his troops, and they quickly move over the difficult terrain to outflank and envelope the forts. The American garrisons are defeated and retreat, abandoning the forts. The British soon

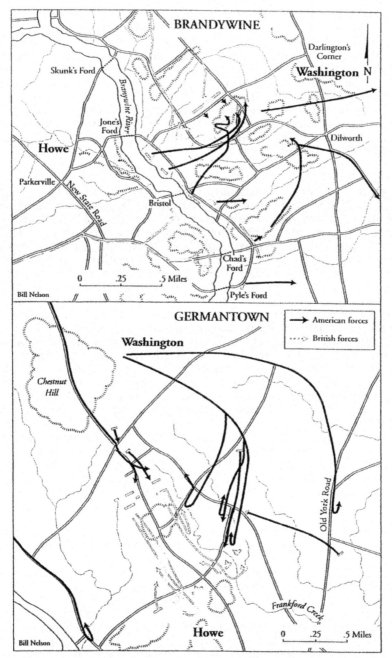

Fig. IV-24: Battles of Brandywine and Germantown, 1777

do likewise, and withdraw, after destroying the chain across the river.

At headquarters, Washington dictates a letter to Sir William Howe, written in the hand of Alexander Hamilton, "General Washington's compliments to General Howe. He does himself the pleasure to return him a dog, which accidentally fell into his hands, and by the inscription on the Collar, appears to belong to General Howe." It seems that the dog, during or shortly after the Battle of Germantown, may have chased after a deer or searching for some food had wandered off. But, since he was "in uniform" with his master's name on the collar, he could not be admitted a spy, and must thus be returned.

7 October 1777:
Tuesday. Near Saratoga, Burgoyne launches his reconnaissance with about 1,700 men, beginning what is called the Battle of Bemis Heights or the 2nd Battle of Saratoga. He divides this force into three columns. They march across rough terrain, and having to halt for the repair or building of bridges to carry the artillery slows the advance. It is about 1:30 o'clock in the afternoon before the troops emerge onto Barber's wheatfield, south of the Breymann Redoubt. Gates now has a total force of about 16,000 men, and orders Morgan to attack the British. Soon, informed that the British thrust is something more than a patrol, Gates adds Dearborn's units to the attack. Poor and Learned are brought up as reinforcements. In less than an hour the British left and right wings are in full retreat. Benedict Arnold, though without a command of his own, appears and energizes the American troops in the center, and is wounded, but his leadership wins the Breymann Redoubt for the Americans. Simon Fraser is mortally wounded. Breymann is shot and killed. Burgoyne's force loses a total of nearly 900 men, a good half the force he used in the attack. The American losses are about 150 men. The battle ends in darkness as the exhausted troops of both sides collapse on the ground. [See Fig. IV-23, p. 275]

8 October 1777:
Wednesday. Burgoyne orders his troops into the Great Redoubt, close to the Hudson River and north of the area of the battlefield.

At York, the Congress, concerned about transmittal of information, goods, services, or supplies to the enemy, resolves "That any person, being an inhabitant of any of these states, who shall act as a guide or pilot by land or water for the enemy, or shall give or send intelligence to them, or in any manner furnish them with supplies of provisions, money, cloathing [sic], arms, forage, fuel, or any kind of stores, be considered and treated as an enemy and traitor to these United States."

In the services of supply for the army, the three most important positions—quartermaster general, commissary general, and clothier general—have been held by persons all to subject to corruption and with poor leadership and organizational skills. Quartermaster General Thomas Mifflin, having largely given up his duties, resigns. Commissary General William Buchanan and Clothier General James Mease have been equally lazy and inefficient.

9 October 1777:
  Thursday. General George Washington makes his headquarters at Towamencin, in eastern Montgomery County, Pennsylvania, at Frederick Wampole's house.
  Washington writes to Brig. Gen. James Potter, "Dear Sir: A person of the name of Patterson, an inhabitant of Wilmington, can give you a particular acct. of the situation, strength & ca. Of the enemy at that place; from whence you may judge of the practicability of attempting something by way of surprise, if your numbers are adequate, upon the garrison. ... that the great object of your expedition is to deprive the enemy of supplies from Chester County and to interrupt their convoys from Chestertown, Wilmington, &ca. whilst our defense upon the river, obliges them to have recourse to a transportation of necessaries by land from their shipping."

10 October 1777:
  Friday. South of Philadelphia, below Hog Island, the British navy is trying to remove the chevaux-de-frise and other obstacles placed in the Delaware River by Pennsylvania Commodore John Hazelwood. Hazelwood, in turn, keeps firing at the British to slow down their work. British warships are unable to reach the annoying American defenders until they can get through the blockages. The British finally open a small gap, but it is not large enough for warships.
  At York, the Congress orders that $12,000 be advanced to the Marine Committee, for public service in Baltimore.

11 October 1777:
  Saturday. The Congress, upon a report of the Board of War, resolves a number of items affecting the operations of the Commissary of Hides; 1.) That the Commissary of Hides be authorized to hire wagons for the use of his department, 2.) That he request guards from the general officers in command of any department for protection of said wagons, as he proposes to travel through that department, 3.) That he make periodic returns to the Board of War of transactions, quantities of hides on hand, leather made therefrom; tallow, offal, and hooves of the cattle belonging to the United States.

12 October 1777:
    Sunday. In York, Thomas Burke writes to Maj. General John Sullivan, "I was present at the action of Brandywine and saw and heard enough to convince me that the fortune of the day was injured by miscarriages where you commanded. I understood you were several days posted with the command on the right wing; that you were cautioned by the Commander-in-Chief early in the day to be particularly attentive to the enemy's motions, who he supposed would attempt to cross higher up the creek and attack your flank; that you were furnished with proper troops for reconnoitering, and yet you were so ill informed of the enemy's motions that they came up at a time and by a route which you did not expect; that you conveyed intelligence to the Commander in Chief which occasioned his countermanding the dispositions he had made for encountering them on the route by which it afterwards appeared they were actually advancing. That when at length the mistake was discovered you brought up your own Division by an unnecessary circuit of two miles, in the greatest disorder, from which they never recovered, but fled from the fire of the enemy without resistance. That the miscarriages on that wing made it necessary to draw off a great part of the strength of the centre, which exposed General Wayne to the superiority of the enemy. I heard officers in the field lamenting in the bitterest terms that they were cursed with such a commander; and I overheard numbers during the retreat complain of you as an officer whose evil conduct was forever productive of misfortunes to the army."

13 October 1777:
    Monday. In the British Camp at Saratoga, William Digby, keeps a Journal, in which he writes, "Their cannon racked our posts very much; the bulk of their army was hourly reinforced by militia flocking in to them from all parts, and their situation, which nearly surrounded us, was from the nature of the ground unattackable in all parts; and since the 7th the men lay constantly upon their arms, harassed and fatigued beyond measure, from their great want of rest. All night we threw up traverse [a means of laying down fire indirectly, laterally, or traversely across from a position] to our works, as our lines were enfiladed or flanked by their cannon."
    At the town of Esopus (now Kingston), New York, a British raiding party, commanded by Major General John Vaughan and transported up the Hudson River by Captain Sir James Wallace, attacks and burns much of this community, in a feeble effort by Henry Clinton at support for Burgoyne.
    On the Delaware River between Hog Island and Billingsport, John Hazelwood brings his fleet of small vessels

down the river to fight the British in a night attack that lights up the sky with fire from cannon and fire rafts burning as they glide over the water.

14 October 1777:
Tuesday. From The Hague, Charles William Frédéric Dumas writes to the Committee of Foreign Affairs, "Our States-General are assembled, and they have begun with labors which by no means please your enemies. The first was to make a claim directly, in the name of their high mightinesses, upon the English minister for the Dutch vessel destined for St. Eustatia, and taken in the Channel by an English vessel of war, under the pretext that the vessel was American built. Our States have sent instructions on this subject to their envoy at London, with orders to have discontinued whatever process has been instituted by the captor before the English judges against this vessel ..."

15 October 1777:
Wednesday. At the American Camp before Saratoga, Benjamin Warren writes in his journal, "All remains still like Sunday." But there is great activity on the peacemaking front, as James Wilkinson and William Whipple for Maj. Gen. Gates and Lt. Col. Nicholas Sutherland and Captain James Craig for Burgoyne prepare articles for capitulation.

John Harvie, a delegate from Virginia, attends the Congress and takes his seat.

16 October 1777:
Thursday. Burgoyne vacillates on details in the capitulation, hoping for a last minute rescue, or a postponement, or a miracle. But Gates is not buying. The treaty must be ratified or he will attack. Burgoyne agrees.

Washington is at Worcester, at Peter Wentz's. At headquarters here a court of enquiry is held to consider the conduct of an expedition upon Staten Island. Major General Sullivan had led an expedition to Staten Island which failed in its mission. After hearing the evidence and the defense the court unanimously concludes that the expedition promised great advantage to the cause, was well concerted, and the orders for its execution were proper. However accidents, which were out of the power of Major General Sullivan to foresee or prevent rendered the expedition abortive. The court concludes that Sullivan's conduct and planning and executing the expedition was such that he deserves the approbation of his country, and not its censure, and he stands honorably acquitted of any unsoldierly conduct in this matter.

General Orders give the parole as Carlisle and the countersigns as Lancaster and York.

17 October 1777:
Friday. The surrender of Major General John Burgoyne and his entire force takes place on the flats by the Hudson River, a bit north of the Schuyler House, in the early afternoon, at the site of the old Fort Hardy, on the northwest confluence of the Fishkill Creek with the Hudson River. This important victory of American arms, will confirm to the French that the new nation truly does have the ability to stand up to their enemy, and will lead to a Treaty of Alliance. However, the terms and provisions of the Convention to which Gates agreed, will not sit well with the Congress, and future actions by the Congress will alter those provisions.

Washington writes to Richard Henry Lee, "General Conway's merit, then, as an officer, and his importance in this army, exists more in his own imagination, than in reality: For it is a maxim with him, to leave no service of his own untold, nor to want any thing which is to be obtained by importunity."

18 October 1777:
Saturday. At Army headquarters at Worcester, Washington, receives the good news of the surrender of John Burgoyne.

From York, Pennsylvania, Benjamin Harrison, a delegate from Virginia, and the Committee of Foreign Affairs writes to the commissioners at Paris, "We have the pleasure of enclosing to you the copy of a letter from General Gates containing the circumstances of a victory gained over General Burgoyne on the 7th. This event must defeat the main views of General Clinton in proceeding up the Hudson River. He has, it is true, got possession of Fort Montgomery, but with much loss, as we hear. Though the enemy should boast much of this acquisition, yet we are persuaded the consequences will be very little profitable to them, as Governor Clinton, of New York, and his brother, General James Clinton, are acting vigorously in concert with General Putnam, who commands in that quarter."

Lafayette is able to leave the hospital at Bethlehem, Pennsylvania, and return to duty with the Army. He arrives in camp at Skippack Road to join Washington's headquarters at the home of Peter Wentz.

19 October 1777:
Sunday. In York, John Hancock, president of the Congress, writes to the New Hampshire Assembly, "Gentlemen: I am so pressed with business that I have only time to cover [send under cover] you the sundry resolves of Congress to which I beg to refer your attention. The judgement of the Court Marshall [Martial] respecting General Sullivan I beg you will order to have printed in your newspapers."

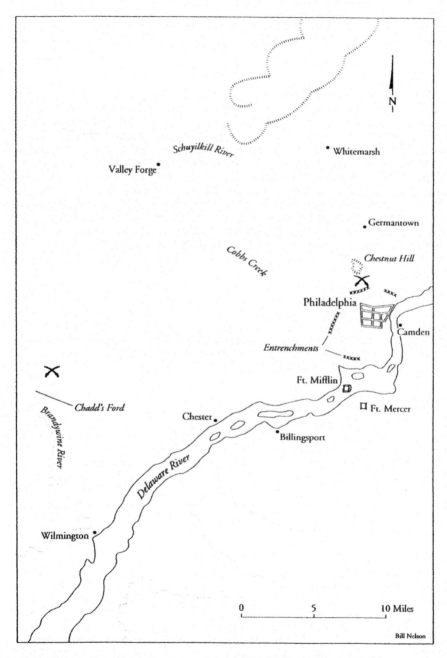

Fig. IV-25: British Occupation of Philadelphia, 1777

Sir William Howe, requiring more troops to deal with the water approaches to Philadelphia, evacuates his camp at Germantown, and pulls his troops back into the city of Philadelphia. He now feels that he needs to capture the two American forts denying him the free use of the Delaware River.

20 October 1777:
Monday. From Braintree, Massachusetts, Abigail Adams writes to her husband John "'Tis not more than three weeks since I thought our affairs looked in a more prosperous train than they had done since the commencement of the war. Though they have not taken the turn I hoped for, yet I doubt not they will finally terminate in our favor. Providence for wise purpose has oftentimes since the commencement of this war brought about our deliverance by ways and means which have appeared to us the most improbable and unlikely; has given into our hands those things which we were destitute of, and in the greatest necessity for, so true it is, Acknowledge Him in all thy ways and He shall direct thy paths."

21 October 1777:
Tuesday. Howe orders Colonel Carl Emil Kurt von Donop, with 2,000 Hessian troops, to attack the Americans in Fort Mercer at Red Bank, New Jersey. In the early hours, Donop crosses the Delaware River to the Jersey side, and marches his troops to attack Fort Mercer from the landward flank, believing that to be lightly defended. They march inland and encamp overnight at Haddonfield, New Jersey.

22 October 1777:
Wednesday. Colonel von Donop lands more of his command, and his artillery at Cooper's Ferry on the New Jersey side of the Delaware River, and makes plans to attack Fort Mercer on the high ground at Red Bank.
In Philadelphia, frustrated by limitations on his requests for troops and supplies in much larger numbers than the Home Office is willing or able to provide, and beginning to recognize that America cannot be returned to the fold of the British Empire by force, William Howe requests to be relieved of his command.

23 October 1777:
Thursday. The Americans have prepared to deny the British the Delaware River as a means of supply support for the British after their occupation of Philadelphia by erecting the fortification near Red Bank, New Jersey they name Fort Mercer. It is commanded by Colonel Christopher Greene, with about 400 men. The Hessians, under von Donop, with about 1,600 of his men attack the fort in two columns. As the first column attacking the northern and eastern sides of the fort gets within range, they are cut down by devastating artillery

and musket fire, and cannot move against the fort's nine-foot high parapet. Suffering heavy casualties, they retreat, falling all the way back to their encampment near the village of Haddonfield, nearly nine miles away. Von Donop, attacking with the second column on the southern parapet, neglects to bring any scaling ladders. He, too, is overwhelmed by massive artillery and musket fire, and receives a mortal wound in the leg. The Hessian losses total more than 400 men, while the Americans lose about 40 men. [See Fig. IV-25, p. 285].

24 October 1777:
    Friday. Howe is less than pleased with von Donop's failure to eliminate Fort Mercer, and requests assistance from the British naval vessels in the Delaware River, below the American forts at Billingsport and Fort Mifflin on Hog Island. Two of these ships, the 64-gun ship-of-the-line HMS *Augusta*, and the sloop of war HMS *Merlin*, run aground as they attempt to avoid the underwater chevaux-de-frise obstacles the Americans have set in the river.
    Sir William Howe, at his headquarters in Philadelphia is seriously concerned about this failure to break through the American defenses below the city, because he cannot supply his army without a ready and easy means of transporting the materials he requires.

25 October 1777:
    Saturday. At the American forts on the Delaware River, the British sloop of war HMS *Merlin*, is not able to be hauled off the shoal onto which it has run aground, so the British, not wanting it to fall into American hands, set it afire. The ship-of-the-line HMS *Augusta*, also stuck on a shoal, is set on fire by artillery from Fort Mifflin. It will explode the next day.
    At York, the Congress hears a Report from the Committee on Indian Affairs, and resolves that the petition from the agents of the Stockbridge Indians that they be employed in the service of the United States be referred to Maj. Gen. Horatio Gates, to whose army they are requested to repair.

26 October 1777:
    Sunday. In York, the Marine Committee writes to the Eastern Navy Board, sending the board warrants for funds, empowering any two members of the board to act in the absence of the third, and stating that the removal of the ships now under construction from the rivers in which they are now located is of great importance. These ships must be sent to sea at all events.

27 October 1777:
    Monday. The Congress again takes up consideration of the Articles of Confederation, particularly Article 14, which deals with the powers of the Congress, and agrees to language that

makes the Congress the final arbiter of disagreements between states on the matter of boundaries.

28 October 1777:
      Tuesday. At York, Pennsylvania, John Adams writes to Abigail, "The people of this country are chiefly Germans, who have schools in their own language, as well as prayers, psalms, and sermons, so that multitudes are born, grow up, and die here, without ever learning the English. In politics they are a breed of mongrels or neutrals, and benumbed with a general torpor. If the people in Pennsylvania, Maryland, Delaware, and Jersey had the feelings and the spirit of some people that I know, Howe would be soon ensnared in a trap more fatal than that in which, as it is said, Burgoyne was taken. Howe is completely in our power, and if he is not totally ruined it will be entirely owing to the awkwardness and indolence of this country. Fighting, however, begins to become fashionable. Colonel Greene [Christopher Greene, 1st Rhode Island Continental Regiment] has exhibited a glorious example in the defense of Red Bank." (See the sketch for 23 October 1777)

29 October 1777:
      Wednesday. At headquarters, Whitemarsh, Pennsylvania, a Council of War is held during which Washington reports that the enemy's force amounts to about ten thousand rank and file, that they have established batteries opposite Fort Mifflin and they are trying to open water communications to Philadelphia. He further informs the members of the council that the last returns of his army yielded 8,313 continental troops and 2,717 militia rank and file. He also notes that General Burgoyne and his whole army have capitulated to General Gates on condition of being permitted to return to Great Britain, and not bearing arms again in North America during the present contest. He then raises four questions to the council; 1.) Is it prudent, in our present circumstances to attempt an attack—it is not, 2.) What disposition of the army is best—to take post on ground nearby, which has been reconnoitered, 3.) Will the office of Inspector-General, for the purpose of establishing one uniform set of Manual and Maneuvers be advisable—yes, 4.) Should regimental promotions extend only to captains, and should soldiers be rewarded for apprehending deserters, as are others—yes. He also wishes to know what help can be drawn from the northern armies at this time.
      President John Hancock begs leave to resign from the Congress, and departs for Boston. The secretary is to serve as presiding officer until a new choice is made for president.

30 October 1777:
      Thursday. From Passy, Benjamin Franklin, Silas Deane, and Arthur Lee write to the Committee of Foreign Affairs,

reporting that the frigate commissioned to be built in Holland
for America's use is nearly finished. It is a vessel of thirty 24-
pounders, but the difficulty of equipping the ships has
caused it to be sold to the King of France. However, he is
gracious enough to engage the captain thereof to remain in
his service.

Washington, now aware that the major remaining threat
to America is the British force at Philadelphia, sends his aide,
Lieutenant Colonel Alexander Hamilton to Albany, to hasten
the units in Gates's now dormant army south to reinforce
American forces around Philadelphia and the Delaware River
forts. Washington feels that if he can choke off the British
supply lines into the city, thus constricting their means of
support, they will be forced to evacuate. It is too bad the
Congress did not see clearly enough the value of many small
whaleboats, rather that the frigates which only cost money.

31 October 1777:
Friday. Colonel James Wilkinson is admitted to the
Congress, to lay papers before them. He requests time to
"digest and arrange them." He indicates, also, that he has
answers to questions relative to the situation at the Northern
Department "... of our army, and those of the enemy, before,
at the time of, and since the capitulation of General
Burgoyne." Wilkinson then withdraws. This is a ploy by him
to allow him time to expand upon his role in the defeat, and
thus seek advancement.

1 November 1777:
Saturday. In York, to fill the chair of the president of the
Congress, Henry Laurens of South Carolina is unanimously
chosen.

At headquarters in Whitemarsh, Washington writes to the
President of Congress, "The enemy still consider the
possession of our posts on the River of great importance, and
from their preparation of fascines ..., and the best information
I have been able to obtain, they will make further efforts to
carry them. After the action of the 4th ulto. at Germantown, I
hoped, we should have been in a situation to attack the
enemy again on those grounds, and with more success than
in the former instance. But this I was not able to effect. The
inclosed return will give Congress a general view of the
strength of this army, when it was made and a particular one
of the forces of each state which compose it. By this, they will
perceive, how greatly deficient the whole are in furnishing
their just quotas. We have not yet come to any determination
respecting the disposition of our troops for the winter;
supposing it a matter of great importance, and that for the
present we should be silent upon it. At the request of Govr.
Clinton, I have transmitted a copy of his letter to me giving an
account of Genl. Vaughan's expedition up the North River,
after the capture of Fort Montgomery, and the destruction

committed by his troops in burning Kingston and the houses and mills on the river. According to the latest advices, they have returned again, and it is reported, that they have destroyed the barracks and fort and gone to New York."

2 November 1777:
Sunday. In York, the North Carolina delegation writes to Richard Caswell reporting the defeat of General Burgoyne and enclosing a copy of the Articles of Convention, they also note that General Clinton had taken Ft. Montgomery and "burned the little town of Kingston."

At Whitemarsh, Pennsylvania, Lafayette removes from the Morris mansion to the home of George Emlen at headquarters, because he wants to be close to Washington and his "family", to gain first-hand information regarding any independent command as it might become available.

Washington begins to fortify his position by constructing redoubts, emplacing cannon, and entrenching to protect and defend against any attack Howe might choose to make.

3 November 1777:
Monday. At York, Colonel James Wilkinson attends and presents the Congress with the papers relative to the convention settled between Burgoyne and Gates at Saratoga on 17 October 1777. He also takes this opportunity to embellish his own role in the Saratoga battles, so as to polish his image. Actually, he did almost nothing but serve as a messenger boy.

At the Delaware River forts, Brig. Gen. James Varnum arrives with his units along the river to strengthen the defenses. He encourages Hazelwood to bring his vessels north of Fort Mifflin, and his floating batteries and Continental ships next to the chevaux-de-frise, at which spot they will best be enabled to fire upon any British vessels that attempt a passage, or at least discourage them.

4 November 1777:
Tuesday. On the Delaware River, Hazelwood brings the brig *Andrew Doria* and the sloop *Fly* to a point near the mouth of the Schuylkill River.

Washington is at Whitemarsh, where he sets up headquarters at the Emlen House, and writes to Sir William Howe, "Sir: I have been informed by Lt. Col. Frazer (Persifor Frazer, of the 5th Pennsylvania Regiment), who is now a prisoner in your possession, that Major Belford (Nisbet Balfour of the 4th Foot, British Army, Aide to Sir William Howe) one your aids, had assured him it was your earnest desire, that a general exchange of prisoners should take place on equitable terms; or if this could not be effected, that the officers on both sides should be released on parole. This I have no doubt was done by your authority, and with an intention that it should be communicated to me. I assure you,

Sir, nothing will afford me more satisfaction, than to carry the first proposition into execution. But lest we should still unhappily disagree about the privates to be accounted for, and that this may not operate to the prejudice of the officers, it is my wish for their mutual relief, that their exchange may immediately take place, so far as circumstance or rank and number will apply." This business of prisoner exchange will consume much of the higher ranking officers time on both sides as the war goes on. It is important for them to relieve the distress of their men.

5 November 1777:
    Wednesday. The Congress wishes to secure the posts on the Hudson River, and passes several resolutions to that effect; 1.) That Maj. Gen. Gates be empowered to apply to the states of Massachusetts, Connecticut, New York, and New Jersey for militia to garrison the posts on the river, 2.) That Maj. Gen. Israel Putnam be called upon to join a detachment from Gates for securing the communication of these posts, 3.) That Gates be empowered to order such a number of gallies, gunboats, fire-rafts, chains, caissons, and chevaux-de-frise, and such fortifications for obstructing and keeping possession of the river.
    On the Delaware River, Varnum orders Captain James Lee with two cannons to a hill downriver from Fort Mercer, near Mantua Creek, where Lee can fire at British warships attempting to work their way up the river.

6 November 1777:
    Thursday. The Congress resolves that General Washington be directed immediately to settle the relative ranks of the officers of the cavalry, and issue their commissions accordingly.
    From headquarters at Whitemarsh, General Orders state "The Colonels or officers commanding regiments are to a point one officer from each regiment, to go with four men to Bethlehem, to get such of their cloathing as is absolutely necessary, and bring the same in waggons to camp. The waggon master general will make the necessary provision or waggons for that end." The parole is given as Warsaw and the countersigns as Berlin and Dresden.

7 November 1777:
    Friday. The Congress accepts the resignation of Maj. Gen. Thomas Mifflin as quartermaster general, but notes that his rank and commission of major general be continued without pay, until further orders. Mifflin has been something less that the best officer of the revolution in this capacity. Too much of the time he is found not at his duty station, and not performing his duties.
    Washington writes to Lieutenant Colonel Peter Adams (of the 7th Maryland Regiment), "The approaching season and the

distresses of the army in the articles of blankets and cloathing make it necessary, that every practicable measure should be pursued to procure supplies. Therefore to relieve, if possible, the wants of the troops, raised by the State of Maryland, in these essential articles, you are to proceed immediately to Govr. Johnson with the letters you have in charge for him, and to receive whatever supplies the State may be in a situation to furnish in these instances, and which they may think proper to deliver. You know the circumstances of the troops and must explain them."

8 November 1777:
Saturday. From his farm near Philadelphia, a Quaker Gentleman, Robert Morton keeps a dairy, in which he notes, "A report prevails that the British have, by orders evacuated Rhode Island. I went this morning to see the floating batteries upon the banks of Schuylkill, one of which had been launched the day before and was found very leaky and insufficient for that purpose. They are now repairing her, expecting to be ready to make the attack in a few days. A proclamation is at last published to prevent the soldiers plundering the inhabitants, and persons appointed to patrol."
The Congress is not too pleased with the Convention that Maj. Gen. Horatio Gates accepted from Burgoyne, so they try to find means of securing that large British force so that it is not available for future use against the United States. They direct Maj. Gen. William Heath to cause to be enumerated the name and rank of every commissioned officer and the name, former place of abode, occupation, size, age, and description of every non-commissioned officer and private soldier and all other persons comprehended in the convention of 16 October 1777. Heath is to transmit an authentic copy thereof to the Board of War, in order that if any such person of said army is hereafter found in arms against these states in North America during the present contest, he may be convicted of the offence and suffer the punishment in such case inflicted by the law of nations.

9 November 1777:
Sunday. In York, Pennsylvania, James Duane, writes to George Clinton, expressing concern over the attacks on Forts Montgomery and Clinton and the burning of Kingston; but joy over the defeat of General Burgoyne. Duane notes that the Congress resolved that every expense to maintain a sufficient force for the protection and security of the passes in the highlands and the communication of the Hudson River be allowed.

10 November 1777:
Monday. From Saratoga Gates writes to the Congress attempting to justify his stupid terms to Burgoyne of the convention he approved. Gates says that he allowed these

terms on the absurd grounds there would be very few British soldiers to embark, because many of them would desert on their march to Boston. How Gates could have possibly thought of such an idea at the time of the convention is not explained. He also advises the Congress to delay embarking these convention troops.

Howe begins a bombardment of the other American fort on the Delaware River, Fort Mifflin. This fort prohibits the free use of that means of supply for his army in Philadelphia. It is located on the Pennsylvania side (west) of the river on the south end of Mud Island. [See Fig. IV-25, p. 285].

The Congress resolves that the Committee of Foreign Affairs be directed to write to the commissioners of the United States, in France and Spain, to purchase and ship, on the continental account, five hundred tons of lead, four hundred tons of powder, one million gun-flints, tents for fifty thousand men, and ten thousand yards of flannel for the making of cartridges.

11 November 1777:
Tuesday. The British step up their bombardment of Fort Mifflin, south of Philadelphia, and almost opposite Fort Mercer at Red Bank, New Jersey. Howe is determined to destroy these American forts that are obstacles to his use of the river as a mode of transport for the supplies and communication he needs. It is his water transport with the other British forces and supplies in New York that is so critical to his ability to maintain a position in Philadelphia.

If the British cannot clear and maintain such a supply line, they will be forced to abandon the city. The American troops at Fort Mifflin courageously endure this long and brutal bombardment, holding out for six days under heavy fire from ships and shore batteries.

Congress takes into consideration new articles to be added to or included in the Articles of Confederation. They agree to some, expunge others, and substitute some. This whole business of the Articles of Confederation has and will continue to consume much of the time of the Congress the remainder of this year.

12 November 1777:
Wednesday. The Congress approves the following resolution: "Freedom of Speech and debate in Congress shall not be impeached or questioned in any court or place out of Congress. The members of Congress shall be protected in their persons from arrests and imprisonments during the time of their going to, and from, and attendance on Congress, except for treason, felony or breach of the peace."

At Fort Mifflin, Varnum rotates a new garrison into the battered fortification. Weary men have been holding up the British for days. He hopes fresh troops will continue the process a little longer.

13 November 1777:
Thursday. From Paris, Arthur Lee writes to the Baron de Schulenburg, reporting that William Lee is appointed commissioner for Berlin, representing the United States of America, and requesting the court's instructions regarding the details of and procedure for his arrival. These matters are punctiliously to be observed in all the European Courts, and the Americans need to be very careful how they tread. He goes on to note, "The entire discomfiture of General Burgoyne and the northern expedition, as well as the untruth of what was circulated about General Howe's success, with the sole view of diverting the public attention from the ill success of the Canadian armament, is now universally acknowledged in England. We have received no dispatches on the subject. But from the place he is in, we are satisfied General Howe will meet with a manly opposition."

14 November 1777:
Friday. At Fort Mifflin, on Mud Island in the Delaware River, with its garrison of about 500 men, is nearly destroyed by the extended British bombardment.
At Whitemarsh, Washington writes to Maj. Gen Horatio Gates, expressing a view that Burgoyne will apply for a change of place of embarkation of the prisoners taken at Saratoga from Boston to Rhode Island or some part of Long Island Sound. He then goes on to point out that any such change would be prejudicial to the American cause because the sooner these convention troops arrive in England the sooner fresh English troops can be sent to America to continue the war.

15 November 1777:
Saturday. In York, the Congress has come to general agreement on the Articles of Confederation, and makes out a commemorative listing of each and every article, ordering that three hundred copies be printed and lodged with the secretary, to be subject to the future orders of Congress. There are still a few sticky issues, mainly relating to western lands, claimed by some states that hold up full approval of the document.

16 November 1777:
Sunday. From Braintree, Massachusetts, Abigail Adams writes to her husband, John "General Burgoyne and his troops arrived last week in Cambridge. All seems to be quietness at present. From the southward we get no very authentic accounts. My brother has had the misfortune to be taken upon his return from a cruise up the Baltic. They had a valuable prize with them loaded with duck and cordage. He was captain of marines on board the *Tartar*, Captain Grimes, Master, and was carried into Newfoundland, since which we have not heard from him. You make no mention of receiving

any letters from me for a long time. I hope none have miscarried."

17 November 1777:
    Monday. At Fort Mifflin, after enduring more than a week of bombardment, Major Simeon Thayer, commanding, orders the fort abandoned. There is nothing left to defend—the walls all battered down, the guns dismounted, many American defenders killed or wounded, no food left in the fort, the troops without a full kit of clothing. Under cover of darkness, and leaving the flag still flying (the fort never officially surrenders), the garrison escapes upriver.
    Francis Dana, a delegate from Massachusetts, and William Ellery, a delegate from Rhode Island, attend and take their seats in the Congress.

18 November 1777:
    Tuesday. The Congress orders that a warrant issue on Thomas Smith, commissioner of the loan office for the state of Pennsylvania, in favor of William Henry of Lancaster for $10,000 for the purchase of shoes and leather for the use of the army.
    Arthur St. Clair, artillery chief Henry Knox, and Brig. Gen. de Kalb make an inspection trip to the Delaware River, reporting that the loss of Fort Mifflin is not the end of the campaign to deny use of the Delaware River to the British.
    Cornwallis leads a detachment of 2,000 troops south of Philadelphia to Chester.

19 November 1777:
    Wednesday. The Congress, having received information, through various channels "... that the American soldiers and other inhabitants of the United States of America, whom the fortune of war hath made prisoners to the British army under command of General Howe, now imprisoned in Philadelphia, are treated with such shocking inhumanity that numbers expire in the prison yard for want of food...", is shocked and notes that such treatment of the American prisoners is not only inconsistent with the practice of civilized nations, but totally the reverse of that humane treatment which the British prisoners have uniformly received in these united states. The Congress resolves "That General Washington be desired to make strict enquiry into the truth of this information, and to report to Congress, as soon as possible, the results of his enquiries."
    Cornwallis and his forces cross the Delaware River to Billingsport, New Jersey, on small craft and rafts. They are joined by a body of 4,500 reinforcements sent down from New York City. The purpose of this body is to advance upon and attack Fort Mercer from the landward side. Winter is coming on, and the British are is serious trouble regarding their supply lines. They need to open up the Delaware River.

20 November 1777:

Thursday. The Congress learns from various reports and letters that inroads have been made on the western frontiers of Virginia and Pennsylvania by savage tribes of Indians, and that a number of helpless persons have been cruelly massacred. Some papers, styled "Proclamation," under the hand and seal of Henry Hamilton, Lieutenant Governor of Fort Detroit, left by the Indians where they committed their murders, now in the possession of the Congress, indicate that these savages have been instigated by British agents, in this barbarous war, particularly by Hamilton. The Congress resolves to request that Washington send Colonel William Crawford to Pittsburg to take command of the continental troops and militia in the Western Department, now under Brigadier General Edward Hand being relieved to go to Albany.

At Whitemarsh, Lafayette leaves headquarters to join with Nathanael Greene in an expedition to Haddonfield, New Jersey, the purpose being to attack Cornwallis, as he may be trying to attack Fort Mercer. Washington is hoping that Cornwallis can be drawn into a trap by Greene and Lafayette. Meanwhile, Varnum and Christopher Greene at Fort Mercer do not feel that the garrison is able to withstand a siege, unless a huge influx of support is immediately available. This not being the case, they decide it is better to abandon the place, and save the troops. The magazine is blown, and most of the men are evacuated, leaving a small contingent as a rear guard.

21 November 1777:

Friday. At Fort Mercer, the rear guard falls back, just ahead of the British vanguard.

At headquarters, Whitemarsh, General Orders state "Those paymasters of regiments, who have drawn pay for any officers or men in Col. Morgan's Rifle Corps, are immediately to pay the same over to the paymaster of that Corps. The officers of the day report that sentries from the picqyets (sic) keep fires by them. This dangerous practice is absolutely forbidden, and all officers of guards are without fail to visit all their sentries between every relief, to see that they are alert, and keep no fires; and in cold and bad weather they are to relieve the sentries every hour. They are also to see that the sentries are well informed of their duty, and to instruct such as are deficient." The parole is given as Brookfield and the countersigns as Springfield and Pomfret.

The Congress resolves to recall Silas Deane from his duties at the Court of Versailles. They defer until Monday the choosing of a commissioner to replace Deane.

22 November 1777:

Saturday. Learning that false and groundless rumors and reports have appeared in Europe indicating that America and

Great Britain have a treaty and that it is probable a reconciliation will take place, the Congress resolves "That all proposals for a treaty between the king of Great Britain, or any of his commissioners, and the United States of America, inconsistent with the independence of the said states, or with such treaties or alliances as may be formed under their authority, will be rejected by Congress. That the Commissioners of the United States at the several courts in Europe be directed to apply to the respective courts and request their immediate assistance in preventing a further embarkation of foreign troops to America, and also to urge the necessity of their acknowledging the independence of these states."

At Fort Mercer, the British march into the place following the American evacuation. The Royal Marines are assigned the task of demolishing the fort, its embrasures, and its embankments. They wish to leave no opportunity for an easy rebuild at some future time by the Americans. Nathaniel Greene now has little chance to attack Cornwallis.

23 November 1777:
Sunday. At headquarters, Whitemarsh, Washington writes to Sir William Howe, "Sir: I am compelled by repeated complaints of the inhuman treatment still shown to the unhappy prisoners in your hands to call upon you for a clear and explicit answer to my letter of the 14th, instant. This I shall expect to receive by Monday evening next. Their sufferings demand immediate redress, and unless, I obtain the most satisfactory assurances on this head, duty will constrain me to retaliate instantly, on the prisoners in my possession."

This problem of the mistreatment of American prisoners of war by the British is a blot and stain upon the heretofore understood honor of the British nation. Washington uses this sense of honor to shame the British commanders into compliance with proper rules of conduct.

In York, Henry Laurens, president of the Congress, writes to Joseph Reed, forwarding Reed's appointment as a commissioner for Indian affairs on the western frontier of Pennsylvania.

24 November 1777:
Monday. Concerned about a shortage of flour for making bread and also the lack of threshed wheat from which to make the flour, the Congress resolves to hire several mills within six miles. They expect to purchase or impress wheat in the sheaf and request soldier assistance for that purpose—then set the mills to work. By these means they expect that a current supply of flour will be obtained and that time will be gained for establishing magazines of flour at Pottsgrove, Reading, and Lancaster. It is believed that this will provide sufficient flour for at least three months, by

which time the Board of War will be able to plan the supplies for the next campaign.

25 November 1777:
    Tuesday. In York, the Congress resolves that the governor and council of Virginia be requested to provide a guard at Continental expense that will provide security and protection to the shipyards building frigates.
    Washington orders Nathaniel Greene to return with his troops to the main army, since he no longer sees any mission for him in New Jersey and needs those troops if Howe should attack him while Washington's forces are divided.

26 November 1777:
    Wednesday. The Congress resolves "That Monsieur Fleury [François Louis, Marquis de Teissedre de Fleury], in consideration of the disinterested gallantry which he has manifested in the service of the United States, be appointed to the rank of lieutenant colonel in the army."

27 November 1777:
    Thursday. The Congress elects three additional members to the Board of War; Major General Horatio Gates, Joseph Trumbull, and Richard Peters, with Gates to be appointed president of the Board of War.

28 November 1777:
    Friday. The Congress resolves unanimously "That a committee of three be appointed forthwith to repair to the army, and in private confidential consultation with General Washington, to consider of the best and most practicable means for carrying on a winter's campaign with vigour [sic] and success, an object which Congress have much at heart, and on such consultation, with the concurrence of General Washington, to direct every measure which circumstances may require for promoting the public service."

29 November 1777:
    Saturday. The Congress forms a committee of three to procure a translation into French of the Articles of Confederation, inviting the inhabitants of Canada to accede to the union of these states.
    Lafayette returns to headquarters at Whitemarsh, following his expedition into New Jersey with Maj. Gen. Greene.

30 November 1777:
    Sunday. In York, William Ellery, a delegate from Rhode Island, writes to Nicholas Cooke, noting that copies of the Articles of Confederation and of Resolves of the Congress have already been transmitted to him. He further reports that

the British have evacuated Fort Ticonderoga and Mount Independence.

At headquarters, Whitemarsh, General Orders state "On the 25th of November instant, the Honorable Continental Congress passed the following resolve: That general Washington be directed to publish in general orders, that Congress will speedily take into consideration the merits of such officers as have distinguished themselves by their intrepidity and their attention to the health and discipline of their men; and adopt such regulations as shall tend to introduce order and good discipline into the army and to render the situation of the officers and soldiery, with respect to cloathing and other necessaries, more eligible than it has hither to been." The parole is given as Northhampton and the countersigns as Greenland and Portsmouth.

1 December 1777:
Monday. In London, Lord Frederick North, receives William Howe's request to be relieved of his command of the British Forces in North America. Neither North nor the King have been truly pleased with the way Germain and Howe have been conducting the war in America. One of them must go. Now, with Howe's request for relief, the problem is solved. It will take awhile before the order is issued and a replacement named.

Nathanael Greene, with his troops, re-crosses the Delaware and joins Washington at Whitemarsh.

The Congress orders that a warrant issue in favor of Colonel Benjamin Flower, Commissary General of military stores for $10,000.

2 December 1777:
Tuesday. The Congress has appointed John Adams to be a commissioner at the Court of Versailles and resolves that a commission be made out for him.

At headquarters in Whitemarsh, Washington writes to Major General Israel Putnam, "The importance of the North River in the present contest and then necessity of defending it, are subjects which have been so frequently and so fully discussed and are so well understood, that it is unnecessary to enlarge upon them. These facts at once appear, when it is considered that it runs thro' a whole State, that it is the only passage by which the enemy from New York or any part of our coast, can ever hope to cooperate with an army that may come from Canada; that the possession of it is indispensibly essential to preserve the communication between the eastern, middle, and southern states; and further, that upon its security, in a great measure, depend our chief supplies of flour for the subsistence of such forces as we may have occasion for, in the course of the war, either in the Eastern or Northern Departments, or in the country lying high up on the west side of it."

3 December 1777:

Wednesday. From Paris, Arthur Lee writes to Dr. Berkehout, a British secret agent, seeking to obtain from the American commissioners in Paris the terms of an accommodation with England. In his letter, Lee notes, "We have powers to receive but not to make overtures. If they therefore stay for overtures from us, I promise you they will not receive them till their faith can move our mountains. I hoped something from this negotiation, and therefore more willingly lent myself to it; but I now see too well their abundant pride and folly to think the public will derive any advantage from it."

4 December 1777:

Thursday. The Pennsylvania Assembly, experiencing the difficulties of continuing to permit substitutes to perform militia duty, resolves "That ... the legislature of the commonwealth of Pennsylvania, forthwith to repeal the clause in the said laws which permits the hiring of substitutes to perform militia duty; and, in lieu thereof, to impose and lay such fines on those persons who neglect, or refuse to march when called forth on duty ..."

After sunset, Howe sends 12,000 troops north out of Philadelphia, in two columns under Cornwallis and Knyphausen, to attack Washington's army at Whitemarsh. About three miles on the road, Cownwallis' units, in the vanguard, are sniped at by militia. They then halt and form a defense line, awaiting reinforcements.

5 December 1777:

Friday. On the road to Whitemarsh, Lord Cornwallis advances his light infantry toward Chestnut Hill, where a Pennsylvania militia detachment of 600 men, under Brig. Gen. James Irvine, engages them. The British repulse the attack, but Irvine is wounded.

At York, Francis Lewis, a delegate from New York, attends and takes his seat in the Congress.

6 December 1777:

Saturday. At headquarters, Whitemarsh, General Orders state "The Commissary General says he has put six day's provisions into the hands of the division and brigade commissaries; if therefore the troops want provisions, it must be the fault of the latter; and this want will be attended with such pernicious consequences, that no excuse will be admitted in behalf of any commissary who fails supplying his division or brigade, but a severe example will be made of him. The troops are to ground their arms at their alarm posts; and as soon as possible, draw and cook their provisions for today and tomorrow, and immediately set about making the best provision they can of wood and huts for tonight." The parole is given as Bennington and the countersigns as Bedford and Bethlehem.

The Congress considers a report of the Board of War concerning correspondence between General Washington and General Howe relative to the exchange and treatment of prisoners. This is a critically important subject, and one which General Washington is most anxious to have regularized and promulgated. After some considerable debate upon the matter, the Congress postpones further consideration until Monday next.

7 December 1777:

Sunday. At Whitemarsh, Pennsylvania, Sir William Howe, still chafing at the fact that he has been unable to bring General George Washington to a battle in which he can destroy the American army, sets out from Chestnut Hill in still another attempt. Having skirmished with American units in several probing actions, he makes a move upon the American left flank. This is quickly picked up by the Americans, and countered by Colonel Daniel Morgan's riflemen and Colonel Mordecai Gist's Maryland militia, who lay a hot fire into Howe's ranks. The next day, Howe returns to Philadelphia.

8 December 1777:

Monday. Resuming consideration of the matter of the exchange and treatment of prisoners, the Congress concludes that Howe is making a distinction of treatment between persons taken in arms and citizens who, due to the fortunes of war, have fallen into his power. The Congress is desirous that Washington request a response from Howe with an explicit explanation of his conduct to prisoners, whether officers, soldiers, or citizens who may be subject to Howe's control. The exchange and treatment of prisoners continues to be an issue between the belligerents throughout the war.

9 December 1777:

Tuesday. Pennsylvania has been quite lax in its responsibilities of providing blankets and support for the hospitals, which laxity, it is decided, by the members of the Congress, needs to be remedied. The "Congress, therefore, submit it to the assembly of the State of Pennsylvania, whether under these critical, distressing circumstances, it would not be advisable to vest the continental Board of War, or such persons as the said Board may, for that purpose, appoint, with full powers to collect clothing, and blankets & agreeable to the restrictions in the ordinances of council."
That would remove the chore of collection from the state's responsibility and control, and place it in the hands of a military officer who might have a more vested interest in seeing to the care of wounded soldiers.

10 December 1777:
 Wednesday. Concerned that supplies for the army under Washington's command have, since the loss of Philadelphia, been drawn from distant places, entailing great expense, irregularity, and scantiness of supplies, the Congress seeks to find a means of correction. Learning also that little of the clothing, food, provisions, and forage that remain in the counties of Philadelphia, Bucks, and Chester get to Washington's troops, who suggests that the Congress nudge Pennsylvania to do something about the problem. It is not that there is an actual shortage of grains and forage, it is that the people are reluctant to part with it, in the face of British hard specie, and fear of retaliation if they do not deal with the British. Therefore, the Congress recommends to the Legislature of Pennsylvania that they enact a law requiring all persons within their state to assist in the provision of such supplies as General Washington may require.

11 December 1777:
 Thursday. At Matson's Ford, near Gulph Mills, Pennsylvania, in the early morning, Lord Charles Cornwallis leads about 3,500 men on an foraging expedition to collect supplies and provisions. He is soon faced with troops under Brigadier Generals James Potter and John Lacey with a body of Pennsylvania militia that halt his progress and force Cornwallis to return to Philadelphia.
 Washington and Lafayette remove with headquarters to Swede's Ford.

12 December 1777:
 Friday. From Passy, Benjamin Franklin, Silas Deane, and Arthur Lee write to Lord North in London, "From motives of duty, an earnest desire of mitigating the calamities of war, we proposed, near a year since, to the King of Great Britain's ambassador here, an exchange of prisoners in Europe. The answer we received must have been made known to your lordship, and the world will judge of its decency. It would have been honorable for that noble lord, and happy for thousands who have since suffered unnecessarily, if he had considered that moderation is a mark of wisdom and humanity an ornament of the highest station. These are the sentiments at least which have governed the Congress and the people of the United States."
 General Washington makes his headquarters at Swede's Ford.

13 December 1777:
 Saturday. The Congress resolves "... as the opinion of this congress, that it is essential to the promotion of discipline in the American army, and to the reformation of the various abuses which prevail in the different departments that an

appointment be made of inspectors general, agreeable to the practice to the best disciplined European armies."

Washington is trying to remove his overworked army to a place of rest. He takes his troops upriver, crosses the Schuylkill on a bridge of wagons, and heads towards Gulph Mills.

14 December 1777:

Sunday. Washington makes his headquarters at Gulph Mills, where the Army, tired after its exertions, rests for several days. Washington writes to the President of Congress, "On Thursday morning we marched from our old encampment and intended to pass the Schuylkill at Madisons Ford, where a bridge had been laid across the river. When the first division and a part of the second had passed, they found a body of the enemy, consisting, from the best accounts we have been able to obtain, of four thousand men, under Lord Cornwallis possessing themselves of the Heights on both sides of the road leading from the river and the defile called the Gulph, which I presume, are well known to some part of your honorable body. This unexpected event obliged such of our troops as had crossed to repass and prevented our getting over till the succeeding night. This maneuver on the part of the enemy, was not in consequence of any information they had of our movement, but was designed to secure the pass whilst they were foraging in the neighboring country ... Enclosed is a copy of a letter from Gen. Burgoyne, by which you will perceive, he requests leave to embark his troops at Rhode Island or some other place in the Sound, and in case this cannot be granted, he may be allowed, with his suite to go there and return from thence to England." He then discusses the problem of the shortage of flour noting that in Bucks and Philadelphia Counties have been pretty well denuded and that millers are unwilling either from fear of lack of payment to grind more "however Congress may be assured, that no exertions of mine as far as circumstances will admit shall be wanting to provide our own troops with supplies on the one hand, and to prevent the enemy from them on the other. I should be happy if the civil authority in the several states thro' the recommendations of Congress, or their own mere will, seeing the necessity of supporting the army, would always adopt the most spirited measures, suited to the end."

15 December 1777:

Monday. The Congress learns that many cattle have been driven into the marshes of Kent County, Delaware and into other parts of that county, which are exposed to the depredations of the enemy. It therefore resolves, "That the Board of War be authorized and directed to give such orders for securing the said stock as they shall deem most effectual. That the owners of the stock so removed be paid for same at reasonable rates." These matters of supply and provisions, in which the Congress continues to involve itself, are better handled by competent officers.

16 December 1777:
    Tuesday. From the Hague, Holland, Charles William Frédéric Dumas, writes to the Committee of Foreign Affairs, "I congratulate you and the honorable Congress, and all you United America with all my heart. This news [Burgoyne's capture] has made the greatest possible sensation in this country: a deep consternation among those who have all their interest in England; a marked joy among those who hate your enemies. This news has made an astonishing impression everywhere; all is considered lost to the English." This is certainly heartening news to the Congress, learning that folks in European states view the war in this light.
    Virginia ratifies the Articles of Confederation, being the first state to do so.

17 December 1777:
    Wednesday. John Witherspoon, a delegate from New Jersey, attends and takes his seat in the Congress. The Congress resolves, "That General Washington be directed to inform General Burgoyne the Congress will not receive nor consider any proposition for indulgence or altering the terms of the convention of Saratoga, unless immediately directed to their own body."

18 December 1777:
    Thursday. In Camp at Gulph Mills, Pennsylvania, the American army celebrates a "Day of Thanksgiving and Praise" for the victory over the British at the Battles of Saratoga.
    In General Orders today, Washington orders all major generals to see that an active field officer is appointed for each brigade to superintend the business of locating and making huts for each regiment, as they will soon be located at Valley Forge. Officers commanding regiments with their Captains are to cause the men to be divided into squads of twelve, each squad to make a hut for themselves.

19 December 1777:
    Friday. The main army under General George Washington marches from Gulph Mills about seven miles west at 10 o'clock in the morning into camp at Valley Forge, where cantonments had been laid out. Washington has been to this site before, and feels that it is close enough to the British to oversee and interdict their foraging, and adequate for defense against any attack they might entertain. Temporary huts are erected from the tentage and covered with leaves and straw. A very great deal has been written about Valley Forge, some of it incorrect. For example, there was little or no shad run to alleviate hunger, nor was it a particularly cold winter.

Brigadier General William Smallwood is ordered to Wilmington, Delaware, to forestall any British attempt to seize the town.

20 December 1777:

Saturday. At Valley Forge, it is learned that Major General Charles Cornwallis has sailed from Philadelphia to return to England.

General Washington issues a proclamation requiring all persons within 70 miles of his headquarters to see that they thresh half of their grain by 1 Feb 1778 and the other half by 1 Mar 1778. Failure to do so will result in having all remaining grain, not so threshed, seized by the quartermasters and paid for as straw, instead of at the higher valued rate for grain. This is, unfortunately, a needful step for the Continental Army, in order to survive and continue to threaten the British Army in Philadelphia.

21 December 1777:

Sunday. At headquarters, Valley Forge, Washington writes to Brigadier General James Potter. "Dear Sir: Major Clark has wrote to me several times about some provision that a Mr. Trumbull was sending into Philadelphia by his permission as a cover to procure intelligence. This provision was seized by Colo. Ranking and has been since detained by him. I desire you will give orders to have it delivered, for unless we now and then make use of such means to get admittance into the City we cannot expect to obtain intelligence. I think it of the greatest consequence to have what hay remains upon the islands above the mouth of Derby Creek destroyed, especially if what you heard of the former magazine of hay being spoiled is true. At any rate, as we cannot remove it, I think it should be done as speedily as possible, as we shall probably oblige them to come out into the County to forage, which will perhaps give us an opportunity of cutting off a party. The mode I leave intirely (sic) to Colo. Morgan and yourself. I am informed that there are parties cutting wood every day on this side the Schuylkill. I do not doubt that they might easily be drove in, but I think destroying the hay ought to be first attended to."

General Orders today give the parole as Cumberland, and the countersigns as Carlisle and Caroline. Field Officers are to call at headquarters to pick up a copy of the hut plans and directions for assembling and emplacing them.

22 December 1777:

Monday. At Valley Forge, Washington writes to Henry Laurens, the president of the Congress, "It is with infinite pain and concern, that I transmit [to] Congress the inclosed (sic) copies of sundry letters respecting the state of the Commissary's department. If these matters are not exaggerated, I do not know from what cause, this alarming deficiency or rather total failure of supplies arise; but unless more vigorous exertions and better regulations take place in that line, and immediately, this army must dissolve."

A large body of British troops march out of Philadelphia, intent upon forage. In an 18th century army, that travels by wagon, horses are essential---and they require a lot of bulky food.

23 December 1777:
Tuesday. At Valley Forge, General Orders report 11,982 men in camp, 2,898 of whom are listed as unfit for duty because of illness, lack of footwear, or otherwise without proper clothing for the winter---naked in the terms of the day. Any idea of a winter campaign is ridiculous under these circumstances. Provisions are also sorely lacking, such as adequate food, clothing, armaments, and gunpowder.

24 December 1777:
Wednesday. Major John Jameson is directed to take command of parties of horse to patrol the roads into Philadelphia, and to cut off intercourse between that city and the British posts east of the Schuylkill River. Also, he is to watch the motions of the enemy, and seize provisions.

25 December 1777:
Thursday. From headquarters, Valley Forge, Washington writes to Governor of North Carolina, Richard Caswell. "A spirit of resigning their commissions, whether resulting from necessary causes of feigned ones, I cannot determine, has been but too prevalent in the army of late. I have discountenanced it as much as possible, especially where the applications were by men of merit and in some such instances have peremptorily refused to grant them. The practice is of a pernicious tendency and must have an unhappy influence on the service. I shall pay due regard to the Resolve of your Honorable House of Commons, and that their views may be more fully answered, I shall deliver a copy of it to the Commanding Officer of your troops, that it may be communicated through their Line."

Washington also writes to Massachusetts delegate Elbridge Gerry. "Dear Sir: Not withstanding my last letters to Congress were very explicit, and expressive of the wants of this Army, the necessity of arranging many matters in it, and making the necessary appointments without a moments loss of time, yet, when I consider the advanced season, and consult my passed experience of delay, I am induced to take the liberty of claiming your particular attention to this business; hoping thereby, that the method suggested by you, of having a Committee of Congress, of from the Board of War, sent to camp to consult with me, or a Committee of my appointing (for it would be impossible for me to give that close attention which the nature of the thing would require) on the best regulations, arrangements, and plans for the next campaign will be approved. Our whole Military system might then be considered, and such alterations as should be found necessary and beneficial, and that circumstances would admit of, be adopted. If this committee should happen to be composed of members from the Board of War, they could fix many matters at the same time with Genl. Knox in the Ordinance Department, which requires as close attention and dispatch; as any thing whatever; in short I can foresee many great advantages which would result from it, without one possible evil."

Washington writes to Richard Caswell, Governor of North Carolina, expressing his concern over the large number of qualified officers resigning their commissions. And goes on to add, "I have nothing that is agreeable or interesting to inform you of in the Military line. The enemy still remain in possession of Philadelphia, and are strongly fortified by a chain of intrenchments (sic) and redoubts from Schuylkill to Delaware. By a letter from the eastward, a ship arrived at Portsmouth, New Hampshire, about the last ulto. in seventy five days from Marseilles with forty eight brass four pounders, 19 nine inch mortars, 4110 stand of arms, 9 tons of gunpowder, and 61,051 lb. of sulphur, 2500 9 inch shells, and 2000 four lb. Balls for the United States. This is an agreeable event, and it is a recent proof of the friendly disposition of the French Nation."

A set of orders for a move that was intended against Philadelphia by way of a surprise, but was never executed is as follows: Guards are to be posted at every avenue to the city to stop and secure every person going in or coming out; a detachment of battalion size to surprise and possess the redoubts of the enemy; the right wing of the Army under Genl. Sullivan to secure all the ferries from the west shore of the Delaware River; the left wing of the Army to march into the city, take possession of the most advantageous parts of the city, release all American prisoners, and demand the surrender of the enemy; four brigades are assigned to form a reserve; the Pennsylvania Militia to pour in and crush Howe before he can recover from the surprise or regain his ships. While the orders are never executed, the notice is interested because it illustrates the method and detail in which orders are issued for most actions.

General Orders give the parole as Springfield and the countersign as Windsor. It snows all day.

26 December 1777:

Friday. At Valley Forge, Albigence Waldo, Surgeon to A Connecticut Continental Regiment, keeps a Diary, in which he comments upon the generalship of Washington, "Because he knows better than to leave his Post and be catch'd like a d----d fool cooped up in the City. [In answer to the query, 'Why does he not rush in & take the City?'] He has always acted wisely. His conduct when closely scrutinized is uncensurable. Were his inferior Generals as skillful as himself, we should have the grandest choir of Officers ever God made. Many country Gentlemen in the interior parts of the States who get wrong information of the affairs & state of our Camp, are very much surprised ... [at the] delay to drive off the enemy, being falsely informed ... it brings disgrace on the Continental Troops, who have never evidenced the least backwardness in doing their duty ... but impartial truth in the future History will clear up these points, and reflect lasting honor on the Wisdom & prudence of Genl. Washington."

General Washington is outraged to learn that a few soldiers have committed robberies and unwarrantable offences against the friends of liberty, and sets up orders to punish those found guilty of any such actions. Washington feels strongly that all such actions are injurious to the cause in which the whole army is engaged.

27 December 1777:

Saturday. At headquarters, Valley Forge, Washington writes to Virginia Governor Patrick Henry. "In several of my late letters, I addressed you on the distresses of the troop for want of cloathing (sic). Your ready exertions to relieve them have given me the highest satisfaction. At the same time, knowing how exceedingly the service has been injured, how great the sufferings and loss of men thro' this want, I cannot but hope every measure will be pursued, that circumstances will admit, to keep them supplied from time to time. No pains, no efforts can be too great for this purpose."

Washington also writes to Robert R. Livingston. "The Regiments, small in the beginning of the campaign and much diminished by service, will not bear a draft without reducing them to mere Companies. I expect a Committee of Congress here in a short time, to confer upon ways and means of new modelling the Army, I shall, among other things, strongly recommend the formation of Corps of Light Infantry, and as your brother [Henry Beekman Livingston] will be on the spot, he will have an opportunity, if such are formed, of putting in his claim for a command."

Washington writes to Brigadier General Anthony Wayne. "General Orders respecting the Camp Regulations you mention have been for the most part issued, and as soon as the state of our clothing will permit I think the mode of foraging you mention to be highly desirable. I wish you not to leave Camp or its vicinity, until the huts are completed and some regulation takes place."

Washington writes to Deputy Quartermaster General, Colonel Henry E. Lutterlough. "Sir: As we have more than probably taken a position for the winter, and every exertion in the different departments should be made to prepare for the next campaign. I take this early opportunity to remind you of the necessity of providing common tents, bell tents for arms, ammunition wagons, and such other essentials in your line as you know will be wanted for the use of the troops next campaign. A moments reflection must convince you that the smallest delay will be injurious, as the season for providing these things is fast advancing, and the difficulty in obtaining them may be great."

General Orders give the parole as Castleton, and the countersigns as Pittsburg and Stanwix.

28 December 1777:
Sunday. At Valley Forge, some (but by no means all) huts are being erected quickly.

Washington writes to Major General John Armstrong, "The method you have adopted for preventing the intercourse and supply of marketing from the country, I think is a good one, and I expect will have the intended effect, though I fear it is impossible to put a total stop to it, even by the greatest exertions of the officers, as there are many avenues to Town which it will be found difficult to guard. Congress had information that there was a great quantity of flour near the British lines which I suppose by what you mention to be groundless. I have, by their desire, issued a Proclamation ordering the farmers to thresh out their wheat and prepare it for mill, and that in case of noncompliance within certain periods, it shall be seized upon for the use of the army and only paid for as straw."

29 December 1777:
Monday. During the night, ice has formed about an inch and a half thick on the Schuylkill River. Concerned by the harsh weather, General Washington exhorts his troops to exert themselves to complete all the hutments, so the men might be more comfortable during the coming months.

At Valley Forge George Washington writes a circular letter to the states, addressed to the executive of the state except for the one to Massachusetts which was sent to the Council. The letter was sent to all the states except Georgia. "Gentlemen. I take the liberty of transmitting to you the enclosed return, which contains a state of such of the Regiments of your state, as are in the army immediately under my command. By this you will discover how deficient, how exceedingly short they are of the compliment of men which of right according to the establishment they ought to have. This information, I have thought it my duty to lay before you, that it may have the attention which its importance demands; and in full hope, that the most early and vigorous measures will be adopted, not only to make the Regiments more respectable, but compleat (sic). The expediency and necessity of this procedure are too obvious to need arguments. Should we have a respectable force to commence an early campaign with, before the enemy are reinforced, I trust we shall have an opportunity of striking a favorable and an happy stroke; but if we should be obliged to defer it, it will not be easy to describe with any degree or precision what disagreeable consequences may result from it. We may rest assured, that Britain will strain every nerve to send from home and abroad, as early as possible, all the troops it shall be in her power to raise or procure. Her views and schemes for subjugating these States and bringing them under her despotic rule will be unceasing and unremitted. (sic). Nor should we, in my opinion, turn our expectations to, or have the least dependence on the intervention of a foreign war. Our wishes on this head have been disappointed hitherto, and I do not know that we have a right to promise ourselves from any intelligence that has been received, bearing the marks of authority that there is any certain prospect of one. However, be this as it may, our reliance should be wholly on our own strength and exertions. If, in addition to these, there should be aid derived from a war between the enemy and any of the European powers, our situation will be so much the better. If not, our efforts and exertions will have been the more necessary and indespensible (sic)."

30 December 1777:
Tuesday. The enemy marches out of Philadelphia to Darby, and a detachment is ordered to observe and harry them. This delays some units from the swift completion of their huts.

Washington writes to Major General Thomas Conway, "You will observe by the Resolution of Congress relative to your appointment, that the Board of War is to furnish a set of instructions, according to which the troops are to be manoeuvred [sic]. As you have made no mention of having received them, I suppose they are not come to you. When they do, I shall issue any orders which may be judged necessary to have them carried into immediate execution ... you may judge what must be the sensations of those Brigadiers, who by your promotion are superceded. I am told they are determined to remonstrate against it; for my own part I have nothing to do in the appointment of General Officers, and shall always afford every countenance and due respect to those appointed by Congress; taking it for granted, that prior to any resolve of that nature, they take a dispassionate view, of the merits of the officer to be promoted, and consider every consequence that can result from such a procedure; nor have I any other wish on that head, but that good attentive officers may be chosen, and no extraordinary promotion take place ..."

31 December 1777:
Wednesday. General George Washington is concerned about the under-strength condition of so many regiments (battalions). The deficiency in numbers of troops for the various Continental units is reported in the muster roll for

December. That muster roll, the official report of troops from each and every state, with a listing of the number of regiments for that state, and the sum of troops missing from that state to fill its quota in all of its regiments, is an absolute reckoning of just how many men are missing from how many regiments for each state.

Those states with the largest number of soldiers required to complete their quota are North Carolina for nine regiments requires 5,044 men; Virginia for 15 regiments requires 4,932 men; Pennsylvania for 12 regiments requires 4,791 men; and Massachusetts for 15 regiments requires 4,670 men. Those states with the lowest number of soldiers to complete their quota are Delaware for one regiment requires 431 men; Rhode Island for two regiments requires 758 men; New York for four regiments requires 1,609 men; and New Hampshire for three regiments requires 1,649 men. It can be quickly seen that this is a large number of soldiers missing from many regiments in the army. Such a large number of missing soldiers throws a burden upon those present and fit for duty.

Major General Thomas Conway, newly appointed Inspector General replies to Washington's letter of yesterday, saying he intends to prepare a set of regulations and have them printed, but leaves these matters incomplete and shifts the responsibility back upon the commander-in-chief. He claims he is getting no support in the laborious duties of an Inspector-General, and is ready to return to France.

Thus ends the Year of the Hangman—so named because the repeated sevens in the year 1777 remind persons of the gibbet, from which so many felons have been executed in the public presence.

The Congress, which had left Philadelphia as the British and Hessian troops were approaching the area in December 1776, reconvenes in Baltimore for three months. Though they return to Philadelphia in early March 1777, they find themselves pressed again by the British advance in September 1777, and meet briefly in Lancaster, then in York, Pennsylvania, while the British occupy Philadelphia.

Burgoyne successfully captures Fort Ticonderoga, Fort Anne, and Fort Edward, but is harried at Bennington, slowed to a crawl, halted at Saratoga, and surrenders in October. Howe, after dithering in New York and finally making a sea voyage into Chesapeake Bay, approaches Philadelphia from the south. He defeats Washington in a series of closely fought battles, at Cooch's Bridge and Brandywine, and enters the city on 26 September 1777. Washington continues to harass the British and Hessian forces, loses another closely fought battle at Germantown, and thrusts at Howe's outposts and redoubts on the periphery of Philadelphia. He finally settles in winter quarters at Valley Forge.

Now comfortably housed in Philadelphia, with the rebels watching him and a forage war being carried on, Sir William Howe comes to realize that, to his surprise and dismay, the capture of the capitol city, the seat of the Congress and the largest city on the American continent, is not decisive, nor even of consequence. The rebel Congress simply moves away, and the patriots still hang all around him. The conquest of America has nothing to do with occupying its towns and cities. He has to defeat its troops, armies, and corps of militia. He has, also, to win over the hearts and minds of a people seeking liberty, not obeisance to monarchy. He fails on all counts!

The Bibliography lists books that a reader may wish to view regarding this year: Pancake, John S., *1777: The Year of the Hangman*; Ketchum, Richard M., *Saratoga, Turning Point of America's Revolutionary War*; Taaffe, Stephen R., *The Philadelphia Campaign 1777-1779*.

V. The Year 1778

1 January 1778:

Thursday. At Wilmington, Delaware, Brigadier General Smallwood reports that his troops have taken a British sloop with a load of flour, pork, and poultry and an armed brig with clothing for four British regiments, more than 1,000 stand of arms, ammunition, pork, butter, and officer baggage.

At Valley Forge, Washington writes to the president of Congress, "You must be sensible, that very little time is left between this and the opening of the next campaign for the provision of field equipage, carriages, horses, and many other articles essentially necessary, towards which I cannot find that any steps have yet been taken. The enemy returned into Philadelphia on Sunday last, having made a considerable hay forage, which appeared to be their only intention. As they kept themselves in close order and in such a position that no attack could be made upon them to advantage, I could do no more than extend light parties along their front and keep them from plundering the inhabitants and carrying off cattle and horses, which had the desired effect." General Orders give the parole as Ulster and the countersign as Salem.

2 January 1778:

Friday. At headquarters in Valley Forge, General Washington, in an effort to prevent unnecessary applications for furloughs, requires that all officers shall apply through their respective major generals of the divisions to which they belong, who, in turn will only grant any such furlough to those officers whose Regiments are in a full and proper state of health, readiness, and discipline to permit the officers' absence from the camp.

3 January 1778:

Saturday. The commander-in-chief approves the sentence of a court martial of Ensign Samuel Carpenter. Carpenter absented himself from camp, knowing that his regiment was about to go into action, and so is cashiered from the service.

Henry Laurens warns that the commissary, quartermaster, and clothier departments are in disarray, and that something needs to be done to correct these conditions.

4 January 1778:

Sunday. General Orders at Valley Forge require that as soon as a hut has been completed, the tents earlier used for shelter are to be turned in to the quarter master general. These orders are the result of many tents being cut up and used by the desperate soldiers for clothing. Many of the huts are being completed, but they are not the perfect answer to protection from the weather. Drafty, windowless, smoky, the huts themselves lead to illness of the occupants. Too many men, crowded together in an airless room is bound to lead to readily passed contagious diseases to the inhabitants of the space.

5 January 1778:
Monday. Captain Walter Butler, who has been in jail in Albany, New York, writes again to Major General Philip Schuyler, requesting that he be paroled or exchanged.

A Commissary (today's Supply Officer) of Maj. Gen. Nathanael Greene's Division is found guilty of theft. His punishment is that he must repay the two persons from whom he has stolen. Then he is mounted backwards on a horse, without saddle, his coat turned, his hands tied behind him, and drummed out of the division. This sentence is to be published in the newspapers as a discouragement to others.

6 January 1778:
Tuesday. At Valley Forge, Washington writes to, William Claton, Benjamin Yard, Rensselaer Williams, and Benjamin VanCleave (Magistrates of Trenton and Mercer counties, New Jersey), "Gentlemen: I received your letter of the 2nd instant pointing out the many inconveniences that will attend Trenton and its neighborhood by quartering the light horse there. Before this step was determined on I made inquiry of the Forage Master Genl., who reported, that plenty of forage could be got convenient to the town. My desire of adding some degree to the security of that neighborhood and the public property thereabouts was also an inducement to its which by your letter I observe you are of opinion, will have a contrary effect. But in this I am satisfied you will find yourselves deceive'd particularly when they will be aided by a body of Infantry on that side Delaware, which probably may be the case after some little time. My duty obliges me to quarter the horse in such places as can afford them the necessary supplies during the winter, and where they may at the same time give some cover to the country. If upon trial, Trenton is not found to answer these intentions, such change must take place as will most probably answer this purpose."

The quartermaster general is ordered to send an iron oven to each brigade at the camp at Valley Forge. General Washington repeats his order of 4 Jan 1778, that all tents be turned in to the quartermaster.

7 January 1778:
Wednesday. The British, in Philadelphia, have attracted a good many vendors to the market stalls from nearby Bucks County, Pennsylvania. It helps that they can pay with specie in pounds sterling, whereas the Americans must rely upon paper currency, that depreciates rapidly.

At headquarters, Valley Forge, Washington writes to Brigadier General William Smallwood, "Dear Sir: The enclosed to Govr. Johnson [Thomas Johnson Governor of Maryland], on the subject of completing the clothing the troops of Maryland,

is left open for your inspection. After reading, be pleased to seal
and transmit it to the Governor with the returns for which I
have referred him to you. We are in the greatest want of blocks
and falls [block and tackle] to raise the bridge over Schuylkill,
the timber is all cut and ready to put up. Enclosed you have a
list of such things as are wanting ..."

8 January 1778:
        Thursday. The issue of the *New Jersey Gazette*, of this date
has the following doggerel regarding Sir William Howe's
expeditions to attack the rebels at Valley Forge:
                "Threat'ning to drive us from the hill,
                Sir William march'd t'attack our men;
                But finding that we all stood still,
                Sir William he-march'd back again."
In York, the Congress again takes under consideration the
matter of the convention entered into by Major General Gates
and Lieutenant General Burgoyne at Saratoga. Members
remain unhappy with the convention and try to find ways to
avoid the more difficult aspects. One item brought up is its
issue of cartouch boxes, carried by the British soldiers. The
Congress believes they are part of one's weaponry, and,
therefore, should have been delivered up at the time of the
convention, but were not. This, they claim is a breach of public
faith.

9 January 1778:
        Friday. At headquarters, Valley Forge, Washington writes to
Baron Von Steuben, "Sir: I yesterday received the honor of
yours from Portsmouth [New Hampshire], enclosing the copy of
a letter from Messrs. Franklin and Deane, the original of which
I shall be glad to receive from your own hands, as soon as it is
convenient for you to undertake the journey. As it will lay solely
with Congress, to make a suitable provision for you in
American Army, you will be under the necessity of prolonging
your journey, in order to lay before them at York, the honorable
testimonials which you bear of your former service. I return you
my thanks for the polite manner in which you express your
desire of serving under me."
        General Orders require that each division and each brigade
shall cause a hospital to be erected upon ground near their
encampment. The officers appointed to superintend this work
are to receive their plans and directions from the adjutant-
general's office.

10 January 1778:
        Saturday. In the camp at Valley Forge, John Reily of the 2nd
Virginia Regiment, who has been found guilty by court martial
of deserting his guard duty and taking two prisoners in irons
with him, is hanged before a captain and 40 men from each
brigade of the Army.

In York, the Congress establishes a committee to travel to Valley Forge, investigate the supply conditions, consult with Washington, and recommend solutions to the problems discovered. This committee will remain in or near the encampment for some while, as its members inspect, review, and consult upon the many problems confronting the Continental Army.

11 January 1778:
Sunday. At headquarters, Valley Forge, General Washington writes to Captain George Lewis (a Virginia gentlemen in the 3rd Continental Dragoons, serving as an aide to Washington), "Dear George: I am sorry to find by your letter to Mr. Harrison [Lieut. Col. Robert Hanson Harrison], that you still continue indisposed. If the state of your health requires leave of absence, I shall not object to your visiting your friends in Virginia to recover it. You will take this in your way as I shall want to see you before you go. I wish you to have every part, and parcel of my baggage removed from Newtown to this place. I do not know in whose care, and possession it is; but as satisfied I ought to have a good deal there. Among other things: a bed, andirons, plates, dishes, and kitchen utensils; however, be it what it will, let the whole come. Pay, or bring an account of the expenses attending the storage &, and hire or impress proper wagons for bringing these things."
General Orders give the parole as Boston and the countersigns as Cambridge and Medford.

12 January 1778:
Monday. At Headquarters, Valley Forge, Washington writes to Doctor Benjamin Rush expressing concern and regret that the medical department seems to be so inadequate to the needs required and the ends proposed. He then goes on to say, "From the peculiarity of our circumstances we cannot expect to be as well furnished with the necessary apparatus of an hospital as we ought to be; but still I believe we might do much better if more order and discipline was observed by the patients. Upon hearing of the many irregularities committed by them I have lately ordered a discreet Field Officer to visit the principle hospitals and endeavor to establish a proper discipline. Among the many necessary reforms in the military line, I suppose that of the regulation of the hospitals will be considered. I shall always be ready to contribute all in my power towards rendering the situation of these unhappy people who are under the necessity of becoming the inhabitants of them, as comfortable as possible."
General Orders gives the parole as Edenton and the countersigns as Savannah and Charleston.

13 January 1778:
Tuesday. To replace Colonel Timothy Pickering, who is called to a seat on the Board of War, General Orders notes that

Colonel Alexander Scammel is now appointed adjutant general of the Continental Army.

14 January 1778:
   Wednesday. At headquarters, Valley Forge, Washington writes to Count Pulaski, reporting that in response to Pulaski's concern about forage he has spoken with the forage master general and believes that the problem may be more with the officers and men of Pulaski's Legion seeking better quarters rather than the availability of forage, saying "... that the barracks and the town together will certainly furnish ample quarters. I must postpone any decision with respect to the horses, until the arrival of the Committee of Congress, as I am in daily expectation of those gentlemen. I hope you will not be long kept in suspense, if you can in the meantime, engage the owners to keep their horses on the spot, you will take every proper step for that purpose. I have no objection to your making trial of the abilities of Mr. Betkin, [Henry Bedkin] as Brigade Major for the present, it will soon be discovered whether he is equal to the Office."
   General Orders state that brigade-majors are to deliver a listing of all the field grade officers (majors, lieutenant colonels, colonels) in their several brigades at orderly time the next day. The parole is Perseverance and the countersigns are Peace and Plenty.

15 January 1778:
   Thursday. At Valley Forge, most of the huts for both the soldiers and the officers are complete. General Orders note, "The works marked out by the engineers for the defense of the Camp are to be executed with all possible dispatch ..." The quartermaster is ordered to erect huts for prisoners under guard of the provost.

16 January 1778:
   Friday. In Berlin, the Baron de Schulenburg writes to Arthur Lee, "As the events of this war become daily more interesting, I must again request, sir, that you will be kind enough to communicate to me regularly the advices you may receive. The king interests himself very much in them, and his majesty wishes that your generous efforts may be crowned with success; and as I have already advised you in my letter of the 18th of December, he will not hesitate to acknowledge your independence whenever France, which is more interested in the event of this contest, shall set the example. As to the muskets and other arms of our manufacturing, you shall be at liberty, sir, to purchase or to command them ..."

17 January 1778:
   Saturday. At headquarters, Valley Forge, Washington writes to Bartram Galbreth (Lieutenant of Lancaster County, Pennsylvania). "Sir: Mr. William Smith, is employed in the

Continental Service as Deputy Waggon Master, Josiah Kittara
as Waggon Conductor, William Smith, Jr. as Sub-Conductor,
and Thomas Edwards and Amos Evans as Waggoners, the
certificates of their being attached to the Continental Army in
these capacities will be delivered to you by Mr. Wm. Smith, who
goes in behalf of the rest, and as it cannot be the intention of
the Legislature to treat persons of this description in the light
of delinquents, I have no doubt that upon receipt of this you
will acquit them from the fines to which they have hitherto
been considered as subject under the Militia Act."

General Orders give the parole as Buckingham and the
countersigns as Boston and Brentwood.

18 January 1778:
Sunday. At Valley Forge, General Washington approves the
sentence of a court martial held on the 12th instant for Ensign
John Foster. Foster is found guilty of challenging Captain
Walter Cruise and behaving in a character unbecoming an
officer and gentleman. Foster is sentenced to be discharged
from the service, however, in consideration of the
circumstances, Washington is pleased to restore Ensign Foster
to his former rank. At the same time, he is sorry to observe that
the dispute between the parties arose from a cause and was
conducted in a manner that does neither of them much honor.

19 January 1778:
Monday. In York, Pennsylvania, Henry Laurens writes to
Major General William Heath, noting that while he is in receipt
of several letters from him, he has not gotten the answers with
which to respond. Committees are still working with the letters,
and he is so burdened with work, he has not had time, as yet,
to address the issues therein, but will endeavor to urge the
business forward.

20 January 1778:
Tuesday. At York, James Lovell writes to John Adams,
acknowledging receipt of Adams' acceptance of his appointment
as commissioner to France. Lovell goes on to say he will send
Adams' papers and clothes, and that the information about
Burgoyne and the capitulation at Saratoga should go speedily
forward.

21 January 1778:
Wednesday. At York, John Witherspoon and James Lovell
write to the commissioners at Paris, "We mean in this letter to
give you a succinct view of the state of our military affairs. You
must, long before this reaches you, have been made acquainted
with the signal success of the American arms in the northern
department, particularly the several engagements in that
quarter previous to the surrender of General Burgoyne and his
whole army to General Gates. Since that time Ticonderoga and
Mt. Independence have been evacuated by the enemy, so that

the whole of that department is now in our possession. The Indians are perfectly quiet, and we have lately received intelligence that those formerly in the interest of our enemies inclined to our side, as also that the inhabitants of Canada, where the enemy have but small force, are in general much disposed to favor us. A part of the enemy's army is still in possession of New Port ... As to the armies in this state General Howe is still in Philadelphia, but possesses no part of the country around it. General Washington's army is in huts to the westward of the Schuylkill, refreshing and recruiting during the winter ..."

22 January 1778:
    Thursday. From Paris, William Lee writes to the president of Congress, pointing out the inadequacy of his commission. "Having lately had a conference with the imperial ambassador of this court [the ambassador representing Vienna and Berlin], he observed immediately an imperfection in my commission, as it only authorizes me to treat with the Emperor of Germany, and not with his mother, who is the reigning and sovereign prince over all the Austrian dominions, as well in Germany and Flanders as elsewhere. She is extremely jealous of her power and authority, not permitting her son to interfere in any manner in the government of her dominions. Her title is, 'The Most Serene and Most Potent Princess Maria Theresa, Queen of Hungary and Bohemia, Arch Duchess of Austria, etc.' The emperor, her son, though heir to her dominions, is at present only commander–in–chief of his mother's army, and as emperor is the head of the German Empire."

23 January 1778:
    Friday. In York, Pennsylvania, Henry Laurens, president of Congress, writes to Lieutenant Colonel William Palfrey, paymaster-general of the Continental Army, "I received & presented immediately to Congress your letter of yesterday, & directions were immediately given to the Treasury Committee to supply you without delay, with a sum of money sufficient for the present demands of the Army at Valley Forge."

24 January 1778:
    Saturday. At Lancaster, Pennsylvania, John Harvie and Gouverneur Morris write to the Pennsylvania Council, noting that charges and fees of publicans (Tavern Keepers, and sellers of alcohol) that deal with any of the Continental services are "... to be determined by Congress only, seeing that no single State ought of right to interfere in compacts which affect the public faith and honor of the Confederacy"

25 January 1778:
    Sunday. In the Bahamas, American Naval Captain John Peck Rathbun, pursuing a view that an opportunity to obtain

gunpowder might present itself, approaches the Island of New Providence in the sloop *Providence*, and scouts the vicinity.

At headquarters, Valley Forge, Washington writes to Major General Israel Putnam, "I begin to be very apprehensive that the season will entirely pass away, before anything material will be done for the defense of Hudson's River. You are well acquainted with the great necessity there is for having the works there finished as soon as possible, and I most earnestly desire, that the strictest attention may be paid to every matter which may contribute to finishing and putting them in a respectable state before spring." Washington also writes to Colonel Lewis La Radiere (French Engineer Officer), "As the majority of the Council were for erecting the new works upon West Point, in preference to the place upon which Fort Clinton was built, I desire that they may be carried on with all dispatch. If we remain much longer disputing about the proper place, we shall lose the winter, which is the only time we have to make preparations for the reception of the enemy. I am afraid, if you leave the works to come down here, that matters will not go on properly in your absence, for I should imagine that the eye of the Engineer is constantly wanting over men not used to such business."

General Orders give the parole as Indostan and the countersigns as Ireland and India.

26 January 1778:

Monday. Henry Laurens, president of the Congress, writes to Isaac Motte, a delegate from South Carolina, noting that, while Benjamin Harrison is the paymaster general for the Southern Department, that office does not give him complete authority over the expenditures some of the states make on their own, even those in Motte's area of the Southern Department. Therefore, the Congress has little control over much of the monies expended by these states, on behalf of the Continental public efforts, and that includes the army.

27 January 1778:

Tuesday. John Henry writes to Thomas Johnson, noting that he is sensible of "... the low state of our own Treasury," and is most thankful for the salt provided by Maryland. He also notes the poor supply situation with the army at Valley Forge, reporting that a Committee is now with that army looking for ways and means to see that it is properly supplied.

In York, Thomas Conway writes to George Washington at Valley Forge, to assure the General that he, Conway, was not a part of any cabal and that the language reported in a letter he had written is not accurate.

At Nassau, New Providence Island, the Bahamas, Captain Rathbun lands a force of Marines and seamen from his sloop *Providence* (12 guns), and seizes the forts, raising the American flag over them.

28 January 1778:
    Wednesday. From Paris, Ralph Izard writes to Benjamin Franklin, discussing the issue of a duty on molasses. He seems to feel that, if the French are allowed or encouraged to place a duty on molasses being exported to America, it might open a door for smuggling and could be an occasion for disruption of the friendship and harmony which is building between France and America. Izard is aware that the decision regarding this matter rests with the American commissioners at the Court of France, but he feels that he needs to express the negative view.
    Major General Lafayette leaves the camp at Valley Forge to travel to York for the purpose of receiving instructions from the Congress and bills of credit for a proposed expedition into Canada.

29 January 1778:
    Thursday. From the Army Camp at Valley Forge, the Congressional Committee writes to Henry Laurens, "In the course of inquiry into the state of the civil Departments of the Army, that of the Commissary General of Purchases has attracted very considerable attention. That there have been very great failures in the necessary supply of provisions is unquestionable, but we are not so clear, as to the causes which have produced this evil. Many have been assigned, it is unnecessary to enumerate them as we understand Congress have made inquiry into this Department, the result of which has not been favourable [sic] to the capacity and abilities of the gentlemen now in office. We beg leave to acquaint Congress of our inquiries into this Department have rather confirmed than changed this opinion. We are, therefore, induced to recommend to the earliest attention of Congress the choice of a suitable successor, a man of abilities, extensive connection & influence."
    In York, the Congress resolves that the prisoners at Winchester, Virginia, apprehended by Pennsylvania troops, may be released upon taking the prescribed oath supporting the United States.

30 January 1778:
    Friday. From Moore Hall, near Valley Forge, Francis Dana writes to Elbridge Gerry, "The Committee were convinced of the absolute necessity of filling that office [Quartermaster General] with a person who thoroughly understands the duties of it, and could not find one equal by any means to Schuyler. They were nevertheless persuaded of the weight of certain objections against him [Schuyler], which they leave for the consideration of Congress."

31 January 1778:
    Saturday. At York, Cornelius Harnett writes to Richard Caswell, "I wish this measure had taken place sooner; the taxes also I hope will be soon collected, this measure of taxation

unless entered into with spirit by the Legislatures of the several States, must end in the ruin of the prodigious quantity of paper money now in circulation. The Grand Army still remain encamped at Valley Forge; unless a large body of Militia of the adjacent States immediately reinforce them, I have little reason to expect any thing decisive can possibly be done this winter, as we are told Genl. Howe's lines are exceeding strong – and should Genl. Howe be reinforced in the Spring, by a strong body of troops I suppose we shall have warm work – unless France & Spain declare War ..." It is interesting to note how Harnett expresses concern over the lack of support the states provide to the central government by not approving a national taxing authorization, yet expecting France to rescue the country.

1 February 1778:
Sunday. At Passy, Benjamin Franklin and Silas Deane write to the Comte de Vergennes, "The news you have received from England [as to alleged reconciliation] can not be true. No treaty would be entered into with Howe by Washington when the congress was to hand; and Howe could have no propositions to make but such as were authorized by the act of Parliament, and had been long since rejected. In short, we esteem the story of a treaty with America to be merely an artifice of the stock–jobbers to keep up the funds."

At headquarters, Valley Forge, Washington writes to Major John Jameson, of a Virginia Dragoon Regiment, "The quantity of provision, flour especially, that is carried into Philadelphia is by all accounts so great that the British Army is well supplied with almost every article. The committee of Congress now here expressed a desire that this pernicious intercourse may be cut off as effectually as possible. I know of no other way to prevent the supply of flour, but disabling the mills, as we have not Guards sufficient to stop all the roads. You are therefore, in concert with Genl. Lacey to fix upon a certain time and attempt to disable all the mills upon Pennepack, Frankfort, and Wissahicken Creeks ..."

Washington writes to Colonel Israel Angell, commander of the 2nd Rhode Island Regiment, "As it is my wish to cut off the intercourse with Philadelphia, as effectually as possible, I desire that no passes may be granted by you to any persons, upon any pretense whatsoever, and that you will do all in your power to apprehend those who attempt to go into the City with marketing."

General Orders give the parole as Rockingham and the countersigns as Richmond and Rutland.

2 February 1778:
Monday. From Versailles, Conrad Alexandre Gerard writes to the American commissioners at Paris, "I have acquainted his majesties ministers with the fresh demand respecting the 11th and 12th of the articles of the treaty of commerce. The king

having approved these two articles agreeable to your unanimous wishes, they can not be submitted to a new examination without inconvenience and considerable delay. I am therefore charged to send you the French copies of the two treaties, that you may have them transcribed side by side with the English translation, and when this is done, I trust you will give me notice."

At headquarters, Valley Forge, Washington, learning by letter of an attempt to assassinate New Jersey Governor William Livingston, writes him "The recent detection of the wicked design you mention gives me the most sensible pleasure; and I earnestly hope you may be alike successful in discovering and disappointing every attempt that may be projected against you, either by your open or concealed enemies. It is a tax, however, severe, which all those must pay, who are called to eminent stations of trust, not only to be held up as conspicuous marks to the enmity of the public adversaries to their country, but to the malice of secret traitors and the envious intrigues of false friends and factions."

John Laurens writes to his father Henry, discussing the issue of the slaves, "You will accuse me perhaps my dearest friend of consulting my own feelings too much; but I am tempted to believe that this trampled people have so much human left in them, as to be capable of aspiring to the rights of men by noble exertions, if some friend to mankind would point the Road, and give them a prospect of Success. If I am mistaken in this, I would avail myself even of their weakness, and conquering one fear by another, produce equal good to the Public. You will ask in this view how do you consult the benefit of the Slaves. I answer that like other men, they are creatures of habit, their cowardly ideas will be gradually effaced, and they will be modified anew; their being rescued from a state of perpetual humiliation, and being advanced as it were in the scale of being will compensate the dangers incident to their new state. The hope that will spring in each mans mind respecting his own escape will prevent his being miserable. Those who fall in battle will not lose much; those who survive will obtain their reward. Habits of subordination, patience under fatigues, sufferings and privations of every kind are soldierly qualifications which these men possess in an eminent degree. Upon the whole my dearest friend and father, I hope that my plan for serving my Country and the oppressed Negro race will not appear to you the Chimera of a young mind deceived by a false appearance of moral beauty, but a laudable sacrifice of private interest to Justice and the Public good."

3 February 1778:
Tuesday. At headquarters, Valley Forge, Washington writes to Elias Boudinot, "Dear Sir: A letter from Congress will accompany this containing two resolutions relative to prisoners. You will perceive by them that Congress go upon the presumption of our furnishing our prisoners in the enemy's

hands wholly and entirely with provisions. Their fixing no rule for liquidating and accounting for the rations heretofore supplied by the enemy, is a proof that they do not intend them to continue, but expect our prisoners will hereafter be altogether victualled by ourselves. This is a matter, it will be necessary to attend carefully to, both that a competent supply be immediately ready for the purpose, and that there be no deficiency in future, otherwise the consequences may be dreadful, for the past conduct of the enemy gives too much reason to apprehend they would not be very apt to relieve want, which we had undertaken wholly to administer to."

Washington writes to Doctor Thomas Bond, denying his request for passes through his lines. "I am sorry to inform you, that however willing to oblige your father and yourself, I do not think I can with propriety comply with your request. I cannot suppose your father would mean to make the least ill use of the privilege he wishes for; but every indulgence of this kind becomes a precedent for others, and you will easily be sensible that it must be inexpedient, to admit any person to a free intercourse with the country, who is actually in the power of the enemy. It is necessary all communication should be intercepted between the County and the City, which I am endeavouring to effect."

Lafayette leaves York, Pennsylvania, returning to Valley Forge for a conference on his mission for another crack at Canada, and will then go to Albany, New York.

4 February 1778:
Wednesday. In Paris, the French Cabinet approves of a firm alliance with the United States of America. This will, in two more days, result in the signing of a treaty between France and the United States of America.

Sir William Howe, not pleased with his duties in America and with a feeling that this rebellion of the American colonies is difficult, if not impossible, to suppress, has requested again to be relieved of his command. (See the sketch for 22 Oct 1777) George Germain, not particularly impressed with Howe's prosecution of the war, is pleased to receive his resignation, and, with the King's consent, writes to Howe, reporting that His Majesty approves of his request and he may return as soon as shipping is found. His replacement is named as Henry Clinton, who is already in America.

5 February 1778:
Thursday. At York, the committee of foreign affairs writes to Ralph Izard, saying the Congress is pleased with his acceptance of his commission and encouraged by the prospect of his obtaining a loan of money in Italy. Due to the emissions of paper money by both the states and the Congress, there has been a great depreciation in its value and the country is starved for specie and seeks loans from Europe. "Therefore, congress have given, in regard to you, the same instructions as to the

gentlemen at the courts of France and Spain, and we doubt not of your best exertions."

At London, in the House of Commons, George Johnstone writes to Robert Morris discussing a possible reconciliation between Great Britain and the American colonies. He goes on to note "... I have heard a hint, and I have good reason to think, a proposition will be made to Parliament in four or five days by administration that may be a ground of reunion." Neither Johnstone, nor almost all the members of Parliament and the ministers of the government of Britain seem to have any clue as to what will be required before serious talks of peace can be entered into by both sides. An acknowledgment of independence must be accepted. There is going to be no "reunion" with Great Britain on the part of the United States of America.

South Carolina becomes the second state to ratify the Articles of Confederation. While ratification is most helpful, it does not allow the national government a taxing authority.

6 February 1778:

Friday. At Versailles, France, the Treaty of Amity and Commerce and the Treaty of Alliance between France and the United States of America are formally signed. This is a real stroke of great good fortune for the embryonic United States of America, which has need of a strong and established naval force.

New York becomes the third state to ratify the Articles of Confederation.

7 February 1778:

Saturday. At Moore Hall, near Valley Forge, Lafayette is in conference with others regarding the needs and requirements of the Congressional approval of an expedition into Canada. The Congress continues to have an unrealistic and uninformed attitude toward a conquest of Canada, and has authorized still another attempt. Lafayette, chosen to head-up such an effort, wishes to lay out what should be the requirements for any such expedition, and pick the brains of those who should know.

8 February 1778:

Sunday. At Passy, Benjamin Franklin and Silas Deane write to the president of Congress, reporting that a treaty of amity and commerce has been completed and signed. They also report that a treaty of alliance with France has been completed and signed. Note that these are two separate treaties, one dealing with the commercial and business aspects, the other with the military and naval aspects of arms to prosecute the war.

9 February 1778:

Monday. At headquarters, Valley Forge, Washington writes to Major General Horatio Gates, discussing the letters relating to the comments, and insidious, back-stabbing remarks in a conspiracy to remove the commander-in-chief by Maj. Gen. Thomas Conway, Gates and others, known as the "Conway Cabal." Washington's letter includes, "Not withstanding the hopeful presages, you are pleased to figure to yourself of General Conway's firm and constant friendship to America, I cannot persuade myself to retract the prediction concerning him; which you so emphatically wish had not been inserted in my last. A better acquaintance with him, than I have reason to think you have had, from what you say, and a concurrence of circumstances oblige me to give him but little credit for the qualifications of his heart; of which, at least, I beg leave to assume the privilege of being a tolerable judge. Were it necessary, more instances than one might be adduced, from his behaviour and conversation, to manifest, that he is capable of all the malignity of detraction, and all the meanness of intrigue, to gratify the absurd resentment of disappointed vanity, or to answer the purposes of personal aggrandizement, and promote the interests of faction."

Lafayette, having crossed the Delaware River at Coryell's Ferry, is at Flemington, New Jersey, from which place he will proceed to Poughkeepsie, New York, as he travels to Albany in pursuit of the Congressionally approved expedition to Canada. Lafayette is no fool, and learning that very little, sometimes nothing has been done, by way of gathering the supplies, arranging magazines, collecting the boats and wagons needed for such an expedition, begins to feel that the support for the expedition will not be readily forthcoming. He is correct. A great deal of procrastination on the part of supply officers, commissary officers, politicians, and contractors is the cause of this unwarranted delay.

10 February 1778:
Tuesday. In York, the Congress resolves "That the Board of War be directed to enquire into the conduct of all strangers or suspicious characters, or whose business is not known and approved, who may come to the place where Congress sits, and to take care that the public receive no damage by such persons."

11 February 1778:
Wednesday. At Moore Hall, Valley Forge the Congressional Committee writes to Henry Laurens, "We lately wrote to you upon the state of the Commissary Department; since which the Marquis Lafayette hath favored us with a visit on his way to the Northern Army." [The Committee makes two points about the Canada Expedition, in their letter: first, that to carry on the enterprise demands a large scale effort which we have neither the men nor the money to invest. Second, if a considerable expedition should fail, as is most likely since we have not Montgomery or a ready means of travel except one road, the

results are likely to be desertion, disgrace to our arms, and disenchantment of our friends in Europe.] The letter goes on to say, "Burgoyne demonstrated the imprudence of distant expeditions across an inhospitable wilderness where there is ... The country from Albany to Montreal is already drained of forage. To subsist two thousand men with the several retainers and followers of an army will require at least four tons of provisions per day. Forty times this quantity must be transported two hundred miles. That alone will employ about four hundred horses ..."

The Congress orders that a warrant issue in favor of Marquis de Teissedre de Fleury for two hundred dollars for the payment of a horse lost in the public service.

12 February 1778:
Thursday. At Passy, Benjamin Franklin writes to David Hartley, noting that America finds itself aligning with France because there the Americans are received with cordiality, respect and affection, which they never experienced in England when it was most deserved. America "... has been forced and driven into the arms of France," by the stubbornness and intransigence of England.

13 February 1778:
Friday. In York, the Congress, learning that there is great danger of the armies being distressed if the exportation of beef and pork from the state of North Carolina be not prohibited by some form of embargo, resolves "That the legislative and executive powers of the State of North Carolina be earnestly requested immediately to lay an embargo on all beef and pork, except so much as may be necessary for the vessel's use for the voyage, and to take the most effectual measures to prevent the embargo from being evaded."

The Congress approves "That there is due to John Dunlap, for printing sundry resolves of Congress from 31 October 1776, to 10 September 1777, a balance of 1,117 69/90 dollars."

The Congress resolves "That there is due to Charles Thomson, Esq. for his services in the office of Secretary to Congress from the 10th of May 1776, to the tenth of the present month, it being one year and nine Months, at 1,200 dollars per Year, 2,100 dollars, and that two thousand dollars per year be hereafter allowed to the Secretary of Congress."

14 February 1778:
Saturday. At headquarters, Valley Forge, Washington writes to Lt. Col. Adam Hubley, "I send you an order for constituting a Court, both for the trial of criminals and of others that may be brought before it. There are, however, some mistakes in the present proceedings, which it will be necessary to rectify in the next. Joseph Rhoad and Windle Myer, being inhabitants, are not triable on the Articles of War, but must be tried on a special

resolution of Congress passed on the 8th of October last and extended by another of December 29th, which are enclosed for the government of the Court. If it can consist of the same members who composed the former, it will save trouble."

Washington writes to Governor William Livingston, "I do myself the honor of transmitting to you a letter from the Committee of Congress now here. These gentlemen have represented the distress of the Army for want of provision so fully and in so just a light, that I shall forbear to trouble you with further observations upon the subject. I shall only observe, that if the picture they have drawn is imperfect it is because the colourings are not sufficiently strong. From your zeal and earnest wishes to promote the service, I am firmly convinced we shall have every relief in your power to give. I should have troubled you before on this interesting and alarming business had I not supposed Congress the proper body to have been informed, and that the means of relief should be under their direction."

Washington writes to Major General John Sullivan, denying Sullivan's request for leave from Valley Forge to visit his family, and explaining the great difficulties under which the army operates at camp, saying "Under such circumstances, to whom am I to look for support, but to my principle officers. Confined to my quarters by an uninterrupted series of business, I am not able to pay that attention to matters in the field which is absolutely necessary and for which I must therefore depend almost wholly upon the officers high in command. I hope I need not make use of further arguments to convince you of the impossibility of granting your request at this time, and I flatter myself you will attribute my refusal to necessity, as I assure you nothing would give me greater pleasure than to indulge you could I possibly do it with consistency."

15 February 1778:
Sunday At headquarters, Valley Forge, Washington writes to Robert Lettis Hooper, deputy quartermaster general, Nathaniel Falconer, and Jonathan Mifflin, deputy commissaries of purchases, "I am constrained to inform you that the situation of the Army is most critical and alarming for want of provision of meat of any kind. Many of the troops four days and some longer, have not drawn the smallest supplies of this article. Their patience and endurance are great, but the demands of Nature must be satisfied. I must therefore, Gentlemen, in the most urgent terms, request and entreat your immediate and most active exertions to procure and forward to camp, as expeditiously as possible, all the provision of meat of any kind which it may be in your power to obtain."

Washington writes to Richard Henry Lee, "I am very glad to find that the Assembly of Virginia have taken matters up so spiritedly; but wish, in stead of attempting to raise so many volunteers, they had resolved at all adventures to complete their regiments by drafting. If all the states would do this, and fall upon ways and means to supply their troops with comfortable clothing upon moderate terms, and Congress would make the commissions of officers of some value to them, every thing would probably go well, making at the same time some reform in the different departments of the Army; nothing standing in greater need of it than the quartermasters and commissaries [two of the most serious problems faced by the Continental Army], as no army ever suffered more by their neglect ..."

Washington writes to the Reverend William Gordon, "I have said, and I still do say, that there is not an officer in the service of the United States that would return to the sweets of domestic life with more heartfelt joy than I should; but I would have this declaration accompanied by these sentiments, that while the public are satisfied with my endeavours I mean not to shrink in the cause; but the moment her voice, not that of faction, calls upon me to resign, I shall do it with as much pleasure as ever the weary traveler retired to rest."

At the American camp in Valley Forge, General Orders give the parole as Gibraltar, and the countersigns as Greene, and Glover.

16 February 1778:

Monday. At Passy, Benjamin Franklin, Silas Deane, and Arthur Lee, write to the Committee of Foreign Affairs, "We have now the pleasure of sending you the treaties of amity and alliance which France completed, after long deliberation, and signed the 6th instant."

Rhode Island becomes the fourth state to ratify the Articles of Confederation.

17 February 1778:

Tuesday. At headquarters, Valley Forge, Washington writes to Henry Champion, "The present situation of the army is the most melancholy that can be conceived. Our supplies of provisions of the flesh kind for some time past have been very deficient and irregular. A prospect now opens of absolute want such as will make it impossible to keep the army much longer from dissolution unless the most vigorous and effectual measures are pursued to prevent it. I have much confidence in your zeal and activity and I trust upon this occasion they will be exerted in a peculiar manner to hurry on to camp all the cattle you may be able to purchase." Lafayette arrives at Albany, New York, to meet with Philip Schuyler and others as they try to find the resources to execute the congressionally ordered expedition into Canada.

18 February 1778:

Wednesday. At headquarters, Valley Forge, Washington prepares an address to the inhabitants of New Jersey,

Pennsylvania, Maryland, and Virginia, commending them upon the efforts so far exhibited by them and indicating that, with adequate support, it might be possible to secure the blessing of peace, liberty, and safety, by assembling a force sufficient to open the next campaign and operate offensively. He requests exertions of the citizens of those states in his address "... to prepare cattle for use of the army during the months of May, June, and July next ..."

Washington writes to Major General Nathanael Greene, "If you have any prospect of making it worth the while, I would by all means have you continue foraging a few days longer. If the matters alleged against Mr. James [Jacob James tried to raise a troop of Tory Dragoons in Chester County, Pennsylvania], are founded in truth, and he is within reach, he ought immediately to be secured."

Washington writes to Brigadier General John Glover, "Your presence, as that of every other General Officer, will be essentially requisite, to aid me in carrying into execution, many important new arrangements, which, there is a prospect, will take place, for the reformation and better establishment of the Army." Washington goes on to refuse to accept Glover's request to resign his commission.

The Congress resolves that Governor George Clinton of New York be authorized and requested to superintend the business of obstructing, fortifying, and securing the passes of the Hudson River.

19 February 1778:
Thursday. In London, the Parliament agrees to legislation that removes the British right to levy direct taxes upon the American colonies, and not to quarter troops there without local consent. These are intended to be proffers of acceptance of the American grievances, leading to accommodation and reunion with the Mother Country. It is largely triggered by the British concern of dealing with their ancient enemy, France.

Congress resolves "That General Mifflin be directed to attend immediately the Board of War, and that he order the several deputies and agents under him in the department of the Quartermaster General to proceed vigorously in executing the business of that department, without attending to the settlement of their respective accounts, until the department is properly arranged, and they can attend to the settlement of their accounts without detriment to the public cause."

20 February 1778:
Friday. At headquarters, Valley Forge, Washington writes to Major General Benjamin Tallmadge, "As you have been successful in contracting for boots and leather breeches, I would not have you confine your views in these articles, to the precise number that may be wanted by your Regiment, but

wish that you would extend them in such a manner, as to be useful to the other Regiments."

In York, the Congress elects two more members to the Committee of Commerce—Elbridge Gerry and Henry Laurens.

21 February 1778:

Saturday. At Valley Forge, Washington writes to the Board of War, reporting that he has requested Henry Knox to bring some of the artillery at or near Albany to a depository closer to the main army, perhaps mostly by water down the Hudson in the spring. Washington also notes that Knox has informed him that the Congress has ordered twenty-five field pieces and two howitzers to Farmington, Connecticut. Washington requests the reason for this action, and asks that those pieces be forwarded to him as soon as possible.

Washington writes to Henry Knox, "I shall immediately write to the Board of War, on the subject of the artillery sent to Farmington ..."

Washington writes to Brigadier General William Smallwood, "When a man is found at an improper distance from camp, or circumstances that indicate an attempt to desert, he is certainly to be considered and treated as a deserter."

Washington writes to Captain Henry Lee, "Your application to the Assessors of the several hundreds [political subdivisions of counties], was extremely judicious, and I have no doubt that by your activity and prudent management, you will avail yourself of all the resources of the country, without giving unnecessary umbrage to the inhabitants."

Washington writes to William Duer, who had informed Washington of an American, John Biddle, a deserter who has made a complete sketch of the Valley Forge encampment, and gone to the enemy. Washington thanks Duer for the information, but reassures him that the Americans are well defended, and the British would have a extremely difficult task in attempting to attack, since they would be quickly exposed to defeat in detail.   The Congress orders that a warrant issue for $500,000 in favor of the delegates of Georgia, for the sole purpose of calling in the Continental currency of that state.

22 February 1778:

Sunday. At headquarters, Valley Forge, Washington writes to Governor William Livingston, "I cannot but be highly sensible of the fresh proofs given, of that zeal which yourself in particular, and the State of New Jersey in general, have so uniformly manifested in the common cause, and of the polite regard you have in repeated instances shown to my applications. I feel with you the absolute necessity of calling forth the united efforts of these states, to relieve our wants, and to prevent in future a renewal of our distresses; and the impossibility of answering these purposes by partial exertions. Nothing on my part has been or will be omitted, that may in the least tend to put our affairs upon this only footing, on which they can have any stability or success."

At Valley Forge, General Orders give the parole as Orkney, and the countersigns as Ormond, and Otway.

23 February 1778:

Monday. At Passy, Benjamin Franklin writes to Arthur Lee, "The enclosed, which you sent me, contained a letter from Mr. Hartley, in which he acquaints me that on the 17th Lord North had made his propositions towards a conciliation with America, and asked leave to bring in two bills, one to renounce all claim of taxation, the other to empower commissioners to treat with any persons or bodies of man in America on a peace ..."

At Valley Forge, the Baron Friedrich Wilhelm von Steuben, arrives in camp. He will soon fill the post of inspector general, prepare regulations for the Continental Army, and train them this winter to enable the American soldier to march, maneuver, and fight effectively against British and Hessian regulars. [See Fig. IV-26, p. 337].

24 February 1778:

Tuesday. The Board of War is asked to provide instructions to Lafayette, charged with an expedition into Canada. Considering the length of the route and the inclement season, he is to be particularly attentive to have his men well-clothed and supplied with provisions so as to guard against any misfortune.

In York, Lieutenant Colonel James Wilkinson, surely an indiscreet officer, and perhaps also a dishonorable one, challenges his former commander, Major General Horatio Gates to a duel, believing that some slight on Gate's part may have injured Wilkinson's reputation. Gates suggests to Wilkinson that they both ought to devote their energies to their duties, and, fortunately, they both agree, thus calling off any duel that might have occurred on such a silly matter.

25 February 1778:

Wednesday. The Assembly of Pennsylvania, meeting in Lancaster, has prepared a letter which is laid before the Congress in York, requesting to be furnished with instructions for superintendents of provisions, plans for superintendents of purchases, and instructions for millers.

26 February 1778:

Thursday. From Passy, Benjamin Franklin writes to David Hartley, the British negotiator, "I received yours of the 18th and 20th of this month, with Lord North's proposed bills. The more I see of these ideas and projects of your ministry, and their little arts and schemes of amusing and dividing us the more I admire the prudent, manly, and magnanimous propositions contained in your intended motion for an address to the king. What reliance can we have on an act expressing itself to be only a declaration of the intention of Parliament concerning the exercise of the right of imposing taxes in America, when in the bill itself, as well as in the title, a right is supposed and claimed which never existed ..."

Georgia becomes the fifth state to ratify the Articles of Confederation.

27 February 1778:

Friday. At Albany, New York, Major General Lafayette is greatly disappointed that in spite of a good bit of discussion upon and approval of his expedition into Canada, nothing appears to have been prepared. Troops have not been assigned, supplies are not stocked and loaded, transport is not ready, no organizational arrangements seem to have been made; in short, he feels that the program is all talk, no action.

In Valley Forge, von Steuben has a conference with General Washington to determine just how this additional foreign officer might be used. Needing a new quartermaster general was an early thought, but, impressed with Steuben's obvious military knowledge and requiring a person who will actually train his troops, Washington assigns him to the task, without naming him inspector general, or agreeing to any actual rank. Since Steuben agrees to serve as a volunteer, this is acceptable.

Connecticut becomes the sixth state to ratify the Articles of Confederation.

28 February 1778:

Saturday. In Paris, Arthur Lee writes to the Committee of Foreign Affairs, "Our joint dispatches of the 28th of December 1777, informed you that Spain had promised us three millions of livres, to be remitted to you in specie, through the Havana. This information we had through the French Court. We have since been informed, through the same channel, that it would be paid to our banker here in quarterly payments. Finding, however, that no payment was made, I applied lately to the Spanish ambassador here for an explanation. From him I learned that, by order of his court, he had informed the court of France that such a sum should be furnished for your use, but in what manner he was not instructed, nor had he received any further communication on the subject. He promised to transmit my application to his court without delay."   This letter demonstrates how very difficult it is to conclude matters of business and finance. There is no e-mail, no rapid means of conveying data or money.

1 March 1778:

Sunday. At Valley Forge in General Orders, Washington addresses "... his warmest thanks to the virtuous Officers and Soldiery of this Army for that persevering Fidelity and Zeal manifest in all their conduct. Their fortitude, not only under the common hardships incident to a military life, but also under the additional sufferings to which the peculiar situation of these States have exposed them, clearly proves them worthy of the enviable privilege of contending for the rights of human nature, the Freedom and Independence of their Country. The recent instance of uncomplaining patience during the scarcity of Provisions in Camp is fresh proof that they possess in an eminent degree the Spirit of Soldiers and the Magnanimity of Patriots."

2 March 1778:
     Monday. In York, Pennsylvania, James Lovell, for the Committee of Foreign Affairs, writes to William Bingham in Martinique, "The committee of secret correspondence, which almost a year ago was denominated the 'Committee for Foreign Affairs' stands indebted to you for your many letters, both of interesting advice and ingenious political speculation. The critical position of Quartermaster General, vacant since Thomas Mifflin quit in October, is filled by Nathanael Greene."

3 March 1778:
     Tuesday. At Valley Forge, General Orders includes a notice that a corps of dragoons is being recruited. A list of items needed for each horseman and a request that gentlemen wishing to serve at their own expense are invited to join is included. Dragoons are cavalry units, and are especially helpful because, being mounted, they can travel faster and farther than foot soldiers. They also become the eyes of an army, quickly able to report what they see.

4 March 1778:
     Wednesday. An American Soldier writes a piece that is published in the *Pennsylvania Packet*, "To The Britons. Your King and Parliament are a spectacle to the world, and their conduct in the American war, will render them immortal in infamy. [The soldier certainly lays it on.] It is hard to say which will be greatest, the astonishment or indignation of mankind, but certain it is, the wise and just will execrate their memory to latest time. With blood and murder, robbery and ravishment, burning and desolation, with every species of cruelty and death, have their hireling savages and butchers marked their steps in America."
     At the suggestion of Philip Schuyler, Major General Lafayette attends an Indian Conference at Johnstown, New York. This should help the young Frenchman to get some grasp of just who and what these Indians are like, how they negotiate, assess their scouting abilities, and learn what their mode of dress and speech is like.
     New Hampshire becomes the seventh state to ratify the Articles of Confederation.

Fig. V-26: Von Steuben and Washington, 1778

5 March 1778
     Thursday. At headquarters, Valley Forge, Washington writes
to Brig. Gen. Samuel Holden Parsons, "I am exceedingly glad to
hear of your determination to remain in the Army at this time,
when too many are withdrawing themselves from the Service ...
The Committee of Congress who are now here have desired that
no Commissions may be filled up till some new general
arrangements of the Army are completed. Inclosed (sic) you
have a letter for Genl. Knox who is expected from the eastward.
If he has not arrived with you, be pleased to forward it to
Springfield with orders if he has not been there to send it on to
Boston."
     Washington writes to Brigadier General Henry Knox, "I
would not have you keep any more of the new arms in the
Magazines to the eastward than you think will be absolutely
necessary for the recruits coming on to the Army, what number
that will probably be you can best judge who are upon the spot.
I do not know what steps Congress intend to recommend to the
States for filling their Regiments, but I am certain that nothing
short of the measure you mention [a draft] will prove effectual.
The Committee now here wrote upon this subject to Congress
very soon after they arrived, and pointed out the necessity of
falling upon some spirited measures for reinforcing the Army,
but they have not yet received any answer, and I very much
fear that the States will each proceed in different ways most of
them feeble and ineffectual."
     Washington writes again to Brigadier General Samuel
Holden Parsons, reporting that he (Washington) has learned the
exact location of Sir Henry Clinton's quarters in New York City
and is hopeful that a practicable means of taking Clinton
prisoner might be set afoot and requests Parsons to look into
the matter, and set it in motion, if possible.
     In York, the Congress resolves to print and emit an
additional $2,000,000 in bills of varying denominations. The
Congress has been forced into this position in order to have
some form of negotiable paper readily available. Inflation
continues to be a serious problem for the fledgling nation,
because there is little specie and no national credit to support
the paper.
     Pennsylvania becomes the eighth state to ratify the Articles
of Confederation.

6 March 1778:
     Friday. At headquarters, Valley Forge, Washington writes to
the Committee from the Congress at Moore Hall, "Gentn:
However inconvenient, and distressing to the Service in this
quarter it may be to part with another Majr. General, yet, in
obedience to a resolve of Congress I must do it, if neither Genl.
Putnam nor Heath, in the judgement of the Comee. Will answer
the purposes of the command at Rhode Island."

Washington writes to the Board of War, "As the neighbourhood of Philadelphia is the place where the Army will rendezvous in the spring, I think it will be necessary to draw the arms from all our remote Magazines to those in our rear, and I have for this reason desired Genl. Knox to send all the new ones from the eastward to this State. The State of Virginia has voted a very considerable number of men, who are to serve for six months, and it is more than probable, that if other States should find it difficult to procure their quota of Continental Troops that they may adopt similar expedients. I take it for granted that they will depend upon public Magazines for arms, and it will be a mortifying and discouraging circumstance should we not be able to supply them."

Washington writes to Major General John Sullivan, "All Continental Officers prisoners with the enemy, either while in confinement or on parole, so long as they continue Officers of the United States, are entitled to their pay and rations, liable to a deduction for what they may have received in confinement.

The Congress orders that Thomas Paine be paid $70 a month for ten months service as secretary to the Committee of Foreign Affairs.

7 March 1778:
    Saturday. At headquarters, Valley Forge, Washington writes to the president of the Congress, "In consequence of the letters which have lately passed between Gen. Howe and myself, copies of which I had the honor to transmit you, I was about to send Commissioners to meet those appointed by Genl. Howe for adjusting the disputed points between us; carrying into execution an exchange of prisoners and improving the old Cartel, as far as it might be practicable, for their better accommodation in future."

The Congress agrees with Washington's appointment of Colonel Nathaniel Gist on a mission to the Indians on the borders of Virginia and the Carolinas he is to undertake, and provides instructions to him. He is authorized and empowered to engage in the service of Virginia and the Carolinas, for the next campaign, a number of Indians, not exceeding two hundred, and interpreters of the Indian languages as Gist shall judge necessary. He is to receive five thousand dollars for defraying expenses he shall incur in this work, and to keep an account of the expenditures, getting vouchers as he proceeds.

8 March 1778:
    Sunday. At headquarters, Valley Forge, Washington writes to Colonel Elias Dayton, "I am very sorry to find from your letter that the ill state of your health added to the situation of your private affairs, renders it highly inconvenient on the last and impossible upon the former to remain in the Service. I am so well convinced that you have no other motives for quitting the service than those you have alleged, that you have my consent

as far as it depends upon me, but Congress having in a late instance seemed to have reserved to themselves the right of accepting the resignations of Officers of your rank, I have not since that time thought myself at liberty to receive such Commissions, before their consent has been obtained. You will, therefore, be pleased to make application to them."

Dayton never does resign. He will serve to the end of the war, rising to the rank of Brigadier General.

General Orders give the parole as Hamden, and the countersigns as Hexham, and Hull.

9 March 1778:

Monday. The Congress resumes consideration of the report of the Committee on the Commissary, and supports the recommendations of Gouverneur Morris on supplies for the army. Among the items approved are 10,000 barrels of pickled fish, 10,000 quintals of Cod, 20,000 barrels of salted pork, 30,000 bushels of peas, 2,000 bushels of onions, and 10,000 beef cattle. An army really does travel on its stomach.

10 March 1778:

Tuesday. Lafayette returns to Albany from his attendance at the Oneida Indian Conference in Johnstown. In addition to learning something of the Indian mode of dress, speech, and warfare, he also arranged to recruit about 50 Oneidas and Tuscaroras for service with Washington in the spring.

Massachusetts becomes the ninth state to ratify the Articles of Confederation. But, unlike the later Constitution, wherein nine states will become sufficient to conclude acceptance of an item, the Articles require full unanimity—all thirteen must ratify. It will not happen until 1 March 1781. This is yet another weakness in the approach written into the Articles of Confederation. The Continental Congress is so weak in its ability to direct and support the War of the American revolution, that it almost fails, and will not be corrected until after the Constitutional Convention in 1787.

11 March 1778:

Wednesday. Congress orders that a warrant for $50,000 issue to Joseph Borden, commissioner of the loan office of New Jersey in favor of Colonel Mark Bird, on the application of General Mifflin, late quartermaster general.

12 March 1778:

Thursday. At Passy, Benjamin Franklin writes to David Hartley, "In the pamphlets you were so kind to lend me there is one important fact misstated, apparently from the writer's not having been furnished with good information; it is the transaction between Mr. Grenville and the Colonies, wherein he understands that Mr. Grenville demanded of them a specific sum; that they refused to grant anything, and that it was on their refusal only that he made the motion for the stamp act. No one of these particulars is true. The fact was this: Some time in the winter of 1763-4 Mr. Grenville called together the agents of the several Colonies, and told them that he proposed to draw a revenue from America, and to that end his intention was to levy a stamp duty on the Colonies by act of Parliament in the ensuing session, agents write this to their respective assemblies and communicate to him the answers ..." But, no attention was paid to the comments of the colonies. Grenville went ahead with compulsion rather than persuasion. "And thus the golden bridge which the ingenious author thinks the Americans unwisely and unbecomingly refused to hold out to the minister and Parliament was actually held out to them, but they refused to walk over it."

In New York, Sir Guy Johnson at British headquarters, writes to Lord George Germain. He reports that a runner has gotten through with dispatches from Lieutenant Colonel Mason Bolton, the commander at Fort Niagara, that state a body of Indians, commanded by a few regulars cannot be assembled nor maintained the way regular forces are, and thus are not useful for raids, especially during the Indians' hunting season.

13 March 1778:
Friday. At Versailles, the French government officially informs the British of their commercial treaty with the United States. This formal recognition of the Independence of America, requires the British to recall their ambassador, which they do this evening.

The Congress affirms a resolution regarding the duties and responsibilities of the various officers in the Commissary Department. While this is a helpful start toward bring that department into a more perfect operating arm, it will not be the sole resolution of the problems confronting the Army.

14 March 1778:
Saturday. In York, the Congress orders that a warrant issue in favor of Joseph Nourse, paymaster to the Board of War and Ordnance, for $5,000 for the board to advance to Colonel Nathaniel Gist for the purpose of recruiting Indians.

15 March 1778:
Sunday. At headquarters, Valley Forge, Washington writes to Brig. Gen. John Glover, "I wrote to you to acquaint you with the important purpose, which indispensibly require the presence of yourself and every other General Officer, in Camp, and from the reasons then mentioned, as well as because those urged in a former letter on the subject, daily acquire more weight, I am induced to avail myself of the opportunity by Colonel Shepard, again to press your return to the Command of your Brigade. The arguments which I have used to dissuade you from quitting the Service, will I flatter myself have their due

influence, and lead you to renounce all thoughts of resigning in our present critical circumstances."

Washington writes to Brig. Gen. George Weedon, requesting Weedon to return to camp as soon as possible; Washington noted that there was no further information regarding the relative ranking of the brigadier generals, but that the Congress has the matter under consideration.

A Grand Parade is formed to witness the drumming out of Lieutenant Enslin. The miscreant is marched through each wing of the army, with all the drums and fifes playing, his coat is turned, and he is finally transported over the Schuylkill River with orders never to be seen in camp in the future.

General Orders give the parole as Portsmouth, and the countersigns as Pitt, and Plato.

In Philadelphia, Ambrose Serle, aide to British Admiral Lord Howe, keeps a Journal, in which he records, "Came on board the [HMS] *Eagle*. A Rebel Colonel (Gabriel Johonot), who came down in a Flag of Truce, dined with the Admiral. A mean-looking fellow, but apparently not destitute of abilities, or rather of that low cunning, which is the characteristic of the New England people. He was very careful to use the term State for the old word Colony, and sat with his Uniform (buff & blue) in all the native confidence of his countrymen. A Commissary came with him from Genl. Burgoyne."

16 March 1778:
Monday. Congress receives letters from General Washington regarding the settlement of accounts of prisoners of war prior to exchange. The Congress appoints a committee of three members to review these matters and make specific recommendations. Selected to this important committee are Francis Lightfoot Lee of Virginia, John Henry of Maryland, and Samuel Huntington of Connecticut.

17 March 1778:
Tuesday. At Versailles, Conrad Alexandre Gérard writes to the commissioners at Paris, "Gentlemen: I am charged to acquaint you that you will be presented to the king next Friday, if you will have the goodness to render yourselves here at 10 o'clock in the morning. Count de Vergennes hopes you will do him the honor to dine with him on the same day."

18 March 1778:
Wednesday. Washington is authorized to conclude an exchange of prisoners, even though the details of the accounts of each and every such prisoner may not yet be fully settled. It is agreed that there will still be a sufficient number of British prisoners in American hands to offset any concern about who is coming out ahead. However, there are still a few folks, overly concerned about these details—they are called nit-pickers, and they exist in every army.

19 March 1778:

Thursday. From Paris, Arthur Lee writes to the president of the Congress, "It is all together uncertain when it will be convenient for Spain to accede to the alliance; and I am apprehensive that the war, which is likely to break out in Germany, will prevent the King of Prussia from declaring so soon, and so decidedly, as he promised. The court of Spain will, I apprehend, make some difficulties about settling the dividing line between their possessions and those of the United States. They wish to have the cession of Pensacola." Lee has been stewing in Europe for some while, and is quite frustrated that issues of diplomacy seem to take forever to come to a conclusion.

20 March 1778:

Friday. At headquarters, Valley Forge, Washington writes to the Board of War, "As soon as Genl. Greene enters upon the Office of Quartermaster General he will attend to the stores at Reading and have all that are not immediately or soon wanted for the Army, removed to a place of greater safety. The enemy cannot possibly march a body of horse or foot from Philadelphia, upon the route mentioned in the information [a recent letter from the Board], without being discovered by our patrols. A few days ago one of our scouting parties fell in with and took four fine teams going into Philadelphia. [The ability to interdict supplies to the British occupying the city is most useful.] Inclosed you have the information of two of the wagoners who were taken. By enquiring who their acquaintances are, some further discoveries may be made."

Congress approves a resolution that Continental naval officers, not in actual service on active duty, shall be entitled to their pay, but not to their rations and subsistence.

21 March 1778:

Saturday. The Franco-American Treaties (one of Alliance, and another of Amity and Commerce) force the British government to rethink their strategy regarding the American War. Now they find themselves in a new world war, with the problems of dealing with their ancient enemy France, who has something the Americans do not, a large and effective naval force. George Germain issues new orders to Sir Henry Clinton: Detach 5,000 troops from the Philadelphia garrison for an attack upon the French West Indies, and plan to evacuate Philadelphia, which cannot be properly defended with the remaining forces.

In York, the Congress, concerned over possible enemy incursions up the Hudson River, resolve that all the forts, posts, and passes in the state of New York, and all the troops and units therein, shall be under the command of a single general officer.

22 March 1778:

Sunday. At headquarters, Valley Forge, Washington writes to Sir William Howe, "You are under a mistake as to the rank of Mr. Ethan Allen, which is only that of Lieutenant Colonel; and as such he has been returned and considered by your Commissary, Mr. Loring. [This is an important matter, relating to the rank of British equivalent officers who might be thus exchanged.] The conduct of Lt. Col. [John] Brooks in detaining John Miller [an American deserter, operating as a King's trumpeter, and under a flag of truce], requires neither palliation nor excuse. I justify and approve it. There is nothing so sacred in the character of the King's Trumpeter, even when sanctified by a flag, as to alter the nature of things, or consecrate infidelity and guilt. He was a deserter from the Army under my command, and, whatever you have been pleased to assert to the contrary, it is the practice of War and Nations, to seize and punish deserters." Notice how upright and straight-forward Washington is in this matter. He tolerates no shading in matters of honor.

General Orders give the parole as Beverly, and the countersigns as Buxton, and Brent.

23 March 1778:

Monday. From Paris, William Lee writes to the President of the Congress, "I have the pleasing satisfaction of congratulating you and my country on the independency of the thirteen United States of America being now openly acknowledged by the court of France, which must soon put a glorious end to all our troubles. About fourteen days ago the French minister in London formally avowed to the British Ministry the treaty which his most Christian majesty had made with you, and on the 20th instant your commissioners were, informed, introduced to the king and his ministers at Versailles, as the representatives of sovereign States, and on Sunday last they were introduced to the Queen and all the royal family."

24 March 1778:

Tuesday. From York, James Lovell for the Committee of Foreign Affairs writes to the commissioners at Paris, bemoaning the fact that the Committee does not receive frequent and regular information from them regarding the affairs the effect foreign policy, nor of the progress of negotiations. This is partly due to dispatches which have been stolen or those that have to be thrown overboard before capture. The reader is reminded once again of just how parlous is the conveyance of information at the time of the revolution, especially over the ocean. These means of communication, subject to all kinds of delays, accidents, and theft, were not the more secure means available to us in our time. There is no such thing as a secure, protected means of passing along information. Not by land, by sea, by river, by horse, it is all subject to attack, weather, fire, loss.

25 March 1778:

Wednesday. At headquarters, Valley Forge, Washington writes to Maj. Gen. William Heath, "I hope no time will be lost in removing Genl. Burgoyne's troops from Boston after the receipt of the Resolution of Congress for that purpose. If they remain within reach of the enemy's force who are at Newport, I think it more than probable that they will make an effort to rescue them. I beg you will exert yourself in forwarding on the recruits for such of the Massachusetts Regiments as are with this Army; they need not remain to be inoculated as that can be done conveniently upon their arrival in Camp, and the Doctors say the men will be much healthier thro' the campaign than if they had been inoculated at home and marched immediately upon recovery. I am particularly pressing in this matter, because I have many reasons for thinking that Genl. Howe means to call in reinforcements and attack us before we receive ours. Four Regiments are actually embarked at New York and reports from Rhode Island say there is an appearance of their evacuating Newport."

Washington writes to Governor William Livingston, "I am much concerned that it is not in my power to afford further aid for checking the incursions of the enemy in Jersey. The situation of this Army will not admit of the smallest detachments to be made from it. It is our misfortune not to have a sufficient force on foot, either for the purposes of offense or defense, and the fatal policy of short inlistments (sic), like an evil genius, is now prosecuting us and marring all our operations."

Congress orders that a warrant issue [an 18th century term for a check] in favor of the Board of War for $200,000 for public service.

26 March 1778:

Thursday. At Valley Forge, Washington writes to Jean Baptiste Ternant, "As you seem to have taken for granted that your services are rejected, and intimate an inconsistency in my not discouraging from the beginning the application you made in your behalf, it is incumbent upon me to assure you, that I have not given up the idea of your becoming one of the Subinspectors [deputy quartermaster general], on the terms expressed in my last letter and acceded to by you."

Washington writes to the Officer Commanding at Albany, "Sir: I desire you will immediately upon receipt of this order Colo. Hazen's Regiment down to Fishkill, where the commanding Officer is to take his orders from Major General McDougall. Congress having particularly directed that Colo. James Livingston's Regiment should be sent to the Highlands, you are also to order that Regiment down, to take orders from Genl. McDougall."

General Orders gives the parole as Feud, and the countersigns as Framingham and Frankfort.

27 March 1778:

Friday. At Chaillot, France, Arthur Lee writes to Benjamin Franklin, "In consequence of what you mentioned to me relative to the German courts, I consulted the Spanish ambassador whether it could be determined with any degree of certainty how long it would be before the business I am pledged for with his court would require my presence. His answer was that it was altogether uncertain. In this situation it appeared to me that, under my present engagements, I could not venture to so great a distance. My brother (William Lee) has therefore set out on his original plan that was settled at Versailles."

28 March 1778:

Saturday. From Versailles, King Louis XVI of France writes to the Congress, "Very Dear and Great Friends and Allies: You will learn, undoubtedly with gratitude, the measure which the conduct of the King of Great Britain has induced us to take, of sending a fleet to endeavor to destroy the English forces upon the shores of North America. This expedition will convince you of the eagerness and their vigor which we are resolved to bring to the execution of the engagements which we have contracted with you. We are firmly persuaded that your fidelity to the obligations which your plenipotentiaries have contracted in your name will animate more and more the efforts which you are making with so much courage and perseverance." The friendliness with which France responded to the American request for aid is a mark of the respect the two nations had for each other.

29 March 1778:

Sunday. At Versailles, the Count de Vergennes prepares a memoir to serve as an Instruction to Conrad Alexandre Gérard, named to be Minister to the United States of America from France. The instructions include; 1.) To guard against the possibility of the Congress making a separate peace with the British; 2.) To dissuade the Congress from any plan that might include the acquisition of the Floridas; 3.) Block any plans the Congress should promote for adding Canada to the thirteen states; 4.) Check, as much as possible, congressional desires for subsides.

At headquarters, Valley Forge, Washington writes to Brig. Gen. George Weedon, enclosing a resolution of the Congress, respecting the rank of the brigadiers in the Virginia Line, and adds in his letter "... that it is my opinion the parties interested should acquiesce in whatever decision might be given concerning it ... and the pressing necessity there is for General Officers in Camp, induces me again to request your most expeditious return."

At the Valley Forge encampment, the Orderly Book of the 2nd Pennsylvania Continental Line includes Brigadier General Anthony Wayne's order for cleanliness, "As there is no greater or surer mark of discipline than Cleanliness, so there is nothing more conductive to health and spirit; it introduces a laudable pride which is substitute for almost every virture; the Genl. therefore, in the most pointed terms, desires the officers to oblige their men to appear clean & decent at all times and upon all occasions: Even punishing that Soldier that appears dirty whether on duty or not."

30 March 1778:
    Monday. At Valley Forge, Washington writes to Colonel William Russell (of the 13th Virginia Regiment), noting that the dispersed condition of the regiment and the number of deserters, requires that some diligent officer return to the part of the country from which the unit was raised for recruiting and collecting deserters. Then the unit is to proceed to Fort Pitt for duty.
    In York, the delegation from South Carolina is named-- William Henry Drayton, John Matthews, Thomas Heyward, Henry Laurens, and Richard Hutson—and their credentials presented.

31 March 1778:
    Tuesday. At Albany, New York, Maj. Gen. Lafayette, having received notice from the Congress that the expedition into Canada has been called off, departs to return to Valley Forge.
    At headquarters, Valley Forge, Washington writes to Maj. Gen. Nathaniel Greene, approving of the locations for magazines to hold the large quantities of grain and hay required.
    Washington writes to Major General Alexander McDougall, noting that the British seem to be preparing for some operations in the Philadelphia vicinity. He then goes on to suggest that this just might offer an opportunity to attack . "We must either oppose our whole force to his [Howe], in this Quarter, or take the advantage of him in some other, which leads me to ask your opinion of the practicability of an attempt upon New York ..."

1 April 1778:
    Wednesday. At Passy, Benjamin Franklin writes to Arthur Lee, "There is a style in some of your letters, I observe it particularly in the last, whereby superior merit is assumed to yourself in point of care and attention to business, and blame is insinuated on your colleagues without making yourself accountable, by a direct charge of negligence or unfaithfulness, which has the appearance of being as artful as it is unkind."

2 April 1778:
    Thursday. Because too many wagons, loaded with supplies, are waylaid, stolen by raiders, or some of the materials removed by the drivers for sale for personal gain, Congress hears a

report from the Board of War respecting the employing of a conductor or wagon master to take charge of the wagons to be sent to the southward. They also order that three members be added to the committee to confer with commissary general Jeremiah Wadsworth—William Henry Drayton, Nathaniel Scudder, and John Banister are chosen for this duty.

3 April 1778:
Friday. At headquarters, Valley Forge, Washington writes to the president of the Congress, "Captain [Henry] Lee of the Light Dragoons and the officers under his command having uniformly distinguished themselves by a conduct of exemplary zeal, prudence, and bravery; I took occasion on a late signal instance of it to express the high sense I entertained of their merit, and to assure him, that it should not fail of being properly noticed. I was induced to give this assurance, from a conviction, that it is the wish of Congress to give every encouragement to merit, and that they would cheerfully embrace so favorable an opportunity of manifesting this disposition. I had it in contemplation at the time, in case no other method, more eligible, could be adopted, to make him an offer of a place in my family [become a member of Washington's staff]. I have consulted the Committee of Congress upon the subject, and we were mutually of opinion, that the giving Capt. Lee the command of two troops of Horse on the proposed establishment with the rank of Major, to act as an independent partisan corps, would be a mode of rewarding him, very advantageous to the service. Capt. Lee's genius particularly adapts him to a command of this nature, and it will be most agreeable to him, of any station, in which he could be placed."

The Congress orders that a warrant issue (an 18th century term frequently used to denote a check or its equivalent that can pass for cash) for $200,000 in favor of William Buchanan, Commissary General of Purchases, for the use of the Middle Department. These warrants, while authorized by the Congress, all too frequently are discounted by the users, as the fiscal power of the Congress declines.

4 April 1778:
Saturday. In answer to an accusatory letter from Arthur Lee at Chaillot, Benjamin Franklin writes to Lee, "Mr. Deane communicated to me his intention of setting out for America immediately as a secret, which he desired I would mention to nobody. I complied with his request. If he did not think fit to communicate it to you also, it is from him you should demand his reasons. This court has an undoubted right to send as ministers whom it pleases and where it pleases, without advising with us, or desiring our approbation. The measure of sending M. Gerard as a minister to Congress was resolved on without consulting me; but I think it a wise one, and, if I did not, I do not conceive that I have any right to find fault with it.

France was not consulted when we were sent here. Your angry charge, therefore, of our 'making a party business of it is groundless. We had no hand in the business."

5 April 1778:
    Sunday. At headquarters, Valley Forge, Washington writes to the President of Pennsylvania. Thomas Wharton, Jr., "Sir: I take the liberty to enclose you a letter to me from Mrs. Mary Pemberton [wife of Israel Pemberton, a Quaker prisoner], requesting a passport for some waggons to be sent out, with articles for the use of her husband and others, who are now in confinement. As the persons concerned are prisoners of the state I did not think proper to comply with her request. I have assured her that I would transmit her letter to you, and did not doubt, but her application would meet with your ready concurrence. If you will be pleased to send the passports required to me, I will convey it by a flag [a method of allowing passage through enemy and friendly lines]. The letter mentions one or more waggons; I dare say, you will extend the indulgence, as far as may be requisite and consistent with propriety."
    General Orders give the parole as Roxbury, and the countersigns as Rumney, and Rindge.

6 April 1778:
    Monday. At Passy, Benjamin Franklin writes to Arthur Lee, chiding him for his censure of the measure that procures clothing for American soldiers in response to the orders of Congress. Lee seems to nit-pick on a number of matters that he feels he is (or should be) privy to because of his position. These are matters he is quite capable of discovering by merely asking Franklin or Deane, but instead, he chooses to complain that he was not informed or finds fault with the manner of doing something.

7 April 1778:
    Tuesday. Papers and a certificate from the commissioners at Fort Pitt, assigned to investigate the charges against Colonel George Morgan, are presented to Congress. These charges may have come mostly from jealous land speculators who resent Morgan's ability to acquire lands in the west. Upon examination, the committee concludes that "... after the clearest and most satisfactory testimonies, wholly acquit the said Colonel George Morgan of the charges against him; and, we testify that we are possessed of the knowledge of various facts and circumstances, evincing not only his attachment to the cause, but also an uncommon degree of diligence in discharging the duties of his employment and of attention to the interests of United States; and therefore are of opinion he ought to be restored to the fullest confidence of his country."

In Philadelphia, Ambrose Serle, writes in his Journal, "Two or three small armed vessels, with troops on board, arrived last night from Egg Harbor, where they had destroyed some Salt Works, erected by the Rebels, and other stores, to the value of near £30,000, without the least inconvenience. Enterprises on te Coast, by small detachments, would annoy the Rebels exceedingly, and with great facility on our part."

8 April 1778:
Wednesday. From Paris, Arthur Lee, after consultation with Franklin, pens a memorial for the Netherlands, expressing to these possible future allies the sense of the American position vis a vis free trade, "When the ancestors of the present inhabitants of the United States of America first settled in that country they did it entirely at their own expense. The public of England never granted one shilling to aid in their establishment. The State of England, therefore, could not justly claim the benefit of an acquisition which it never made. Upon this principle the first settlers conceived they had a right to exchange and sell produce of their labor to all nations, without control."

9 April 1778:
Thursday. From his headquarters at Valley Forge, Washington writes to Brigadier General James Mitchell Varnum, who has submitted his request to resign "However contrary to my wish and inclination it is to refuse the requests of my Officers, there are cases in which duty requires a sacrifice of my feelings, it is upon this principle that I find myself under the disagreeable necessity of disapproving the application which you have made for leave of absence, for I cannot think myself warranted in suffering the Army to be deprived of its best bulwark, good Officers, at a time when we cannot from one moment to another, assure ourselves of inactivity on the part of the enemy. General [Jedediah] Huntington's leave of absence was partly obtained because your stay was regarded as certain. If you were to go at this time, your Division would be without a single General officer, when our circumstances rather demand the presence of them all. For these reasons I hope you will renounce all thoughts of quitting camp, and endeavor to conciliate your happiness with the public interest and the good of the Service."
Congress orders $4,000 for the use of Colonel Daniel Morgan for the building of armed boats on the Ohio River. The purpose of the boats is to interdict British-Indian raids across the Ohio to attack Patriot settlements on its southeast side.
10 April 1778:
Friday. At Passy, Benjamin Franklin and Arthur Lee write to Charles William Frédéric Dumas, "We have now the pleasure of acquainting you that Mr. John Adams, a member of Congress, appointed to succeed Mr. Deane in this commission, is safely

arrived here. He came over in the *Boston*, a frigate of thirty guns, belonging to the United States. In the passage they met and made prize of a large English letter of marque ship of fourteen guns, the *Martha*, bound to New York, on whose cargo £70,000 sterling were insured in London."

11 April 1778:

Saturday. In France the newly appointed minister plenipotentiary to the United States of America, Conrad Alexandre Gérard, departs from Toulon.

At headquarters, Valley Forge, Washington writes to Colonel Stephen Moylan, "Your return [a unit's report of persons present, sick, or on leave] of the Cavalry is really vexatious, but what can be expected when Officers prefer their own ease and emolument to the good of their Country or to the care and attention which they are in duty bound to pay to the particular Corps they command. I desire you will make strict inquiry into the conduct of every officer present and find out whether those absent have gone upon furlough regularly obtained. And if it appears that they have been negligent in point of duty or are absent without leave, arrest and have them brought to trial; for I am determined to make examples of those to whom this shameful neglect of the cavalry has been owing."

Congress orders that Joseph Reed be granted a leave of absence for a few days to remove his family to a place of security.

12 April 1778:

Sunday. At headquarters, Valley Forge, Washington writes to Brig. Gen. William Smallwood, "Upon a full consideration of all circumstances, I have determined to withdraw the main body of your division from Wilmington, and to have a field Officer and two good Captains with about 150 men who can be depended upon, to act as patrols from Wilmington to Duck Creek, and, in conjunction with the Militia, cut off the trade between the enemy and the disaffected in the lower Counties. I would have you begin to file off your baggage and stores immediately upon receipt of this, without giving the true reason and when you have fixed upon a day to march, give me notice, that I may order preparations to be made to receive your men. You had better make a small circuit, than march directly across to Camp, to avoid all possibility of being interrupted."

General Orders give the parole as Bemis and the countersigns as Burlington and Bennington.

13 April 1778:

Monday. From Passy, John Adams writes to Abigail, "The reception I have met in this kingdom has been as friendly, as polite, and as respectful as was possible. It is the universal opinion of the people here, of all ranks, that a friendship between France and America is the interest of both countries, and the late alliance so happily formed, is universally popular; so much so, that I have been told by persons of good judgment that the government here would have been under a sort of necessity of agreeing to it, even if it had not been agreeable to themselves. The delights of France are innumerable. The politeness, the elegance, the softness, the delicacy, are extreme. In short, stern and haughty republican as I am, I cannot help loving these people for their earnest desire and assiduity to please."

In Philadelphia, Ambrose Serle, writes in his Journal, "This afternoon the [HMS] *Andromeda*, Capt. Bryne, arrived at Sandy hook in 7 weeks from Portsmouth [England], and brought Expresses to the Admiral & General, the substance of which were, a Declaration of the Parliament relative to the exercise of the right of taxation in America, and a Bill for empowering H.M. [His Majesty] to send out Commissioners with full powers to treat with the Rebels, to suspend certain Acts of Parliament, to cause a cessation of Hostilities, by land, to grant pardons, and to make & unmake Governors. Lord & General H. [Howe] are nominated among the Commissioners."

14 April 1778:

Tuesday. At The Hague, Holland, Charles William Frédéric Dumas writes to the Committee of Foreign Affairs, "I have the satisfaction of being able to apprise you that since the declaration of France, made here the 18th of March, affairs have taken in this country a most favorable turn. My last journey to Amsterdam has not been useless. But I can not trust to paper and to the vicissitudes of so long a voyage the detail of my operations. I constantly give information to your honorable commissioners, to whom I write almost every post. I will say only in general that the cabal of your enemies fails in all the attempts it has made to engage this republic to put herself in the breach for them. We are preparing a third piece upon credit. I will add copies of it to my packet when it is printed."

At Valley Forge, Ebenezer Crosby, Surgeon in Commander-in-Chief's Lifeguard at the Flying Hospital, writes to Norton Quincey, "It would please you to see this Log-City, part of which is as regular as Philadelphia and affords much better quarters than you would imagine, if you consider the materials, season, and hurry in which it was built. The front line is built on a ridge, near a mile and a half in length, having a breastwork thrown up from one end to the other of it. The left wing of the whole is supported by Schuylkill, and the right by a very large height, extending itself just in the rear of the center-line, quite to the river, this is also fortified. It was necessary to fortify the Camp, as we could not move for want of horses, having kill'd hundreds and rendered, I might say thousands, useless at present through the great scarcity of forage and badness of the roads. Not only the horses but the men were obliged to fast several times, once for near a week, there not being any meat in Camp for that time. This could not be owing to a real scarcity in the Country, but to a defect in the Commissary Department, yet they bore it with the greatest patience."

15 April 1778:
Wednesday. In York, the Congress takes a good bit of time to work out the details of a new Board of Treasury. It is designed to handle all the fiscal affairs of the nation, not just bits and pieces, but everything: funds, loans, lottery, bills of exchange, bills of credit, direct the affairs of the Loan and Lottery Office, hire and fire personnel, prepare reports on the Public expenses, provide estimates of budget monies to the future, audit accounts, pay bills, and secure contracts. This becomes the embryonic Department of the Treasury.

16 April 1778:
Thursday. In London, Lord North, offers the idea of a peace commission, which does not include the power to recognize the independence of the colonies. Named to this three-person commission are: Frederick Howard, Earl of Carlisle, from whom the group gets its name as the Carlisle Commission, William Eden, and William Johnstone, the latter the former Governor of West Florida.
Congress resolves that all the personnel in the Commissary Department be bonded.

17 April 1778:
Friday. At headquarters, Valley Forge, Washington writes to President Thomas Wharton, Junior, of Pennsylvania, "I have long been convinced that one great cause of the backwardness of the people to supply us with articles in the Qr.Masters and Commissary's departments, has been owing to the impudent choice of deputies in these departments, who have not only personally abused the inhabitants, but have defrauded them of a great part of their dues. So glaring an instance, of one of those improper appointments, has lately presented itself to me, that I thought it my duty to take the deputation away from the person to prevent his doing mischief, and as he was empowered to act by Mr. Thomas Edwards the Commissioner of Lancaster County, I thought it highly expedient to give you information of it, with the character of Patrick Maguire, the person named in the inclosed (sic) extensive Commission. He was hired about twelve months ago, to act as steward in my family, in which station he continued until a few weeks past, when I was obliged to dismiss him. I hope you will attribute this representation of facts to be the true motive, which is, my desire of delivering the people from the oppression which they have too long labored under, by being harassed and abused by persons of Mr. Maguire's stamp."

Congress orders that $1,500,000 be advanced to Jeremiah Wadsworth, Commissary General, for the use of that department. Wadsworth had built a rather full and generally complete staff of buyers and distributors of all kinds of military supplies for both the American Army and the French forces. In order to do so, he recruited an English and French speaking fellow, John Church.

18 April 1778:
Saturday. At headquarters, Valley Forge, Washington learning of an uprising by local Tories near Dover, Delaware, writes to Brig. Gen. William Smallwood, "Suffering so audacious an insurrection as that you mention to go unpunished or to gain head, will be of so dangerous a tendency, that I desire you will immediately take the most effectual means to suppress it. The Act of Congress against persons supplying the enemy with provision continued in force until the 10th of this month; but if you succeed in your intended expedition, perhaps some more worthy of being made examples of may fall into your hands, and therefore I would have you suspend the execution of any of those convicted, til you see the issue of the disturbance in Kent."

The Congress, concerned over the loss of the frigate *Virginia*, resolves, "That the navy board in the middle district ... make a strict enquiry and examination into the causes of the loss of said frigate ... and examine all persons, evidences, and papers necessary, and make a report of such their enquiry, together with the evidences, to the Marine Committee, to be laid before Congress."

19 April 1778:
Sunday. From Valley Forge, Washington writes to Sir William Howe, "Mr. [Stephen] Lowry was never a principal commissary of ours, but only acted occasionally as a Deputy, for purchasing provisions where he lived. I do not know whether he was employed, at the time of his capture, even in this line. From this state of facts, you can readily agree with me, that I can not with propriety accede to your offer. However, in order to put the fair Lady, in whose case you so obligingly interest yourself, in the possession of her husband, I would propose that an exchange should take place between Mr. Higgins and Mr. Lowry. I am ready, as far as it depends on me, to comply with the Lady's wishes, and it remains with you to lend your aid for their completion. I request that your flags in the future may cross the Schuylkill near Philadelphia, and proceed to our posts, by the Lancaster Road. By taking the route east of Schuylkill they may meet with accidents from parties of Militia, for which I cannot be responsible."

Washington writes to Governor Patrick Henry of Virginia, "I hold myself infinitely obliged to the Legislature for the ready attention which they paid to my representation of the wants of the Army and to you, for the strenuous manner in which you have recommended to the people an observation of my request for fattening cattle. Congress have just made a change in the Commissary General's department by the appointment of Mr. Jeremiah Wadsworth of Connecticut, in the room of Mr. Buchanan. Mr. Wadsworth is a man of most extensive influence in the Eastern States, has a thorough knowledge of the resources of those States, and possesses that most useful quality of great activity and address in business. I shall take the first opportunity of acquainting him with your appointment of Mr. Hawkins, that he may co-operate with him."

General Orders give the parole as Independence and the countersigns as Ipswich and Jamaica.

20 April 1778:

Monday. In York, the Congress prepares detailed instructions to Major General Gates, who is to command the Northern Department. They lay heavy emphasis upon the security of the Hudson River, since it is the means by which goods and supplies are brought across from east to west, and troops are transported in a like manner. It is a vital link in connecting the states, one with another. Its interruption by the enemy would be a disaster.

21 April 1778:

Tuesday. In England, the three members of the Carlisle Commission, along with newly promoted Lieutenant General Charles Cornwallis, slip anchor aboard the HMS *Trident* to sail for America.

Captain Walter Butler, a Tory leader, had been captured by the Americans at the Battle of Oriskany on 6 Aug 1777. During his confinement in Albany, New York, Butler has requested parole or exchange several times, but the Americans view him as much too dangerous to release. Today, he manages to escape his jailers.

22 April 1778:

Wednesday. Congress is disturbed by a printed paper, circulating among the people, that purports to offer a treaty and a cessation of hostilities between America and Great Britain. It is apparent that this "paper" is a product of the British peace seekers who really want to ease up on the British military efforts in American so they can invest more in home island defense, and against French offensive actions in the West Indies. The Congress doesn't buy, and issues their own well-reasoned rebuttal.

23 April 1778:

Thursday. From Paris, David Hartley writes to Benjamin Franklin, "God bless you, my dear friend. No exertion or endeavor on my part shall be wanting that we may sometime or other meet again in peace. Your powers are infinitely more influential than mine. To those powers I trust my last hopes. I will conclude, blessed are the peacemakers."

At York, the Congress, believing that persuasion and influence, coupled with the example of the deluded and fear of danger may have induced some of the subjects of the states to aid and abet the occupying British forces in several places, and are probably desirous of returning to their duty, but could be put off by fear of punishment when the Americans regain control of a territory or city. Therefore, the Congress resolves that it be recommended to the legislatures of the several states to pass laws offering pardon to any such citizens, who shall surrender themselves and return to the state to which they belong. It is further recommended that the good and faithful citizens of these states receive such returning penitents with compassion and mercy, and forgive and bury their past failings. It is ordered that 500 copies in English and 200 in German be printed for circulating.

24 April 1778:

Friday. At headquarters, Valley Forge, Washington writes to Governor George Clinton, "In the affair if Princeton the winter before last, a box was taken from the enemy, which by appearances was supposed to contain a quantity of hard money. It was put into a small ammunition cart, on the spur of the occasion and has ever since disappeared. I am informed there were some suspicions at the time against one and [Joseph] Crane, a Capt. Lieutenant in the artillery, who it was imagined had converted the box and its contents to his own use. The enclosed letter to Mr. Hamilton, gives some reason to believe those suspicions were not without foundation: and if any method could be fallen upon to detect the villainy and recover the money, or some equivalent for it, it would not be amiss. I am not able to give you any clue to the discovery further than to refer you to Mr. Kip whom I have desired to communicate to you all the information he may be possessed of on the subject. Crane it seems lives in Orange County, within your government."

Washington writes to Horatio Gates, "It being indispensibly necessary that some general plan of operation should be settled for the present campaign; and perceiving that Congress have been pleased to appoint you to command on the North River; I am to request, if you should not find it too inconvenient, that you will make a digression from your route thither, and favor me with a call at this Camp, that we may enter upon a discussion of the point, and form some general system. The propriety of this measure, particularly at this advanced period, will be so obvious to you, that it is unnecessary to add upon the subject."

Washington writes to Major General Thomas Mifflin, "In conformity to a resolve of Congress, of which the enclosed is a copy, I am to inform you that a Council of War at which I request your attendance, will be held at this place to deliberate and determine upon the measure recommended by Congress. As the meeting of the Council, will depend upon the arrival Gen. Gates, to whom I have written, you will be pleased to enquire of him when he will be here, and regulate yourself accordingly."

The Congress takes some time to consider a matter of protocol. Two of its members, being called to a session, do not respond in a timely or gentlemanly manner. It is a cause of concern among the body of delegates, who react by enquiring closely about the ways in which the two answered the messengers calling them to their duty. The Congress takes itself seriously when it comes to matters of procedure.

North Carolina becomes the tenth state to ratify the Articles of Confederation.

25 April 1778:
Saturday. At Versailles, Count de Vergennes writes to Benjamin Franklin, "I have made known to the king, sir the substance of the letter which you did me the honor of writing to me yesterday, and I am directed by his majesty to express to you the satisfaction he has experienced from the information which you have communicated on your conferences with Mr. Hartley. The grand principle of the English policy has always been to excite divisions, and it is by such means she expects to sustain her empire; but it is not upon you, nor upon your colleagues that she can practice such art with success. I entertain the same sentiments of confidence in the United States. As to the rest, it is impossible to speak with more dignity, frankness, and firmness than you have done to Mr. Hartley ..."

26 April 1778:
Sunday. From Versailles, de Sartine writes to the Count de Vergennes, "I have received your letter of the 20th instant, accompanied by the translation of the representations addressed to you by the American commissioners relative to the fears of the merchants of Bordeaux and Nantes, who have hitherto transacted business with America, and by the request of the commissioners with regard to the protection of that commerce. For nearly a month the French coast along the bay of Biscay, and a part of that on the Channel, have been guarded by twenty frigates and corvettes, distributed in the open sea, as well as along the entrances of harbors and rivers. Those stations at the latter places take under their protection the French and American ships which sail from those points, and convoy them beyond the capes. If they meet any vessels inward bound, they convoy them to the entrance of the harbors. The frigates stationed farther out at sea are employed in chasing away the Guernsey and Jersey privateers which are

a great interruption to commerce. The same orders have been issued in the Colonies where the frigates there stationed convoy the French and American vessels from the coasts. The reports made to me assure that these orders are promptly executed, and that the protection is extended as fully to American as to French vessels."

27 April 1778:
        Monday. At headquarters Valley Forge, Washington writes to the President of Congress thanking him for the resolution of the Congress that renewed and extended to 10 August 1778 the powers vested in the General by them on the occasion of the British attack and capture of Philadelphia. He goes on to express in language as follows, "... and they may rest assured that whatever powers are entrusted to me, shall be unvariably directed to promote the interest of these States. If in any case there should be a misapplication or failure in the execution, there will be the effect of mistake and not of design."
        Congress resolves that the Board of War and Ordinance transmit proper instructions to General Heath by which he is to send the treasurer the hard money (specie) belonging to the United States.

28 April 1778:
        Tuesday. At York, Henry Laurens writes to his son John, in which he says, "I wish the States & the People of the States could be roused to fill a reputable Army. You have thousands of men scattered over the country in the character of servants to Officers. Why are not they collected. There is amazing laxness of discipline somewhere or perhaps too generally in your army."
        Major General Gates is empowered to appoint two more officers from the line to act as aides-de-camp.

29 April 1778:
        Wednesday. At headquarters, Valley Forge, Washington writes to Major General William Heath, "It is astonishing that officers will, in direct violation of the Resolution of Congress, my recruiting instructions, and the most evident principles of policy, founded in experience, persevere in enlisting deserters from the British Army. Supposing it might be done in any case, yet there is every possible objection to the measure in the instance of deserters from General Burgoyne's Army. These troops did not originally come into our hands through choice, they were conquered, brought to our possession by compulsion. Those apprehensions of punishment in case of return, which may operate on the minds of deserters, they feel nothing of. So far from the most distant chance of punishment they will be applauded by the commanders of the British Army, for their fidelity and attachment to their prince ..."

The Congress elects three of its members to serve on the Marine Committee in the place of those who are absent—Nathaniel Scudder, George Plater, and Thomas Adams.

30 April 1778:
    Thursday. At headquarters, Valley Forge, Washington writes to Governor of New York, George Clinton, "I should be extremely sorry if the incursions you apprehend, should take place. From the defeats and disappointments the Indians met with the last campaign, when pushed on and supported by a formidable regular army, we had reason to hope, that they would remain peaceable, at least for some time. However, there is no reasoning with precision from the past to the future conduct of these people. Their own disposition to ravage, with the artifices of the enemy may possibly induce them to commit some outrages in order to alarm and divert a part of our force, from the points at which it will be materially wanted. Securing the north river is an object of the first magnitude and appears to be a principal one in the opinion of Congress, yet his [Gates] instructions extend to the protection of the northern and western frontiers of the State against any ravages that may be attempted."
    Washington writes to Henry Laurens, "I think with you, that a most important crises is now at hand; and that there cannot be too much wisdom in all our Councils for conducting our affairs to a safe and happy issue. There should in my opinion, be a full representation of the States in Congress, which I have often regretted has not been the case for a long time past. I also concur with you in sentiment, that gentlemen any where, whose abilities might be of essential service in case of treaty with the British Commissioners, ought to be called forth for the purpose. It will be a work of infinite importance and the result may lead to happiness or to misery; to freedom or to slavery."
    Washington writes to the President of Congress, "The extensive ill consequences arising from a want of uniformity in discipline and manoeuvres throughout the Army, have long occasioned me to wish for the establishment of a well organized inspectorship, and the concurrence of Congress in the same views as induced me to set on foot a temporary institution, which from the success that has hitherto attended it, gives me the most flattering expectations, that will, I hope obtain their approbation."
    Washington is, of course, talking about Baron Von Steuben and highly recommends him to the Congress and that they extend to him the rank of Major General.
    In York, the Congress passes a resolution that no commissioned officer who shall be honored with a brevet commission shall be entitled, by virtue of such brevet, to any higher rank in the unit to which he belongs than he held before. That the brevet rank entitles him only to serve in detachments from the line, or in courts martial.

<u>1 May 1778:</u>
    Friday. At headquarters, Valley Forge, Washington writes to the Board of War, discussing prisoner exchange and the state of the armourer (sic) department, adding, "I make no doubt but every thing has been done and will be done to put matters in the best state of preparation. I am exceedingly glad to hear that so active a man as Mr. [William] Henry [Superintendent of Armourers] is universally represented to be, has succeeded Butler in the Armourer's department, which had been long shamefully conducted."
    Congress orders $150,000 be paid John Collins for him to transmit to the governor of the state of Rhode Island, Nicholas Cooke, at Cooke's request as an advancement for payment of military provisions that the state supplies to the Continental forces in the state.

<u>2 May 1778:</u>
    Saturday. In Manheim, Pennsylvania, Robert Morris writes to James Lovell, reporting Simeon Deane's arrival at Lancaster from France. Deane delivered five packets directed to Morris as chairman of the Committee of Foreign Affairs. Morris is hoping there might be some private letters enclosed, but there are none. He forwards the papers to Lovell, also a member of the committee.
    At Valley Forge, news of the French Treaty of Alliance reaches headquarters. Washington is pleased, and plans to set aside an occasion to formally acknowledge this important event and inform the troops.

<u>3 May 1778:</u>
    Sunday. In York, John Banister writes to his brother-in-law, Theodorick Bland, Jr., reporting the arrival of the Treaties of Alliance and of Amity and Commerce between France and the United States. Banister goes on to outline the contents of these treaties, noting the mutual responsibilities of the two nations. Many very similar letters are sent to persons throughout the states, and the information is published in many newspapers.

<u>4 May 1778:</u>
    Monday. The Congress consider the two Treaties between the King of France and the United States of America, and after having them fully read and discussed, ratifies both. There is a Treaty of Amity and Commerce, containing 33 articles; a form of the passports, according to the 27th Article; a Treaty of Alliance, Eventual and Defensive containing 12 articles; and an Act Separate and Secret. A committee of three is chosen to prepare the form of ratification. They also pass a resolution, "That this Congress entertain the highest sense of the magnanimity and wisdom of his most Christian majesty, so strongly exemplified in the treaty of amity and commerce, and the treaty of alliance, entered into on the part of his majesty, with these United

States at Paris, on the 6th day of February last; and the commissioners, or any of them, representing these States at the court of France, are directed to present the grateful acknowledgements of this Congress to his most Christian majesty, for his truly magnanimous conduct respecting these states, in the said generous and disinterested treaties, and to assure his majesty, on the part of this Congress, it is sincerely wished that the friendship so happily commenced between France and these United States may be perpetual."

5 May 1778:
Tuesday. Congress approves that a passport be granted Mrs. Prevost, wife of Brigadier Prevost, Commander in East Florida, and now at Augustine (St. Augustine), that she may return to Europe.

The committee appointed to prepare the form of ratification of the treaties agreed to, approved, and ratified yesterday, bring in their report, which is read and approved. Six copies are to be made for transport by different conveyances.

After a number of weeks of working with the American troops, on intensive training, and very effectual forming, marching, maneuvering, firing, and assembling, von Steuben is rewarded by the Congress, upon recommendation of Washington, to be the inspector general of the Army with the rank of major general.

At Valley Forge, Major General Charles Lee, who has been exchanged for the British Major General Richard Prescott, returns to duty and enters the encampment to present himself for assignment to General Washington. Lee has been seen by many as the most experienced and knowledgeable officer in the American Army. He is not, as will soon appear.

6 May 1778:
Wednesday. At Valley Forge, a Feu de Joie (a volley musket firing from end to end, in rapid sequence along a line of troops) to celebrate the news of the French alliance is performed at parade, reviewed by Washington, Lafayette, Stirling, and Greene.

General Orders state "The Commander-in-Chief being more desirous to reclaim than to punish offenders and willing to show mercy to those who have been misled by designing traitors and that as many as can may participate the pleasures of the truly joyful day is pleased to pardon William McMarth of the artillery and John Morrel of Colo. Henry Jackson's Regiment now under sentence of death and orders their immediate release from confinement, hoping that gratitude to his clemency will induce them in future to behave like good soldiers." The parole is given as France and the countersigns are Franklin and Frederick.

7 May 1778:

Thursday. Congress resolves that the Commissioners appointed for the Courts of Spain, Tuscany, Vienna, and Berlin should live in such style and manner as supports the dignity of their public character. They are empowered to draw bills of exchange upon the commissioners at the Court of Versailles.

At Bordentown, New Jersey, British Major John Maitland leads a light infantry battalion, on flat boats, convoyed by a schooner and a brig, up the Delaware River to sink, burn, and destroy the American vessels there. He is very successful, destroying 44 vessels, including the frigates *Washington* and *Effingham*, along with tents, tar, pitch, and other valuable stores.

8 May 1778:

Friday. The Congress prepares an address to the citizens of the United States, recommending that it be read by every minister of the Gospel in their places of worship. It is a wonderful exposition of the ideals of American freedom and liberty.

Henry Clinton arrives at Philadelphia, to take over as commander of the British forces in America.

At Valley Forge, General George Washington holds a conference, mandated by Congress, of all the Army's highest ranking officers. Gates, Greene, Stirling, Mifflin, Lafayette, de Kalb, Armstrong, Steuben, Knox, and Duportail are brought together to solicit their views on the coming campaign. This assembly recommends that the army remain on the defensive and await events.

9 May 1778:

Saturday. From Paris, Arthur Lee writes to the Committee of Foreign Affairs, "Spain, and the German powers are yet undecided with regard to us. I do not think our enemies will succeed with Holland. We shall endeavor to establish a fund for the purposes you desire."

The Congress approves of a proclamation regarding American armed vessels. It appears that in a few cases such vessels have done violence to neutral ships, contrary to the usage and custom of nations. These actions reflect poorly upon the United States, and are to cease. Officers and seamen of the United States are to govern themselves strictly and in all things agreeably to their commissions and instructions.

10 May 1778:

Sunday. At headquarters, Valley Forge, Washington writes to Richard, Lord Howe, "I would take the liberty to offer your Lordship my request for the release of John Chance, who is a prisoner on board one of the ships under your Lordship's command. In the case of this man, I find myself peculiarly interested, as his long suffering and present confinement may perhaps, in some degree, be ascribed to me." (Because of the long delay in the transmittal of prisoner exchange protocols.)

In York, Jonathan Bayard Smith writes to George Bryan, reporting that the Congress has ratified the treaties between France and the United States. He also reports upon the destruction of the Continental currency issued from 22 June 1775 of $20,010,000 dollars, to be replaced by Loan Office Certificates.

11 May 1778:
Monday. The Congress is presented with a problem of a captured Portuguese vessel, a snow *Our lady of Mt. Carmel and St. Anthony* (a type of two masted square sail sailing vessel, something like a brig with an auxiliary mast abaft the main mast, usually with a trysail, rather than a square sail and a boom), en route from the Brazils to Fayal on the high seas by an armed American vessel. The snow is taken into Massachusetts, and the master sent home in another vessel, at his request. The cargo of the snow is perishable and damage may arise from continuing at dock or even returning to her destination. The Congress resolves that Massachusetts, with all speed, make sale of the cargo of the snow and the vessel and deposit the net proceeds thereof to the United States. If an owner steps forward he may recover such funds upon proper proof of same.

12 May 1778:
Tuesday. At headquarters, Valley Forge, Washington writes to Governor William Livingston of New Jersey, "There are several matters, which render the drawing together a large body of forces, just at this time, impracticable. The deranged state of the Commissary and Quartermaster Generals' departments, with which you are well acquainted, are sufficient obstacles. Everything is doing, to put the Qur.Mastership upon a proper and respectable footing; and I hope the new Commissary General, with the assistance of the States, will be able to make such arrangements, that we shall, some time hence, be able to victual a very considerable body of men."

Washington writes to the President of Congress, "I have appointed Genl. [Lachlan] McIntosh to command at Fort Pitt in the Western Country for which he will set out, as soon as he can accommodate his affairs."

The Board of War is directed to make inquiry into the causes of the loss of boats on the Ohio.

In Philadelphia, Ambrose Serle, writes in his Journal, "Lord Howe after breakfast, called me aside, and gave me a long & full account of the discussed which government had conceived from his Brother's conduct, and of his own intentions to resign his Command, though the Admiralty had expressed strong wishes for his continuing in a service, where he had been so eminently & undeniably useful. He then told me, that as the Commission, we came out with, was now at an end, our attendance in this Country was no longer necessary, & therefore that Mr. Strachey would embark with the General, and that I might sail in the next Ship-of-War for England ..."

13 May 1778:
     Wednesday. At headquarters, Valley Forge, Washington writes to William Heath, "The Court of Versailles has announced her alliance, with the United States, to that of London, upon which the ambassadors were immediately withdrawn from the respective Courts. The Houses of Lords and Commons have addressed the King upon the subject, and seem to resent the matter highly. We have this by a Philadelphia paper of the 9th. A war I suppose will be the inevitable and speedy consequence."
     Washington writes to Major General Philemon Dickinson, "With our present force it is impossible to take a fixed post in Jersey. I first detached Colo. [Israel] Shreve with his own Regt. Since that I have reinforced him with Colo. [Matthias] Ogden's, and as my numbers increase here, I shall strengthen the party in Jersey. They must for the present content themselves with moving about and acting according to circumstances."
     General Washington forwards a letter from General Howe to the Congress regarding an exchange of prisoners. The same is referred to a committee of three; William Duer, Richard Henry Lee, and Charles Carroll.

14 May 1778:
     Thursday. At York, Richard Henry Lee and James Lovell for the Committee for Foreign Affairs write to the commissioners at Paris, "Gentlemen: Our affairs have now a universally good appearance. Everything at home and abroad seems verging towards a happy and permanent period. We are preparing for either war or peace. For although we are fully persuaded that our enemies are wearied, beaten, and in despair, yet we shall not presume too much on that persuasion, and the rather, because it is our fixed determination to admit no terms of peace but such as are full in character with the dignity of independent States, and consistent with the spirit and intention of our alliances on the Continent of Europe."

15 May 1778:
     Friday. The Congress, having received information regarding infractions of the convention of Saratoga by British officers who, it is reported, are compelling some of these British prisoners to bear arms against the United States, since their return to Canada, requests that Governor Clinton look into this matter. Congress has never fully accepted the convention articles, feeling that the arrangements Horatio Gates made with Burgoyne are much too lenient.

16 May 1778:
  Saturday. At Valley Forge, disgusted with the lack of performance by the clothier general, Washington writes to James Mease, "I am now to inform you that the complaints against your department have become so loud and universal, that I can no longer dispense with your presence in camp to give satisfaction on the many subjects of discontent that prevail in the army from that source, and to relieve me from those difficulties in which I am involved in by your absence."
  Congress orders $100,000 to be delivered to Dr. Jonathan Potts, for use in the hospitals of the middle district.

17 May 1778:
  Sunday. At headquarters, Valley Forge, Washington writes to the Marquis de Lafayette, in which he reviews an issue that has arisen among some officers making objection to the taking of an oath. Those objections were; 1.) The oath seems an indignity to some, 2.) Some concerned about rank do not wish to swear an oath since they feel it would be improper if promoted, 3.) Some fear the taking of an oath might debar them from resigning, 4.) The taking of the oath might restrain them in a change of the army. Washington concludes that these objections are not valid because the oath itself is not new, it is substantially the same as required in all governments and does not imply any indignity. Nor would it effect any unsettled rank of the officers, or their resignations, and the fourth objection reveals the impropriety of the whole proceeding.
  Washington writes to Philip VanRensselaer, Commissary of military stores at Albany, "Sir: General Knox informs me that he gave you directions to send from Albany two thousand arms with bayonets for the use of this army; as we are in the most pressing want of these articles, I am to desire that you will exert yourself to have them forwarded with all possible expedition and to commit them to the care of an attentive, active person in your department, who may provide as well for security as dispatch in their transportation."
  General Orders give the parole as Ramapan and the countersigns as Rochester and Rome.

18 May 1778:
  Monday. From Braintree, Massachusetts, Abigail Adams writes to her husband John , "Difficult as the day is, cruel as this war has been, separated as I am, on account of it, from the dearest connection in life, I would not exchange my country for the wealth of the Indies, or be any other than an American, though I might be queen or empress of any nation upon the globe."
  At Valley Forge, Washington assigns a large detachment of 2,200 men and five guns to Maj. Gen. Lafayette, all of whom parade and march off from camp for an expedition to Barren Hill, Pennsylvania.

In occupied Philadelphia, the British officers put on an elaborate, massive, and very expensive, show for their departing commander, Sir William Howe. It is called the Meschianza.

19 May 1778:
Tuesday. Lafayette takes up his position at Barren Hill near Matson's Ford in Montgomery County, Pennsylvania. He is about equidistant between his Valley Forge support and the British in Philadelphia. The British are not unaware of this force, and plan an attack. They march out in the evening with plans to encircle the American position, pin them against the Schuylkill River and attack in the morning.

20 May 1778:
Wednesday. At Barren Hill, the British, under Howe, Clinton, Grey, and Grant, with a total of about 5,000 men and fifteen guns, heavily outnumbering Lafayette's force, attack at dawn. Grant and Grey's units quickly overrun the militia units, but a company of American riflemen provide a needed delaying action. Aware that he is outnumbered, Lafayette, withdraws by a back road, that the British have not scouted, and departs with all his troops from what might otherwise have been a serious loss.

The British were, as usual, overconfident and foolish. The Americans were cool, and their training under von Steuben surely bolstered their actions this day. The Americans camp near Swede's Ford. The British march back to Philadelphia, a 40-mile return journey that exhausts the men, for no good purpose.

21 May 1778:
Thursday. At Passy, John Adams writes to Samuel Adams, "The situation of the general affairs of Europe is still critical and of dubious tendency. It is still uncertain whether there will be war between the Turks and the Russians, between the Emperor and the King of Prussia, and indeed between England and France, in the opinion of many people. My own conjecture, however, is that a war will commence and that soon."

Lafayette re-crosses the Schuylkill River with his detachment, and marches back to Barren Hill, now abandoned by the British.

22 May 1778:
Friday. At headquarters, Valley Forge, Washington writes to Brig. Gen. Charles Scott, "Sir: I want to obtain a very particular account of the number of men who have come from Virginia under the old and new draught law. You are therefore to order the commanding Officers of the different Regiments in your Brigade to make you, as soon as possible, an exact return of the men in their respective corps who came out as draughts or

substitutes, distinguishing those of the old from the new. If you can obtain a return of those who either died or deserted after they joined their regiments, I should be glad to have it. After the returns have been made to you, be pleased to examine them carefully, and send them to me. Let the County be mentioned from whence the draughts came."

Washington writes to Brigadier General William Smallwood, "It is very far from improbable that the enemy will endeavor to fulfill their threats against your post. I am informed they have now a considerable detachment actually embarked, which they give out as intended for New York; but which may be destined against you. I am convinced you will be at all times upon your guard, and will omit no precaution to prevent a surprise. In case any attempt should be made as it will in all likelihood be with a force superior to your own, I would wish you to embrace the safest part and not materially risk your detachment, for objects of inferior magnitude. I commit, however, the whole to your own prudence."

The Congress resolves that the legislatures of the respective states enact laws for exempting from militia duty all persons who have deserted or shall hereafter desert from the British army or navy during the present war. The members of the Congress have been made aware of the unsteady adherence of such persons to the cause.

23 May 1778:
Saturday. At headquarters, Valley Forge, Washington writes to Colonel Israel Shreve, "The enemy seem to be preparing for some general movement: among others, it is possible they may make a push across the Jerseys, towards Amboy. You will keep the troops under your command in the most compact order, to act according to circumstances. In case they [the British] should make a general embarkation, you will not enter the City; but hold yourself in readiness to march on receiving orders from me for that purpose."

The Barren Hill detachment, under Lafayette, having accomplished their purpose of dissuading the British from further foraging, returns to Valley Forge.

24 May 1778:
Sunday. At Passy, John Adams writes to the Commercial Committee, "Gentlemen: I find that the American affairs on this side of the Atlantic are in a state of disorder very much resembling that which is so much to be regretted on the other, and arising as I suppose, from the same general causes, the novelty of the scenes, the inexperience of the actors, and the rapidity with which great events have succeeded each other. Our resources are very inadequate to the demands made upon us, which are perhaps unnecessarily increased by several irregularities of proceeding."

25 May 1778:
        Monday. At Passy, Benjamin Franklin writes to David
Hartley, member of Parliament, old friend of Franklin's, and
minister plenipotentiary of Great Britain, "I wish to know
whether your ministers have yet come to a resolution to
exchange the prisoners they hold in England, according to the
expectations formerly given you. We have here above two
hundred, who are confined in the *Drake*, where they must be
kept, as we have not the use of prisons on shore, and where
they can not be so conveniently accommodated as we could
wish. But as the liberal discharge we have given to near five
hundred prisoners taken on your coast has wrought no
disposition to similar returns, we shall keep these and all we
take hereafter till your counsels become more reasonable."

26 May 1778:
        Tuesday. At headquarters, Valley Forge, Washington writes
to Maj. Gen. Horatio Gates, "In my letters to the Board of War
some time ago, I informed them that I should draw about 4000
stand from the eastward and Albany for the use of this Army,
and that I had ordered a sufficient number to be left on the
other side of the North River for the Eastern Levies. General
Knox informs me, that he has left 3000 stand for that purpose.
There are now at least 2500 men consisting of those whose
arms are out of repair, and the Levies of New York, New Jersey,
Pennsylvania, and Maryland, who are unable to do duty for
want of arms. The 10th. Carolina Regiment lately arrived at
camp, have not a musket. I therefore desire that 728 stand may
be immediately sent down, and that all the arms which General
Knox by my orders directed to be sent from Springfield and
Albany to this quarter may come on without the least delay.
You will consider the above as an order not to be dispensed
with in the present situation of affairs."
        Congress asks the quartermaster general to furnish Baron
von Steuben with two good horses for his use.

27 May 1778:
        Wednesday. At sea off the North American coast, HMS
Trident, with the three Carlisle commissioners and Lieutenant
General Charles Cornwallis on board, is hailed by the brig HMS
Stanley, informing the former that both Howe and Clinton are
now not in New York, but in Philadelphia. Thus, they sail for
that port.
        Congress orders that $200,000 be paid to Joseph Nourse,
paymaster to the Board of War and Ordinance, for transmittal
to William Palfrey, paymaster general, for the use of that
department. The Congress also adjusts the establishment of the
American Army. Each battalion of infantry is to consist of nine
companies. The strength of each company and the pay of each
officer and enlisted man are set forth in a table.

28 May 1778:
Thursday. The Congress increases the size of Major Henry Lee's Corps of Light Dragoons from two troops to three. One of the army's major weaknesses has been it's inability to quickly learn, and then transmit, information about enemy actions to higher headquarters. Horsemen help, because cavalry are the eyes of an army. They can range far and wide, sometimes in small patrols, seeking out the enemy, and quickly reporting his whereabouts to higher authority.

29 May 1778:
Friday. At Valley Forge, Washington writes to Governor George Clinton, "I am happy to find by a letter from General Schuyler of the 22nd, which came to hand last night, that the Indian Nations, which had discovered an unfriendly disposition, seem to be well affected, and to afford grounds to hope for a friendly alliance between us. If this can be effected, or we can only keep them from falling upon our frontiers it will be a fortunate circumstance; as we may not only then employ nearly the whole of the Continental Force wherever Sir Henry Clinton's movements require it ... That the enemy mean to evacuate Philadelphia, is almost reduced to a certainty. It is as much so as an event can be that is contingent. Their baggage and stores are nearly, if not all embarked, and from our intelligence, there is reason to conclude that many days will not elapse before they abandon it. All accounts concur, that New York will be the place of their first destination. Whether they will move by sea or land cannot be ascertained; but the weight of circumstances is in favor of the latter."
The Congress grants the prayer of some men who have brought the sloop *Tryal* into Beaufort, North Carolina, that the sums adjudged to the use of the United States may be given up to the use of the litigants.

30 May 1778:
Saturday. At headquarters, Valley Forge, Washington prepares instructions to Major General Charles Lee, "Sir: Poor's, Varnum's, and Huntington's Brigades are to march in one division under your command to the North River. The Quartermaster General will give you the route, encampments, and halting days to which you will conform as strictly as possible to prevent interfering with other troops and that I may know precisely your situation on every day. Leave as few sick and lame on the road as possible such as are absolutely incapable of marching with you are to be committed to the care of proper officers with directions to follow as fast as their condition will allow. Be strict in your disciple, suffer no rambling, keep the men in their ranks and the officers with their divisions, avoid pressing horses, as much as possible and punish severely every officer or soldier who shall presume to press without proper authority. Prohibit the burning of fences,

in a word you are to protect the persons and property of the inhabitants from every kind of insult and abuse. Begin your marches at four o'clock in the morning at latest that they may be over before the heat of the day, and that the soldiers may have time to cook, refresh, and prepare for the ensuing day."

John Wentworth, Jr. a delegate from New Hampshire, attends, and takes his seat in the Congress.

A band of about 300 Iroquois Indians, instigated by British leaders, attack and burn the settlement of Cobleskill, New York, in a terror assault upon the frontier settlements. Many of these Indians are living in and near Fort Niagara, located on the east side of the Niagara River near its mouth at Lake Ontario. From this fort, where the British have a depot for Indian goods, a great number of Indian raids begin.

31 May 1778:
Sunday. At headquarters, Valley Forge, Washington writes to John Augustine Washington "I am mistaken if we are not verging fast to one of the most important periods that ever America saw; doubtless before this reaches you, you will have seen the draughts of two bills intended to be enacted into Laws, and Lord North's speech upon the occasion; these our accounts from Philadelphia say, will be immediately followed by the commissioners; and Lord Amherst, Admiral Keppel, and General Murray are said to be the Commissioners. These gentlemen I presume, are to move in a civil and military line, as Genl. Howe is certainly recalled, and report is, Lord Howe also. Be this as it may, it will require all the skill, the wisdom, and policy, of the first abilities of these states, to manage the helm, and steer with judgment to the haven of our wishes through so many shelves and rocks, as will be thrown in our way. This, more than ever, is the time for Congress to be replete with the first characters [Washington notes quite correctly that the quality of many current members of the Congress is not up to the abilities of earlier members.] in every state, instead of having a thin Assembly, and many States totally unrepresented, as is the case at present."

1 June 1778:
Monday. In Paris, Arthur Lee writes to the Committee of Foreign Affairs, "The appearance of things between this country and Great Britain, and the Emperor and the King of Prussia has been so long hostile, without an open rupture, that it is not easy to say when either war will begin. The King of Prussia has found it so necessary to cultivate the aid of Hanover, Hesse, Brunswick, etc., that he has declined receiving your deputy or following the example of France, as he promised."

2 June 1778:
Tuesday. At headquarters, Valley Forge, Washington writes to the Board of General Officers, "Gentlemen: The business of

your meeting this morning is to take into consideration and report your opinion concerning Lt. Colonel DuPlessis' claim of rank and service in the corps of artillery, to which he was annexed by an order of Congress: Colonel DuPlessis will produce to the Board the papers on which his pretensions are founded. There are herewith my answer to a memorial from the officers of Artillery, on this subject, and a second memorial from them in reply. In the issue to which the matter is now brought, whatever may be contained in my answer, can only be considered as declarative of my opinion, and can have no influence in deciding the question. I wish to have the sentiments of the Board accurately and explicitly, as to the nature and operation of Mr. DuPlessis' appointment, specifying the particular species of service, in which he ought to be employed in the corps of Artillery, in giving which they will no doubt pay proper attention to former decisions of a similar kind."

Washington writes to the President of Congress, "I sincerely wish the Legislatures of the various States had passed Laws, adopting the generous policy, recommended by Congress in their Resolution of the 23rd of April. (For which see the sketch for that date). I am assured by authority not to be questioned, that for want of this, hundreds, nay, thousands of people, and among them valuable artisans, with large quantities of goods will be forced from Philadelphia, who otherwise would willingly remain." Major General Horatio Gates, commander in the Northern Department, guarding the Hudson Highlands, and the numerous small fortifications up and down the river, is requesting a deputy adjutant general. The Congress elects Colonel William Malcolm to the post.

3 June 1778:
Wednesday. At Passy, John Adams writes to his wife, Abigail, "It would be endless to attempt a description of this country. It is one great garden. Nature and art have conspired to render everything here delightful. Religion and government, you will say, ought to be excepted. With all my heart. But these are no afflictions to me, because I have well fixed it in my mind as a principle, that every nation has a right to that religion and government which it chooses, and as long as any people please themselves in these great points, I am determined they shall not displease me."

4 June 1778:
Thursday. In Quebec, Captain Walter Butler prepares a report to Sir Guy Carleton regarding his trip to Niagara. In it he states that the six nations (Iroquois) seem well disposed to the Crown. He also says that raids are planned upon the frontier settlements.

At York, the Congress, considering the problems of safety and property protection that might ensue from the expected British evacuation of Philadelphia, resolves, "That should the city of Philadelphia be evacuated by the enemy, it will be expedient and proper for the Commander-in-Chief to take effectual care that no insults, plunder, or injury of any kind, may be offered to the inhabitants of the said city. That in order to prevent public or private injury from the operations of ill disposed persons, the General be directed to take early and proper care to prevent the removal, transfer, or sale of any goods, wares, or merchandise in possession of the inhabitants of the said city, until the property of the same shall be ascertained by a joint committee, consisting of persons appointed by Congress and of persons appointed by the supreme executive council of the State of Pennsylvania, to wit, so far as to determine, whether any, or what part thereof may belong to the king of Great Britain or to any of his subjects."

5 June 1778:
Friday. The Congress, concerned about the incomplete and sometimes unavailable records of their former actions, wishes to examine and extract the resolutions from their journals. The secretary is ordered to deliver to the auditor general all the journals of the Congress required for the extracting of such resolutions. This will provide the delegates with a ready and easy reference as future debates on the variety of subjects they deal with are brought up for discussion, modification, or amendment.

6 June 1778:
Saturday. In York, Pennsylvania, Thomas Heyward, Jr., a delegate from the state of South Carolina, attends and takes his seat in the Congress.
Letters are received from Lord Richard Howe and Lieutenant General Henry Clinton stating that they are two of the commissioners appointed by the Parliament, on the Carlisle Commission, to discuss the possible means of a peace between Britain and her colonies.

7 June 1778:
Sunday. In York, Josiah Bartlett, a delegate to the Congress from New Hampshire, writes to his wife Mary, "Yesterday Congress Receivd [sic] letters from Lord Howe & Genl. [sic] Clinton informing us that they were two of the Commissioners appointed by Parliament to Settle the Dispute with America. But as it appears by the act of Parliament which they sent us they are not authorised [sic] to acknowledge our Independence I Suspect a peace will not soon take place tho [sic] I believe that the fighting Business is chiefly over."

8 June 1778:
Monday. At headquarters, Valley Forge, Washington writes to Major General Nathanael Greene, "As the removal of the troops from General Smallwood's command will leave our stores at the Head of Elk (now Elkton, Maryland) exposed, and their only protection will be such as they may derive from the Militia of the country; you are without loss of time to have everything of value in your magazines thereabouts, transported to the most convenient place for the purpose of the Army. As Genl. Smallwood with his Brigade is expected in Camp this afternoon, you will give immediate orders for marking his ground."

Washington writes to William Fitzhugh, "We have been in daily expectation of an evacuation of the City of Philadelphia, why it has not taken place before this, as the baggage, stores, and everything else belonging to the enemy is on board transports I cannot undertake to say unless the arrival of the long talked of Commissioners has been the cause. These gentlemen have at length appeared in the characters of Lord Carlisle, Govr. Johnstone, and Mr. William Eden."

The Congress resolves that a company of foot be raised in Northumberland County, Pennsylvania, for its defense, and the assistance of its neighboring counties, against the Indians who may attack the frontiers in this northern area of the state. The troops so organized are to be local militia forces, and as such will be subject to local military authority, not Continental officers.

9 June 1778:
Tuesday. At Paris, Arthur Lee writes to the Committee of Foreign Affairs, "The British ministry have agreed to an exchange of prisoners with us, by which we shall immediately release upwards of two hundred. War is not commenced in Germany, but is talked of as inevitable. The deputy of Congress for Vienna is at his destination, to feel the disposition of that court. But I understand that their attention is so engaged with the approaching war that other propositions proceed slowly."

In Philadelphia, Ambrose Serle, writes in his Journal, "At a meeting, which Loring our Commissary held with Boudinot the Rebel Commissary, it was this day agreed, that we should receive in exchange above 2200 of our men, which were due to us upon the Cartel Account from the Rebels; but none of them belonging to the Convention, made with Genl. Burgoyne."

10 June 1778:
Wednesday. At headquarters, Valley Forge, Washington writes to Brig. Gen. Lachlan McIntosh, "I am sorry to find that more vigorous measures have not been pursued for promoting the objects of your command. From the apprehensions which seemed to prevail of inroads by the Savages and the desire to repel them, I hoped by this, that things would have been in a

much better train. I assure you, Sir, I would willingly give you every justifiable aid from this Army. At present, the situation of affairs will not permit my doing more than what I have already, The enemy are yet in Philadelphia with a respectable force, and ours but very little if any increased, since you left us. [To go to Fort Pitt] From what reason I shall not pretend to determine, but certainly there is an unaccountable kind of lethargy in most of the States in making up their quota of men. It would seem from their withholding their supplies or not sending them into the field, that they consider the war as quite at an end. Colo. [Daniel] Brodhead will march tomorrow with his Regiment, and Major Campbell in consequence of your request will also set out to serve with you."

The Congress writes again to the several states to meet their quotas of men for the reinforcement of the army, and to exercise their powers to effect the embargo on provisions wanted by the army, so as to reduce the demands upon the treasury.

11 June 1778:
Thursday. Information received by the Congress from Philip Schuyler indicates that the cruelties lately exercised by the savages on the frontiers of New York, Pennsylvania, and Virginia are the commencement of an Indian war which threatens, with extensive devastation, the frontiers of these United States. The Indian nations identified as carrying on these incursions are the Senecas, Cayugas, Mingoes, and Wyandots, acting contrary to the voice of their nations. With the presence of Mr. Butler and Mr. Magee, British agents working with the Indians, it appears incontestably that this cruel war has been industriously instigated, and is still being prosecuted with unrelenting perseverance by the principle officers in the service of the King of Great Britain including Lt. Colonel Hamilton, commanding officer of the garrison of Detroit. The Congress resolves that there be an expedition to reduce the garrison of Detroit and to compel the Indian nations now in arms to come to terms of peace.

12 June 1778:
Friday. At headquarters, Valley Forge, Washington writes to Horatio Gates, "Whether the intention of the enemy is to make the present campaign offensive or defensive, time alone must discover. But if the former, I cannot think they mean to operate against the Eastern States [by which he means New England] in any manner, than by laying waste their coast, and destroying their seaport towns. They will never venture into a Country full of people, and who they have always found ready to give them the most spirited opposition. Should the North River be their object, I can, as I have mentioned in my former letters, march such a part of this Army thither, by the time they can reach it, that they will not be able to effect anything by coup de main. The arrival of the Commissioners from Great

Britain, upon the 7th instant, seems to have suspended the total evacuation of Philadelphia. The transports, except a few storeships and victuallers, have fallen down the River, and many of the troops are in Jersey, where they have thrown over a number of their horses and waggons (sic). They seem to be waiting until the Commissioners have announced themselves to Congress and found whether a negotiation under their present powers, can be brought about."

The Congress is informed that Philip Livingston, a delegate from New York and a signer of the Declaration of Independence, has died the previous night. Members resolve that the Congress will attend the funeral, in a body, this evening.

13 June 1778:
Saturday. The Congress resolves that the delegates from the states of New Hampshire, Massachusetts, and Connecticut, be requested, in the name of this Congress, to write to their respective states, setting forth the urgent necessity of their immediately raising the quota of troops by them respectively agreed upon, to be under the command of Major General Sullivan, for the relief of the State of Rhode Island, and to prevent further depredations of the enemy in that state.

14 June 1778:
Sunday. At Valley Forge, Washington writes to Colonel Thomas Hartley, "It appears to me from a consideration of the respective proceedings, that both [John] King [private] and [Christopher] Shockey [private] might be executed agreeably to their sentences [a Court Martial for desertion], without the imputation of a rigorous severity. However as the Court Martial have interposed a petition in favor of the former, which has also received a sort of countenance from Congress, by their suspending his sentence, I grant him a pardon, I also pardon Shockey, as the crime of which he has been convicted, altho' clearly proved according to the proceedings, does not seem to me to deserve death more than King's. Indeed, in the conduct of King, there were some circumstances leading to consequences of greater political criminality."

General Orders give the parole as Almanze and the countersigns as Arms and Art.

15 June 1778:
Monday. At Passy, Benjamin Franklin, Arthur Lee, and John Adams, write to de Sartine, "Whatever is due for necessaries furnished to Captain Jones by the Caisse de la Marine at Brest, either from the Magazine or for the subsistence of his people, we shall also readily and thankfully pay as soon as we have seen and approve of the accounts; but we conceive that, regularly, the communication of accounts should always precede demands of payment."

In Philadelphia, a woman who washed clothes for the Carlisle Commissioners, has heard a conversation indicating that the British intend to leave the city in a few days. She relays this intelligence to Washington through her son.

At Valley Forge, in General Orders, the parole is given as Bohemia, and the countersigns as Boston and Bolton.

General Washington reminds the Army of former orders to be in readiness to march. While he does not yet have definitive information, strong hints of what the British are up to are filtering into headquarters. It seems that they may be planning to evacuate Philadelphia.

16 June 1778:
Tuesday. The Carlisle Commission prepares a letter to the Congress which mentions France as an enemy of Britain and neglects or does not include an ackowledgement or recognition of the independence of the United States of America. The Congress resumes consideration of the letter from these commissioners, orders a reply and affirms the same, "That this Congress cannot hear any language reflecting upon the honor of his most Christian majesty, the good and faithful ally of these states." Coupled with the lack of recognition of America, this cuts off the Carlisle Commission efforts to discuss any peace proposals before they begin.

In Philadelphia, before dawn, Sir Henry Clinton, intending to evacuate the city, orders his artillery removed from the redoubts. During the day, several British regiments are ferried across the Delaware River.

Three captured British deserters are brought into camp and interrogated. They confirm that movements are afoot to ship out the heavy baggage, and, with Loyalists sailing them down the River, and to evacuate the city within the next few days.

At Valley Forge, General Orders gives the parole as Connecticut and the countersigns as Cambridge and Coventry.

17 June 1778:
Wednesday. In York, Congress resumes consideration of the draft of a letter, in answer to the letter and papers of the Carlisle Commission, as follows: "The acts of the British parliament, the commission from your Sovereign, and your letter, suppose the people of these states to be subjects of the crown of Great Britain, and are founded on an idea of dependence, which is utterly inadmissible. I am further directed to inform your Excellencies, that Congress are inclined to peace, notwithstanding the unjust claims from which this war originated, and the savage manner in which it hath been conducted; they will therefore be contented to enter upon a consideration of a treaty of peace and commerce, not inconsistent with treaties already subsisting, when the King of Great Britain shall demonstrate a sincere disposition to that purpose. The only solid proof of this disposition will be an

explicit acknowledgment of the independence of these states, or the withdrawing his fleets and armies."

The Congress orders that $600,000 be advanced to the Board of War and Ordnance for carrying on an expedition against the Indians.

In Philadelphia, more of the British and Hessian occupation troops cross the Delaware River. Heavy equipment, invalids, a number of Tories, and some supplies are shipped down the river. Thus, traveling with less baggage, with light troops, and unburdened by the sick and wounded, Sir Henry Clinton is hopeful of marching through New Jersey with his army of about 10,000 men to the safety of the British-held port of New York. By the next day he will have his entire garrison out of Philadelphia and on their way to Haddonfield, New Jersey.

At Valley Forge, Washington calls a Council of War, during which he outlines several proposals regarding how the army should deal with the expected British evacuation of Philadelphia. Major General Charles Lee opposes attacking the enemy, believing they are too strong and much too well-trained to be defeated by the Americans. He seems to be totally unaware of the transformation wrought on Washington's Continental Army by the rigorous training of von Steuben during the winter.

18 June 1778:
Thursday. At Valley Forge, Washington writes to Baron Von Steuben, granting him permission to go to York in order to review with the Congress the details of the inspector general's department. The trip will promote the service and allow Steuben to lay before the Congress such a plan of organization as will eliminate causes of disagreement and settle any misunderstanding still lingering with some of the delegates about the value of a quality inspector general department. Washington further notes, "I am perfectly satisfied with the conduct of the officers who have acted as your assistants, and think that the army has derived every advantage from the institution under you, that could be expected in so short a time. With your plan of uniting the offices of Brigade Major and Brigade Inspector, I am of opinion with you that many advantages would result from it. The taking the Brigade Majors from the line of Majors would be contrary to our present arrangement of the Army, and therefore can only be effected by the authority of Congress."

Washington learns that the British have or are finally planning to evacuate the city of Philadelphia, and orders an advance troop to scout the British route and strength.

19 June 1778:
Friday. At headquarters, Valley Forge, Washington writes to Benedict Arnold, "You are immediately to proceed to Philadelphia and take command of the troops there. The

principal objects of your command you will find specified in the enclosed resolve of Congress of the 4th instant [for which see the sketch of that date], which you will carefully execute. You will take every prudent step in your power, to preserve tranquillity and order in the city, and give security to individuals of every class and description; restraining, as far as possible, 'til the restoration of civil government, every species of persecution, insult, or abuse, either from the soldiery to the inhabitants, or among each other. I leave it to your own discretion, to adopt such measures, as shall appear to you most effectual and, at the same time, least offensive, for answering the views of Congress, to prevent the removal, transfer, or sale of any goods, wares, or merchandize (sic), in possession of the inhabitants of the city, 'til the property of them can be ascertained in the mode directed."

The American Army marches out of its winter encampment at Valley Forge in pursuit of British Lieutenant General Sir Henry Clinton. The first units to leave are the brigades of Jedediah Huntington, Enoch Poor, and James Mitchell Varnum. By about 3 o'clock, Anthony Wayne marches out with his units. Brig. Gen. William Maxwell and Colonel Daniel Morgan are instructed to harass the enemy, and proceed to find and attack their rear guard. While some information about the British whereabouts is known, Washington does not have an exact location, nor a grasp of the direction they will take.

20 June 1778:
Saturday. Washington writes to the president of the Congress, "I have the honor to inform you, that I am now advanced with the main body of the Army within ten miles of Coryell's Ferry, and shall halt to refresh the troops, for the night. Genl. Lee with the six Brigades mentioned in my former letter, will reach the ferry this evening. My last accounts from Jersey were from Genl. Dickinson, dated yesterday at 3 o'clock. These say, the enemy had then advanced to Eyerstown, three miles below Mount Holly, and were busily engaged in repairing the bridge which had been destroyed."

At York, the Congress takes up again the matter of the Articles of Confederation. Richard Henry Lee writes to John Adams, "The friends to the future happiness and glory of America are now urging the Confederation to a close, and I hope it will be signed in a few days."

21 June 1778:
Sunday. Washington, following notice of the British evacuation of Philadelphia, has broken camp at Valley Forge to catch up with and fight the British as they retreat. His troops are at Coryell's Ferry on the Delaware River, about 30 miles north and west of the British line of march.

Washington writes to the president of the Congress, reporting that some Indians of the Seneca Nation desire the release of one Astiarix, a Seneca warrior, who has been captured on the frontiers of Virginia. An exchange has been suggested and Washington is agreeable to it, but requests that the Congress will order it to be accomplished. Washington goes on to note that he has treated the Indians with civility but at the same time has warned them "... to cease hostilities against Americans and become our friends, or at least neutral, or he will turn his whole force against them as soon as he is clear of the British Army."

22 June 1778:
Monday. At headquarters in Coryell's Ferry, General Orders require that a field return of all troops is to be made by each brigade, under the inspection of the brigadiers. Commanding officers of companies will see that their men fill their canteens before they begin the march. Each brigade is to furnish twenty-five of its best marksmen, with an active, spirited officer, to join Colonel Morgan's corps of riflemen, and continue under his command until the enemy passes through the Jerseys. These orders are designed by Washington to harass and delay the enemy in their march across New Jersey, and, If possible, bring them to a general action in a battle.

At York, the Congress debates more emendations from several states to the Articles of Confederation, especially those relating to western lands.

23 June 1778:
Tuesday. George Washington is at Hopewell, New Jersey at the home of John Hunt.

General Orders state "When the general beats the order for march, all Regiments are to be ready and fall in quickly. Colonels of regiments will send to the artillery park for arms required to complete their men now on the ground fit for duty." The Americans under Maxwell are reinforced by the troops of Brig. Gen. Charles Scott, and are ordered to harass the flanks of the marching British troops. The parole is given as Philadelphia and the countersigns as Brunswick and Boston.

A British detachment seizes intact the bridge over the Crosswick Creek in New Jersey. This action, plus the British occupation of Allentown, New Jersey, the next day helps fix the route of march of the British towards New York. Rather than try the Raritan River, Clinton now selects the Sandy Hook route, which is further east and provides less opportunities for flanking attacks. He feels that his troops can beat off almost any size American attack, but he does have concern for his rather extensive baggage train, which is much more vulnerable to spoiling attacks. There is also no way in which this British commander can have detailed knowledge of the extent to which the training Von Steuben has imparted to the American Continental Army has made it much more effective. Sir Henry Clinton may get a surprise.

24 June 1778:
Wednesday. Throughout the northeastern parts of North America, this day, most folks pause in what they are doing, to view a total eclipse of the sun.

At Hunt's House, near Hopewell, General Orders require that officers are on no account to be absent from their encampment, and they are to be particularly vigilant in preventing their men from straggling.

Washington calls a Council of War to request whether to engage in an active offensive attack upon Clinton or to proceed with a more passive strategy. Charles Lee, Hamilton, and Knox vote for the passive approach, feeling that the British troops are too well-trained and too professional for the Americans to confront in a pitched battle. Nathaniel Greene, Wayne, Steuben, Duportail, and Lafayette vote for attempting a major offensive attack. The outcome of the council is to avoid a general engagement, but seek a nipping action on Clinton's flanks and rear. Colonel Charles Scott, commanding a detachment of 1,500 men is ordered to harass the enemy's left flank, while Colonel Daniel Morgan does the same to the right flank and rear.

25 June 1778:
Thursday. The Congress takes into consideration the report from the state of New Jersey upon the various sections in the Articles of Confederation and Perpetual Union, and upon motion determines to reconsider the suggestions offered by New Jersey and present them to the other states as well. This whole business of trying to gain approval and acceptance of the Articles of Confederation consumes a great part of the time and energy of the Congress throughout this year of 1778.

Washington's army is now at Kingston, but he is still unaware of Clinton's exact location. Lafayette moves to Hightstown, New Jersey, with the detachments of Maxwell, Morgan, Scott, and Wayne.

26 June 1778:
Friday. Washington is at Cranberry, New Jersey. New intelligence reports that the enemy is now moving toward Monmouth County. Colonel Charles Scott's command has been enlarged, and Maj. Gen. Lafayette is given command of this large detachment, now numbering more than 5,000 troops, to attack the British rear guard and flanks, now approaching the village of Freehold.

27 June 1778:
Saturday. General Washington is at Englishtown, New Jersey. General Orders note that "As we are now nigh the Enemy and of consequence Vigilance and Precaution more essentially necessary, the Commander in Chief desires and enjoins it upon all Officers to keep their Posts and their

soldiers compact so as to be ready to form and march at a moments warning as circumstances may require."

Although Major General Charles Lee has been quite negative about the American troops' abilities to successfully attack the British army, upon learning that the detachment assigned to Lafayette is now rather large, he requests the command of it. Having seniority of rank, Lee is given that command. Washington instructs Lee to attack the rear guard the next day, and says he will be bringing up the rest of the army in support as quickly as possible. Washington is concerned that if he does not attack the British vigorously now, he may not have another opportunity, before they are safely enclosed and protected in and near New York. The British are encamped east of Freehold, near Monmouth Court House, prepared for a defense, if necessary, or for offense, as needed, or to continue their march north and east to a place of safety under the guns of English ships.

At York, the Congress revisits the Articles of Confederation. And having received comments from New Hampshire, Massachusetts, Rhode Island, Connecticut, New York, Pennsylvania, Virginia, North Carolina, South Carolina, and Georgia, make comparison and order that a new, engrossed copy be prepared and that the delegates of the respective states lodge copies with the secretary their powers for ratifying the same. The Congress then adjourns to meet again on 2 July 1778 in Philadelphia.

28 June 1778:
Sunday. In the Wyoming Valley of Pennsylvania, Colonel Zebulon Butler, with about 300 patriot troops occupies Forty Fort. Major John Butler with a body of Tory rangers and Seneca and Delaware Indians burn a mill and take three prisoners, in a related attack just a few miles further east.

Near Freehold, about 3 o'clock in the morning, Major General Lee orders Scott's brigade towards Monmouth. Lieutenant Colonel John Laurens reports that the British are pulling out of Monmouth. The American advance corps under Colonel Daniel Morgan skirmishes with the British rear guard and right flank as they are leaving Monmouth.

Colonels Wayne, Scott, and Maxwell have been told they will attack the British left flank. However, Lee issues no definitive orders to the various units under his command, so there is little by way of co-ordinated efforts, leaving the units to engage the enemy as they are able. When Lee tries to get units into position, too many of them are in a small space with little room to deploy. Soon, the British counterattack, and some of the American units fall back to find support from other units.

Wayne scatters some British cavalry, but is not properly reinforced to attack them further. The British lunge between Wayne's unit and other American units, to attack both of the American flanks. However, the Americans quickly recover and deliver a deadly fire that halts the attacks, and forces the British back. Lee learns that there are about 1,800 British troops in these skirmishes. To him, that seems about the right size as a rear guard to protect the British forces, while Clinton makes his getaway. But, Clinton also seeks to get units in proper order to attack or defend as opportunity might be revealed.

While these units on both sides are deploying into position, Lee spots large numbers of Redcoats coming from the north down the Middletown road to the relief of their rear guard. These are the troops Clinton has ordered to return with the purpose of effecting a defeat on the scattered American units. With the increasing pressure on their fronts, some Americans begin to withdraw. Lee, who has orders to attack the British at the first opportunity, sees only units falling back, and believes the Americans are being forcefully attacked. He orders a general retreat. An artillery duel takes place, and is partially successful in slowing the British attacks.

Washington comes upon the scene, and is horrified to see his American troops in such disarray. He orders the troops to halt, brings up more artillery, reinforces the regiments and brigades, sees that the Americans return fire upon the enemy, and soon has the situation more firmly in hand. As additional American units come onto the field, Washington inserts them into gaps so as to reinforce and extend his lines. The battle rages on in the heat of the day, and numbers of troops are overcome by the extreme heat and many suffer from heat stroke.

Clinton, now feeling the pressure from the American attacks, sends for additional reinforcements from Knyphausen and Cornwallis whose troops are north on the way to Sandy Hook. Both sides are struggling to build superior forces at the point of attack in order to defeat the other. The fight continues until sunset, without a clear winner. The British break off and gather to depart the field in the dark, and will quickly march away, leaving the field to the Americans, who then claim the victory . This is the Battle of Monmouth, New Jersey. [See Fig. V-27, p. 381].

29 June 1778:

Monday. Clinton is able to withdraw his army in the small hours of the night from the field of battle and slips away to Middletown. The Americans, exhausted by yesterday's battle, rest. There are the dead and wounded to find, bury, care for, and move. Supplies are brought up, and the army awaits concentration, as the more scattered units arrive. The days are very hot.

At headquarters in the fields near Monmouth Court House, Washington writes to the president of the Congress, "Sir: I have the honor to inform you that about seven o'clock yesterday morning both Armies advanced on each other.

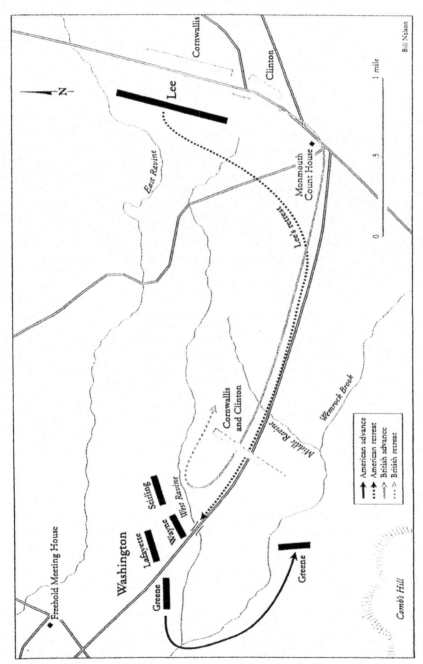

Fig. V-27: Battle of Monmouth, 28 June 1778

About noon they met on the grounds near Monmouth Court House, when an action commenced. We forced the enemy from the field and encamped on the ground. They took a strong post in our front, secured on both flanks by morasses and thick woods, where they remained 'til about 12:00 at night, and then retreated. I cannot at this time go into a detail of matters. When opportunity will permit I shall take the liberty of transmitting Congress a more particular account of the proceedings of the day."

General Orders state "The Commander-in-Chief congratulates the Army on the Victory obtained over the arms of his Brittanic Majesty yesterday and thanked most sincerely the gallant officers and men who distinguished themselves upon the occasion and such others as by their good order and coolness gave the happiest presages of what might have been expected had they come to action. General Dickinson and the militia of this State are also thanked for the noble spirit which they have shown in opposing the enemy on their march from Philadelphia and for the aid which they have given by harassing and impeding their motions so as to allow the Continental troops time to come up with them. A party consisting of two hundred men to parade immediately to bury the slain of both armies. The Officers of the American Army are to be buried with military honors due to men who have nobly fought and died in the cause of Liberty and their Country. Colo. Martin is appointed to superintend collecting the sick and wounded on the army's route through Jersey between Coryell's and Monmouth and send them to Princeton hospitals, he will call immediately at the orderly office for further orders. It is with peculiar pleasure in addition to the above that the Commander-in-Chief can inform General Knox and the Officers of Artillery that the enemy have done them the justice to acknowledge that no artillery could be better served than ours." The parole is given as Monckton and the countersigns as Bonner and Dickason.

30 June 1778:
Tuesday. Washington, aware that he cannot catch the British forces with his tired and exhausted troops, rests his men in and near Monmouth Court House. Hospitals are set up, and the wounded men, both American and British, are treated by all the available help that can be found. He sends Daniel Morgan and William Maxwell to keep an eye on the retreating British, making certain they do not turn about to attack the Americans.

Washington claims the victory, because he holds the ground. However, very many of the officers hold a view that the battle should have been and could have been a much more decisive victory for American arms, had it not been for the inability of Charles Lee to coordinate his attacks, issue orders, and follow through with the leadership, vigor, and elán expected. Lee writes to Washington, and requests a Court Martial to clear his name. Washington responds, "As soon as circumstances will permit, you shall have an opportunity of justifying yourself to the army, to Congress, to America, and to the world in general; or of convincing them that you were guilty of a breach of orders, and of misbehavior before the enemy, on the 28th instant in not attacking them as you had been directed, and in making an unnecessary, disorderly, and shameful retreat."

1 July 1778:
Wednesday. At Passy, Benjamin Franklin writes to Charles Weissenstein, "You endeavor to impress me with a bad opinion of French faith: but the instances of their friendly endeavors to serve a race of weak princes who, by their own imprudence, defeated every attempt to promote their interest, weigh but little with me, when I consider the steady friendship of France to the thirteen united states (cantons) of Switzerland, which has now continued inviolate for two hundred years."
After resting from the Battle of Monmouth, and tending to the many wounded and burying the dead from both armies, the American Army marches towards New Brunswick, New Jersey.

2 July 1778:
Thursday. The president and a number of members of the Congress meet at the state house as they return to Philadelphia. But, there not being sufficient members present for a quorum, they adjourn from day to day until 7 July 1778. This non-attendance seems to plague the Congress, as too many of its members do not adhere to their duty.
At New Brunswick, the general court martial of Major General Charles Lee sits with Major General William Alexander (Stirling) as president. The charges are: 1.) Disobedience of orders, in not attacking the enemy as instructed, 2.) Misbehavior before the enemy, in a disorderly and shameful retreat, and 3.) Disrespect to the commander-in-chief. This court martial will convene again in a few days, and begin a lengthy calling of witnesses for both the prosecution and the defense.

3 July 1778:
Friday. General George Washington makes his headquarters at Brunswick, New Jersey. The American troops wash and bathe in the Raritan River.
In the Wyoming Valley, Pennsylvania, Major John Butler and his Tory and Indian raiders attack Forty Fort, defended by American Colonel Zebulon Butler and about 300 men and boys. The Tory forces are being supported and supplied by a local Tory family, the Wintermots, who have a fort-like house nearby. The Tories set fire to the place, giving the Americans

the impression they are withdrawing. The Americans take the bait, and come out of their enclosure of Forty Fort in pursuit. They quickly run into a waiting ambush of Tories and Indians, who rush upon them after the first musket firing. The poorly trained Americans flee, are set upon by the enemy, and very many are killed, scalped, burned. This becomes known as the Wyoming Valley Massacre.

4 July 1778:
     Saturday. At headquarters, Brunswick, New Jersey, Washington writes to Governor Patrick Henry, "I take the earliest opportunity of congratulating you on the success of our arms over the British on the 28th June near Monmouth Court House. I have in a letter to Congress, given a very particular account of the manoeuvres of both Armies preceding the action, and of the action itself; and as this will be published I must take the liberty of referring you to it for the matter at large. The enemy left 245 dead upon the field and 4 Officers among whom was Colo. Monkton of the Grenadiers, the above were buried by us, but we found besides, several graves and burying holes in which they had deposited their dead before they were obliged to quit the ground. Our loss amounted to 60 rank and file killed and 130 wounded. We lost but two Officers of rank, Lt. Col. Bonner of Pennsylvania and Major [Edmund B.] Dickinson of the 1st Virginia Regt. We made upwards of one hundred prisoners while the enemy remained within our reach, but desertions since they left Philadelphia have been prodigious, I think I may without exaggeration assert that they will lose near one thousand men in this way before they quit Jersey, and that their Army will be diminished two thousand by killed, wounded, desertions, and fatigue."
     Lieutenant Colonel George Rogers Clark, with 175 Virginia volunteers, captures the British outpost at Kaskaskia, protected by a work called Fort Gage, located on the east bank of the Mississippi River, in what is now Randolph County, Illinois. The place has been under the command of a Frenchman, Sieur de Rocheblave, who, learning from Clark of the French alliance and the generous terms offered, surrenders without a shot being fired. Clark is a most enterprising officer, taking full advantage of opportunities in a timely manner.

5 July 1778:
     Sunday. At New Brunswick, New Jersey, at the home of Lucas Voorhees, a general court marital is reconvened as Major General Charles Lee attempts his own defense. Many officers are called as witness, as the case moves with the army for the next few weeks.
     Lieutenant General Sir Henry Clinton, having escaped from Washington's forces at the Battle of Monmouth Courthouse,

has marched his army north and east to Middletown, New Jersey. This morning these nearly 10,000 soldiers march down from the hills of where they have bivouacked to cross over on a pontoon-like bridge to Sandy Hook (now an Island, resulting from the storms of the previous winter). There they board flatboats and row out to transports that take them to Staten Island, from whence so many of them had started nearly a year ago to crush this colonial rebellion once and for all. Clinton believed, as did many Britons, that the capture of a major city would force the collapse of the countryside. Thus, by defeating Washington's army and capturing the capital city of Philadelphia, he expected to win. He is found to be wrong.

At Kaskaskia, Clark sends a small body of about 30 mounted men, under Captain Joseph Bowman, north to secure the small trading outposts along the east bank of the Mississippi River. They successfully capture St. Philip and Prairie du Rocher, and continue towards Cahokia, riding all night without sleep.

6 July 1778:
Monday. At Philadelphia, Titus Hosmer writes to Richard Law, reporting that he is lodged with Roger Sherman at his former place with Mrs. Cheeseman. He notes that he had a difficult time traveling first to York, and then to Philadelphia in extreme heat. He also notes that the members of the Congress, before they left York, "... had gone thro and considered all the Objections & Amendments proposed by the different states respecting the Articles of Confederation, and upon the whole, to deal impartially, rejected them all and determined to adhere to the Articles as they were settled. Nine States will ratify them as they stand, the remaining four have yet neglected to Instruct & Impower [sic] their Delegates to ratify, but it is expected they will soon do it."

Captain Bowman arrives at Cahokia (located nearly opposite St. Louis in what is now St. Clair County, Illinois, about 60 miles north of Kaskaskia), and captures the place of about 100 residents without a fight. These places help secure the Illinois country to the United States.

7 July 1778:
Tuesday. In Philadelphia, ten states appearing to make a quorum, the Congress assembles for business. They resolve unanimously "That the thanks of Congress be given to General Washington for the activity with which he marched from the camp at Valley Forge, in pursuit of the enemy; for his distinguished exertions in forming the order of battle; and for his great good conduct in leading on the attack and gaining the important victory of Monmouth over the British grand army, under the command of   Lieutenant General Sir Henry Clinton, in their march from Philadelphia to New York."

8 July 1778:
Wednesday. In Philadelphia, Henry Laurens writes to Israel
Putnam, "Until yesterday a sufficient number of States had not
been convened to form a house for business, and the
accumulation of papers between our adjournment from York
and meeting in this City has prepared more work than we shall
be able to accomplish in two or three days." Laurens also
noting to Putnam, who had enquired about the results of the
investigation into the loss of Forts Clinton and Montgomery to
the British in October 1777, while Putnam was in command,
that the Board of War has not yet unpacked their papers, and
the Report is not accessible, but he (Laurens) will procure a
copy and transmit it to Putnam as soon as it becomes available.

The Congress resolves, "That the Board of War be directed
to send for and confer with the Seneca chiefs who have lately
quitted the city of Philadelphia to inquire in what character and
with what views they have come among us, whether as
representatives or ambassadors of the Seneca nation; and
whether the Seneca nation, as such, have committed hostilities
against us, and report specially and immediately to Congress."

9 July 1778:
Thursday. At Passy, John Adams writes to James Lovell,
"There is no declaration of war as yet at London or Versailles,
but the ships of the two nations are often at sea, and there is
not the smallest doubt but war will be declared, unless Britain
should miraculously have wisdom given her to make a treaty
with the Congress like that which France has made. Spain has
not made a treaty; but be not deceived nor intimidated; all is
safe in that quarter."

In Philadelphia, Andrew Adams, a delegate from
Connecticut, attends and takes his seat in the Congress.

10 July 1778:
Friday. In Paris, France declares war against Great Britain.
This brings the alliance with America to a point of physical,
visible, and welcome support. No longer will there be a need to
"hide" the aid given by the French to the Americans. It is now
all out in the open. The major value to America is the French
naval arm. It can keep the English quite busy trying to
blockade American ports.

Washington is at Paramus, New Jersey at Mrs. Theodosia
Prevost's home. The Court Martial of Charles Lee continues, as
more officers are called to give evidence.

11 July 1778:
Saturday. In Philadelphia, a letter written the day before
from Silas Deane reports that he arrived yesterday in Delaware
Bay on board the *Languedoc*, commanded by his excellency the
Count d'Estaing, with a fleet of twelve ships of the line and four
frigates that sailed from Toulon on 10 April 1778.

At headquarters, Paramus Church, Washington writes to Maj. Gen. Horatio Gates, reporting where he is, and indicating that he intends that Baron de Kalb will move tomorrow towards the Hudson River at King's Ferry. He goes on to request Gate's opinion on the disposition of the army, considering the needs for forage and provisions. "After considering the state of the fortifications, water defences and other matters necessary to be attended to, I request to be favored with your opinion, whether the whole or a principal part of the Army with me, can remain on this side the river and be in a condition to act properly and in time, in case the enemy should direct their operations up the river and against those places; and if it can, what place will be most suitable for it to occupy as a Camp."

12 July 1778:
Sunday. Henry Laurens, instructed by Congress and with the advice and full support of General Washington and the Board of War, writes to certain states, "The present circumstances of public affairs afford me barely time for referring you to the inclosed [sic] Act of Congress of yesterday's date empowering General Washington to call on the state of New Hampshire and other States therein enumerated for such Militia as he shall think requisite for co-operating with the Count d'Estaing, commander of the French Fleet, arrived on this Coast against the Enemy, and earnestly recommending in each State the forwarding with utmost dispatch such forces as shall be called for by the Commander- in- Chief."

13 July 1778:
Monday. At Passy, Benjamin Franklin writes to David Hartley, "Enclosed is the list of our prisoners which by an accident was long in coming to us. There are supposed to be about fifteen more remaining in the hospital, whose names we have not yet obtained, and about as many who, being recovered of their wounds, have been suffered to go home to England. If you continue in the opinion of making the exchange at Calais, you will send us the papers necessary to secure the vessel that shall transport the men from the ports where they are to that place against capture; as the marching them thither would be attended with great inconveniences, and many of them might desert on the way from and apprehension of being put on board Men-of-War on their arrival in England."

14 July 1778:
Tuesday. In Philadelphia, the Sieur Conrad Alexandre Gérard having arrived and delivered to the president of the Congress a copy of a letter from "... his most Christian Majesty signed, Louis," and underneath the signature of Gravier de Vergennes. The letter is read and Congress resolves that his excellency le Sieur Gérard be received as minister plenipotentiary "... from his most Christian Majesty to the Congress of the United States of America."

At Headquarters, Paramus, New Jersey, Washington writes to the Comte d'Estaing, congratulating him upon his arrival and assuring him of the warmest wishes for success. Washington also advises d'Estaing of his own whereabouts, suggests that they work out some signals, and reports that the enemy are expecting a fleet from Cork. "With respect to the number or force of the British Ships of War, in the Port of New York, I am so unhappy as not to be able to inform you of either, with the precision I could wish as they are constantly shifting their stations. It is probable, and I hope it is the case, that your advices on the subject, from some captures you may have made, are more certain than those of Congress, or any I can offer. The number of their transports is reported to be extremely great, and I am persuaded that it is. If possible, I will obtain an accurate state of their Ships of War, which I shall do myself the honor of transmitting to you."

15 July 1778:
    Wednesday. At headquarters, Haverstraw, New York, Washington writes to Jeremiah Wadsworth, "I desire you immediately to select fifty of your best bullocks, and give orders to have two hundred sheep, if to be procured and a quantity of poultry purchased in the most convenient part of the country. They are intended as a present to the Count D'Estaing, Admiral of the French Fleet now laying off Sandy Hook. You are to send them to the coast as expeditiously as possible, and by giving notice to the Admiral, he will contrive means of taking them off. A letter from me will be delivered to you for the Count, which you are to forward with the provision. You are to write to him in your public character and offer him any assistance that he may want in victualing the Fleet under his command."

Washington writes to Captain William Dobbs, a coast pilot, requesting assistance for the French naval forces arriving of New York, pointing out that these French have no pilots with knowledge of the harbor and shoals in that area. "A considerable fleet of french men of war, chiefly Ships-of-the-Line, has just arrived at Sandy Hook, under the command of Admiral Count D'Estaing. As the Admiral is a stranger to our coast, and is come for the purpose of cooperating with us against the enemy, it is absolutely necessary that he should be immediately provided with a number of skillful pilots, well acquainted with the coast and harbors and of a firm attachment to our cause. I am assured by Governor Clinton and General McDougal, that you answer this description in every part, I must therefore request the favor of you to see me as early as possible, when I would flatter myself you will not have the smallest objection to going on board the fleet on so essential and interesting occasion. I will not at this time say anything of your pay, but I doubt not we shall readily agree on a sum that will not only be just but generous and if we should not, that your services will be liberally considered and rewarded by the

States. I wish you to come prepared to go as the situation of affairs will not admit of delay."

16 July 1778:
Thursday. At Passy, Benjamin Franklin, Arthur Lee, and John Adams write to the Council of Massachusetts, enclosing a letter from M. de Sartine, the Minister of State for the Marine of France, who has requested assistance from America with provisioning the French Islands of St. Pierre and Miquelon. The commissioners point out that it might be easier and more effective for American ships to do this, since they are much closer, than for French vessels. That would also free the French vessels to assist more directly on the American coast. They close their letter, "We have the honor to request that this letter and its enclosure may be laid before the general court, and that such measures may be taken as their wisdom shall dictate to the accomplishment of so desirable a purpose."

17 July 1778:
Friday. At headquarters, Haverstraw, New York, Washington writes to Maj. Gen. John Sullivan, "I have the pleasure to inform you, of what you have probably heard before this time, that the Admiral Count D'Estaing has arrived upon the coast, and now lays off Sandy Hook, with a fleet of twelve Ships-of-the-Line and four Frigates belonging to his most Christian Majesty. The design of this fleet is to cooperate with the American Armies, in the execution of any plans, which shall be deemed most advantageous of our mutual interests, against the common enemy. No particular plan is yet adopted, but two seem to present themselves; either an attack upon New York, or Rhode Island. Should the first be found practicable, our forces are very well disposed for the purpose; but should the latter be deemed most eligible, some previous preparations must be made. That we may therefore be ready at all points, and for all events, I desire that you may immediately apply in the most urgent manner in my name, to the States of Rhode Island, Massachusetts, and Connecticut to make up a body of 5,000 men inclusive of what you already have; establish suitable magazines of provisions, and make a collection of boats proper for a descent. You should engage a number of pilots well acquainted with the navigation of the harbor of New Port and of the adjacent coast, and have them ready to go on board upon signals which will be thrown out by the French Admiral, and of which you will be advised. That you may have the earliest intelligence of his arrival, you should establish a chain of Expresses from some commanding view upon the coast to your quarters. I need not recommend perfect secrecy to you, so far as respects any assistance from the French Fleet. Let your preparations carry all the appearance of dependence upon your own strength only. Lest you may think the number of 5,000 men two few for the enterprise, I will just hint to you, that there

are French troops on board the Fleet, and some will be detached from this Army should there be occasion."

In Philadelphia, John Penn is appointed by the Congress to be a member of the Marine Committee for the state of North Carolina.

18 July 1778:
Saturday. At headquarters, Haverstraw, New York, Washington writes to Brig. Gen. John Glover, "You are hereby directed to march the Brigade under your command to Fort Clinton on West Point, where you are to use every exertion for carrying on and completing the works, Upon your arrival, you are to instruct the troops now there, immediately to proceed to the Army and join their respective corps therein."

Washington writes to Governor William Greene of Rhode Island, noting the arrival of the French fleet under Admiral D'Estaing, and apprising Greene of the British fleet expected from Cork, indicating that it might take a course through Long Island Sound. "If this should be the case, it might answer the most valuable intentions, were the Eastern States to collect immediately all their frigates and privateers to rendezvous at some convenient place for intercepting their (the British fleet's) passage that way. Could the whole or any considerable part of this (British) fleet be taken or destroyed, it would be a fatal blow to the British army ..."

Joseph Brandt, with a band of Tories and Indians, sacks the village of Andrustown, New York.

19 July 1778:
Sunday. Washington makes his headquarters in White Plains, about seven miles from King's Ferry, New York, at Elijah Miller's House, from which place he writes to Maj. Gen. Horatio Gates, enclosing details of the arrangement of the army. Washington orders Gates to draw off three regiments to march for West Point and another to secure the Tarrytown area.

In Philadelphia, Joseph Reed, a delegate from Pennsylvania writes to his brother-in-law, Dennis DeBerdt, a Loyalist hoping to ease the terror of war and alluding to the efforts of the Carlisle Commission. Reed notes "America will endure the extremity of human woe before she will ever submit to the Sovereignty of that power [England] which has so oppressed, insulted & distressed her. My opinion is with my countrymen fully upon this point & therefore I cannot give the Commissioners the smallest encouragement. As I have not nor shall see Governor [George] Johnstone [a member of the Carlisle Commission] in his public character I shall feel a real concern if he should be found to be one in the long list of Apostates from virtue & public Honour (sic) which have blackened the English History for 50 years past. You [Great Britain] have made a sufficient sacrifice of human blood & treasure on the altar of false dignity–the further you proceed the more disgraceful will be your fall–for nothing short of omnipotence can now check the rising glory of this Western World. Your truest policy is therefore to call home your Fleets & Armies, acknowledge our Independence & as you have been such unfortunate gamesters try now for a saving game of your Islands in the West Indies & your debts in this country."

20 July 1778:
Monday. From Philadelphia, Samuel Adams writes to James Warren, referring to the actions of the Carlisle Commission, "This shuts the door and it will remain shut till they will be pleased to open it again. [by which he means the Carlisle Commission]. Governor [George] Johnstone has acted so base a part as to hint the offer of bribes to the President and every other Member of Congress, as well as the General [Washington] by this he has in my opinion the just contempt of the world. I have lately been well assured that a bribe of ten thousand guineas [a British gold coin of 21 shillings] has been offered to a gentleman of station & character here. He refused it, as you might well suppose, with proper resentment, telling the lady who negotiated this dirty business, that the British King was not rich enough to purchase him."

21 July 1778:
Tuesday. At headquarters, White Plains, New York, Washington writes to the Officer Commanding at West Point, "Captain [John] Clark will deliver you this, with eight persons, two with families, who have been sent from Bennington [Loyalist prisoners] under sentence of banishment into the enemy's lines. As I have received a letter from Governor Clinton, with a copy of a petition from the prisoners and of a letter from the Committee of Albany, all remonstrating against the proceedings had against these men. As I am determined not to involve myself in any dispute about matters, with which I have nothing to do, I have resolved to lay the affair before Congress by the first opportunity, that they may determine upon it, as they shall think proper. In the meantime, you will take charge of the prisoners and supply them with provisions, allowing them such indulgencies as may be reasonable. I do not wish or mean that their confinement should be close or rigorous. Yet they must not be suffered to escape."
From Philadelphia, Gouverneur Morris writes to the Earl of Carlisle (he of the Carlisle Commission), "My Lord, as you, in conjunction with your brother Commissioners have thought proper to make one more fruitless negotiatory essay, permit me, through your Lordship, once more to address the brotherhood. It is certainly to be lamented that gentlemen so accomplished should be so unfortunate. Particularly, my Lord, it is to be regretted that you should be raised up as the topstone to a pyramid of blunders. On behalf of America I have to entreat that you will pardon their Congress for any want of politeness in not answering your letter. You mistake the matter exceedingly when you suppose that any person in

America wishes to prolong the calamities of war. But the fault lies on you or your master, or some of the people he has about him. Congress when Sir William Howe landed on Staten Island, met him with their Declaration of Independence. They adhered to it in the most perilous circumstances. They put their lives upon the issue; nay their honor. Now in the name of common sense how can you suppose they will relinquish this object in the present moment? Nay my Lord, eventually Great Britain must acknowledge just such an independence as Congress think proper ..."

In the Congress, pursuant to the powers vested in them, the delegates of North Carolina sign the ratification of the Articles of Confederation on behalf of their state.

22 July 1778:
Wednesday. At Passy, Benjamin Franklin writes to James Lovell, noting that he has not yet received all of the resolutions of the Congress. He points out that, "Commerce among nations as well as between private persons should be fair and equitable, by equivalent exchanges and mutual supplies. The taking unfair advantage of a neighbor's necessities, though attended with temporary success, always breeds bad blood. To lay duties on a commodity exported, which our neighbors want, is a knavish attempt to get something for nothing. The statesman who first invented it had the genius of a pickpocket ..."

23 July 1778:
Thursday. At White Plains, New York, Lafayette prepares to leave for a journey to Providence, Rhode Island, in order to cooperate with the French Fleet under Admiral d'Estaing, and American forces under Major General John Sullivan.

Washington writes to Brig. Gen. John Glover, "Upon Colo. [William] Malcolm's arrival at West Point, you are to join your Brigade, now upon its march to Providence. As the Colo. Commandant has his orders, you need not come down here, but go directly across the country. There is the greatest necessity for the speedy arrival of these troops at Providence and therefore, if you find your baggage any incumbrance, leave it to come on under a small Guard of men who may perhaps be fatigued by the march."

Washington writes to George Clinton, Governor of the State of New York, "Accounts of the ravages of the Indians upon the frontier of this state are distressing. I wish it were in my power to afford an adequate relief, but as you are well acquainted with our force, and what we have to oppose, I am certain you will think that I have done all in my power. Colo. Butler having shifted his ground before my orders got to his hands, has been the occasion of some delay, he is however to go this day up to New Windsor by water."

24 July 1778:
    Friday. At headquarters, White Plains, New York, Washington writes to Gouverneur Morris, in which he discusses the appointment of so many foreigners to offices of high rank and trust in the service. "The lavish manner, in which rank has hitherto been bestowed on these gentlemen, will certainly be productive of one or the other of these two evils: either to make it despicable in the eyes of Europe, or become a means of pouring them in upon us like a torrent, and adding to our present burden. But it is neither the expense nor the trouble of them that I most dread; the driving of all our own officers out of the service, and throwing not only our army, but our military council's, entirely into the hands of foreigners."
    Lafayette is at Stamford, Connecticut, en route to Rhode Island.

25 July 1778:
    Saturday. In Paris, Ralph Izard writes to Henry Laurens, president of the Congress, "You will find by my letter to the committee of this day's date, that the situation of affairs has not allowed me yet to go into Italy. My own inclinations, if they alone had been consulted, would have carried me there long ago."

26 July 1778:
    Sunday. At headquarters, White Plains, New York, Washington writes to the President of Congress, concerning the situation of Baron Von Steuben. Lacking enough general officers to command divisions and brigades, because so many of them were on temporary duties at courts martial either as members or as witnesses, Washington gives temporary command of a division to Von Steuben on their march from Monmouth Courthouse to White Plains. Von Steuben desires to retain a field command position which would exclude other general officers from such a field command. Not wishing to lose Von Steuben, Washington requests the Congress to solve the problem which they will do in a few weeks.
    In Philadelphia, Henry Laurens writes to Patrick Henry, governor of Virginia, noting that the several resolutions of the Congress enclosed are full explanations of the expedition to Detroit, and the raising a reinforcement of infantry and cavalry in Virginia. Since it is Virginia that is hosting this expedition to eliminate or reduce the Indian threat to the frontier, Laurens feels that Henry need not require further information from him.

27 July 1778:
    Monday. About 100 miles west of Ushant, in the Bay of Biscay, a naval battle is fought between the French, under Admiral Louis Guillouet, the Comte d'Orvilliers with 29 ships-of-the-line and the British, under Admiral Augustine Keppel

with 30 ships-of-the-line. Both fleets suffer serious damage, and each quickly returns to port, the battle being inconclusive.

On the New York frontier, Charles Smith, a Tory, writes to Captain Walter Butler, saying that it is difficult to get recruits. "Men are struck with terror, the Northern Army, I understand, having given them a sad strike." This letter never reaches Butler, but, instead, is captured by American forces and forwarded to New York Governor George Clinton.

28 July 1778:
Tuesday. At Florence, Italy, Signor Niccoli writes to Ralph Izard, reporting that the possibility of loans from Florence are not likely. He also points out that Tuscany is just emerging from an inactive commerce and is not in a position to consider loans. The only dim possibility for loans that Niccoli sees is perhaps the City of Genoa. It has a goodly trade business, and might be interested in learning about the commercial possibilities in this new country of America.

29 July 1778:
Wednesday. The French fleet, under the Comte d'Estaing arrives off Point Judith, Rhode Island, to cooperate with an American force, under Major General John Sullivan to attack and defeat the British force believed to consist of 3,000 troops, under the command of Major General Sir Robert Pigot.

30 July 1778:
Thursday. In Philadelphia, Roger Sherman, a delegate from Connecticut, writes to Jonathan Trumbull, Jr., paymaster general of the Northern Department, acknowledging receipt of Trumbull's request to resign that office. Sherman then goes on to enquire of Trumbull if he would be willing to accept a new position as a commissioner of the treasury board. "Our public affairs at present seem to be in a favorable situation–except that of the currency which demands immediate attention and I think measures may be devised to put it on a better footing. I think our enemies can have but little prospect of success in subduing us, and I believe they wish for peace on almost any terms."

At headquarters, White Plains, New York, Washington writes to Colonel Stephen Moylan, "I approve of the step you took to drive off the stock from Bergen, but if it appears to you that the families will be distressed by keeping their milch cattle, you have liberty to restore them to such persons and in such numbers as you think proper. I desire you will, upon receipt of this, come over with all your Cavalry except about twenty-four, who are to act on concert with the detachment of foot. Colo. [John Graves] Simcoe [of the British Queen's Rangers] told Captain [Winthrop] Sargent [3rd Continental Artillery], who went down with a flag yesterday, that Admiral [John] Byron [of the British Navy] was arrived. Be pleased to endeavour (sic) to find out the truth of this. Leave orders with your Officer to keep a good look out from Fort Lee and if he perceives any extraordinary movement to make report to me."

Lafayette is at Norwich, Connecticut, with the troops of Brigadier Generals John Glover and James Mitchell Varnum, en route to Providence to reinforce Sullivan.

31 July 1778:

Friday. In Amsterdam, Holland, E. T. Van Berckel writes to Charles William Frédéric Dumas, thanking him for a copy of the Treaty of Amity and Commerce between France and the United States of America. He is hopeful that this sample will assist in providing the same mark of distinction between the Dutch provinces and the United States.

From White Plains, Washington writes to the Marquis De Lafayette, "I had last night the pleasure of receiving yours of the 28th dated at Saybrook. I hope your next will inform me of your arrival at Providence, and of your having seen the Count D'Estaing's Fleet off the Harbour of Newport, an event, of which I am most anxious to hear."

Washington writes to Brig. Gen. James Clinton, ordering him to move his units towards King's Bridge and the enemy's lines nearby, so as to provide protection for American parties making maps in the area, with the additional view of alarming the British, who may be too comfortable, and that a perceived attack could have the added benefit of distressing those among the enemy who are inclined to defect. "The Principal objects in view are, to cover the Engineers and Surveyors, while they reconnoitre, and as far as time will permit, survey the ground and roads in your rear, and in front of this Camp. Also to encourage that spirit of desertion [among the enemy] which seems so prevalent at present."

1 August 1778:

Saturday. At New York harbor, British Admiral Richard Howe, now reinforced by ships of Vice Admiral John Byron, departs for Rhode Island to confront the French fleet there.

In Philadelphia, the Marine Committee writes to John Wereat, Continental agent in Georgia, who has complained that the proceeds from a sale of the captured vessel *Hinchinbrook* had been improperly delivered to the Continental officer responsible for its capture, rather than to him. The Marine Committee notes that the regulations in such cases do seem to give that approach [payment to the capturing officer] as the correct method. They go on to say that the matter has been turned over to the governor and state for resolution.

2 August 1778:

Sunday. Major General John Sullivan arrives aboard the flagship of the Comte d'Estaing for the purpose of conferring on their joint attack upon the British forces. Unfortunately, Sullivan speaks no French, and d'Estaing is put off by

Sullivan's forwardness that the Frenchman views as his crude manners. Little is accomplished.

3 August 1778:
Monday. Major General Lafayette, with the reinforcements of the Brigades of Glover and Varnum, arrives at Sullivan's Camp, west of Providence, Rhode Island. He is attached to the staff of Maj. Gen. John Sullivan to assist in the joint operation with the French against the British at Newport.

In Philadelphia, the Congress formally notifies the French minister, Conrad Alexandre Gerard that they will receive him at noon on 6 August.

4 August 1778:
Tuesday. At Passy, John Adams writes to James Warren, noting that the various resolutions of Congress, treaties, and letters from America are read in Europe with avidity. He further points out that these publications "... seem to excite the ardor of the French nation, and of their fleets and armies, as much as if they were Americans."

Lafayette meets with the Comte d'Estaing aboard his flagship, Languedoc (90 guns), in the outer harbor of Newport.

5 August 1778:
Wednesday. At headquarters, White Plains, New York, Washington writes to Brig. Gen. John Stark, "I cannot determine what is to be done respecting the State prisoners at Albany who draw continental provision. Govr. Clinton says those at Poughkeepsie are furnished with provision by the state. I would have you enquire of the magistrates of Albany and know of them how it first happened that those prisoners drew from the continental store. The Commissary should keep an exact account of what he issues. I cannot see why the soldiers wives in Albany should be supported at public expense. If they would come down and attend as Nurses to the Hospitals they would find immediate employ."

Congress orders that a warrant issue in favor of Joseph Nourse, paymaster to the Board of War and Ordinance, for $6,000 to pay for draughts for the use of the Baking Department.

6 August 1778:
Thursday. In the Congress, the committee charged with preparing the protocol for receiving the Sieur Gérard, Minister Plenipotentiary of France to the United States, formally introduce him to the Congress. The entire process has been carefully worked out among the members of Congress. Anxious to be seen as doing things correctly. Being seated in a chair, the minister's secretary delivers to the president of the Congress his letter confirming him as minister. This is read in both French and English, after which Gerard arises and addresses the Congress in both French and English. The

president of the Congress then returns a short answer in English, after which the secretary of the Congress delivers the same to the minister, who is then conducted to his home.

7 August 1778:
    Friday. Maj. Gen. John Sullivan's army in Rhode Island is now considerably enlarged by the addition of militia units, more of whom arrive at his encampments every day. He marches his forces from Providence to Howland Ferry, near Tiverton, closer to his objective—the British army on the island of Rhode Island. He is planning an attack upon the British, hoping with his now enlarged body of men he will be able to defeat them. But, Sullivan, while a faithful officer, is slow about taking advantage of opportunities.

8 August 1778:
    Saturday.   At headquarters, White Plains, Washington writes to the Comte D'Estaing, conveying intelligence that Lord Richard Howe has sailed from Sandy Hook but the design of this movement is unknown. Washington states that while it is not known where he may be intended, perhaps "... stimulated by a hope of finding you divided in your operations, he may choose to go to Rhode Island. It is more likely he may hope by making demonstrations towards you to divert your attention from Rhode Island and afford an opportunity to withdraw their troops and frustrate the expedition we are carrying on. I shall not trouble you with any further conjectures, as I am persuaded you will be able to form a better judgment than I can, of his intentions, and of the conduct it will be proper to pursue in consequence."
    The Board of Treasury having recommended a number of persons as signers of the Continental currency (to make them legal tender), the Congress proceeds to the election of the same. Twenty persons are chosen for these positions. As the Continental paper money continues to decline to worthlessness, the inability of the Congress to provide for some funding, probably by means of some form of taxing is required.

9 August 1778:
    Sunday. Sullivan crosses Howland Ferry and entrenches his troops upon Rhode Island near its northern tip. The British fleet arrives off its coast, while the French fleet is held inside the harbor because of contrary winds.
    In Paramus, New Jersey, the court martial of Charles Lee concludes the portion of the trial insofar as the hearing of testimony of the many officers called as witnesses. A military court martial is serious business, and must be conducted according to stated rules and regulations.

10 August 1778:
      Monday. At White Plains, Washington writes to the Marquis
De Lafayette, "The common cause, of which you have been a
zealous supporter, would I know, be benefitted by Genl.
Greene's presence at Rhode Island, as he is a native of that
State, has an interest with the people, and a thorough
knowledge of the country. Therefore I accepted his proffered
services, but was a little uneasy lest you should conceive that
it was intended to lessen your command.   Your cheerful
acquiescence to the measure [of Greene taking command of
some brigades], after being appointed to the Command of the
Brigades that marched from this army, obviated every
difficulty, and gave me singular pleasure."
      The French Comte d'Estaing, with a favorable wind from
the north, ups anchor, and sails his fleet out of Narragansett
Bay, Rhode Island, near noon to do battle with the British
fleet. It takes some while to get all the ships out of the narrow
reaches of the harbor, and ordered in line, before it is dark.

11 August 1778:
      Tuesday. Both the British and French ships in the two
fleets maneuver during the day to obtain the weather-gage. By
night, a violent gale comes up and scatters the ships of both
fleets, with much damage. Howe withdraws to New York.
D'Estaing slowly limps in to Newport, arriving on the 20th.

12 August 1778:
      Wednesday. The Congress resolves "That every officer in
the army of the United States, whose duty requires his being
on horseback in time of action, be allowed a sum not
exceeding five hundred dollars, as a compensation for any
horse he shall have killed in battle."
      In Paramus, the court martial of Maj. Gen. Charles Lee
finds him guilty of all three charges brought against him. (See
sketch for 2 July 1778). They sentence him to suspension of
command for a year.

13 August 1778:
      Thursday. In Madrid Spain, James Gardoqui writes to
Arthur Lee, reporting that proposals for borrowing monies
through the hands of noblemen are impossible for the present.
He further points out that Spain has provided provisions
through various channels and will continue to do so as much
is possible.
      At headquarters, White Plains, Washington writes to
Brigadier General John Stark, "I am favored with yours of the
10th enclosing a letter from Colo. [Richard] Butler, whose
presence I hope will curb the disaffected and stop the ravages
upon your frontier. If an expedition of any consequence should
be carried on, a proper supply of light artillery shall be
furnished, in the meantime let me know whether you want all

or any artillery that you already have. I think you had better inform civil authority that they must in future supply their State prisoners with provision."

Washington writes to Brigadier General William Maxwell, "I have your favor of the 10th enclosing a list of the French Fleet. I am informed that Lt. [Aaron] Lane of your Brigade, who was the officer that received the flag at Second River, opened the packet from the British Commissioners to Congress, read the contents and made them known to several persons, one of whom is ready to prove the fact. I therefore desire that Mr. Lane may be arrested and sent up here, to be tried for so unofficer like a procedure."

14 August 1778:
    Friday. Congress resolves that the vice president and supreme executive council of Pennsylvania be requested to station a vessel, under the command of a vigilant officer, near the mouth of the Cape May channel, with orders to search all vessels that may be outward bound, either through Cape May Channel or the Delaware; and if any such shall be found exporting provisions contrary to the embargo, they are to be brought before government officials to answer for their misconduct.

15 August 1778:
    Saturday. American Major General John Sullivan, who is pushing his army toward Sir Robert Pigot's lines on Rhode Island, starts digging regular approaches. For the next several days, both armies are preparing for battle.

    From White Plains Washington writes to Lund Washington, bemoaning the high prices of things and the depreciation of continental money. He goes on to note his inability, not his unwillingness, to purchase additional lands in the vicinity of his property. Since he has little money, Washington suggests to Lund that perhaps land could be purchased by way of barter for the exchange of other lands or for his Negroes, of which Washington says he would "... every day long more and more to get clear of."

    Then alluding to a specific parcel of land Washington writes, "For this land also I had rather give Negroes, if Negroes would do. For to be plain I wish to get quit of Negroes. I should not incline to sell the land I had of [Daniel Jenifer] Adams unless it should be for a price proportioned to what I must give for others. I could wish you to press my Tenants to be punctual in the payment of rents, right and justice with respects to myself requires it, and no injury on the contrary a real service to themselves as the man who finds it difficult to pay one rent will find it infinitely more so to pay two, and his distresses multiply as the rents increase."

16 August 1778:

Sunday. In Philadelphia, Gouverneur Morris writes to John Jay, noting that Arthur Lee seems to be forever criticizing and defaming people. Morris reports several such events, including Lee's accusation of William Carmichael, who has been fully exonerated, subsequently, by the Congress.

General George Washington forwards the results of the Charles Lee court martial to the Congress, without comment.

17 August 1778:

Monday. The Congress has reviewed a report of the Court of Enquiry in respect to Major General Putnam and the posts of the Hudson Highlands, which were captured by the British. Upon careful examination of the facts and consideration of the evidence, it appears that those posts were lost, not from any fault, misconduct, or negligence of the commanding officers, but solely through the want of an adequate force under their command to maintain and defend them. Therefore, the Congress approves the report. A good example of too little too late. It is the responsibility of the Congress to see that the commanders they chose, have the means to execute the wishes they express.

18 August 1778:

Tuesday. At Passy, Benjamin Franklin, Arthur Lee, and John Adams write to de Sartine, noting that they are in agreement with him regarding two of the articles of proposed regulations for prizes and prisoners.

In Philadelphia, William Duer writes to George Clinton, "When I first received it [a sum of public money due to the State of New York], my determination was to proceed to the State of New York within a few days--but the foreign affairs becoming interesting [by which he means compelling] from the arrival of the French Minister, and the necessity of getting a decision of Congress upon the conduct of the State of Vermont. I have endeavored in vain to get several trusty persons to take the charge of this money in order to deliver it to you for the purpose of its being paid into the treasury of our State. But one or two of that number, who might with some inconvenience to themselves have carried at least part of it did not choose to run the risque. I am not willing to hazard it with a person at my own risque, unless I should find a very trustworthy character, who will consent to take the trouble. I have, therefore, to request that your Excellency will be pleased to direct some person who may be depended upon, and who may be coming to Philadelphia, to call upon me for the money."

19 August 1778:

Wednesday. The Congress resolves that the respective Navy boards be authorized and empowered to appoint and constitute courts of enquiry and courts martial, under the direction of the

Marine Committee, to examine and determine all offenses and misdemeanors in the Marine Department, according to law martial.

20 August 1778:
Thursday. D'Estaing, with the French fleet, returns to Newport. However, he can not be induced to land his troops. This leaves Sullivan without the expected support of these French soldiers.

The Congress sets up the regulations for the office of the Inspector General of the Armies of the United States. Among the items included are "That the Duty of the Inspector General shall consist in forming a System of Rules and Regulations for the Exercise of the Troops in the Manual Maneuvers and Evolutions, for the purpose of service in Guards and Detachments, and for Camp and Garrison Duty."

21 August 1778:
Friday. In Philadelphia, the New York delegates write to Governor George Clinton, reporting that Virginia has informed Congress that until their Continental accounts are adjusted Virginia will not pay any proportion of their quota until these accounts are settled. They go on to wonder whether New York should do the same and also report that many states have received large advances from the continent (by which they mean both foreign loans and United States funds) for which there has been an inadequate accounting. They go on to say that they do not censure or condemn any sister state and have great confidence in the wisdom the New York State Legislature knowing that they will pursue a correct line of conduct.

At midnight, d'Estaing sails off to Boston in order to repair his dismasted vessels.

22 August 1778:
Saturday. Without the expected French support, and the lack of control over the waters around Newport Island, the Americans are not in the best shape to attack and defeat the British, who are now well entrenched and reinforced to a level of nearly 6,000 men. What had, only a few days before, seemed like an easy conquest, with about 10,000 men, is now seen as a possible disaster, and large numbers of the militia forces depart. Had Sullivan acted with more vigor, he might have won a great victory—he certainly had all the forces available to do so.

23 August 1778:
Sunday. Henry Laurens writes to Lachlan McIntosh, commenting upon events at Rhode Island. He dwells at some length on Maj. Gen. John Sullivan's recent reports, saying that he has about 9,000 troops, the British about 6,500, and that he (Sullivan) is preparing to attack Pigot.

Henry Laurens writes to James Graham, a Georgia Loyalist, in response to Graham's request to return from New York to Georgia, via Charleston, "Were it as inoffensive, Sir, without further enquiry to grant the free passage to yourself, I would with great pleasure remove the difficulties you complain of, and add every means in my power for the happy prosecution of your wishes, but your application is met by a question which you have not enabled me to determine; is the gentleman a Citizen of any of these states? If sir, you are a subject of His Britannic Majesty, the moment you pass the line of usurpation you will consider yourself and be considered as in an enemy's Country, libel to penalties common in such cases, unless you are guarded by a special license from the Representatives of the good people of the Union. All therefore that I can at present contribute toward your relief, is to lay your letter before Congress, and you shall be presently advised of the result." The Congress refers Graham's letter to Georgia and South Carolina.

24 August 1778:
Monday. In Philadelphia, the Congress resolves that the Commissary General of Purchases procure 20,000 barrels of flour, and, to obtain vessels for the transportation of these barrels, confer with the Marine Committee, so that convoy may be obtained and the destination thereof directed and adequately protected.

Josiah Bartlett writes to his wife, Mary, "My Dear, This day your two letters of the 24th & 31st of July were brought me by the Eastern Post, and am very happy to hear you were all well & that Rhoda [his daughter] in particular had in a great measure recovered her health. The very irregular manner in which I receive your letters, sometimes 2 or 3 at once & then missing 2 or 3 weeks without receiving any, makes me suspect that the Post has left off riding to Exeter as usual. Does my letters come to you in the same irregular manner. I have no news of importance to write to you. Rhode Island the French Fleet are the great objects from which we expect the first news of consequence. This State have made a law for confiscating all the Estates real & personal of those inhabitants who joined the enemy. Monsr. Gerard the French embassador has given all the members of Congress an invitation to dine with him tomorrow being the Birth Day of his most Christian Majesty French King. The ambassador has paid visits in form to all the Delegates; he began with New Hampshire and paid me the first visit about ten days ago."

25 August 1778:
Tuesday. At Paris, Ralph Izard writes to the commissioners at Paris, reporting that he has information from some merchants in Leghorn, Italy, who express an interest in entering into the American trade. However, Izard notes that these merchants seem apprehensive of meeting African

cruisers on the Mediterranean and that this danger may also deter many Americans from entering into the trade.

26 August 1778:
Wednesday. The Congress orders that William Bedlow, deputy paymaster to William Palfrey, be allowed an additional $35 per month in consideration of the extra services and circumstances under which he operates.

At headquarters, White Plains, Joseph Reed writes to his wife Esther, "My dear Hetty, we did not reach this place before Sunday evening owing to the heat of the weather. Our quarters are hot & very dirty. I think I never met with such a combination of smells & everyone offensive. This Army seems at present to be stationary & indeed both main armies appear to be looking at Rhode Island where there is hourly expectation of something important. The French Fleet have returned, but very much shattered by the late storm which has handled both Squadrons pretty severely. Two frenchmen of war are dismasted & one missing. I shall forward the business here with all possible expedition that I may return to Philadelphia where I am much wanted & where my interest evidently calls me. I shall have the pleasure of seeing you on the way & staying with you as long as I can. In the mean time I must bid my Dear Girl Adieu & assure her that I am with unalterable affection ..."

27 August 1778:
Thursday. In Paris, Arthur Lee writes to James Gardoqui in Italy, "We are a young people, and have had fourteen civil governments to settle during the heat and pressure of a violent war, accompanied with every possible circumstance that could augment the expense and difficulty usually attending a state of warfare. It is in this moment of distress that our real friends will show themselves in enabling us to prevent those calamities which, though they cannot subdue, will yet injure us infinitely. Our industry, were peace and commerce once established, would soon enable us to repay them, and they would be sure of a gratitude more lively and lasting."

Lafayette is in Boston for an interview with the Comte d'Estaing, to try to persuade him to return to Newport and complete the joint operation against the British. Sullivan has been undiplomatic with this French officer, and very unwise in his approach to defeating the British under Pigot. Sullivan had an opportunity to win a great victory, but let it slip.

28 August 1778:
Friday. At Newport, Sullivan is now aware that he may be in a most difficult position, and begins to withdraw from Newport Island.

At headquarters, White Plains the Committee on Arrangement (The process of determining the relative rankings of specific grades of officers within units of the Continental

Army, involving the needs of the service) writes to George Clinton, "The Committee of Congress for the Arrangement of the Army, had flattered themselves that they should meet with little or no difficulty in the New York line; but find themselves mistaken & under a necessity of requesting Information & Advice from you on this head. Col. Gansevort's Regiment not being on the ground, we have no materials nor the requisite assistance to arrange it, but we are informed it has been arranged agreeable to the Establishment, by the Authority of the State. If so, we should be glad to be favored with a Report of it. We also find disputes of Rank subsisting both as to the rank of the Regiment, & the Officers. Col. DuBois claims of all under than Van Schaick in both points; but we have had a Rank Role as settled by the authority of the State contrary to his claims. We wish you to explain it, as his Commission bearing date the 25 June 1776 will apparently give him rank over Cortlandt, Livingston, & Gansevort. There will be several vacancies in the Regiments which the commanding officers propose to give no recommendations for, but as it is not only a point of propriety and policy—but conformable to a Resolve of Congress that the States should fill up all vacancies except in cases of ordinary succession, we have not received any of these recommendations."

29 August 1778:
     Saturday. British Maj. Gen. Robert Pigot is no fool. His scouts have quickly picked up on the American withdrawal, and the British are after them. Sullivan has a fortified position on a rise called Butts Hill at the north end of Newport Island, near Bristol Ferry. There, the Americans try to make a stand, but the enemy is allowed to form up on hills just to the south. Artillery duels and British naval gunfire continue as the Americans attempt to hold off the attacking forces. This becomes known as the Battle of Rhode Island. Because the Americans leave the field, it is a British victory.

30 August 1778:
     Sunday. The besieged Americans on Butts Hill manage to evacuate to Tiverton, Rhode Island, with the help of Glover's Marblehead sailors.
     Lafayette leaves Boston, and hurries to return to Rhode Island, late in the evening, where he resides in camp at Tiverton.
     At headquarters, White Plains, the General Court Martial writes to General George Washington, "It is submitted by the Committee to your Excellency's judgment, whether it would not be better to direct an adjournment of the Court Martial, which is composed of the principal part of the General Officers, for a few days until the Arrangement of the Army shall be completed, as all information and subject matter for the Committee to proceed upon is derived from these officers. The

Committee also request your Excellency to order the attendance of Generals Poor, Patterson, and Nixon, tomorrow."

In Philadelphia, John Mathews, a delegate from South Carolina, writes to Thomas Bee, Speaker of the South Carolina House of Representatives, "It is true I did oppose the Embargo act, as I shall uniformly do, every act of Congress, where I perceive an attempt to step over that constitutional line which has been chaulked out to them even independent of the Confederation, for if they can exceed their powers in one instance, they may claim an equal right to do it in any; and which was the case in this affair for the favors of the measure claimed a right to do it, because they had done it before. This proves to what dangerous lengths precedents may be carried. Never suffer the plea of Necessity to justify the Act, for a specious pretext can never be wanted, by artful men, to cover even the most arbitrary measure, under the guise of necessity."

31 August 1778:
Monday. In Paris, Arthur Lee, writes to the Committee of Foreign Affairs, "Gentlemen: It has been hinted to me that there will be two important subjects of negotiation with the Spanish court, upon which I beg to have the orders of Congress. First. Providing the Spanish navy with masts at a stipulated and as reasonable price as possible. Second. The cession of Florida, should it be conquered to them. For this they would stipulate, whenever peace is concluded, to furnish the funds for redeeming all or a great part of the paper." (By which he means the loans or advances made by Spain to America.)

1 September 1778:
Tuesday. In Paris, Ralph Izard writes to Signor Niccoli, bemoaning the views regarding possible loans from Tuscany, "...affords no very flattering prospects to us from Tuscany. My expectations and hopes from that quarter were high, and I confess that I am disappointed. All Europe appears to me to be interested in the success of our cause, and Italy will certainly receive no inconsiderable share of the benefits resulting from the establishment of the independence of the United States. It is, therefore, not a little to be wondered at that she should refuse to stir a finger towards the accomplishment of that event."

Sir Henry Clinton arrives at Newport with 5,000 troops to support Pigot.

At headquarters, White Plains, Washington writes to the Marquis De Lafayette, concerning the departure of the French fleet from Rhode Island, and the reaction of some Americans to it, "I feel that every thing that hurts the sensibility of a gentleman; and consequently, upon the present occasion, feel for you and for our good and great allies the French. I feel myself hurt also at every illiberal and unthinking reflection which may have been cast upon Count D'Estaing, or the conduct of the Fleet under his command; and lastly I feel for my Country. Let me entreat you therefore my dear Marquis to take no exception at unmeaning expressions, uttered perhaps without consideration, and in the first transport of disappointed hope. Every body Sir, who reasons, will acknowledge the advantages which we have derived from the French Fleet, and the zeal of the Commander of it, but in a free, and republican Government, you cannot restrain the voice of the multitude; every man will speak as he thinks, or more properly without thinking, consequently will judge of effects without attending to the causes."

2 September 1778:
     Wednesday. In Paris, Ralph Izard writes to the Count de Vergennes, "I am directed by the Congress to endeavor to procure a loan of money in Italy, and have in consequence done everything in my power to obtain proper information on the subject. My correspondent in Tuscany gives me no hopes of procuring any there, as that country is just beginning to emerge from a state of languor, under which it has suffered for two centuries. No other part of Italy seems to afford a more agreeable prospect except Genoa, and I am told that even there the security of the court of France will probably be expected for any sum which the inhabitants of that republic may have it in their power to lend to the United States."
     Lafayette moves to a camp near Bristol, Rhode Island.

3 September 1778:
     Thursday. The Congress resolves, "That any person who has been or shall be appointed a brigade chaplain, and previous to his appointment shall have acted in that capacity, be allowed for the time of such service, after the date of the certificate of the brigadier or colonel commandant of his brigade to Congress, recommending him to the said office, the pay and rations or subsistence of such a chaplain, deducting the sums received as regimental chaplain."

4 September 1778:
     Friday. Forty-five British warships and 4,000 troops make raids upon Buzzards Bay and Martha's Vineyard, destroying shipping, naval stores, and homes.
     At headquarters, White Plains, Washington writes to the President of Congress, "I had the pleasure to hear this morning, by a letter from General Sullivan of the 31st ulto. that he had effected a retreat to the main, the preceding night, without any loss, either of men of stores. As he has written to Congress fully upon the subject, and I feel their anxiety to hear it, I shall not detain Major Morris longer than to observe, that I think the retreat a most fortunate, lucky and well timed event. Major Morris informs me that he has heard that Lord [Richard] Howe was off Boston with his fleet, and it appears by a New

York paper of the 2nd, that Rear Admiral [Peter] Parker arrived at Sandy Hook this day a week, with six Ships-of-the-Line of seventy four guns each, which is corroborated by other accounts. I transmitted the intelligence to His Excellency, Count D'Estaing yesterday and the day before, as it acquired more and more the appearance of certainty."

5 September 1778:
    Saturday. At headquarters, White Plains, Washington writes to Maj. Gen. John Sullivan, congratulating him on a successful retreat in the face of a reinforced British army at Rhode Island. "I have been informed that you were obliged to draw all the arms from the magazine at Springfield to put into the hands of the Militia. If this has been the case, I entreat you to make use of all possible means to have them returned, when the Militia are disbanded, and lodged again in the magazine. A large Regiment arrived a few days ago from North Carolina, unarmed, and we have none to supply them. I beg you will upon no account or pretense suffer them [the Militia] to turn their backs upon you, before they have delivered their arms and other stores, for if they once carry them out of your sight, it will be impossible to recover them."
    The Congress orders that a warrant issue for $400,000 for payment to the state of North Carolina for the purpose of raising, equipping, and marching the men voted by said state to complete their Continental battalions. This payment is actually a reimbursement to the state for their support of the continental efforts that are deemed to be the fiscal responsibility of the Congress. It would be nice if the States more fully supported that responsibility with the funds to do so.

6 September 1778:
    Sunday. In Philadelphia, Gouverneur Morris writes to George Clinton, Governor of New York, expressing concern over an act of the state legislature that requires all hitherto neutral persons to take an oath acknowledging the state "... to be of right a free and independent state," or else to be banished behind British lines. Morris feels that such language is too stern and harsh, and that it is not good policy to banish useful citizens. Perhaps, he recommends "... it is better to bend the spirit of the legislation than to scatter the riches and strength of the state among the enemy."

7 September 1778:
    Monday. At headquarters, White Plains, Washington writes to Captain Edward Norwood, "I have already given my reasons in General Orders, for disapproving the proceedings of the Court Martial in your case, and therefore I need not repeat them. I will only observe that they appear to me, to be contrary to precedent and common usage, and totally irregular and incomplete. Under this persuasion I could not but continue

your arrest. The matters in charge against you had never been tried."

Washington writes to Charles Pettit, Deputy Quartermaster General, "I imagine you must stand in need of assistance in your office at this time, by reason of Genl. Greene's absence. I therefore think it advisable and expedient that Colo. [Udny] Hay should be immediately called down from the Highlands, more especially as it is probable that the army may be under the necessity of changing its present position in a short time. If the enemy continue in New York this winter, we shall be obliged to quarter a considerable force at and in the vicinity of the Highland posts. I would therefore have you immediately contract for a quantity of boards, plank, scantlin [framing timber] and nails for the purpose of building barracks."

The Congress hears an extract from the minutes of the General Assembly of Pennsylvania, applying for funds to pay for clothing purchased for their continental troops, and refers the matter to the Board of Treasury.

8 September 1778:
Tuesday. The Congress trying to find ways and means to augment the continental forces resolves "That General Washington be authorized, if he shall judge it for the interest of the United States, to augment the continental bounty to recruits, inlisting [sic] for three years or during the war. To a sum not exceeding ten dollars, and that he use his discretion in keeping this matter secret as long as he shall deem necessary. And in applying the augmentation of bounty, as circumstances may require."

9 September 1778:
Wednesday. At headquarters, White Plains, Washington writes to the Officer Commanding the Militia at Hackensack New Bridge, "Sir: Major Clough who commands at Hackensack, is under the necessity of some times allowing persons to carry small matters into New York, and to bring a few goods out, that he may the better obtain intelligence. The persons employed in that way are sometimes stopped by your guards, under suspicion that they are carrying on a contraband trade. You will therefore be pleased to give orders to your officers not to detain or molest any person showing a pass from Maj. Clough."

Washington writes to Charles Pettit, "I have more reason for thinking that the Army will have occasion to remove from its present position shortly, than when I wrote you two days ago. I, therefore desire you will immediately send off all the supernumerary stores of your department. I think it would save land carriage if they were transported by water above the posts in the Highlands, and removed from thence more inland, at leisure. The ox teams you mentioned should be collected as quick as possible, as I mean to remove the sick, and all the spare stores of every department from this ground."

Washington writes to Doctor William Shippen, Junior, "It is more than probable, from some late manoeuvres of the enemy, that the Army will have occasion to move from its present position to the Eastward. I therefore desire that the most immediate measures may be fallen upon to remove the sick of the army at least as far as Danbury. The Hospital established at Bedford will for the above reasons be too much exposed and should therefore be immediately removed also as far as Danbury. The Quarter Master General will, upon application, afford all the assistance in his power, towards procuring wagons for the removal of the patients and hospital stores."

The Congress resolves that an enquiry be made into the causes and failure of the expedition at Rhode Island, and that General Washington be requested to cause the enquiry to be made as soon as possible.

10 September 1778:
Thursday. At Passy, Benjamin Franklin, Arthur Lee, and John Adams, write to the Comte de Vergennes, noting that the Congress wishes to settle accounts with the house of Roderique Hortalez & Co., and the compensation, if any, which should be allowed them on all merchandise and warlike stores that have been shipped by them for the use of the United States in the past. They are applying to Vergennes and seeking his advice in how best to proceed with this task, since the secret company is a creature of French origin.

11 September 1778:
Friday. At headquarters White Plains, Washington writes to Lieutenant Colonel William Butler, "I am glad to find by your letters of the 31st August that matters continued so quiet upon the frontier. It appears to me, that the money arising from the sale of cattle belonging to those in the interest of the enemy, belongs to the captors. But I beg you will proceed in these matters with the caution which you have used in the first instance, otherwise the soldiers for the sake of plunder will seize everything under the denomination of its being Tory property."

The Committee of Commerce reports that the sum of $2,000 should be transmitted to Stephen Steward of Maryland to enable him to purchase cable and running rigging for the ship Chase., and that it would be improper to purchase the ship Defense on the public account.

12 September 1778:
Saturday. At White Plains, Washington writes to Maj. Gen. John Sullivan, offering thoughts and suggestions about how to distribute his troops since both the British fleet and now the British army under Major Charles Grey have left Rhode Island. Washington recommends that Sullivan be careful about dividing his forces in the possible presence of a superior

enemy force. He also warns against placing any large detachment into necks of land which the enemy can surprise by sea and offering the view that small guards posted at the most likely places of descent are all that may be needed to warn of enemy movements.

The Congress resolves that the eastern states be requested to call out such number of militia as General Sullivan shall require, in cases of great emergency, to check the ravages of the enemy, or to repel any invasion they may attempt into any of the eastern states.

13 September 1778:
Sunday. In Philadelphia, Henry Laurens writes to the Massachusetts Council, enclosing several acts of the Congress, i.e., for making up clothing for the Army; expressing the high sense of patriot exertions of the eastern states in the Rhode Island expedition; for removing the convention troops (those captured at Saratoga), and for reinforcing General Sullivan.

14 September 1778:
Monday. At Albany, New York, Brig. Gen. John Stark writes to General George Washington, reporting the return of a scout from Unadilla, New York, who has brought in three prisoners, and also notes that Captain Walter Butler and Joseph Brandt are planning another raid of the Tories and Indians upon the Mohawk Valley villages.

15 September 1778:
Tuesday. Washington writes to Maj. Gen. Israel Putnam, "You are to march precisely at the hour appointed tomorrow morning, with two divisions, the one under your own immediate command, and the other under the immediate command of Baron de Kalb you will take the route by Young's Tavern and Stephen Danford's to Croton Bridge. Near Croton's bridge the two divisions will separate. With the one under your immediate command, you are to proceed to West Point to reinforce the garrisons in the Highlands, and aid in the completion of the works with all possible expedition. Baron de Kalb will proceed with his division towards Fredericksburgh to join the second line. You are to regulate your particular order of march agreeable to the principles established in a General Order issued at Valley Forge the first of last June and to the General Order of this day; to both which you will without doubt pay the most exact attention. You will attend carefully to the accommodation of your men on the march; keep your column always compact, prevent straggling, and use every other precaution which distinguishes a well ordered march; discouraging by the strictest discipline all injury or abuse, either to the persons or properties of the inhabitants, on any pretense whatever."

The Congress resolves that John Hooper and James Murray, two men in Pulaski's Legion, being charged with robbery of a Delaware citizen, be sent, under guard, to Wilmington, to be dealt with according to law.

16 September 1778:
Wednesday. Washington is at Reuben Wright's Mill, in White Plains, New York, from which he writes to Sir Henry Clinton, "Sir: I transmit you the inclosed [sic] copies of sundry Resolutions of Congress, by their order, and take the liberty to request your answer to the last of them, on the subjects of passports [for American transport vessels to bring food and fuel to the Convention prisoners at Boston] by the earliest opportunity. I was much concerned to hear, that one of my patrols fired on a Flag coming from your lines on Monday evening. I shall do every thing in my power to prevent the like mistake on any future occasion."

17 September 1778:
Thursday. At Passy, Benjamin Franklin, Arthur Lee, and John Adams write to M. de Sartine, Minister of Marine for the Court of France, regarding the issue of a French brigantine, *Isabella*, retaken by the American privateer, *General Mifflin*, from a Guernsey privateer. "We have the honor to agree perfectly with your excellency in your sentiments of justice and policy of the principle of reciprocity between the two nations, and that this principle requires that French ships of war or privateers should have the same advantage, in case of prizes and recaptures, that the American privateers enjoy in France."

Washington is in Fredericksburg, in the southeastern part of Dutchess County, New York.

At German Flats, New York, Loyalist Captain William Caldwell and Mohawk Indian Joseph Brant lead an attack in the early morning with a body of 300 Tories and 150 Indians against patriot settlers in the area. Many of the residents make it safely to either Fort Herkimer or Fort Dayton, but the attacking force puts most of the homes, farms, and barns to the torch. This raid incenses many Americans, who press for some form of retaliation. More than 700 head of livestock, including cattle, horses, and sheep, are driven off. Nearly 720 people, including more than 385 children are left homeless by this brutal raid upon defenseless citizens.

18 September 1778:
Friday. Lafayette moves with Sullivan's army from their encampment near Bristol to a camp near Warren, Rhode Island.

At Philadelphia, Robert Morris writes to John Hancock, "I heard with great satisfaction of your joining, as a Volunteer, the army at Rhode Island and was sanguine in my hopes &

expectations that Mars wou'd have been propitious and sent you home crowned with laurels. The brave & virtuous know how to deserve success and although they cannot command it when they please, yet the appointed hour will come when merit must have its reward. It may be wise not to enquire into the causes that operated the failure of that expedition, but look forward & try to get rid of those troublesome enemies, that tease & harass us from one end of the Continent to the other. I hope they will not dare, to undertake an expedition against Boston, or if they do, my firm persuasion is that they will smart severely for it, but the situation of the British affairs in general is such, that I cannot help thinking they must quit the United States very soon, in order to take care of those territories they have some title to."

19 September 1778:

Saturday. Congress takes into consideration the affairs of the treasury and finance. The report of the committee on these matters is read, in which are made a number of recommendations. Among these are to negotiate a loan of £5,000,000 in Europe, borrow $20,000,000 on loan, borrow $10,000,000 on loan office certificates; call upon the states to pay in their quotas of $10,000,000, enact a poll tax to develop revenue, enact a duty of 2% on all imported commodities. Only sixty copies of this report are to be printed, and the delegates are pledged to silence upon these matters for the present.

At Fort Clinton, in West Point, New York, Washington writes to Brigadier General Louis LeBeque DuPortail, "Colo. Kosciuszko who was charged by Congress with the direction of the forts and batteries has already made such a progress in the construction of them as would render any alteration in the general plan a work of too much time, and the favorable testimony which you have given of Colo. Kosciuszko's abilities prevents uneasiness on this head; but whatever amendments subordinate to the general disposition shall occur as proper to be made, you will be pleased to point out to Col, Kosciuszko that they may be carried into execution."

20 September 1778:

Sunday. At Passy, Benjamin Franklin, Arthur Lee, and John Adams write to the American prisoners in Plymouth, England, expressing their interest in their comfort and their liberty. They go on to report that their efforts to free them may bear fruit, as the British government is now willing to make a cartel to exchange prisoners. This issue of prisoner exchange is only a minor, but important part of the endless work of the American envoys in Europe. The French government has a passport, allowing these prisoners to come from England to Nantes or L'Orient with American captives, there to take British prisoners back to Great Britain in exchange.

21 September 1778:

Monday. In Philadelphia, the Congress, concerned about the problem of the depredations of the Floridians and Indians into Georgia, and aware that the state has little by way of resources to provide for their security, resolves "That a warrant issue to the State of Georgia for $1,000,000 for the purpose of establishing a military chest."

22 September 1778:

Tuesday. At headquarters, Fredericksburgh, New York, Washington writes to Major General William Heath, "Whatever may be the future intentions of the enemy, it is evident that they have lain aside all designs against Boston for the present: Lord Howe having returned to the Hook with his fleet and the troops under Genl. Grey have come down the Sound again and have landed at White Stone upon Long Island. I am pleased to hear, by a letter from Genl. Greene of the 16th that the affray mentioned in yours of the 10th [a fight between a number of American and French sailors] has terminated in such a manner as to convince the French gentlemen that no public harm or insult was intended by the people of the town of Boston. All possible means should now be taken to cultivate harmony between the people and seamen, who will not be so easily reconciled as their Officers ..."

Congress, concerned about letters, and rumors, and accusations of and about their commissioners in European courts, resolves that William Carmichael be directed to attend at the bar of the house (meaning the rail that separates the judges, attorneys, and their secretaries from the general public) and there to be examined upon his knowledge of both the uses of the public money by Silas Deane and the dissensions among the American commissioners in Europe.

23 September 1778:

Wednesday. At Passy, John Adams writes to Benjamin Franklin, noting that some of the articles in the accounts of their expenditures had been formerly paid by him out of his account while traveling to France from America, and that these monies should, therefore, be adjusted, so that the public is not charged twice for items already covered.

24 September 1778:

Thursday. At headquarters, Fredericksburgh, Washington writes to Lord Stirling, "I have just received intelligence of the enemy's having thrown a body of about 5000 men over to Paulus Hook, and of their advancing about five miles on the road toward the English neighborhood. I have also gotten intelligence that about 3000 men with artillery were advancing from King's Bridge. The design of these movements is, probably a forage, and the gathering of stock. It may also be something else, and, as our Posts in the highlands are of infinite importance to us, I desire your Lordship will immediately detach General Clinton's Brigade towards Peekskill ..."

Conrad Alexander Gérard, the Minister Plenipotentiary of France, having notified Congress, pursuant to his powers, has appointed Martin Oster, Vice Consul of France in the Port of Philadelphia.

25 September 1778:
Friday. At Passy, Benjamin Franklin writes to Ralph Izard, thanking him for his detailed explanation of the French view and background upon their concern over certain fishing rights. Because the American seek to include the right to fish in areas on and near the Grand Banks, this information becomes an important part of the negotiations regarding the avenue toward peace.

26 September 1778:
Saturday. The Congress resumes consideration of the report of the Committee on the Arrangement of the Treasury, and approves a lengthy resolution that includes that a house be provided at the place where Congress shall sit where all the several offices of the Treasury are to be located. These offices include comptroller, auditor, treasurer, and clerks.

27 September 1778:
Sunday. From Versailles, France, the Comte de Vergennes writes to the commissioners at Paris, reporting that he has transmitted their request regarding protection of American vessels from the Barbary States to M. de Sartine of the French Ministry of Marine, who is pursuing the matter.

Lafayette leaves Rhode Island to make a short trip to Boston.

In Penobscot Bay, the American frigate *Raleigh*, having run aground after a three-day chase, is captured by the British.

28 September 1778:
Monday. In Paris, Ralph Izard writes to John Adams, regarding the fisheries of New England, and the luxury and vanity introduced by the very high profits they gain, which he believes is the fault of the people not the fisheries. "The passion for ribbons and lace may easily be checked by a few wholesome sumptuary laws; and the money that has hitherto been employed on these articles will be found very useful toward sinking our enormous national debt."

From Boston, Lafayette writes to General George Washington, requesting a leave to return to France.

29 September 1778:
Tuesday. At Headquarters, Fredericksburgh, Washington writes to the President of Congress, in which he reports, "I

have just rec'd an account from Jersey, which I fear is too true, that Colo. [George] Baylor's Regt. of Dragoons were surprised in their quarters [at Old Tappan, Bergen County] the night before last, and most of them killed or taken. They [stragglers] think the Colonel and most of the Officers were made prisoners, and that the privates were put to the sword."

The Congress proceeds to the election of a commissioner of Accounts at the Treasury Office and selects Resolve Smith.

30 September 1778:

Wednesday. The Congress orders that letters between Major General Heath and Major General Phillips respecting the settlement of accounts for supplies for the convention prisoners of Saratoga be referred to a committee of three, whose members are Elbridge Gerry, William Duer, and Meriwether Smith.

1 October 1778:

Thursday. General George Washington is at Fishkill, New York, at Brinkerhoff's house, from which he writes to Maj. Gen. Horatio Gates, "I do not find that the enemy are advancing on the west side of the River. From the latest accounts they were at the liberty pole , and at the Newbridge near Hackensack; and from many circumstances and the conjectures of the officers in their neighborhood, it would seem that foraging is the principal object of their expedition."

At Boston, Lafayette departs to return to Philadelphia.

2 October 1778:

Friday. Due to the shortages of crops of wheat and other grain in the states of New York, New Jersey, Pennsylvania, Delaware, Maryland and Virginia, and the "wicked arts" of speculators and engrossers who are industriously purchasing grain and flour and thus rendering it impracticable for the Army to obtain timely and sufficient supplies for their operations, the Congress resolves that the legislative powers of these states authorize the civil magistrates within their jurisdictions to issue warrants to military commissaries to seize such supplies for the public use.

3 October 1778:

Saturday. At headquarters, Fishkill, New York, Washington writes to Henry Laurens, "Your favor of the 23rd Ultmo. came to my hands at Fredericksburgh the evening before I left it for this place. I am well convinced myself that the enemy, long ere this, are perfectly well satisfied that the possession of our Towns, while we have an Army in the field, will avail them little. It involves us in difficulty, but does not, by any means, insure them conquest. They will know, that it is our arms, not defenceless Towns, they have to subdue, before they can arrive at the haven of their wishes, and that, till this end is accomplished, the superstructure they have been endeavouring (sic) to raise, 'like the baseless fabric of a vision' falls to nothing."

The Congress orders the Board of War to enquire into claims for clothing and equipment for his legion, charged by Brigadier Count Pulaski to the Continental clothier general for payment, contrary to procedure. This has led to Pulaski's arrest, but the Congress feels that the problem may lie with his unfamiliarity with the army procurement procedure, rather than willful disobedience, and orders the Board to procure bail for Pulaski, and settle the bills as seems reasonable.

4 October 1778:
Sunday. At headquarters, Fishkill, New York, Washington writes to Maj. Gen. William Heath, "The intelligence given you by Mr. [William] Colvill [formerly an Ensign in the Royal Scotch Emigrants] is very interesting if it can be depended upon, and particularly to Count D'Estaing, to whom no doubt you have communicated it. Your distribution of the twelve hundred Militia men ordered out by the Council of State, exactly coincides with my wishes. Their labor if it has not its immediate use, will remain a permanent security to the town, and as you observe give confidence and tranquility to our allies. Every intelligence of progress of clothing, is very acceptable to me, as it diminishes my anxiety and opens the prospect of a happy completion of our wishes, in this important article; the stopping a sufficient quantity for the invalids was perfectly right. The enemy in the Jerseys continue nearly in the same position as when I last had the pleasure of writing to you and will probably retire as soon as they have secured their plunder. A packet is arrived at New York which will probably determine General Clinton's plans."

In Philadelphia, Cornelius Harnett, delegate from North Carolina writes to Richard Caswell, Governor of North Carolina, sending funds by express and requesting instructions from the State Assembly to the North Carolina delegation in the Congress.

5 October 1778:
Monday. At headquarters, Fishkill, New York, Washington writes to Edward Rutledge, member of the South Carolina Assembly, Congress I presume, are suspicious of the enemy having an eye for your State, by the measures they are taking for its defense; but I have no idea myself of the enemy's detaching part of their land or sea force on an enterprise of this kind while a respectable French Fleet hovers on this coast. You will have the whole or none of them. Though there is no telling; for they have done, and left undone things, so contrary to common conceptions, that they puzzle at all times and upon all occasions, even conjecture. The bearer Maj. Gen. Lincoln is nominated by Congress to take Command of the Southern department, and I take the liberty of recommending

him to your civilities as a worthy character, a brave, and an attentive officer."

The Congress orders that a warrant issue in favor of the delegates of the state of New Hampshire for $150,000 for the use of said state.

6 October 1778:
     Tuesday. From Paris, Arthur Lee writes to James Gardoqui in Spain, "If to prevent the effusion of human blood, and all the shocking calamities attending a war like this, be worthy of a pious prince; if to prevent the chances of war from having any influence in preventing the dismemberment of the British Empire, and the humiliation of their pride, be an object worthy of a political prince; if to drive the English immediately from America, and receive a portion of her independent commerce, be an advantage to the crown and people of Spain, this is the moment for its monarch to decide and enforce those events by an immediate declaration of our independence and a union of force which must be irresistible."

7 October 1778:
     Wednesday. General George Washington has not established a fixed headquarters, but rather makes a constant circuit of his units in and around the Highlands of the Hudson River, because he quite properly has a concern about potential British attempts to sever the line of the Hudson River which could separate the New England states from the Mid-Atlantic states.

Washington writes to Maj. Gen. Horatio Gates, "The capture, or destruction of the French fleet appears to be the most important object, they [the British] can have on the continent; and it is very possible, they may have it in contemplation, though the time they have lost, since they have had the superiority at sea and the advanced season of the year are strong arguments against it. Our present disposition was formed on the possibility of such an event, at the same time, that it does not lose sight of the security of the North River, or the concentration or our force to repel any attempt upon the army. Though it may not be probable that the enemy have at present any design against either of these, it would be imprudent to offer them a temptation by diminishing our strength in a considerable detachment, so far Eastward as to be out of supporting distance. If they were able to possess themselves of the Highland passes and interrupt the navigation of the River, the consequences on the score of subsistence would be terrible as well to the fleet as the army. It is supposed the enemy have lost all hopes of effecting any thing material against these states, and this supposition is upheld by powerful reasons; but after all, the truth of it depends so much upon the contingencies of naval operations and European politics, that it would be very unwise to let it essentially influence our military arrangements."

8 October 1778:
     Thursday. At Paris, the Ambassador of Naples writes to the American commissioners in that same city, "Gentlemen: I am persuaded that you already know that the King of the Two Sicilies, my master, has ordered the ports of all his dominions to be kept open to the flag of the United States of America, for which reason, to avoid every possible mistake at this time, when the seas are covered with the privateers of different nations, and likewise with pirates, I request you to inform me of the colors of the flag of the United States of America, and likewise the form of the clearances, the better to know the legality of the papers which it is customary to present in ports to gain free admission."

9 October 1778:
     Friday. At Passy, Benjamin Franklin and John Adams write to the Ambassador of Naples expressing their pleasure at receiving a letter informing them that the King of the Two Sicilies has ordered the ports of his dominions to be open to the flag of the United States of America. They request a copy of the edict for the purpose of forwarding it to the Congress, and go on to say, "It is with pleasure that we acquaint your excellency that the flag of the United States of America consists of thirteen stripes alternately red and white; a small blue square field the upper angle, next the flag staff, with thirteen white stars, denoting a new constellation."
     Washington makes his headquarters again at Fredericksburgh, New York.

10 October 1778:
     Saturday. At Fredericksburgh, New York, Washington writes to John Park Custis noting that he consents to the sale of lands which he holds in rights of Dower and discusses other properties. He goes on to state to Custis that "A moments reflection must convince you of two things. First that Lands are a permanent value, that there is scarce a possibility of their falling in price, but almost a moral certainty of their rising exceedingly in value. Secondly, that our paper currency is fluctuating, that it has depreciated considerably, and that, no human foresight can, with precision, how low it may get as the rise or fall of it depends upon contingencies which the utmost stretch of human sagacity can neither foresee, nor prevent. My design in being thus particular with you, is to answer two purposes; first, to show my ideas of the impropriety of parting with your own lands faster than you can vest the money in other lands, and secondly, to evince to you the propriety of my own conduct, in securing to myself and to your Mother the intrinsic value, neither more nor less, of the Dower Estate."
     The Congress orders that a warrant issue to James Reed, paymaster to the Navy Board in the Middle District, for $2,666

60/90 for two years' wages. (See the Sketch for 13 September 1776 for an explanation of these odd fractions, p. 154.)

11 October 1778:

Sunday. In Philadelphia, Samuel Adams writes to James Warren, commenting upon a newspaper article, that attempts to link Arthur Lee with a known double agent in the British employ. He also notes that Silas Deane (who, it turns out, is the author of the accusing newspaper article about Lee), considerably exceeded his instructions and powers and without authority sent so many unqualified persons to America with expectations of high commissions.

12 October 1778:

Monday. In Paris, Arthur Lee writes to the Comte de Vergennes, noting that he (Lee) is charged with full powers to conclude a treaty with Spain, and he has been in Spain and had conferences with the Marquis de Grimaldi. He goes on to state, "All the objections which were then alleged against an immediate declaration are now removed. The consistency of our cause is unquestionable. France is ready and has actually declared." He requests the advice and assistance of Vergennes in dealing with the court of Spain.

13 October 1778:

Tuesday. At headquarters, Fredericksburgh, New York, Washington, anxious to keep his French allies informed of events, as well as to be seen as friendly and open to them, writes to the Comte D'Estaing, "I have the honor to send your Excellency the British account of the late engagement between the two fleets [the naval battle off Ushant, see sketch of 27 July 1778] respectively under the command of Monsieur D'orvillers and Admiral Keppel, contained in a letter from the latter; published by authority, which I have just received from New York. The insipid terms of this letter, the frivolous pretext assigned were not renewing the engagement, the damage confessed to have been received, the considerable number of the killed and wounded announced to the public in the shape of an official report, which from the customary practice can not be suspected of exaggeration, and the acknowledged necessity of returning immediately into Port, are circumstances that prove at least the enemy have had no great cause of triumph in this affair."

14 October 1778:

Wednesday. At Fredericksburgh, New York, Washington writes to the Major and Brigadier Generals, "I have been waiting impatiently for the movements of the enemy to come to an issue that might ascertain their intentions for the Winter, which has hitherto prevented my taking the present step; but the uncertainty in which they still continue involved, and the advanced season of the year, will not longer admit of delay in

420   V. The Year 1778

fixing upon a plan for the general disposition of the Army in winter quarters. In determining this, it will readily occur to you that the following particulars are to be considered. The security of the Army itself, its subsistence and accommodation, the protection of the Country, the support of our important posts, the relation which ought to be preserved with the french fleet should it remain where it is, depending on the degree of probability of a Winter operation against it, and the succour it may derive from the troops under Genl. Sullivan and the Militia of the Country. After a full consideration of these points, and of any other matters requiring attention, you will be pleased to favor me with your opinion as speedily as possible. The main questions to be decided are, whether the Army shall be kept in a collected State and where, whether it be distributed into cantonments and in what manner and places, how soon it shall enter into quarters, and what precautions shall be used in respect to covering provisions and forage."

In Philadelphia, a letter from Jeremiah Wadsworth, commissary general, is read, with an account of his receipts and expenditures, amounting to $6,500,000, and orders that the letter be referred to the Board of Treasury.

15 October 1778:

Thursday. At Frankfurt, Germany, William Lee writes to the Committee on Foreign Affairs, "Gentlemen: I have the honor of forwarding to you herewith a third copy of the plan of a treaty of amity and commerce between the Seven United Provinces of The Netherlands, and the United States of America, which you will perceive was settled by M. de Neufville, as representative of Mr. Van Berckel, counselor pensionary of the city of Amsterdam, and myself."

16 October 1778:

Friday. From Fredericksburgh, New York, Washington writes to the Council of War, "The Commander-in-Chief informs the Council, that the enemy's whole force in these States still continue two principal divisions; one at New York and its dependencies consisting of about thirteen thousand, the other on Rhode Island consisting of about five thousand. That a considerable detachment from the former sent three or four weeks since into Bergen County, in the Jerseys, have hitherto been employed in a forage, part are said to have lately returned and the remainder it is given out, intend to cut a quantity of wood before they leave the Jerseys. That an officer of ours, prisoner with the enemy, just exchanged brings an account of the actual embarkation of a large body of troops, on Saturday night and Sunday last, said to be destined for the Southward, of which however, no confirmation has been received from any other quarter. That our whole force in this quarter is about fifteen thousand rank and file, fit for duty; including the two brigades in the Jerseys, and the garrison at

West Point, a considerable part of which have completed and will soon complete the term of service, for which they are engaged."

The Congress, aware that the convention troops (those British and Hessian prisoners given up at Saratoga), cannot be properly cared for or continued to be kept in Massachusetts, resolves that General Washington be directed to take the necessary measures to remove these prisoners to Charlottesville, Virginia.

17 October 1778:

Saturday. At headquarters, Fredericksburgh, New York, Washington writes to Lord Stirling, "I have undoubted intelligence, that a very considerable embarkation is making from New York. It is of the utmost importance that we should ascertain the numbers as near as possible, their destination, the time of their sailing, and above all how they are convoyed as to numbers and force of Ships of War. Upon this, and a certain account of what Ships of War remain in New York the Count D'Estaing will probably form his plan of Operations. I therefore entreat your Lordship to leave no means untried to come at a knowledge of these facts. I would not wish you to take up any vague reports, because I shall forward your intelligence to the Count. You may always distinguish in your letters what you think may be depended upon, and what is dubious. If an Officer acquainted with marine affairs was stationed at Bonumtown he would have an opportunity of seeing every thing going in or out of the Hook and could give intelligence of the time of the fleets sailing; endeavoring to distinguish the men of war from the transports. Major [Ebenezer] Howell will have an opportunity of counting the exact number from his Station at Black Point. Be pleased to give him notice that a fleet is upon the point of sailing, desire him to be attentive and inform him of the importance of being particular, and expeditious in communicating his intelligence."

The Congress orders Governor Patrick Henry of Virginia to forward 1,000 troops and Governor Richard Caswell of North Carolina to forward 3,000 troops for the defense of Charleston, South Carolina.

18 October 1778:

Sunday. From Marley, France, M. de Sartine writes to the commissioners in Paris, reporting upon the handling of the prize money resulting from an American capture of a British vessel "The capture of the Nile and of her cargo has been declared good. To order a particular restitution, and deprive the captors of property which they have acquired provisionally, at least would be an interference of the government with the laws, and would introduce a dangerous precedent in the proceedings established by His Majesty relative to prizes. The more firmly you are convinced that the claims of Mr. Izard are conformable to the treaty, the more ready you should be to believe that they will be favorably received, and the expenses of a suit are inconsiderable."

19 October 1778:
    Monday. At headquarters, Fredericksburgh, Washington writes to Governor George Clinton, "The advices which I have just received from different quarters bear the strongest marks of an immediate evacuation of New York. These considerations induce me, should it be deemed expedient, to make an addition to Colo. Cortlandt's command by sending up the whole of Genl. Clinton's Brigade, except Van Schaick's Regt. which is to relieve Gansevoort's at Fort Schuyler. I do not know the situation of Chemung, the place which Colo. [Thomas] Hartley advises to be possessed by us, and cannot therefore say, whether the same body of men which are to be employed upon the Anaquaga [an Indian village] expedition, could afterwards break up the settlement at Chemung. I shall send General Hand to take command at Albany in the room of General Stark who goes to Rhode Island. That there may be a more free and full communication upon this subject I have desired Genl. Clinton, Genl. Hand, and Colo. Cortlandt to wait upon you. As your Legislature are now sitting, there must be Gentlemen from every part of the State well acquainted with the frontier, the different routes, the resources of the country, and many matters conducive to the conduct and success of such an expedition."
    The Congress is not being completely funded by the states as required by the Articles of Confederation. In that document it is specified that central funding shall be supplied by the several states in proportion of all their lands, and resolves that the delegates of each state fix a time for making the evaluation of such lands in their state. Too many states have failed to do so, or have done it only partially.

20 October 1778:
    Tuesday. At headquarters, Fredericksburgh, Washington writes to Major General John Sullivan, "An intelligent officer stationed at Amboy reports that the 16th Octor. about twelve ships fell down to the Hook, and the 17th early in the morning about one hundred ships of war and transports also fell down to the Hook. Thus we see very circumstance supposes an evacuation at hand, though the enemy's object or destination cannot be investigated from these circumstances. The preparations or movements in your quarter if well known I would think more immediately tend to this discovery at least they may serve to ascertain with more certainty whether a general evacuation of the States be intended. For this purpose you will take every method to discover what is going forward in the garrison, among the shipping, whether it is employed in the embarkation of stores and of what kind. In short every minute motion and circumstance should be collected. You will

spare no reasonable expense to gain this information nor make any delay in its communication."

Washington writes to Royal Flint, Deputy Commissary of Purchases, there is the strongest reason to suppose that a great part of the Army will continue this Winter upon the east side of Hudson's River. The season approaches fast when it will be next to impossible, on account of the roads, to bring forward a sufficiency of flour even for daily consumption. The distress to which we were reduced last Winter at Valley Forge, for want of a proper magazine, makes me extremely solicitous to see such an one established in time, as will, with what can be brought on from time to time, supply the exigencies of the Army without difficulty. I therefore desire you immediately to set every engine at work, to get as much flour as possible brought from the southward and stored upon the east side of the River, near Fishkill. It will there be convenient to the Highland posts, to the Army should it be barracked anywhere upon the River, or be ready for transport to the eastward should there be occasion to move to that quarter. Whatever flour may be purchased upon the head of Hudson's river should be brought down while the navigation continues open. Genl. Schuyler, who is well acquainted with the River, informs me that it is no uncommon thing, to have it froze over by the middle of November. You therefore see the necessity of losing no time in having the flour from thence brought down."

The Congress resolves that $100,000 be transmitted to Benjamin Harrison, deputy paymaster general, for paying the arrears due the Continental troops, and the militia of Virginia.

21 October 1778:
Wednesday. At headquarters, Fredericksburgh, Washington writes to Brigadier General Edward Hand, "I have furnished Genl. Schuyler with the resolve of Congress directing the Expedition to Chemung, and desired him in conjunction with Gov. Clinton and yourself to take the matter fully into consideration, that if thought practicable at this season of the year it may be undertaken, if not, that I may stand justifiable to Congress for laying it aside. You have in my opinion put the present supply of the inhabitants of the German Flats upon the proper footing, I will lay their distressed situation before Congress and if they approve of their being supply at public expense, it may be continued until they can settle themselves again and procure the means of livelyhood."

Washington writes to Governor George Clinton, concerning the supply of flour to the army, "I would, therefore, request the favor of your Excellency to lay the proposal before your Assembly, and endeavor to obtain the nomination of a suitable person in each district or township producing wheat and flour throughout the state, to procure as exact a return as possible of what remains of either, in the hands of every person within his district. As this will be for the general advantage, I do not think the state should bear the expense of the inquiry. I will therefore engage for the payment of such wages, as shall be by the Assembly deemed adequate for the trouble. Both the Quartermaster and the Commissary General are anxious to know what they may depend upon with certainty in this quarter."

In Philadelphia, the Congress resolves "That the Marquis de la Fayette, Major General of the United States, have leave to go to France and that he return at such time as it be most convenient to him ..."

22 October 1778:
Thursday. The Congress creates a plan of attack upon Quebec and orders that the members be under the injunction of secrecy with regard to it. They also resolve "That General Washington be directed to procure from Canada and Nova Scotia, as speedily as possible, the most exact intelligence that can be obtained respecting the number of troops in those provinces, and their stations; and also the number of vessels of war, their force and stations, with the number, state and strength of the fortifications."

23 October 1778:
Friday. At camp near Fredericksburgh, Washington writes to the president of the Congress, "I have reason to hope that Lt. Col. Butler has already destroyed the town [Anaguaga]. I am now consulting Gov. Clinton and General Schuyler, who are much better acquainted with the frontiers in this quarter than I am, upon the practicability of an expedition of a large scale, against Chemung. I don't know what will be the result; but I am apprehensive from the advanced season of the year and the daily increase of the rivers and creeks, it will be found impracticable or at least extremely difficult in the execution. I have written to General Heath to take immediate measures for carrying into effect, the intention of Congress, respecting the removal of the Convention Troops, in case, Sir Henry Clinton has not furnished supplies of provision and fuel ..."

The Congress orders that a warrant issue in favor of Major General Lincoln, for $3,000, to bear the expenses of himself and suite to South Carolina. The Congress also begins discussion of the Charles Lee court martial. While a general court martial is a serious military matter, the Congress has been requested to review the court's opinion in this case.

24 October 1778:
Saturday. At Versailles, the Comte de Vergennes writes to Arthur Lee, "I have received with great sensibility, the news which you have obtained by the way of Spain. It is a very great fatality that the unlucky gale of wind separated the squadrons just as Count d'Estaing had joined the English. He then had a superiority, which he must have lost if the capital admirals Byron and Parker have joined Lord Howe. We are very

impatient to receive some direct accounts from our vice-admiral. We flatter ourselves that the favorable winds will bring some dispatches from him. I request you, in the meantime, sir, to communicate whatever news you may receive through other channels."

25 October 1778:
Sunday. At headquarters, Fredericksburgh, Washington writes to the Comte D'Estaing, reporting recent information of the British fleet at Sandy Hook which seems to now consist of invalids and merchantmen taking the protection of a convoy since several regiments still remain in the harbor. Washington further sends this information to the following officers; Israel Putnam in the Highlands, Horatio Gates at Hartford, William Heath at Boston, John Sullivan at Providence, Alexander McDougall at Hartford, The Baron De Kalb at Fishkill, and James Clinton at Peekskill.

The Marine Committee writes to the Eastern Navy Yard at Boston, expressing the expectation that the vessels *Boston*, *Providence*, *Ranger*, and *Warren*, have arrived, and that the Navy Yard will immediately get these vessels ready for sea. Likewise, they expect the frigate *Alliance* to be used to carry Lafayette to France, and forewarn the yard to have her ready to sail.

26 October 1778:
Monday. At headquarters, Fredericksburgh, Washington writes to the President of Congress, "I advised your Excellency of the measures I had taken to ascertain the practicability of an enterprise against Chemung. [This is the embryonic idea that will mature into the Sullivan Expedition against the Iroquois Indians.] I have the honor to enclose you the report of Governor Clinton, General Schuyler, and General Hand on the subject, I cannot help concurring with these gentlemen in opinion, and am persuaded from a number of considerations that we must lay aside all thoughts of an expedition against that place for the present."

The Congress resolves that Brigadier Count Pulaski's legion, and all other cavalry units at or near Trenton, New Jersey, repair to Sussex Court House. The president of the Congress will inform General Washington of this resolve, pointing out the necessity of ordering the cavalry to some place or places where men and horses may be easily supplied with food and forage.

27 October 1778:
Tuesday. From the Hague, Holland, Charles William Frederic Dumas writes to the commissioners at Paris, reporting that he is trying mightily to secure a treaty of Amity and Commerce, but unanimity is necessary to agree on any such treaty in the Netherlands.

Lafayette takes his leave of the Congress, and departs for Boston, to take ship for France.

28 October 1778:

Wednesday. From Fredericksburgh, George Washington writes to George Measam, "The cold season advances so rapidly and the necessities of the troops are so distressingly great, that it is of infinite importance to the service to have the clothing of every kind brought to camp and distributed as speedily as possible. It begins to be high time to enter into Winter quarters; and we shall be obliged to adopt the same expedient and submit to the same inconveniences with respect to quarters this Winter as we did the last. To reconcile the men's minds to the drudgery and sufferings they have before them, nothing can contribute so powerfully as to have them well clad, before they begin, in doing this we have not a moment to loose. I am, therefore, to desire you will exert yourself to the utmost to forward the clothing with all possible dispatch. Provided it come on in some tolerable order, we must dispense with the nice punctilios of exact method which at another time might be very proper. The great and pressing object now is to have the clothing put upon the men's backs to shelter them from the inclemencies of the season. I enclose you a certificate which will show what colored clothing the troops of each state are to have as determined by lot. In any issues you make, you must govern yourself by this."

In Philadelphia, Richard Henry Lee and James Lovell write to Ralph Izard in France, "You will be pleased [because the British have failed completely in their efforts at peace offerings, since without first acknowledging independence, the Americans are not going to proceed with any negotiations with anyone] at knowing that the British commissioners are convinced of their folly of their errand to America and are returning home."

29 October 1778:

Thursday. At headquarters, Fredericksburgh, Washington writes to the President of Congress discussing the embarkation of British troops at New York which gathered at Sandy Hook and have since left in a convoy to a destination not known. Washington also points out the problem of the supply of provisions and forage to the troops and that, under the Quartermaster General Nathanael Greene, operations in that department have been very smooth. Washington further notes that the problem of determining the location and size of magazines for provisions and the erection of barracks for the housing of troops is difficult to determine without a grasp of intelligence as to the proposed operations of the enemy.

The Congress proceeds to the nomination of a commissioner and a secretary for the Board of War. They also fix the salaries of various officers in the Continental departments.

30 October 1778:
  Friday. At Versailles, the Comte de Vergennes writes to the commissioners at Paris regarding the arrangements to be made with the Barbary powers for the protection of the American flag in the Mediterranean. He reports that before France can proceed it is proper that the commissioners be provided with full powers from the Congress, that these powers should include using funds for presents expected to be bestowed. When all these preliminaries are complied with Vergennes feels the King will hasten to forward the American views to the Barbary States.

31 October 1778:
  Saturday. From Fredericksburgh, Washington writes to Brig. Gen. Louis Le Béque du Portail, "I have received your remarks on the state of the fortifications already erected for the defense of the Town of Boston, and on such amendments and additions as appear to you necessary to render them effectual. Your reasonings and observations appear to be strong and well founded; but at this distance, and without so perfect a knowledge of the local circumstances of the place, as I could wish, I cannot undertake to judge absolutely of the plan you propose. I have referred the consideration of it to General Gates, who is appointed by Congress to take the command at Boston, and who will no doubt adopt every measure proper to be taken on the occasion. You will be pleased to communicate with him on the subject. I have it much at heart that the security of Philadelphia should be better provided for than it now is, so that as soon, as the question concerning Boston is decided, I shall be glad to see you, that you may repair to Philadelphia."
  Incursions by Indians upon the frontier areas of New York State are increasing, resulting in requests to the Congress and to Governor George Clinton for relief. However, there are currently too many other problems facing the army, the state of New York, and the Congress to properly address this issue, which is postponed until the following year.

1 November 1778:
  Sunday. At headquarters, Washington writes to Maj. Gen. Horatio Gates, sorry to learn by a letter of the 28th October that Gates is low on flour "I had a letter written immediately to the Commissary upon the occasion, and from his account, I hope you have obtained a supply before this. He says three or four parcels had gone from Danbury for Hartford in the course of the week, and that more was on the road from Fredericksburgh. As to seizing flour belonging to private persons, I have no authority for the purpose. When the wants of the Army absolutely compel the measure, it must be justified on the principle of necessity."

Lafayette is taken quite seriously ill at Fishkill, New York, on his way to Boston, and is housed at the Brinkerhoff house for care, where he remains for the rest of the month.

2 November 1778:
    Monday. At headquarters, Fredericksburgh, Washington writes to Maj. Gen. Israel Putnam, "General Gates having been ordered by Congress to repair to Boston and take command of the Eastern district; I have thought it best, that you should proceed to Hartford and take command of the division late General Gates, consisting of Poor's, Patterson's, and Learned's brigades. This you will, therefore, be pleased to do without delay. The standing order for that division is that it is to remain at Hartford 'til further orders from me, or till the arrival of the enemy's fleet to the Eastward shall demonstrate that they intend a serious land operation that way; in which case you are to advance and give me instant notice of it, as it is my intention on such an event to proceed immediately eastward."
    Washington writes to George Clinton, Governor of New York, "I am honored with yours of yesterday enclosing an Act of the legislature of your state empowering the Commissary, under certain restrictions to seize all Wheat, Flour, or Meal in the hands of Forestallers, or Wheat of the year 1777 and years preceding. I have, immediately in the absence of the Commissary General, transmitted this salutary law to the Asst. Commy. General who is with the Army, that he may without loss of time, proceed to put it into execution. I have also recd. the report of the Senate, setting forth their suspicions of the real-practices of some of the deputies in the Commissary's office, and recommending an inquiry into their conduct."
    The Congress resolves that a chaplain be appointed to the garrisons in the Posts at the Highlands of the Hudson River, with entitlement to the pay and subsistence of a brigade chaplain. The Rev. John Mason is elected to this position, in which office he remained to the end of the War.

3 November 1778:
    Tuesday. At headquarters, Washington writes to Maj. Gen. William Heath, "With respect to the removal of the Convention troops, the Resolution of Congress which was transmitted you, requires the measure and points out the only condition, on which they could have remained. I was nothing more than a mere vehicle, an instrument in forwarding of it, that it might have the intended operation. It will be certainly best for their baggage to go by water into James River, from whence it may be transported to the Falls and from thence to the places where the Troops are to quarter. [Charlottesville] My letter of the 29th enclosed a Copy of a Resolve of Congress appointing General Gates to command in the Eastern district. I transmitted him a Copy of the Resolution directing the removal of the Convention Troops, and write him by this

conveyance upon the subject of their baggage, in case he should be at Boston."

4 November 1778:
Wednesday. From the Hague, Holland, Charles William Frédéric Dumas writes to the American commissioners in Paris, reporting that the British have presented a memorial to the Dutch, demanding commissioners to settle treaties, and that the court of Great Britain does not wish the Dutch republic to grant free convoy to the Americans. These arrogant demands by the English court irritate the peacekeeping, quiet Dutch.

5 November 1778:
Thursday. The Congress resolves that the three companies on the posts of western Pennsylvania be re-enlisted, and their full complement completed, with their period of duty being one year from 15 December 1778. These companies shall all receive a bounty, a suit of clothes, and not be removed from the frontiers of the state, except on expeditions against the Indians.

6 November 1778:
Friday. At headquarters, Fredericksburg, Washington writes to Maj. Gen. William Phillips, British Second in Command to Burgoyne, "The several packets which he [Captain Richard Masters of the British Army] had in charge have been set into New York, but from recent and particular resolve of Congress I could not comply with your intention respecting Captain Masters's interview with General [Henry] Clinton. He has however made his application in writing for an exchange, and waits in this neighborhood for his excellency's answer. Your cares for the troops of Convention on their present march, are such as discover the attentive commander; while your expressions of politeness claim my personal respect. I shall endeavor, during the continuance of their march to confine its inconveniences to such as are unavoidable, or that cannot be obviated by any arrangement of ours at this season of the year. For this purpose I have appointed an officer of rank to attend the march, and commissaries and quartermasters to meet the troops, with such other dispositions as appear necessary on the occasion. The resolution of Congress directing the removal of the Convention troops to Charlottesville, includes in my opinion, its officers under every description; and in this sentiment I have written to Major General Gates who now commands at Boston."
Congress orders that a warrant issue for $260,538 and 48/90 to Michael Hillegas, Treasurer. This odd fraction of ninetieths appears many times in Congressional authorizations, as a means of noting small fractions of the larger denominations of Continental currency. It is mostly a

book-keeping arrangement by the several government departments.

7 November 1778:
Saturday. At headquarters, Fredericksburgh, General Orders state that at a brigade general court martial held near Camp Hartford, Lieutenant David Gilman of the 2nd New Hampshire regiment was tried for ungentlemanlike behavior in requesting private soldiers to steal horses for him, is found guilty and sentenced to be cashiered from the service. The orders also report a brigade general court martial held at the corp of artillery in which Captain [Andrew] Moody was tried for contemptuous behavior and is reprimanded in brigade orders. The parole is given as Carthagena and the countersigns as Cambray and Condé.

The Congress resolves that the Commissary General of Prisoners be directed to take proper measures, until further order of the Congress, for the temporary supply of the British prisoners of war captured by the United States, with such quotas of rations as are furnished our prisoners in the hands of the enemy by the British commissaries.

8 November 1778:
Sunday. At headquarters, Washington writes to Colonel Theodorick Bland, "You are hereby appointed to superintend the removal of the convention troops from the State of Massachusetts to Charlottesville in Virginia. You will therefore proceed immediately on the shortest route to Enfield, or to where the first division of the troops may have arrived, and announce yourself to the Officer commanding. You will then dispatch Major Jamison, who is directed to assist you in the execution of this duty, to the rear of the troops, to see that the necessary provisions and arrangements are made for the intermediate and successive divisions. During the march you will have respect to the quartermasters who are appointed to attend the troops and see that their halting places are convenient for cover and accommodation. You will also have regard to the Commissaries, so that good provisions be distributed and at the proper times. You will accommodate the stages of march to the state of the weather, the condition of the troops, and the nature of the country through which they travel."

Washington writes to Maj. Gen. Alexander McDougall, "As I am obliged to go from Head Quarters this morning on business of consequence, I am under the necessity of giving a very short answer to your letter of the 3rd inst. which was only presented to me just now. Your reasoning as to the improbability of the enemy's operating to the Eastward was very strong, and your views of the difficulties that would attend the quartering of the Whole Army on this side of the North River, are certainly well founded and coincide much with my own. If the troops are ordered to move to the

Westward, I shall not have the smallest objection to your visiting Mrs. McDougall, or if from her indisposition, for which I am extremely sorry, you prefer going now, it will be perfectly agreeable to me. As to myself, I had rather you should go immediately than wait the event of the Troops marching. The proceedings of the Court Martial cannot have my attention till I return."

In Philadelphia, William Whipple writes to Richard Henry Lee a mostly social note expressing his hope that they will soon again be together in Congress (Lee is currently on leave), and reporting that he (Whipple) is now on the Marine Committee.

9 November 1778:
Monday. In Philadelphia, the Congress approves a moderation of the parole exchanges among the prisoners, that benefits both sides, in that it relieves the pressure on scarce supplies. Maj. Gen. Heath is informed that he may give passes and extend paroles to several British prisoners, and to officers' wives and families.

10 November 1778:
Tuesday. The Congress, determined to settle the issues of finance, orders "That the plan of finance be an order for tomorrow, and that Congress proceed on the consideration of that business every day after, precisely at one o'clock, until the same be finished, and this rule be not broken unless by unanimous consent."

11 November 1778:
Wednesday. Joseph Brant and a body of Mohawk and Seneca Indians attack the scattered homes in New York's Cherry Valley. A new fort, recently completed, is not used as it should be and the Indians, after skirmishing, turn on the defenseless inhabitants in their homes. Women and children are killed, men are butchered, many farmhouses are burned. More than thirty settlers are killed, seventy or more are taken prisoner. The wanton killing of unarmed citizens, the burning of homes, the pillaging of property and person, serves to add to the bitter indignation over these massacres on the New York frontier and increases the pressure for an armed campaign upon the Indian nations.

Washington, having made somewhat of a circuit of the Highland Posts, in an inspectional and supervisory mode, returns to his headquarters in Fredericksburgh, Westchester County, New York.

12 November 1778:
Thursday. At Passy, Benjamin Franklin, Arthur Lee, and John Adams write to M. de Sartine, "It gives us great pleasure to find so large a number of vessels going out upon this occasion. Their cargoes are much wanted to enable our

countrymen to sustain the war. We therefore most cheerfully join with the subscribers to the letter, who have also petitioned your excellency in requesting a large convoy to protect those ships quite home to America."

13 November 1778:
     Friday. At headquarters, Fredericksburgh, Washington writes to the President of Congress "Baron De Steuben will have the honor of delivering this to you. He waits upon Congress on the subject of the Inspectorship, which he is extremely anxious should be put upon some decided footing. He appears to be sensible of some difficulties in the plan formerly proposed and which I had the honor sometime since to transfer my observations upon; and desirous, that they should not prove an obstruction to the progress of an institution, which, if accommodated to the circumstances and sentiments of the Army, promises very great advantages to the service. The success of Baron had in the beginning and the benefits derived from it makes me regret the obstacles that have so long suspended his exertions; and I should wish he may have it in his power to resume them on principles most advancive (sic) of the service."
     The Congress resolves that three members be added to the Board of Treasury. Those chosen are Richard Hutson, Oliver Ellsworth, and Francis Lightfoot Lee.

14 November 1778:
     Saturday. In Philadelphia, pleased with the conduct and bravery of Major Silas Talbot and the men under his command in boarding and taking the armed schooner HMS *Pigot* of eight twelve-pounders and forty-five men, in the east passage between Rhode Island and the mainland, the Congress presents Talbot with a commission as lieutenant colonel.

15 November 1778:
     Sunday. At Passy, Benjamin Franklin, Arthur Lee and John Adams write to M. de Sartine, the French impresario and major factotum of marine matters, reporting to him that they have ventured, without orders or permission from the United States, to lend small sums of money to prisoners in dungeons in Great Britain, in order to assist them with their expenses to Nantes, L'Orient, and Bordeaux. The three American gentlemen further state that they will consider every Frenchman taken by the English on board of any American vessels in the same light as if he were an American. This manner of dealing with the French authorities is very well received, as it breathes of good-will and friendliness.

16 November 1778:
     Monday. At headquarters, Washington writes to Maj. Gen. Philip Schuyler, noting that he had received the disagreeable intelligence that the enemy had committed many outrages in

the settlements of Cherry Valley. "These incursions and depredations of one settlement after another are infinitely distressing, and if possible, I should be happy to check them effectually. I have ordered the remainder of Clinton's Brigade to move immediately to Albany. I have directed the Quarter Master Genl. to set the saw mills to work about Fort Ann and Fort Edward, and shall be happy in your advice to Colo. Lewis upon the occasion. The enemy still remain in New York and at Rhode Island, and it would seem from the lateness of the season, and other circumstances, that they mean to winter there, yet there are some things which favor a hope to the contrary."

The Congress is still consumed with problems of finance. Members order that resumption of consideration of the first four propositions of the report of the Committee on Finance be referred to the Committee of the Whole. The motion is approved, and the next day agreed as the occasion to do so.

17 November 1778:

Tuesday. The Congress informs the president of the South Carolina Assembly that the resolution of the Congress relative to appointments extends only to regimental officers, not to officers on the general staff.

Progress is made upon the propositions brought to the Committee of the Whole on the matters of finance, (See sketch of 19 September 1778) but the committee having come to no conclusion on these matters, desires leave to sit again.

18 November 1778:

Wednesday. At headquarters, Fredericksburgh, Washington writes to the Board of War, "The troops of the Convention have advanced considerably towards the North River. They will be guarded to that place by the Militia of Connecticut and from thence to the Delaware by an escort of Continental troops. As I cannot with any degree of convenience send the Continental troops beyond the Delaware, I am under the necessity of desiring the Board to make a requisition to the Executive Council of Pennsylvania, to give orders to the County Lieutenants of Northampton Burkes, Lancaster, and York to hold four or five hundred of the Militia of each of those Counties ready as they shall be called upon by Colo. Bland...who is appointed by me to superintend the march of the troops the whole way. I could wish that no time may be lost in giving the orders, lest there should be some unnecessary delay on the roads at this advanced season. The troops have hitherto come on in very good order and with great expedition and I hope they will continue so to do through their whole march."

The credentials for the delegates of the state of Maryland are laid before the Congress. The delegates duly elected by legislature of that State are George Plater, William Paca,

William Carmichael, James Forbes, and Daniel of St. Thomas
Jenifer.

19 November 1778:
    Thursday. The Congress orders that a warrant issue for
$1,485 for Maj. Gen. Robert Howe. The credentials for the
state of New York are presented to the Congress, naming the
following delegates elected to serve from that state: James
Duane, Gouverneur Morris, Philip Livingston, William Floyd,
and Francis Lewis.

20 November 1778:
    Friday. The Congress, according to order, resolves itself
into a Committee of the Whole to further consider the
propositions regarding finance. After some time spent in this
debate, the president resumes the chair and Francis Lightfoot
Lee reports that the committee have had the matter under
consideration, not having come to a conclusion, sit again.

21 November 1778:
    Saturday. At Fredericksburgh, Washington writes to Maj.
Gen. Philip Schuyler, in which he discusses winter campaigns,
concluding that they are generally destructive to troops,
require extensive preparation, and concluding that nothing
but pressing necessity can justify them. Washington goes on
to say that America should acquire mastery of Lake Champlain
and offers a suggested plan to Schuyler requesting his
opinions and comments upon it. Washington also requests an
opinion from Schuyler upon the idea of a possible attack upon
and reduction of the British post at Fort Niagara. This place, a
center of British activity with the Indian Tribes, if conquered,
will help insure the security and safety of the frontiers of
Pennsylvania and Virginia, as well as New York, from the
many incursions those citizens suffer from the raids
originating from Fort Niagara.
    Congress appoints Daniel Roberdeau to Marine Committee.

22 November 1778:
    Sunday. In Philadelphia, Henry Laurens writes to Lt. Col.
Francis Huger, deputy quartermaster general for South
Carolina, informing him that his request to resign that office
will be accepted by the Congress, and the new officer to fill
that position is likely to be Stephen Drayton.

23 November 1778:
    Monday. From Fredericksburgh, Washington writes to
Colonel Theodorick Bland, setting forth the route for the officer
commanding the march of the convention troops beyond the
Hudson River. They are to go by way of New Windsor, New
York, to Sussex Court House New Jersey, thence west to
Lancaster and York, Pennsylvania, then to Frederick,
Maryland and Leesburg, Virginia. "The distance of the seat of

government in Virginia, from those parts through which you pass, prevents my calling in the usual way for the escorts of Militia through that state. I have written a circular letter to the Commanding Officers in the several counties, which you will transmit as you advance in the time and manner you judge most convenient. I send you herewith a warrant for two thousand dollars towards bearing the expense of your command ..."

The Congress resolves that $10,000 be advanced to Lieutenant Colonel Benjamin Temple, of the 1st Regiment of Light Dragoons, for the purpose of payment of arrears to the troops of said regiment due them.

24 November 1778:

Tuesday. The Congress resolves a lengthy set of rules to govern the means of ranking officers in the army. It then orders the Committee of Arrangement to transmit to the Board of War lists of all the officers of the Army, arranged in the several regiments and corps.

25 November 1778:

Wednesday. At headquarters, Fredericksgurgh, Washington writes to Brig. Genl. Anthony Wayne, "You will be pleased to detach a Captain, ... and fifty men who are to lay at Robinson's Mills near Mahopack Pond [New York] till the rear of the Pennsylvania Troops are about passing the North River, then they are to follow and join their respective corps. The intention of this party is to prevent any of the Convention Troops under pretense of desertion, from passing that way to New York. The Captain will detach a Subaltern and sixteen men to Issac Beddoes about half a mile from Robinson's Mills, and at the coming in of another road, for the same purpose. The party of 50 to be furnished with six days provision."

Washington writes to Colonel Daniel Morgan, "You are to remain at Pompton until the rear division of the Convention Troops has passed Chester on the route to Sussex Courthouse. You are then to march to Middlebrook and receive directions from the Quarter Master General for the position of the Brigade under your command in the line of encampment."

The credentials for the delegates of Pennsylvania are presented. Those elected for the ensuing year are Daniel Roberdeau, William Clingan, Edward Biddle, John Armstrong, William Shippen, Samuel Atlee, and James Searle.

26 November 1778:

Thursday. At headquarters, Washington writes to the President of Congress, informing the President by means of a letter being delivered by John Dodge, "... that this fellow Dodge is a strong patriot who has carried on a commercial business on the Indian Frontiers between Pittsburgh and Detroit was captured by the British, jailed in Detroit for a time, then sent to Quebec from which place he escaped and came into our lines. Washington goes on to note that Dodge is well acquainted with the Indian tribes and their languages and knows his way around both Lake Erie and Lake Ontario and would be a very important addition in our dealings with frontier." Washington, therefore, recommends to the President that the Congress find some position for him that will be useful to America in trying to secure the frontier.

In Philadelphia, the delegates of New Jersey, sign and ratify the Articles of Confederation., making New Jersey the 11th state to ratify. The holdouts are Delaware and Maryland.

27 November 1778:

Friday. At headquarters, Washington writes to Sir Henry Clinton, "In order to negotiate an exchange on the principles contained in your letter of the 10th, Lieutenant Colonels Harrison and Hamilton of the Army under my command, will meet Colonels [Charles] O'Hara and [West] Hyde at Amboy, on Monday the seventh of December at 11 o'clock, with proper powers. I would propose as the means of expediting business that our respective Commissaries of prisoners should attend at the same time and place, to carry into execution what shall be determined by the Commissioners."

Washington writes to the president of the Congress, reporting that he is preparing his army to go into winter quarters. The disposition of these encampments are that nine brigades will be stationed on the west side of the Hudson River one of which is to be near Smith's Clove to secure that pass. Another brigade will be at Elizabethtown. The remaining six brigades will be at Middlebrook. Six brigades will be left on the east side of the Hudson River and at West Point. The artillery park will be at Pluckemin New Jersey. "In order as much as possible to reduce the demand of forage and facilitate the supplies, I have given directions when the several divisions arrive at their cantonments, to send away to convenient places at a distance from them, all the horses not absolutely requisite to carry on the ordinary business of the army. It is unnecessary to add, that the Troops must again have recourse to the expedient of hutting, as they did last year." Experience has taught the American Army how it must shelter itself when barracks are not available—which is most of the time.

The Congress avers that officers appointed by the Congress to raise regiments previous to 7 October 1776 ought to receive additional pay from that time. It, therefore, resolves that the paymaster general see that such officers be paid the sums due them under these previous resolutions and appointments of the Congress.

28 November 1778:

Saturday. At headquarters, Fredericksburgh, Washington writes to Brig. Genl. Anthony Wayne, "Genl. [John Peter Gabriel] Muhlenberg had directions not to move from his ground until the 2nd division of the Convention Troops had passed the North River. This I imagine was effected on the 26th and that the Virginia Troops would march yesterday morning; if so, they will have passed you before this reaches you. If they should not, be pleased to send to Genl. Muhlenberg and know the reason of his delay. If you find him in such a situation that you can reach the ferry before him, you may move down, pass over and continue your march to Middlebrook. You did well to see to the order of the boats."

The Congress orders that a warrant for $100,000 be advanced to Colonel Benjamin Flower, Commissary General of Military Stores, for the use of that department.

29 November 1778:
Sunday. At Passy, Benjamin Franklin writes to David Hartley in England, "I have heard nothing from you lately concerning the exchange of prisoners. Is that affair dropped? Winter is coming on apace. I understand that your charitable contribution is near expended and not likely to be renewed. Many of those unfortunate people must suffer greatly. I wish to have a line from you informing me what may be depended on."

Washington is at Fishkill, New York, on the east side of the Hudson River opposite the town of Newburgh, making his headquarters there.

30 November 1778:
Monday. The Congress orders that information on the Convention troops (those British and Hessian units captured under the convention of Saratoga in October 1777) "... be referred to a committee of three, and that the said committee be directed to take measures for collecting evidence relative to the infractions made by the enemy on the convention of Saratoga; and that all the evidence heretofore collected be committed to the said committee."

1 December 1778:
Tuesday. In Philadelphia, the Congress resolves that Colonel George Morgan, commissary of purchases for the western district, be furnished with $204,000 to enable him to form magazines of provisions for the use of that department in the year ensuing.

The New York delegates write to Governor George Clinton, reporting that they have recovered printed copies of the Constitution of the State left behind in Philadelphia when they departed for York. They enclose several for the governor's use, as well as copies of the treaties of Alliance, and of Amity and Commerce between America and France. "While we lament the reiterated sufferings of our fellow citizens from the depredations of the savages and disaffected, we agree with your Excellency that every defensive system in a predatory war must prove vain and chimerical and that a vigorous irruption into the enemy's country can alone promise advantage and safety. To this great object we shall extend our views and endeavour (sic) to have it carried into effect as soon as the season will permit. In the mean time, if the whole of the New York Brigade which is ordered to march for the defence of our frontiers is not thought a sufficient force, be pleased to inform us, and it shall be our care to obtain the aid you may require and to promote any measures which may be recommended for the immediate protection and future security of the State we represent."

2 December 1778:
    Wednesday. Washington is at Elizabethtown, New Jersey.
    Lafayette, now recovered from his bout of illness, leaves Fishkill, to continue his travel to Boston.
    At Philadelphia, James Duane writes to Governor George Clinton, regarding what the Congress considers to be a breach of the Convention of Saratoga "It is the desire of Congress that this perfidious procedure [allowing Burgoyne's army to leave America under any excuse or pretense or convention whatsoever] may be exposed in the fullest light, and they, therefore, request that your Excellency will endeavor to procure further evidence, and, if possible, one of General Carlton's proclamations or orders requiring those troops [British and Hessian soldiers from the Saratoga surrender] to join their respective corps. One thousand dollars in specie are now delivered to Mr. Bancker for the purpose of making the necessary discoveries, to be employed in such manner as your Excellency shall be pleased to direct; when it is expended you will be pleased to remit the account to the Treasury board that you may be properly discharged. I do not think it necessary to send the continental money directed to be paid into your hands, for the above purpose."   The Marine Committee writes to Abraham Whipple "We have received your letter dated November last giving an account of your proceedings in your late voyage which we approve of. At that time you had command of the ship *Columbus*. There was on board her a seaman named John Gallard who says he lost his arm in the engagement with the enemies ship the HMS *Glasgow* and has applied to the Congress for half-pay which by the resolve of Congress he is entitled to during his life. If you know this to be a fact we request that you will transmit to us a Certificate thereof by the first opportunity."

3 December 1778:
    Thursday. At Passy, John Adams writes to the President of Congress enclosing the latest newspapers and stating that while rumors have circulated that the enemy intends to withdraw from the United States, the reverse is too apparent. "We may call it obstinacy or blindness if we will; but such is the state of parties in England, so deep would be the disgrace, and perhaps so great the personal danger to those who have

commenced and prosecuted this war, that they can not but persevere in it at every hazard; and nothing is clearer in my mind than that they never will quit the United States until they are either driven or starved out of them."

4 December 1778:
Friday. The Congress resolves that Lieutenant Henry P. Livingston be promoted to the rank of Captain of the commander-in-chief's guard, replacing Captain Gibbs, lately promoted to Major.

5 December 1778:
Saturday. The Congress resolves that the sentence of the general court martial upon Major General Lee be carried into execution, and orders that the proceedings of the courts martial and the trials of Major General Schuyler and Major General Lee be published.

6 December 1778:
Sunday. Washington is at Paramus, New Jersey, from which he writes to Brig. Gen. Peter Muhlenburg, "You will be pleased upon receipt of this letter, immediately to put the troops under your command in motion with their field artillery and ammunition for Sufference at the mouth of Smith's Clove, and there wait further orders. You will divest yourself of your baggage, which is to be ordered on to the place appointed for winter quarters. You may bring a few tents in some of the strongest wagons to serve in case of very bad weather for the security of the arms but you are not to encumber yourself with many, but to travel as light in every respect as possible."

At Elizabethtown, New Jersey, at 9 o'clock in the evening, Washington writes to Maj. Gen. Nathanael Greene, regarding quartering of troops, "This minute Colo. Hamilton received a letter from Doctor McHenry dated today at Paramus, with the following paragraph, 'desire Colo. Harrison to write to Genl. Greene on the subject of his letter respecting a change of ground for hutting. He may tell Genl. Greene, that the situation marked out in the first instance seems to his Excellency the most eligible; but that Genl. Greene must be a more competent judge, to which place the preference should be given.' With respect to the movements of the enemy the said McHenry writes thus. 'We are informed by a Major of Militia that the enemy's vessels are near King's ferry, and it is said that a body of about 2,000 men are as high up as Tarrytown. Their object would appear forage and provision to be collected between Kingsbridge and the posts at the Highlands.' Genl. Wayne is ordered to Sufferans, Genl. Muhlenburg to the same place; we shall move that way immediately."

7 December 1778:
    Monday. The Congress resolves "That Silas Deane, report to Congress, in writing, as soon as may be, his agency of their affairs in Europe, together with any intelligence respecting their foreign affairs which he may judge proper."

8 December 1778:
    Tuesday. At Passy, John Adams writes to the President of the Congress reporting upon some speeches of Parliament and debates flowing from them. These all indicate efforts on the part of Great Britain to menace the frontiers of the colonies, to reinforce Canada, and to bombard and pillage the coastal towns. Adams believes that concerned British citizens fear losing the war might incur a train of consequences that might include the loss of the West Indies, a part of their East India trade, perhaps also parts of Canada, Nova Scotia, the Floridas and the American Fisheries as well as a diminution of their naval power and national bankruptcy.

9 December 1778:
    Wednesday. The President of the Congress, Henry Laurens, takes his seat, but before entering upon any business, rises and, having assigned several reasons as to why he could not continue any longer to execute the office, resigns as president. The next day is designated for the election of a new person to fill that office.
    The reasons Laurens gives for resigning are that he has already served for more than thirteen months, while the Articles of Confederation, although not yet ratified by all the states, indicates a one year term. Perhaps more importantly he feels that a letter published in the newspaper by Silas Deane "... is a sacrifice of the peace and good order of these states to the personal resentments of Deane," and that he (Laurens) sitting in the chair of the Congress would feel it dishonorable to hear him as he (Deane) presents his case to the Congress. In his speech to the Congress announcing his resignation, Laurens also adds "... I am determined to continue a faithful and diligent laborer in the cause of my country, and at the hazard of life, fortune, and domestic happiness, to continue, by every means in my power to the perfect establishment of our Independence."

10 December 1778:
    Thursday. According to order, the Congress proceeds to the election of a president to replace Henry Laurens, who has resigned. The ballots being taken, John Jay is elected.
    James Duane, a delegate from New York writes to George Clinton, Governor of New York, "Mr. President Laurens, who has been in the Chair 13 months yesterday resigned, sated with honor, and worn down with fatigue. A respect as to the confederacy had a influence on this measure. You remember this grand instrument of our federal union restrains the same

member from serving more than a year at a time. A great majority of the Congress immediately determined that one of the New York Delegates should succeed in the Chair. We held up General Schuyler, which seemed to be very agreeable. On account of his absence, Mr. Jay was prevailed on to take the chair with a resolution on his part to resign in favor of General Schuyler as soon as he attends."

11 December 1778:

Friday. Lafayette arrives at Boston from Fishkill, New York.

At headquarters, Middlebrook, New Jersey, Washington writes to the President of Pennsylvania, Joseph Reed, reporting upon two major recent events. The first of these is Sir Henry Clinton's manoeuver up the Hudson River, as far as King's Ferry. Washington feels that perhaps this was an attempt upon the enemies part to rescue the convention troops. This British incursion lasted less than a day and the British burned only three small houses and nine barrels of spoiled herrings, re-embarked and returned to New York. But it took the time of General Washington to attend to what might have been a serious matter.

The other event is General Charles Lee's publication in Dunlap's Gazette of his (Lee's) actions at the Battle of Monmouth, in an attempt to justify his actions that brought about his court martial. Washington will not respond nor enter into a discussion of these matters by means of a newspaper and feels that Lee "... has misrepresented many facts and thrown out insinuations that have no foundation in truth." Washington's views of Lee is that Lee wants "... to have the world believe that he was a persecuted man ..."

12 December 1778:

Saturday. The Congress receives a petition and representation of Robert Hardie; a petition of Elizabeth Wright; a petition of Mary Werts; and a memorial of the Rev. Adam Boyd, which are read, and referred to the Board of Treasury.

In Philadelphia, John Jay writes to Washington, "Among the various duties incident to the appointment with which Congress has been pleased to honor me, that of corresponding with those public characters whom I most esteem, will be particularly agreeable. This consideration, added to those of a public nature, will constantly press my attention to everything which may respect your Excellency; and permit me to assure you of my endeavor to render the ease and honor of your station and department equal to the high obligations America owes you."

William Paca writes to Thomas Johnson, "I enclose you a few blank Commissions & Bonds. Congress have lately ordered a new Form for Commissions which soon will be published and therefore I send a few only of the old. By a letter from Genl. Washington of the 7th instant we are informed that Clinton & his armament have turned back without being able to effect anything except burning a house or two at Kings Ferry. The General conjectures that Clinton was misinformed of the strength of the Highland Forts. Our army are moving into Winter Quarters."

13 December 1778:
Sunday. In Philadelphia, Samuel Adams writes to his wife Elizabeth, commenting upon some of the political concerns he has. One of these is the feeling he observes in the minister plenipotentiary of France to America, Conrad Alexandre Gérard. Adams believes that Gérard holds a view that he (Adams) would violate the Franco-American Treaty, which includes an article requiring the allies to consult and agree to any conditions of a peace settlement, by agreeing to a separate peace with Britain. Actually, Adams does not hold such a view, except in the case that if the French go behind the American commissioners to quickly conclude a peace for their own purposes, without their knowledge and consent.

14 December 1778:
Monday. The Congress resolves that a new Committee of Commerce be appointed, to consist of five members, and that any three of them be empowered to transact business. The Committee is further to be empowered to employ clerks and bookkeepers, take charge of all the books and paper of the Secret Committee, the Late Committee of Commerce, and call to account the said committees and all other persons entrusted with public moneys for commercial purposes, and in general to conduct the commercial affairs of the United States. This embryonic committee much later in the history of the United States of America will become the Department of Commerce.

15 December 1778:
Tuesday. Eliphalet Dyer and Jesse Root, delegates from the state of Connecticut, attend and produce their credentials and take their seats in the Congress.
At headquarters, Middlebrook, New Jersey, Washington writes to Major General Nathanael Greene, requesting Greene to provide materials for ship-building at Albany, form magazines for forage, entrenching tools, and a number of other items required to build batteaux, wagons, and other means of transport in preparation for an expedition by next April. These preparations will be for the use of the Sullivan Expedition against the Iroquois Indians on the frontier areas of upstate New York.

16 December 1778:
Wednesday. At Middlebrook (now part of Bound Brook), New Jersey, Jacob Weiss, deputy quartermaster writes an order for tools to be used by the army for making their huts

"Broad axes, adzes, claw or carpenter's hammers, 12 or 15 cross-cut saws with cross-cut and hand saw files ... "

Washington had sized up this area of Somerset County on earlier occasions, and deemed it a good place for a winter encampment. More importantly, he wishes to be able to protect New Jersey, continue to threaten the British in New York and Staten Island, and support troops against any enemy advance upon the Highlands.

The Congress resolves "That a convenient furnished dwelling house be hired, and a table, carriage, and servants provided, at the public expense, for the President of Congress for the time being; that the Committee on the Treasury appoint and agree with a steward, who shall have the superintendance [sic] of the household of the President and of the necessary expenditures, and be accountable for such monies as shall, from time to time, be advanced for the purpose aforesaid."

17 December 1778:

Thursday. At Paris, Arthur Lee writes to Floridablanca, enclosing a copy of the proclamation and manifesto issued in America by the British commissioners, which has a plan of desolation and cruelty announced in it and approved by the Parliament. "The intentions of Great Britain, derogatory at once of all the sacred rights of humanity and of the honor God and of the established laws of civilized nations are thus declared in the manifesto."

18 December 1778:

Friday. At Albany, New York, Brigadier General James Clinton writes to General George Washington, reporting that smallpox has made its appearance among the inhabitants of Canajoharie. He also reports that Colonel Peter Gansevoort's regiments have come into Schenectady for the purpose of inoculation.

19 December 1778:

Saturday. At headquarters, Middlebrook, New Jersey, Washington writes to the Baron Von Steuben, "I am much obliged to you for the polite assurances you give; and in my turn, I beg you will believe, that when the institution [Inspector General], at the head of which you have been placed can once be established upon a footing mutually agreeable to you and to the army, to which end all measures I have taken in it have been directed, I shall be happy to give you every support in my power to facilitate your operations. In doing this I shall equally consult the personal consideration I have for you, and the improvement and benefit of the army, which I am persuaded will be greatly promoted by the full exertion of the same talents, experience, and activity, of which you have Already given the most satisfactory proofs."

An extract from the minutes so far as relates to the actions of the Congress on the proceeding and sentence of the general court martial in the trial of Major General Lee, is laid before the Congress and read, whereupon a motion is made that the secretary be directed to furnish Major General Lee with a certified copy of the said extract.

20 December 1778:
Sunday. In Philadelphia, Thomas Burke, a delegate from North Carolina writes to Richard Caswell, Governor of that state, reporting that he arrived on 9 December 1778, and found the Congress much involved in fiscal matters. Burke disapproves of the proposal to call in the Continental paper currency and replace the currency with Loan Certificates.

21 December 1778:
Monday. At headquarters, Middlebrook, Washington issues instructions to Brig. Gen. William Maxwell, "You are appointed to the command at Elizabethtown at which place you are to remain with the New Jersey Brigade; but should you be of opinion that the troops can be more conveniently quartered by removing part to Newark, you may order a Regiment or as many to that place as circumstances shall require. The principal object of your position is to prevent the enemy stationed upon Staten Island from making incursions upon the main and also to prevent any traffic between them and the inhabitants."

Washington writes to Lord Stirling, "Congress having been pleased to require my attendance at Philadelphia for a few days, the immediate command of the troops at this place will devolve upon your leadership. The hutting the troops in the most speedy and commodious manner, and the preservation of order and discipline, I doubt not will receive your Lordship's particular attention."

The Congress agrees to a resolution that Continental currency be received into the continental loan offices, there to be exchanged for certificates to be registered and given to the owners by the commissioners of said offices.

22 December 1778:
Tuesday. Not all Revolutionary persons are the most wonderful, virtuous, upstanding, righteous, patriotic, and disinterested people we have come to believe is the general description of the people of this era. A good example of the lack of these attributes is the matter of Silas Deane. It split the Congress more deeply and violently than any other issue that came before it during the War of the Revolution. Deane is recalled to the Congress to explain his actions and the conduct of his office as a Commissioner of the United States to France. Bitter rivalries develop. Anger, frustration, charges and counter charges are thrown about, most without any support whatsoever. Henry Laurens, the former president of

Congress, is unbelieving that supposed "gentlemen" could behave in such a manner. Deane is left to stew, month after month, and finally takes to the public press in a fit of anger.

23 December 1778:
Wednesday. Washington is in Philadelphia, the guest of Henry Laurens, in order to attend the Congress the next day, to which he has been called for the purpose of discussing future plans and army requirements.

The Maryland Delegates write to Governor Thomas Johnson, "The Expedition against Florida, always was, and still is, in our opinion a dangerous and ruinous project, attended with a certain considerable loss and expense, without the smallest hope of success or advantage. And although Congress have not re-considered or in any way countermanded their former orders and recommendations, yet we think it not improper privately and in confidence to inform you, that there does not appear to us any hope of success in prosecuting this Expedition."

24 December 1778:
Thursday. In Philadelphia, the Commander-in-Chief attends the Congress, in conformance with a Congressional request, in order to confer with them upon specific operations for the next campaign.

John Fell, Delegate from New Jersey, reports in his diary that a committee is appointed to consult with General Washington respecting the ensuing campaign. The remainder of the day was taken in debate upon a number of matters especially the issue of a breach of privilege against General [William] Thompson.

John Jay writes to Joseph Reed, "The President of Congress presents his compliments to the President of the state [Pennsylvania], and sends him by Mr. James Trumbull twelve Commissions for private vessels of war, with an equal number of Bonds & Instructions." These Commissions are for the authorizing of privateers, who will thus be enabled to legally chase, fight, capture, and bring into Port for sale any enemy vessel they may encounter.

25 December 1778:
Friday. At Middlebrook, New Jersey, William Alexander, Lord Stirling writes to George Washington, reporting that he is sending Hessian Major General the Baron Friedrich von Riedesel, with an escort from Sussex Court House to Virginia.

26 December 1778:
Saturday. The Congress resumes consideration of the report of the Committee of the Whole on the subject of finance, and approves an amendment, "That the commissioners of the loan offices make returns to the Treasury Board immediately after the 1st day of June next, of the amount of bills received

into their respective offices, to be exchanged as aforesaid, and that proper bills to exchange the same be furnished and ready to be delivered out at their said offices within sixty days from and after the said first day of June."

27 December 1778:
Sunday. At headquarters in Middlebrook, New Jersey, General Orders state that Captain Abraham Kirkpatrick is appointed brigade major in General Scott's Brigade. The parole is given as Brutus and the countersigns as Berwick and Beverly.

At Philadelphia Washington writes to President Joseph Reed of Pennsylvania, "I am extremely sorry that it is not in my power to inform the Council, with precision, in the several points of their inquiry. The State supplies of clothing hitherto sent to Camp, have been but small and partial. These, I believe, have been generally issued by Officers appointed by the respective states, and conformably to their instructions. It is probable the Genl. Officers of their line have had some direction in the matter, to promote a fair and proper distribution."

28 December 1778:
Monday. In Albany, New York, Brigadier General James Clinton writes to George Washington, reporting that some units do not have a correct return of troops and equipment, that most items of clothing issue are in short supply, and that powder and ball is wanting. This Clinton is the older brother of the Governor of New York, George Clinton, and the father of De Witt Clinton, he of Erie Canal fame. This family is not to be confused with the English family from which Sir Henry Clinton springs.

In Philadelphia, Washington writes to Benjamin Franklin, "The Marquis de Lafayette having served with distinction as Major General in the Army of the United States, two campaigns, has been determined by the prospects of an European War to return to his native Country. It is with pleasure that I embrace the opportunity of introducing to your personal acquaintance a gentlemen whose merit cannot have left him unknown to you by reputation. The generous motives which first induced him to cross the Atlantic; the tribute which he paid to gallantry at Brandywine, his success in Jersey before he had recovered of his wound, in an affair where he commanded Militia against British Grenadiers; the brilliant retreat by which he eluded a combined manoeuver of the whole British force in the last campaign, his services in the enterprise against Rhode Island are such proofs of his zeal, military ardour, and talents as have endeared him to America, and must greatly recommend him to his Prince."

29 December 1778:

Tuesday. At Philadelphia Washington writes to the Marquis de Lafayette, "This will be accompanied by a letter from Congress, which will inform you, that a certain expedition [Canadian expedition], after a full consideration of all circumstances, has been laid aside. I am sorry, however, for the delay it has occasioned you by remaining so long undecided. I am persuaded, my dear Marquis, there is no need of fresh proofs to convince you either of my affection for you personally, or of the high opinion I entertain of your military talents and merit. Yet as you are on the point of returning to your native country, I cannot forbear indulging my friendship by adding to the many honorable testimonies you have received from Congress, the enclosed letter from myself to our minister at your court." (Washington's letter to Franklin of yesterday).

Near Savannah, at Brewton Hill, Georgia, American Major General Robert Howe, with a force of about 700 troops, is attacked by British Colonel Archibald Campbell with 3,000 regulars, and defeated.

30 December 1778:

Wednesday. At headquarters, Middlebrook, Washington writes to Benjamin Harrison, discussing briefly some of his Virginian properties, and dwelling more fully upon the British reactions to the French alliance, and the consequent concern with the area of the West Indies and the large trade from that part of the world. Washington also asks that Virginia send her best men to Congress "... they must not content themselves in the enjoyment of places of honor or profit in their own country, while the common interests of America are mouldering and sinking into irretrievable ..."

In Philadelphia, there not being a sufficient number of states present to proceed to business, the Congress adjourns to 10 o'clock the next day.

31 December 1778:

Thursday. The Congress resolves "That, in addition to the fifteen millions of dollars to be paid the year ensuing, the states be called on to pay in their quotas of six million dollars, annually, for eighteen years, commencing with the year 1780, as a fund for sinking the loans and emissions of the United States to the 31 numeral day of December 1778, inclusive."

This year of 1778 is a critical year in the War of the American Revolution. The main Army, under General George Washington at Valley Forge, had to endure hardships and shortages that sorely tested their ability to survive and function. But they did so, to their everlasting glory! What is more, the arrival of Baron Frederick William Augustus de Steuben (usually styled Von Steuben, and also styled Friedrich Ludolf Gerhard Augustin), provided the Army with the training and discipline it so badly needed. During the winter months, and into the spring of 1778, Steuben trained and organized the American Army, by using small unit samples, each of them then teaching others. The things Von Steuben instills are; position of the soldier, weapon drills, weapon firings, marching in line and column, and maneuvering in the field from one position to another rapidly.

Unlike the previous winter, when the main Army was in New Jersey and had the wonderful help of the forage war assisted by militia to deny supplies to the British, while providing them to the Americans, the British now occupy Philadelphia, and the Americans do not have enough local support from militia to harass them. Thus, provisions, forage, footware, clothing, and ammunition are in short, frequently critical, supply.

As the spring returns, Sir William Howe discovers that merely occupying a city or large town in America, does nothing by way of truly controlling the countryside around it, and applies to resign. He is actually trapped in the city of Philadelphia. Receiving orders acknowledging his request to be relieved, he is delighted to turn over the command to Sir Henry Clinton, whose army, retiring across New Jersey to New York City, is nearly beaten and captured at the Battle of Monmouth Courthouse.

The French enter into a strong alliance with the United States. Other treaties are pursued with other nations by American ministers. The Tories and Indians, based at Fort Niagara, raid the Cherry Valley and the Wyoming Valley, in south central New York and north central Pennsylvania. The British reaction to the French alliance with America causes a shift in both policy and focus of British military actions. Requirements to protect the West Indies sugar islands and the inability of the British land forces to contain, control, or defeat Washington, require new plans in the south.

The Bibliography lists books for further review of the events of this year: Ward, Christopher, *The War of the Revolution*; Busch, Noel F., *Winter Quarters: George Washington and the Continental Army at Valley Forge*; Jackson, John, Valley Forge: *The Pinnacle of Courage*; Stryker, William S., *The Battle of Monmouth*.

APPENDIX 1

ROSTER of MILITIAMEN in CAPT JOHN PARKER'S COMPANY at LEXINGTON on 19 APRIL 1775

OFFICERS:

Capt Parker, John
Ens Munroe, Robert

Lt Tidd, William
Ens Simons, Joseph

NCO's:

Clerk Harrington, Daniel
Cpl Munroe, John
Cpl Sanderson, Samuel
Dummer Diamond, William

Sgt Munroe, William
Cpl Parker, Ebenezer
Cpl Viles, Joel
Fifer Harrington, Jonathan

PRIVATES:

Bowman, Ebenezer
Brown, James
Brown, Solomon
Chandler, John, Jr.
Douglas, Robert
Estabrook, Prince, Wd
Green, Isaac
Harrington, Caleb, KIA
Harrington, Jonathan, KIA
Harrington, Moses, Jr.
Harrington, Thomas
Hastings, Samuel
Hadley, Thomas, Jr.
Hosmer, John
Lock, Ebenezer
Mead, Abner
Munroe, Jedediah, Wd
Munroe, Nathan
Mulliken, Nathaniel
Muzzy, John
Parker, Jonas, Jr.
Pierce, Solomon, Wd
Reed, Joshua
Reed, Nathan
Russell, Philip
Simons, Joshua
Smith, Phineas
Stearns, Phineas
Todd, John, Wd
Underwood, Joseph
Wellington, Enoch
Winship, Thomas, Wd

Bridge, John, Jr.
Brown, John – KIA
Chandler, John
Comee, Joseph, Wd
Durant, Isaac
Farmer, Nathaniel, Wd
Grimes, William
Harrington, John
Harrington, Moses, III
Harrington, Thaddeus
Hastings, Isaac
Hadley, Samuel, KIA
Hagar, Micah
Lock, Benjamin
Lock, Reuben
Munroe, Ebenezer, Jr., Wd
Munroe, John, Jr.
Munroe, William, III
Muzzy, Isaac, KIA
Parker, Jonas, KIA
Parkhurst, Nathaniel
Porter, Asahel, KIA
Reed, Joshua, Jr.
Robbins, John, Wd
Sampson, Benjamin
Smith, John
Snow, Simeon
Stone, Jonas, Jr.
Tidd, Samuel
Wellington, Benjamin
Winship, John
Wood, Sylvanus

Wyman, James

The source for this list is in Coburn, Frank Warren, *The Battle of April 19, 1775*, (Lexington Historical Society, 1922), pp. 60-61

APPENDIX 2

SIGNERS of the DECLARATION of INDEPENDENCE

New Hampshire:

Josiah Bartlett
William Whipple
Matthew Thornton

Massachusetts:

John Hancock
Samuel Adams
John Adams
Robert Treat Paine
Elbridge Garry

Rhode Island:

Stephen Hopkins
William Ellery

Connecticut:

Roger Sherman
Samuel Huntington
William Williams
Oliver Wolcott

New York:

William Floyd
Philip Livingston
Francis Lewis
Lewis Morris

New Jersey:

Richard Stockton
John Witherspoon
Francis Hopkinson
John Hart
Abraham Clark

Pennsylvania:

Robert Morris
Benjamin Rush
Benjamin Franklin
John Morton
James Smith
George Taylor
James Wilson
George Ross

Delaware:

Ceasar Rodney
George Read
Thomas McKean

Maryland:

Samuel Chase
William Paca
Thomas Stone
Charles Carroll

Virginia:

George Wythe
Richard Henry Lee
Thomas Jefferson
Benjamin Harrison
Arthur Middleton
Thomas Nelson, Jr.
Francis L. Lee
Carter Braxton

North Carolina:

William Hooper
Joseph Hewes
John Penn

South Carolina:

Edward Rutledge
ThomasHeyward, Jr.
Thomas Lynch, Jr.

Georgia:

Button Gwinnett
Lyman Hall
George Walton

The Congress, on 2 July 1776, approved a resolution of Richard Henry Lee, presented on 7 June 1776, that "these Colonies are, and of right ought to be, independent States". But it was 4 July 1776 when they finally approved of the language in the Declaration, presented by the five (5) person Committee they had appointed on 10 June 1776. The signing took place on and after 2 August 1776.

APPENDIX 3

MAJOR BATTLES of the WAR of THE AMERICAN REVOLUTION

Listed in this Appendix are many, but not all the battles, skirmishes, fights, and conflicts that took place during that portion of the period of the American Revolution in this Volume 1 from Lexington/Concord through the year 1778. The criteria for inclusion has to do more with the importance of the outcome, rather than the number of men involved. For example, the rather small numbers of men in the George Rogers Clark Expedition, that invaded and secured the Illinois country for the future United Sates, recommends the inclusion of the captures of Kaskaskia, Cahokia, and Vincennes. Each included battle is listed in chronological order, with the date or dates of the engagement, and the page or pages on which the reader will find the sketch for that battle.

Battle	Date	Page
Lexington-Concord, MA	19 Apr 1775	9
Ticonderoga, NY	10 May 1775	17
Crown Point, NY	12 May 1775	18
Siege of Boston, MA	20Apr 1775,17 Mar 1776	12,107
Bunker Hill, MA	17 Jun 1775	28
Chambly, Canada	19 Oct 1775	61
Fort St. John's PQ	2 Nov 1775	66
Montreal, Canada	13 Nov 1775	71
Siege of Quebec, Canada	15 Nov 1775, 6 May 1776	71,120
Ninety-Six, SC	20, 21 Nov 1775	74
Great Bridge, VA	9 Dec 1775	78
Great Canebrake, SC	22 Dec 1775	82
Quebec, PQ	31 Dec 1775	84
Moore's Creek Bridge, NC	27 Feb 1776	102
The Cedars, Canada	19 May 1776	123
Trois Rivieres, PQ	8 Jun 1776	127
Sullivan's Island, SC	28 Jun 1776	131
Lyndley's Fort, SC	15 Jul 1776	138
Esseneccatown, SC	1 Aug 1776	142
Tugaloo River, SC	10 Aug 1776	144
Tamassy, SC	12 Aug 1776	145
Long Island, NY	26-29 Aug 1776	148-150
Kip's Bay, NY	15 Sep 1776	155
Harlem Heights, NY	16 Sep 1776	155
Coweecho River, NC	19 Sep 1776	157
Valcour Island, NY	12 Oct 1776	162
Throg's Neck, NY	13 Oct 1776	162
White Plains, NY	28 Oct 1776	168
Fort Washington, NY	16 Nov 1776	172
Fort Lee, NJ	20 Nov 1776	173
Long Retreat, NJ	21 Nov-7 Dec 1776	174-180

Trenton, NJ	26 Dec 1776	188
Assunpick Creek, NJ	2 Jan 1777	193
Princeton, NJ	3 Jan 1777	195
King's Bridge, NY	17 Jan 1777	199
Millstone, NJ	20 Jan 1777	200
Quibbletown, NJ	8 Feb 1777	205
Bonhamtown, NJ	8 Mar 1777	212
Peekskill, NY	22 Mar 1777	215
Bound Brook, NJ	13 Apr 1777	220
Woodbridge, NJ	19 Apr 1777	222
Ridgefield, CT	27, 28 Apr 1777	224
Thomas Creek, FL	17, 18 May 1777	230
Short Hills, NJ	26 Jun 1777	240
Fort Ticonderoga, NY	6 Jul 1777	244
Hubbardton, Vt	7 Jul 1777	245
Skenesborugh, NY	7 Jul 1777	245
Fort Anne, NY	8 Jul 1777	246
Fort Stanwix, NY	18 Jul 1777	249
Oriskany, NY	6 Aug 1777	255
Bennington, NY	16 Aug 1777	260
Cooch's Bridge, DE	3 Sep 1777	266
Brandywine, PA	11 Sep 1777	269
Freeman's Farm, NY	19 Sep 1777	272
Paoli, PA	21 Sep 1777	273
Diamond Island, NY	23 Sep 1777	274
Philadelphia, PA	25,26 Sep 1777	274
Germantown, PA	4 Oct 1777	278
Fort Montgomery, NY	6 Oct 1777	280
Bemis Heights, NY	7 Oct 1777	280
Kingston, NY	13 Oct 1777	283
Fort Mercer, PA	22 Oct 1777	287
Fort Mifflin, PA	14 Nov 1777	294
Whitemarsh, PA	6,7 Dec 1777	301
Gulph Mills, PA	11 Dec 1777	302
Bordentown, NJ	7 May 1778	359
Monmouth, NJ	28 Jun 1778	379
Kaskaskia, IL	4 Jul 1778	384
Cahokia, IL	6 Jul 1778	385
Butts Hill, RI	29 Aug 1778	405
Brewton Hill, GA	29 Dec 1778	447

454

ACKNOWLEDGMENTS

No historian works alone---and I am no exception.

Many, many writers and diggers in the field of the American Revolution have gone before me and ploughed the ground that makes my efforts easier. During the period of our Bicentennial, with children in tow, I visited all the major sites of the Revolutionary War. Great credit is due the National Park Service, their Rangers and their programs for the wonderful gift they give to the people who learn what happened there.

Very many Libraries have been visited, among which are: The New England Historic Genealogical Society Library, The Connecticut State Library, the New York Genealogical and Biographical Society Library, The New York Historical Association Library, The Library at the United States Military Academy, The David Library of the American Revolution, especially Katie Ludwig; The Library of Congress, the DAR Library, The Library of the Society of the Cincinnati at Anderson House, the SAR Library, The Swem Library, the Williamsburg Foundation Library, The South Carolina Historical Society Library.

Maps are a critically important and useful part of a work of this nature. The mapmaker for this book is Bill Nelson of Accomac, Virginia. Primary proofing of the work was done by David Marsh, the polished copyediting by Diane Nye, and a final proof reading by Harriette Morgan. The Index was prepared by Roxanne Carlson at Flintlock Press. Reviews of parts of this work were read and commented upon by Michael A. Christian, Librarian of the Sons of the American Revolution at Louisville, KY. His valuable suggestions have been most helpful, and many are included.

Fiscal Grant-in-Aid support for this book has been most graciously provided by The Maryland Society of the Sons of the American Revolution (MDSSAR), including a bequest of Wilson King Barnes (Former P-G of the NSSAR, and President of the MDSSAR), by the SGT Lawrence Everhart Chapter of the MDSSAR, and by a member and former President of the Chapter, Dr. Henry Laughlin. The Descendants of the Signers of the Declaration of Independence [DSDI] also contributed to funding for outside contractors for this book.

ABOUT THE AUTHOR

Born into a military family at William Beaumont General Hospital, Fort Bliss, El Paso, Texas on 19 August 1926, Frederick Wallace Pyne, was the eldest child of Frederick Cruger Pyne and Helen Louise Wallace.

His father was a 1924 Graduate of the United States Military Academy at West Point, New York. He resigned his active Commission, kept up a National Guard and Army Reserve status, and joined the Alcoa Company as a Sales Engineer.

Pyne went to public schools in Elizabeth, New Jersey; Pittsburgh, Pennsylvania; and Highland Falls, New York. He enlisted in the Army on 6 June 1944 (D-Day), took his basic training, and went to OCS at Fort Benning, Georgia but, along with all other 18 and 19 year old non-college students, was dismissed after VE day (8 May 1945).

He continued in the Army, including a full year's service in Panama, from which he was selected as a Candidate for West Point, and was transferred to the Army Preparatory School, then at Stewart Field New York. There he took the physical and entrance examinations, and was admitted as a Cadet on 1 July 1948 (Class of 1952).

However, he later resigned from West Point, and completed his undergraduate education at Tri-State College (now re-named Trine University), in Angola, Indiana, earning a B.S.C.E. degree. He married Jo Ann Rammes in Birmingham, Michigan on 18 July 1952. They removed to Maryland in June 1954, and had four children. He was employed as an Engineer by the State and the Army for a total of 34 years. He earned a Master's Degree from Johns Hopkins University in 1966 (M.S.E.), and a PhD from Canbourne University in London, England in 2005.

Retiring from the DOD as a biomedical engineer in 1988, he took a position as an Adjunct Professor of Mathematics at the Frederick Community College. He still teaches occasional courses in History and English Literature through the Institute for Learning in Retirement [ILR].

456

Fig. XI-51: The Rev. Frederick W. Pyne, Author

Coming late in life to Holy Orders, he was ordained in the United Episcopal Church of North America [UECNA], served as the Rector of a congregation in Frederick, Maryland, and retired in 2000. Pyne is very interested in English and Early American History, and has published several works on genealogy, which he considers the handmaiden of history.

During his "working" life, he had been a Professional Registered Engineer in Maryland, Pennsylvania, Delaware, and New York; and a Fellow of the American Society of Civil Engineers (F.A.S.C.E.) He was a Registered Sanitarian, and a Registered Land Surveyor in the State of Maryland. He is a Professional Genealogist, and had been Certified by the Board for Certification of Genealogists. He was also listed in Marquis Who's Who in America, 1999, 54th Edition.

He is a member of many Lineage Societies, including: Society of Mayflower Passengers (Maryland Elder), Ancient and Honorable Artillery Company of Massachusetts, Colonial Clergy, Descendants of the Illegitimate Sons and Daughters of the Kings of Britain, The Crown of Charlemagne, National Society Americans of Royal Descent, Sons of the Revolution (PA), Sons of the American Revolution (MD, Former State Registrar, Former Chapter President), New York State Society of the Cincinnati, Descendants of the Signers of the Declaration of Independence (Former President-General, Former Registrar-General, current Chaplain-General), Society of Early Quakers, National Society of the Sons and Daughters of the Pilgrims, Society of Colonial Wars, Society of the War of 1812.

He now resides in a Continuing Care Retirement Community (CCRC), "Buckingham's Choice", near Buckeystown, Maryland, with is wife of more than 56 years. There he devotes much of his time to genealogy, historical writing, and teaching.

BIBLIOGRAPHY

Aaron, Larry G., *The Race to the Dan: The Retreat that Rescued the American Revolution,* (Warwick House, Lynchburg, VA, 2007)

Abernethy, Thomas Perkins, *Western Lands and the American Revolution,* (Russell & Russell, Inc., NYC, 1959)

Alden, John R., *A History of the American Revolution,* (Alfred A. Knopf, 1969, Reprint Da Capo)

Alden, John R., *The Revolution in the South, 1763-1783,* (Baton Roughe, LA, 1954)

Allen, Gardner W., *A Naval History of the American Revolution,* (Williamstown, MA, 1913), 2 vols.

Almon, John, *The Parliamentary Register, or History of the Proceedings and Debates of the House of Lords, 1775 - 1784,* (London), 17 vols.

Anderson, Fred, *Crucible of War: The Seven Years' War and the Fate of Empire in British North America, 1754-1776,* (Alfred Knopf, 2000)

Anderson, Lee Patrick, *Forty Minutes by the Delaware: The Story of the Whitalls, Red Bank Plantation, and the Battle for Fort Mercer,* (Upublish.com, 1999)

Augur, Helen, *The Secret War of Independence,* (New York, 1955)

Babits, Lawrence E., *A Devil of a Whipping: The Battle of Cowpens,* (University of North Carolina, 1998)

Bailyn, Bernard, *Faces of Revolution: Personalities and Themes in the Struggle for American Independence,* (Alfred A. Knopf, New York, 1990)

Bailyn, Bernard, *To Begin the World Anew; The Genius and Ambiguities of the American Founders,* (Alfred A. Knopf, New York, 2003)

Bakeless, John, *Background to Glory: The Life of George Rogers Clark,* (Philadelphia, 1957)

Baker, William S., *Itinerary of General Washington from June 15, 1775 to December 23, 1783,* (Hunterdon House, Lambertville, New Jersey, Reprint, 1970)

Barefoot, Daniel W., *Touring North Carolina's Revolutionary War Sites*, (John F. Blair, Publisher, Winston-Salem, NC, 1998)

Barefoot, Daniel W., *Touring South Carolina's Revolutionary War Sites*, (John F. Blair, Publisher, Winston-Salem, NC, 1999)

Barnhart, John D., Ed., *Henry Hamilton and George Rogers Clark in the American Revolution*, (Crawfordsville, IN, 1951)

Barnes, Ian, *The Historical Atlas of the American Revolution*, (Routledge, NY, 2000)

Barthomees, James B., Jr., *Fight or Flee: The Combat performance of the North Carolina Militia in the Cowpens-Guilford Courthouse Campaign, January to March 1781*, (PhD. Dissertation, Duke University, 1978)

Bass, Robert D., *Gamecock: The Life and Campaigns of General Thomas Sumter*, (Holt, Rhinehart and Winston, New York, 1961)

Bass, Robert D., *Ninety-Six: The Struggle for the South Carolina Back Country*, (Sandlapper Press, Lexington, South Carolina, 1978)

Bass, Robert D., *Swamp Fox: The Life and Campaigns of General Francis Marion*, (Henry Holt and Co., New York, 1959)

Bass, Robert D., *The Green Dragoon*, (Paperback, 2003)

Becker, Carl, *The Declaration of Independence*, (Vintage Books, 1970)

Bemis, Samuel Flagg, *The Diplomacy of the American Revolution*, (New York, 1935)

Berg, Fred Anderson, *Encyclopedia of Continental Army Units: Battalions, Regiments, and Independent Corps*, (Harrisburg, 1972)

Bill, Alfred Hoyt, *The Campaign of Princeton, 1776-1777*, (Princeton University Press, 1948)

Bill, Alfred Hoyt, *New Jersey and the Revolutionary War*, (Van Nostrand Company, 1964)

Billias, George Athan, *George Washington's Generals and Opponents: Their Exploits and Leadership*, (Da Capo Press, 1994)

Bird, Harrison, *Navies in the Mountains*, (Oxford University Press, 1962)

Bird, Harrison, *Attack on Quebec*, (Oxford University Press, 1968)

Birnbaum, Louis,, *Red Dawn at Lexington; "If They Mean to Have a War, Let It Begin Here."*, (Houghton Mifflin Company, Boston, 1986)

Black, Jeremy, *War for America: The Fight for Independence, 1775-1783*, (New York, St. Martin's Press, 1991)

Blake, John Ballard, *Public Health in the Town of Boston, 1630 - 1822*, (Harvard University Press, 1959)

Blanco, Richard L.,Editor, *The American Revolution 1775 - 1783 An Encyclopedia*, (Garland Publishing, Inc., New York, 1993), 2 vols.

Bliven, Bruce, *Battle for Manhattan*, (New York, 1956)

Boatner, Mark Mayo, III, *Landmarks of the American Revolution*, (Stackpole Books, 1973)

Boatner, Mark Mayo, III, *Encyclopedia of the American Revolution*, (Stackpole Books, 1994)

Bodle, Wayne K., *Valley Forge Winter: Civilians and Soldiers in War*, (University Park, 2002)

Borick, Carl P., *A Gallant Defense: The Siege of Charleston, 1780*, (University of South Carolina Press, 2003)

Borneman, Walter R., *The French & Indian War; Deciding the Fate of North America*, (HarperCollins, 2006)

Boudinot, Elias, *Journal or Historical Recollections of American Events During the Revolutionary War*, (1894)

Bowen-Hassel, Gordon E., et als., *Sea Raiders of the American Revolution: The Continental Navy in European Waters*, (Naval History Center, Washington, DC, 2003)

Boyle, Joseph Lee, *Writings from the Valley Forge Encampment of the Continental Army, December 19, 1777 - June 19, 1779*, (Heritage Books, 2002 - 2004), 5 vols.

Breeden, Robert L., Ed, *The Revolutionary War, America's Fight for Freedom*, (National Geographic Society, 1967)

Bridenbaugh, Carl, *Cities in Revolt*, (Alfred A. Knopf, Inc. New York, 1955)

Buchanan, John, *The Road to Guilford Courthouse: The American Revolution in the Carolinas*, (John Wiley and Sons, 1997)

Buchanan, John, *The Road to Valley Forge; How Washington Built the Army That Won the Revolution*, (John Wiley & Sons, Inc., 2004)

Buel, Richard Jr., *Dear Liberty: Connecticut's Mobilization for the Revolutionary War*, (Wesleyan University Press, Middletown, Connecticut, 1980)

Buker, George E., *The Penobscot Expedition: Commodore Saltonstall and the Massachusetts Conspiracy of 1779*, (Naval Institute Press, Annapolis, 2002)

Busch, Noel F., *Winter Quarters: George Washington and the Continental Army at Valley Forge*, (PhD. Dissertation, University of Pennsylvania, 1987)

Burgoyne, Bruce E., Editor, *Enemy Views: The American Revolutionary War as Recorded by the Hessian Participants*, (Heritage Books, 1996)

Burnet, Edmund C., Editor, *Letters of Members of the Continental Congress*, (Carnegie Institution of Washington, DC, 1921-1936), 8 Volumes

Caldwell, E. I., *Fort St. Jean on the Richelieu River*, (Bulletin of the Fort Ticonderoga Museum, Vol. IV, No. 7, July 1938)

Callahan, North, *Henry Knox, General Washington's General*, (Reprint, Friends of Montpelier, 1989)

Calloway, Colin G., *The Scratch of a Pen: 1763 and the Transformation of North America*, (Oxford University Press, 2006)

Carp, Benjamin L., *Rebels Rising: Cities and the American Revolution*, (Oxford University Press, 2007)

Carrington, Henry B., *Battles of the American Revolution, 1775-1781*, (Reprint, Promontory Press, 1972)

Cashin, Edward J., *William Bartram and the American Revolution on the Southern Frontier*, (University of South Carolina Press, 2000)

Caughey, John W., *Bernardo de Galvez in Louisiana, 1776 - 1783*, (Berkely, CA, 1934)

Chandler, Allen D., Editor, *The Revolutionary Records of the State of Georgia*, (1908, Reprint New York, 1972), 3 vols.

Chadwick, Bruce, *The First American Army: The Untold Story of George Washington and the Men Behind America's First Fight for Freedom*, (Sourcebooks, Inc, 2005)

Chadwick, Bruce, *George Washington's War; The Forging of a Revolutionary Leader and the American Presidency*, (Sourcebooks, Inc, 2005)

Chidsey, Donald Barr, *July 4, 1776, The Dramatic Story of the First Four Days of July, 1776*, (Crown Publishers, Inc., 1967)

Chidsey, Donald Barr, *The War in the North: An Informal History of the American Revolution in and Near Canada*, (Crown Publishers, Inc., 1967)

Chidsey, Donald Barr, *The War in the South: The Carolinas and Georgia 9in the American Revolution*, (Crown Publishers, Inc., 1969)

Clark, Malcolm C., *The Coastwise and Caribbean Trade of the Chesapeake Bay, 1696-1776*, (PhD. Dissertation, Georgetown University, 1970)

Clark, William Bell, Editor, *Naval Documents of the American Revolution*, (Washington, DC, DON, Naval History Division, 1964 - 1976), 10 Vols.

Clarke, William Butler, Editor, *Col. John Brown's Expedition Against Ticonderoga and Diamond Island, 1777*, (Boston, New England Historical and Genealogical Register, v. 74, Oct. 1920, pp. 284-293)

Clary, David A., *Adopted Son: Washington, Lafayette, and the Friendship That Saved the Revolution*, New York, Bantam Books, 2007)

Clement, Justin, *Philadelphia 1777, Taking the Capital*, (Osprey Publications, 2007)

Clinton, Henry, *The American Rebellion: Sir Henry Clinton's Narrative of his Campaigns, 1775-1782*, (Edited by William Willcox, Hampden, CT, Archon Books, 1971)

Closen, Ludwig, *The Revolutionary Journal of Baron Lugwig Von Closen, 1780-1783*, (Translated and edited by Evelyn M. Acomb, University of North Carolina Press, 1958)

Coburn, Frank Warren, *The Battle of 19 April 1775*, (Lexington Historical Society, 1922)

Coggins, Jack, *Ships and Seamen of the American Revolution,* (Dover Publications, 2002)

Cohen, Sheldon, *Yankee Sailors in British Gaols: Prisoners of War at Forton and Mill, 1777-1783,* (Newark, DE, 1995)

Coffin, Howard, Curtis, Jane and Will, *Guns Over the Champlain Valley: A Guide to Historic Military Sites and Battlefields,* (The Countryman Press, Woodstock, VT, 2005)

Commanger, Henry Steele & Morris, Richard B., *The Spirit of Seventy-Six: The Story of the American Revolution as Told by its Participants,* (1958, Reprint, Castle Books, 2002)

Conrad, Dennis M., *Nathanael Greene and the Southern Campaigns, 1780-1783,* (PhD. Dissertation, Duke University, 1979)

Cook, Fred J., *Dawn Over Saratoga: The Turning Point of the Revolutionary War,* (Doubleday, 1973)

Conway, Stephen, *The British Isles and the War of American Independence,* (New York, 2000)

Corwin, Edward S., *French Policy and the American Alliance of 1778,* (Gloucester, MA, 1969)

Countryman, Edward, *A People in Revolution:The American Revolution and Political Society in New York, 1760-1790,* (Johns Hopkins University Press, Baltimore, 1981)

Cox, Caroline, *A Proper Sense of Honor: Service and Sacrifice in George Washington's Army,* (Chapel Hill, 2004)

Curtis, Edward M, III, *The Organization of the British Army,* (New Haven, 1926)

Dameron, J. David, *Kings Mountain: The Defeat of the Loyalists,* (Da Capo Press, 2003)

Dann, John C., *The Revolution Remembered: Eyewitness Accounts of the War for Independence,* (University of Chicago Press, 1980)

Daughan, George C., *If by Sea; The Forging of the American Navy, from the Revolution to the War of 1812,* (Basic Books, New York, 2008), especially Chapters 1 - 7

Daughters of the American Revolution, *Forgotten Patriots—African American and American Indian Patriots of the*

Revolutionary War: A Guide to Service, Sources, and Studies, Washington, DC, 2008), 2nd Edition

Davies, K. G., Editor, *Documents of the American Revolution 1770-1783*, (Shannon, Irish University Press, 1976)

Davis, Burke, *The Cowpens-Guilford Courthouse Campaign*, (J. B. Lippincott Company, Philadelphia, 1962

Davis, Burke, *The Campaign That Won America: The Story of Yorktown*, (Dial Press, New York, 1970)

Davis, Burke, *George Washington and the American Revoultion*, (Random House, 1975)

Davis, David Brion, *The Problem of Slavery in the Age of the American Revolution*, (Ithaca, New York, 1973)

Davis, David Brion and Mintz, Steven, Editors, *The Boisterous Sea of Liberty: A Documentary History of America from Discovery through the Civil War*, (Oxford University Press, 1998), especially pp. 173-218

Davis, Robert P., *Where a Man Can Go: Major General William Phillips, British Royal Artillery, 1731-1781*, (Westport, CT, 1999)

Draper, Lyman C., *King's Mountain, it's Heroes. History of King's Mountain, October 7, 1780*, (Overmountain Press, Johnson City, TN, Reprint, 1996)

Dearborn, Henry, *Revolutionary War Journals of Henry Dearborn, 1775-1783*, (Books for Libraries Press, Freeport, NY, 1969)

Denny, Ebenezer, *Military Journal of Major Ebenezer Denny, an Officer in the Revolutionary and Indian Wars*, (Philadelphia, Historical Society of Pennsylvania, 1859)

Desjardin, Thomas A., *Through a Howling Wilderness: Benedict Arnold's March to Quebec, 1775*, (St. Martin's Press, New York, 2006)

Diamant, Lincoln, *Chaining the Hudson: The Fight for the River in the American Revolution*, (Fordham University Press, New York, 2004)

DiIonno, *A Guide to New Jersey's Revolutionary War Trail*, (Barnes & Nobel, 2000)

Doddridge, John, *The Settlement and Indian Wars of the Western Parts of Virginia and Pennsylvania, 1763-1783*, (Heritage Books, 2004)

Draper, Theodore, *A Struggle for Power: The American Revolution*, (New York, 1995)

Dukes, Richard Sears, Jr., *Anatomy of a Failure: British Military Policy in the Southern Campaign of the American Revolution, 1775-1781*, (PhD. Dissertation, University of South Carolina, 1993)

Dull, Jonathan R., *The French Navy and American Independence: A Study of Arms and Diplomacy, 1774-1787*, (Princeton University Press, 1975)

Dull, Jonathan R., *A Diplomatic History of the American Revolution*, (Yale University Press, 1985)

Dupuy, Trevor Nevitt, *The Military History of Revolutionary War: Naval Battles*, (Franklin Watts, Inc., 1970)

Dupuy, Trevor Nevitt & Hammerman, Gay M., *People and Events of the American Revolution*, (R.R. Bowker, Company, New York, 1974)

Dwyer, William, *The Day is Ours! November 1776-January 1777; An Inside View of the Battles of Trenton and Princeton*, (Rutgers University Press, 1998)

Eckenrode, H.J., *The Revolution in Virginia*, (Archon Books, 1964)

Edgar, Walter B., *Partisans And Redcoats: The Southern Conflict That Turned the Tide of the American Revolution*, (HarperCollins, 2003)

Edler, Friedrich, *The Dutch Republic and the American Revolution*, (The Johns Hopkins Press, 1911)

Eller, Ernest McNeill, Editor, *Chesapeake Bay in the American Revolution*, (Tidewater Publishers, Centreville, MD, 1981)

Ellis, Davis M., *The Saratoga Campaign*, (McGraw, 1969)

Ellis, Joseph J., *Founding Brothers: The Revolutionary Generation*, (New York, 2000)

Ellis, Joseph J., *America Creation; Triumphs and tragedies at the Founding of the Republic*, (Alfred A. Knopf, New York, 2007)

Elting, John R., *The Battles of Saratoga*, (Philip Freneau Press, Monmouth, NJ, 1977)

Esposito, Vincent J., Brigadier General, Chief Editor, *The West Point Atlas of American Wars; Volume I 1689-1900*, (Henry Holt and Company, Inc., 1995)

Evans, Elizabeth, *Weathering the Storm: Women of the American Revolution*, (Scribner's, 1975)

Everest, Allan S., *Moses Hazen and the Canadian Refugees in the American Revolution*, (Syracuse University Press, 1976)

Fenn, Elizabeth A., *Pox Americana: The Great Smallpox Epidemic of 1775-1782*, (Hill and Wang, 2001)

Ferguson, Clyde R., *General Andrew Pickens*, (PhD. Dissertation, Duke University, 1960)

Ferling, John, *The Loyalist Mind: Joseph Galloway and the American Revolution*, (Pennsylvania State University, 1977)

Ferling, John, *A Wilderness of Miseries: War and Warriors in Early America*, (Greenwood Publishing Group, 1981)

Ferling, John, Editor, *The World Turned Upside Down: The American Victory in the War of Independence*, (Greenwood Press, New York, 1988)

Ferling, John, *Struggle for a Continent: The Wars of Early America*, (Harlan Davidson, 1993)

Ferling, John E., *Setting the World Ablaze: Washington, Adams, Jefferson and the American Revolution*, (Oxford University Press, 2000)

Ferling, John, *A Leap in the Dark: The Struggle to Create the American Republic*, (Oxford University Press, 2004)

Ferling, John E., *Almost a Miracle: The American Victory in the War of Independence*, (Oxford University Press, 2007)

Fischer, David Hackett, *Albion's Seed: Four British Folkways in America*, (Oxford University Press, 1989)

Fischer, David Hackett, *Paul Revere's Ride*, (Oxford University Press, 1994)

Fischer, David Hackett, *Washington's Crossing*, (Oxford University Press, 2004)

Fischer, Joseph R., *A Well-Executed Failure: The Sullivan Campaign against the Iroquois, July-September 1779*, (Columbia, University of South Carolina Press, 1997)

Fitzpatrick, John C., *The Writings of George Washington, from the Original Manuscript Sources 1745 - 1799*, (Washington, DC, 1931 - 1944, 39 vols., especially vols. 3 - 27

Fleming, Thomas J., *Now We Are Enemies: The Story of Bunker Hill*, (St. Martin's Press, 1960)

Fleming, Thomas, J., *Beat the Last Drum: The Siege of Yorktown, 1781*, (St. Martin's Press, 1963)

Fleming, Thomas J., *The Forgotten Victory; The Battle for New Jersey - 1780*, (Reader's Digest Press, 1973)

Fleming, Thomas J., *Downright Fighting, The Story of Cowpens*, (National Park Service Handbook, 135, Superintendent of Documents, Government Printing Office, Washington, DC, 1988)

Fleming, Thomas J., *1776: Year of Illusions*, (Castle Books, Edison, NJ, 1996)

Fleming, Thomas J., *Liberty! The American Revolution*, Viking; The Penguin Group, 1997)

Fleming, Thomas J., *The Perils of Peace: America's Uncertain Fate After Yorktown*, (HarperCollons Publishers, Inc., 2007)

Flexner, James Thomas, *Washington, The Indispensable Man*, (Little, Brown and Company, 1974)

Flood, Charles Bracelem, *Rise, and Fight Again: Perilous Times Along the Road to Independence*, (Dood, Mead, 1976)

Foner, Eric, *Tom Paine and Revolutionary America*, (New York University Press, 2005)

Foote, Allan B., *Liberty March: The Battle of Oriskany*, (North Country Books, 1999)

Force, Peter, Editor, *American Archives, 3 Series*, (Washington, 1853) 9 volumes

Ford, Worthington Chauncey, editor, *Journals of the Continental Congress, 1774-1789*, (Washington, DC, 1904-1937; Reprint New York, 1971), 34 volumes; especially volumes 2 -25

Fortescue, Sir John, *A History of the British Army*, (Macmillian, London, 1902), 13 Volumes, in particular v. 3. 1763-1793.

Fortescue, Sir John, *The War of Independence; The British Army in North America, 1775-1783*, (Stackpole Books, 2001)

Forthingham, Richard, *History of the Siege of Boston and the Battles of Lexington, Concord, and Bunker Hill, Also, an Account of the Bunker Hill Monument with Illustrative Documents*, (Scholars Bookshelf, 2005)

Fowler, David J., *Guide to the Sol Feinstone Collection of the David Library of the American Revolution*, (Washington Crossing, PA, 1994)

Fowler, William M, Jr., *Rebels Under Sail: The American Navy During the Revolution*, (Scibners, 1976)

Fredriksen, John C., *Revolutionary War Almanac*, (Facts on File, 2006)

Freeman, Douglas Southall, *George Washington*, (Charles Scribner's Sons), 1951), 7 volumes, particularly 3, 4, 5.

French, Allen, *The Day of Lexington and Concord*, (Little Brown & Company, Boston, MA, 1925)

French, Allen, *The First Year of the American Revolution*, (Boston, 1934)

Frey, Sylvia R., Water from the Rock: *Black Resistance in a Revolutionary Age*, (Princeton, NJ, 1991)

Frothingham, Richard, *History of the Siege of Boston*, (Reprint Da Capo Press, 1970)

Furcron, Thomas B., *Mount Independence, 1776-1777*, (Bulletin of the Fort Ticonderoga Museum, Vol. IX, No.4, 1954)

Gallagher, John J. *The Battle of Brooklyn*, (Da Capo Press, 2001)

Galloway, Colon G., *The Scratch of a Pen: 1763 and the Transformation of North America*, (Oxford University Press, 2006)

Galvez, Bernardo de, *Yo Solo*, (Journal # 587p, His battle journal during the American Revolution, David Library of the American Revolution, Washington's Crossing, PA)

Galvin, John R. [General], *The Minutemen: The First Fight: Myths and Realities of the American Revolution*, (1989)

Gardiner, Robert, ed., *Navies and the American Revolution*, (Naval Institute Press, 1996)

Gardner, W. Allen, *A Naval History of the American Revolution*, (1913, Reprint Williamstown, MA, 1970), 2 Volumes

Gerlach, Don R., *Philip Schuyler and the American Revolution in New York*, (Lincoln, NE: University of Nebraska Press, 1964)

Gibson, Lawrence Henry, *The Coming of the Revolution*, (Harper & Row, 1954)

Glatthaar, Joseph T. And Martin, James Kirby, *Forgotten Allies: The Oneida Indians and the Amer8ican Revolution*, (New York, 2006)

Godfrey, Carlos E., *The Commander-in-Chief's Guard*, (1904; Reprint, Clearfield Press, Baltimore, MD, 2001)

Golway, Terry, *Washington's General: Nathanael Greene and the Triumph of the American Revolution*, (Henry Holt and Co., 2005)

Gordon, John B., *South Carolina and the American Revolution: A Battlefield History*, (University of South Carolina Press, 2003)

Gordon, John W., *South Carolina and the American Revolution; A Battlefield History*, (University of South Carolina, 2003)

Graymont, Barbara, *The Iroquois in the American Revolution*, (Syracuse University Press, 1972)

Greene, Jack P., Editor, *Colonies to Nation, 1763-1789: A Documentary History of the American Revolution*, (W.W. Norton & Company, Ndew Yoerk, 1975)

Greene, Jack P.& Pole, J.R., Editors, *The Blackwell Encyclopedia of the American Revolution*, (Cambridge, MA, 1991)

Greene, Jerome A., *The Guns of Independence: The Siege of Yorktown, 1781*, (Savas Beatie, NY, 2005)

Grenier, John E., *The Other American Way of War: Unlimited and Irregular Warfare in the Colonial Military Tradition*, (PhD. Dissertation, University of Colorado, 1999)

Hallahan, William H., *The Day The American Revolution Began, 19 April 1775*, (William Morrow and Company, 2000)

Hallahan, William H., *The Day The Revolution Ended, 19 October 1781*, (John Wiley & Sons, Inc, 2004)

Halsey, Francis Whiting, *The Old New York Frontier: Its Wars with Indians and Tories, Its Missionary Schools, Pioneers and Land Titles, 1614-1800*, (1901, Reprint, Heritage Books, 1996)

Hamilton, Edward Pierce, *Fort Ticonderoga; Key to a Continent*, (Little, Brown and Company, 1964)

Hannings, Bud, *Chronology of the American Revolution: Military and Political Actions Day by Day*, (McFarland & Company, 2008)

Harvey, Robert, *A Few Bloody Noses: The Realities and Mythologies of the American Revolution*, (Overlook Press, New York, 2003)

Hatch, Louis Clinton, *The Administration of the American Revolutionary Army*, (New York, 2004)

Hawke, David Freeman, *A Transaction of Free Men*, (Da Capo Press, 1988)

Hearn, Chester G., *George Washington's Schooners*, Naval Institute Press, Annapolis, 1995)

Heitman, Francis B., *Historical Register of Officers of the Continental Army During the War of the Revolution*, (Clearfield Press,2000)

Hendrickson, Robert, *Hamilton I (1757-1789)*, New York, Mason/Charter, 1976)

Herkimer, Gil, *Roads to Oriskany*, (Alfa Publications, 1996)

Hibbert, Christopher, *Redcoats and Rebels; The War for America, 1770-1781*, (London, The Folio Society, 2006)

Hielscher, Udo, *Financing the American Revolution*, (Museum of American Financial History, New York, 2003)

Higginbotham, Don, *Daniel Morgan, Revolutionary Rifleman*, (University of North Carolina Press, 1961)

Higginbotham, Don, *The War of the American Independence: Military Attitudes, Policies, and Practice, 1763-1789*, (The Macmillan Company, New York, 1971)

Higginbotham, Don, *George Washington and the American Military Tradition*, (University of Georgia Press, Athens, 1985)

Hill, Ralph Nading, *Lake Champlain: Key to Liberty*, (Countryman Press, 1995)

Hilowitz, Harry, *Revolutionary War Chronology and Almanac*, (Hope Farm Press, 1995)

Hoffer, Edward E., *Operational Art and Insurgency War: Nathanael Greene's Campaign in the Carolinas*, (Command and General Staff College, Fort Leavenworth, KS, 1988)

Hollinshead, Byron, *I Wish I'd Been There*, (New York, 2006)

Hudson, Ruth Strong, *The Minister from France: Conrad Alexander Gérard*, (Euclid, Ohio, 1994)

Huston, James H., *The Sinews of War: Army Logistics, 1775-1783*, (Washington, DC, 1966)

Ippel, Henry P., *Jeffery, Lord Amherst, British Commander-in-Chief, 1778-1782*, (PhD. Dissertation, University of Michigan, 1957)

Isaacson, Walter, *Benjamin Franklin, an American Life*, (Simon & Schuster, New York, 2003), particularly Chapters 12, 13, 14.

Isenberg, Nancy, *Fallen Founder: The Life of Aaron Burr*, (Viking Press, New York, 2007)

Jackson, John, *Valley Forge: Pinnacle of Courage*, (Gettysburg, PA, Thomas Publications, 1999)

Jackson, John W., *The Delaware Bay and River Defenses of Philadelphia, 1775-1777*, (Rutgers University Press, 1974)

Jackson, John W., *With the British Army in Philadelphia, 1777-1778*, (Presidio Press, Ann Rafael, California, 1979)

Jennings, Francis, *Empire of Fortune*, (W.W. Norton & Company, 1988)

Jenson, Merrill, *The Founding of a Nation*, (Oxford University Press, 1968)

Johnson, Paul, *A History of the American People*, (HarperCollins Publishers, 1997), especially Part Two

Johnston, Elizabeth Bryant, *George Washington; Day by Day*, (Cycle Publishing Company, 1895)

Johnston, Henry Phelps, *Campaign of Seventeen Seventy Six in and Around New York and Brooklyn*, (Da Capo Press, 1971)

Johnston, Henry Phelps, *The Yorktown Campaign and the Surrender of Cornwallis, 1781*, (Eastern Acorn Press, 1997)

Kajencki, Francis Casimir, *Casimir Pulaski: Cavalry Commander of the American Revolution*, (El Paso, Texas, 2001)

Kaplan, Sidney and Kaplan, Emma Nogrady, *The Black Presence in the Era of the American Revolution*, (Amherst, MA, 1989)

Karapalides, Harry J. *Dates of the American Revolution*, (Burd Street Press, (1998)

Keegan, John, *Fields of Battle: The War for North America*, (New York, 1996)

Kennett, Lee, *The French Forces in America, 1780-1783*, (Greenwood Press, Westport, CT, 1977)

Ketchum, Richard M., *Decisive Day: The Battle of Bunker Hill*, (Henry Holt and Company, 1974)

Ketchum, Richard M., *Divided Loyalties: How the American Revolution Came to New York*, (Henry Holt and Company, 2002)

Ketchum, Richard M., *Saratoga, Turning Point of America's Revolutionary War*, (Henry Holt and Company, 1997)

Ketchum, Richard M., *The Winter Soldiers; The Battles for Trenton and Princeton*, (Doubleday, 1973)

Ketchum, Richard M., *Victory at Yorktown, the Campaign That Won the Revolution*, (Henry Holt Company, NY, 2004)

Kirkwood, Robert, *The Journal and Order Book of Captain Robert Kirkwood of the Delaware Regiment of the Continental Line*, (Edited by Joseph Brown Turner, Port Washington, NY, Kennikat Press, 1970)

Knouff, Gregory T., *The Soldiers' Revolution: Pennsylvania in Arms and the Forging of Early American Identity*, (University Park, PA, 2004)

474   Bibliography

Krueger, John W., *Troop Life at the Champlain Valley Forts During the American Revolution*, (Bulletin of the Fort Ticonderoga Museum, Vol. XIV, No. 4 & 5, 1984)

Kwasny, Mark Vincent, *Washington's Partisan War, 1775-1783*, (Kent State University Press, 1996)

Lancaster, Bruce, *From Lexington to Liberty, The Story of the American Revolution*, (Doubleday & Company, 1955)

Landers, H.L., *The Battle of Camden, S.C., August 16, 1780*, (Kershaw County Historical Society, 1997)

Langguth, A.J., *Patriots: The Men Who Started the American Revolution*, (Simon & Schuster, 1988)

Larrabee, Harold Atkins, *Decision at the Chesapeake*, (Clarkson A. Potter, NY, 1964)

Leckie, Robert, *George Washington's War: The Saga of the American Revolution*, (Harper Collons Publishers, 1992)

Lefkowitz, Arthur S., *The Long Retreat: The Calamitous American Defense of New Jersey, 1776*, (Rutgers University Press, 1999)

Lefkowitz, Arthur S., *George Washington's Indispensable Men: The 32 Aides-de-Camp Who Helped Win American Independence*, (Stackpole Books, Mechanicsburg, PA, 2003)

Lefkowitz, Arthur S., *Benedict Arnold's Army*, (Savas Beatie, 2008)

Leiby, Adrian C., *The Revolutionary War in the Hackensack Valley*, (Rutgers University Press, 1992)

Lengel, Edward George, *General George Washington A Military Life*, (Random House, New York, 2005)

Lengel, Edward George, *The Glorious Struggle: George Washington's Revolutionary War Letters*, (HarperCollins, New York, 2008)

Lengyel, Cornel Adam, *Four Days in July*, (Doubleday & Company, Inc., (NYC, 1958)

LeRoy, Perry Eugene, *Sir Guy Carleton as a Military Leader During the American Revolution; Invasion and Repulse, 1775 - 1776*, (PhD. Dissertation, Ohio State University, 1960)

Lesser, Charles H., *The Sinews of Independence. Monthly Strength Reports of the Continental Army*, (Chicago, 1975)

Lipscomb, Terry W., *Battles, Skirmishes, and Actions of the American Revolution in South Carolina*, (South Carolina Department of Archives and History, 2003)

Lord, Philip, Jr., *War Over Walloomscoik; Land Use and Settlement Pattern on the Bennington Battlefield - 1777*, (New York State Museum Bulletin No. 473, Albany, NY, 1989)

Lossing, Benson John, *The Pictorial Field-Book of the Revolution*, (Harper & Bros., 1859; Reprint, Charles E. Tuttle Company, Rutland, VT, 1972), 2 Volumes

Lowenthal, Larry, *Days of Siege: A Journal of the Siege of Fort Stanwix in 1777*, (Journal # 938p, David Library of the American Revolution, Washington's Crossing, PA)

Lumpkin, Henry, *From Savannah to Yorktown: The American Revolution in the South*, (University of South Carolina Press, 1981)

Lundeberg, Philip K., *The Gunboat Philadelphia and the Defense of Lake Champlain in 1776*, (Basin Harbor, VT: Lake Champlain Maritime Museum, 1995).

Lundin, Leonard, *Cockpit of the Revolution: The War for Independence in New Jersey*, (Princeton, 1940)

Luzader, John, *Saratoga: A Military History of the Decisive Campaign of the American Revolution*, (Savas Beatie, 2007)

Mackesy, Piers, *The War for America, 1775-1783*, (Harvard University Press, 1964)

MacLeod, Normand, *Detroit to Fort Sackville, 1778-1779; The Journal of Normand MacLeod*, (Journal # 1364, David Library of the American Revolution, Washington's Crossing, PA)

Maquire, Thomas J., *The Surprise of Germantown: Or, the Battle of Clivden, October 4th, 1777*, (Thomas Publications, 1996)

Mahan, Alfred T., *Major Operations of the Navies in the War of the American Revolution*, (Boston, 1913)

Malone, Dumas, *The Story of the Declaration of Independence*, (Oxford University Press, 1975)

476   Bibliography

Maier, Pauline, *American Scripture: Making the Declaration of Independence*, (Alfred A. Knopf, New York, 1997)

Martin, David G., *The Philadelphia Campaign: June 1777 - July 1778*, (Combined Books, Conshohocken, PA, 1993)

Martin, James K. and Louden, Mark E., *A Respectable Army: The Military Origins of of the Republic, 1763-1789*, (Harlan Davidson, Wheeling, Il, 2006)

Mattern, David B., *Benjamin Lincoln and the American Revolution*, (University of South Carolina Press, 1995)

McCowen, George Smith, Jr., *The British Occupation of Charleston 1780-1782*, (Columbia University Press, 1981)

McCrady, Edward, *History of South Carolina in the Revolution 1775 - 1780*, (Columbia, SC, 1901)

McCullough, David, *1776: America and Britain at War*, (Simon & Schuster, 2005)

McCullough, David, *John Adams*, (Simon & Schuster, 2001)

McGuire, Thomas J., *Battle of Paoli*, (Stackpole Books, Mechanicsburg, PA, 2000)

McGuire, Thomas J., The *Philadelphia Campaign, Volume I: Brandywine and the Fall of Philadelphia*, (Stackpole Books, Mechanicsburg, PA, 2006)

McGuire, Thomas J., The *Philadelphia Campaign, Volume II: Germantown and the Roads to Valley Forge*, (Stackpole Books, Mechanicsburg, PA, 2007)

Middlekauff, Robert, *The Glorious Cause*, (Oxford University Press, 1982)

Miller, Nathan, *Sea of Glory: A Naval History of the American Revolution*, (Nautical and Aviation Publishing Company, Mount Pleasant, SC, 2000)

Mintz, Max M., *The Generals of Saratoga*, (Yale University Press, 1990)

Mintz, Max M., *Seeds of Empire, The American Revolutionary Conquest of the Iroquois*, (New York University Press, 2001)

Mires, Charlene, *Independence Hall in American Memory*, (University of Pennsylvania Press, 2002)

Mitchell, Broadus, *The Price of Independence: A Realistic View of the American Revolution*, (Oxford, New York, 1974)

Mitchell, Joseph B., *Decisive Battles of the American Revolution*, (G.P. Putnam's Sons, NY, 1962)

Montross, Lynn, *The Story of the Continental Army*, (Barnes and Noble, New York, 1967; Originally published in 1952 as *Rag, Tag and Bobtail*)

Morgan, Edmund S., *Benjamin Franklin*, (Yale University Press, 2002)

Morgan, William James, Ed., *Naval Documents of the American Revolution*, (Washington, 1970)

Morris, Richard B., *The Peacemakers: The Great Powers and American Independence*, (New York, 1965)

Morison, Samuel Eliot, *John Paul Jones: A Sailor's Biography*, (boston, 1959)

Morrissey, Brendan, *Monmouth Courthouse 1778: The Last Great Battle in the North*, (Osprey Publishing, 2005)

Muir, Dorothy Troth, *General Washington's Headquarters 1775-1783*, (Troy University Press, Alabama, 1977)

Murray, Stuart, *Washington's Farewell to His Officers After Victory in the Revolution*, (Images from the Past, Bennington, VT, 1999)

Myers, Joseph P., *Inventing the Republic: The Continental Congress, Institutional Formation, and the Revolution of American National Identity*, (PhD. Dissertation, Temple University, 1999)

Myers, Minor, Jr., *Liberty Without Anarchy: A History of the Society of the Cincinnati*, (Reprint, University of Virginia Press, 2004)

Namier, Lewis B., *England in the Age of the American Revolution*, (London, 1930)

Nash, Gary B., *The Unknown American Revolution: The Unruly Birth of Democracy and the Struggle to Create America*, (Viking, New York, 2005)

National Park Service, *Signers of the Declaration*, (U.S. Government Printing Office, 1973)

478 Bibliography

Nelson, James L., *Benedict Arnold's Navy; The Ragtag Fleet that Lost the Battle of Lake Champlain but Won the American Revolution*, (McGraw Hill, 2006)

Nestor, William R., *The Frontier War for American Independence*, (Stackpole Books, 2004)

Newlin, Algie I., *The Battle of New Garden: The Little Known Story of One of the Most Important 'Minor Battles' of the Revelutionary War in North Carolina*, (North Carolina Friends Historical Society, 1995)

Ney, Diane, *Illustrated Guide to Sites of the American Revolution*, (Barnes & Noble, 2004)

Nolan, James Bennett, *Lafayette in America: Day by Day*, (Johns Hopkins Press, 1934)

Norton, Mary Beth, *Liberty's Daughters: The Revolutionary Experience of American Women*, (Reprint, Ithaca, Cornell University Press, 1996)

O'Brien, Michael Joseph, *The Commander-In-Chief's Guard*, (American Irish Historical Society, Boston, 1928)

O'Kelley, Patrick, *Nothing but Blood and Slaughter, the Revolutionary War in the Carolinas, Volume One, 1771 – 1779*, (Blue House Tavern Press, nd)

O'Kelley, Patrick, *Nothing but Blood and Slaughter, the Revolutionary War in the Carolinas, Volume Two, 1780*, (Blue House Tavern Press, nd)

O'Kelley, Patrick, *Nothing but Blood and Slaughter, the Revolutionary War in the Carolinas, Volume Three, 1781*, (Blue House Tavern Press, nd)

O'Kelley, Patrick, *Nothing but Blood and Slaughter, the Revolutionary War in the Carolinas, Volume Four, 1782*, (Blue House Tavern Press, nd)

Pancake, John S., *This Destructive War, The British Campaign in the South, 1780 - 1782*, (University of Alabama Press, 1985)

Pancake, John S., *1777: The Year of the Hangman*, (University of Alabama Press, 1984)

Palmer, Dave Richard, *The Way of the Fox: American Strategy in the War for America, 1775-1783*, (Westport, CT, Greenwood Press, 1975)

Palmer, Dave Richard, *George Washington, First in War*, (2002)

Palmer, Dave Richard, *George Washington and Benedict Arnold: A Tale of Two Patriots*, (Regnery Publications, Washington, DC, 2006)

Patterson, Richard S. and Dougall, Richardson, *The Eagle and the Shield"; A History of the Great Seal of the United States*, (GPO, Washington, DC, 1976)

Patton, Robert H., *Patriot Pirates: The Privateer War for Freedom and Fortune in the American Revolution*, (Pantheon Books, New York, 2008)

Pearson, Michael, *These Damned Rebels: The American Revolution as Seen Through British Eyes*, (Da Capo Press, 1972)

Peckham, Howard H., *The War for Independence, A Military History*, (Chicago, 1958)

Peckham, Howard H., Editor, *The Toll of Independence: Engagements and Battle Casualties of the American Revolution*, (University of Chicago Press, 1974)

Peebles, John, *John Peebles' American War: The Diary of a Scottish Grenadier, 1776-1782*, (Journal # 4727, The David Library of the American Revolution, Crossing, PA)

Pell, Joshua, *Diary, 1776 - 1777*, (Bulletin, Fort Ticonderoga Museum, Vol. III, No. 6)

Perrault, Gilles, *La Revanche américain: Le Secret du Roi*, (Paris, 1996)

Peterson, Harold L., *The Book of The Continental Soldier*, (Harrisburg, PA, 1968)

Phillips, Kevin, *The Cousin's Wars, Religion, Politics, and the Triumph of Anglo-America*, (Basic Books, 1999)

Pula, James S., *Thaddeus Kosciuszko, The Purest Son of Liberty*, (Hippocrene Books, New York, 1999)

Puls, Mark, *Henry Knox, Visionary General of the American Revolution*, (Palgrave Macmillian, 2008)

Purcell, Edward L., & Burg, David F., *The World Almanac of the American Revolution*, (Pharos Books, NY, 1992)

Purcell, Edward L., *Who Was Who in the American Revolution*, (Facts On File, NY, 1993)

Purcell, Sarah J., *Sealed with Blood: War, Sacrifice, and Memory in Revolutionary America*, (Philadelphia, 2002)

Pyne, Frederick Wallace, The Rev., *The Genealogical Register of the Descendants of the Signers of the Declaration of Independence*, (Picton Press, Rockland, ME, 1997-2002), 7 vols.

Quarles, Benjamin, *The Negro in the American Revolution*, (Chapel Hill, North Carolina, 1996)

Raphael, Ray, *A People's History of the American Revolution: How Common People Shaped the Fight for Independence*, (The New Press, New York, 2001)

Rankin, Hugh F., *The North Carolina Continentals*, (Chapel Hill, NC, 1971)

Rankin, Hugh F., *Francis Marion: The Swamp Fox*, (Thomas Y. Crowell, New York, 1973)

Raynor, George, *Patriots and Tories in Piedmont Carolina*, (The Salisbury Post, 1990)

Reed, John F., *Campaign to Valley Forge, July 1, 1777-December 19, 1777*, (Reprint, Pioneer Press, 1980)

Rhodehamel, John H., Editor, *The American Revolution: Writings from the War of Independence*, (Library of America, New York, 2001)

Roberts, Kenneth, Editor, *March to Quebec: Journals of the Members of Arnold's Expedition*, (New York, Doubleday and Company, 1938)

Rodger, N.A.M., *The Command of the Ocean: A Naval History of Britain, 1649-1815*, (W.W. Norton and Company, 2004), especially Chapters 21, 22, 24-27

Royster, Charles, *A Revolutionary People at War: The Continental Army and American Character, 1775-1783*, (1779)

Salley, A. S., Jr., *The Georgia-Florida Campaigns in the American Revolution: 1776, 1777, and 1778*, (PhD. Dissertation, Tulane University, 1979)

Sampson, Richard, *Escape in America: The British Convention Prisoners, 1777 – 1783*, (Anglo Press, 1995)

Savas, Theodore P. & J. David Dameron, *A Guide to the Battles of the American Revolution*, (Savas Beatie, NY, 2005)

Schama, Simon, *Rough Crossings: Britain, The Slaves and the American Revolution*, (HarperCollins Publishers, 2006)

Schecter, Barnet, *The Battle for New York: The City at the Heart of the American Revolution*, (Walker & Company, New York, 2002)

Schiff, Stacy, *A Great Improvisation: Franklin, France, and the Birth of America*, (Henry Holt and Company, New York, 2005)

Schuyler, Major General Philip, *Report to the Continental Congress, November 6, 1776*, (Bulletin, Fort Ticonderoga Museum, Vol. III, No. 6)

Scoggins, Michael C., *The Day it Rained Militia: Huck's Defeat and the Revolution in theSouth Carolina Backcountry, May-July 1780*, (The History Press, Charleston, SC, 2005)

Scribner, Robert L., and Tarter, Brent, Editors, *Revolutionary Virginia: The Road to Independence*, (Charlottesville, University of Virginia Press, 1979), 17 Volumes

Searcy, Martha, *The Georgia-Florida Contest in the American Revolution 1776-1778*, (University of Alabama Press, 2003)

Selby, John E., *The Revolution in Virginia, 1775-1783*, (The Colonial Williamsburg Foundation, 1988)

Selesky, Harold E., *Encyclopedia of the American Revolution*, (Thompson Gale, 2006)

Selig, Robert, *March to Victory, Washington and Rochambeau and the Yorktown Campaign of 1781*, (Chief of Military History Publication, CMH Pub 70 – 104-1)

Seymour, William, *A Journal of the Southern Expedition, 1780-1783*, (Journal # 1288p, The David Library of the American Revolution, Washington's Crossing, PA)

482   Bibliography

Shea, J. G., Editor, *The Operations of the French Fleet Under the Count de Grasse in 1781-1782 as Described in Two Contemporaneous Journals*, New York, 1894, Reprint, Da Capo Press, 1971)

Shelton, Hal T., *General Richard Montgomery and the American Revolution*, (New York University Press, 1996)

Shy, John, *Toward Lexington: The Role of the British Army in the Coming of the American Revolution*, (Princeton, NJ, 1965)

Shy, John, *A People Numerous and Armed: Reflections on the Military Struggle for American Independence*, (University of Michigan Press, 1976)

Skaggs, David Curtis, *The Old Northwest in the American Revolution, An Anthology*, (State Historical Society of Wisconsin, Madison, WI, 1977)

Smith, George, *An Universal Military Dictionary*, (1779, Reprint Museum Restoration Service, Ottawa, Ontario, 1969)

Smith, Page, *A New Age Now Begins*, (McGraw-Hill Book Company, 1976), 2 volumes

Smith, Paul H., Editor, *Letters of Delegates to Congress, 1774-1789*, (Library of Congress, 1977-1989), 25 Volumes, particularly vols. 1-21.

Smith, Samuel E., *The Battle of Brandywine*, (Monmouth, NJ, Philip Freneau Press, 1976)

Smith, William, *Historical Memoirs of William Smith, 1778 - 1783*, (Edited by William H.W. Sabine, Arno Press, New York, 1971)

Snapp, James Russell, *Exploitation and Control: The Southern Frontier in Anglo-American Politics in the Era of the American Revolution*, (PhD. Dissertation, Harvard University, 1988)

Sosin, Jack M., *The Revolutionary Frontier, 1763-1783*, (Reprint, University of New Mexico Press, 1974)

Stalker, Michael D., *George Rogers Clark and the Revolutionary War in the Northwest*, (Master's Thesis, East Stoudsburg University, 2002)

Stein, Alan, Ed., *Orderly Books of the American Revolution in the Morristown Historical Park*, (Morristown, NJ, 1994)

Stember, Sol, *The Bicentennial Guide to the American Revolution*, (E.P. Dutton, 1974), 3 volumes

Stephenson, Michael, *Patriot Battles: How the War of Independence Was Fought*, (New York, Harper Collins Publishers, 2007)

Stockley, Andrew, *Britain and France at the Birth of America: The European Powers at the Peace Negotiations, 1782-1783*, (University of Exeter, UK, 2001)

Stoudt, John Joseph, *Ordeal at Valley Forge, a Day-by- Day Chronicle from December 17, 1777 to June 18, 1778*, (University of Pennsylvania Press, 1963)

Stryker, William S., *The Battles of Trenton and Princeton*, (1858, Reprint, Spartanburg, SC, 1967)

Stryker, William S., *The Battle of Monmouth*, (Princeton, NJ, 1927)

Sweeney, Jerry K, *A Handbook of American Military History*, (Westview Press, Boulder, CO, 1996)

Swager, Christine R., *Come to the Cow Pens!*, (Hub City Writers Project, Spartansburg, SC, 2002)

Swiggert, Howard, *War Out of Niagara, Walter Butler and the Tory Rangers*, (New York, 1933)

Symonds, Craig L., *A Battlefield Atlas of the American Revolution*, (The Nautical & Aviation Publishing Company of America, Inc. (1986)

Sypher, Francis J., Jr., *Biographies of Original Members & Other Continental Officers*, (New York State Society of the Cincinnati, Fishkill, NY, 2004)

Sypher, Francis J., Jr., *Histories of New York Regiments of the Continental Army*, (New York State Society of the Cincinnati, Fishkill, NY, 2008)

Syrett, David, Editor, *Commissioned Sea Officers of the Royal Navy, 1660-1815*, (Aldershot, England, 1994)

Taaffe, Stephen R., *The Philadelphia Campaign 1777-1779*, (University of Kansas Press, 2003)

Tarleton, Lieutenent Colonel, *A History of the Campaigns of 1780 and 1781 in the Southern Provinces of North America*, (1787, Reprint, Arno Press, 1968)

484 Bibliography

Tatum, Edward H., Editor, *The American Journal of Ambrose Serle, Secretary to Lord Howe, 1776-1778*, New York, 1940, Reprint, Arno Press, 1969)

Taylor, Alan, *The Divided Ground: Indians, Settlers, and the Northern Borderland of the American Revolution*, (Alfred A. Knopf, New York, 2006)

Taylor, Robert J., Editor, *Papers of John Adams*, (Belknap Press of Harvard University Press, 1983), v. 5

Thacher, James, *Military Journal of the American Revolution from the Commencement to the Disbanding of the American Army, Comprising a Detailed Account of the Principal Events and Battles of the Revolution With Their Exact Dates and a Biographical Sketch of the Most Prominent Generals*, (Hartford, CT, Hurlbut, Williams and Co., 1862, Reprint, Corner House Historical Publications, Gansevoort, NY, 1998)

Thane, Elswyth, *The Fighting Quaker: Nathanael Greene*, (Mattituck, Amereon House, 1972)

Toll, Ian W., *Six Frigates: The Epic History of the Founding of the U.S. Navy*, (W. W. Norton & Company, New York, 2006)

Toth, Charles W., Editor, *The American Revolution in the West Indies*, (Port Washington, NY, 1975)

Tourtellot, Arthur Bernon, *Lexington and Concord: The Beginning of the War of the American Revolution*, (Norton, 2000)

Tucker, Glenn, *Mad Anthony Wayne and the New Nation*, (Stackpole Books, 1973)

Tuchman, Barbara W. *The First Salute: A View of the American Revolution*, (1958)

Tussell, John, *Birthplace of the Army: A Study of the Valley Forge Encampment*, (Pennsylvania Historical and Museum Commission, Harrisburg, PA, 1998)

Valley Forge Orderly Book of General George Weedon, (Dodd, Meade and Company, New York, 1902)

Van Buskirk, Judith L., *Generous Enemies: Patriots and Loyalists in Revolutionary New York*, (Philadelphia, 2002)

Van Powell, William Nowland, *The American Navies of the Revolutionary War*, (G.P. Putnam's Sons, New York, 1974)

Walker, Anthony, *So Few The Brave: Rhode Island Continentals 1775-1783*, (Seafield Press, 1981)

Waller, George Macgregor, *The American Revolution In The West*, (Nelson - Hall, Chicago, IL, 1976)

War Office, 4th of June 1779, *A List of all the Officers of the Army: The General and Field Officers of the several Troops, Regiments, Independent Companies, and the Garrisons; with an Alphabetical Index to the Whole*

Ward, Christopher, *The War of the Revolution*, (The Macmillian Company, 1952), 2 Volumes

Ward, Christopher, *The Delaware Continentals 1776-1783*, (The Historical Society of Delaware, 1941)

Ward, Harry M., *The Department of War, 1781 – 1795*, (University of Pittsburgh Press, 1962)

Ward, Harry M., *Between the Lines: Banditti of the American Revolution*, (Westport, CT, 2002)

Ward, Harry M., *George Washington's Enforcers: Policing the Continental Army*, (Carbondale, IL, 2006)

Warren, Mercy Otis, *History of the Rise, Progress and Termination of the American Revolution*, (1805, Reprint Edited by Lester H. Cohen, Indianapolis: Liberty Fund, 1988)

Weigley, Russell F., *The Partisan War: The South Carolina Campaign of 1780-1782*, (University of South Carolina Press, Columbia, 1970)

Weintraub, Stanley, *General Washington's Christmas Farewell; A Mount Vernon Homecoming, 1783*, (Simon & Schuster, 2003)

Weintraub, Stanley, *Iron Tears: America's Battle for Freedom, Britain's Quagmire: 1775-1783*, (Simon & Schuster, 2005)

Wharton, Francis, *The Revolutionary Correspondence of the United States*, (Government Printing Office, 1889), 6 Volumes

Wilbur, C. Keith, *Pirates & Patriots of the Revolution*, (Chelsea House, Philadelphia, 1973)

Willcox, William B., *Portarit of a General; Sir Henry Clinton in the War of Independence*, (Alfred A. Knopf, New York, 1964)

486

Williams, Glenn F., *Year of the Hangman: George Washington's Campaign Against the Iroquois*, (Westholme Publishing, Yardley, PA, 2005)

Williams, John, *The Battle of Hubbarton, The American Rebels Stem the Tide*, (Vermont Division for Historic Preservation, 1988)

Williams, Samuel, *Tennessee During the Revolutionary War*, (Nashville, 1944)

Wilson, Barry K., *Benedict Arnold: A Traitor in Our Midst*, (McGill-Queen's University, 2001)

Wilson, David K., *The Southern Strategy: Britain's Conquest of South Carolina and Georgia, 1775-1780*, (University of South Carolina Press, 2005)

Wilson, Ellen Gibson, *The Loyal Blacks*, (New York, 1976)

Wilson, Howard McKnight, *Great Valley Patriots: Western Virginia and the Struggle for Liberty*, (McClure Press, 1976)

Wood, Gordon S., *The Creation of the American Republic, 1776-1783*, (University of North Carolina Press, 1969)

Wood, Gordon S., *The Radicalism of the American Revolution*, (Alfred A. Knopf, NY, 1992)

Wood, Gordon S., *The American Revolution; A History, 1776-1783*, (Modern Library, 2002)

Wood, Gordon S., *Revolutionary Characters; What Made The Founders Different*, (Penguin Books, Ltd., 2006)

Wood, W.J., *Battles of the Revolutionary War, 1775-1781*, (Da Capo Press, 1995)

Wood, Virginia Steele, *The Georgia Navy's Dramatic Victory of April 19, 1778*, (The Georgia Historical Quarterly, Vol. XC, Number 2, Summer 2006), pp. 165 - 195.

Woodward, Joel A., *A Comparative Evaluation of British and American Strategy in the Southern Campaigns of 1780-1781*, (Command and General Staff College, Fort Leavenworth, KS, 2002)

Wright, Robert K., Jr., *The Continental Army*, (Center of Military History, United States Army, Washington, DC, 1986)

Zeiler, Harris R., *The Maddest Idea in the World: The Origins of the United States Navy during the Revolution*, (Master's Thesis, East Stroudsburg University, 1996)

Zobel, Hiller B., *The Boston Massacre*, (W. W. Norton and Co., New York, 1970)

INDEX

Lightning Source UK Ltd.
Milton Keynes UK
UKOW01f1200040817
306699UK00002B/334/P